BirdLife Conservation Series No. 2

IMPORTANT BIRD AREAS IN THE MIDDLE EAST

compiled by

M. I. Evans

a joint project with

Ornithological Society of the Middle East

OSME

in cooperation with

International Waterfowl and Wetlands Research Bureau

IWRB

sponsored by

Royal Society for the Protection of Birds

RSPB

BirdLife® INTERNATIONAL

Wellbrook Court, Girton Road, Cambridge CB3 0NA, U.K.
tel. 01223-277318 fax 01223-277200 (code 0223- until April 1995)
email birdlife@gn.apc.org

ISBN 0 946888 28 0

A catalogue record for this book is available from the British Library

Series editor Duncan Brooks
Design CBA (Cambridge) and Duncan Brooks
Layout and text preparation Duncan Brooks, Michelle Hines, Regina Pfaff

Text set in Times (9/11 pt) and Optima

Imageset by Spire Origination (Norwich)
Printed and bound by Page Bros (Norwich) Ltd

Cover illustration Crab Plover *Dromas ardeola,* by Norman Arlott.

IMPORTANT BIRD AREAS IN THE MIDDLE EAST

■

MAIN CONTRIBUTORS

S. C. Madge (Afghanistan); Dr S. Mohamed, Environmental Protection Committee, E. Hirschfeld (Bahrain); Department of the Environment, Dr D. A. Scott (Islamic Republic of Iran); Dr K. Y. Al-Dabbagh, Dr H. Y. Siman, Dr P. Ctyroký, Dr D. A. Scott, S. Marchant (Iraq); S. Blitzblau, Dr R. Frumkin, Dr R. Yosef (Israel, West Bank, Gaza, Golan Heights); A. Budieri, I. Andrews, Dr D. M. Shafei, A. Sutari, K. Irani, Dr A. Dajani, Dr M. Masseti (Jordan); Prof. C. W. T. Pilcher, M. Shehab, Environment Protection Council (Kuwait); A. Serhal (Lebanon); R. H. Daly, M. D. Gallagher, Dr J. Eriksen, Ministry of Regional Municipalities and Environment (Sultanate of Oman); R. Nation, Environmental Protection Committee (Qatar); S. F. Newton, A. V. Newton, P. Symens, A. Suhaibani, M. Shobrak, M. al-Salamah, M. C. Jennings, P. Gaucher, B. S. Meadows, A. J. Stagg (Kingdom of Saudi Arabia); Dr I. Hanna, Dr A. M. Agha, Dr R. Sabbagh, Dr M. A. Kabbani, A. M. Macfarlane, S. Zaiane, Dr M. Masseti, W. Attar, B. Attar, M. Abbasi, J. J. Dumas, M. Kasparek (Syria); C. Richardson, S. Aspinall, P. Hellyer (United Arab Emirates); R. F. Porter, K. Shaw, C. Bradshaw, F. Stone, D. Showler, M. C. Jennings (Yemen); D. J. Brooks (BirdLife International).

■

PROJECT STEERING COMMITTEE

Dr C. J. Bibby   Dr N. Burgess   R. F. A. Grimmett
R. P. Martins   C. Perennou   R. F. Porter
Dr M. R. W. Rands (Chairman)   Dr D. A. Scott

■

LINE DRAWINGS

S. M. Andrews

MAPS

A. J. Long

CONTENTS

NATIONAL INVENTORIES

ACKNOWLEDGEMENTS

THIS INVENTORY is based on the fieldwork of hundreds of birdwatchers and keen amateur and professional ornithologists. I heartily thank all observers in the region, past and present, who have taken the time to write down what they saw at particular sites, and who thus made possible the compilation of this book.

I thank especially the main contributors in each country (some of whom became unofficial 'coordinators'), who participated with energy and enthusiasm in the work of providing all the material which has been compiled in this book. I hope that the book will reflect their outstanding contributions: S. C. Madge (Afghanistan); Dr S. Mohamed, Environmental Protection Committee, E. Hirschfeld (Bahrain); Dr D. A. Scott, S. A. Ayafat (on behalf of the experts of the Department of the Environment) (Islamic Republic of Iran); Dr K. Y. Al-Dabbagh, Dr H. Y. Siman, Dr P. Ctyroký, Dr D. A. Scott, S. Marchant (Iraq); S. Blitzblau, Dr R. Frumkin, Dr R. Yosef (Israel, West Bank, Gaza and Golan Heights); I. Andrews, A. Budieri, A. Sutari, Dr D. M. Shafei, K. Irani, Dr A. Dajani, Dr M. Masseti (Jordan); Prof. C. W. T. Pilcher, M. Shehab, Environment Protection Council (Kuwait); A. Serhal (Lebanon); R. H. Daly, M. D. Gallagher, Dr J. Eriksen, Ministry of Regional Municipalities and Environment (Sultanate of Oman); R. Nation, Environmental Protection Committee (Qatar); S. F. Newton, A. V. Newton, P. Symens, A. Suhaibani, M. Shobrak, M. al-Salamah, M. C. Jennings, P. Gaucher, B. S. Meadows, A. J. Stagg (Kingdom of Saudi Arabia); Dr I. Hanna, Dr A. M. Agha, Dr R. Sabbagh, Dr M. A. Kabbani, A. M. Macfarlane, Dr M. Masseti, W. Attar, B. Attar, M. Abbasi (Syria); C. Richardson, S. Aspinall, P. Hellyer (United Arab Emirates); R. F. Porter, K. Shaw, C. Bradshaw, F. Stone, M. C. Jennings, D. Showler (Yemen).

The impetus for this project lay with M. R. W. Rands who, as Programme Director at the BirdLife International Secretariat and as Chairman of the Ornithological Society of the Middle East (OSME), was instrumental in setting up and initiating the project. The financial support of the International Department of the Royal Society for the Protection of Birds (RSPB—the BirdLife Partner in the U.K.), arranged through A. B. Gammell, has been critical in the smooth functioning and completion of this project in just over two years, and OSME also made a very substantial financial contribution relative to their resources.

As Coordinator, I was greatly aided by the Project Steering Committee: Dr M. R. W. Rands (Chairman), Dr C. J. Bibby, Dr N. Burgess (RSPB), R. F. A. Grimmett, R. P. Martins (OSME), C. Perennou (IWRB), R. F. Porter (RSPB) and Dr D. A. Scott. In addition I am grateful to M. R. W. Rands, C. J. Bibby and R. F. A. Grimmett for day-to-day advice and supervision at the BirdLife International Secretariat. J. Barnes and L. Serubula were a constant and dependable source of secretarial support and good humour, and were instrumental in helping to keep the project going.

The initial design and development of the project was assisted by comments and constructive criticism from S. B. el Din, C. Richardson, Dr R. J. Hornby (National Avian Research Center, Abu Dhabi), Dr S. Mohamed (Dept of Biology, University of Bahrain), E. Hirschfeld, and Dr H. Mohammadi (on behalf of the experts of the Department of the Environment, Islamic Republic of Iran), and I am most grateful to them.

During my travels in the region I was indebted by the great help and hospitality shown by friends and colleagues: A. and Z. Serhal, A. Chamas, S. Saidi and family, H. Hicham, N. El-Hassnieh, T. Hassanieh, and Dr M. Hallab (Lebanon); A. and T. Budieri, M. Abu Ja'fer, J. Al-Joundi, K. Irani, A. Sutari, and D. M. Shafei (Jordan); Dr A. Khatib, Dr R. Sabbagh, Dr M. A. Kabbani, W. and B. Attar, Dr M. al-Nimeh, and Dr E. Bailey (Syria); R. H. Daly, M. Gallagher, and J. and H. Eriksen (Oman). In particular I am grateful to the Office of the Adviser for Nature Conservation, Diwan of Royal Court, for its generous sponsorship of my visit to the Sultanate of Oman.

At the Secretariat of BirdLife International, D. J. Brooks provided a great deal of assistance in compiling many of the texts at a crucial time when the backlog of work threatened to grow unmanageable.

I thank the organizations collaborating on this project who have provided members of the Steering Committee and whose staff have shared their data and provided help in numerous other ways: the International Waterfowl and Wetlands Research Bureau (Dr M. Moser, C. Perennou, Dr T. Jones, Dr P. Rose, P. Gorbutt), the World Conservation

Monitoring Centre (G. Drucker, Dr C. Magin, T. Inskipp), OSME (F. E. Warr, H. and G. Welch) and the RSPB (J. O'Sullivan). I thank here again those 38 observers who contributed their data-sheets to the OSME Sites Register Scheme (coordinated initially by N. J. Collar and then M. R. W. Rands), providing an invaluable baseline of data; their names are listed in the relevant issues of the *OSME Bulletin* (see p.12).

Other staff at the BirdLife International Secretariat assisted in numerous ways, especially R. Pfaff and I. Hughes with their meticulous word-processing skills, as well as Dr G. Allport, M. J. Crosby, J. Loughlin, A. J. Long, M. Langeveld, Z. Waliczky and T. Salathé.

I am grateful to S. Zaiane and D. Raydan for their immediate help, at very short notice, in rapidly and carefully translating a large mass of data-sheets and other material from the Arabic.

A diverse variety of assistance was also provided by F. Parakatil (IUCN), M. Smart (Ramsar Bureau), G. Archibald (International Crane Foundation), A. L. Rao (IUCN–Pakistan), Dr M. F. Mörzer Bruyns, Dr F. Al-Timimi, Dr S. J. Darroze (FAO), R. Slothouwer, J. Wattel, Y. Achich (UNEP Regional Activity Centre, Tunis), I. Andersen (Regional Bureau of Arab States, UNDP) and Prof. W. Büttiker.

A. J. Long, S. M. Andrews and N. Arlott provided the excellent maps, text line drawings and cover drawing (respectively) at short notice, the RSPB Design Section was kind enough to organize the scanning of drawings, and in the final stages of the project Dr J. W. Duckworth and M. O'Sullivan helped greatly with editing and analysis and provided much-needed moral support.

M. I. Evans

INTRODUCTION

MANKIND has inhabited the Middle East continuously for hundreds of thousands of years. The domestication of wild plants and animals and the invention of agriculture were key developments in human history which originated in the Middle East and which have had far-reaching consequences for the natural environment worldwide during the last 10,000 years. The emergence of farming and nomadic pastoralism in the region greatly increased the carrying capacity of the land, and the rapid spread of these new land-use practices led to a gradual and relentless modification of Middle Eastern habitats and landscapes over thousands of years, in which natural, and perhaps even man-made, climate changes were also inextricably linked. These changes were characterized by widespread deforestation of uplands and river valleys and general degradation of soils and vegetation cover on the lowlands and plateaus. Such overall trends were exacerbated by a more-or-less continuous growth in human populations. However, long experience with resource scarcity has also led to the evolution of some of the most striking and successful examples of sustainable land-use practices anywhere in the world.

Notwithstanding the traditional conservation of natural resources that still exists in some areas of the Middle East, overall human population levels in the region continue to grow, agricultural practices continue to intensify, industrial capacity continues to expand, and traditional ways of life are consequently coming under increasing pressure. The growing need for fresh water, food, raw materials and land has led to increased levels of wetland drainage and pollution, deforestation for fuelwood and timber, coastal land-claim, lowering of water-tables, over-exploitation of marine resources and 'desertification' (land degradation) in the Middle East, as in many areas of the world. However, there is now a widespread and increasing understanding and agreement amongst most governments of the world that conservation of the environment and its biodiversity is essential for the long-term welfare of their peoples, as demonstrated by the 157 countries which signed the Convention on Biological Diversity at the United Nations Conference on Environment and Development (UNCED) in Rio de Janeiro in June 1992.

Despite the perceptions of many of those unfamiliar with the region, the Middle East has a relatively high level of biodiversity on a global scale, generally higher than the more temperate areas of the northern hemisphere. Its complex patchwork of environments—some of the largest and most diverse wetland, steppe, desert and marine ecosystems in the world are found within the region—provide habitats for more than 800 species of bird. More than 60 of these species are endemic, being wholly or largely restricted to the Middle East, with the majority concentrated into four globally important centres of endemism (south-west Arabia, Socotra, Mesopotamia and West Himalayas). Many millions of birds depend on the ecosystems of the Middle East for breeding, staging or wintering sites; these sites' very high value to birds reflects their overall ecological importance, since birds are an excellent indicator group for detecting areas of more general importance for their high overall biodiversity or productivity, and for monitoring these areas' status—birds are the only large and easily observable class of organisms that are relatively well-known on a global scale as well as being found in most habitats and regions on earth.

Given the situation outlined above, the need to give decision-makers up-to-date information on the priority areas for conserving birds and habitats in the Middle East is now urgent.

AIMS OF THE STUDY

The conservation of biodiversity and natural resources, including birds, can generally be approached in the following three ways.

- Protection of species from direct threats, for example direct persecution or unsustainable hunting, trading or harvesting, usually by legislation but sometimes also through active management of populations in the case of globally threatened or highly economically valuable species.

- Protection of sites by designating areas for the conservation of natural resources, and regulating and managing them according to the needs of the biodiversity they contain.
- Protection of the wider environment and ensuring sustainable use of natural resources, by regulating economic activities that modify habitats and landscape (e.g. agriculture, water supply, industry), and by controlling pollution of air, soil and water.

All are of importance and are complementary in the maintenance of a country's natural resources and biodiversity, as an insurance for the well-being of its people in the long term. Any attempts to maintain the existing distribution and abundance of the Middle East's biodiversity, including that of its birds, will only be successful if all of these approaches are followed. This study is aimed at the promotion of the second approach by providing, in handbook form, key information on sites of regional and international importance for the conservation of the Middle East's birds and other wildlife. This edition is intended primarily for use by national nature conservation organizations, national and sectoral land-use planners, and international agencies.

This book, the result of a two-year study, identifies 391 of the most important sites in the region for conservation of birds and biodiversity, and provides an indication of the degree to which they are protected or under threat. It represents perhaps the first comprehensive basis for the promotion of a network of sites for bird and biodiversity conservation throughout the Middle East, from the shores of the Mediterranean to the western Himalayas, and from the mountains of Iranian Azarbayjan to the island of Socotra.

Specifically, this inventory of sites is intended to serve six functions.

- To contribute towards the development and implementation of national strategies for the conservation of biodiversity, in line with the spirit of the Biodiversity Convention, and in particular to assist the development by national organizations and agencies of programmes to identify and conserve areas of high biodiversity value.
- To inform political decision-makers and their advisors at local, national and international levels of the existence and importance of these vital sites, so that policies and proposals for use of land and natural resources can be formulated or modified, as necessary and appropriate.
- To assist governments in the implementation of, and active participation in, international and regional agreements, such as the Biodiversity Convention and the Ramsar Convention.
- To serve the conservation activities of, and promote coordination among, international organizations, particularly:

  – United Nations Educational, Scientific and Cultural Organization (UNESCO), especially the UNESCO World Heritage Convention Committee, the National Committees of the UNESCO Man and Biosphere Programme, and the UNESCO Regional Office for Science and Technology–Arab States (ROSTAS–ECO);

  – United Nations Environment Programme (UNEP), especially its Regional Seas programme, including the Regional Activity Centre for [Mediterranean] Specially Protected Areas (RAC/SPA), the Regional Organization for the Protection of the Marine Environment (ROPME), and the Programme for the Environment of the Red Sea and the Gulf of Aden (PERSGA);

  – Arab League Educational, Cultural and Scientific Organization (ALECSO);

  – IUCN–The World Conservation Union and the World Wide Fund for Nature (WWF–International);

  – Global Environment Facility (GEF) of the United Nations Development Programme (UNDP), the World Bank and UNEP;

  – UN Food and Agriculture Organization (FAO);

  – UN Economic and Social Commission for Western Asia (ESCWA).
- To help to identify future priorities for action in bird conservation and research in the Middle East, in terms of important sites, species, habitats and threats, in order to motivate the scientific community to continue providing data as well as to stimulate them to fill gaps in knowledge.
- To provide relevant and useful material to national education and training experts.

The aim has been to identify sites of importance for the following four priority groups of birds.

- Species threatened with global extinction (where the danger of biodiversity loss is most immediate).
- Species which concentrate in large numbers at, and are dependent on, particular sites either when breeding, on migration, or during the winter (these sites are especially important in sustaining population levels for a wide range of species).
- Species which are threatened or declining throughout all or large parts of their range in the Middle

East (their declines point to approaching biodiversity loss).

- Species that have relatively small total world ranges with important populations in the Middle East (the region has a special responsibility for maintaining these endemic populations as part of any contribution to conserving the planet's biodiversity).

In addition, the following more habitat- or ecosystem-based, and less single-species-oriented, categories of site were selected.

- Sites for rare, threatened or unique habitats, or outstanding representative examples of natural habitats, which support characteristic associated assemblages of bird species.
- Sites important for the conservation of wild bird populations because of their proven or potential value for increasing environmental awareness, for carrying out appropriate research, or for sustainable eco-tourism.

THE NEED AND OPTIONS FOR IMPORTANT BIRD AREA PROTECTION

This inventory is a list of sites in the Middle East which require effective protection where necessary. The great majority of the sites listed here are not just important because of their bird species, but have their own intrinsic value as ecosystems with a great variety of other animal and plant species.

The preparation of this inventory comes at a time when 24 species of the Middle East avifauna are considered to be threatened with global extinction (Collar and Andrew 1988, Groombridge 1993; see also the chapter on 'Site selection', p. 20). A further 40 species, many with populations which are clearly decreasing, are considered to be threatened throughout all, or a major part, of their range in the Middle East. If action is not taken across the Middle East, then the region's biodiversity could be significantly impoverished by the beginning of the twenty-first century.

Most countries in the Middle East have frameworks for the designation of protected areas, although not actively implemented in every country. The existence of such areas is crucial for effective conservation of natural resources and biodiversity in the long term.

The type of action needed will vary from site to site, but the options immediately available will largely be dictated by the protected-area legislation already in force in each country. Appropriate protection will vary from protected landscapes where the management objective is to maintain the landscape character whilst sustaining traditional land-uses and ecological diversity, to strictly protected nature reserves, where man-made disturbances are minimized. The inventory is not, therefore, a list of sites which should all be strictly protected. At many of the sites, some economic activities are compatible with conservation and in some cases may be vital in the maintenance of particular habitats. In such cases, existing land-uses may need to be supported rather than restricted, and regulation of factors such as grazing and other uses of specified habitats may be more important than designating strictly protected areas.

Most countries in the Middle East are party to one or more of the international conventions (described in the next chapter) set up to conserve wildlife and its habitats in particular areas. This inventory of Important Bird Areas (IBAs) should be regarded as a list of sites which need to be considered for protection under the terms of one or more of these agreements. There are several international programmes which are also significant for the conservation of sites important for biodiversity; these include UNESCO's Man and the Biosphere Programme, and the UNEP Regional Seas Programme. The conservation activities of international governmental organizations such as the Arab League Educational, Scientific and Cultural Organization, and the Gulf Cooperation Council, could also contribute to the welfare of these sites.

This inventory is not an end in itself but an aid for effective regional planning of nature conservation areas. It could also be the basis for something more important and more ambitious than has so far been attempted—the development of a scientifically planned network of potentially protectable areas for birds and biodiversity throughout the Middle East, transcending national frontiers, and designed to safeguard a significant proportion of the Middle East's bird populations throughout the next century. Such a network can only be set up if there is cooperation between Middle Eastern countries and if the promotion of such a network is given a high priority. The existing international and regional measures summarized in the next chapter already provide a good framework for taking the first steps towards this goal.

LIMITS TO THE IMPORTANT BIRD AREA CONCEPT

There are problems in selecting IBAs and defining their boundaries when dealing with large tracts of homogeneous habitats such as steppes and deserts where important bird species are dispersed at low densities and in rather homogeneous communities, but in highly significant overall numbers. The conservation importance of these extensive habitats cannot be in doubt, yet in many cases it is difficult or inappropriate to identify smaller areas or sites of particular value within these habitats. This is because:

- Fragmentation and partitioning of primeval habitats by mankind in 'marginal' and pastoralist lands is not as obvious as in more fertile areas, which have been more radically altered by cultivation, and where remaining small fragments of semi-natural bird- and biodiversity-rich habitat can be much more clearly identified.
- Even where the bird communities are not as homogeneous as the habitat seems, the important areas for birds cannot be identified due to a lack of detailed information on bird distribution.

As a consequence, sites selected for steppe and desert species in this study tend to be large, in order to incorporate a sufficiently representative tract of habitat. However, the nomadism of certain desert birds means that a particular area of desert may be very important for breeding or wintering of these species in one particular year (i.e. after good rain has fallen there) but may not become 'important' again for up to 100 years. When even the vegetation 'moves' around from year to year, it may be that any particular area, fixed and static as it is, can never be large enough to accommodate a self-sustaining community of nomadic desert bird species, and even a network of such areas will still be subject to the fugitive nature of the fauna and flora.

Thus a proportion of the Middle East's bird species, because of their highly dispersed or nomadic distribution, cannot be protected fully by the appropriate management of the sites in this inventory, in some cases at any time in their life-cycle. While some Important Bird Areas have been listed which hold significant numbers of such species, only a small proportion of their total population can ever be covered by a network of appropriately managed areas. Not only steppe and desert birds such as larks and sandgrouse, but also some birds of prey, as well as many passerines, fall into this category. Furthermore, most species that do concentrate in numbers at particular sites, and which benefit most from the identification and appropriate management of sites, do not do so throughout the year.

It is therefore clear that the appropriate management of the sites listed in this inventory goes only some way towards the objective of maintaining the diversity, abundance and distribution of the Middle East's bird fauna and its habitats. It is essential not to neglect the need for positive conservation measures in the wider countryside surrounding IBAs, based on sound ecological principles, and as part of national and sectoral land-use strategies aimed at maintaining a 'biodiversity-rich' Middle East. Furthermore, sites can be seriously affected by the pollution of water and air, sometimes of international origin. A Middle East with a high level of biodiversity not only requires a comprehensive network of sites and appropriate land-use strategies, but also effective international controls on pollution.

The need to regulate rangeland use, and farming and forestry practices, is of particular importance, and generally is more relevant than the protection of individual sites in countries with vast expanses of relatively uniform rangeland, agricultural land or forests. The protection of individual sites in such regions, in the sense of setting them aside as protected areas, is less important than introducing effective regulations ensuring that whatever use is made of such ecosystems by man does not affect their long-term ecological integrity and change their natural characteristics, for example through major loss of vegetation cover, soil degradation or salinization of groundwater.

Despite these provisos, the 'important areas' concept is an essential corner-stone of conservation planning and implementation, if ongoing losses of biodiversity and natural resources are to be stemmed, and should represent a major component of any strategy to conserve the natural heritage of the Middle East.

THE MIDDLE EAST REGION

The region covered by this study (Figure 1, p. 31) includes Afghanistan, Bahrain, Iran, Iraq, Israel and the Occupied Territories, Jordan, Kuwait, Lebanon, Oman, Qatar, Saudi Arabia, Syria, the United Arab Emirates and Yemen.

BirdLife International recognizes the global value of biodiversity and has no view on the location of political boundaries within the region. Important Bird Areas identified in the occupied territories of West Bank and Gaza, as well as in occupied Syria (Golan Heights), are included within the Israel inventory for purely practical reasons, given that country's current administration of these areas (as at December 1993).

BACKGROUND TO THE STUDY

This study is the second in a global programme by the BirdLife International partnership to identify all of the Important Bird Areas in the world, following the publication of *Important Bird Areas in Europe* (Grimmett and Jones 1989), which listed and described 2,444 sites in 32 countries, including Turkey and the Azerbaijan Republic on the north-west border of the Middle East as defined and covered in this book. The countries of North Africa, with an avifauna closely related to the Middle East region, are participating in the ongoing *Important Bird Areas in Africa* project, with results due for publication by 1998.

This project has closely followed the methodology of the European IBA project, including the criteria for the selection of sites, and thus the results are integrated and comparable to a high degree. More detail on the similarities to, and differences from, the European IBA project can be found in the chapters on 'Site selection' (p. 20) and 'Data presentation' (p. 28).

This is the first comprehensive and detailed compilation of information on areas important for birds in the Middle East region, covering all species and countries, using objective criteria for site selection, and based on the gathering of much previously unpublished, original information as well as a review of the literature. However, the following, previous studies (with a regional rather than national scope) have been of value to this project.

The earliest compilation of data on important bird areas in the Middle East was an overview in 1967 of the wetlands, covering 53 sites in Afghanistan, Iran, Iraq, Israel, Jordan, Lebanon and Syria (Savage 1968a,b,c, Savage and Firouz 1968). Information on the wetlands in these countries was updated and expanded by Carp (1980), who gave preliminary details of those qualifying as 'Wetlands of International Importance' under the criteria of the Ramsar Convention. Luther and Rzóska (1971) compiled general information on a few of these sites as part of the International Biological Programme. In 1975 an important regional conference on the promotion of the establishment of marine protected areas in the region was held in Tehran, and the proceedings included inventories of important sites for marine wildlife (including birds) for several countries in the region (IUCN 1976). A comprehensive review of the breeding seabirds of the region in 1982 (Gallagher *et al.* 1984) included an inventory of all of the important sites. Summers *et al.* (1987) discussed the importance of wetlands in western Asia as staging and wintering areas for migratory shorebirds, and included a preliminary list of sites important for shorebirds. Bijlsma (1987) included an inventory of the important migratory 'bottleneck' sites for large soaring birds (raptors and storks) in the Mediterranean zone of the Middle East.

In 1983, the Ornithological Society of the Middle East (OSME) initiated the Sites Register Scheme, which collected information on important areas in the Middle East, covering all the countries in this study as well as some neighbouring ones, up until 1991. There were no criteria for site selection, and any site which contributors considered worthy was incorporated. Data-sheets for 181 sites were received from 38 contributors, making a valuable contribution to ornithological knowledge of the region based on original data, much of it previously unpublished. However, the scheme's success in gathering information on a country-by-country basis was determined by the distribution and level of activity of OSME's members, and results were accordingly biased in that no site-information was received for Bahrain, Iran, Kuwait and Oman, and very few data-sheets were submitted for some other important countries such as Afghanistan and Iraq. In addition, the information was held as an archive and was not published (Collar 1985, 1986, Evans 1988, 1992).

Since the 1960s the International Waterfowl and Wetlands Research Bureau (IWRB) has compiled information on waterfowl count sites in Israel, Lebanon, Jordan and Syria as part of its Western Palearctic Waterfowl Census (e.g. Rose 1992), and in 1987 the initiation of the Asian Waterfowl Census extended more-or-less regular site-coverage to the rest of the Middle East as defined here (e.g. Perennou and Mundkhur 1992). Programmes for the compilation and publication of detailed site information are being carried out by the UNEP Regional Activity Centre for Specially Protected Areas (RAC/SPA 1987; a new edition is in press) for Mediterranean coastal sites of nature conservation importance (including Syria, Lebanon and Israel), and by the World Conservation Monitoring Centre for internationally recognized protected areas in all countries of the region (WCMC 1991).

METHODS

The compilation of this inventory has involved the collection of data by two principal methods:

- The circulation of a data-sheet questionnaire to BirdLife International's Sections and Representatives, and to numerous additional experts, throughout the Middle East and elsewhere. This sometimes resulted in the establishment of an unofficial 'coordinator', who in turn consulted appropriate sources in his or her area of responsibility. Emphasis was given to engaging maximum participation by governmental and non-governmental conservation bodies and academic institutions in the region. In the event, information was gathered from many sources, including national environmental organizations, individuals, scientists, protected areas' staff, hunters, natural history museums, research institutions, universities, and cartographic centres.
- The analysis of published and unpublished material held by BirdLife International, OSME and

IWRB, including data from previous surveys such as OSME's Sites Register Scheme, and IWRB's database of winter waterfowl counts. Draft inventories for some countries were compiled by BirdLife International and were then circulated to experts for comments and updating of information.

Because of time constraints on the project and lack of financial resources, it was not possible to promote field surveys, although a complete review of the literature was possible for most countries, usually undertaken by the 'coordinators', for their particular countries or regions.

Further information on methods is given in the chapters on 'Site selection' (p. 20) and 'Data presentation' (p. 31).

UPDATING AND ADDING TO THE INVENTORY

This publication is intended to be an exhaustive inventory based on current knowledge. Inevitably there are sites which are probably of equal importance to some of those listed here which are missing because of a lack of sufficient information. BirdLife International and the relevant national organizations would be pleased to receive corrections or up-to-date information regarding the sites included in this inventory. Persons wishing to submit data for new sites are asked to complete the data-sheet which can be found at the back of this book. Data will be held in the World Bird Database of the BirdLife International partnership, and will be maintained and updated by national partners and globally as new information becomes available.

A Middle East Wetland Inventory is now under way, a joint venture of IUCN, WWF, the Ramsar Bureau, IWRB and BirdLife International. The wetland inventory is covering the same area as this study, and publication of the *Directory of Wetlands in the Middle East* is expected in mid-1995. It is anticipated that the Middle East Wetland Inventory will benefit greatly from the present study, which will provide a starting point from which a broader account of wetland attributes, functions and values can be developed.

REFERENCES

BIJLSMA, R. G. (1987) *Bottleneck areas for migratory birds in the Mediterranean region: an assessment of the problems and recommendations for action.* Cambridge, U.K.: International Council for Bird Preservation (Study Rep. 18).

CARP, E. (1980) *A directory of western Palaearctic wetlands.* Nairobi: United Nations Environment Programme/Gland, Switzerland: International Union for Conservation of Nature and Natural Resources.

COLLAR, N. J. (1985) OSME Sites Register Scheme. Progress Report no. 1. *Orn. Soc. Middle East Bull.* 14: 8–10.

COLLAR, N. J. (1986) OSME Sites Register Scheme. Progress Report no. 2. *Orn. Soc. Middle East Bull.* 16: 8–11.

EVANS, M. I. (1988) OSME Sites Register Scheme. Progress Report no. 3. *Orn. Soc. Middle East Bull.* 21: 12–14.

EVANS, M. I. (1992) OSME Sites Register Scheme. Progress Report. *Orn. Soc. Middle East Bull.* 29: 20.

GALLAGHER, M. D., SCOTT, D. A., ORMOND, R. F. G., CONNOR, R. J. AND JENNINGS, M. C. (1984) The distribution and conservation of seabirds breeding on the coast and islands of Iran and Arabia. Pp. 421–456 in J. P. Croxall, P. G. H. Evans and R. W. Schreiber, eds. *Status and conservation of the world's seabirds.* Cambridge, U.K.: International Council for Bird Preservation (Techn. Publ. 2).

GRIMMETT, R. F. A. AND JONES, T. A. (1989) *Important Bird Areas in Europe.* Cambridge, U.K.: International Council for Bird Preservation (Techn. Publ. 9).

IUCN (1976) *Promotion of the establishment of marine parks and reserves in the northern Indian Ocean including the Red Sea and Persian Gulf. Papers and proceedings of the regional meeting held at Tehran, Iran, 6 to 10 March 1975.* Morges, Switzerland: International Union for Conservation of Nature and Natural Resources.

LUTHER, H. AND RZÓSKA, J. (1971) *Project Aqua: a source book of inland waters proposed for conservation.* Oxford: Blackwell Scientific (International Biological Programme Handbook 21).

PERENNOU, C. AND MUNDKHUR, T. (1992) *Asian Waterfowl Census 1992.* Slimbridge, U.K.: International Waterfowl and Wetlands Research Bureau.

RAC/SPA (1987) *Directory of marine and coastal protected areas of the Mediterranean region.* Tunis: Regional Activity Centre for Specially Protected Areas/Gland, Switzerland: International Union for Conservation of Nature and Natural Resources.

ROSE, P. M. (1992) *Western Palearctic Waterfowl Census 1992.* Slimbridge, U.K.: International Waterfowl and Wetlands Research Bureau.

SAVAGE, C. D. W. (1968a) The wildfowl and wetland situation in Afghanistan. Pp. 119–122 in: *Proceedings of a technical meeting on wetland conservation, Ankara-Bursa-Istanbul, 9–16 October 1967.* Morges, Switzerland: International Union for Conservation of Nature and Natural Resources.

SAVAGE, C. D. W. (1968b) The wildfowl and wetland situation in Iraq. Pp. 128–133 in: *Proceedings of a technical meeting on wetland conservation, Ankara-Bursa-Istanbul, 9–16 October 1967.* Morges (Switzerland): International Union for Conservation of Nature and Natural Resources.

SAVAGE, C. D. W. (1968c) The wildfowl and wetland situation in the Levant. Pp. 134–138 in *Proceedings of a technical meeting on wetland conservation, Ankara-Bursa-Istanbul, 9–16 October 1967.* Morges, Switzerland: International Union for Conservation of Nature and Natural Resources.

SAVAGE, C. D. W. AND FIROUZ, E. (1968) The wildfowl and wetland situation in Iran. Pp. 115–119 in: *Proceedings of a technical meeting on wetland conservation, Ankara-Bursa-Istanbul, 9–16 October 1967*. Morges, Switzerland: International Union for Conservation of Nature and Natural Resources.

Summers, R. W., Underhill, L. G., Pearson, D. J. and Scott, D. A. (1987) Wader migration systems in southern and eastern Africa and western Asia. *Wader Study Group Bull.* 49/*IWRB Spec. Publ.* 7: 15–34.

WCMC (World Conservation Monitoring Centre) (1991) *Protected areas of the world*, 2: *Palaearctic*. Gland, Switzerland: International Union for Conservation of Nature and Natural Resources.

INTERNATIONAL MEASURES FOR SITE CONSERVATION

THE VARIOUS international and regional conventions and programmes represent a strong basis for international cooperation in the protection of natural resources in the Middle East. This section briefly describes those which are relevant to the protection of Important Bird Areas in the Middle East. The inventory of sites in this book should be viewed as a technical companion to such conventions and programmes, since a proper understanding of the location and importance of valuable sites is essential for their effective implementation.

INTERNATIONAL CONVENTIONS AND PROGRAMMES

Five international conventions (four global, one Mediterranean) adopted since 1975, and two international programmes, are particularly relevant to the conservation of sites.

Convention concerning the Protection of the World Cultural and Natural Heritage (World Heritage Convention)

This convention, generally referred to as the World Heritage Convention, came into force in December 1975, its objective being the protection of cultural and natural heritage of outstanding universal value. Its scope is limited in that it confers protection on a relatively small number of areas of outstanding universal value from the point of view of science, conservation or natural beauty. For the purposes of the Convention the following is considered as 'natural heritage' (Article 2):

- natural features consisting of physical and biological formations or groups of such formations, which are of outstanding universal value from the aesthetic or scientific point of view

and

- geological and physiographical formations and precisely delineated areas which constitute the habitat of threatened species of animals and plants of outstanding universal value from the point of view of science or conservation

and

- natural sites or precisely delineated areas of outstanding universal value from the point of view of science, conservation or natural beauty.

Article 4 of the Convention states that each Party recognizes its duty to ensure the identification, protection, conservation, presentation and transmission to future generations of the natural heritage situated on its territory, and requires that it does all it can do to further this end. Each Party identifies sites of natural heritage as described in Article 2 and is required, in so far as is possible, to:

> submit to the World Heritage Committee an inventory of property forming part of the cultural and natural heritage, situated in its territory and suitable for inclusion in the list (Article 11).

The 'list' is the World Heritage List which is managed by the World Heritage Committee (drawn from the State Parties), and an appropriate proposal from a Party is required before a site can be considered for selection. Parties to the Convention accept a legal duty to do all they can to protect sites which are on the list. Each party must contribute to a fund to assist Parties to discharge their obligations in respect of listed sites; contributions are set at 1% of contributions to the annual budget of UNESCO, currently totalling approximately US$2 million. The World Heritage Fund has been extremely successful, initiating a system whereby the world community acknowledged its duty to contribute financially to the conservation of biological diversity in developing countries. The World Heritage Committee's 'List of World Heritage in Danger' covers sites threatened by serious and specific dangers. By the end of 1992, there were 129 Parties to the Convention, making it the most widely applicable area-based conservation treaty in the world, and the List contained a total of

87 natural sites and 15 'mixed' cultural and natural sites. However no natural World Heritage Sites have been designated by the 11 Middle Eastern Contracting Parties (Table 1). There are clearly many sites in the Middle East, identified by this inventory, which potentially qualify for listing.

Convention on Wetlands of International Importance especially as Waterfowl Habitat (Ramsar Convention)

This convention was signed in Ramsar, Iran, on 2 February 1971 and came into force in December 1975. It was the first global treaty to concern itself exclusively with habitat conservation, although coverage is limited to wetlands, albeit broadly defined. The main undertakings accepted by the Contracting Parties are to:

- designate suitable wetlands within (their) territory for inclusion in a List of Wetlands of International Importance (Article 2,1)

and

- formulate and implement their planning so as to promote the conservation of the wetlands included in the List, and as far as possible, the wise use of wetlands in their territory (Article 3,1)

and

- promote the conservation of wetlands and waterfowl by establishing nature reserves on wetlands whether they are included in the list or not, and provide adequately for their wardening (Article 4,1).

There is no obligation on States to establish protected areas, but each Contracting Party must designate at least one site for inclusion in the List at the time it joins the Convention (Article 2,4).

As of January 1994, Iran and Jordan, the two Contracting Parties in the Middle East (Table 1), had 19 sites on the List covering 1,364,922 ha, all of which are ornithologically very important and are included in this inventory. In addition, Israel had signed the Convention subject to ratification. Of the five international conventions covered here, Ramsar is the second most widely applicable in terms of global geographical coverage, with 81 Contracting Parties and 645 sites worldwide, and it has had a very positive impact on wetland conservation in many states. The 'wise use' concept, which applies to all wetlands whether or not they are included in the List, is receiving increasing attention globally. In 1990, the Parties to the Ramsar Convention set up a Wetland Fund, to assist Parties financially to discharge their obligations to conserve Ramsar sites.

The 'Overview and recommendations' chapter contains a review of this site inventory with respect to the Ramsar Convention, highlighting those sites that qualify as candidate Ramsar sites in the Middle East (see pp. 35–36).

Convention on the Conservation of Migratory Species of Wild Animals (Bonn Convention)

This convention, generally known as the Bonn Convention, came into force in November 1983. Its fundamental objective is to protect migratory species (not only birds, but mammals, fish and invertebrates) in recognition of the fact that protection is needed

Table 1. Conventions relevant to the conservation of Important Bird Areas in the Middle East (as at December 1993).

					UNEP Regional Seas Programme		
	Wetlands (Ramsar 1971)	World Heritage (Paris 1972)	Migratory species (Bonn 1979)	Biodiversity (Rio de Janeiro 1992)	Mediterranean (Barcelona 1976)	The Gulf (Kuwait 1978)	Red Sea and Gulf of Aden (Jiddah 1982)
Afghanistan		CP		+			
Bahrain		CP		+		CP	
Iran	CP	CP		+		CP	
Iraq		CP				CP	
Israel	+		CP	+	CP*		
Jordan	CP	CP		CP			CP
Kuwait				+		CP	
Lebanon		CP		+	CP*		
Oman		CP		+		CP	
Qatar		CP		+		CP	
Saudi Arabia		CP	CP			CP	CP
Syria		CP			CP		
UAE				+		CP	
Yemen		CP		+			CP

CP Contracting Party (has ratified or acceded to the Convention)
\+ Signatory (has signed but not ratified the Convention)
* Has ratified the Protocol concerning Mediterranean Specially Protected Areas (1982)

throughout every part of their migratory range, and that this requires international cooperation and action in the form of international conservation agreements. If a Party to the Convention is a Range State of a migratory species listed in Appendix I or Appendix II it accepts an obligation to provide strict protection for species in Appendix I and to endeavour to conclude Agreements with other Range States for the conservation and management of species in Appendix II. Appendix I species are in danger of extinction throughout all or a major part of their range, and Appendix II species are those which would benefit from international cooperation in their conservation and management.

For Appendix I species, Parties that are Range States are obliged to endeavour, amongst other things, to

- 'conserve and, where feasible and appropriate, restore those habitats of the species which are of importance in removing the species from danger of extinction (Article III 4a)'

and with regard to the Agreements which Parties are obliged to sign for Appendix II species, each Agreement should, where appropriate and feasible, provide for the

- 'maintenance of a network of suitable habitats appropriately disposed in relation to the migration routes.'

As of January 1994, two countries in the Middle East were Contracting Parties to the Convention (Israel and Saudi Arabia) and there were 43 Contracting Parties and nine Signatories worldwide (Table 1). A number of globally threatened species occurring in significant numbers in the Middle East are on Appendix I and some of their Range States have ratified the Convention (e.g. *Geronticus eremita*, Saudi Arabia; *Larus leucophthalmus*, Saudi Arabia). To date, no Agreements between Range States have been concluded for bird species on Appendix II, although a draft African–Eurasian Migratory Waterbirds Agreement and a draft Agreement on *Chlamydotis undulata* (Asian populations) are both currently being developed. Important Bird Areas in the Middle East which support Appendix I species are listed in Appendix 3 of this book.

Convention on Biological Diversity (Biodiversity Convention)

This convention, generally known as the Biodiversity Convention, came into force in December 1993. Threats to biological diversity have increased almost everywhere in the world during recent decades, mainly as a result of the continuing destruction of natural habitats. Requirements for the conservation of biodiversity have therefore developed far beyond what was envisaged when the first conservation conventions were concluded. As part of a global approach to conservation, this Convention accordingly places far greater emphasis upon the conservation of ecosystems than upon the protection of species as such. In the Preamble, the Contracting Parties note that:

- 'the fundamental requirement for the conservation of biological diversity is the *in situ* conservation of ecosystems and natural habitats and the maintenance and recovery of viable populations of species in their natural surroundings ...'

Under Article 8 dealing with *in situ* conservation, Parties are required, as far as possible and as appropriate, to

- 'establish a system of protected areas or areas where special measures need to be taken to conserve biological diversity'

and

- 'develop, where necessary, guidelines for the selection, establishment and management of protected areas or areas where special measures need to be taken to conserve biological diversity'

and

- 'regulate or manage biological resources important for the conservation of biological diversity whether within or outside protected areas, with a view to ensuring their conservation and sustainable use'

and

- 'promote the protection of ecosystems, natural habitats and the maintenance of viable populations of species in natural surroundings'

and

- 'promote environmentally sound and sustainable development in areas adjacent to protected areas with a view to furthering protection of these areas'

and

- 'rehabilitate and restore degraded ecosystems and promote the recovery of threatened species, *inter alia*, through the development and implementation of plans or other management strategies'

and

- 'prevent the introduction of, control or eradicate those alien species which threaten ecosystems, habitats or species.'

The Convention contains no obligation for Parties to protect the areas which are most important for the conservation of biological diversity. Instead, Annex I to the Convention provides guidance for area selection in the form of an indicative list of components of biological diversity important for its conservation and sustainable use. However, the list is so broad that it may be difficult to use it in practice to establish priorities. The Parties are therefore free to protect whatever areas they choose, and the inventory published in this book is intended to contribute to that process.

There are no provisions for the establishment of a worldwide network of areas protected because of their importance for global biodiversity, or for the compilation of a list of areas protected in this way. However, these are matters which may be covered subsequently through the adoption of a Protocol or by decisions of the Conference of the Parties. The conservation of ecosystems is also promoted through general obligations for the identification and monitoring of important components of biological diversity (Article 7). Parties are required to identify processes and categories of activities which may have significant adverse impacts on the conservation and sustainable use of biological diversity. Environmental impact assessment obligations are set out in Article 14.

As of April 1994, at least 160 countries around the world had signed the Biodiversity Convention (including 10 Middle Eastern countries) and more than 50 countries had also ratified the Convention, including Jordan (see Table 1).

Convention for the Protection of the Mediterranean Sea against Pollution (Barcelona Convention)

In 1976, the governments of countries surrounding the Mediterranean Sea signed this Convention, generally referred to as the Barcelona Convention, which is part of the UNEP Regional Seas Programme (see below). One important Protocol associated with the Convention was adopted in 1982 and is entitled the Protocol concerning Mediterranean Specially Protected Areas. It was adopted to provide special protection to endangered Mediterranean species as well as to habitats considered vital for their conservation. Contracting Parties which have ratified this Protocol have agreed to:

- 'take all appropriate measures with a view to protecting those marine areas which are important for the safeguarding of the natural resources and natural sites of the Mediterranean Sea Area (Article 1)'

and

- 'establish protected areas and ... endeavour to undertake the action necessary in order to protect those areas and, as appropriate, restore them, as rapidly as possible.'

Such areas are to be established in order to safeguard in particular: (1) sites of biological and ecological value (the genetic diversity, as well as satisfactory population levels, of species, and their breeding grounds and habitats; representative types of ecosystems, as well as ecological processes); (2) sites of particular importance because of their scientific, aesthetic, historical, archaeological, cultural or educational interest (Article 3). The establishment of buffer zones is provided for. However the Protocol is not a binding obligation.

As of December 1993, there were three Contracting Parties in the Middle East (Israel, Lebanon and Syria) and the Protocol had been ratified by Israel and Lebanon, and signed by Syria. By December 1993, about 123 Mediterranean Specially Protected Areas had been designated and notified to the UNEP Regional Activity Centre for Specially Protected Areas (the secretariat for the Protocol, based in Tunis), including seven designated by Israel and one by Lebanon. The 'Overview and Recommendations' chapter contains a review of the site inventory with respect to this Protocol, identifying all sites that are candidate Specially Protected Areas (see p. 37).

UNESCO's Man and the Biosphere (MAB) Programme

This Programme of the United Nations Educational, Scientific and Cultural Organization) was launched in 1970 and aimed, amongst other things, to:
develop within the natural and social services a basis for the rational use and conservation of the resources of the biosphere.

The MAB Project 8 (one of 14 international themes or projects in the Programme) is 'the conservation of natural areas and the genetic material they contain'. The objective was to create a worldwide network of reserves (Biosphere Reserves), with each reserve qualifying under one or more of the following four categories.

- Representative examples of natural biomes.
- Unique communities or areas with unusual natural features of exceptional interest such as a population of a globally rare species.
- Examples of harmonious landscapes resulting from traditional patterns of land-use.
- Examples of modified or degraded ecosystems capable of being restored to more natural conditions.

Each Biosphere Reserve needs to be large enough to comprise an effective conservation unit. Unlike sites on the World Heritage List which must each be of exceptional value, Biosphere Reserves are selected because they are representative of different types of ecosystems. Their purpose is the conservation of these ecosystems and the species they contain, scientific research, monitoring, education and training. In addition, Biosphere Reserves must be integrated into their social, economic and cultural environment and for that purpose local populations should be involved as much as possible in their conservation and management. Biosphere Reserves must be zoned, with a core area devoted to strict protection and a buffer zone in which human activities may only be authorized to the extent that they are compatible with the conservation objectives of the area. Around the buffer zone, there must be a transition zone where specific cooperative links with the local populations should be developed and maintained. It follows that Biosphere Reserves are usually inhabited areas except for the core zone.

The Biosphere Reserve network is the only specific programme undertaken by an international organization for the establishment and conservation of protected areas which has a worldwide coverage. As there is no treaty or any legally binding obligations governing the network, designations of Biosphere Reserves are made on a purely voluntary basis. Proposed designations by individual States must, however, be approved by the MAB Coordination Council. Unsuitable areas may therefore be refused. However, there are no criteria that require some degree of legal protection to be accorded to an area before it can be listed, nor is there any legal obligation to protect an area once it has been listed. There is, though, a strong moral obligation to protect these areas, in view of the prestige of the network and its major scientific importance. In 1992, there were 313 Biosphere Reserves located in 76 countries. A number of countries in the Middle East are active in the MAB programme and a total of nine Biosphere Reserves (totalling 2,609,731 ha) have been designated in the region, all by Iran. As the network in the Middle East grows, it will make an increasingly important contribution to the conservation of ecosystems and improve the conservation standing of existing protected areas.

UNEP's Regional Seas Programme

The United Nations Environment Programme has established a marine conservation programme which currently covers 11 seas or coastal regions. The procedure in each case is for UNEP to prepare an Action Plan upon which a framework Convention is then based. A certain number of Protocols are then adopted to amplify each of the framework Convention's basic provisions.

These Regional Seas instruments are designed to achieve a global approach by the States bordering a given sea to its particular environmental problems. Pollution is usually given priority as the main problem, but most of the Regional Seas Conventions also emphasize the need to preserve natural habitats. The legal basis on which the Protocols to these Conventions were developed to deal with protected marine and coastal areas is to be found at article 194.5 of the United Nations Convention on the Law of the Sea of 1982 (still not in force), which creates a general obligation to protect

rare or fragile ecosystems as well as the habitat of depleted, threatened or endangered species and other forms of marine life.

The successful implementation of these conventions depends upon the cooperation amongst, and policing by, all the countries bordering the regional sea in question. Three framework Conventions have been developed in the Middle East, covering all of the seas in the region. The Mediterranean is covered by the Barcelona Convention (described above), and the Red Sea/Gulf of Aden and the Arabo-Persian Gulf regions also have their own conventions. The Barcelona Convention has an associated Protocol covering area-based conservation of natural resources, while the other two conventions do not. The latter two are briefly described below however.

Convention for Co-operation on the Protection of the Environment from Marine Pollution

The governments of Bahrain, Iran, Iraq, Kuwait, Oman, Qatar, Saudi Arabia and the United Arab Emirates adopted the Regional Convention for Co-operation on the Protection of the Marine Environment from Pollution, together with the Action Plan for the Protection and Development of the Marine Environment and the Coastal Areas, in Kuwait in 1978. The secretariat is provided by the Regional Organization for the Protection of the Marine Environment (ROPME) in Kuwait. ROPME has supported a series of ecological studies with IUCN.

Convention for the Conservation of the Red Sea and Gulf of Aden Environment

In 1982 the Regional Conference of Plenipotentiaries on the Conservation of the Marine Environment and Coastal Areas in the Red Sea and Gulf of Aden was convened in Jiddah at the invitation of the government of Saudi Arabia by the Arab League Educational, Cultural and Scientific Organization (ALECSO). The Conference adopted the Action Plan for the Conservation of the Marine Environment and Coastal Areas in the Red Sea and Gulf of Aden (Programme for the Environment of the Red Sea and Gulf of Aden, PERSGA), together with the Regional Convention for the Conservation of the Red Sea and Gulf of Aden Environment. The Convention incorporates five General Obligations, which do not include any specific statements concerning area-based conservation of natural resources, and no further Protocols concerned with site protection have since been agreed. In the Middle East, the Convention has been ratified by Jordan, Saudi Arabia, Palestine represented by the Palestine Liberation Organization, and Yemen.

REFERENCES

Boere, G. C. (1991) The Bonn Convention. Pp. 345–360 in T. Salathé, ed. *Conserving migratory birds*. Cambridge, U.K.: International Council for Bird Preservation (Techn. Publ. 12).

de Klemm, C. and Shine, C. (1993) *Biological diversity conservation and the law*. Gland, Switzerland: International Union for Conservation of Nature and Natural Resources.

SITE SELECTION

AN IMPORTANT BIRD AREA was defined in the following terms for project participants—for guidance only, in order that they might bear the definition in mind when determining the approximate area of interest of, or boundary for, a particular IBA where this had not previously been demarcated. As far as possible the site should:

- Exist as an actual or potential protected area, with or without buffer zones, or be an area which can be appropriately managed for wildlife conservation

and

- Provide all the requirements of the birds that it is important for, alone or with other sites, at the appropriate season.

Not all Important Bird Areas have met the second of these requirements (e.g. for many seabird breeding sites, the critical feeding areas in neighbouring seas have not yet been identified and thus cannot be defined and incorporated within the IBA). No limits were placed on the minimum or maximum size of sites chosen, other than those given above, and the size range of Important Bird Areas in the Middle East is consequently very large. The definition above is not applicable to the identification of 'bottleneck' sites where large numbers of migratory birds concentrate due to a site's geographical location or physical structure.

CRITERIA USED TO SELECT IMPORTANT BIRD AREAS

The following six categories of site were selected, using the criteria outlined below. The criteria were developed from those used in the *Important Bird Areas in Europe* project (Grimmett and Jones 1989), with help from the Project Steering Committee, Middle Eastern wildlife conservation organizations and individual experts. Any particular site has often met several different criteria.

CATEGORY 1: Sites supporting globally threatened species

Criterion:

- The site regularly holds the species.

Twenty-four species have been considered when applying the criterion (see List 1), based on their inclusion in the *1994 IUCN Red List of threatened animals* (Collar and Andrew 1988, Groombridge 1993). Subspecies have not been considered when applying the criterion. The decision to exclude subspecies from the third edition of the ICBP/IUCN Bird Red Data Book, explained at length by Collar and Stuart (1985), was taken on the grounds that, with so many threatened species still requiring conservation attention, subspecies had to take second place at a global level.

LIST 1 Species occurring in significant numbers in the Middle East and threatened with worldwide extinction according to IUCN criteria (Collar and Andrew 1988, Groombridge 1993).

Phalacrocorax pygmeus	Pygmy Cormorant
Pelecanus crispus [1,2]	Dalmatian Pelican
Geronticus eremita [1]	Northern Bald Ibis
Anser erythropus [2]	Lesser White-fronted Goose
Branta ruficollis [2]	Red-breasted Goose
Marmaronetta angustirostris [2]	Marbled Teal
Oxyura leucocephala [2]	White-headed Duck
Haliaeetus leucoryphus [2]	Pallas's Sea-eagle
Haliaeetus albicilla [1]	White-tailed Eagle
Aegypius monachus [2]	Cinereous Vulture
Aquila heliaca [2]	Imperial Eagle
Falco naumanni [2]	Lesser Kestrel
Crex crex	Corncrake
Grus leucogeranus [1]	Siberian White Crane
Tetrax tetrax	Little Bustard
Chlamydotis undulata [2]	Houbara Bustard
Otis tarda [2]	Great Bustard
Vanellus gregarius [2]	Sociable Plover
Numenius tenuirostris [1]	Slender-billed Curlew
Larus leucophthalmus [1]	White-eyed Gull
Larus audouinii [1]	Audouin's Gull
Saxicola macrorhyncha	Stoliczka's Bushchat
Turdus menachensis	Yemen Thrush
Cisticola haesitatus	Island Cisticola

[1] Species or population on Appendix I of the Bonn Convention
[2] Species or population on Appendix II of the Bonn Convention

For those globally threatened species which are widely dispersed at low density in the Middle East (e.g. wintering *Aegypius monachus*, migrating *Chlamydotis undulata*), it has usually only been possible to choose a selection of representative sites, after consideration of:

- the number of the species at the site;
- the density of the species at the site;
- the completeness/intactness of the site.

NB After the analysis for this book was finalized, a revision of the list of globally threatened bird species was completed (Collar *et al.* 1994). As a result, certain species in List 1 above are no longer considered to be globally threatened: *Phalacrocorax pygmeus*, *Haliaeetus albicilla*, *Aegypius monachus*, *Tetrax tetrax*, *Chlamydotis undulata* and *Larus audouinii*. This change will not result in the disqualification of any sites in the inventory, since all of the above species should still be treated as threatened on a regional, Middle Eastern scale (i.e. should be moved to List 3 of this book, see below), at least provisionally. In addition, the revision of Collar *et al.* (1994) leads to other birds (with significant populations in the Middle East) being added to the list of globally threatened species: *Aythya nyroca* (Ferruginous Duck), *Aquila clanga* (Greater Spotted Eagle), *Columba eversmanni* (Eastern Stock Dove), *Parisoma buryi* (Yemen Warbler), *Onychognathus frater* (Socotra Starling) and *Emberiza socotrana* (Socotra Bunting). Apart from *Aquila clanga*, all of these species were already considered to be regionally threatened (i.e. included in List 3, below) or are restricted wholly or largely to the Middle East (i.e. included in List 4, below), and thus have already been incorporated into the site-selection process.

CATEGORY 2: Sites where birds concentrate in important numbers, either when breeding, or on passage, or in winter

Criteria:

- The site holds an average of 1% or more of a seabird or waterfowl species' biogeographical, flyway or Middle Eastern population;

or

- The site holds an average of 20,000 or more waterfowl;

or

- The site is a migratory bottleneck where, on average, more than 5,000 storks or 3,000 raptors or 2,000 cranes pass during spring and/or autumn migration.

See Lists 2a and 2b for the 1% levels of population sizes of seabird and waterfowl species in the Middle East which were used in this study. These 1% figures have been developed in connection with the Ramsar Convention, and follow a draft document which was prepared for the Conference of the Contracting Parties of the Ramsar Convention at Kushiro (Japan) in June 1993 on behalf of IWRB, the Asian Wetland Bureau and Wetlands for the Americas (Rose and Scott 1993). The conference officially approved the figures, subject to further revision, and they will shortly be published in their revised state.

Two types of 1% population estimate are provided in the draft Ramsar document: specific, single-figure estimates for the better-studied species, and a range (maximum–minimum) estimate for those less well-known. The present study used the first type of figure where provided (List 2a), and for the minority of less well-known species, the minimum figure of the range provided was used (List 2b). No estimate at all was given for a few biogeographical populations of waterbirds occurring in the Middle East (e.g. *Numenius phaeopus*).

In the absence of any comprehensive source of breeding population data, 1% figures (in pairs) for breeding populations have been obtained (for both types of 1% figure) by dividing the non-breeding population estimates (described above) by three. For seabird species not included in Rose and Scott (1993), 1% figures were obtained from the literature, mainly Gallagher *et al.* (1984) and Cooper *et al.* (1984), for Red Sea/Arabo-Persian Gulf populations.

The numerical criteria for bottleneck sites cause the inclusion of most of the important sites in this category. Birds using these sites are particularly vulnerable because they concentrate in large numbers, and at some of these sites they are subject to human disturbance, unregulated exploitation or persecution.

CATEGORY 3: Sites for species which are threatened or declining throughout all or large parts of their range in the Middle East

Criterion:

- The site is one of the five most important for the species in the Middle Eastern country in question.

See List 3 for the relevant species.

The importance of a site was determined, where possible, after consideration of:

- the numbers of the species at the site;
- the density of the species at the site;
- the completeness/intactness of the site.

The list of species is provisional, and represents a first attempt at a general overview of the conservation status of birds in the Middle East that are not globally threatened. The list includes the following.

- Species/subspecies in danger of extinction or de-

LIST 2a Estimated 1% population sizes for seabird and waterfowl species that congregate in the Middle East.

	c.1% breeding (pairs)	c.1% non-breeding (birds)	Region applicable
Tachybaptus ruficollis	3,300	10,000	South-west Asia/Africa
Podiceps nigricollis	330	1,000	Europe
	85	250	Caspian Sea
Phaethon aethereus	15	40	Middle East
Sula dactylatra	80	240	Middle East
Sula leucogaster	55	160	Middle East
Phalacrocorax carbo	330	1,500	Black Sea/Mediterranean
	300	1,000	South-west/Southern Asia
Phalacrocorax nigrogularis	1,300	4,000	World
Anhinga rufa	1	1	South-west Asia
Pelecanus onocrotalus [1]	30	100	Caspian Sea
	270	800	Black Sea/Eastern Mediterranean
Egretta gularis	55	170	South-west/Southern Asia
Casmerodius albus	15	50	Eastern Mediterranean/Black Sea
Ardea goliath	1	1	Asia
Ciconia nigra [2]	—	200	Central/Eastern Europe
	30	100	South-west Asia
Ciconia ciconia [2]	—	4,000	Central/Eastern Europe
Plegadis falcinellus [2]	65	200	Africa/South-west Asia
Threskiornis aethiopicus	1	2	Iraq/Iran
Platalea leucorodia [2]	5	15	Red Sea (*P. l. archeri*)
	75	230	South-west/Southern Asia
Phoenicopterus ruber [2]	1,800	5,500	South-west/Southern Asia
Cygnus olor [2]	—	250	Caspian Sea
Cygnus columbianus [2]	—	3	Caspian Sea
Anser albifrons [2]	—	2,500	Black Sea
	—	150	Caspian Sea
Anser anser [2]	—	250	Black Sea
	—	800	Western Siberia/Caspian Sea
Tadorna ferruginea [2]	70	200	Black Sea
	100	300	South-west Asia
Tadorna tadorna [2]	—	600	Black Sea
	—	800	Caspian Sea
Anas penelope [2]	—	6,000	Black Sea/Mediterranean
	—	2,500	South-west Asia
Anas strepera [2]	—	750	Black Sea/Mediterranean
	—	1,300	South-west Asia
Anas crecca [2]	—	10,000	Black Sea/Mediterranean
	—	15,000	South-west Asia
Anas platyrhynchos [2]	—	20,000	Black Sea/Mediterranean
	—	8,000	South-west Asia
Anas acuta [2]	—	3,000	Black Sea/Mediterranean
	—	7,500	South-west Asia/Africa
Anas clypeata [2]	—	2,200	Black Sea/Eastern Mediterranean
	—	1,400	South-west Asia
Netta rufina [2]	—	2,000	South-west Asia
Aythya ferina [2]	—	12,500	Black Sea/Mediterranean
	—	3,500	South-west Asia
Aythya fuligula [2]	—	6,000	Black Sea/Mediterranean
	—	2,000	South-west Asia
Aythya marila [2]	—	500	Black Sea/Caspian Sea
Aythya nyroca [2]	3	10	South-west Asia
Clangula hyemalis [2]	—	100	Caspian Sea
Melanitta fusca [2]	—	100	Black Sea/Caspian Sea
Bucephala clangula [2]	—	200	Black Sea/Mediterranean
Mergellus albellus [2]	—	650	Black Sea/Mediterranean
	—	300	South-west Asia
Mergus serrator [2]	—	500	Black Sea/Mediterranean
	—	50	South-west Asia
Mergus merganser [2]	—	100	Black Sea/Mediterranean
	—	50	South-west Asia
Porphyrio porphyrio	30	100	South-west Asia
Fulica atra	—	20,000	Black Sea/Mediterranean
	—	20,000	South-west Asia
Grus grus [2]	—	100	Turkey (*G. g. lilfordi*)
	—	200	South-west Asia
Haematopus ostralegus	—	250	South-west/Southern Asia

cont.

LIST 2a *cont.*

	c.1% breeding (pairs)	c.1% non-breeding (birds)	Region applicable
Recurvirostra avosetta [2]	100	300	Black Sea/Eastern Mediterranean
Dromas ardeola	140	430	World
Glareola pratincola [2]	100	300	South-west Asia
Charadrius hiaticula [2]	—	2,000	*C. h. tundrae*
Charadrius mongolus [2]	—	250	South-west Asia/Africa (*C. m. pamirensis*)
Charadrius leschenaultii [2]	30	100	Western Asia (*C. l. columbus*)
	220	650	Central Asia (*C. l. crassirostris*)
Charadrius asiaticus [2]	—	200	World
Pluvialis squatarola [2]	—	440	South-west Asia/Africa
Vanellus indicus [2]	20	50	South-west Asia
Calidris tenuirostris [2]	—	15	South-west/Southern Asia
Calidris alba [2]	—	1,200	South-west Asia/Africa
Calidris minuta [2]	—	1,200	Western Asia/Africa
Calidris ferruginea [2]	—	3,100	Western Asia/Eastern Africa
Calidris alpina [2]	—	1,500	Western Asia/Eastern Africa (*C. a. alpina*)
Gallinago gallinago [2]		10,000	Western Siberia
Limosa lapponica [2]	—	1,000	South-west Asia/Africa
Tringa cinerea [2]	—	440	Western Asia/Africa
Arenaria interpres [2]	—	500	Western Asia/Eastern Africa
Larus hemprichii	130	400	World
Larus minutus	—	500	Black Sea/Western Asia
Larus ridibundus	—	4,500	Mediterranean
	—	2,500	Western Asia/Africa
Larus genei	800	2,400	Mediterranean
	500	1,500	South-west/Southern Asia
Larus canus	—	500	Black Sea/Caspian Sea
Larus fuscus	—	1,250	North-east Europe
Larus cachinnans	1,200	3,500	*L. a. michahellis*
Larus armenicus	100	300	World
Sterna nilotica	80	250	Black Sea/Eastern Mediterranean
Sterna bergii	130	400	South-west Asia/Africa
	7	20	Mediterranean
Sterna bengalensis	200	600	South-west/Southern Asia
Sterna sandvicensis	—	850	Black Sea/Mediterranean
	170	500	South-west/Southern Asia
Sterna dougallii	100	300	Eastern Africa/Madagascar
Sterna repressa	2,000	6,000	World
Sterna anaethetus	500	1,500	Red Sea/Arabo-Persian Gulf
Sterna albifrons	250	750	Black Sea/Eastern Mediterranean
	40	120	Caspian Sea
Sterna saundersi	100	300	World
Chlidonias hybridus	330	1,000	Eastern Mediterranean
Chlidonias leucopterus	830	2,500	Africa

[1] Species or population on Appendix I of the Bonn Convention [2] Species or population on Appendix II of the Bonn Convention

clining in numbers or reducing their range in the Middle East.

- Species which are threatened in an important or representative part of their range in the Middle East.
- Species with a restricted range within the Middle East which are vulnerable to particular changes in habitat.
- Species which are confined, when breeding, wintering, on passage, or when roosting, to particular habitats which are threatened throughout all or large parts of the Middle East.

The list includes those Middle Eastern species classified as 'near-threatened' by Collar and Andrew (1988), and consists mostly of non-passerines, often large (with associated low breeding productivity) and/or specialized to vulnerable/rare/dwindling habitats or unusual diets, as well as biogeographical 'relict' species with very small populations, some colonial-breeding waterbirds and seabirds, and species particularly subject to pressures from hunting, trapping or persecution. For some species, population declines have been documented in several different areas of the Middle East, and for other species there is much anecdotal, or unpublished, or published but unsynthesized, information that points towards declines. Species with a small breeding population in the Middle East but widely distributed elsewhere, and which are apparently not declining or not immediately threatened by habitat changes or human persecution, are not included.

NB Following the new listing of globally threatened bird species (Collar *et al.* 1994; see List 1, above),

LIST 2b Estimated absolute minimum 1% population sizes for seabird and waterfowl species that congregate in the Middle East.

	c.1% breeding (pairs) (minimum)	c.1% non-breeding (birds) (minimum)	Region applicable
Podiceps cristatus	—	100	Caspian Sea
Podiceps cristatus	—	100	Southern Asia
Podiceps grisegena	—	100	Caspian Sea
Podiceps auritus	—	100	Caspian Sea
Puffinus persicus	30	100	World
Pelecanus rufescens	330	1,000	World
Botaurus stellaris	30	100	South-west Asia
Ixobrychus minutus	80	250	South-west Asia
Nycticorax nycticorax	30	100	South-west Asia
Ardeola ralloides	30	100	South-west Asia/Africa
Ardeola grayii	330	1,000	South-west/Southern Asia
Bubulcus ibis	30	100	South-west Asia
Egretta garzetta	80	250	Eastern Europe/South-west Asia
Casmerodius albus	30	100	South-west Asia
Ardea cinerea	30	100	Western Asia
Ardea purpurea	330	1,000	Eastern Europe/South-west Asia
Ciconia abdimii	80	250	World
Ciconia ciconia [2]	80	250	Western Asia
Cygnus cygnus [2]	—	100	Western Asia
Anas querquedula [2]	—	1,000	Asia/Eastern Africa
Bucephala clangula [2]	—	100	South-west Asia/Caspian Sea
Rallus aquaticus	—	100	South-west/Southern Asia (*R. a. korejewi*)
Grus grus [2]	—	250	Eastern Europe (nominate)
Grus virgo [2]	—	250	South-west Asia/Eastern Africa
Himantopus himantopus [2]	80	250	Black Sea/Eastern Mediterranean
	30	100	South-west Asia
Glareola pratincola [2]	30	100	Eastern Mediterranean
Glareola nordmanni [2]	30	100	World
Charadrius alexandrinus [2]	80	250	Black Sea/Eastern Mediterranean
	80	250	Africa/South-west Asia
Eudromias morinellus [2]	—	100	Asia/Eastern Africa
Vanellus leucurus [2]	30	100	South-west Asia/Africa
Vanellus vanellus [2]	—	250	Western Asia/Eastern Africa
Calidris temminckii [2]	—	100	Western Asia/Africa
Limicola falcinellus [2]	—	100	Western Asia/Eastern Africa
Philomachus pugnax [2]	—	1,000	South-west Asia/Africa
Lymnocryptes minimus [2]	—	100	Western Siberia
Gallinago media [2]	—	100	Western Siberia
Limosa limosa [2]	—	250	South-west Asia/Africa
Numenius arquata [2]	—	250	Western Asia/Eastern Africa
Tringa erythropus [2]	—	100	Western Asia/Eastern Africa
Tringa totanus [2]	—	250	Western Asia/Eastern Africa
Tringa stagnatilis [2]	—	250	Western Asia/Eastern Africa
Tringa nebularia [2]	—	250	Western Asia/Eastern Africa
Tringa ochropus [2]	—	250	Western Asia/Eastern Africa
Tringa glareola [2]	—	1,000	Western Asia/Eastern Africa
Tringa hypoleucos [2]	—	1,000	Eastern Europe/Western Asia
Phalaropus lobatus [2]	—	1,000	Eurasia
Larus ichthyaetus	80	250	Western Asia/Eastern Africa
Larus cachinnans	30	250	Black Sea/Caspian Sea
Larus argentatus	30	100	*L. a. taimyrensis*
	30	100	*L. a. heuglini*
	30	100	*L. a. omissus*
Sterna nilotica	30	100	South-west Asia
Sterna caspia	30	100	South-west Asia/Africa
Sterna hirundo	80	250	Africa/Western Asia
Chlidonias hybridus	80	250	South-west /Southern Asia
Anous stolidus	100	300	Red Sea/Arabo-Persian Gulf

[1] Species or population on Appendix I of the Bonn Convention [2] Species or population on Appendix II of the Bonn Convention

which was completed after this site inventory had been finalized, certain species in List 3 are now considered to be threatened on a global scale (and should be moved to List 1 in this book, see above): *Aythya nyroca*, *Columba eversmanni* and *Parisoma buryi*. Also, *Prunella fagani* (Arabian Accentor) should be added to List 3 (being already on List 4, see below), due to its new classification as near-threatened (Collar *et al.* 1994).

LIST 3 Species which are threatened or declining throughout all or large parts of their range in the Middle East.

Bulweria fallax	Jouanin's Petrel
Phalacrocorax nigrogularis	Socotra Cormorant
Anhinga rufa	African Darter
Botaurus stellaris	Great Bittern
Ardea goliath	Goliath Heron
Ciconia ciconia [2]	White Stork
Threskiornis aethiopicus	Sacred Ibis
Anser indicus [2]	Bar-headed Goose
Aythya nyroca [2]	Ferruginous Duck
Pernis apivorus [2]	European Honey Buzzard
Elanus caeruleus	Black-winged Kite
Gypaetus barbatus	Lammergeier
Neophron percnopterus [2]	Egyptian Vulture
Gyps fulvus [2]	Griffon Vulture
Torgos tracheliotus	Lappet-faced Vulture
Terathopius ecaudatus	Bateleur
Micronisus gabar	Gabar Goshawk
Accipiter brevipes [2]	Levant Sparrowhawk
Aquila pomarina [2]	Lesser Spotted Eagle
Falco concolor [2]	Sooty Falcon
Falco biarmicus [2]	Lanner
Falco cherrug [2]	Saker
Tetrao mlokosiewiczi	Caucasian Black Grouse
Francolinus francolinus	Black Francolin
Phasianus colchicus	Common Pheasant
Grus virgo [2]	Demoiselle Crane
Ardeotis arabs	Arabian Bustard
Gallinago media [2]	Great Snipe
Sterna dougallii	Roseate Tern
Columba eversmanni	Eastern Stock Dove
Ketupa zeylonensis	Brown Fish Owl
Caprimulgus poliocephalus	Mountain Nightjar
Todirhamphus chloris	Collared Kingfisher
Dendrocopos dorae	Arabian Woodpecker
Parisoma buryi	Yemen Warbler
Carpodacus synoicus	Sinai Rosefinch

[1] Species or population on Appendix I of the Bonn Convention
[2] Species or population on Appendix II of the Bonn Convention

CATEGORY 4: Sites for species which have relatively small total world ranges with important populations in the Middle East

Criterion:

- The site is one of the five most important for the species in the Middle Eastern country in question.

Sixty-two species have been considered when applying the criterion (see List 4). Some of these species are globally threatened, or threatened or declining within the Middle East (see Lists 1 and 3 respectively). The Middle East has a major responsibility for the conservation of these species.

The importance of a site was determined, where possible, after consideration of:

- the numbers of the species at the site;
- the density of the species at the site;
- the completeness/intactness of the site.

Some of the species in List 4 (e.g. *Ammoperdix heyi*, *Pycnonotus xanthopygos* and *Sylvia minula*) are, in parts of their range, numerous and are unlikely to be

LIST 4 Species which have relatively small total world ranges with important populations in the Middle East.

Bulweria fallax	Jouanin's Petrel
Puffinus persicus	Persian Shearwater
Phalacrocorax nigrogularis	Socotra Cormorant
Tetraogallus caspius	Caspian Snowcock
Alectoris melanocephala	Arabian Partridge
Alectoris philbyi	Philby's Partridge
Ammoperdix griseogularis	See-see Partridge
Ammoperdix heyi	Sand Partridge
Dromas ardeola	Crab Plover
Burhinus recurvirostris	Great Thick-knee
Glareola nordmanni [2]	Black-winged Pratincole
Larus leucophthalmus [1]	White-eyed Gull
Larus hemprichii	Sooty Gull
Sterna repressa	White-cheeked Tern
Sterna saundersi	Saunders' Little Tern
Otus brucei	Striated Scops Owl
Strix butleri	Hume's Tawny Owl
Apus berliozi	Forbes-Watson's Swift
Dendrocopos assimilis	Sind Pied Woodpecker
Dendrocopos dorae	Arabian Woodpecker
Pycnonotus xanthopygos	Yellow-vented Bulbul
Hypocolius ampelinus	Grey Hypocolius
Prunella ocularis	Radde's Accentor
Prunella fagani	Arabian Accentor
Irania gutturalis	White-throated Robin
Oenanthe finschii	Finsch's Wheatear
Oenanthe xanthoprymna	Red-tailed Wheatear
Oenanthe picata	Eastern Pied Wheatear
Oenanthe lugentoides	South Arabian Wheatear
Oenanthe monacha	Hooded Wheatear
Oenanthe alboniger	Hume's Wheatear
Turdus menachensis	Yemen Thrush
Parisoma buryi	Yemen Warbler
Cisticola haesitatus	Island Cisticola
Cisticola incanus	Socotra Cisticola
Acrocephalus griseldis	Basrah Reed Warbler
Hippolais languida	Upcher's Warbler
Sylvia mystacea	Ménétries' Warbler
Sylvia leucomelaena	Arabian Warbler
Sylvia minula	Desert Lesser Whitethroat
Sylvia althaea	Hume's Lesser Whitethroat
Phylloscopus neglectus	Plain Leaf Warbler
Turdoides altirostris	Iraq Babbler
Turdoides squamiceps	Arabian Babbler
Nectarinia balfouri	Socotra Sunbird
Podoces pleskei	Pleske's Ground Jay
Onychognathus tristramii	Tristram's Grackle
Onychognathus frater	Socotra Starling
Passer moabiticus	Dead Sea Sparrow
Passer euchlorus	Arabian Golden Sparrow
Passer insularis	Socotra Sparrow
Carpospiza brachydactyla	Pale Rock Sparrow
Montifringilla theresae	Afghan Snowfinch
Estrilda rufibarba	Arabian Waxbill
Serinus syriacus [1]	Syrian Serin
Serinus rothschildi	Arabian Serin
Serinus menachensis	Yemen Serin
Rhynchostruthus socotranus	Golden-winged Grosbeak
Carduelis yemenensis	Yemen Linnet
Rhodopechys sanguinea	Crimson-winged Finch
Emberiza cineracea	Cinereous Bunting
Emberiza socotrana	Socotra Bunting

[1] Species or population on Appendix I of the Bonn Convention
[2] Species or population on Appendix II of the Bonn Convention

threatened, and in these regions to attempt the selection of important sites for these species would be unrealistic and also of limited value. This has been taken into account in the site-selection process (see the 'Comments on the inventory' section in the relevant national chapters for lists of such 'common' species).

This list was compiled by selecting species with c.50% or greater of their breeding or wintering range within the Middle East as defined here, after reference to maps and descriptions of ranges and abundance in Hüe and Etchécopar (1970), Ali and Ripley (1971–1983), Cramp *et al.* (1977–1993), Harrison (1982) and Hollom *et al.* (1988).

In addition, a number of species have a significant proportion of their world population (conservatively estimated to be less than 50%, but sometimes a borderline case) breeding in, wintering in or migrating through the Middle East as defined in this study, including *Marmaronetta angustirostris* (included in List 1 of this book), *Circus macrourus* (Pallid Harrier), *Accipiter brevipes* (List 3), *Falco concolor* (List 3), *Tetrao mlokosiewiczi* (List 3), *Glareola nordmanni* (List 3), *Charadrius caspius* (Caspian Plover), *Vanellus gregarius* (List 1), *V. leucurus* (White-tailed Plover), *Limicola falcinellus* (Broad-billed Sandpiper), *Larus ichthyaetus* (Great Black-headed Gull), *Columba eversmanni* (List 3), *Caprimulgus mahrattensis* (Sykes's Nightjar), *Dendrocopos syriacus* (Syrian Woodpecker), *Pycnonotus leucotis* (White-eared Bulbul), *Hippolais olivetorum* (Olive-tree Warbler), *H. rama* (Sykes's Warbler), *Sylvia rueppelli* (Rüppell's Warbler), *Sitta tephronota* (Eastern Rock Nuthatch), *S. neumayer* (Western Rock Nuthatch), *Nectarinia habessinica* (Shining Sunbird), *N. osea* (Palestine Sunbird), *Lanius nubicus* (Masked Shrike), *Petronia xanthocollis* (Yellow-throated Sparrow) and *Emberiza caesia* (Cretzschmar's Bunting). An attempt was made to include details in the national inventories of the status of these species at sites where they occurred.

CATEGORY 5: Sites for representative, rare, threatened or unique habitats possessing characteristic associated bird communities

Criteria:

- The site is a particularly good representative example of a natural or near-natural habitat with a characteristic bird community, in the appropriate biogeographical region; or
- The site is an example of a habitat (with a characteristic bird community, in the appropriate biogeographical region) which is rare, and/or unusual, and/or vulnerable to detrimental change.

CATEGORY 6: Sites important for bird conservation because of their value for education, research or tourism

Criteria:

- The site is a centre for education/research/tourism which generates benefits for bird conservation; or
- The site has excellent potential to become a centre for education/research/tourism which would benefit bird conservation.

In addition, if contributors felt that a site was important for bird conservation but did not qualify under the above criteria, they were encouraged to complete a data-sheet on the site, stating the reasons why the site was felt to be important. All the values of these proposed Important Bird Areas were considered, and for those sites included in the national inventories, the reasons are described in the section 'Comments on the inventory' at the beginning of the site inventory for each country.

COMPARISON WITH PREVIOUS STUDIES ON IMPORTANT BIRD AREAS

Readers familiar with *Important Bird Areas in Europe* (Grimmett and Jones 1989) will note slight differences in the approach to site selection. In the 'Definition of an IBA', an IBA has not been defined as 'different in character or habitat or ornithological importance from the surrounding land', because in large parts of the Middle East there are extensive tracts of homogeneous habitats (of nature conservation importance) such as steppe and desert where only the characteristics listed in the present definition could apply. Two extra categories of site have been chosen, in addition to the single-species-oriented categories, in order to give some emphasis to sites holding important assemblages of bird species, and to sites which are indirectly important for the conservation of bird populations. No sub-sites have been identified, in order to streamline data collection and presentation. For Category 2 sites, the migratory 'bottleneck' criterion was expanded to include cranes (Gruidae) as well.

CONFIDENTIALITY

Some sites which hold species vulnerable to egg-collection or hunting are included in the inventory. Such sensitive data have not been disclosed without evaluation of the factors affecting each site or species. As a result, confidentiality has been sacrificed because threats such as habitat loss are considered to exceed the risks involved in publishing site details.

REFERENCES

ALI, S. AND RIPLEY, S. D. (1971–1983) *Handbook of the birds of India and Pakistan*, 1–4 (second edition), 5–10 (first edition). Oxford: Oxford University Press.

COLLAR, N. J. AND ANDREW, P. (1988) *Birds to watch: the ICBP world checklist of threatened birds.* Cambridge, U.K.: International Council for Bird Preservation (Techn. Publ. 8).

COLLAR, N. J., CROSBY, M. J. AND STATTERSFIELD, A. J. (1994) *Birds to watch 2: the world list of threatened birds.* Cambridge, U.K.: BirdLife International (BirdLife Conservation Series no. 4).

COLLAR, N. J. AND STUART, S. N. (1985) *Threatened birds of Africa and related islands: the ICBP/IUCN Red Data Book, part 1.* Third edition. Cambridge, U.K.: International Council for Bird Preservation.

COOPER, J., WILLIAMS, A. J. AND BRITTON, P. L. (1984) Distribution, population sizes and conservation of breeding seabirds in the Afrotropical region. Pp. 403–419 in J. P. Croxall, P. G. H. Evans and R. W. Schreiber, eds. *Status and conservation of the world's seabirds.* Cambridge, U.K.: International Council for Bird Preservation (Techn. Publ. 2).

CRAMP, S. AND SIMMONS, K. E. L., EDS. (1977) *The birds of the western Palearctic*, 1. Oxford: Oxford University Press.

CRAMP, S. AND SIMMONS, K. E. L., EDS. (1980) *The birds of the western Palearctic*, 2. Oxford: Oxford University Press.

CRAMP, S. AND SIMMONS, K. E. L., EDS. (1983) *The birds of the western Palearctic*, 3. Oxford: Oxford University Press.

CRAMP, S., ED. (1985) *The birds of the western Palearctic*, 4. Oxford: Oxford University Press.

CRAMP, S., ED. (1988) *The birds of the western Palearctic*, 5. Oxford: Oxford University Press.

CRAMP, S., ED. (1992) *The birds of the western Palearctic*, 6. Oxford: Oxford University Press.

CRAMP, S. AND PERRINS, C. M., EDS. (1993) *The birds of the western Palearctic*, 7. Oxford: Oxford University Press.

GALLAGHER, M. D., SCOTT, D. A., ORMOND, R. F. G., CONNOR, R. J. AND JENNINGS, M. C. (1984) The distribution and conservation of seabirds breeding on the coast and islands of Iran and Arabia. Pp. 421–456 in J. P. Croxall, P. G. H. Evans and R. W. Schreiber, eds. *Status and conservation of the world's seabirds.* Cambridge, U.K.: International Council for Bird Preservation (Techn. Publ. 2).

GRIMMETT, R. F. A. AND JONES, T. A. (1989) *Important Bird Areas in Europe.* Cambridge, U.K.: International Council for Bird Preservation (Techn. Publ. 9).

GROOMBRIDGE, B., ED. (1993) *1994 IUCN Red List of threatened animals.* Gland, Switzerland: International Union for Conservation of Nature and Natural Resources.

HARRISON, C. (1982) *An atlas of the birds of the western Palaearctic.* London: Collins.

HOLLOM, P. A. D., PORTER, R. F., CHRISTENSEN, S. AND WILLIS, I. (1988) *Birds of the Middle East and North Africa: a companion guide.* Calton, U.K.: T. and A. D. Poyser.

HÜE, F. AND ETCHÉCOPAR, R. D. (1970) *Les oiseaux du proche et du moyen orient.* Paris: N. Boubée and Cie.

ROSE, P. M. AND SCOTT, D. A. (1993) Waterbirds as indicators of wetlands of international importance: an application of the 1% criterion. Draft report presented at Fifth Conference of the Contracting Parties to the Ramsar Convention, 9–16 June 1993, Kushiro, Japan. Slimbridge, U.K.: International Waterfowl and Wetlands Research Bureau.

DATA PRESENTATION

THE NATIONAL INVENTORIES, which make up the major part of this book, each consist of a short introduction to bird conservation in the country concerned, a country map showing the location of the Important Bird Areas, and a series of detailed site accounts (site inventory).

INTRODUCTION

The text proceeds under the following headings.

General information

The introduction to the site inventory starts with a brief overview of the country, covering location, human population, topography, main vegetation and land-use.

Ornithological importance

This provides a brief overview of bird habitats and populations in a Middle Eastern context, and covers breeding species and the importance of the site during migration periods and in winter.

Conservation infrastructure and protected-area system

Covers the protected areas referred to in the inventory (with, where known, a brief explanation of legal protection provided, as well as an indication of the main authority responsible for nature conservation).

International measures relevant to the conservation of sites

Information is given regarding the main international conventions which have relevance to site conservation (Ramsar, World Heritage, Biodiversity, Bonn and Barcelona), whether or not sites have been designated according to UNESCO's Man and the Biosphere Programme; also an indication of involvement in the UNEP Regional Seas Programme.

Overview of the inventory

This provides an overview of the sites included in the inventory, and the extent to which they are protected, unprotected or experiencing changes or problems. If certain types of species or important bird habitats have not been adequately covered, this is also discussed.

Acknowledgements

Mention is made of all persons and organizations known to have contributed data.

The following references have been widely used in preparing the introductions to the inventories.

ABOU JA'FER, M. (1984) [*National parks and national reserves in the Arab countries.*] Tunis: Arab League Educational, Cultural and Scientific Organization. (English translation from Arabic by M. Geha.)

BEAUMONT, P., BLAKE, G. H. AND WAGSTAFF, J. M. (1976) *The Middle East: a geographical study*. London: Wiley.

CARP, E. (1980) *A directory of western Palaearctic wetlands.* Nairobi: United Nations Environment Programme/Gland, Switzerland: International Union for the Conservation of Nature and Natural Resources.

IUCN (1986) *Plants in danger: what do we know?* Gland, Switzerland: International Union for the Conservation of Nature and Natural Resources.

KETENE, M. S. (1991) *Training and manpower requirements for wildlife and protected areas in the Arab world.* Rome: UN Food and Agriculture Organization.

THE TIMES ATLAS OF THE WORLD: COMPREHENSIVE EDITION. Sixth edition. (1980). London: Times Books.

WCMC (WORLD CONSERVATION MONITORING CENTRE) (1991) *Protected areas of the world*, 2: *Palaearctic*. Gland, Switzerland: International Union for the Conservation of Nature and Natural Resources.

UNEP/IUCN (1988) *Coral reefs of the world*, 2: *Indian Ocean, Red Sea and Gulf.* Gland, Switzerland: International Union for the Conservation of Nature and Natural Resources/Nairobi: United Nations Environment Programme (Regional Seas Directories and Bibliographies).

SITE INVENTORY

The site inventory for each country has the following components.

Table of sites (with summary of criteria used in selection)

Includes the site number, the site name and the name of the administrative region of the country in which the site lies. Columns numbered 1 to 6 refer to the different categories of site selected in this study, and the • in these columns indicates where sites have met the relevant criteria for inclusion in the inventory. The • in column 0 (for some countries only) indicates that the site has been selected for other reasons, and the reasons for inclusion are noted in the section 'Comments on the inventory'. A summary of the criteria used to select the six different categories of site accompanies each table (see 'Site selection', p. 20, for details).

It must be stressed that many of the sites in this book are important for reasons additional to the justification given in the tables of sites, and if further data were available some sites would certainly qualify by meeting other criteria.

Site accounts

Following the table of sites, an account (effectively a summary of the data held on file at the BirdLife International Secretariat) is given for each site. For a large proportion of the sites, BirdLife International has more data than that published, which sometimes includes a map of the site showing at least its approximate boundaries. Each site account is presented in a standard format, described below.

Site name

This has been transliterated from the national (or regional) language into Latin script, and is generally the most widely used name. For some countries the contributors have chosen to give the name of the site in English only. For some sites, an alternative site name(s) is also given, below. A glossary is provided, giving English translations of commonly used geographical terms (e.g. wadi, jabal, etc.) as well as the meanings of any acronyms used. For most countries, the site name is followed by the name of the relevant administrative or geographical region(s) of the country in parentheses.

Coordinates

These are the geographical coordinates (latitude and longitude, Greenwich) of the approximate centre of the site, expressed in degrees and minutes. If the site is large, the coordinates of the site's boundary (north-south and east-west spans) are sometimes also given.

Area

The area of the site in hectares (100 ha = 1 km^2), usually taken from returned data-sheets. Many of the areas given are estimates because the boundaries of the site have not been defined, and are usually rounded to the nearest 100 ha, 1,000 ha or even 10,000 ha. For the same reasons, no area is given for some sites.

International protection status

This refers to the site's designation (entirely or partly) either as a Ramsar Site (Ramsar Convention), natural World Heritage Site (World Heritage Convention), Biosphere Reserve (UNESCO's Man and the Biosphere Programme) or Mediterranean Specially Protected Area (Barcelona Convention's Protocol concerning Mediterranean Specially Protected Areas), as at December 1993. Where no area (ha) is given alongside the designation, the protection status, as far as is known, applies to the whole site (but see 'Comments on the inventory' for some countries).

National protection status

This refers to the site's legal protection status at a national level. For most countries, only the English translation of the protected-area category is given, and, where possible, an explanation of the protection afforded is given in the introduction to the inventory. Some sites are covered by two or more types of protected area and often it has not been possible to determine whether they overlap or are complementary. Where no area (ha) is given alongside the designation, the protection status, as far as is known, applies to the whole site (but see the 'Comments on the inventory' for some countries).

Site description

This covers three principal aspects: description of location and of main habitats, and information on main land-use(s) and management. The site descriptions are generally those provided in returned data-sheets, although some incorporate comments from reviewers.

Birds

A summary of the ornithological importance of each site is provided. Information on key species is highlighted in tinted boxes, covering globally threatened species, species occurring in internationally important numbers as defined by the criteria, species which are threatened throughout all or major parts of their Middle Eastern range, and species with ranges wholly or largely restricted to the Middle East. The reader should assume that a variety of other species (some of interest in a Middle Eastern context) also occur at most sites, at some in large numbers. The data were, for most countries, compiled in 1992 and 1993.

English names of birds mentioned in the text are given in Appendix 1 (p. 392). The scientific nomenclature (full species only) largely follows Monroe and Sibley (1993) (see p.392). The order of species follows Hollom *et al.* (1988).

In the case of most non-waterfowl species, the total numbers occurring at the site are not known; hence the repeated use of terms such as 'common', 'fairly common' and 'scarce'. Occasionally a maximum count is also given, representing the maximum number of individuals seen on any one day, but this is given as an indication of abundance only, and should not be taken to imply a population level.

Data for breeding species are usually given as the number of 'pairs'. The great majority of bird species form pairs when breeding, but a few Middle Eastern species are polygamous (e.g. *Circus aeruginosus*) or form no bond (e.g. *Chlamydotis undulata*) and the use of the word 'pair' should be interpreted with caution with these species. The terms 'resident' and 'summer visitor' are used to mean breeding resident and breeding summer visitor, with breeding either proven or assumed. If breeding is in doubt, this is stated.

Data for wintering species are either expressed as the maximum count recorded on a single day (or cumulatively over a few consecutive days in the case of systematic surveys of very large sites), or as an average or a range of this over a number of years (generally the last 3–5 years for which a series was available). In order to standardize data and allow its comparability between sites, data for January are quoted wherever possible, this being the month when wintering populations at sites are most stable and least likely to perform confusing movements between IBAs. The month of the count is only stated for counts outside January. As far as is known the data refer to the number of the species occurring at any one time.

An attempt has been made to standardize data for species occurring at sites on migration (spring and/or autumn passage). For most countries the information is given as the maximum count recorded on a single day, or an average of this over a number of years, but for some species (generally migratory raptors, storks and other waterbirds that concentrate in 'bottlenecks') in some countries the figure given is the total number occurring during a season. Where necessary, an explanation regarding counts of migrating birds is given in the section 'Comments on the inventory' preceding the site inventories.

The data are provided in order to give a general impression of the importance of a site, and to provide a basis for comparison between sites (both within and between countries). It has been impossible to be more consistent given that the project did not have the time or financial resources to promote field surveys and that it has been necessary to rely on data from many different sources (with quite different approaches to data-gathering, analysis and storage amongst individuals, organizations and countries).

Other threatened/endemic wildlife

Other important animal and plant species occurring at the site are also mentioned (where known to BirdLife International), of the following three types: (1) globally threatened species according to the *1994 IUCN Red List of threatened animals* (Groombridge 1993); their threat status is indicated according to the standard IUCN abbreviations: E = Endangered, V = Vulnerable, I = Indeterminate, K = Insufficiently known; (2) narrowly endemic species; (3) 'rare' species (in the sense of species known from few records and/or with highly fragmented ranges and/or low populations, but not considered globally threatened). English names of mammals mentioned in the text are given in Appendix 2.

Conservation issues

A summary of the conservation measures already taken, the main problems, changes or threats, and the conservation measures that have been proposed.

Further reading

In a work of this scale and scope, it has proved impossible to provide references for all of the information presented; however, the most important site-specific references have been listed in abbreviated form at the end of each site account.

Main references

A full list of the main references used, and all of those cited, is provided at the end of each national inventory.

REFERENCES

CARP, E. (1980) *A directory of western Palaearctic wetlands*. UNEP and IUCN, Nairobi and Gland.

CRAMP, S. AND SIMMONS, K. E. L., EDS. (1983) *The birds of the western Palaearctic*, 3. Oxford University Press, Oxford.

GRIMMETT, R. F. A. AND JONES, T. A. (1989) *Important Bird Areas in Europe*. Cambridge, U.K.: International Council for Bird Preservation (Techn. Publ. 9).

GROOMBRIDGE, B., ED. (1993) *1994 IUCN Red List of threatened animals*. Gland, Switzerland: International Union for the Conservation of Nature and Natural Resources.

HOLLOM, P. A. D., PORTER, R. F., CHRISTENSEN, S. AND WILLIS, I. (1988) *Birds of the Middle East and North Africa: a companion guide*. Calton, U.K.: T. and A. D. Poyser.

MONROE, B. L. AND SIBLEY, C. G. (1993) *A world checklist of birds*. New Haven: Yale University Press.

OVERVIEW AND RECOMMENDATIONS

A TOTAL of 391 sites have been identified as Important Bird Areas (IBAs) in the Middle East (Figure 1), in all covering more than 300,000 km^2 or about 5% of the land area of the Middle East. The percentage of each country covered by IBAs varies widely (Figure 2).

The sites were carefully selected according to criteria which confirmed that they held regionally or globally important populations of birds. Figure 3 shows that the majority of sites are important for globally or regionally threatened bird species, and for 'endemic' birds—those species which are confined wholly or largely to the Middle East and for which the Middle East has a special responsibility. A large number of sites also support 1% or more of the population of individual waterbird or seabird species.

Seven main habitat-types can be distinguished in the Middle East: woodland, bushland, grassland, agricultural, desert, wetland and marine. IBAs have been identified in all of these ecosystems, in varying numbers (Figure 4). Wetlands dominate the inventory, comprising half of all IBAs, and one third of wetland sites are coastal, thus featuring also in the

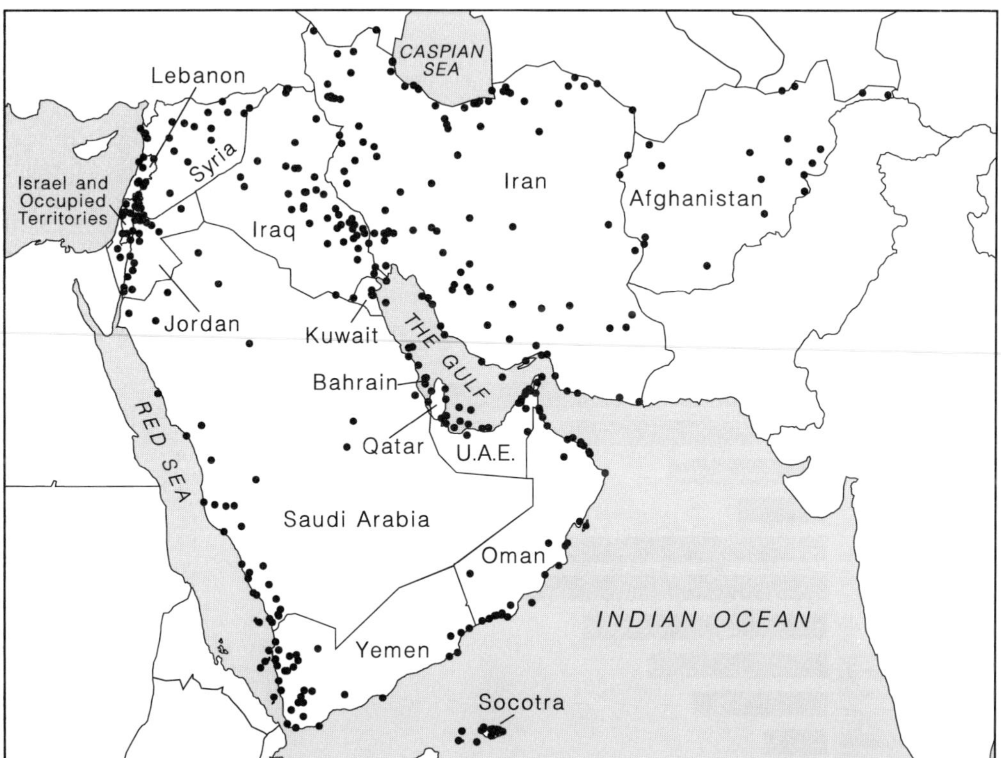

Figure 1. Distribution of Important Bird Areas in the Middle East.

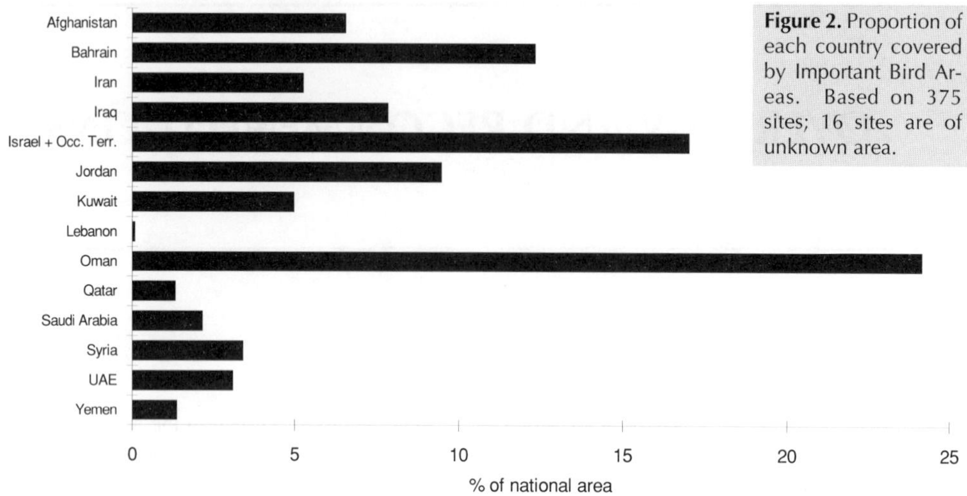

Figure 2. Proportion of each country covered by Important Bird Areas. Based on 375 sites; 16 sites are of unknown area.

marine category. Other habitat-types are represented by lower, but roughly similar, numbers of sites (about 15–25% of the total for each). The large number of wetlands selected as IBAs reflects their great importance to birds and other wildlife in a region where water resources are usually scarce. It is also relatively easy to identify and define wetlands compared to more homogeneous and extensive habitats.

About a quarter of the sites have some form of legal protection of their biodiversity, representing more than a third of the total area covered by IBAs, where known (Figure 5). Thus the majority of all IBAs in the Middle East are unprotected by law. Legal measures do not always guarantee protection on the ground, but they do demonstrate, to all branches of government and to all sectors of society, the official recognition of the importance of a site, so that severe changes or problems can be avoided in advance if possible.

RECOMMENDATION More official recognition of these sites at local, national and regional levels is required, for example through designation under international conventions, through national legal protection measures or through other forms of zonation, such as incorporation in national and local development plans.

About two-thirds of IBAs in the Middle East are not immediately threatened, or are under a low degree of threat of destruction or degradation of their habitats or their value for birds (Figure 6). However, this still means that over a quarter of the most important sites for birds in the Middle East are under a moderate to high degree of threat of immediate destruction, or are facing an unknown level of threat.

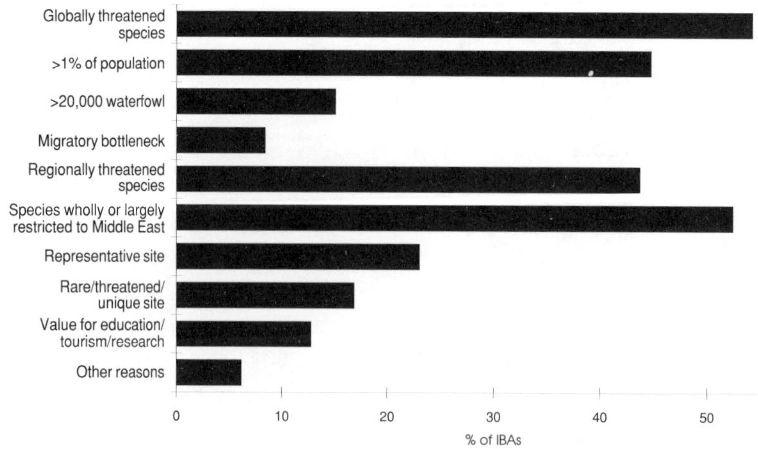

Figure 3. Reasons for choosing Important Bird Areas. The criteria for site selection are explained in more detail in the 'Site selection' chapter (see p. 20).

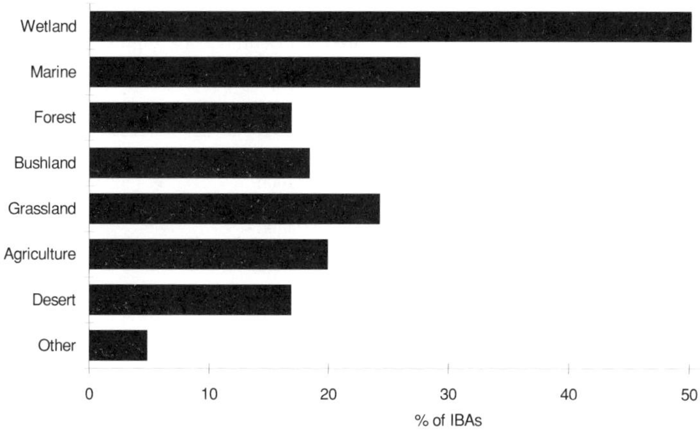

Figure 4. Main habitats of the Important Bird Areas. Note that these totals are not additive: a particular site (especially a large one) can have more than one main habitat represented.

RECOMMENDATION National and local agencies should pay particular attention to the most threatened sites in their country, as these are where the loss of biodiversity is most imminent. In addition, gaps in knowledge of site status should be filled, preferably through carrying out national inventories of Important Bird Areas, improving and expanding upon the versions in this book where necessary.

The IBAs in most urgent need of attention are those whose important habitats or bird populations are under a high degree of threat of destruction or elimination, and where most if not all of the habitat(s) or population(s) are likely to be irreversibly lost unless immediate action is taken. According to the information gathered in this inventory, there are at least 31 such sites in the Middle East (see Table 1). The majority are wetlands or forests which are in the process of being rapidly destroyed or grossly modi-

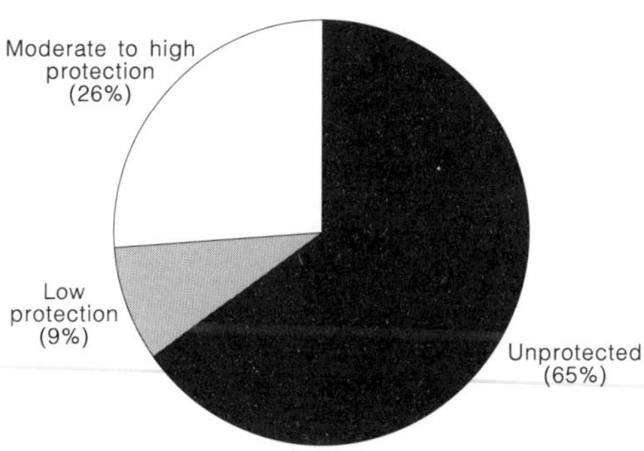

Figure 5. Protection of Important Bird Areas by national laws.

- Unprotected: no legal protection.
- Low protection: partly or wholly included in a reserve with a low level of legal protection of biodiversity values, e.g. grazing reserve, forest reserve, rangeland reserve, resource-use reserve, no-hunting zone, etc. (approximating to IUCN protected-area categories V to VIII).
- Moderate to high protection: partly or wholly protected by law within a nature reserve, wildlife sanctuary, national park, etc. (approximating to IUCN protected-area categories I to IV).

This analysis is based on the areas of 375 sites (16 sites are of unknown area and are excluded) . Only the *legal* protection of *sites* is considered: no account is taken of the level of actual protection currently afforded to a site, nor of any protection (guarding) afforded to particular species living within a site.

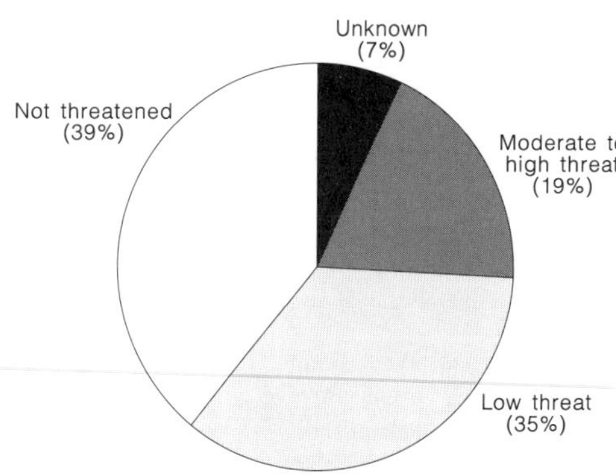

Figure 6. Severity of threats to Important Bird Areas.

- Unknown: no information from within the last 10 years.
- Not threatened: no threat known.
- Low threat: minor threats reported (generally fairly easily reversible and not destructive to fabric of site, e.g. some grazing, hunting, etc.).
- Moderate threat: some serious threats and damage to important habitats or bird populations alike, but irreparable damage not inevitable.
- High threat: serious threat of destruction of important habitats or elimination of important bird populations; most if not all of habitat/population likely to be lost unless immediate action taken.

For little-known sites, the level of threat has sometimes been inferred by extrapolation from recent or past trends, except where the information is too old to be currently reliable.

Table 1. Important Bird Areas in most urgent need of conservation attention in the Middle East. The following 31 sites are under a high degree of threat of immediate destruction (see Figure 6 for definition of 'high'). Sites with little or no legal protection at the national level are separated from those with a higher level of protection.

	Site no. & name	Area (ha)	Main habitats	Threats	Other wildlife
No, or low level of, legal protection					
Afghanistan	001 Darqad	20,000	Wetland, forest	Deforestation	T
	002 Imam Sahib	20,000	Wetland, forest	Deforestation	
	007 Pech and Waygal Valleys	120,000	Forest	Deforestation	T
	012 Safed Koh	200,000	Forest	Deforestation	
	014 Khost	150,000	Forest	Deforestation	
	016 Hamun-i-Puzak	35,000	Wetland	Upstream dams/river diversion	T
Iran	042 Hari Rud Valley near Sarrakhs	8,000	Wetland, agriculture, grassland	Deforestation, disturbance	
	087 Hamoun-i Sabari and Hamoun-i Hirmand	250,000	Wetland, agriculture, desert	River diversion, canal-building, introduction of grass carp	T
	088 South end of the Hamoun-i Puzak	14,900	Wetland	Upstream dams/river diversion	
Iraq	015 Al Jadriyah and Umm Al Khanazeer island	310	Wetland, agriculture	Urban development	
	036 Haur Al Hawizeh	250,000	Wetland	Upstream dams/river diversion	T
	037 Haur Lafta	20,000	Wetland	Upstream dams/river diversion	
	038 Central Marshes	300,000	Wetland	River diversion/drainage	T
	039 Haur Al Hammar	1,350,000	Wetland	Upstream dams/river diversion	T
Jordan	008 Qa Hanna	4,500	Wetland, desert	Water extraction	
Lebanon	004 Ammiq	280	Wetland	Drainage	
Saudi Arabia	010 Tarut Bay	41,000	Wetland, marine	Land-claim	T
	020 Jiddah South Corniche and Port	900	Wetland, marine	Land-claim	
	028 Al-Habrow al-Arabi	250,000	Bushland, grassland, agriculture	Illegal hunting	T
	037 Jizan Bay	200	Wetland, marine	Land-claim	
Syria	003 Tual al-'Abba	30,000	Wetland, grassland, agriculture	Agricultural intensification	
	016 Buhayrat al-Laha	50	Wetland, marine	Drainage, pollution	
UAE	009 Khor Dubai	300	Wetland, marine	Afforestation	
Yemen	020 Ta'izz Wadis	11,000	Wetland, bushland	Drainage	T
Moderate to high level of legal protection					
Afghanistan	009 Kole Hashmat Khan	191	Wetland	Drainage, pollution, disturbance	
Bahrain	001 Tubli Bay	2,500	Wetland, marine	Land-claim, aquifer depletion	
Iran	013 Lavandavil Marsh	949	Wetland, forest	Sea-level rise	
Jordan	009 Azraq Oasis	12,000	Wetland, agriculture, desert	Aquifer depletion	T
Kuwait	006 Al-Jahra Pool Nature Reserve	250	Wetland	Drainage	
Lebanon	001 Palm Islands	500	Marine	Illegal hunting, disturbance	
	002 Ehden Forest	?	Forest	Illegal hunting, disturbance	E

T Globally threatened sp(p). E Narrowly endemic sp(p)

fied, and which have only a low level of legal protection at the national level or none at all. This book does not attempt any more detailed prioritization of the site inventory in order to guide site protection and other kinds of conservation actions, since this will depend on many factors including economic, political and strategic concerns at the national level.

RECOMMENDATION Immediate action is required at these 31 sites if losses to biodiversity at the national, Middle Eastern and world level are to be averted.

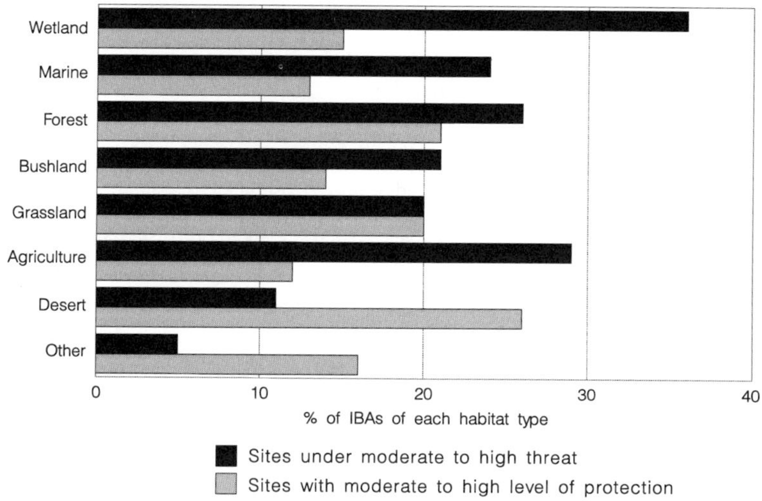

Figure 7. Legal protection of, and threats against, Important Bird Areas of different habitats. See Figures 5 and 6 for definitions 'moderate' and 'high'.

The most threatened sites by habitat-type are wetland IBAs (Figure 7), and the threats here are mostly to do with gross modification or destruction of habitat, often irreversible in practice. The gap between the high percentage of threatened wetland IBAs and the low percentage of protected wetland IBAs is larger than for any other habitat-type, indicating the urgent need for action to halt this degradation and destruction, and to reverse it wherever possible. There is an international agreement which covers the conservation of wetlands at the regional and international level: the Ramsar Convention.

The Ramsar Convention originated within the Middle East, at a conference held in the town of Ramsar in Iran in 1971. It has been successful in promoting the ideas of wetland conservation and the 'wise use' of wetlands in many parts of the world. This inventory has identified at least 99 IBAs in the region which could potentially be designated as 'Wetlands of International Importance' according to the criteria of the Convention, but which are not currently (see Box 1). There is no doubt that these are wetlands of major importance at the Middle Eastern or even global level. However, only two of the countries in the region are Contracting Parties to the Convention, and only 19 sites have been designated so far. The majority of the 118 designated or candidate Ramsar sites have little or no legal protection, and more than 50% are either under a moderate to high degree of threat of immediate destruction, or the degree of threat is completely unknown (Figure 8). Both of these parameters—level of overall protection and degree of threat suffered—are much worse than the average for IBAs in general.

RECOMMENDATION BirdLife International urges governments to accede to the Ramsar Convention, in view of the numerous benefits that unpolluted and productive wetlands produce for mankind. The Ramsar Convention Bureau should vigorously pursue increased representation in the region, given the high levels of threat demonstrated here.

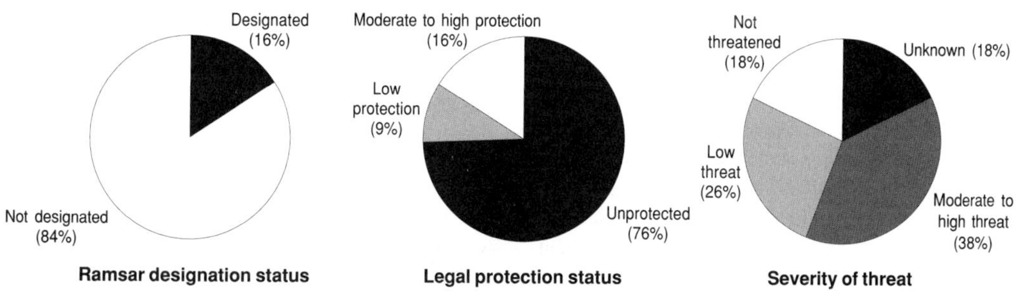

Figure 8. Status of Important Bird Areas which qualify as 'Wetlands of International Importance' under the Ramsar Convention. See Box 1 for a listing of these sites. See Figures 5 and 6 for definitions of 'low', 'moderate' and 'high'.

Box 1. Candidate Ramsar sites.

Currently, Iran and Jordan are the only Contracting Parties to the Ramsar Convention in the Middle East, having designated 19 Ramsar sites ('Wetlands of International Importance') covering more than 13,000 km² of very important wetland habitat.

Two of the Convention's quantitative criteria for selecting Ramsar sites were incorporated into the criteria for selecting Important Bird Areas:

- the site regularly supports 1% or more of a waterfowl species' population;
- the site regularly supports 20,000 or more waterfowl.

As a result, the following 118 wetland sites (as defined by the Ramsar Convention) were selected in the Middle East as IBAs according to these criteria, including all 19 existing Ramsar sites (in *italics*); all sites qualify according to the 1% criterion*, but those that also hold at least 20,000 waterfowl are in **bold** type.

Afghanistan: 013, **015**, **016**.

Bahrain: 001.

Iran: 004, *005*, ***006***, ***007***, 008, **009**, ***010***, 011, **012**, 013, 014, ***016***, ***017***, ***018***, **019**, **020**, ***022***, ***023***, **024**, ***025***, 026, 027, 028, 037, 043, **047**, 052, 054, 057, **059**, **060**, **061**, **062**, **063**, ***064***, **065**, 066, 067, ***068***, **071**, **072**, 073, ***074***, **076**, ***077***, 078, 079, ***087***, ***088***, **090**, 092, **093**, ***096***, 098, *099*, ***100***, 101, 104, 105.

Iraq: 005, 007, 008, **011**, 013, 016, **018**, 020, **021**, **025**, 028, 030, 032, 033, 035, **038**, **039**, 040, 042.

Israel: **002**, 004, 005, 007, **008**, 009.

Jordan: 007, ***009***.

Oman: **016**, **017**, 020, 023, 027.

Saudi Arabia: 005, 008, **009**, **010**, **012**, **013**, 014, 020, 021, 035, **037**, 038.

Syria: 003, **006**, **007**, **017**, 021.

United Arab Emirates: 001, 005, **009**, 017.

Yemen: 020, 033.

These sites are by definition the most important wetlands for birds in the Middle East, and it is stressed that most if not all have a much broader environmental and economic value because of the diversity of other animal and plant species that they support and because of the ecological functions that they perform. Of the 118 IBAs listed above, 99 (84%) qualify as Ramsar sites according to the quantitative criteria for waterfowl, but have not been designated under the Convention. Note that other wetlands in the Middle East, IBAs as well as non-IBAs, are also likely to qualify as candidate Ramsar sites according to the Convention's other, non-waterfowl criteria (dealing with other fauna and flora, and more qualitative aspects). The forthcoming *Directory of Wetlands in the Middle East* (see p. 12) will produce an updated and comprehensive list of candidate Ramsar sites by 1996, taking into account all values of all wetland sites in the region, not just importance for waterfowl. In the meantime, this is the first published analysis to identify and highlight candidate Ramsar sites in the region in a systematic way.

* For analysis of 1% levels, only those species/populations for which there is a single-figure population estimate (not a range) have been considered (Rose and Scott 1993); see p. 21.

The second most threatened sites by habitat-type are agricultural IBAs (Figure 7). These tend to be on plains or plateaus that were formerly semi-natural dry grasslands, shrub-steppes or savannas. Where rain-fed cultivation is possible, virtually all such relatively level areas have long since been converted to cultivation, often thousands of years ago, but so long as farming has remained non-intensive all but the most sensitive bird species characteristic of these areas were able to survive. However, the ongoing adoption of intensive agricultural methods throughout the region is now threatening these sites, and may have led to major declines in many steppeland birds and other wildlife with only limited ability to adapt to irrigation, new cropping regimes and specializations, high pesticide inputs, and mechanization.

The disparity between the high proportion of agricultural IBAs that are threatened and the low proportion that are protected is wider than for any other dry-land habitat-type. However, the threats facing agricultural IBAs are unlikely to be most successfully alleviated by site-protection measures alone, since the main land-use is by definition agriculture, and few countries in the region can afford to take a significant extent of agricultural land out of production, a move which in any case might not meet nature conservation aims. Instead, for many or most agricultural IBAs, the optimum path may lie in enabling rural communities to continue practising non-intensive farming (for example through financial incentives), which would result in the maintenance not only of the sites' value to birds and to biodiversity in general, but also of rural societies. This underlines the need for measures (e.g. financial, legal) which encourage sustainable agricultural land-use in the wider environment, through promoting non-intensive agricultural practices and regulating against unsustainable activities which lead to land degradation ('desertification').

Table 2. Shadow list for Mediterranean Specially Protected Areas. The following marine and coastal IBAs have been designated as Mediterranean Specially Protected Areas (MSPAs), or can be considered as candidate MSPAs (some have already been proposed), according to the criteria of the Barcelona Convention's Protocol on MSPAs (see p. 17).

Country	Site no. & name		Principal habitat	Area (ha)	Area protected nationally (ha)	Area MSPA (ha)	Threats
Israel	007	Carmel Coast	Wetland, islands	2,400	490	120	No major threats
Lebanon	001	Palm Islands	Islands	500	?20	?20	Illegal hunting, gen. disturbance
Syria	009	Umm al-Tuyyur	Woodland	12,000	0	0	Fire, sand extraction
Syria	017	Buhayrat al-Laha	Wetland	50	0	0	Drainage, pesticides, hunting

Two other habitat-types are also priorities for conservation effort, in that high proportions of sites are threatened and low proportions are protected: forest IBAs and marine IBAs (Figure 7). Natural or semi-natural woodlands are very important resources for local people as well as for birds and other wildlife, e.g. for building material, fuelwood, livestock fodder, fruits, medicine and a multiplicity of other benefits, material or otherwise. The scale of human use of trees and woodland is consequently high almost everywhere, and in particular has become unsustainable in the forests of commercial-grade timber in some areas in the north of the region. At present there are no regional agreements which would cover the conservation of the biodiversity and natural resources of Middle Eastern forests and woodlands, as the emphasis to date has been on more tropical areas.

The pressure being exerted on natural habitats by the increasing concentration of human populations in coastal areas of the Middle East is the major reason for the high proportion of threatened marine IBAs (Figure 7). On offshore islands, important for breeding seabirds, the threats come mainly from excessive human disturbance and the introduction of non-native fauna, both of which have direct impacts on the important bird populations and often involve little physical destruction of the site itself. These threats are thus theoretically, and sometimes practically, reversible, given the means to carry out the necessary conservation measures such as protection from disturbance, eradication or control of non-native fauna, and regular monitoring. However, the main threats to coastal sites such as mudflats, lagoons and inlets are land-claim and dredging for housing, municipal recreational areas and industry. Especially since about 20 years ago, these processes have been eating away at the fabric of coastal IBAs in the Middle East, rapidly and irreversibly, and are of great concern in those coastal regions with high human population density.

Table 3. Overview of completeness of inventory.

	Completeness 1	2	3	4
Afghanistan				•
Bahrain	•			
Iran	•			
Iraq				•
Israel/Occupied Territories	•			
Jordan		•		
Kuwait		•		
Lebanon			•	
Oman	•			
Qatar			•	
Saudi Arabia		•		
Syria			•	
United Arab Emirates			•	
Yemen				•

1 Good national inventory: location of most if not all IBAs known, and only a few areas if any remain poorly known.

2 Good information is available on most of the major IBAs, but some regions are still inadequately surveyed, and perhaps many nationally important sites remain to be discovered.

3 Information is available on many of the IBAs, but large areas of the country remain poorly known.

4 No systematic attempt has been made to document the major IBAs; only a few of the most important sites have been surveyed, and most IBAs remain poorly known.

Marine site-protection at a regional level has been successfully promoted in the Mediterranean Sea by the Barcelona Convention, in particular by its Protocol concerning Mediterranean Specially Protected Areas (see Table 2). However, the great majority of the marine and coastal IBAs in the Middle East are located in the Arabo-Persian Gulf, the Red Sea and the Gulf of Aden, where there are no site-based nature conservation protocols attached to the relevant UNEP 'Regional Seas' conventions.

RECOMMENDATION There is an urgent need for the member states of the UNEP 'Regional Seas' conventions for the Red Sea and Gulf of Aden and for the Arabo-Persian Gulf to adopt site-based nature conservation protocols, and to enact them rapidly as part of the Programme for the Environment of the Red Sea and the Gulf of Aden (PERSGA) and as part of the Kuwait Action Plan (KAP).

Completeness of the inventory has varied from country to country (see Table 3), and more comprehensive surveys will be needed for some poorly covered habitat-types (such as woodland) in some countries. Thus it should be noted that this inventory is dynamic: new sites of importance are likely to be discovered as survey work progresses, and in addition some sites may be damaged beyond recovery and lose their value for birds in the future.

RECOMMENDATION Further field surveys are needed in some countries where the present inventory is provisional in character. In other countries, preparation and publication of a revised national inventory in the local language for wide distribution to decision-makers within the country may be the next logical step.

In conclusion, it is hoped that this book will assist owners and managers of land, and decision-makers in central and local governments, in other statutory bodies and in conservation organizations, to advance the conservation of these sites, and to be more aware of the significance of the list as a whole and of their responsibilities in safeguarding the natural heritage of the Middle East.

ADDRESS FOR CORRESPONDENCE

BirdLife International, Wellbrook Court, Girton Rd, Cambridge CB3 0NA, U.K.

NATIONAL INVENTORIES

▪ REPUBLIC OF AFGHANISTAN

Eastern Stock Dove *Columba eversmanni*

GENERAL INFORMATION

Afghanistan has an area of 652,263 km^2 and is a mountainous country, bounded by the Republics of Turkmenistan, Uzbekistan and Tajikistan in the north, Iran in the west, and Pakistan to the south and east. Additionally the slim 'finger' of Wakhan projects to the Chinese frontier in the extreme north-east.

The human population density is low, merely 0.04 persons per km^2, but the barren nature of the countryside makes large tracts uninhabitable; the 1989 estimate of 17.1 million included some 5 million displaced refugees and 1.5 million nomads. The country is divided into 28 provinces, with Kabul as the largest city and the administrative capital.

The climate is continental, typical of a Central Asian land-locked country, with extreme differences between summer and winter temperatures. Summer is especially hot in the lower-lying plains of the north and south, where there is an average July temperature of 32–35°C. Winters are cold, reaching –15°C and often lower in the high Pamir mountains; the lower-lying Amu Darya plains have an average January temperature of 2°C, while further south in the low-lying Seistan basin and in the Jalalabad region of the subtropical east it is milder, with an average January temperature of 9–10°C. Rainfall is low, the wettest region being the extreme east which receives summer rains of up to 1,000 mm per year from the influence of the Indian monsoon; this is in contrast to most of the rest of the country where average annual rainfall is generally less than 100 mm away from the influence of the mountains.

Afghanistan has been ravaged by war and political turmoil over the past 20 years, but for a far longer period man has degraded the landscape through millennia of heavy grazing and wood-cutting; there is evidence to suggest that in far distant times relatively extensive areas of the country were covered by forests and woodlands. The situation is very different today: in 1989 only an estimated 2.6% of the land area contained forests. Most of the country is grazed by sheep and goats, with only 5% actively cultivated. The rugged ranges of the Hindu Kush and Pamirs cover the central and eastern regions, where there are many peaks above 6,000 m, with the highest, Mount Zebak in the Pamirs, at 7,484 m. To the north of the Hindu Kush lie the seasonally hot plains of Turkestan, flanking the Amu Darya (Oxus) river at a meagre 400 m elevation. Most of the southern third of the country is composed of desert plains sloping gradually down into the lowlands of the Seistan basin in the far south-west at 500 m.

Afghanistan can be divided into seven biogeographical regions with distinct geological, climatic, floral and faunistic characteristics.

Hindu Kush region

This consists of two parallel east–west mountain

ranges which form the backbone of the country. The more northerly extends as the Paropamissus (Safed Koh) range almost to the Iranian border in the north-east. The more southerly Koh-i-Baba range penetrates south-west into the heart of the country. These ranges receive little rainfall, but snow-melt water and the resulting seasonal river systems have created a rich variety of vegetation. The upper slopes of the Hindu Kush are clothed in scrubby *Pistacia* woodland, being replaced by *Amygdalus* lower down in the foothills, and the northern slopes are dominated by *Juniperus* scrub. However, these wooded habitats have been largely degraded by very heavy grazing and wood-cutting. Within the central and northern Hindu Kush a unique, subalpine dwarf-scrub community has formed between 3,600 and 4,000 m, with a high degree of endemism. The numerous valleys within the mountains have allowed lower altitude cultivation to develop, particularly in the Bamyan valley; not far from here are the scenically impressive lakes of Bande Amir. Water flowing south out of the Koh-i-Baba forms two high-plateau, saline lakes, Dashte Nawar and Ab-i-Istada.

Pamir–Tien Shan region

In the extreme north-east the Hindu Kush region merges with the Pamir mountains, which form part of the Karakorum range of Pakistan to the east and which extend northwards to meet the Tien Shan range of Central Asia. This region contains the highest peaks in the country, with several glaciers. The valley of the Wakhan river forms the Wakhan Corridor. The climate is very harsh with snow cover from October to April or May. There are two relatively large lakes in the Pamir mountains, which are the source of rivers which flow north to form the mighty Amu Darya river of Turkestan. Damp valley bottoms consist of alluvial deposits with overlying peat. Vegetation is sparse: *Salix* thickets grow in lower valley bottoms, and *Carex*-dominated bogs occur by glacial lakes.

Himalayan Highland region

The forested mountains of eastern Afghanistan are a lush contrast to the rest of the country. This region receives a relatively high rainfall from the extreme western influence of the Indian monsoon; oaks (chiefly *Quercus baloot*) predominate between 1,200 and 2,000 m, with a rich shrub understorey; from 2,200 to 2,500 m a belt of *Pinus gerardiana* is found, above which *Cedrus deodara* is the dominant forest tree up to 3,100 m, with *Picea smithiana* and *Abies webbiana* in the more humid upper levels to 3,300 m. Felling and logging have decimated these West Himalayan forests, even in the more remote areas, and little now remains: they are the most severely threatened of all habitats in Afghanistan. The fast-flowing mountain streams and rivers merge with the Kabul river which flows east into Pakistan and eventually joins the Indus river; it is the only Afghan river to eventually reach the sea.

Indus–Ganges Monsoon Forest region

This region covers only a small area of the country: the lower valley of the Kabul river, east of the Kabul gorge, down through Jalalabad towards the Khyber Pass. Little remains of the original tree and shrub cover, but the vegetation and the birds are basically of Indo-Malayan origin.

Turanian region

North of the Hindu Kush, the lowland desert and steppe meadows of the Amu Darya river plains form the Turanian region, which formerly included extensive areas of *Elaeagnus* riverine swamp woodland and reedbeds *Phragmites*, remnants of which hopefully still survive at Darqad and Imam Sahib. Elsewhere the natural vegetation of this fertile plain has been largely turned over to cultivation and grazing.

Anatolian–Iranian Desert region

The medium altitude (600–1,000 m) western desert plains are classed as the Anatolian–Iranian Desert region; the scanty vegetation varies according to local conditions but is basically dominated by *Artemisia* dwarf-shrub steppe.

Iranian Desert region

The low-lying area of the south-west, centred on the Seistan basin and including the Registan desert, is termed the Iranian Desert region. The Seistan basin is dominated by salt plains but formerly drained several major rivers flowing from the Hindu Kush. Extensive wetlands with surrounding lush vegetation existed until recent times, but damming of major rivers has resulted in the drying-up of most of these and the increasing aridity of Seistan. However, Hamun-i-Puzak is fed by the still undammed Khosh river and remains an exceedingly important wetland of international importance for wintering and passage waterfowl. The Registan desert has received little study but supports an impressive range of desert biotopes from sand-dunes to gravel plains and semi-desert scrub.

ORNITHOLOGICAL IMPORTANCE

Considering that Afghanistan is landlocked and mostly quite arid, its avifauna is remarkably rich. Of the 460 species recorded in the country some 235 breed or are assumed to breed; this diversity is due to the Himalayan and Indian-subcontinent species composition of the avifauna over the eastern part of the country, and to the predominantly Central Asian aspect over the northern plains and the Hindu Kush. Despite this Oriental influence the avifauna is predominantly Palearctic, with the division between the two faunal regions being approximately the Sulaiman Mountains.

Three wetlands are especially important on an international scale. Hamun-i-Puzak, in the Seistan basin in the extreme south-west, may support as many as 1,000,000 waterfowl in winter, as well as a resident population of the globally threatened *Marmaronetta angustirostris* of some hundreds of pairs. It also seems likely that a population of up to c.1,000 birds of the globally threatened *Oxyura leucocephala* may breed in Hamun-i-Puzak, wintering there in wetter years (the species was noted as being 'common' in winter at Hamun-i-Puzak in 1904/05) and moving to winter in Pakistan in drier years. Two other lakes, Dashte Nawar and Ab-i-Istada, are of specific importance in supporting a somewhat mobile population of some 10,000 *Phoenicopterus ruber*, which move between them. Ab-i-Istada is also a very important stopover site for migrating waterfowl, in particular for the tiny 'central' population of the globally endangered *Grus leucogeranus* which is known to winter at Keoladeo National Park (Bharatpur) in India; the lake can also be important for wintering waterfowl, depending on the extent of open water. Other wetlands in Afghanistan are few and do not appear to support internationally important concentrations of waterfowl; due to their high altitude most are covered with ice and snow during the winter months.

Afghanistan has one endemic bird species, *Montifringilla theresae*, and in a global context contains a significant proportion of the breeding range of six others which could be considered as near-endemics: *Columba eversmanni*, *Phylloscopus neglectus*, *P. subviridis*, *Oenanthe picata* and *Passer moabiticus*. The population of *Columba eversmanni* is of particular conservation significance since the species is rare and declining throughout its Central Asian range and may become globally threatened if apparent trends continue. Although no population studies have been made, Afghanistan probably supports significant numbers of breeding *Gypaetus barbatus*, *Neophron percnopterus*, *Aegypius monachus* and other birds of prey.

The Himalayan region in general seems to provide a formidable barrier to migrant small birds en route to their winter quarters in the Indian subcontinent, consequently Afghanistan, situated at the lower western end of the Himalayan chain, witnesses a massive passerine migration throughout the country. Raptors also move through, seemingly on a broad front, although no detailed studies have yet been made. More well-known, but again little studied, is the migration of *Grus grus*, which passes over the Salang Kotal and up the Wakhan valley in considerable numbers.

CONSERVATION INFRASTRUCTURE AND PROTECTED-AREA SYSTEM

In 1991 there was apparently no overall enabling legislation which provided for the establishment and management of protected areas. Prior to military hostilities in 1979, the Directorate of Wildlife and National Parks of the Department of Forests and Range of the Ministry of Agriculture and Land Reform was responsible for the management and protection of the country's protected areas and wildlife. There are at least two categories of protected area.

Waterfowl Reserve or Sanctuary These are individually decreed, and gazetted through individual government orders by the Head of State. Following legal protection, management plans are prepared. Principal objectives include protecting birds from adverse influences of human origin.

National Park The long-term objectives are to conserve natural landscapes through a system of zonation and to develop the tourist potential of the area. The majority of the protected areas that were established and officially declared in the 1970s were published in the official Government Gazette by the Ministry of Justice and, therefore, apparently have no legal status.

Following the onset of military conflict in 1979, there has been extremely limited activity in the field of conservation and protected-area management and administration (MacPherson 1991).

INTERNATIONAL MEASURES RELEVANT TO THE CONSERVATION OF SITES

Afghanistan is a Contracting Party to the World Heritage Convention and has signed the Biodiversity Convention. No natural World Heritage Sites have been designated.

OVERVIEW OF THE INVENTORY

The political turmoil which has enveloped Afghanistan over the past 15 years has prevented an accurate assessment of the country's potential sites of ornithological importance. The bulk of even the most recent information is already nearly 20 years out-of-date. A total of 17 sites have been included in this inventory, covering a wide spectrum of Afghanistan's natural habitats. The delimitation of several sites has proved difficult due to lack of basic information, in particular the Registan desert, Safed Koh, Khost, Hari Rud valley and the north-western steppe. These areas, however, are of such great potential for bird conservation that attention has to be drawn to them, through the designation of representative sites, to emphasize the need to identify and protect more precise areas of intact habitat within them, since some have hardly been investigated at all.

The most vulnerable sites are the forests of the east, typified by the Pech and Waygal valleys, the Safed Koh and Khost. Situated close to the border these forests are being cleared at an accelerating rate, the timber being taken by road into Pakistan. It is quite likely that no significant forest will remain in Afghanistan by the end of this century.

The low-lying, fertile plains of Afghan Turkestan have long been cultivated, but relics of the native Turanian swamp woodland survived until relatively recently, particularly at the two former Royal Hunting Preserves of Darqad and Imam Sahib. These two superb sites had never been surveyed for birds, but if their value has not already been destroyed by conversion to agriculture and indiscriminate hunting, they would repay intense field work.

Afghanistan is not renowned for its wetlands, but the formerly extensive lakes, scrub woodland and reedbeds of the Seistan basin in the south-west of the country must have once been an ornithological paradise. Much has been destroyed by reed-cutting and burning, wood-chopping for fuel, overgrazing and by the damming of feeder rivers; even by 1950 large tracts of this region had become a barren wilderness. However, the waters of Hamun-i-Puzak continued to support vast numbers of passage and winter waterfowl well into the 1970s. The somewhat seasonal wetlands of Dashte Nawar and Ab-i-Istada are also important for passage waterfowl and support an isolated breeding colony of *Phoenicopterus ruber*.

The mountainous northern and central parts of the country contain some of the most spectacular mountain scenery anywhere; the variety of montane habitats and birds are encompassed by the sites of Bande Amir, the Salang Kotal, Small Pamir and Pamir-i-Buzurg.

Although several of the most vulnerable sites may already be very severely damaged, it can be predicted that future field surveys in such a large and mountainous country will reveal many important tracts of habitat yet to be discovered and documented.

ACKNOWLEDGEMENTS

The site accounts and introduction were compiled from information supplied by S. C. Madge, who acknowledges the impressive series of detailed reports compiled principally by Dr R. G. Petocz and Dr J. A. Sayer, team leaders of the National Parks and Wildlife Management Project, which was initiated at the request of the Government of Afghanistan and administered by the Food and Agriculture Organization under the United Nations Development Programme, and which ran from 1972 to 1980, although most ornithological data were collected in the latter years. Waterfowl counts are based mostly on data collected for the International Waterfowl and Wetlands Research Bureau, chiefly by F. J. Koning, during brief winter and early spring visits in 1970–1972. A. Jamil carried out a survey of Ab-i-Istada for this project, with invaluable assistance from A. Fitzherbert and J. Harris (International Crane Foundation). E. Smith supplied valuable information for the site accounts, and Dr K. Habibi reviewed the first draft of the inventory.

SITE INVENTORY

Site no.	Site name	Region	Criteria used to select site									
			1	2i	2ii	2iii	3	4	5i	5ii	6	0
001	Darqad	TK	—	—	—	—	•	—	—	•	—	—
002	Imam Sahib	KD	—	—	—	—	•	—	—	•	—	—
003	Pamir-i-Buzurg	BK	—	—	—	—	•	—	•	—	•	—
004	Small Pamir	BK	—	—	—	•	•	—	•	—	•	—
005	Salang Kotal	BG	•	—	—	•	•	•	•	—	•	—
006	North-western Steppe	HT,BS	•	—	—	—	•	•	•	—	—	—
007	Pech and Waygal Valleys	KR	•	—	—	—	•	•	—	•	•	—
008	Bande Amir	BM	•	—	—	—	•	•	•	—	•	—
009	Kole Hashmat Khan	KB	•	—	—	—	•	•	—	•	•	—
010	Jalalabad Valley	NG	—	—	—	—	•	•	•	—	—	—
011	Hari Rud Valley	HT	•	—	—	—	•	—	—	—	—	—
012	Safed Koh	NG,PK	—	—	—	—	•	•	—	•	—	—
013	Dashte Nawar	GZ	—	•	—	—	•	•	—	—	—	—
014	Khost	PK	—	—	—	—	•	—	—	•	—	—
015	Ab-i-Istada	GZ	•	•	•	—	—	—	—	—	—	—
016	Hamun-i-Puzak	NZ	•	•	•	—	•	•	—	•	—	—
017	Registan Desert	KH	•	—	—	—	—	•	•	—	—	—

Key to regions

BG	Baghlan
BK	Badakhshan
BM	Bamyan
BS	Badghis
GZ	Ghazni
HT	Herat
KB	Kabul
KD	Kunduz
KH	Kandahar
KR	Kunar
NG	Nangarhar
NZ	Nimroz
PK	Paktia
TK	Takhar

Key to criteria

1 Regularly holds a significant number of a globally threatened species.

2i Regularly holds 1% or more of a species' biogeographical or flyway or Middle Eastern population (waterbirds and seabirds only).

2ii Regularly holds 20,000 or more waterbirds.

2iii Migratory 'bottleneck' site: more than 3,000 raptors or more than 5,000 storks or more than 2,000 cranes pass in a season.

3 Regularly holds a significant number of a species which is threatened or declining within the Middle East. Only the top five sites for each such species in the country are considered to qualify as IBAs.

4 Regularly holds a significant number of a species whose world population is wholly or largely restricted to the Middle East. Only the top five sites for each such species in the country are considered to qualify as IBAs.

5i Representative example of a habitat, associated with a characteristic assemblage of bird species.

5ii Rare/threatened/unique habitat, associated with a characteristic assemblage of bird species.

6 Site important for bird conservation through education/research/tourism.

0 Selected for other reasons. See 'Comments on the inventory'.

Comments on the inventory

1. Figures in brackets after species' names, and in boxes, are the maximum daily counts of individuals recorded (not pairs), unless otherwise stated. All counts of wintering birds are from the month of January, unless otherwise stated.
2. The regions given in brackets after the site names are the provinces.
3. All of the sites are believed to meet the criteria. Sites 001 and 002 are so critically threatened that they may have lost their importance through widespread habitat-destruction; however, these sites are also included because of their exceptional importance for threatened mammals and presumably for other life-forms. Sites 012 and 014 are particularly poorly known, but the former supports characteristic West Himalayan species with very restricted world ranges, such as *Phylloscopus subviridis*, *P. tytleri*, *Aegithalos leucogenys* and *Sitta cashmirensis* (together with site 007), and it is suspected that the latter may do so as well.
4. The great majority of information in the site accounts (including bird counts and that on threats) dates from the 1970s, with a much smaller amount from the 1940–1969 period. However it was necessary to use bird information from the last century for sites 012 and 017, and some 1993 information was incorporated for site 015. The

scarcity of ornithological information has led to a bias towards better explored areas, therefore the inventory should be regarded as preliminary.

5. No area is given for a number of sites because their boundaries have not been determined, usually because fieldwork is required before this can be done.
6. The application of the criteria in categories 3 and 4 as shown in the above table is provisional only. Some landbird areas have been chosen to include a representative cross-section of bird habitats.
7. One proposed site (Koh Daman, c.35°05′N 69°15′E) did not qualify according to the criteria, due to lack of sufficient information; further survey and investigation is recommended.

Glossary

FAO, Food and Agriculture Organization of the United Nations
ab, water(body)
dasht, desert
hamun, marsh
kol(e), lake
kotal, pass
koh, mountain (range)
rud, river

001 Darqad (Takhar)

Unprotected

37°25′N 69°30′E
c.20,000 ha

Site description

Lowland flood-plains of the Amu Darya (Oxus) river, interspersed with tributaries and islands, c.80 km north of Taloqan, at 400–450 m. Extensive swamp woodland formerly dominated this region: vast tracts of reeds *Phragmites* interspersed with thickets of *Tamarix* and *Salix* trees and quite large stands of *Elaeagnus* woodland. However in recent years no doubt much has been destroyed and turned into cultivation as it has been on the north side of the river in Tajikistan and elsewhere on the river.

Birds

See box for key species. The site is virtually unstudied ornithologically but, together with Imam Sahib (site 002) further west along the river, it was known in the 1970s to contain the last remnants of *Phasianus colchicus bianchii* in Afghanistan. Other (probable) breeding species include *Vanellus leucurus*, *Dendrocopos leucopterus*, *Acrocephalus concinens* (possible), *A. melanopogon*, *Panurus biarmicus* and *Riparia paludicola*. Large numbers of unspecified wildfowl utilize the area on migration.

Globally threatened species
Marmaronetta angustirostris Probably breeds.

Regionally threatened or declining species
Phasianus colchicus See text.

Other threatened/endemic wildlife

Mammals: in the 1970s the area was extremely important for the last remnants of two endangered subspecies: *Cervus elaphus bactrianus* and *Panthera tigris virgatus* (E; last record was of tracks found in 1967). However, the continued presence of the latter is now highly unlikely, and it is considered extinct.

Conservation issues

Although formerly declared a Royal Hunting Preserve in the early part of the century, with restrictions on settlement, access, conversion to agriculture and hunting, it was never gazetted as such and no conservation measures were formally proposed. Habitat destruction is a very great threat which has probably reached critical proportions: the swamp woodland was being severely deforested and converted to cultivation by settlers in the late 1970s, following the overthrow of the monarchy. The area is currently a war zone. The lack of protected areas severely compromises the survival of any remaining significant areas of woodland. Both *Phasianus colchicus bianchii* and *Cervus elaphus bactrianus* were hunted extensively and without control in the 1970s, and their survival is in doubt unless surveys are carried out and hunting regulated. In the future, the potential damming of the Amu Darya river upstream in Tajikistan is also a threat to the integrity of the site, of unknown magnitude.

Further reading

Sayer and van der Zon (1981).

002 **Imam Sahib** (Kunduz)

Unprotected

37°15′N 68°50′E
c.20,000 ha

■ Site description

Lowland flood-plains of the Amu Darya (Oxus) river in northern Afghanistan, c.60 km north of Kunduz, at c.500 m. Extensive swamp woodland formerly dominated this region: vast tracts of reeds *Phragmites* interspersed with thickets of *Tamarix* and *Salix* trees and quite large stands of *Elaeagnus* woodland. However in recent years no doubt much has been destroyed and turned into cultivation as it has been on the north side of the river in Tajikistan and elsewhere on the river.

■ Birds

Virtually unstudied ornithologically but, together with Darqad (site 001) further east along the river, the site was known in the 1970s to harbour the last remnants of *Phasianus colchicus bianchii* in Afghanistan. Other (probable) breeding species include *Marmaronetta angustirostris* (not proven but likely), *Vanellus leucurus*, *Acrocephalus concinens*, *A. melanopogon*, *Panurus biarmicus* and *Riparia paludicola*. Large numbers of unspecified wildfowl utilize the area on migration.

Regionally threatened or declining species	
Phasianus colchicus	Rare resident; possibly extinct.

■ Other threatened/endemic wildlife

Mammals: in the 1960s the area was extremely important for the last remnants of the threatened subspecies *Cervus elaphus bactrianus*.

■ Conservation issues

Although formerly declared a Royal Hunting Preserve in the early part of the century, with restrictions on settlement, access, conversion to agriculture and hunting, it was never gazetted as such. No conservation measures have been formally proposed. Habitat destruction is a very great threat which may already have reached dramatic proportions: the swamp woodland was being destroyed and turned into cultivation by settlers in the late 1970s, following the overthrow of the monarchy, and the area is currently a war zone. The lack of protected areas severely compromises the survival of any remaining significant areas of woodland. Both *Cervus elaphus bactrianus* and *Phasianus colchicus bianchii* were hunted extensively and without control in the 1970s, and their survival is in doubt unless surveys are carried out and hunting regulated. In the future, the potential damming of the Amu Darya river upstream in Tajikistan is also a threat to the integrity of the site, of unknown magnitude.

■ Further reading

Sayer and van der Zon (1981).

003 **Pamir-i-Buzurg (Big Pamir)** (Badakhshan)

Wildlife Sanctuary

37°10′N 73°00′E
67,938 ha

■ Site description

Spectacular, rugged, barren mountains in the north-east extremity of Afghanistan (the northern side of the Wakhan Corridor) between 3,250 and 6,103 m, with glaciers, glacial lakes and scree slopes. The reserve encompasses a glaciated block of the high Pamirs, within which the valleys of Sargaz, Tulibai, Manjulak and Abakhan drain into the Pamir river to the north (which forms the border with Tajikistan). To the south lies the wide valley of the Wakhan river. A small icefield with associated glaciers is found above 4,600 m. Vegetation is sparse: damp, lower valley bottoms consist of alluvial deposits with overlying peat on which *Salix* thickets grow; flatter areas by glacial lakes up to 5,000 m support extensive and luxuriant boggy meadows dominated by *Carex* and *Kobresia*, growing in hummocks on peaty deposits, whilst dry slopes support a sparse alpine-steppe vegetation up to 4,600 m, and above 4,300 m an alpine-heath zone also occurs. In the 1970s an estimated 75 families used to encamp in the reserve area with c.3,500–4,500 sheep and goats and c.900 yaks and cows during the short summer for grazing.

■ Birds

See box for key species. The precise status and the sizes of populations present are not known. At least 117 species have been recorded from the Afghan Pamir (which has a Tibetan-type avifauna); 75 of these are recorded from the Pamir-i-Buzurg, and probable breeding species among them include *Buteo rufinus*, *Aquila chrysaetos*, *Gyps himalayensis* (possibly, though recorded as *G. fulvus*), *Tetraogallus himalayensis*, *Bubo bubo*, *Eremophila alpestris*, *Motacilla citreola*, *Prunella himalayana*, *P. fulvescens*, *Phoenicurus erythrogaster*, *Tichodroma muraria*, *Cinclus cinclus*, *C. pallasii* (possible), *Montifringilla nivalis*, *Carpodacus rubicilla*, *Leucosticte brandti* and *L. nemoricola*.

Globally threatened species	
Falco naumanni	Passage migrant.
Regionally threatened or declining species	
Anser indicus	Summer visitor to Zor Kol (a lake outside the reserve).
Neophron percnopterus	Passage migrant.
Gypaetus barbatus	Probably breeds.
Gyps fulvus	Probably breeds, but may be misidentification of *G. himalayensis*.
Falco cherrug	Possible summer visitor, but recorded as *F. jugger*.

Other threatened/endemic wildlife

Mammals: *Lynx lynx* (rare), *Uncia uncia* (E), *Ursus arctos* (rare), *Canis lupus* (V), *Capra ibex sibericus* (685 in 1972) and *Ovis ammon poli* (rare: 750 in the reserve area in the 1970s, out of 2,000+ in the Afghan Pamirs).

Conservation issues

Designated as a reserve on account of its population of the endangered sheep *Ovis ammon poli*, and gazetted as a Wildlife Sanctuary in September 1978. Current on-the-ground protection is presumed to be non-existent. In the 1970s there appeared to be no threats to birdlife due to the remoteness of the area and the low human population density. The reserve area does not extend to cover the *Anser indicus* breeding colonies at Zor Kol (see site 004), leaving these highly sensitive sites vulnerable and without any protection. Hunting tours were allowed in the 1970s and uncontrolled hunting of wild ungulates may have occurred in recent years. The remoteness of the region prevents mass tourism but there is potential for trekking tours to develop in the future. The site was recommended for designation as a National Park and natural World Heritage Site in the 1970s (Petocz 1978, Sayer and von der Zon 1981).

Further reading

Nogge (1973), Petocz (1978), Sayer and van der Zon (1981).

004 Small Pamir (Badakhshan)

Unprotected

37°05′N 74°20′E
c.200,000 ha

Site description

This area forms the eastern tip of the Wakhan Corridor, separating China, Pakistan and Tajikistan and encompassing the valleys of the Aksu and Waghir rivers at 4,000–6,000 m. The Aksu flows east out of Chaqmatin lake and joins the Pamir river in Tajikistan; the Waghir drains the adjoining mountains and eventually flows into the Wakhan river a little further west. The mountains are more smoothly rounded on the Tajikistan border but are more rugged to the south bordering Pakistan and China. The area is surrounded by the impressive barren Pamir mountains and contains the lakes of Zor Kol and Chaqmatin. The northern mountains lack the dramatic glaciers and icefields of the Pamir-i-Buzurg (see site 003) but these are present in the mountains bordering China. Vegetation seems to be similar to that of Pamir-i-Buzurg (see site 003). The people of the Small Pamir are Kirghiz and numbered c.2,000 in the 1970s. Much of the lower part of the area has long been heavily grazed by their livestock. The region is one of the great historical crossroads of Central Asia, with numerous passes to the south into Pakistan.

Birds

See box for key species. Zor Kol and Chaqmatin lake are particularly important features ornithologically. The precise status and population sizes of important bird species present in the area are not known. At least 117 species are recorded from the Afghan Pamir, which has a Tibetan-type avifauna, and 65 of these are recorded from the Small Pamir, of which the following breed or probably breed: *Tadorna ferruginea*, *Netta rufina*, *Mergus merganser*, *Aquila chrysaetos*, *Gyps himalayensis* (presumably; recorded as *G. fulvus*), *Falco pelegrinoides*, *Tetraogallus himalayensis*, *Charadrius mongolus*, *Columba leuconota*, *C. rupestris*, *Bubo bubo*, *Eremophila alpestris*, *Motacilla citreola*, *Prunella himalayana*, *P. fulvescens*, *Phoenicurus erythrogaster*, *Phylloscopus collybita sindianus*, *Luscinia svecica*, *Oenanthe deserti*, *Tichodroma muraria*, *Cinclus cinclus*, *Montifringilla nivalis* and *Leucosticte brandti*. The area is a flyway for *Grus grus* ('hundreds'), and *Aquila nipalensis* is a passage migrant in unspecified numbers. Although it has been suggested that the last few Indian-wintering *Grus leucogeranus* may migrate through with *G. grus* (Petocz 1978), based on local people's reports of the species in western Nuristan (Petocz and Larsson 1978; see site 007), it seems more likely that the species migrates through the mountains of northern Afghanistan via Salang Kotal (see site 005) given the known pattern of records north of this region (K. Habibi, pers. comm.).

Globally threatened species

Falco naumanni	Passage migrant.

1% or more of population

	Breeding (pairs)	Wintering	Passage
Grus grus	—	—	hundreds

Regionally threatened or declining species

Anser indicus	Summer visitor with important breeding colonies at Chaqmatin lake and Zor Kol.
Gypaetus barbatus	Probably breeds.
Neophron percnopterus	Passage migrant.
Gyps fulvus	See text.
Falco cherrug	Possibly breeds.

Other threatened/endemic wildlife

Mammals: the Afghan Pamir is very important for *Uncia uncia* (E), *Capra ibex sibericus* and *Ovis ammon poli* (rare).

Conservation issues

No formal conservation measures have been taken, but there are few threats due to the remoteness of the area and the sparse human population. The most obvious threat to birds is human predation of *Anser indicus* eggs, which were widely taken by local people in the 1970s. Very heavy grazing and the cutting of *Artemisia* bushes for fuel has resulted in some degradation of the fragile alpine-steppe vegetation. Hunting tours were allowed in the 1970s and uncontrolled hunting of wild ungulates may have occurred in recent years. The remoteness of the region deters tourism but there is good potential for trekking tours.

Further reading

Nogge (1973), Petocz (1978), Sayer and van der Zon (1981).

005 Salang Kotal (Baghlan)

Unprotected

35°24′N 69°08′E
2,000 ha

Site description

Ten kilometres of valley north from Salang Kotal, the highest pass (3,658 m) on the main road from Kabul to the north of Afghanistan, down to the town of Khinjan (1,500 m). These north-facing slopes are part of the watershed of the Amu Darya (Oxus) river of Turkestan, and are penetrated by a long road-tunnel at 3,200 m. The areas around the tunnel are alpine, boulder-strewn slopes with scant plant growth and grassy areas around patches of snow-melt. Barren crags surround the pass itself. The road drops north down the valley through *Juniperus*-covered slopes, with extensive patches of *Salix* by the fast-flowing Kunduz river; towards Khinjan the valley widens out onto the plains of the Amu Darya valley and there are a few, scattered villages with extensive mulberry *Morus* orchards. The alpine zone is quite heavily grazed by nomads, who cut *Juniperus* and *Salix* bushes for fuel.

Globally threatened species

Aegypius monachus	Scarce passage migrant (1).
Falco naumanni	Scarce passage migrant (6).
Grus leucogeranus	The last few Indian-wintering birds are most likely to migrate through the Hindu Kush at this point, flying over with *G. grus* (K. Habibi pers. comm.).

1% or more of population

	Breeding (pairs)	Wintering	Passage
Grus grus	—	—	>250

Regionally threatened or declining species

Gypaetus barbatus	Resident (1 pair).
Neophron percnopterus	Summer visitor (3 pairs).

Species restricted wholly or largely to the Middle East

Irania gutturalis	Probably breeds among *Juniperus*.
Oenanthe xanthoprymna	Probably breeds in the valley bottom.
Sylvia althaea	Summer visitor among *Juniperus*.
Phylloscopus neglectus	Summer visitor among *Juniperus*.
Rhodopechys sanguinea	Breeds above the treeline.

Birds

See box for key species. An easily accessible area with an excellent diversity of Himalayan breeding birds (at least 33 species), including all Afghan species characteristic of the Turkestan region (*Dendrocopos leucopterus*, *Phylloscopus neglectus*, *P. griseolus*, *Parus flavipectus*, *P. bokharensis*, *Mycerobas carnipes*, *Carpodacus rhodochlamys grandis*, *C. rubicilla* and *Emberiza stewarti*). *Phylloscopus trochiloides nitidus* is a summer visitor to the valley bottom. The area has a marked passage of *Grus grus* but no counts have been made. This account is based on information collected in July 1970.

Other threatened/endemic wildlife
None known to BirdLife International.

Conservation issues
No formal conservation measures are known to have been taken. It is not known whether there are any current problems, but if any, they are likely to be overgrazing and excessive cutting of bushes for fuel. However, extensive areas of shrubby mountainside remained in 1970 and population pressure did not seem great. The woodland on the slopes may have suffered from military activities during the war, due to the site's strategic importance.

Further reading
Madge (1978).

006 North-western Steppe (Herat, Badghis)
Unprotected

35°10′N 62°00′E
80,000 ha

Site description
Barren, hot, desert-steppe plains lying west of the town of Qala-i-Nau in north-west Afghanistan, rising to rounded barren foothills of the Paropamissus (Safed Koh) range to the south, and bordered by Turkmenistan to the north and Iran to the west. The area is between 500 and 1,000 m above sea-level, and fingers of hills project into the plains from the south. *Artemisia* steppe predominates on the plains, with *Pistacia* woodland in the hills; patches of *Juniperus* occur on hills nearer the Paropamissus. Land is mainly used for grazing; *Pistacia* woodland provides seasonal income to local people.

Birds
The region is little explored but could perhaps produce species which are associated with the deserts of adjacent Turkmenistan. See box for key species; other known or possible breeding species include *Accipiter badius*, *Merops superciliosus*, *Melanocorypha bimaculata*, *Calandrella acutirostris*, *Saxicola caprata* and *Scotocerca inquieta*. Just south of the region around Sabzak Kotal, *Certhia himalayana* and *Parus rufonuchalis* breed in *Juniperus* scrub.

Globally threatened species	
Falco naumanni	Summer visitor (in 1972, c.15 pairs at Kushk and c.10 pairs at 'Gozara').
Chlamydotis undulata	May breed (one bird, July 1949).
Regionally threatened or declining species	
Neophron percnopterus	Summer visitor, possibly breeding.
Falco cherrug	May breed.
Columba eversmanni	Nesting at Qala-i-Nau in 1949.
Species restricted wholly or largely to the Middle East	
Oenanthe picata	Resident.
Phylloscopus neglectus	Summer visitor to *Juniperus* just south of Sabzak Kotal.
Carpospiza brachydactyla	Probable summer visitor.

Other threatened/endemic wildlife
Mammals: *Equus hemionus onager* (V) may wander from reserves over the Turkmen border, and likewise *Gazella subgutturosa* (rare); even *Acinonyx jubatus* (V) could still survive.

Conservation issues
No conservation measures have been taken. Overgrazing by livestock, leading to excessive erosion and degradation of soil locally, and uncontrolled hunting are likely to be serious problems. The lack of more detailed information on the state of habitats and on wildlife inventories will inhibit any attempts at protecting areas in the future. The area was proposed as a potential reserve region in 1981.

Further reading
Paludan (1959), Sayer and van der Zon (1981), Smith (1974).

007 Pech and Waygal Valleys (Kunar)
Unprotected

35°00′N 70°50′E
60,000 ha

Site description
Relatively steep-sided valleys, typical of Nuristan and the western Himalayas in general; they are tributaries of the Kunar river in eastern Afghanistan, north of Jalalabad, at c.1,100–3,000 m. The Kunar in turn flows into the Kabul river near Jalalabad. Nuristan is a mountainous region, with granitic peaks of up to 6,300 m. The lower slopes of the valleys contain *Quercus* forest up to c.2,000 m, being replaced by coniferous forest up to c.3,000 m, above which is a narrow *Juniperus* zone. The highest, alpine zone receives little rain and is relatively barren.

The whole region has been somewhat isolated until relatively recently, and the Nuristanis have maintained their distinct cultural heritage to a certain extent. The architecture in many villages is also unique.

■ Birds

A typical and representative west Himalayan breeding avifauna, with at least 53 breeding species. See box for key species; other notable breeding species (some with very restricted world ranges) include *Lophophorus impejanus*, *Pucrasia macrolopha*, *Phylloscopus subviridis*, *P. tytleri*, *Aegithalos leucogenys* and *Sitta cashmirensis*. *Phylloscopus trochiloides nitidus* is a passage migrant.

Globally threatened species

Grus leucogeranus	In the 1970s local people knew the bird and stated that 1–3 individuals occurred on passage with *Grus grus* in the Chaman valley in late March (Petocz and Larsson 1977: 40–41).

Regionally threatened or declining species

Gypaetus barbatus	Resident.
Neophron percnopterus	Summer visitor.
Gyps fulvus	Resident.

Species restricted wholly or largely to the Middle East

Oenanthe picata	Passage migrant.
Sylvia althaea	Summer visitor.

■ Other threatened/endemic wildlife

Mammals: the Nuristan region contains important populations of *Ursus arctos* (rare), *Selenarctos thibetanus* (V), *Uncia uncia* (E), *Panthera pardus* (rare), *Lynx lynx* (rare), *Canis lupus* (V), *Capra falconeri* (E) and *Macacca mulatta* (rare); *Moschus sifanicus* (E) is thought to be extinct. Other notable species include *Prionailurus bengalensis*, *Capra ibex sibericus*, *Petaurista petaurista* and *Hylopetes fimbriatus*.

■ Conservation issues

No formal conservation measures have been taken. Critical problems are the uncontrolled deforestation and widespread hunting (particularly of the two pheasant species, *Lophophorus impejanus* and *Pucrasia macrolopha*, which must be severely depleted). The alpine meadows have been heavily overgrazed. Trekking tourism may develop in the future, given the area's great potential. In 1977 the headwaters of the Pech and Waygal valleys and adjacent areas of upland woodland were proposed as a National Park.

■ Further reading

Paludan (1959), Petocz and Larsson (1977).

008 Bande Amir (Bamyan)

Unprotected

34°52´N 67°10´E
41,000 ha

■ Site description

A string of deep lakes set in a sheer, steep-sided valley in the Hindu Kush range, 60 km west of Bamyan town; the lakes are situated at c.2,900 m but the valley rises to a high mountain escarpment at c.3,800 m. The series of lakes rises in altitude from west to east, with natural limestone dams forming barriers between them. The boundary of the national park encompasses the entire watershed. The climate is strongly continental and extremely severe, the lakes freezing over in winter. The lakes are mostly too deep and steep-sided for waterfowl, and the surrounding cliffs and escarpment are very barren, but the valley bottom west of the lakes is well vegetated. The small shallow lower lake (Gholaman) has fringing beds of *Phragmites* and lies in a grazed meadow-like area. The extensive limestone dam between the two largest lakes (Haibat and Zulfiqar) is covered in *Salix* bushes. To the south is rolling, semi-desert plateau with patches of damp, snow-melt meadow. Large numbers of nomads arrive in spring to graze their flocks in the valley west of the lakes (the only area supporting sufficient vegetation for grazing, where there are also some crops). In the 1970s several thousand tourists per year visited the site which is scenically very beautiful and a natural extension to a visit to the nearby Bamyan valley.

■ Birds

See box for key species. Other breeding species include *Falco jugger* (possibly), *Falco pelegrinoides*, *Tetraogallus himalayensis*, *Bubo bubo*, *Calandrella acutirostris*, *Motacilla citreola*, *Montifringilla nivalis*, *Carpodacus synoicus* (possibly), *Rhodopechys mongolica* and *Emberiza buchanani*. An excellent migration study area, with 152 species recorded (mostly during August–September 1970); species include *Phylloscopus griseolus* and *P. trochiloides nitidus*.

Globally threatened species

Aquila heliaca	Passage migrant.
Falco naumanni	Passage migrant.

Regionally threatened or declining species

Gypaetus barbatus	Breeds.
Falco cherrug	Passage migrant.

Species restricted wholly or largely to the Middle East

Oenanthe xanthoprymna	Possible breeder; passage migrant.
Oenanthe picata	Possible breeder; passage migrant.
Sylvia minula	Passage migrant.
Sylvia althaea	Passage migrant.
Montifringilla theresae	Breeds.
Rhodopechys sanguinea	Breeds.

Other threatened/endemic wildlife

Mammals: *Ovis orientalis* (rare), *Capra ibex* (rare) and *Canis lupus* (V).

Conservation issues

The area was declared Afghanistan's first National Park in 1973, but the declaration was not gazetted and still has no legal status. Current on-the-ground protection of the Park is presumed to be non-existent. No immediate threats to birdlife were apparent in the 1970s. Nomads and their flocks exert heavy pressure on the somewhat thin and fragile vegetation of the valley west of the lakes, through grazing and cutting of *Phragmites* and *Salix* for fuel. Future tourism (e.g. around former tourist areas at the extreme west end of Bande Haibat), if uncontrolled, may damage fragile mountain habitat and disturb sensitive breeding bird species. It has been suggested that the lakes be stocked with rainbow trout *Salmo irideus*; this would not affect the birds but might affect any native fish species present.

Further reading

Madge (1970), Petocz and Skogland (1974), Shank and Larsson (1977).

009 Kole Hashmat Khan (Kabul)

also known as Lake Chaman
Waterfowl Sanctuary

34°30′N 69°12′E
191 ha

Site description

The only wetland remaining from the once extensive Kabul marshes, on the south-east outskirts of Kabul city on the Kabul–Gardez highway, at c.1,800 m. Kole Hashmat Khan is a small, shallow (c.1.5 m max. depth) L-shaped lake, c.2.5 km long and 300–1,000 m wide. It lies in a basin surrounded by the foothills of the Hindu Kush, and the north-east shore opens into the Logar valley, being connected to the Logar river by a small stream; to the east the hills slope down into the subtropical Jalalabad valley, whereas to the west the hills rise steeply into the Paghman mountains (5,000 m). Past drainage and irrigation have reduced the water in both the lake and the Logar river. Both may become virtually dry in hot summers and the lake is typically frozen for two to three months during winter. In the 1970s the edges of the lake incorporated quite extensive *Phragmites* reedbeds and were grazed by livestock. There was a large area of basic cultivation between the lake and the village (c.300 people). Southern fields were property of the public bath and the northern fields were owned by local residents. Nomads moved through with their animals each spring, and the area was quite popular for picnicing. Nearby are the popular shrine of Jubur Ansar and the old fortress of Qala-i-Hashmat Khan.

Birds

See box for key species. The site is used as a migration staging post by waterfowl en route from Pakistan/India to Central Asia and Siberia. A figure of over 30,000 waterbirds has been implied (Day 1988), but this misinterprets data of Niethammer (1967) who states that a total of 32,700 individual birds were seen during a two-year study. Figures quoted below are typical, and at least 157 species have been recorded. Small numbers of waterbirds breed. Other breeding species in the 1960s and/or 1970s included *Podiceps nigricollis* (30 pairs), *Netta rufina* (possibly), *Aythya ferina* (2 pairs) and *Porzana pusilla* (probable). *Acrocephalus scirpaceus* apparently bred in 1967, which would be the sole known Afghan site (nests were found but identification needs confirma-

Globally threatened species

Marmaronetta angustirostris	Passage migrant (1, May 1965).
Oxyura leucocephala	In the 1970s recorded between April and August (e.g. 5, April–May) and possibly bred.
Aegypius monachus	Passage migrant (1, April).

Regionally threatened or declining species

Botaurus stellaris	Possibly breeds.
Aythya nyroca	Scarce passage migrant (1, March).
Neophron percnopterus	Fairly common non-breeding summer visitor and passage migrant; small numbers probably breed in hills nearby.

Species restricted wholly or largely to the Middle East

Oenanthe finschii	Small numbers breed.
Oenanthe picata	Small numbers breed.

tion). Moderate numbers of waterfowl occur on passage and in winter, including *Podiceps nigricollis* (233, March), *Anas clypeata* (471, March), *Aythya ferina* (2,210, March), *Fulica atra* (10,000, March), *Tringa glareola* (500, August) and *Chlidonias hybridus* (150, May). The lake is frozen in winter and its value for waterfowl then is limited; species include *Fulica atra* (5,000 in winter).

■ Other threatened/endemic wildlife

None known to BirdLife International.

■ Conservation issues

Previously a 'royal hunting preserve', it was declared a waterfowl reserve in the 1930s, with restricted hunting. When the monarchy was abolished in 1973 the site was placed under control of the Republican Guard and the Department of Forests and Range. By 1978 the lake was administered by the Presidential Office (Department of Ceremonies of Arg-i-Jamhouriat) and was state property. Current protection of the area is presumed to be nonexistent. Human pressures in the 1970s included water-diversion from the source stream for irrigation, excessive hunting, pollution from commercial laundry businesses, indiscriminate shooting, egg-collecting, reed-cutting and much general disturbance of birds (some deliberate), especially severe and widespread in summer when water levels were low. Cyprinid fish have been introduced, including Carp *Cyprinus carpio*. The site has excellent potential for conservation education. Conversion of the old fort on the site into a hotel, restaurant or visitors' centre is a possibility in the future, with an attendant risk of pollution or excessive disturbance of wildlife locally if development is not carried out with care.

■ Further reading

Day (1988), Niethammer (1967), Puget (1971), Rahim and Larsson (1978).

010 Jalalabad Valley (Nangarhar)

Unprotected

34°27′N 70°25′E
25,000 ha

■ Site description

The city of Jalalabad in the low-lying valley of the Kabul river at 500 m, together with the lakes of Duronta and Sarobi further west along the valley. Almost subtropical, low-altitude climate more akin to the Indian subcontinent than to the rest of the country. Some 50 km west of Jalalabad the river drops from the uplands of Central Asia through the dramatic Kabul gorge. All along the valley there is dry cultivation with plantations of trees, gradually becoming more arid towards the Pakistan border. Around the city itself there are orchards and good tree cover, gardens and some parks. Lake Duronta is an open, freshwater lake c.20 km long with reedbeds at west end, not far from the town (34°25′N 70°27′E), and is generally ice-free in winter. Lake Sarobi is smaller and much further west (34°40′N 69°46′E), a man-made lake, c.2 km across.

■ Birds

See box for key species. The site holds a representative assemblage of characteristically lowland Indo-Malayan species not found elsewhere in Afghanistan: species presumed to breed in or near the area include *Falco jugger*, *Riparia paludicola* (common at Sarobi lake), *Hirundo smithii*, *H. fluvicola* (Sarobi lake), *Anthus similis*, *Prinia criniger*, *Lanius vittatus*, *L. schach*, *Dicrurus macrocercus*, *Sturnus pagodarum* and *Emberiza striolata*. Wintering species include *Pericrocotus ethologus*, *Prunella atrogularis*, *Phoenicurus erythronota*, *Rhyacornis fuliginosus*, *Chaimarriornis leucocephalus*, *Myiophonus caeruleus*, *Turdus ruficollis*, *Certhia himalayana*, *Zosterops palpebrosus*, *Dicrurus leucophaeus*, *Garrulus lanceolatus*, *Serinus pusillus*, *Leucosticte nemoricola*, *Emberiza leucocephalos*, *E. stewarti* and *E. pusilla*, some being hill forest species that have moved to lower ground. Duronta lake supports small numbers of wintering and passage wildfowl (up to 500 birds) and fields around Sarobi lake attract finches and buntings in winter. It is likely that other lowland Indo-Malayan species, new to the Afghan avifauna, will be discovered in future.

Regionally threatened or declining species	
Gypaetus barbatus	May breed.
Neophron percnopterus	Summer visitor, possibly breeding.
Gyps fulvus	May breed.
Falco jugger	May breed.
Species restricted wholly or largely to the Middle East	
Oenanthe finschii	Winter visitor.
Oenanthe xanthoprymna	Winter visitor.
Oenanthe picata	May breed.

■ Other threatened/endemic wildlife

None known to BirdLife International.

Conservation issues

No conservation action has been taken, but there appear to be few threats. There is a possibility of Duronta lake being developed as a recreational area; although it seems to be of only minor importance to waterfowl, at least the western end of the lake, which is furthest from the town and has reedbeds, could be kept as a reserve.

011 Hari Rud Valley (Herat)

Unprotected

34°21′N 62°38′E
35,000 ha

Site description

A 112-km stretch of valley running from Obeh (1,830 m) west to Herat city (1,050 m) in north-west Afghanistan. The valley widens considerably towards Herat and even as far east as Obeh it is c.15 km wide, and comprises barren, desert hills and plains with sparse vegetation and cultivation. Along watercourses stands of *Tamarix* prevail and there are *Populus* groves and some apricot orchards.

Birds

See box for key species. Other interesting breeding species include *Accipiter badius* (Herat), *Picus squamatus flavirostris* (Herat and Obeh), *Alauda gulgula*, *Motacilla citreola* and *Saxicola caprata*. *Phasianus colchicus principalis* formerly occurred in the valley, mainly to the west of Herat, but is probably extinct in Afghanistan through hunting and habitat destruction. The following are also likely to breed, given their presence 100 km further down the valley by the river and on the plains around Kohsan: *Ixobrychus minutus*, *Buteo rufinus*, *Porzana porzana*, *Cursorius cursor*, *Sterna albifrons*, *Melanocorypha bimaculata*, *Calandrella acutirostris*, *Acrocephalus stentoreus*, *Hippolais rama* and *Rhodopechys githaginea*.

Globally threatened species	
Falco naumanni	Summer visitor (16 pairs in 1972).
Regionally threatened or declining species	
Neophron percnopterus	Summer visitor, possibly breeding.
Falco cherrug	May breed.
Columba eversmanni	Large colony at Herat, 10–20 pairs at Obeh.
Species restricted wholly or largely to the Middle East	
Ammoperdix griseogularis	Probably occurs since resident 100 km further down the valley.
Oenanthe picata	May breed.

Other threatened/endemic wildlife

None known to BirdLife International.

Conservation issues

No conservation measures are known to have been taken. Current threats are not known, but the apparently rapid decline of the global *Columba eversmanni* population since c.1980 gives rise for concern for the colonies at this site, the current state of which remains completely unknown. Herat is one of the largest cities in Afghanistan thus the pressure on the surrounding semi-desert vegetation by grazing or agricultural improvement, together with the effects of years of war may mean that the *C. eversmanni* colonies no longer exist.

Further reading

Paludan (1959).

012 Safed Koh (Nangarhar, Paktia)

Unprotected

34°00′N 69°50′E
200,000ha

Site description

The upper zone of a range of mountains south-east of Kabul and bordering the North-West Frontier province of Pakistan, from 2,000 m to over 3,000 m. There are forests of *Cedrus deodara*, *Pinus gerardiana* and *P. excelsa*.

Birds

A poorly studied region at the western limit of many Himalayan forest birds. See box for key species; others known to occur and presumed to breed are *Buteo rufinus*, *Tetraogallus himalayensis*, *Lophophorus impejanus*, *Psittacula himalayana*, *Picus squamatus*, *Anthus similis*, *A. roseatus* (breeds over Pakistan border), *Prunella strophiata*, *Turdus rubrocanus*, *Phylloscopus chloronotus* (breeds over Pakistan border), *P. occipitalis*, *P. subviridis*, *Muscicapa sibirica*, *M. ruficauda*, *Ficedula superciliaris*, *Aegithalos leucogenys*, *Parus melanolophus*, *P. rufonuchalis*, *Sitta leucopsis*, *S. cashmirensis*, *Certhia himalayana*, *Garrulus lanceolatus*, *Nucifraga caryocatactes*, *Corvus macrorhynchos*, *Dicrurus leucophaeus*, *Mycerobas carnipes* and *M. icterioides*. Most of above is based on Wardlaw-Ramsey (1879) during his stay in the Hariab valley. Koelz made a brief visit in 1937 (to Khudi Khel). Other species known to occur just over the border in Pakistani Safed Koh include *Delichon dasypus*, *Tarsiger cyanurus*, *Phylloscopus magnirostris* and *Carpodacus thura*; the occurrence of *Garrulax albogularis*, *Carduelis spinoides* and *Callacanthis burtoni* in the Safed Koh range needs confirmation.

Regionally threatened or declining species

Gypaetus barbatus	Probably breeds.

Species restricted wholly or largely to the Middle East

Oenanthe xanthoprymna	Probably breeds.

Other threatened/endemic wildlife

None known to BirdLife International.

Conservation issues

No formal conservation measures are known to have been taken. Up-to-date knowledge of the condition of habitat and fauna is completely lacking. However, deforestation is almost certain to be a critical problem, and *Lophophorus impejanus* has probably already disappeared through hunting. The lack of protected areas severely compromises the survival of any remaining significant areas of forest.

Further reading

Wardlaw-Ramsey (1879, 1880).

013 Dashte Nawar (Ghazni)

Waterfowl Sanctuary (7,500 ha)

33°50′N 67°45′E
70,000 ha

Site description

Dashte Nawar is a high desert plateau in south-east Afghanistan, c.55 km north-west of Ghazni. It is surrounded by the Kohe Baba range which rises above 4,800 m. In the centre of this desert at 3,200 m is Ab-i-Nawar, a shallow, brackish, alkaline lake of c.3,500 ha, being c.14 × 3 km; the lake contains c.40 small islands of 35–500 m^2. The water comes primarily from snow-melt of the surrounding mountains. The climate is hot and dry in summer and very cold in winter, with only three months of the year having mean minimum temperatures above freezing. The lake bottom supports a dense cover of algae Characeae, but the surrounding mudflats are barren except where they approach the meadows and grasses of the 'Dasht', an upland steppe plateau of meadow grasses and herbs, interspersed with shallow, mostly dry stream beds. The land is state-owned, but semi-nomadic people have grazing rights. In the 1970s some 25 villages supported c.1,200–1,500 people within the area of the Dasht, additionally c.1,300 nomads used the area as summer grazing for c.5,000–7,000 sheep and goats and 700 camels.

Birds

See box for key species. The site holds the highest known breeding colony of *Phoenicopterus ruber* (12,000 birds in 1970; 10,000 birds plus 400 young in 1975); with increasing disturbance and consistently low water levels during the 1970s at the flamingo colony at Ab-i-Istada (see site 015), that population seemed to be breeding increasingly at this site. Little other ornithological information is available. Other breeding species include *Charadrius leschenaultii*, *Pterocles orientalis* and *Rhodopechys mongolica*. Together with Ab-i-Istada these wetlands are of extreme importance to migratory waterfowl, the nearest comparable habitat being 600 km away in Seistan. The site was listed as a wetland of international importance by Carp (1980).

1% or more of population

	Breeding (pairs)	Wintering	Passage
Phoenicopterus ruber	max. 6,000	—	—

Regionally threatened or declining species

Falco cherrug	Possibly breeds.
Columba eversmanni	Passage migrant (May 1977).

Species restricted wholly or largely to the Middle East

Montifringilla theresae	Breeds.

Other threatened/endemic wildlife

Mammals: *Canis lupus* (V).

Conservation issues

The site was approved as a Wildlife and Waterfowl Sanctuary in 1977 by the Head of State, following its establishment as a National Flamingo and Waterfowl Sanctuary by the Directorate of Wildlife and National Parks in 1974; however it is not clear whether the site was ever formally gazetted. It was wardened from 1974 to 1978, with assistance from a WWF grant, and a management plan was prepared (Shank and Rodenburg 1977). Excessive disturbance of breeding birds by graziers and their livestock occurs and is a major threat: most is unintentional but some egg-collection occurs.

■ Further reading

Carp (1980), Petocz and Habibi (1975), Sayer and von der Zon (1981), Shank and Rodenburg (1977).

014 **Khost** (Paktia)

also known as Rost or Matoon

Unprotected

33°22′N 70°01′E

150,000 ha

■ Site description

Foothills of the Safed Koh range, which become higher to the north in adjacent Nangarhar province; situated east of Gardez along Pakistan border, at 1,100–3,000 m. In the hills are remnants of *Quercus baloot* forest, replaced at higher altitudes by forests of *Cedrus deodara*, *Abies webbiana*, *Picea morinda* and *Pinus excelsa*. The steppe around Khost itself has groves of the palm *Chamaerops ritchienna*.

■ Birds

See box for key species. A poorly studied region at the western limit of many Himalayan forest birds. Species known to occur, and presumably breeding, include *Halcyon smyrnensis*, *Anthus similis*, *Cercotrichas galactotes*, *Scotocerca inquieta*, *Muscicapa ruficauda*, *Myiophonus caeruleus*, *Parus melanolophus*, *Sitta leucopsis*, *Dicrurus macrocercus*, *Garrulus lanceolatus*, *Nucifraga caryocatactes*, *Serinus pusillus*, *Mycerobas icterioides* and *Emberiza cia*.

Regionally threatened or declining species	
Gypaetus barbatus	Presumably breeds.

■ Other threatened/endemic wildlife

No information.

■ Conservation issues

No conservation measures are known to have been taken. Deforestation is presumably a critical problem, since a report in 1969 suggested that the forests of Paktia region could be destroyed by the mid-1970s (Sayer and von der Zon 1981). Overgrazing and excessive hunting are also critical problems. Nothing is known of the state of remaining forests, and their lack of protection poses a great threat to their continued existence.

■ Further reading

Puget (1969), Sayer and van der Zon (1981).

015 **Ab-i-Istada** (Ghazni)

Wildlife Sanctuary

32°30′N 67°55′E

27,000 ha

■ Site description

A large, very shallow, alkaline lake situated on a gently rolling plateau at the foot of the Kohe Baba and Kohe Paghman ranges in south-east Afghanistan, c.130 km south of Ghazni, at 2,100 m. The following description is based on observations in the 1970s. The lake's size varied considerably from year to year, being recharged mainly by snow-melt water flow once per year in spring, when it was most extensive (usually c.16 km at the widest point, and up to c.13,000 ha). Summers are very hot and winters very cold: the lake shrank through evaporation during the summer, in some years becoming completely dry by October, but in other years water lasted through the winter, although often freezing apart from a few tiny pools. Extensive mudflats surrounded the lake, extending for 7 km on the east side but only 0.5 km on the west; normally three islands were visible. The lake was fed by a river entering in the north-east and formed by a confluence of the Gardez, Ghazni and Nahara rivers. Extensive semi-desert steppe surrounded the lake and mudflats; characteristic shrubs were *Amygdalus*, *Cousinia*, *Artemisia* and *Tamarix*. *Carex* predominated in a small marsh at the river mouth in the north-east corner, but otherwise there was little plant life in the lake proper or on the mudflats, apart from *Ruppia*. There were no fish in the lake. There were 2,500 people in 15 villages within 10 km of the lake area, concentrated 8 km to the north-east, as well as c.200–300 semi-nomadic people living in the area, with traditional grazing rights for their livestock on the plains. Following a survey in November 1993, the following changes are apparent. Average water levels are higher than in past years, and the water is fresher, due apparently to much water being released from the Band-i-Sardeh dam upstream by local Mujahideen commanders. Fish now occur in the lake. Most villagers left as refugees during the war, but the semi-nomadic people remained. The site is important archaeologically, having several early dwelling mounds and accompanying artefacts. Roads to the area are usually not passable in winter.

■ Birds

A very important wetland for migrating waterfowl and *Grus leucogeranus* in particular, as well as for breeding *Phoenicopterus ruber*. See box for key species. The whole of the tiny, remaining 'central' of the three known breeding populations of *G. leucogeranus* depends on the site as a key 're-fuelling' area whilst on spring migration en route between the Ganges plain in India and Siberia; the species almost certainly uses the site on autumn passage in some years as well, since there is a record of 3 birds in December 1970, although a one-month survey in November 1993 did not locate the species. Since at least the late 1960s, numbers have been declining steadily (e.g. max. 76 at Ab-i-Istada in March 1970, compared to only 5 in India in winter 1992/3), with uncontrolled crane-hunting in Pakistan and Afghanistan being the prime suspect for the decline. *P. ruber* breeds on the islands: 2,900–9,000 birds were present in the three springs of 1969, 1970 and 1974 (an average of c.5,700 birds) but the colony fluctuates markedly in size and in many years no breeding takes place; when conditions are unsuitable the birds shift to Dashte Nawar (see site 013), where breeding was more frequent than at Ab-i-Istada during 1966–1975. Other breeding species include *Tadorna tadorna* (100 pairs), *Recurvirostra avosetta*, *Charadrius alexandrinus*, *C. leschenaultii* and *Larus genei* (100+ birds, June). Large numbers of waterfowl occur on spring passage (when water levels are highest), and several thousand ducks can be present in winter in years of high spring-melt water flow and if the lake does not freeze over; other winter counts include *Recurvirostra avosetta* (285). Over 60 bird species have been recorded. The site was listed as a wetland of international importance by Carp (1980).

Globally threatened species

Oxyura leucocephala	Recorded in May 1977.
Grus leucogeranus	Very rare passage migrant (see text).

1% or more of population

	Breeding (pairs)	Wintering	Passage
Ardea cinerea	—	263	—
Casmerodius albus	—	188	60
Phoenicopterus ruber	c.2,850	—	—
Anser anser	—	1,457	—
Anas clypeata	—	—	1,600
Aythya ferina	—	—	15,000
Himantopus himantopus	breeds	—	594
Calidris minuta	—	—	6,300
Philomachus pugnax	—	—	1,300
Sterna nilotica	breeds	—	580

Species restricted wholly or largely to the Middle East

Glareola nordmanni	Summer visitor, presumed to breed (2+ birds, June 1972).

■ Other threatened/endemic wildlife

None known to BirdLife International.

■ Conservation issues

Game guards were employed during the summer from 1974 to 1979. A management plan was prepared in 1977, and the area was approved as a Wildlife Sanctuary by the Head of State in 1977. Damming and water extraction from feeder rivers (especially the Ghazni and Gardez) for irrigation projects during the 1980s no doubt led to lower-than-average water levels and possibly to an increase in salinity; theoretically, this may have reduced or eliminated the sedge tubers on which *Grus leucogeranus* depends for food, and will also have reduced the likelihood of the site providing an autumn migration staging post for this species. The higher-than-average water levels observed in November 1993 had submerged at least two of the three islands and *Phoenicopterus ruber* did not breed in that year. Hunting of waterfowl in 1993 is occurring only at a low, subsistence level but may still pose a significant threat for *Grus leucogeranus*; local people are not aware of the species or its endangered status. Grazing pressure is heavy in places. During the 1980s the Air Force occasionally used the lake for bombing practise. The site was proposed as a National Park in 1981.

■ Further reading

Carp (1980), Jamil (1994), Petocz and Habibi (1975), Shank and Rodenburg (1977).

016 Hamun-i-Puzak (Nimroz)

Unprotected

31°36′N 61°48′E
35,000 ha

Site description

A very large, permanent, shallow, fresh to brackish lake, lying in the Seistan desert in extreme south-west Afghanistan at 500 m, and surrounded by vast *Phragmites* reedbeds. It derives its waters from the Khashrud river, which is dry in summer but in spring carries meltwater from the central highlands of Afghanistan; formerly the Helmand river was also important but since construction of Kajaki Dam this river has carried little water into the Puzak. The wetland has always been subject to wide fluctuations in size according to variations in rainfall and snowfall in the mountains. About a third of the swampland is in Iran but by far the most permanent wetland is in Afghanistan, where at least formerly the habitat probably never dried out completely, even in the driest years. The wetland is fringed by *Tamarix* scrub, and surrounding desert is dominated by *Artemisia* steppe. In the 1970s the human population was relatively small (a total of c.1,000 in several villages).

Birds

This is the most important wetland in Afghanistan and of major international importance, estimated to hold up to one million wildfowl in winter. A total of 357,000 birds was counted in January 1976 during an aerial survey organized jointly with the Iranian government: see box for key species. Other wintering species in the 1970s included *Tadorna tadorna* (211), *Circus aeruginosus* (51) and *Porphyrio porphyrio*. Little is known of breeding or passage species as most visits have been in mid-winter; former breeding species included *Phoenicopterus ruber*, *Anser anser*, *Cygnus olor*, *Netta rufina* (possibly), and currently may still include *Picus squamatus flavirostris* (although possibly now extinct in Seistan through destruction of trees), *Caprimulgus mahrattensis* (reported as common by Cumming 1905 but not found subsequently, even by Paludan in 1949) and *C. aegyptiacus* (probable).

Globally threatened species

Pelecanus crispus	Probable winter visitor, since regular on the Iranian side.
Anser erythropus	Winter visitor, at least formerly (Savage 1968); no records in 1970s.
Marmaronetta angustirostris	Recorded in winter (63, February 1971) but also probably still breeds (possibly several hundred pairs).
Oxyura leucocephala	Recorded in winter: 'common' in 1904/5, and a count of 10 in the 1970s. However, up to c.1,000 birds which winter in nearby Pakistan (especially in drought years) may well originate from this site, suggesting a breeding population of up to 300 pairs.
Aegypius monachus	Winter visitor (max. 2).
Haliaeetus albicilla	Winter visitor (max. 11).
Aquila heliaca	Winter visitor (max. 7).
Chlamydotis undulata	Probably a regular winter visitor in surrounding deserts (cf. Iranian side).

1% or more of population

	Breeding (pairs)	Wintering	Passage
Pelecanus onocrotalus	—	1,260	—
Ardea cinerea	—	425	—
Casmerodius albus	—	1,826	—
Anser anser	?	3,150	—
Anas acuta	—	15,600	—
Anas clypeata	—	10,100	—
Anas crecca	—	27,220	—
Anas penelope	—	11,050	—
Anas platyrhynchos	—	21,326	—
Anas strepera	—	12,050	—
Marmaronetta angustirostris	hundreds?	63	—
Netta rufina	—	2,500	—
Aythya ferina	—	50,000	—
Aythya fuligula	—	2,500	—
Aythya nyroca	?	100	—
Oxyura leucocephala	300?	10	—
Fulica atra	—	175,000	—
Limosa limosa	—	895	—
Tringa nebularia	—	290	—
Larus ichthyaetus	—	100	—

Regionally threatened or declining species

Aythya nyroca	Winter visitor (see above); possibly breeds.
Francolinus francolinus	Resident.

Species restricted wholly or largely to the Middle East

Hypocolius ampelinus	Probable summer visitor.
Passer moabiticus	The subspecies *P. m. yatii* is endemic to, and a scarce resident in, the Seistan basin.

Other threatened/endemic wildlife

Mammals: *Canis lupus* (V) is said to be common. The entire Seistan area is a unique ecosystem, but is very poorly known.

Conservation issues

No formal conservation measures are known to have been taken, and no part of the area is legally protected for nature conservation despite its ecological uniqueness and global importance. Extensive dam-building, water diversion and irrigation schemes in Afghanistan and Iran extract water from the feeder rivers, especially the Helmand, in an unregulated way (contrary to the nature of existing bilateral agreements dating from the previous century) and have reduced the flow of water into the lake. In severe periods of drought, its area can contract alarmingly, although in the drought years of the mid- to late

1980s, when the Iranian wetlands dried out completely, satellite imagery showed that the Afghani sector still remained flooded with vast reedbeds. In addition, according to recent reports from FAO in Islamabad, the exceptional floods of early 1991 destroyed the Kajaki Dam and damaged other irrigation systems on the Helmand in Afghanistan, so for the present there seems to be no problems of water supply in the Helmand river—though there is apparently a proposal to build a new dam in Afghanistan (the Kamal Khan Dam). *Phragmites* beds are used extensively for fuel, fodder and house and boat construction and are also widely burnt (to encourage regeneration), affecting breeding bird populations. A critical threat in the future may be a proposal (first made in 1976) to construct a paper factory in adjacent Helmand Province which would use reeds from Seistan; the impact of such a scheme on the functioning of the ecosystem is unknown but potentially very severe. In the 1970s wildfowl hunting was uncontrolled but only practised by local people, and was therefore sustainable. Without the creation of protected areas, expansion and commercialization of hunting might pose a major threat however. The site was proposed as a National Park before 1979.

■ Further reading

Green (1993), Petocz, Rodenburg and Habibi (1976).

017 Registan Desert (Kandahar)

Unprotected

30°30′N 65°00′E
3,000,000 ha

■ Site description

The largest desert area of Afghanistan, due south of Kandahar at 800–1,200 m; it extends over a vast tract of southern Afghanistan to the borders of Pakistani Baluchistan, bordered by the Helmand river to the west and its tributary the Arghestan to the north. The desert contains a wide cross-section of desert biotopes from free-moving sand to gravel plains. The area is very cold in winter, very hot in summer. There is no precise information available on habitats and vegetation, but these are potentially rich and varied.

■ Birds

This vast region is virtually unstudied ornithologically, and species listed are based on observations made during the nineteenth century, so no confident comments can be made on present status. See box for key species. Other breeding species probably include *Francolinus pondicerianus* (possibly), *Cursorius cursor*, *Pterocles coronatus*, *P. senegallus*, *P. alchata*, *Caprimulgus mahrattensis* (possibly), *Ammomanes cincturus*, *Alaemon alaudipes*, *Calandrella rufescens*, *Hippolais rama*, *Turdoides caudatus*, *Petronia xanthocollis* and *Rhodopechys githaginea*. Passage and/or wintering species probably include *Phoenicurus erythronota* and *Rhodopechys mongolica*.

Globally threatened species	
Chlamydotis undulata	Probably breeds.
Saxicola macrorhyncha	Possibly resident (2 specimens from April 1891, British Museum).
Species restricted wholly or largely to the Middle East	
Ammoperdix griseogularis	Probably breeds.
Hypocolius ampelinus	Probably breeds.
Oenanthe finschii	Occurs on passage and/or in winter.
Oenanthe xanthoprymna	Occurs on passage and/or in winter.
Oenanthe picata	Occurs on passage and/or in winter.
Oenanthe alboniger	Said by Ticehurst (1927) to occur in winter in Kandahar district, but all published sight records in Afghanistan are suspect due to possible confusion with *O. picata*.
Sylvia minula	Occurs on passage and/or in winter.

■ Other threatened/endemic wildlife

Mammals: older reports recorded large herds of *Gazella subgutturosa* (rare), *Equus hemionus onager* (V) and possibly *Gazella bennetti* (V), but these populations have no doubt been decimated. Larger predators included *Acinonyx jubatus* (V; now surely extinct) and *Caracal caracal* (rare).

■ Conservation issues

No official conservation measures are known to have been taken. Over-hunting, overgrazing and destruction of the desert crust are thought to be ubiquitous problems. The population sizes of remaining *Chlamydotis undulata* and the larger mammals are completely unknown.

■ Further reading

Sayer and van der Zon (1981), Ticehurst (1927).

MAIN REFERENCES

CARP, E. (1980) *A directory of western Palaearctic wetlands.* Nairobi: United Nations Environment Programme/Gland (Switzerland): International Union for Conservation of Nature and Natural Resources.

DAY, S. I. (1988) Directory of Protected Areas: Afghanistan. Unpublished report by Protected Areas Data Unit of the World Conservation Monitoring Centre, Cambridge, U.K.

GREEN, A. J. (1993) *The status and conservation of the Marbled Teal* Marmaronetta angustirostris. Slimbridge, U.K.: International Waterfowl and Wetlands Research Bureau (Spec. Publ. 23).

JAMIL, A. (1994) Mission to the Ab-i-Estada, Ghazni Province, Afghanistan, 23.10.93 to 23.11.93. Unpublished report to International Crane Foundation and BirdLife International.

MADGE, S. C. (1970) Notes on the migration of birds through Bande Amir. Unpublished report.

MADGE, S. C. (1978) Birds of the Salang Pass, central Afghanistan. *Bull. Orn. Soc. Middle East* 1: 2–5.

NIETHAMMER, J. (1967) Zwei Jahre Vogelbeobachtungen an stehenden Gewassern bei Kabul in Afghanistan. *J. Orn.* 108: 119–164.

NOGGE, G. (1973) Ornithologische Beobachtungen im afghanischen Pamir. *Bonn. Zool. Beitr.* 24: 254–269.

PALUDAN, K. (1959) On the birds of Afghanistan. *Vidensk. Medd. Dansk naturh. For.* 122: 1–322.

PETOCZ, R. G. (1978) Report on the Afghan Pamir. Unpublished FAO report. FO/DP/AFG/74/016.

PETOCZ, R. G. AND HABIBI, K. (1975) The flamingoes of Ab-i-Estada and Dashte Nawar. Ghazni Province, Afghanistan. Unpublished FAO report. FO/DP/AFG/72/005.

PETOCZ, R. G. AND LARSSON, J. Y. (1977) Ecological reconnaissance of western Nuristan with recommendations for management. Unpublished FAO report. FO/DP/AFG/74/016.

PETOCZ, R. G., RODENBURG, W. F. AND HABIBI, K. (1976) The birds of Hamun-i-Puzak. Unpublished FAO report. FO/DP/AFG/72/005.

PETOCZ, R. G. AND SKOGLAND, T. (1974) Report on the status of Band-e Amir National Park. Unpublished FAO/UNDP report. FO/DP/AFG/72/005.

PUGET, A. (1969) Contribution à l'étude des oiseaux du nord-est de l'Afghanistan. Thesis. University of Toulouse, France.

PUGET, A. (1971) Observations sur l'avifaune nidificatrice de l'étang de Binihesar (Chamane Qala Hachmatran) dans la proche banlieue de Kaboul en Afghanistan. *Alauda* 39: 139–144.

RAHIM, A. AND LARSSON, J. Y. (1978) A preliminary study of Lake Hashmat Khan with recommendations for management. Unpublished FAO report. FO/DP/AFG/74/016.

SAYER, J. A. AND VAN DER ZON, A. P. M. (1981) National Parks and wildlife management, Afghanistan. A contribution to a conservation strategy. Unpublished FAO report. FO/DP/AFG/78/007.

SHANK, C. C. AND LARSSON, J. Y. (1977) A strategy for the establishment and development of Band-e-Amir National Park. Unpublished FAO report. FO/DP/AFG/74/016.

SHANK, C. C. AND RODENBURG, W. F. (1977) Management plan for Ab-i-Estada and Dashte-Nawar flamingo and waterfowl sanctuaries. Unpublished FAO report. FO/DP/AFG/74/016.

SMITH, E. C. (1974) Some additional information on birds in Afghanistan. *Ardea* 62: 226–235.

TICEHURST, C. B. (1927) The birds of British Baluchistan. *J. Bombay Nat. Hist. Soc.* 31 (in 3 parts).

WARDLAW-RAMSAY, R. G. (1879) Ornithological notes from Afghanistan. *Ibis* (4) 3: 444–449.

WARDLAW-RAMSAY, R. G. (1880) Ornithological notes from Afghanistan. *Ibis* (4) 4: 45–71.

■ STATE OF BAHRAIN

Grey Hypocolius *Hypocolius ampelinus*

GENERAL INFORMATION

Bahrain is an archipelago of 33 low-lying, desert islands with a total land area of c.693 km^2, situated half-way down the Arabian Gulf, c.30 km east of Saudi Arabia, c.30 km west of Qatar and c.100 km south of Iran. Most of the islands are small apart from the main island of Bahrain, and the highest point is Jabal ad Dukhan at 134 m. The total human population in 1991 was about 516,400, with an annual growth rate of 3.5%. The country has a high average population density of c.745 persons per km^2, with most people residing in urban areas in northern, coastal Bahrain. Public access to southern Bahrain is restricted and it remains for the most part uninhabited, undeveloped desert, relatively free from human pressure.

The clear, shallow seas surrounding Bahrain are highly productive, being mostly less than 10 m deep and with much of the substrate being muddy or seagrass-dominated. Extensive reefs occur, especially north and east of Bahrain. The intertidal zone is also productive and extensive, especially in the north and east of the main island where it can be up to 3 km or more in width at low tide. Mangrove *Avicennia* occurs locally in the north-east of the main island, and fringing saltmarsh vegetation is locally common on more sheltered coasts. There is a low diversity of terrestrial habitats due to the harsh environment, lack of contrasting physical features and limited freshwater resources. The vegetation is mainly low, desert shrubland with many salt-tolerant species and no known endemics. There are extensive date-palm gardens in the north of the island, sustained by the good groundwater supply there.

ORNITHOLOGICAL IMPORTANCE

Of the 294 species recorded in the country (excluding escapes and introductions), 20 are resident (mostly Palearctic desert species), eight are summer visitors, 70 are winter visitors and 117 are regularly occurring passage migrants (mostly birds moving along the Palearctic–African flyway, and to a much lesser degree along the Palearctic–Indian flyway). The rest are irregular migrants or vagrants.

One globally threatened species occurs regularly in Bahrain: *Chlamydotis undulata* is an uncommon passage migrant in autumn and a rare winter visitor to the open desert in the south of the island. The offshore islands and shallow seas which surround Bahrain are globally important for breeding *Phalacrocorax nigrogularis* (40,000–100,000 pairs, on the

Hawar Archipelago), and also support internationally important breeding populations of *Egretta gularis* (100 pairs), *Sterna repressa* (2,250–3,250 pairs; mostly on mainland beaches in the south-west) and *Sterna saundersi* (125+ pairs). The intertidal mudflats of the northern and eastern coast of Bahrain provide feeding and roosting sites for important numbers of migrating and wintering coastal waterbirds, especially *Charadrius mongolus*, *Limicola falcinellus*, *Tringa cinerea* and *Larus genei*. Large numbers of *Hypocolius ampelinus* feed and roost in date-palm gardens in the north and central regions during autumn passage and to a lesser extent in winter.

CONSERVATION INFRASTRUCTURE AND PROTECTED-AREA SYSTEM

The Environmental Protection Committee (EPC) is the government body which controls and coordinates environmental matters including site protection for nature conservation. The EPC is supported by the Environmental Protection Technical Secretariat (EPTS), which prepares information for the Committee, including on the identification of key sites, and implements its decisions, including the protection of sites. There is no nature conservation legislation nor overall environmental Act in Bahrain, nor is the creation of protected sites for nature conservation covered under any extant legislation. However areas can be protected for nature conservation by individual Amiri decree. Two types of area have been protected thus far:

Wildlife Reserve

Two sites. Defined as an area left essentially in its natural state, although some Arabian wildlife can be reintroduced to augment existing populations. Management is by the EPC (both sites) and the Al-Areen Wildlife Park Authority (one site), and aims to encourage restoration of natural communities and to minimize the planting or spread of foreign vegetation. Public access is prohibited; entry is restricted to scientific researchers and authorized personnel.

Hema (Wildlife Park)

One site. Established for visitor use by the general public with the aim of increasing awareness of wildlife conservation, and administered by the Al-Areen Wildlife Park Authority and the EPC.

The southern part of the main island and most subsidiary islands are out-of-bounds except for fishermen and people with special permission, which affords considerable protection. The Land Use and Planning Act (1971), Water Act (1971) and Public Health Act (1975) may also provide some planning protection for sites which are threatened by proposed activities involving land-claim/construction/quarrying, groundwater extraction and pollution, respectively.

INTERNATIONAL MEASURES RELEVANT TO THE CONSERVATION OF SITES

Bahrain has ratified the World Heritage Convention and has signed the Biodiversity Convention and the Regional Convention for Cooperation on the Protection of the Marine Environment from Pollution, including the Kuwait Action Plan, but is not a signatory to the Ramsar or Bonn Conventions. The EPTS is currently studying this issue.

OVERVIEW OF THE INVENTORY

Four sites are contained in the following inventory, comprising c.85 km^2, or about 12% of the land area of the country, and covering most of the major habitats of importance for bird conservation: offshore islands and undisturbed sand beaches for breeding seabirds, intertidal wetlands for wintering and migrating waterfowl, and palm scrub in the interior for the Middle East endemic *Hypocolius ampelinus*. However in the case of the globally threatened *Chlamydotis undulata*, which is thinly dispersed over large areas of southern Bahrain, it has not been possible to identify sites of moderate size which are particularly important. The conservation of such dispersed species may be better achieved by more extensive measures than by a sites approach.

Part of one site in the inventory is formally protected for nature conservation, and one site receives some *de facto* protection through being in a restricted, military area. At least two of the four sites are largely free of immediate problems, but the extent and quality of important coastal habitats in north-east Bahrain have been, and continue to be, severely reduced by land-claim and dredging (driven by population increase and industrial expansion), and one site (Tubli Bay) can be considered seriously threatened by these activities.

ACKNOWLEDGEMENTS

The site accounts were compiled from information supplied mainly by Dr S. Mohamed (Vice-Chairman, Bahrain Natural History Society), with assistance from E. Hirschfeld (Bird Recorder, Bahrain Natural History Society). The introduction was compiled partly from information supplied by Dr Khalid Fakhro (Vice-Chairman, Environmental Protection Committee). T. Nightingale helped with advice and information.

SITE INVENTORY

Site no.	Site name	1	2i	2ii	2iii	3	4	5i	5ii	6	0
		Criteria used to select site									
001	Tubli Bay	—	•	—	—	—	—	—	•	•	—
002	Maqabah	—	—	—	—	—	•	—	•	•	—
003	South-west Coast	—	•	—	—	—	•	—	—	—	—
004	Hawar Islands	—	•	•	—	•	•	•	•	•	—

Key to criteria

1 Regularly holds a significant number of a globally threatened species.
2i Regularly holds 1% or more of a species' biogeographical or flyway or Middle Eastern population (waterbirds and seabirds only).
2ii Regularly holds 20,000 or more waterbirds.
2iii Migratory 'bottleneck' site: more than 3,000 raptors or more than 5,000 storks or more than 2,000 cranes pass in a season.
3 Regularly holds a significant number of a species which is threatened or declining within the Middle East. Only the top five sites for each such species in the country are considered to qualify as IBAs.
4 Regularly holds a significant number of a species whose world population is wholly or largely restricted to the Middle East. Only the top five sites for each such species in the country are considered to qualify as IBAs.
5i Representative example of a habitat, associated with a characteristic assemblage of bird species.
5ii Rare/threatened/unique habitat, associated with a characteristic assemblage of bird species.
6 Site important for bird conservation through education/research/ tourism.
0 Selected for other reasons. See 'Comments on the inventory'.

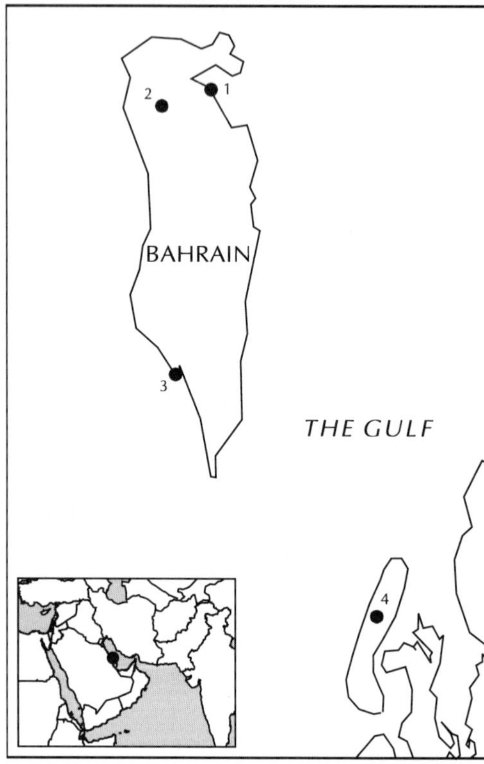

Comments on the inventory

1. All counts are maximum daily counts of individuals (not pairs), unless otherwise stated.
2. All winter counts are from January unless otherwise stated.
3. All counts are post-1979 unless otherwise stated.
4. The Hawar Islands have been very little visited in high summer, therefore the actual breeding population sizes of terns are likely to be higher than the counts given here.

001 Tubli Bay

Wildlife Reserve (250 ha)

26°11´N 50°34´E
2,500 ha

■ Site description

A shallow, sheltered bay in an urban/industrial area, with saltmarsh vegetation, extensive mudflats (mainly on the east side) and a large area of mangrove *Avicennia* (the last remaining area in the country) in the south-west corner of the bay at Sanad. Tidal amplitude is up to 2.5 m and salinity exceeds 4.0%. There are many freshwater springs offshore and onshore, the latter associated with *Phragmites* reedbeds and date-palm gardens. The bay is an important spawning and nursery area for fish and prawns. It receives irrigation run-off from the date gardens and also fully treated sewage effluent.

■ Birds

The most important site in the country for migrating

and wintering coastal waterbirds. See box for key species. Other wintering species include *Egretta garzetta* (100), *Charadrius hiaticula* (300), *Calidris minuta* (1,000), *Arenaria interpres* (250), *Larus ichthyaetus* (150) and *Larus ridibundus* (2,000).

1% or more of population

	Breeding (pairs)	Wintering	Passage
Ardea cinerea	—	218	—
Charadrius alexandrinus	100	500	1,500
Charadrius mongolus	—	500	2,000 (Aug)
Pluvialis squatarola	—	—	500 (Apr)
Limicola falcinellus	—	300	800 (Aug/Nov)
Larus genei	—	1,000	3,000

Other threatened/endemic wildlife
None known to BirdLife International.

Conservation issues
The entire mangrove area at Ras Sanad is a Wildlife Reserve, and there is a mangrove re-planting programme. Land-claim and dredging are a critical problem: since 1975 most of the original mangrove and other intertidal and shallow subtidal habitats (as well as date-palm gardens) have been lost to housing, roads and other urban and industrial development, especially along the northern shore of the Bay. Irresponsible hunting, excessive disturbance of birds by recreational activities, and oil pollution are all major problems at the site.

002 Maqabah
Unprotected

26°10′N 50°30′E
500 ha

Site description
An inland, semi-arid, sandy desert site, with 60% cover of scattered date-palm *Phoenix dactylifera* scrub. Privately owned and currently left uncultivated, unlike nearby areas.

Birds
See box for key species. The palm scrub is the main roost-site for *Hypocolius ampelinus* in Bahrain. The birds feed in date-palm gardens elsewhere.

Species restricted wholly or largely to the Middle East

Hypocolius ampelinus	Common autumn passage migrant (av. max. 500, November–December); very rare in spring. Rare but regular winter visitor (av. max. 35).

Other threatened/endemic wildlife
None known to BirdLife International.

Conservation issues
Some cutting of date-palm scrub and disturbance of *Hypocolius* roosts occurs locally. Lack of human disturbance is essential for roosts, but recently agricultural and housing development has intensified close to the site. The site has been proposed as a Wildlife Reserve.

003 South-west Coast
Unprotected

25°57′N 50°31′E
250 ha

Site description
Long, sand beach on the south-west coast of the main island. An isolated area, relatively undisturbed by humans.

Birds
See box for key species. Important numbers of *Sterna repressa* breed along the mainland coast in several colonies.

1% or more of population

	Breeding (pairs)	Wintering	Passage
Sterna repressa	2,000–3,000	—	—

Species restricted wholly or largely to the Middle East

Sterna repressa	Common summer visitor (see above).

Other threatened/endemic wildlife
Mammals: introduced *Gazella* spp. (some indigenous) are free-living in the desert inland.

Conservation issues
Although no formal protected area for nature conservation exists, public access to most of southern Bahrain is restricted to people with special permission, thus affording considerable protection. Disturbance from human activities remains a threat however, and the colonies are vulnerable to oil pollution of the beaches (as happened in 1980).

004 Hawar Islands

Unprotected

25°40´N 50°50´E
5,300 ha

Site description

A group of 16 small, limestone, desert islands and islets in the Gulf of Salwah, some with cliffs up to 20–30 m high. There is c.20% vegetation cover of saltmarsh bushes, and very extensive seagrass beds in the shallow, clear sea offshore. A highly productive nursery and feeding area for fish. The islands are uninhabited apart from a military garrison.

Birds

See box for key species. The islands support the largest known breeding concentration in the world of *Phalacrocorax nigrogularis*. The main breeding site is on Suwad al Janubiyah island, where 200,000 to 300,000 adults were conservatively estimated to be present in November 1992, along with thousands of nests with eggs. Other breeding species include *Sterna caspia* (max. 10 pairs), *S. anaethetus* (max. 100 pairs) and *Pandion haliaetus* (max. 9 pairs). Wintering species include *Podiceps cristatus* (min. 50) and *Phoenicopterus ruber* (750).

1% or more of population

	Breeding (pairs)	Wintering	Passage
Phalacrocorax nigrogularis	100,000–150,000	—	—
Egretta gularis	100	—	200 (Oct)
Larus cachinnans/L. argentatus	—	500	—
Sterna saundersi	100	—	—

Regionally threatened or declining species

Falco concolor — Summer visitor (max. 13 pairs).

Species restricted wholly or largely to the Middle East

Phalacrocorax nigrogularis — Abundant breeding species (see above); the majority moves elsewhere after breeding.

Sterna repressa — Summer visitor (max. 100 pairs); 2,000 recorded in October.

Sterna saundersi — Summer visitor (see above).

Other threatened/endemic wildlife

Mammals: the second largest population in the world of *Dugong dugon* (V) occurs here (700+); unspecified *Gazella* spp. on Hawar island (apparently introduced). Reptiles: the sea-turtles *Chelonia mydas* (E), *Eretmochelys imbricata* (E), *Dermochelys coriacea* (E) and *Caretta caretta* (V) occur, and *Chelonia mydas* may breed.

Conservation issues

The islands are a restricted military area and access by the general public is prohibited, thus they receive some unintentional protection from non-military disturbance. However, over-collection of eggs and capturing of birds (especially chicks of *Phalacrocorax nigrogularis*) by fishermen is a problem, although the scale has not been quantified. Disturbance by human visitors also greatly facilitates predation of *P. nigrogularis* chicks by gulls, e.g. *Larus cachinnans/L. argentatus*. The site has been affected by major oil spills in the past (e.g. during the 1980–1988 Iran–Iraq war), and this is a critical potential threat, especially during the breeding season. Sovereignty over the islands is formally disputed with Qatar, and the issue is currently before the International Court of Justice. The Hawar islands have a fauna and flora which is perhaps typical and representative of the few remaining unspoilt islands in the whole Arabian Gulf, and they are thus increasingly unique in the region. The islands have been proposed as a Wildlife Reserve.

MAIN REFERENCES

El-Hinnawi, E., ed. (1988) *Bahrain. State of the Environment report.* Nairobi: United Nations Environment Programme.

Hallam, T. J., ed. (1980) *Wildlife in Bahrain.* Bahrain: Bahrain Natural History Society.

Hill, M. and Nightingale, T., eds. (1984) *Wildlife in Bahrain.* Bahrain: Bahrain Natural History Society (Third Biennial Report).

Nightingale, T. and Overy, M., eds. (1987) *Wildlife in Bahrain.* Bahrain: Bahrain Natural History Society (Fourth Biennial Report).

Hirschfeld, E., Mohamed, S. A. and Stawarczyk, T. (1992) *Bahrain wader study 1991.* Zeist, Netherlands: Foundation Working Group International Wader and Waterfowl Research (WIWO report no. 42).

Nightingale, T. and Hill, M. (1993) *The birds of Bahrain.* London: Immel.

Tucker, G. (1985) Autumn wader migration in Bahrain. *Wader Study Group Bull.* 44: 30–32.

■ ISLAMIC REPUBLIC OF IRAN

Siberian White Crane *Grus leucogeranus*

GENERAL INFORMATION

The Islamic Republic of Iran has a land area of 1,648,184 km^2 and is bordered by Iraq, Turkey, Armenia, Azerbaijan, Turkmenistan, Afghanistan and Pakistan. The country has over 2,000 km of coastline in its southern region, about two-thirds of which faces the Persian Gulf with the remainder lying east of the Strait of Hormoz in the Gulf of Oman. The human population was 54,607,000 in 1990, with a natural annual increase of 2.01%.

Iran supports some 7,000 plant species, of which about 20% are endemic. Most endemics are found in mountains; centres of endemism include the peaks of the Alborz and Zagros massifs, solitary peaks in the central plain, the mountain ridges south of Kashan and Yazd, and to the north and south of Kerman. The central plateau is species-poor. Lying as a bridge between four major plant geographical regions (Irano-Turanian, Euro-Siberian, Saharo-Arabian and Sudanian), Iran is one of the largest speciation centres of Holarctic desert flora, with Irano-Turanian plants predominating. Approximately 60% of the country is classified as desert and semi-desert. Hot desert in the south-east supports sparse open scrub of *Acacia*, *Ziziphus* and *Prosopis* on rocky slopes; there are herbaceous communities with *Atriplex* and *Heliotropium* in sandy depressions, and steppes and deserts with *Artemisia* and *Astragalus* occur over most of the centre and east of the country. There are up to 3.75 million ha of woodland, with dry, deciduous forests in the west, *Pistacia–Amygdalus* steppe forest in the south and west, *Juniperus* steppe woodland in the north, and broad-leaved temperate forest with *Alnus*, *Quercus*, *Fagus* and *Carpinus* in the north up to 2,500 m, as well as c.8,900 ha of *Avicennia* mangrove along the Gulf coast. Between 1967 and 1980, 12,000 ha of forest plantation had been established and almost 70,000 ha of desert lands planted or seeded. Up to 11.5% of the land area is under cultivation, although more than half of the country is classified as uncultivable.

The coastal zone is predominantly limestone with some shales and salt- domes. Annual rainfall in the coastal region ranges from 100 to 300 mm, mostly falling between November and April. Temperatures reach 45°C in summer and fall to 5–10°C in the winter. There is a rich and diverse marine fauna, seagrass beds and coral. The western half of Iran's coastline contains estuarine conditions, sand-dunes, extensive tidal flats and mangroves, with an area of cliffs near the Strait of Hormoz. The easternmost part of the Gulf coast has eight offshore islands extending west to Bandar Abbas in the Strait. All are rocky and sparsely populated. In the Gulf of Oman, offshore depths increase to over 50 m and the coastline has extensive sand-dunes, sand beaches and areas of cliffs. The large bays at Chahbahar and Pozam in south-east Baluchistan are two of the finest bays along Iran's south coast and lie in a region with an extremely rich and diverse marine fauna. There is a large artisanal fishery in Iran. Very little oil pollution was reported in the mid-1970s, with the exception of localized concentrations.

ORNITHOLOGICAL IMPORTANCE

Iran possesses a very rich and diverse bird fauna, despite the fact that large portions of the country are arid to semi-arid; 491 species have been recorded. Two main factors are responsible for this: the great range of habitats—from permanent snows to deep deserts and from lush deciduous forest in the north to palm groves and mangrove in the south—and Iran's position at a crossroads between three major faunal regions. The bulk of the country lies within the Palearctic realm. Lying along the southern edge of this region, Iran's bird fauna includes a large western Palearctic faunal element, reaching its eastern extremity in the central Alborz and Zagros mountains, and a smaller, but still marked, eastern Palearctic element, which extends into north-east Iran in the highlands of Khorasan. In southern Iran, two other faunal regions have a pronounced influence on the avifauna: the Indo-Malayan realm in the south-east and the Afrotropical realm in the south-west.

Of 324 breeding species, 131 occur widely in the Palearctic region. Eighty-one are western Palearctic species, reaching the easternmost extremities of their ranges in Iran, while 19 are typically eastern Palearctic species, reaching the westernmost tip of their ranges in Iran. A further 25 species are characteristic of the great Saharo-Sindian desert belt which stretches along the southern edge of the Palearctic region from North Africa through the Middle East to Mongolia, while another 24 are Palearctic species with restricted ranges in the Middle East. The bird fauna of southern Iranian Baluchistan and the southern Persian Gulf coast is predominantly Indo-Malayan, with some 29 breeding species of Indo-Malayan origin reaching the north-west extremities of their ranges in Iran, while in south-west Iran there is a small Afrotropical influence with six breeding species of African origin. Finally, there are nine species of seabird and shorebird of the Indian Ocean, which breed on islands in the Persian Gulf and the Strait of Hormoz.

Eight major habitat types may be identified, each with its own characteristic bird fauna, as follows:

True desert and semi-desert

The desert environment occurs throughout the central desert basin from the region of Tehran through the great Dasht-e Kavir and Dasht-e Lut deserts to the Jaz Murian basin in central Baluchistan and locally along the southern coastal lowlands from north-west Khuzestan to Baluchistan. Rather few species occur in true desert, and densities are very low, but most of those species which have become adapted to this hostile environment have large ranges both in Iran and in the southern Palearctic as a whole. Examples include *Chlamydotis undulata*, *Cursorius cursor*, *Pterocles senegallus* and *P. coronatus*, *Ammomanes deserti* and *A. cincturus*, *Alaemon alaudipes*, *Sylvia nana*, *Oenanthe deserti*, *O. monacha* and *Rhodopechys githaginea*. Although Iran possesses no true endemic species, one species, *Podoces pleskei*, which occurs widely in the deserts of central and eastern Iran, is almost confined to the country, and is known elsewhere only from extreme western Pakistan.

Semi-arid steppe of the desert rim and foothills

Much of Iran's land surface, lying between 1,500 and 2,000 m in elevation and with an annual rainfall of between 100 and 300 mm, supports a steppe vegetation dominated by the low shrub *Artemisia herba-alba*. Large tracts have been modified by man, either through the grazing of domestic animals or irrigation and cultivation, particularly for cereals. The resulting patchwork is now the home of many of Iran's commonest and most widespread birds. Characteristic species include *Buteo rufinus*, *Falco tinnunculus*, *Pterocles orientalis*, *Coracias garrulus*, *Merops apiaster*, several species of lark including the ubiquitous *Galerida cristata*, *Oenanthe isabellina* and *Emberiza melanocephala*.

High mountains

The alpine zones of the Alborz and Zagros mountains and the higher peaks of mountain ranges in Azarbayjan, Khorasan, Kerman and Baluchistan provinces support a montane fauna typical of all high mountain ranges from the Pyrenees and Alps in western Europe to the Himalayas. Characteristic species include *Aquila chrysaetos*, *Gypaetus barbatus*, *Tachymarptis melba*, *Hirundo rupestris*, *Eremophila alpestris*, *Pyrrhocorax graculus*, *Prunella collaris*, *Monticola saxatilis*, *Phoenicurus ochruros*, *Tichodroma muraria* and *Montifringilla nivalis*. *Tetraogallus caspius*, which is confined to high mountain ranges in Turkey and Iran, is still locally common on the highest peaks in the Alborz and Zagros.

Forests and woodland

Although of rather limited extent, Iran's forested regions possess a very rich bird fauna, which is largely western Palearctic in affinities. The luxuriant forests of northern Azarbayjan and the south Caspian region have a bird fauna scarcely different from that of a central European woodland, with common species including *Columba palumbus*, *Picus viridis*, *Dendrocopos major*, *Anthus trivialis*, *Lanius collurio*, *Garrulus glandarius*, *Troglodytes troglodytes*, *Prunella modularis*, *Sylvia atricapilla*, *Hippolais icterina*, *Erithacus rubecula*, *Luscinia megarhynchos*, several species of *Turdus*, several species of *Parus* and *Fringilla coelebs*. The drier and more open oak woodlands of the western Zagros lack some of the true forest species and have a Mediterranean element which includes species such as *Dendrocopos syriacus*, *Lanius nubicus*, *Oenanthe hispanica* and *Emberiza cineracea*. In the even drier mixed *Pistacia*, *Acer* and *Amygdalus* woodlands of the eastern Zagros, the Kerman highlands, and isolated mountains in northern Baluchistan, only a handful of western Palearctic species occur. Characteristic birds here include a mixture of Middle eastern specialities, e.g. *Irania gutturalis* and *Phylloscopus neglectus*, eastern Palearctic species, e.g. *Lanius isabellinus* and *Sylvia althaea*, Indo-Malayan species, e.g. *Lanius vittatus* and western Palearctic species at the extreme edge of their ranges, e.g. *Turdus merula*. Finally, throughout the remoter mountain ranges of Iran there still exist good stands of juniper *Juniperus* woodland with specialities such as *Serinus pusillus* and, in the north-east, *Mycerobas carnipes*.

The hot southern lowlands

The arid tropical climate of the southern coastal lowlands supports a flora and fauna quite unlike that of the rest of Iran. From north-west Khuzestan to eastern Iranian Baluchistan, open park-like stands of *Acacia*, *Prosopis* and *Tamarix* and extensive date-palm groves provide suitable habitat for a variety of Indo-Malayan/Afrotropical species, such as *Streptopelia senegalensis*, *Coracias benghalensis*, *Merops orientalis*, *Pycnonotus leucotis*, *Prinia gracilis*, *Turdoides caudatus*, *Nectarinia asiatica* and *Petronia xanthocollis*. A number of species of Indo-Malayan origin, such as *Calandrella raytal*, *Acridotheres tristis* and *Passer pyrrhonotus*, are confined to extreme south-east Iranian Baluchistan, while several others extend only as far west as the Bandar Abbas region, e.g. *Butastur teesa*, *Francolinus pondicerianus* and *Dendrocopos assimilis*. In the west, the riverine poplar thickets and marsh-edge habitat of Khuzestan hold several specialities, such as *Hypocolius ampelinus*, *Turdoides altirostris* and *Passer moabiticus*.

The wetlands

Although much of Iran is extremely dry, there are several very extensive wetland systems of great importance for a wide variety of waterfowl species. The south Caspian Sea, its 700 km of sandy shoreline, and the freshwater lakes, marshes and brackish lagoons in central Gilan, the Gorgan Bay area, and the Turkoman steppes provide a complex of breeding and wintering areas for waterfowl almost unequalled in the western Palearctic. The region is best known for its wintering waterfowl and the traditional commercial duck-harvesting which this has supported. Regular censuses in recent years have estimated the mid-winter population of ducks, geese, swans and coots at well over a million birds, with perhaps as many birds again occurring on passage in spring and autumn. In addition, there are large wintering populations of *Pelecanus crispus*, *Phoenicopterus ruber*, grebes, herons and egrets, shorebirds and gulls. During the spring and autumn migration seasons, large numbers of shorebirds pass through the south Caspian on their way between breeding grounds in the Arctic and wintering grounds in the Persian Gulf and eastern and southern Africa, and in summer the marshes teem with breeding *Phalacrocorax carbo*, herons, egrets, gallinules including *Porphyrio porphyrio*, and *Chlidonias hybridus*.

The other major wetland areas in Iran are hardly any less spectacular. The wetlands of the Uromiyeh basin in Azarbayjan, centred on the very large and highly saline Lake Uromiyeh, support large breeding colonies of waterfowl, notably *Phoenicopterus ruber* (20,000–25,000 pairs), *Pelecanus onocrotalus* (1,000–1,600 pairs), *Platalea leucorodia*, *Plegadis falcinellus*, *Ciconia ciconia*, *Tadorna tadorna*, *T. ferruginea*, *Recurvirostra avosetta*, *Himantopus himantopus*, *Larus armenicus* and *L. genei*. These wetlands are extremely important for passage shorebirds and in mild winters can hold over 50,000 wintering ducks and geese.

The flood-plains of the Dez, Karun and Karkheh rivers in Khuzestan, the complex of fresh, brackish and saline lakes at the inland delta of the Hirmand river in Sistan of the Afghan border, and the network of fresh and saline lakes in central Fars, particularly Lake Bakhtegan, Lake Tashk, Lake Maharlu, Lake Parishan and the Dasht-e Arjan marshes all provide habitat for many hundreds of thousands of wintering waterfowl. In addition to a wide range of ducks, geese and shorebirds, these wetlands are particularly important for wintering *Pelecanus onocrotalus* (Fars and Sistan), *Threskiornis aethiopicus* (Khuzestan), *Ciconia ciconia* (Khuzestan and Fars), *Phoenicopterus ruber* (Fars) and *Grus grus* (all three areas). In years of good rainfall, wetlands in all three regions can be of great importance for breeding waterfowl, particularly herons, egrets, *Platalea leucorodia*, *Plegadis falcinellus*, *Vanellus indicus*, *V. leucurus* and *Glareola pratincola*.

Coastal habitats of the Persian Gulf and Makran coast

The tidal mudflats, mangrove, sand beaches, rocky shores and sea-cliffs of Iran's south coast support a variety of breeding and wintering waterfowl and seabirds. Breeding species include *Dromas ardeola*, *Burhinus recurvirostris* (only in the east), several species of herons and egrets such as *Ardeola grayii*, *Egretta gularis* and *Ardea goliath* (in mangrove), and several species of terns. Wintering species include *Pelecanus crispus*, *Phalacrocorax carbo*, *Platalea leucorodia*, *Pandion haliaetus*, *Haliaeetus albicilla*, many shorebirds notably *Haematopus ostralegus*, *Limosa lapponica*, *Numenius arquata* and *Charadrius* spp., *Stercorarius* spp., *Larus* spp. and *Sterna* spp.

Offshore islands

The many small and uninhabited islands in the Persian Gulf and Strait of Hormoz provide ideal breeding grounds for large colonies of seabirds. The main species are *Sterna bergii*, *S. bengalensis*, *S. repressa* and *S. anaethetus*, but small colonies of *Phaethon aethereus*, *Phalacrocorax nigrogularis* and *Sterna saundersi* have been found, and *Puffinus persicus* probably breeds.

Of the 491 species which are known to have occurred in Iran at least 324 breed regularly, and 103 are almost if not entirely sedentary, remaining on or near their breeding grounds throughout the year. A few undertake short altitudinal migrations, moving down from the highest mountain ranges during periods of hard weather, and 123 species can be classed as 'partial migrants'. Ninety-eight species are breeding summer visitors, with the great bulk of the Iranian breeding population migrating in autumn either south-west to winter in the Arabian peninsula and Africa or south-east to winter in the Indian subcontinent.

The most important breeding waterfowl populations in Iran in the 1970s were as follows. Globally threatened species comprised *Pelecanus crispus* (5–10 pairs), *Marmaronetta angustirostris* (common), *Oxyura leucocephala* (small numbers) and *Haliaeetus albicilla* (20–30 pairs). Regionally threatened species comprised *Ardea goliath* (several pairs), *Botaurus stellaris* (fairly common) and *Aythya nyroca* (150–300 pairs). Other important species included *Pelecanus onocrotalus* (1,000–1,600 pairs), *Phalacrocorax carbo* (5,200–6,000 pairs), *Ardea purpurea* (250 pairs), *Egretta gularis* (90–100 pairs), *E. garzetta* (800 pairs), *Ardeola ralloides* (1,200 pairs), *Nycticorax nycticorax* (650–700 pairs), *Ixobrychus minutus* (common), *Ciconia ciconia* (3,150–3,400 pairs), *Plegadis falcinellus* (130–200 pairs), *Platalea leucorodia* (210–390 pairs), *Phoenicopterus ruber* (15,000–25,000 pairs), *Tadorna ferruginea* (common), *T. tadorna* (common), *Dromas ardeola* (1,500+ pairs), *Himantopus himantopus* (1,000–1,500 pairs), *Recurvirostra avosetta* (2,000–2,500 pairs), *Burhinus oedicnemus* (common), *Glareola pratincola* (1,000–1,500 pairs), *Vanellus vanellus* (common), *V. leucurus* (300–500 pairs), *V. indicus* (common), *Charadrius alexandrinus* (common), *Tringa totanus* (common), *Larus armenicus* (4,000–5,000 pairs), *L. genei* (4,000–5,500 pairs), *Sterna nilotica* (200–400 pairs), *S. caspia* (30–50 pairs), *S. hirundo* (225–360 pairs), *S. repressa* (300,000 pairs), *S. anaethetus* (25,000–27,000 pairs), *S. saundersi* (130–150 pairs), *S. albifrons* (800–1,150 pairs), *S. bergii* (many thousands), *S. bengalensis* (many thousands), *Chlidonias hybridus* (3,600–7,000 pairs) and *Pandion haliaetus* (25–50 pairs).

Of the non-breeding visitors to Iran 86 species are winter visitors from breeding grounds to the north, mainly Russia and Kazakhstan. Two-thirds of these are waterfowl (particularly ducks, geese, swans and shorebirds) and birds of prey. Ringing (banding) studies have shown that the bulk of ducks wintering in Iran originate from breeding grounds in the basin of the Ob and Irtysh rivers in western Siberia.

The most important populations of wintering waterfowl in the 1970s were as follows (those populations marked with an asterisk (*) are highly variable, depending on the severity of winter in the North Caspian region and/or in Iran). Globally threatened species comprised *Pelecanus crispus* (1,000–1,250), *Phalacrocorax pygmeus* (800–1,100), *Anser erythropus* (4,000–7,500), *Marmaronetta angustirostris* (9,000–30,000), *Oxyura leucocephala* (25–100*; 500–700 in 1971/72), *Grus leucogeranus* (9–14) and *Haliaeetus albicilla* (200–250). Regionally threatened species comprised *Ardea goliath* (15–30), *Botaurus stellaris* (fairly common), *Threskiornis aethiopicus* (50–100) and *Aythya nyroca* (200–1,000). Other important species included *Podiceps cristatus* (5,000–7,000), *P. nigricollis* (3,500–4,500), *Pelecanus onocrotalus* (500–2,300, depending on condition of Sistan basin), *Phalacrocorax carbo* (25,000–30,000), *Ardea cinerea* (2,750–3,600), *Casmerodius albus* (4,500–6,500), *Egretta gularis* (700–1,000), *E. garzetta* (600–1,400), *Ciconia nigra* (50+), *C. ciconia* (750–2,050), *Platalea leucorodia* (700–1,200), *Phoenicopterus ruber* (35,000–70,000), *Anser albifrons* (2,500–5,000), *A. anser* (15,000–32,000), *Cygnus cygnus* (25–900*), *C. columbianus* (20–100*), *C. olor* (100–550*; 8,500–9,000 in 1971/72), *Tadorna ferruginea* (7,000–11,000), *T. tadorna* (15,000–25,000), *Anas penelope* (100,000–150,000), *A. strepera* (30,000–80,000), *A. crecca* (800,000–1,350,000), *A. platyrhynchos* (250,000–700,000*), *A. acuta*

(230,000–600,000), *A. clypeata* (25,000–120,000), *Netta rufina* (500–1,000*; 15,000–20,000 in 1971/72), *Aythya ferina* (55,000–85,000), *A. fuligula* (20,000–65,000*), *Bucephala clangula* (400–2,500*), *Mergellus albellus* (100–250*; 2,500–3,000 in 1971/72), *Grus grus* (2,000–3,200), *Porphyrio porphyrio* (500–1,000), *Fulica atra* (300,000–500,000), *Haematopus ostralegus* (9,000–12,000), *Himantopus himantopus* (2,500–3,000), *Recurvirostra avosetta* (1,500–2,500), *Dromas ardeola* (1,250–1,750), *Vanellus vanellus* (25,000–35,000), *V. leucurus* (1,200–1,600), *V. indicus* (5,000+), *Pluvialis squatarola* (1,000–2,000), *Charadrius hiaticula* (2,500–6,000), *C. alexandrinus* (5,000–10,000), *C. mongolus* (2,500–5,000), *C. leschenaultii* (5,000–10,000), *Eudromias morinellus* (500–1,000), *Limosa limosa* (10,000–15,000), *L. lapponica* (25,000–35,000), *Numenius arquata* (15,000–25,000), *Tringa totanus* (15,000–25,000), *T. stagnatilis* (500–1,000), *T. cinerea* (2,000–3,000), *Arenaria interpres* (500–1,500), *Scolopax rusticola* (5,000+), *Gallinago gallinago* (10,000+), *Lymnocryptes minimus* (1,000+), *Calidris alba* (10,000–15,000), *C. alpina* (50,000–90,000), *Limicola falcinellus* (500–1,000), *Larus cachinnans/L. argentatus* (20,000–35,000), *L. ichthyaetus* (800–4,000*), *L. ridibundus* (35,000–60,000), *L. genei* (35,000–55,000), *L. minutus* (100–3,000*), *Sterna nilotica* (1,000–3,000), *S. caspia* (750–1,500), *S. bergii* (many thousands), *S. bengalensis* (many thousands), *S. sandvicensis* (many thousands), *Chlidonias hybridus* (100–400) and *Pandion haliaetus* (150–200).

In many cases the number of birds overwintering represents only a small proportion of the total present during the migration seasons, indicating that a large through-passage is taking place. Twenty-four species occur in Iran only as passage migrants in spring and autumn, breeding to the north of Iran and wintering to the south-west or south-east. The remaining 57 non-breeding species include vagrants and rare stragglers. Many species of waterfowl are common on migration, and *Anas querquedula*, *Calidris minuta* and *Philomachus pugnax* are particularly abundant.

On the whole, there seems no reason to believe that there have been widespread changes in bird populations in Iran since the 1970s. There have been some quite dramatic changes in numbers of waterfowl at certain wetlands, related to increased hunting/disturbance or rise in Caspian Sea level, and there appear to have been some shifts in distribution (e.g. there are now more *Anser anser* wintering in the south and fewer in the north than there used to be). Some species of waterfowl appear to have increased significantly (e.g. *Tadorna ferruginea*, *Phoenicopterus ruber*, *Grus grus* and possibly even *Pelecanus crispus*). Other species of waterfowl, notably some *Anas* species, might appear from recent counts to have decreased substantially. However, in the 1970s aircraft were used extensively to census waterfowl in the huge wetlands in the south (Khuzestan, Fars and Sistan/Baluchistan) and it was only this way that the large wintering concentrations of *Anas crecca* and *A. acuta* were discovered and counted. No aerial censuses have been carried out since the revolution, and thus the relatively low counts of some species in recent years are quite understandable. (A thorough comparison of ground and aerial counts in the 1970s revealed that even the best ground counts were finding only about 10% of the birds in the Khuzestan wetlands.)

For other groups of waterfowl (shorebirds, gulls, terns, etc.) and most landbirds, there is no evidence on population trends one way or another. A doubling of the human population since the early 1970s, coupled with increased deforestation, increased overgrazing, etc., has undoubtedly resulted in a decline in many bird species, at least locally, but on the whole, the reserve network has fared quite well. The only serious problems are likely to have been with some of the game species, notably the bustards. All three bustards appear to have declined dramatically since the 1970s.

CONSERVATION INFRASTRUCTURE AND PROTECTED-AREA SYSTEM

The Environmental Protection and Enhancement Act (1974) is the main law covering nature conservation. Four categories of protected natural area can be established and protected; any previously designated sites have been re-classified under this law. The law is administered by the Department of the Environment. As of December 1991, the protected areas system in the Islamic Republic of Iran comprised 77 sites totalling at least 8,041,265 ha and covering over 4.8% of the country. The following are the four categories of protected area (number of sites as of December 1991).

National Park (Park-e-Melli)

Seven sites. Relatively large areas of natural or semi-natural land. They must represent outstanding examples of the nation's geological, ecological, geographic, historical, archaeological and scenic features, to be set aside in perpetuity for their preservation, protection, conservation and recreational potential. Notable requirements include possession of unique flora and fauna and/or of relatively pristine remnants of the regional flora representative of particular geographical zones.

An area is considered to be of national significance if: it is of sufficient scenic beauty; has unique geomorphological and scenic beauty; has unique geomorphological and landscape features; possesses diverse and/or unique examples of biotic communities or ecosystems; and is of sufficient size to permit public use, management, research, zoning and protection.

Management includes minimal measures necessary for essential conservation of the area, controls being required to limit damage from visitor use through zoning of recreational areas. Many parks permit human occupation, livestock grazing and agriculture, although attempts are being made for them to be phased out. Permitted activities include provision for culling of wildlife by authorized hunters.

Wildlife Refuge (Panahgah-e-Hayat-e-Vahsh)

23 sites. Areas of representative habitat-types set aside for conservation and management of native wildlife and the protection and management of its habitat; including breeding, spawning, wintering and other areas. Management practice includes restoration of these resources.

Recreational use by the public is secondary to the purpose of management for wildlife and vegetation restoration. Wildlife refuges include public-use zones in which farming, livestock grazing, vegetation cutting or other land-use activities are permitted and sometimes encouraged to enhance the wildlife values of the reserves.

Hunting, fishing, trapping, poisoning, or capturing of wildlife and collection of flora is prohibited except where such activities are consonant with management practices. Settlements and human activity are restricted, eliminated or prohibited according to Department of the Environment regulations.

Protected Area (Maneqe-ye-Hefazat Shode)

43 sites. Established to serve various environmental conservation and protection needs. The sites are set up with multiple-use and single-use objectives, including ecological, scientific, economic, educational, cultural and recreational needs. Selection criteria differentiate 20 categories ranging from protection of unique, unusual or representative flora and fauna, to unusual habitats or species at extremes of their range, to sites where the influence of man on natural ecosystems can be measured. Areas are established to provide conditions conducive to the regeneration and amelioration of representative habitats and/or endangered species. Such regions are also envisaged as centres of breeding stock for the re-population of wildlife species that are on the decline in adjacent areas.

Unlicensed hunting is prohibited. The utilization of rangeland and forest within the boundaries of protected areas are subject to restrictions promulgated with the cooperation of the Ministry of Agriculture. If livestock grazing, woodcutting or other activities are likely to alter the natural environment they can be curtailed in accordance with legislation of 1974.

Human populations are often present, but in practice an effort has been made to exclude villages and other habitations. Policies include attempts to phase out human settlement, grazing and agriculture. In a number of cases, research and limited tourism occur. Protected areas often act as buffer zones encompassing national parks, ensuring that development can be regulated and limit or avoid management problems.

National Nature Monument

Four sites. Small areas designated for the preservation of special features illustrating typical, unique or unusual phenomena of geological, scientific, historical and/or natural history interest. Prospective sites for this category have no minimum size. To be considered of national significance a site must contain at least one of the following: outstanding geological formations or features illustrating a specific geological process; specialized physiographic areas; aquatic or terrestrial ecosystems containing representative, unique or unusual characteristics; habitats supporting endangered species; examples of scenic grandeur; individual specimens or groups of specimens representing the nation's zoological, botanic, geological or natural history. Such sites may or may not be open to visitors depending on the requirements of the feature for protection and preservation. Management to maintain certain species or to expose features for study is considered acceptable.

In addition to these reserves, as of December 1991, there were five Protected Rivers under the jurisdiction of the Department of the Environment: the Chalus, Karadj, Lar/Haraz, Sardab and Jajerud.

INTERNATIONAL MEASURES RELEVANT TO THE PROTECTION OF SITES

Iran is a party to the Ramsar Convention and World Heritage Convention and, as of December 1993, had designated 18 Ramsar sites (covering a total of 1,357,550 ha) but no natural World Heritage Sites. All the Ramsar sites are very important for birds and other wildlife and are included in this directory. Iran has signed (but not ratified) the Biodiversity Convention. It participates in the UNESCO Man and the Biosphere Programme and, as of December 1993, had designated nine Biosphere Reserves (covering a total of 2,609,731 ha), all of which are included in this directory. Iran has ratified the Regional Convention for Cooperation on the Protection of the Marine Environment from Pollution and the Action Plan for the Protection and Development of the [Gulf] Marine Environment and the Coastal Areas. A joint agreement was signed with the USSR in 1973 to combat pollution in the Caspian Sea.

OVERVIEW OF THE INVENTORY

This inventory contains 105 sites, covering a total area of c.87,000 km^2 or about 5% of the area of the country. A relatively high proportion of the sites receive some form of legal protection for nature conservation. Coverage of all the major habitat-types which are important for birds is considered to be good, reflecting the large amount of ornithological fieldwork which has been carried out in the last 30 years in the country. The more extensive and homogeneous habitats, such as deserts and steppes, are covered by a number of representative sites. However, many bird species which Iran has important populations of, such as raptors, gamebirds, sandgrouse and many passerines, tend not to congregate but to have scattered distributions. Therefore only a small proportion of their total populations is covered by the inclusion of some representative sites. To conserve these dispersed species it is necessary to consider the integration of conservation measures for the wider environment into regulations governing important land-uses such as agriculture and forestry.

ACKNOWLEDGEMENTS

The site accounts were compiled from information supplied by Dr D. A. Scott and by experts at the Department of the Environment, coordinated by Mr S. A. Ayafat (Head, Director's Office, Public and International Affairs). Information on categories and surface areas of protected areas is based on the Department of the Environment's official list of protected areas dated 1370 (1991/92) together with comments from Mr B. Riazi (Habitat Specialist, Natural Environment Bureau, Department of the Environment) to Dr D. A. Scott, as well as further revisions provided to BirdLife by the Department of the Environment (received in December 1993). The introduction was compiled from information in IUCN (1991), apart from the section on 'Ornithological importance' which was compiled from information provided by Dr D. A. Scott (especially Scott 1990). D. J. Brooks assisted with the compilation of data.

SITE INVENTORY

Site no.	Site name	Region	Criteria used to select site									
			1	2i	2ii	2iii	3	4	5i	5ii	6	0
001	Akh Gol	AZ	•	—	—	—	—	—	—	—	—	—
002	Kiamaki	AZ	—	—	—	—	—	•	—	—	—	—
003	Arasbaran	AZ	—	—	—	—	•	•	—	•	—	—
004	Dasht-e-Moghan	AZ	•	•	—	—	—	—	—	—	—	—
005	Gori Gol	AZ	•	•	—	—	—	—	—	—	—	—
006	Lake Uromiyeh	AZ	•	•	•	—	•	—	•	—	—	—
007	Shur Gol, Yadegarlu and Dorgeh Sangi Lakes	AZ	•	•	•	—	—	—	—	—	—	—
008	Gordeh Git and Mamiyand	AZ	•	•	—	—	—	—	—	—	—	—
009	Ghara Gheshlaq Marshes	AZ	•	•	•	—	—	—	—	—	—	—
010	Lake Kobi	AZ	•	•	•	—	—	—	—	—	—	—
011	Nowruzlu and Ghazanlu	AZ	•	•	—	—	—	—	—	—	—	—
012	South Caspian Shore	GL,MZ	•	•	•	—	•	—	—	—	—	—
013	Lavandavil Marsh	GL	•	•	—	—	—	—	—	—	—	—
014	Abbas-abad Dam	GL	•	•	—	—	—	—	—	—	—	—
015	Lisar	GL,AZ	•	—	—	—	•	•	•	—	—	—
016	Anzali Mordab Complex	GL	•	•	•	—	•	—	—	—	—	—
017	Bandar Kiashar Lagoon and Mouth of Sefid Rud	GL	•	•	•	—	—	—	—	—	—	—
018	Amirkelayeh Lake	GL	•	•	•	—	—	—	—	—	—	—
019	Fereidoonkenar Marshes	MZ	•	•	•	—	—	—	—	—	—	—
020	Seyed Mohalli, Zarin Kola and Larim Sara	MZ	•	•	•	—	—	—	—	—	—	—
021	Dasht-e Naz	MZ	•	—	—	—	—	—	—	•	—	—
022	Lapoo-Zargmarz Ab-bandans	MZ	•	•	•	—	—	—	—	—	—	—
023	Miankaleh Peninsula and Gorgan Bay	MZ	•	•	•	—	•	—	—	—	—	—
024	Gomishan Marshes and Turkoman Steppes	MZ	•	•	•	—	—	—	—	—	—	—
025	Lake Alagol, Lake Ulmagol and Lake Ajigol	MZ	•	•	•	—	—	—	—	—	—	—
026	Incheh Borun Lake and Marshes	MZ	•	•	—	—	—	—	—	—	—	—
027	Voshmigir Dam	MZ	—	•	—	—	—	—	—	—	—	—
028	Lake Bibishervan and Lake Eymar	MZ	•	•	—	—	—	—	—	—	—	—
029	Central Alborz Region (Alborz-e Markazi)	MZ	•	—	—	—	•	—	—	—	—	—

Site no.	Site name	Region	Criteria used to select site									
			1	2i	2ii	2iii	3	4	5i	5ii	6	0
030	Upper Lar Valley	TH	—	—	—	—	•	•	—	—	—	—
031	Lashgarak and Latian Dam	TH	•	—	—	—	•	—	—	—	•	—
032	Kavir Region	TH	•	—	—	—	•	•	•	—	•	—
033	Parvar Protected Area	SM	—	—	—	—	•	•	•	—	—	—
034	Khosh-Yeilagh	MZ	•	—	—	—	—	—	•	—	—	—
035	Golestan	MZ	•	—	—	—	•	•	•	—	—	—
036	Touran	SM	•	—	—	—	—	•	•	—	—	—
037	Rud-i Jowin and Rud-i Kalshur	KR	•	•	—	—	—	—	—	—	—	—
038	Shirvan Area	KR	•	—	—	—	—	—	—	—	—	—
039	Sarani	KR	•	—	—	—	—	—	•	—	—	—
040	Tandoureh	KR	•	—	—	—	—	—	•	—	—	—
041	Lotfatabad and Darregaz Area	KR	—	—	—	—	—	—	—	•	—	—
042	Hari Rud Valley near Sarrakhs	KR	•	—	—	—	—	—	—	•	—	—
043	Tayebad Plains at Ghoomi and Sarhad	KR	•	•	—	—	—	—	—	—	—	—
044	Namakazar Basin	KR	—	—	—	—	—	•	—	—	—	—
045	Sahlabad Area	KR	—	—	—	—	—	•	—	—	—	—
046	Divandareh/Zarrineh Owbatu	KD	•	—	—	—	—	—	—	—	—	—
047	Lake Zaribar	KD	•	•	•	—	—	•	—	—	—	—
048	Western Zagros North of Nowsud	KD	—	—	—	—	•	•	•	—	—	—
049	Dasht-i Gaz	KD	•	—	—	—	—	—	—	—	—	—
050	Plains near Ghorveh	HD	•	—	—	—	—	—	—	—	—	—
051	Assadabad Plain	HD	•	—	—	—	—	—	—	—	—	—
052	Hashelan Marsh and Doh Tappeh Plains	KS	•	•	—	—	—	—	—	—	—	—
053	Telesm Plain	KS	•	—	—	—	—	—	—	—	—	—
054	Ilam Area	IM	—	•	—	—	—	•	—	—	—	—
055	Oshtrankuh	KS	—	—	—	—	•	•	•	—	—	—
056	Mooteh	IF	•	—	—	—	—	—	•	—	—	—
057	Dez Dam	KZ	•	•	—	—	—	—	—	—	—	—
058	Karkheh River Marshes	KZ	•	—	—	—	—	•	—	—	—	—
059	Dez River Marshes and Plains	KZ	•	•	•	—	•	•	—	•	—	—
060	Karun River Marshes	KZ	•	•	•	—	•	—	—	—	—	—
061	Horeh Bamdej (Sadi Shavour Marshes)	KZ	•	•	•	—	•	—	—	—	—	—
062	Hamidieh (Omidiyeh) Plains	KZ	•	•	•	—	—	•	—	—	—	—
063	Susangerd Marshes (Horeh Sosangerd)	KZ	•	•	•	—	—	—	—	—	—	—
064	Shadegan Marshes, Khor-al Amaya, Khor Musa	KZ	•	•	•	—	•	—	—	—	—	—
065	Izeh and Sheikho Lakes	KZ	—	•	•	—	—	—	—	—	—	—
066	Cheghakor Marsh	CM,BK	•	•	—	—	—	—	—	—	—	—
067	Gandoman Marsh	CM,BK	•	•	—	—	—	—	—	—	—	—
068	Gavekhoni Lake, Marshes of Lower Zaindeh Rud	IF	•	•	•	—	—	—	—	—	—	—
069	Kalmand	YZ	•	—	—	—	—	—	—	—	—	—
070	Kuh-i Dena, and Yasuj and Sisakht Area	FR	—	—	—	—	—	•	•	—	—	—
071	Dorudsan Dam	FR	—	•	•	—	—	—	—	—	—	—
072	Kaftar Lake	FR	•	•	•	—	—	—	—	—	—	—
073	Haft Barm	FR	•	•	—	—	—	—	—	—	—	—
074	Dasht-e Arjan and Lake Parishan	FR	•	•	•	—	•	•	•	—	—	—
075	Bamou	FR	•	—	—	—	•	—	—	—	—	—
076	Lake Maharlu	FR	•	•	•	—	—	—	—	—	—	—
077	Lake Bakhtegan, Lake Tashk and Kamjan Marshes	FR	•	•	•	—	—	—	—	—	—	—
078	Harm Lake	FR	•	•	—	—	—	—	—	—	—	—
079	Hormod	FR	•	•	—	—	—	•	—	—	—	—
080	Bahram-e-Gour	FR	•	—	—	—	—	•	—	—	—	—
081	Khabr-va-Rouchoon	KM	•	—	—	—	—	•	—	—	—	—
082	Deh Bakhri Area	KM	—	—	—	—	—	•	•	—	—	—
083	Mehrouyeh	BA	•	—	—	—	—	•	—	—	—	—
084	Kuh-i Bazman	SB	•	—	—	—	—	—	•	—	—	—
085	Hamoun-i Gabi	SB	•	—	—	—	—	•	—	—	—	—
086	Kuh-i Taftan	SB	•	—	—	—	—	—	•	—	—	—
087	Hamoun-i Sabari and Hamoun-i Hirmand	SB	•	•	•	—	•	•	—	—	—	—
088	South end of the Hamoun-i Puzak	SB	•	•	•	—	•	•	—	—	—	—
089	Kharku Island	PG	—	•	—	—	—	—	—	—	—	—
090	Hilleh River Delta	PG	•	•	•	—	—	—	—	—	—	—
091	Bushire Bay	PG	—	—	—	—	—	—	•	—	—	—
092	Monde River Delta	PG	•	•	—	—	—	—	—	—	—	—
093	Nakhilu, Morghu and Ummal Karam Islands	PG	—	•	•	—	—	—	—	—	—	—
094	Sheedvar Island	PG	—	•	•	—	—	—	—	—	—	—
095	Faror Islands	PG	—	—	—	—	—	•	—	•	—	—
096	Khouran Straits	BA	•	•	•	—	•	•	•	—	—	—
097	Geno	BA	—	—	—	—	—	—	•	—	—	—

Site no.	Site name	Region	Criteria used to select site 1	2i	2ii	2iii	3	4	5i	5ii	6	0
098	Hormoz Island	BA	—	•	—	—	—	•	—	—	—	—
099	Rud-i-Shur, Rud-i-Shirin and Rud-i-Minab Deltas	BA	•	•	—	—	•	•	—	—	—	—
100	Rud-i-Gaz and Rud-i-Hara Deltas	SB	•	•	•	—	•	•	—	—	—	—
101	Khor Jask	SB	•	•	—	—	•	•	—	—	—	—
102	Rud-i-Jagin and Rud-i-Gabrik Deltas	SB	•	—	—	—	•	•	—	—	—	—
103	Pozam–Maytab Coast	SB	•	—	—	—	—	—	—	—	—	—
104	Chahbahar Bay and Khor Konarak	SB	•	•	—	—	—	•	—	—	—	—
105	Lower Sarbaz River and Khor Govater	SB	•	•	—	—	•	•	•	—	—	—

Key to regions

AZ Azarbayjan
BA Bandar Abbas
BK Bakhtiari
CM Chaharmahal
FR Fars
GL Gilan
HD Hamadan
IF Isfahan
IM Ilam
KD Kurdistan
KM Kirman
KR Khorasan
KS Kermanshah
KZ Khuzestan
MZ Mazandaran
PG Persian Gulf Coast
SB Sistan/Baluchistan
SM Semnan
TH Tehran
YZ Yazd

Key to criteria

1 Regularly holds a significant number of a globally threatened species.

2i Regularly holds 1% or more of a species' biogeographical or flyway or Middle Eastern population (waterbirds and seabirds only).

2ii Regularly holds 20,000 or more waterbirds.

2iii Migratory 'bottleneck' site: more than 3,000 raptors or more than 5,000 storks or more than 2,000 cranes pass in a season.

3 Regularly holds a significant number of a species which is threatened or declining within the Middle East. Only the top five sites for each such species in the country are considered to qualify as IBAs.

4 Regularly holds a significant number of a species whose world population is wholly or largely restricted to the Middle East. Only the top five sites for each such species in the country are considered to qualify as IBAs.

5i Representative example of a habitat, associated with a characteristic assemblage of bird species.

5ii Rare/threatened/unique habitat, associated with a characteristic assemblage of bird species.

6 Site important for bird conservation through education/research/tourism.

0 Selected for other reasons. See 'Comments on the inventory'.

Comments on the inventory

1. Persian place names of sites generally follow the English versions in use at the Department of the Environment in the 1970s. In some cases, many different versions of the same Persian name have appeared in the literature or in reports from Iran.
2. The official names of some of the Ramsar sites are slightly different to the site names used in this inventory.
3. For all but a few sites, geographical coordinates have been taken from the 1:1,000,000 Operational Navigation Charts.
4. Precise areas are given only for protected areas and some of the wetlands (e.g. Ramsar Sites) which have been well documented. Boundaries have not been defined for the non-protected sites, and any areas given in these cases are only crude estimates.
5. It has not been possible to use the 'Top 5 site: species restricted wholly or largely to the Middle East' criterion for the following species: *Ammoperdix griseogularis*, *Prunella ocularis*, *Irania gutturalis*, *Oenanthe finschii*, *O. xanthoprymna*, *O. picata*, *O. alboniger*, *Sylvia mystacea*, *S. althaea*, *Phylloscopus neglectus*, *Carpospiza brachydactyla* and *Rhodopechys sanguinea*. All of these are common and widespread over much of Iran, and occur commonly in many of the listed sites. However, their presence is always listed, where known.
6. Most sites qualify as either a 'representative bird community' or a 'rare/threatened/unique bird community', but have only been explicitly selected on these criteria when they are weak on the other criteria.
7. Under the section 'Birds', an attempt has been made to summarize the status of all globally threatened species, regionally threatened species and 'endemic' species (whose ranges are wholly or largely restricted to the Middle East) which are known to have occurred at each site, even if they have been recorded only as vagrants.

   The listing of waterfowl counts equal or greater than 1% of population size is restricted to maximum counts: generally single-day counts but occasionally derived from two or more consecutive days when different parts of a large site were covered on different dates (for example, most of the counts at site 023 were derived from surveys lasting 2 to 3 days).

   The great majority of the 'Wintering' counts were made in January, during the Department of the Environment's annual mid-winter waterfowl census. However, these mid-winter counts usually

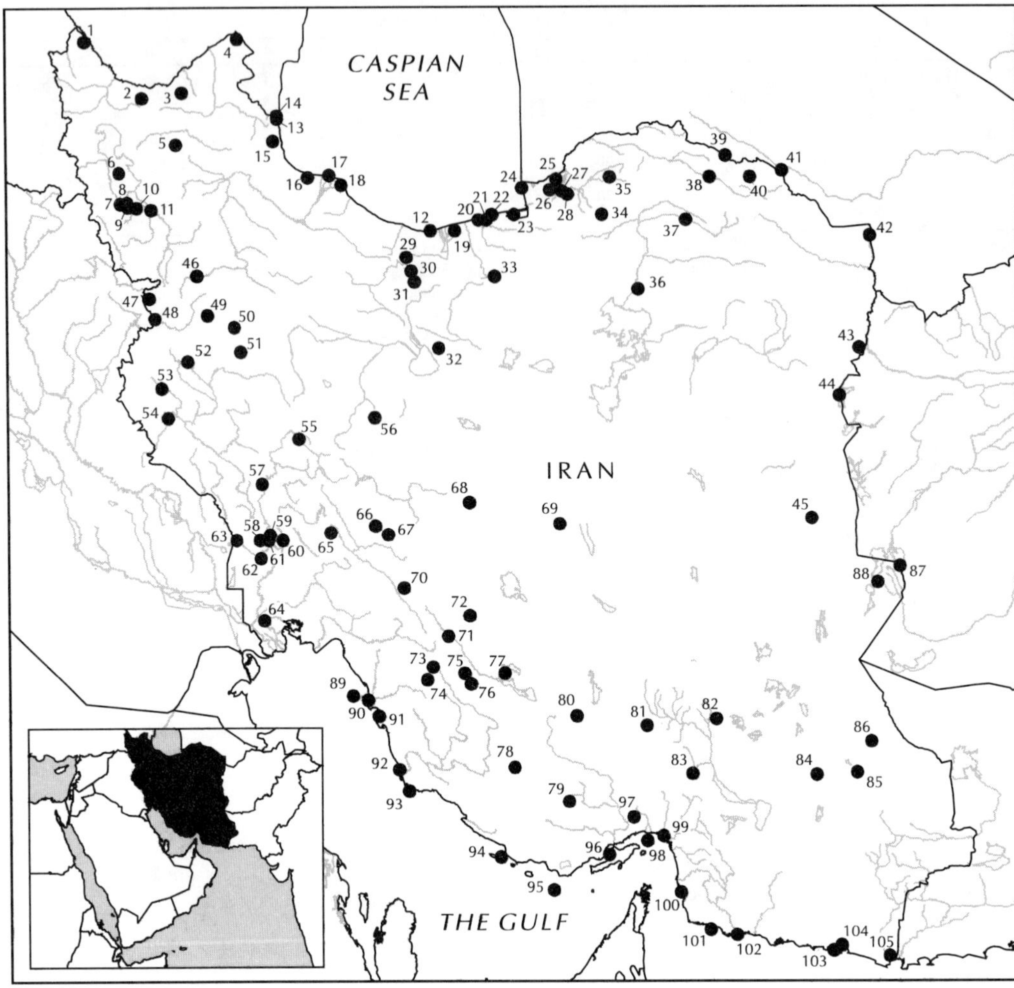

began during the last few days of December and continued until the end of the first week of February. Thus a few December and February figures have been included, although only when it was apparent that these were truly wintering birds.

8. Other interesting species recorded at the site have often been listed in the site accounts, and include local specialities (e.g. *Tetrao mlokosiewiczi*), species with a very restricted distribution in Iran (e.g. *Parus bokharensis*), species at the edge of their range within Iran (e.g. *Parus ater* in Sarani, Khorasan), species which are generally rather scarce or local in Iran (e.g. *Anthus similis*, *Lanius nubicus*), species which occur in unusually high numbers at the site (e.g. a colony of 1,000+ *Streptopelia turtur* in the Dez Reserve, Khuzestan) and rarities (e.g. *Larus brunnicephalus* at two sites), as well as an assortment of other species which typify the bird community in question (e.g. *Ammomanes cincturus*, *Monticola saxatilis*).

9. Source of bird data. For all species except certain waterfowl (flamingos, ducks, geese and cranes) and some of the gamebirds and bustards, the ornithological information is based almost entirely on the personal records (about 60,000) of D. A. Scott, dating from the 1970s. Extensive use has been made of Department of the Environment (DOE) reports from the 1970s for data from the mid-winter waterfowl censuses and bustard surveys, and of some material from L. Cornwallis (1976 and 1977). DOE wintering waterfowl census data from the 1980s have been incorporated into the '1% or more of population' section of the boxes in site accounts; often counts from the 1970s are appended to these in square brackets, for comparison.

10. For the 'Other threatened/endemic wildlife' section, lists of mammals are taken from Department of the Environment reports in the 1970s and may now be considerably out of date.

11. Due to major changes in the environment and lack of current information, no comments were received on the following sites from the Department of the Environment, pending further surveys and investigation: 011, 014, 026, 027, 028, 030, 031, 034, 037, 039, 041, 044, 048, 049, 057, 058, 059, 060, 061, 063, 071, 076, 079, 081, 082, 083, 084, 085, 086, 089, 091, 093, 098 and 102.
12. Other important sites such as Iolkadan wetlands, Nong Galak, Koh Birag and the Jaz Murian wetlands have not been included in this inventory due to lack of time and information, but they strongly deserve consideration for inclusion in any future edition of this book.
13. All three bustards appear to have declined dramatically since the 1970s (see site 023 for *Tetrax tetrax*). All the main sites for *Otis tarda* in the 1970s have been included, but many of these may no longer have any bustards, and if so, should be deleted from future editions of this book. Most of the *Chlamydotis* sites would probably still qualify, even without bustards, as they are interesting desert areas.

Glossary

DOE, Department of the Environment
FAO, United Nations Food and Agriculture Organization
ab-bandan, irrigation pond
bandar, harbour, anchorage
dasht, desert
gol, lake
hamoun, marsh
khor, tidal inlet, coastal lagoon
kol, lake
kuh, mountain
rud, river

001 Akh Gol (Azarbayjan)

Unprotected

39°33′N 44°47′E
600 ha

Site description

A small fresh to brackish lake and marshes set at 820 m in an amphitheatre of rugged lava hills on the south side of the Aras valley in extreme north-west Iran, 115 km north of Khoy near the border with Armenia. The lake is fed by small springs and local run-off, and drains eastwards into the Aras river c.5 km away. The small western portion of the lake retains water all summer, but the main eastern section dries out in late summer, exposing extensive mudflats. The lake is generally frozen and snow-covered in mid-winter. There are extensive reedbeds *Phragmites* around the lake's western margins, and a large area of brackish *Salicornia* flats with scattered clumps of *Phragmites* and *Tamarix* on the plains to the east. The hills to the north and south support shrub–steppe vegetation dominated by *Artemisia*. Livestock are grazed in the area and there is probably some waterfowl hunting. Land ownership is public.

Birds

See box for key species. The site is primarily important for its breeding waterfowl which include many *Himantopus himantopus* and smaller numbers of five other species of shorebirds.

Globally threatened species

Marmaronetta angustirostris	At least one pair bred in 1974.
Oxyura leucocephala	May have bred in recent years.

1% or more of population

	Breeding (pairs)	Wintering	Passage
Himantopus himantopus	100–150	—	—

Regionally threatened or declining species

Neophron percnopterus	May breed.

Species restricted wholly or largely to the Middle East

Oenanthe finschii	Common summer visitor in adjacent hills.
Carpospiza brachydactyla	Common summer visitor in adjacent hills.

Other threatened/endemic wildlife

None known to BirdLife International.

Conservation issues

No conservation measures have been taken. Some changes in the area have had adverse effects on the vegetation and avifauna, and further survey is required.

Further reading

Scott (1976a).

002 **Kiamaki** (Azarbayjan)

Wildlife Refuge

38°40′N 46°00′E
84,400 ha

Site description

A rugged range of mountains south of the Aras river in northern Azarbayjan about 70 km north-west of Tabriz. It extends from the steppic plains at the base of the foothills at an elevation of c.1,500 m to the highest peak at 3,347 m. Sparse *Artemisia* steppe is the main vegetation. Land ownership is public.

Birds

See box for key species. The refuge is one of the best localities in Iran for *Tetraogallus caspius*, and *Perdix perdix* also occurs; other breeding species include *Aquila chrysaetos*, *Falco tinnunculus*, *F. subbuteo*, *Alectoris chukar*, *Athene noctua*, *Cuculus canorus*, *Merops apiaster*, *Coracias garrulus*, *Eremophila alpestris*, *Turdus torquatus* (presumed summer visitor), *Pyrrhocorax pyrrhocorax*, *Sturnus roseus* (summer visitor or passage migrant) and *Emberiza melanocephala*. Winter visitors include *Asio flammeus*.

Globally threatened species

Aegypius monachus	Resident.

Regionally threatened or declining species

Gyps fulvus	Resident.

Species restricted wholly or largely to the Middle East

Tetraogallus caspius	Department of the Environment personnel have recorded counts of up to 75 in October.

Other threatened/endemic wildlife

Mammals: *Canis lupus* (V), *Ursus arctos* (rare), *Lynx lynx* (rare), *Panthera pardus* (rare), *Capra hircus aegagrus* (rare) and *Ovis ammon* (rare).

Conservation issues

The entire area was established as a Wildlife Refuge in 1974. No conservation measures are known to have been proposed.

003 **Arasbaran** (Azarbayjan)

Protected Area

38°45′N 46°50′E
72,460 ha

Site description

The site comprises the Kalibar Mountains, to the south of the Aras river in northern Azarbayjan c.90 km north-east of Tabriz. It extends from the semi-arid steppic foothills at c.1,500 m in the south, over the mountain tops at c.2,500 m, and down into the valley of the Aras river (in the Caspian drainage basin) at c.700 m in the north. The relatively dry, southern slopes are covered with steppic vegetation. The northern slopes are deeply dissected into parallel ridges and steep-sided valleys. Moisture-laden winds from the Caspian support deciduous forest up to c.2,000 m, and lush alpine meadows above the tree-line. There are numerous perennial springs and streams draining north into the Aras river. This rather isolated patch of deciduous forest forms an outlier of the extensive forests of the Caucasus to the north. Summers are generally warm and pleasant, but winters are extremely cold with heavy snow. There are many small villages, but access has remained difficult because of the absence of all-weather roads. The wide range of habitats in the Protected Area includes *Artemisia* steppe and wheat cultivation on southern slopes, alpine tundra on the rocky summits, alpine meadows above the tree-line, and deciduous forest and scrub dominated by *Quercus* and *Rosa* on the northern slopes. Large areas of forest have been cleared for the cultivation of cereals and vegetables and for orchards and pastureland, and much of the remaining forest has been degraded by grazing and cutting of fuelwood. Land ownership is public.

Birds

See box for key species. This is Iran's only locality for *Tetrao mlokosiewiczi*, which is restricted to the upper deciduous forest and alpine meadow zones in the south-central part of the reserve at 1,800–2,100 m. This population was discovered in 1971, and was estimated to number 200–300 birds, but there has since been some decline due to forest clearance in the early 1970s. By 1977, the grouse were confined to two areas (Dogorun valley and an area north of Kharil), and the population was thought to be only c.110 birds. The reserve supports a diverse forest and montane avifauna, including a number of species with very restricted breeding ranges in Iran, such as *Turdus philomelos*, *T. merula*, *Locustella naevia*, *Acrocephalus palustris*, *Sylvia curruca*, *Saxicola rubetra*, *Parus caeruleus*, *Pyrrhula pyrrhula*, *Serinus pusillus* and *Emberiza hortulana*.

Phylloscopus trochiloides nitidus is particularly common in the forest. *Aquila chrysaetos* is resident. At least 104 species have been recorded in the reserve.

Regionally threatened or declining species	
Gypaetus barbatus	Probably breeds.
Neophron percnopterus	Probably breeds.
Gyps fulvus	Probably breeds.
Francolinus francolinus	Resident along Aras river in north.

Species restricted wholly or largely to the Middle East	
Tetraogallus caspius	Occurs on the highest peaks.

Other threatened/endemic wildlife

Mammals: unusually high densities of *Ursus arctos* (rare) and *Canis lupus* (V), as well as populations of *Lynx lynx* (rare), *Ovis ammon* (rare) and *Capra hircus* (rare).

Conservation issues

The entire area was declared a Restricted Region (no hunting allowed) in 1971, but this gave no habitat protection. In 1975, the southern half of the Restricted Region (including the entire range of the population of *T. mlokosiewiczi*) was given full protection as a Wildlife Refuge (38,320 ha), while the remainder was reclassified as a Protected Area (34,145 ha). The Wildlife Refuge has since been downgraded to Protected Area, leaving a single Protected Area of 72,460 ha (wrongly given as 7,240 ha in IUCN 1991). 52,000 ha of the Protected Area were designated as a Biosphere Reserve in 1976. No conservation measures are known to have been proposed. Hunting has probably never posed a serious threat to *T. mlokosiewiczi*: shepherds and farmers rarely molest it, and the area has remained remote and difficult of access. The principal threat is the progressive clearance of forest for agriculture, particularly at lower elevations, and overgrazing by domestic livestock. The clearance of forest on steep slopes and subsequent terracing for wheat cultivation in the 1970s led to severe soil erosion, loss of topsoil, and exposure of bare rock over large areas of former grouse habitat.

Further reading

Argyle (1977c), Eftekhar (1973c), Gharamani (1971), Mansoori (1974), Scott (1973c, 1976d), Scott and Howell (1976).

004 Dasht-e-Moghan (Azarbayjan)

Unprotected

39°35′N 48°00′E
3,000 ha

Site description

The site comprises cultivated lowland plains near the town of Parsabad, c.160 km north of Ardabil in extreme north-east Azarbayjan. The area is bordered in the north-west by the Aras river and in the north-east by the frontier with Azerbaijan. At this point, the Aras river flows in a broad valley c.1.5–2.0 km wide and 10 m below the level of the adjacent plains; it is wide and meandering, with many braided channels and shingle banks. The riverine habitats include stagnant pools with emergent marsh vegetation, open *Tamarix* scrub (mainly on the many small islands) and grassy areas. The plains are densely populated, with many small villages, and are almost entirely cultivation with cotton and wheat, though there are some areas of short grassland and *Artemisia* steppe in the east and *Populus* stands around the villages. There is some livestock grazing. Land ownership is public.

Birds

See box for key species. An important wintering area for geese and ducks; one of the best areas in Iran for *Anser albifrons*. The goose flocks feed at dawn and dusk on the cultivated plains of the Dasht-e-Moghan and spend much of the day loafing on shingle banks in the river. Small numbers of *Mergus merganser* occur along the river, and *Phalacrocorax carbo* also winters.

Globally threatened species	
Anser erythropus	Up to 4 have occurred in late autumn.
Tetrax tetrax	Has occurred in small numbers in late autumn.

1% or more of population	Breeding (pairs)	Wintering	Passage
Casmerodius albus	—	188 [40]	—
Cygnus olor	—	274 [–]	—
Anser albifrons	—	320	—
Anser anser	—	1,371 [714]	—
Tadorna ferruginea	—	149	—
Vanellus vanellus	—	400	—

Other threatened/endemic wildlife

None known to BirdLife International.

Conservation issues

The geese are subject to high levels of disturbance from farm workers when feeding on the cultivated plains, and there is some waterfowl hunting.

Further reading

Scott (1976a).

005 Gori Gol (Azarbayjan)

also known as Gory Gol
Unprotected

37°50′N 46°40′E
120 ha
Ramsar Site

Site description

Lake Gori is a fresh to brackish, eutrophic lake lying at 1,950 m on the north side of the main Tabriz–Tehran highway, c.40 km east-south-east of Tabriz. It is fed by local rainfall, springs and small streams, receiving the bulk of its water after the spring snow-melt, and overflows at its north-east corner into a small stream; there is little fluctuation in water level. The bottom is a mud deposit on shale and rocks. The lake is generally frozen by late December and remains so, often under deep snow, all winter. There are extensive areas of *Phragmites*, *Juncus*, *Carex* and *Scirpus* around the shore and abundant underwater vegetation. The surrounding area is semi-arid steppe with one small settlement and wheat cultivation on the west and damp grassland on the south-west. Sport fishing, grazing, reed-cutting and wildfowl hunting occur.

Birds

See box for key species. An important site for breeding waterfowl, notably *Podiceps nigricollis* and *Oxyura leucocephala*, and the only known breeding locality in Iran for *Podiceps grisegena*; *Pelecanus onocrotalus* occurs in some years, presumably feeding birds from Lake Uromiyeh. Other breeding species include *Fulica atra* (1,500–2,000 birds) and *Himantopus himantopus* (50–100 birds). A wide variety of waterfowl occurs on passage, especially *Anas querquedula* and *Fulica atra*, and including *Tadorna tadorna* and *T. ferruginea*, but the lake has no value for wintering waterfowl as it is completely frozen for most of the winter.

Globally threatened species

Oxyura leucocephala — Several pairs breed.

1% or more of population

	Breeding (pairs)	Wintering	Passage
Podiceps nigricollis	125–150	–	–
Anas querquedula	–	–	1,000 (Aug)
Aythya nyroca	several	–	40 (Sep)
Oxyura leucocephala	several	–	15 (Oct)

Regionally threatened or declining species

Aythya nyroca — See above.

Other threatened/endemic wildlife

None known to BirdLife International.

Conservation issues

The lake was designated a Ramsar Site in 1975, but no conservation measures are known to have been proposed. Although unprotected, the area is under the supervision of the Department of the Environment. Lying by a main road and so close to Tabriz, it is used intensively for recreation, including shooting, which causes considerable disturbance to breeding waterbirds.

Further reading

Carp (1980), Ramsar Convention Bureau (1993), Scott (1976a,c).

006 Lake Uromiyeh (Azarbayjan)

also known as Lake Uromieh, formerly Lake Rezaiyeh
National Park (463,600 ha)

37°30′N 45°30′E
483,000 ha
Ramsar Site, Biosphere Reserve

Site description

Lake Uromiyeh lies at 1,280 m in an inland drainage basin in western Azarbayjan, 60 km south-west of Tabriz. At c.140 km long (from north-west to south-east) and up to 55 km wide near the southern end, it is a vast hypersaline lake of great scenic beauty with extensive salt-encrusted flats and shingle beaches. The average depth is c.5 m, the level fluctuating by c.1–2 m depending on winter rains. The bottom is mud or silt, often covered by salt crystals. Salinities range from 80 to 280 p.p.t. and the water temperature from 3 to 30°C. There are several large areas of fresh to brackish marsh with abundant aquatic vegetation in the deltas of the many small rivers and streams which flow into the lake. The most extensive of these marshes is in the south at the mouth of the Jogatu Chay river. The lake includes 56, mostly small, uninhabited islands. The largest, Kabudan (Ghoyoon Daghi), comprises 3,125 ha of hilly steppe with scattered trees. The climate is semi-arid, with very hot summers and extremely cold winters (temperatures below –25°C). The lake supports an abundant growth of the alga *Enteromorpha* and there is a very rich algal bloom and build up of brine shrimp *Artemia salina* between early June and the end of September, but the lake itself is too saline to support any other plants or animals. The marshes and shorelines have typical saltmarsh plant communities of *Suaeda*, *Atriplex* and *Frankenia* with *Juncus*, some *Phragmites* at river mouths, and occasional stands of *Tamarix*. Remnant stands of *Pistacia* forest survive on the larger islands, notably Kabudan and Ashk, together with *Rhamnus* bushes and *Artemisia* shrubs. There are rolling wheat-lands to the west and south, and semi-arid steppe and hills to the north and east. There are villages on the shore, with small steamer ferries operating between them. The lake has little value for conventional outdoor recreation because of its extremely high salinity, but has exceptionally high values for eco-tourism because of its great scenic beauty and spectacular concentrations of waterbirds.

Birds

See box for key species. The lake is extremely important for breeding *Pelecanus onocrotalus*, *Plegadis falcinellus*, *Platalea leucorodia*, *Phoenicopterus ruber*, *Tadorna ferruginea*, *T. tadorna*, *Himantopus himantopus*, *Recurvirostra avosetta*, *Larus armenicus*, *L. genei* and many other species. The pelicans, spoonbills, *Egretta garzetta* and many of the gulls breed on a group of small islands (Dowguzlar Islands) near the south end of the lake, feeding on the extensive brackish and freshwater wetlands on the plain to the south. Flamingos are known to have bred in large numbers every year since at least the early 1960s, and appear to be increasing steadily; in some years there are several large colonies. After hatching, the chicks form large creches and swim to the south end of the lake to feed in the extensive shallows. Most other species of waterfowl breed on the mudflats round the lake or in the extensive fresh to brackish marshes at the main river mouths. The vast mudflats surrounding the lake are the most important autumn staging area for migratory shorebirds and *Anas querquedula* in Iran, while the open waters of the lake occasionally support huge numbers of passage *Podiceps nigricollis*. An estimated 146,000 small shorebirds (probably mostly *Calidris minuta* and *C. ferruginea*) were located on the mudflats during an aerial survey on 29–31 August 1973, along with over 21,000 *A. querquedula* and 13,600 *Recurvirostra avosetta*. The lake appears to be an important moulting area for *Tadorna tadorna* (with up to 35,000 in August), and in mild winters may support large numbers of wintering waterfowl. *Alectoris chukar* is a common resident. At least 187 species have been recorded in the reserve.

Globally threatened species

Anser erythropus	One recorded in winter.
Marmaronetta angustirostris	Several pairs breed.
Haliaeetus albicilla	Winter visitor (max. 2).
Otis tarda	A regular visitor to the plains around the lake in the 1970s, with up to 19 recorded in August, but the birds were not known to breed in the area.

1% or more of population

	Breeding (pairs)	Wintering	Passage
Podiceps nigricollis	—	—	8,225 (Aug)
Pelecanus onocrotalus	1,000–1,600	—	—
Egretta garzetta	90	—	—
Casmerodius albus	—	123 [—]	—
Ciconia ciconia	common	—	—
Plegadis falcinellus	100+	—	—
Platalea leucorodia	50–100	—	—
Phoenicopterus ruber	15,000–25,000	19,000	—
Cygnus columbianus	—	63 [—]	—
Anser albifrons	—	118	265 (Nov)
Anser anser	several	80 [4,500]	—
Tadorna ferruginea	300–500	224 [3,500]	—
Tadorna tadorna	4,000–5,000	64,000 [16,140]	35,000 (Aug)
Anas querquedula	—	—	21,200 (Aug)
Aythya nyroca	several	—	—
Himantopus himantopus	300–500	—	—
Recurvirostra avosetta	1,500–2,000	—	13,600 (Aug)
Glareola pratincola	50–100	—	—
Charadrius alexandrinus	250+	—	—
Vanellus vanellus	500–1,000	—	3,000 (Aug)
Calidris minuta	—	—	10,000+ (Aug)
Philomachus pugnax	—	—	9,440 (Aug)
Tringa totanus	2,000–3,000	7,080	8,330 (Aug)
Tringa stagnatilis	—	—	1,395 (Aug)
Tringa ochropus	—	—	428 (Jul)
Larus genei	3,000–4,000	—	19,565 (Aug)
Larus armenicus	4,000–5,000	—	—
Sterna albifrons	40–70	—	—
Chlidonias hybridus	100–200	—	—
Chlidonias leucopterus	—	—	1,140 (Aug)

Regionally threatened or declining species

Aythya nyroca	Several pairs breed.
Neophron percnopterus	At least 10 pairs breed on the islands.
Falco biarmicus	The islands are the only known breeding locality in Iran (at least 5 pairs).

Other threatened/endemic wildlife

Mammals: *Ovis ammon* of the western red race have been introduced to Kabudan Island (estimated 1,150 in 1973/74), and *Dama mesopotamica* (E) to Ashk Island. *Panthera pardus* (rare) was introduced to Kabudan in about 1970 in an attempt to control *Ovis* numbers; it is known to have bred there, but is believed to have died out towards the end of the decade.

Conservation issues

Kabudan Island was established as a Protected Region in February 1960. This was enlarged to cover the entire lake and all its islands (483,000 ha) in 1967. The Protected Region was reduced in size to 465,000 ha and given National Park status in the early 1970s; it has since been reduced to its present size of 463,600 ha. The entire lake was designated a Ramsar Site in 1975, and 462,600 ha of the National Park were designated a Biosphere Reserve in 1976.

Cornwallis (1976) recommended that the boundaries of the National Park be extended to the upper limit of the inundation zone of the lake. This would involve no conflict with agricultural interests, and would incorporate the Gordeh Git and Mamiyand marshes (see site 008), the Talab-e-Garrous marshes, and Ghopi Bob Haydar (a small lake and freshwater marsh c.4 km south-east of Talab-e-Garrous). Freshwater discharge into the marshes at the south end of the lake was reduced in the early 1970s following the construction of a dam on the Mahabad river, but this was partially compensated for by discharge from the irrigation scheme through two main drains emptying into one of the marshes (Talab-e-Garrous). These drains provide water to the marsh through the summer and have improved its value for nesting birds (Cornwallis 1976). The most serious threat is likely to be water-borne pollution from towns in the catchment area, especially the large city of Tabriz to the north-east and the town of Uromiyeh to the west, and pollution with toxic chemicals used in the surrounding agricultural land.

■ Further reading

Carp (1980), Cornwallis (1976), Firouz (1974), Firouz *et al.* (1970), Ramsar Convention Bureau (1993), Savage (1964), Scott (1973b, 1975c, 1976a,b,c, 1991, in press), Summers *et al.* (1987).

007 Shur Gol, Yadegarlu and Dorgeh Sangi Lakes (Azarbayjan)

Unprotected

37°01´N 45°31´E
2,500 ha
Ramsar Site

■ Site description

The lakes lie at 1,290 m on the plains to the south of Lake Uromiyeh, 7–10 km south of the south-east corner of the lake and c.30–35 km north-west of Mahabad. Shur Gol and the associated Hassanlu marshes (37°01´N 45°28´E, 2,000 ha) consist of a shallow, brackish to saline lake and marshland fed by local rainfall, springs, seepages and small streams. Flooding occurs in autumn and winter, but drainage is virtually closed and the complex dries out completely only in very dry years. The much smaller wetlands of Yadegarlu (37°02´N 45°32´E, 350 ha) and Dorgeh Sangi (36°59´N 45°34´E, 150 ha) lying a few kilometres to the east and south-east are shallow freshwater lakes with peripheral eutrophic marshes. Both are subject to wide fluctuations in water level, and are often completely frozen in winter. The extensive marshes at Shur Gol and Yadegarlu are dominated by *Carex* and grasses. There is relatively little aquatic vegetation at Dorgeh Sangi, where extensive bare mudflats are exposed when water is low. The surrounding land includes wheat fields on the rolling hills and plains to the north, and more intensive agriculture in the vicinity of the villages to the south.

■ Birds

See box for key species. The wetlands are especially important for breeding waterfowl, notably *Plegadis falcinellus*, *Marmaronetta angustirostris*, *Oxyura leucocephala* and *Glareola pratincola*, and passage ducks, *Fulica atra* and shorebirds, and large numbers of waterfowl visit to feed in summer, including

Globally threatened species

Anser erythropus	In the 1970s up to 70 wintered, with up to 175 on autumn passage.
Marmaronetta angustirostris	Breeds (10–15 pairs) and winters (max. 10).
Oxyura leucocephala	Several pairs breed.
Haliaeetus albicilla	Regular in winter (max. 3).
Otis tarda	Occasional visitor to surrounding plains in the 1970s (maximum 6).

1% or more of population

	Breeding (pairs)	Wintering	Passage
Podiceps cristatus	20–30	100	—
Pelecanus onocrotalus	1,000 birds (feeding only)	—	—
Plegadis falcinellus	50–75	—	—
Cygnus columbianus	—	57	—
Tadorna ferruginea	—	2,350 [—]	1,855 (Nov)
Anas crecca	—	2,500	45,100 (Nov)
Anas querquedula	—	—	1,370 (Aug)
Anas clypeata	—	—	5,500 (Nov)
Marmaronetta angustirostris	10–15	10	—
Aythya ferina	—	484	15,000
Aythya nyroca	several	—	—
Oxyura leucocephala	several	—	—
Fulica atra	—	2,500	120,000
Himantopus himantopus	—	—	1,500 (Aug)
Recurvirostra avosetta	—	—	500 (Jul)
Glareola pratincola	50–80	—	—
Vanellus vanellus	breeds	—	1,460 (Jun)
Philomachus pugnax	—	—	2,500 (Aug)
Limosa limosa	—	—	500 (Aug)
Tringa totanus	breeds	—	1,700 (Aug)
Tringa stagnatilis	—	—	350 (Aug)

Regionally threatened or declining species

Aythya nyroca	Several pairs breed.

Pelecanus onocrotalus (see box), *Ciconia ciconia* (150; also breeds in the area), *Platalea leucorodia* (100) and *Phoenicopterus ruber* (1,000). When not frozen, the lakes also support large numbers of wintering waterfowl, mainly dabbling ducks and *F. atra*. A small flock of *Cygnus columbianus* occurred regularly in the early 1970s (the only regular wintering site in Iran), but there have been no confirmed records of the species at the site since then. *Anser albifrons* and *A. anser* have been present in winter.

Other threatened/endemic wildlife
None known to BirdLife International.

Conservation issues
All three wetlands were designated as a single Ramsar Site of 2,500 ha in 1975 but there is no legal protection. Cornwallis (1976) recommended that Wildlife Refuges be established at Yadegarlu and Dorgeh Sangi lakes. There have been reports of wetland drainage for agriculture at Yadegarlu.

Further reading
Carp (1980), Cornwallis (1976), Ramsar Convention Bureau (1993), Scott (1976a,c).

008 Gordeh Git and Mamiyand (Azarbayjan)

37°02′N 45°40′E
500 ha

also known as Girdeh Git and Meimand
Unprotected

Site description
The site comprises two adjacent areas of freshwater marsh, Gordeh Git and Mamiyand, on the plains 10 km south of Lake Uromiyeh and c.30 km north of Mahabad. Most of the wetland is covered with tall stands of *Phragmites*. Land ownership is public.

Birds
See box for key species. Breeding birds include *Ciconia ciconia* (common summer visitor), *Oxyura leucocephala*, *Circus aeruginosus* and *Glareola pratincola*. Large numbers of wintering waterfowl have been recorded in recent years, and *Chlidonias leucopterus* is a common passage migrant.

Globally threatened species

Marmaronetta angustirostris	May have bred in the 1970s, but no evidence since then.
Oxyura leucocephala	One or two pairs bred in the 1970s, but not confirmed since then.
Otis tarda	Up to 20 have occurred on the surrounding plains in winter.

1% or more of population

	Breeding (pairs)	Wintering	Passage
Tadorna ferruginea	—	2,500 [—]	—
Tadorna tadorna	—	3,000 [—]	—
Oxyura leucocephala	1–2	—	—
Glareola pratincola	50+	—	—

Other threatened/endemic wildlife
None known to BirdLife International.

Conservation issues
Cornwallis (1976) recommended that the boundaries of Lake Uromiyeh National Park be extended to the upper limit of the inundation zone of the lake, thus including the Gordeh Git and Mamiyand marshes. There is no information on threats to the site.

Further reading
Cornwallis (1976), Scott (1976a).

009 Ghara Gheshlaq Marshes (Azarbayjan)

37°10′N 45°50′E
40,000 ha

No-hunting Area

Site description
The site comprises c.400 ha of permanent freshwater marshes on the plains 12 km south of Lake Uromiyeh, c.20 km north of Mahabad. The marshes are usually frozen and under snow in winter. There are extensive *Phragmites* beds and little open water, surrounded by a belt of seasonally flooded sedge and grassland. Peripheral areas of the wetland have been drained and converted to agricultural land. There is livestock grazing. Land ownership is public.

Birds
See box for key species. The marshes are important for breeding waterfowl, notably *Plegadis falcinellus*

Globally threatened species
Marmaronetta angustirostris Summer visitor (10–20 pairs).
Oxyura leucocephala Current status uncertain.

1% or more of population

	Breeding (pairs)	Wintering	Passage
Anser anser	—	3,280 [—]	—
Tadorna tadorna	—	15,000 [—]	—
Anas acuta	—	—	10,000
Aythya fuligula	—	2,700 [—]	—

and *Marmaronetta angustirostris*; other breeding species include *Buteo rufinus*, *Circus aeruginosus* and *Falco tinnunculus*. *Pelecanus onocrotalus* visits to feed in summer from colonies at Lake Uromiyeh. Large numbers of ducks occur during the migration seasons, as well as *Circus pygargus*, *Pandion haliaetus* and *Limosa limosa*. In most winters, the wetland is frozen and devoid of birds, but in mild years it may support large numbers geese and ducks, as well as *Aquila chrysaetos*, *Circus cyaneus* and *Accipiter nisus*.

■ Other threatened/endemic wildlife

None known to BirdLife International.

■ Conservation issues

The marshes have recently been designated a No-hunting Area, and are likely to be given Protected Area status by about 1998. The Department of the Environment has proposed that the area be designated a Ramsar Site. Large portions of the marsh were drained by the Mahabad Multipurpose Drainage and Irrigation Project in the 1970s. Since the early 1980s, several large-scale die-offs of waterfowl have occurred during the breeding and migration seasons; up to 100,000 waterfowl are believed to have died in a single year, possibly from botulism.

■ Further reading

Cornwallis (1976), Scott (1976a,c).

010 Lake Kobi (Azarbayjan)

Unprotected

36°57′N 45°30′E
1,200 ha
Ramsar Site

■ Site description

Lake Kobi (Ghopi Bob Ali) is a shallow, eutrophic, fresh to brackish lake with seasonally flooded marshes, on the plains 30 km south of Lake Uromiyeh and c.25 km north-east of Mahabad. The wetland receives its water from local rainfall, several springs, seepages and temporary watercourses fed by snowmelt, overflowing when full into marshland to the north and west. It regularly freezes in winter. The lake supports abundant submerged vegetation; there are extensive sedge marshes around much of the shore, and *Phragmites* beds occur in the south and to the north-west, together with some grassland. The whole area is surrounded by rolling steppic hills, with scattered settlements and cultivation to the north and south. Grazing of livestock and wildfowl hunting occur. Land ownership is public.

■ Birds

See box for key species. The marshes support a variety of breeding waterfowl, notably *Nycticorax nycticorax*, *Ardeola ralloides*, *Egretta garzetta*, *Plegadis falcinellus* and *Aythya nyroca*, and there was a breeding colony of *Podiceps nigricollis* at the lake in 1972. The lake is an extremely important staging area for ducks, *Fulica atra* and shorebirds in autumn, regularly holding in excess of 100,000 birds. Species in especially high numbers have included

Globally threatened species

Branta ruficollis	Flock of 16 recorded January 1970.
Marmaronetta angustirostris	One recorded in August.
Oxyura leucocephala	Occurs in summer, apparently as a non-breeder (33 birds loafing).
Haliaeetus albicilla	Regular winter visitor (max. 1).
Otis tarda	Occasional visitor (max. 6) to surrounding plains.

1% or more of population

	Breeding (pairs)	Wintering	Passage
Nycticorax nycticorax	100	—	—
Ardeola ralloides	100	—	—
Egretta garzetta	100	—	—
Ciconia ciconia	243 birds feeding	—	—
Plegadis falcinellus	100–150	—	—
Phoenicopterus ruber	—	—	6,600
Anser anser	—	7,000 [—]	—
Tadorna ferruginea	—	2,890	—
Tadorna tadorna	—	1,300 [—]	—
Anas querquedula	—	—	3,000 (Aug)
Anas clypeata	—	1,395	5,000 (Nov)
Aythya ferina	—	2,300	20,000
Aythya nyroca	several	—	—
Oxyura leucocephala	33 birds	9	100+ (Nov)
Fulica atra	—	15,000	50,000 (Nov)
Himantopus himantopus	—	—	600 (Aug)
Vanellus vanellus	breeds	—	300 (Aug)
Tringa totanus	—	—	300 (Aug)

Regionally threatened or declining species
Aythya nyroca Several pairs breed.

Phoenicopterus ruber, *Anas querquedula*, *A. clypeata*, *Aythya ferina* and *F. atra*. Large numbers of ducks and *F. atra* stay on through very mild winters when the lake remains unfrozen. However the figures for *F. atra* given below date from the 1970s, and in recent years less than 2,000 have been recorded, a major decline.

Other threatened/endemic wildlife

None known to BirdLife International.

Conservation issues

The lake was designated a Ramsar Site in 1975, but there is no legal protection. No threats to the site are known.

Further reading

Carp (1980), Cornwallis (1976), Ramsar Convention Bureau (1993), Scott (1976a,c, 1978a).

011 Nowruzlu and Ghazanlu (Azarbayjan)

Unprotected

36°55′N 46°10′E
17,000 ha

Site description

An area of undulating plains set at 1,260 m between ranges of stony hills on either side of the Zarrineh Rud, lying between the villages of Nowruzlu and Ghazanlu, 15–32 km south-east of Miandoab and c.45 km east-north-east of Mahabad. The site also includes Nowruzlu Dam, a small water storage reservoir of c.1,000 ha on the Zarrineh Rud in the north-west. The plain is fairly heavily populated, with several villages and a complex network of gravel and dirt roads. A line of high-tension power cables crosses the site. The plains are cultivated (primarily wheat) and the adjacent rolling hills are *Artemisia* steppe. There is a small marshy area with some reedbeds and shrubby vegetation where the river enters Nowruzlu Dam. Livestock (mainly sheep and goats) graze on fallow land and the adjacent hills.

Birds

See box for key species. The site is known to have been an important breeding area for *Otis tarda* in the 1960s, and there were still several nesting there in the 1970s; the plains are regularly visited by flocks in spring and autumn, with a maximum of 37 in November 1972. Nowruzulu Dam is an important feeding area for *Pelecanus onocrotalus* and *Platalea leucorodia* from the breeding colonies at Lake Uromiyeh, and occasionally holds large numbers of waterfowl during the spring and autumn migration seasons. Flocks of *Anser albifrons* and *A. anser* frequent the area in winter.

Globally threatened species

Marmaronetta angustirostris	Recorded in winter (max. 1).
Haliaeetus albicilla	One record in November.
Otis tarda	Present spring to autumn, and breeds (see text).

1% or more of population
(counts from Nowruzulu Dam)

	Breeding (pairs)	Wintering	Passage
Pelecanus onocrotalus	830 feeding	—	—
Anser albifrons	—	156	—
Tadorna ferruginea	—	—	650 (Nov)
Anas querquedula	—	—	5,000 (Aug)

Other threatened/endemic wildlife

None known to BirdLife International.

Conservation issues

High levels of disturbance from farming activities render much of the area unsuitable for bustards, and the high-tension power lines may constitute a hazard to them in flight.

Further reading

Adhami (1972a), Fotoohi and Mansoori (1974), Fotoohi and Scott (1975), Scott (1971a,b, 1976a).

012 South Caspian Shore, from Astara to Gomishan

36°35′N 52°00′E
650 km

(Gilan, Mazandaran)
Unprotected

■ Site description

The entire 650-km length of shore and inshore waters of the Caspian Sea in Iran, from Astara on the border with Azerbaijan in the west (38°25′N 48°52′E) to the border with Turkmenistan, c.35 km north-north-west of Gomishan, in the east (37°21′N 53°57′E). The shore is almost entirely a narrow, hard, sand beach backed by low sand-dunes, except in the extreme west where there are stretches of shingle, and at one point to the west of Alamdeh (central coast) where there is a small area of rocky shore. The salinity of the Caspian is c.12–13 p.p.t. and the inshore waters are shallow. Between 1866 and 1933 the water level fluctuated between 25.2 and 26.0 m below sea-level. In the early 1930s, however, following the construction of several major dams on the River Volga in the former U.S.S.R., the level started to fall and this continued almost without break (other than seasonal fluctuations) until 1977–1978, when the level had reached 28 m below sea-level. Then began a sudden and rapid rise, averaging over 10 cm per year. By the end of 1991, the water had risen by c.1.8 m, bringing the level back almost to that of the 1930s. In the mid-1970s, when the sea was at its lowest, the beach was generally 30–50(–100) m wide, but by 1992 most of the beach had been submerged and the sea was invading the adjacent vegetated dunes. There remains considerable uncertainty about the cause of this sudden rise in level. It has been argued that it was deliberately engineered by the Government of the former U.S.S.R. in an effort to restore the sea to its original level. Two major engineering works could have contributed: the closing of Karabogaz Bay in the east Caspian in 1978 (thereby reducing the loss of water through evaporation), and the diversion of two Siberian rivers into the Ural river (thereby increasing the inflow of fresh water). According to some calculations the closing of Karabogaz Bay could alone have been responsible for a rise in sea-level of 40–45 cm, but there is also a strong body of opinion that the rise in sea-level is a natural phenomenon and merely part of a long-term cycle. The Caspian supports a major fishery. Land ownership is public.

■ Birds

See box for key species. The area is important for a wide variety of migratory waterfowl, notably grebes, cormorants, diving ducks and gulls in winter, and terns on passage. The sea is used extensively as a day roost for wintering surface-feeding ducks which feed at night on freshwater marshes and rice fields on the coastal plain. Large numbers of shorebirds stop over briefly along the beach in spring and autumn, but rather few winter. The most important stretches of shoreline for waterfowl are the Miankaleh Peninsula (see site 023) and the coast north of Gomishan (see site 024). *Haliaeetus albicilla* remains fairly common throughout the South Caspian region, especially in winter, and frequently scavenges along the shore or fishes in inshore waters. Small numbers of *Plegadis falcinellus* occur on passage. Land ownership is public.

Globally threatened species

Pelecanus crispus	Winter visitor (see below).
Marmaronetta angustirostris	One recorded, December.
Oxyura leucocephala	One recorded in winter.
Haliaeetus albicilla	Common along entire coast.

1% or more of population

	Breeding (pairs)	Wintering	Passage
Podiceps cristatus	—	8,875	—
Podiceps nigricollis	—	760	—
Phalacrocorax carbo	—	3,500	—
Pelecanus crispus	—	83	—
Anas penelope	—	12,900	—
Anas strepera	—	3,250	—
Anas crecca	—	171,000	—
Anas platyrhynchos	—	170,000	—
Anas clypeata	—	4,350	—
Netta rufina	—	2,385	—
Aythya fuligula	—	39,900	—
Bucephala clangula	—	813	—
Charadrius alexandrinus	—	220	340 (Dec)
Vanellus vanellus	—	—	510 (Nov)
Calidris alba	—	90	2,070 (Sep)
Calidris minuta	—	—	2,300 (Sep)
Numenius phaeopus	—	—	310 (Apr)
Larus minutus	—	700	—
Larus ridibundus	—	7,600	—
Larus canus	—	960	—
Larus cachinnans	—	900	—
Sterna albifrons	—	—	1,100 (Aug)

Regionally threatened or declining species

Aythya nyroca	Winter visitor (max. 8).

■ Other threatened/endemic wildlife

None known to BirdLife International.

■ Conservation issues

The falling level of the Caspian in the 1960s and 1970s was becoming a cause of concern to fishing and shipping interests, as important fish spawning areas in coastal wetlands were drying out, and much of the very shallow northern Caspian was becoming too shallow for shipping. Thus the recent rapid rise in sea-level has been welcomed. Significant changes have occurred at coastal wetlands in the South Caspian, including three Ramsar Sites (the Miankaleh/ Gorgan Bay complex, the Anzali Mordab complex and the Bandar Kiashahr/Sefid Rud complex), but on the whole the rise in sea-level has probably had more positive than negative effects. There seems widespread agreement that the 'optimum' level for the Caspian Sea is c.26 m below sea-level, i.e. a little higher than at present. Fisheries departments and the shipping industry are undoubtedly benefiting from the higher level, and few of the towns, ports and coastal installations around the Caspian have been adversely affected, since most were established in the early part of the century when the sea-level was still high. The major economic losses have been in beach development and tourism, the rising level having almost obliterated the extensive sandy beaches and caused considerable damage to recreational facilities.

Further reading

Ferguson (1972), Scott (1976a,c).

013 Lavandavil Marsh (Gilan)

formerly Astara Wildlife Refuge
Protected Area

38°20′N 48°50′E
949 ha

Site description

A small area of swampy woodland and freshwater marshes adjacent to the Caspian beach c.10 km south of Astara. The site is bordered to the west by the main coast road from Astara to Bandar Anzali. The narrow coastal plain comprises a series of old beach ridges, with swampy woodland dominated by *Alnus*, permanent pools with extensive stands of *Juncus* in the depressions, and scrub on high ground. Land ownership is public.

Birds

See box for key species. A pair of *Haliaeetus albicilla* bred in the area in the 1970s, and may still do so. The wetlands support small numbers of waterfowl in winter, for example *Egretta garzetta* (120), while the adjacent beach occasionally holds substantial numbers of shorebirds for short periods during migration. Situated on the west coast of the Caspian, at a point where the coastal plain is almost at its narrowest, the site lies in a bird migration corridor, and is thus an excellent locality for observing migration. Large numbers of herons and egrets have been observed migrating south over the site and adjacent Caspian Sea in autumn (including 1,320 in a single day in September), while a wide variety of migrant landbirds occur in the woodlands and marshes. At least 167 species have been recorded in the reserve.

Globally threatened species

Phalacrocorax pygmeus	Winter visitor (see below).
Milvus milvus	Vagrant (1, September).
Haliaeetus albicilla	Resident; one pair breeds locally.

1% or more of population

	Breeding (pairs)	Wintering	Passage
Phalacrocorax pygmeus	—	146	—
Ardeola ralloides	—	—	360 (Sep)
Casmerodius albus	—	168	—
Ardea cinerea	—	—	340 (Sep)

Other threatened/endemic wildlife

None known to BirdLife International.

Conservation issues

The entire area was designated a Wildlife Refuge in about 1975. No conservation measures are known to have been proposed. Since the 1970s, the area has become threatened by major sea-level rise and land-use changes in recent years.

Further reading

Scott (1976a).

014 Abbas-abad Dam (Gilan)

Unprotected

38°23′N 48°50′E
45 ha

Site description

A small reservoir (used for irrigation) in an area of deciduous woodland on the narrow coastal plain of the Caspian Sea, c.7 km south of Astara. The dam lies at the foot of the forested coastal ranges, west of the Astara to Bandar Anzali highway. In late winter and spring parts of the surrounding woodland are flooded, while at low water level in late summer some mudflats are exposed. There is some emergent marsh vegetation, numerous tall dead trees and an adjacent area of swampy woodland.

Birds

See box for key species. The swampy woodland and dead trees in the lake support a large breeding colony of *Phalacrocorax carbo* plus much smaller numbers of four species of herons and egrets.

Other threatened/endemic wildlife

None known to BirdLife International.

Globally threatened species

Phalacrocorax pygmeus	Regular in winter (max. 3).
Haliaeetus albicilla	Resident; up to 2 pairs breed locally.

1% or more of population

	Breeding (pairs)	Wintering	Passage
Phalacrocorax carbo	1,200–1,500	—	—
Nycticorax nycticorax	70	—	—
Ardeola ralloides	50	—	—

Conservation issues

No conservation measures are known to have been proposed. Much of the surrounding forest has been cleared for pasture and cultivation (mainly fruit and vegetables).

Further reading

Scott (1976a, 1978a).

015 Lisar (Gilan, Azarbayjan)

Protected Area

37°59′N 48°15′E
33,050 ha

Site description

The site lies in the north-west Alborz (Elburz) Mountains c.50 km south of Astara and includes the entire watershed of the Lisar river from its source near the crest of the Alborz in the west to the Caspian shore in the east (c.30 km), and also part of the much drier western slope of the Alborz. There is a freshwater lake (Nur Gol or Neur Gol, 38°00′N 48°33′E) of c.200 ha with extensive sedge marshes in a depression at 2,300 m on the western slope of the divide. The lake drains north into a tributary of the Aras river and provides some breeding habitat for waterbirds, but is frozen for about half the year. There are many villages and farming areas at low elevations in the main valley, but the upper regions of the reserve remain sparsely populated and relatively undisturbed. The site includes the full range of Caspian forest types from lowland *Alnus* in the coastal zone to the tree limit, as well as alpine meadows on the Caspian slope of the divide, montane steppe on the dry western slopes and rocky crags near the summit (3,197 m). Land ownership is public.

Birds

See box for key species. The area supports a good variety of breeding species of Caspian forest and the high Alborz, including *Pernis apivorus*, *Aquila pomarina*, *Phasianus colchicus*, *Oenanthe xanthoprymna* and *Phylloscopus trochiloides nitidus*. *Pandion haliaetus* and *Haliaeetus albicilla* are resident in the coastal zone and presumably breed in the reserve. *Ciconia nigra* has been recorded at Nur Gol in summer and may breed. *Tetraogallus caspius* occurs on the high crags. Other breeding species include *Falco tinnunculus*, *Alectoris chukar*, *Oriolus oriolus* and *Garrulus glandarius*, and winter visitors include *Rallus aquaticus*, *Emberiza citrinella* and *E. schoeniclus*. At least 111 species have been recorded in the reserve.

Globally threatened species

Haliaeetus albicilla	Resident; probably 2 pairs.

Regionally threatened or declining species

Pernis apivorus	Summer visitor.
Aquila pomarina	Summer visitor.

Species restricted wholly or largely to the Middle East

Tetraogallus caspius	Resident.
Oenanthe xanthoprymna	Summer visitor.

Other threatened/endemic wildlife

Mammals: *Canis lupus* (V), *Ursus arctos* (rare), *Lynx lynx* (rare), *Panthera pardus* (rare), *Capra hircus aegagrus* (rare) and *Ovis ammon* (rare).

Conservation issues

A Protected Area of 31,250 ha was established in 1970 and subsequently enlarged to its present size of 33,050 ha. No conservation measures are known to have been proposed. Large areas of forest at low elevations have been cleared for cultivation and pasture, and much of the remaining forest has been degraded by cutting for fuelwood and by grazing. There has been some illegal logging in the reserve.

Further reading

Scott (1976b).

016 Anzali Mordab Complex (Gilan)

Wildlife Refuge (360 ha) and Protected Area (4,500 ha)

37°25´N 49°28´E
15,000 ha
Ramsar Site

Site description

The Anzali Mordab lies in the western part of the broad deltaic plains around the city of Rasht in the south-west Caspian region; the town of Bandar Anzali is situated at the mouth of the main Mordab lagoon. The site, which includes Siahkesheem Marsh (37°24´N 49°22´E, 6,700 ha), comprises a large, shallow, eutrophic, freshwater lagoon, fed by several rivers rising in the Alborz Mountains to the south, and separated from the Caspian Sea by a sandy barrier, c.1 km wide, with open grassland, *Punica* scrub and sand-dune vegetation. Mid-way along its length the lagoon empties into the Caspian through a narrow channel straddled by the busy fishing port of Anzali Mordab. Much of the centre and east of the Mordab supports vast stands of *Phragmites* (up to 6 m high) while the western part is mainly open water. The partially enclosed basin of the Rud-e-Esfand (Siahkesheem Marsh) in the south-west is almost entirely overgrown with dense reedbeds. The permanent wetland area is surrounded by a broad belt of flood meadows and ab-bandans (shallow impoundments which retain water for summer use in irrigation). These largely seasonal wetlands are bordered by arable land to west, south and east. Selke Ab-bandan (37°24´N 49°29´E, 360 ha) is situated on the southern edge of the main Mordab, and comprises 360 ha of shallow freshwater marsh and flood meadows with tall reedbeds to the north and arable land to the south. The wetland is surrounded by a low embankment and was originally created as a water storage pond and duck-hunting area. Other similar shallow marshes along the southern edge of the Mordab and around its eastern end continue to be maintained as private duck-hunting reserves. Open-water areas support extensive beds of the water lily *Nelumbium maciferum* and a very rich growth of other floating and submerged vegetation including *Lemna*, *Potamogeton*, *Hydrilla*, *Myriophyllum* and *Ceratophyllum*. The marshes and flood meadows to the south support similar vegetation with the addition of *Trapa natans*, *Juncus* and *Carex*. The Mordab is a very important spawning and nursery area for economically important species in the Caspian Sea fishery and also supports a major local fishery. Duck-hunting is an important activity in winter, including both sport hunting and market hunting for sale in local markets and export to Tehran. Many of the ab-bandans surrounding the Mordab are managed as duck-hunting areas in winter. The duck hunters employ a traditional dazzling and hand-netting technique. Elsewhere in the Mordab, hunting is by shotgun. The protected areas are in the public domain.

Birds

See box for key species. The Anzali Mordab and its satellite wetlands such as Siahkesheem Marsh and Selke Ab-bandan are extremely important for a wide variety of breeding, passage and wintering waterfowl. The wetlands support a very large breeding colony of *Chlidonias hybridus*, small colonies of six species of herons and egrets, up to 25 pairs of *Circus aeruginosus* and (at least formerly—see below) a large resident population of *Porphyrio porphyrio*. They also support huge wintering concentrations of ducks, geese, swans and coots. The wetland is the most important wintering area in Iran for *Phalacrocorax pygmeus* (see box), and one of the most important sites for wintering *Haliaeetus albicilla*. At least 144 species have been recorded in Siahkesheem Protected Area and at least 157 species in Selke Wildlife Refuge, including *Jynx torquilla* (fairly common passage migrant).

Due to great hunting pressure the number of waterfowl wintering in Anzali Mordab in recent years has been much lower than in the 1970s, when the total count of ducks and *Fulica atra* usually exceeded 200,000. The great majority of waterfowl are

Globally threatened species

Phalacrocorax pygmeus	Over 500 regularly present in mid-winter.
Pelecanus crispus	Up to 6 recorded in winter.
Anser erythropus	Up to 32 recorded in winter.
Oxyura leucocephala	Passage migrant (see below).
Haliaeetus albicilla	Common winter visitor (max. 20) and probably breeds locally.
Aquila heliaca	Winter visitor (max. 6).
Vanellus gregarius	Passage migrant (see below).

1% or more of population

	Breeding (pairs)	Wintering	Passage
Podiceps cristatus	20	260	—
Podiceps nigricollis	—	300	—
Phalacrocorax carbo	—	950	4,200 (Mar)
Phalacrocorax pygmeus	—	410 [650]	—
Nycticorax nycticorax	20	250	—
Ardeola ralloides	150	—	900 (Sep)
Bubulcus ibis	20	16	620 (Oct)
Egretta garzetta	150	300	585 (Sep)
Casmerodius albus	—	170	200 (Aug)
Ardea cinerea	20	100	110 (Oct)
Plegadis falcinellus	—	55	—
Cygnus olor	—	2,530 [2,200]	—
Cygnus columbianus	—	16 [51]	—
Cygnus cygnus	—	849 [711]	—
Anser albifrons	—	500	—
Anas penelope	—	30,000	—
Anas strepera	—	14,900 [7,850]	—
Anas crecca	—	540,000	—
Anas platyrhynchos	—	67,800	—
Anas acuta	—	55,000	—
Anas querquedula	—	—	3,850 (Apr)
Anas clypeata	—	24,300	—
Aythya ferina	—	65,000	—
Aythya fuligula	—	34,500	—
Aythya nyroca	—	51	130 (Nov)
Bucephala clangula	—	120	—
Mergellus albellus	—	382	—
Oxyura leucocephala	—	—	25 (Mar)
Rallus aquaticus	—	common	—
Porphyrio porphyrio	common	135 [40]	—
Fulica atra	—	106,400	—
Vanellus gregarius	—	—	8 (Apr)
Vanellus vanellus	—	5,630 [2,710]	—
Philomachus pugnax	—	—	2,500 (Mar)
Limosa limosa	—	1,380	—
Tringa totanus	—	—	700 (Dec)
Larus minutus	—	1,750	—
Larus ridibundus	—	2,510 [1,000]	—
Larus cachinnans	—	—	300 (Sep)
Chlidonias hybridus	2,000–4,000	—	—

Regionally threatened or declining species

Botaurus stellaris	Recorded in winter; visitor.
Aythya nyroca	Passage migrant and winter visitor (see above).

now confined to the well protected Selke Wildlife Refuge, Siahkesheem Marsh and a chain of private duck-netting marshes along the south side of the Mordab.

Selke Wildlife Refuge continues to support large numbers of birds, but there is evidence of a change in species composition, with more diving ducks and *F. atra* and fewer dabbling ducks and geese than in the 1970s. This is undoubtedly a result of the higher water levels in the Refuge caused by the rise in level of the Caspian Sea.

There has been a dramatic decline in the population of *P. porphyrio* at Anzali Mordab in recent years. The reasons for this decline are unknown, as the extent of suitable habitat appears to have increased enormously during the last decade, but may be related to the great increase in water depth and/or spread of *Azolla*.

Other threatened/endemic wildlife

Mammals: *Canis lupus* (V) has been recorded during severe winters.

Conservation issues

There are two reserves in the Anzali Mordab complex. The central portion of Siahkesheem Marsh (3,515 ha) was first established as a Protected Region in 1967, enlarged to 6,701 ha and upgraded to Wildlife Refuge in 1971, and reduced to 4,500 ha and downgraded to Protected Area in the 1980s. Selke Ab-bandan (360 ha) has been protected as a Wildlife Refuge since 1970. In an effort to increase the level of protection afforded to waterfowl in the Anzali Mordab, the Department of the Environment has recently taken steps to establish a non-hunting area at Sorkhan Kol in the central Mordab. The whole Anzali Mordab complex, including Siahkesheem Marsh, Selke Ab-bandan and several other ab-bandans bordering the marshes, was designated a Ramsar Site in 1975. The Department is currently undertaking a major programme of research at the Anzali Mordab to measure changes in water level, water quality, physico-chemical characteristics, etc.

The Department of the Environment should investigate a variety of possibilities for conserving waterfowl populations in the Mordab while at the same time maintaining hunting opportunities for the general public. These might include the following:

- imposing stricter controls on the number of hunters, number of days when hunting is permitted, bag limits, hunting techniques, etc.;
- giving greater encouragement to duck hunting communities using traditional hunting techniques to manage and patrol their hunting areas (e.g. as occurs at Gasghiasheh Ab-bandans in the eastern Mordab);
- encouraging sport hunters (using shot-guns) to form their own hunting clubs or societies to manage their activities more wisely;
- improving the protection of Siahkesheem Protected Area;
- creating a buffer zone around Selke Wildlife Refuge to reduce poaching around the edge of this

extremely important reserve;

- establishing additional non-hunting areas in other parts of the Anzali Mordab (e.g. at Sorkhan Kol).

Several major changes have occurred in the ecological character of the Anzali Mordab complex since about 1970, most strikingly the greatly increased extent of *Phragmites* which now almost entirely covers the east and centre of the main mordab. Rapid spread of *Phragmites* had already become a problem in the mid-1970s, and was attributed to falling water levels in the Mordab, as a result of the then-continuing fall in the level of the Caspian, and to increased inflow of sewage, fertilizers, etc. However, the 1.8 m rise in the level of the Caspian since 1978 has resulted in a 1 m rise in the water level in the main Anzali Mordab and increased salt water intrusion during the summer (when the Caspian is at its highest and inflow of fresh water is least). These increases in water depth and salinity will probably check the expansion of *Phragmites* but there are no signs yet of die-back.

Perhaps a more serious problem has been the massive spread of *Azolla*, which was introduced into the Caspian wetlands by rice-farmers in the 1970s and now covers much of the water within the reedbeds and quieter backwaters. The ecological consequences are not yet clear, but the greatly reduced abundance of *Nelumbium maciferum* and *Trapa natans* (both valuable waterfowl food plants) seems partly attributable to the spread of *Azolla*.

Hunting of waterfowl in the Anzali Mordab has increased greatly since the 1970s. The number of licensed hunters in Gilan Province rose from c.6,000 in the 1970s to c.20,000 in the early 1990s. Traditional hunting by dazzling continues at a high level, and is thought to account for at least 100,000 waterfowl per season. Hunting with shotguns has increased considerably, and there are now c.1,000 such hunters at Anzali Mordab, thought to account for another 100,000 waterfowl per season. Poaching is reported to have been a very serious problem in the reserves in the first few years after the revolution, but the situation has improved considerably, especially at Selke Wildlife Refuge where there is a new Game Guard Station and protection is excellent.

Further reading

Carp (1980), Ferguson (1972), Firouz *et al.* (1970), Fotoohi (1974), Howell (1976), IUCN (1991), Nielsen (1969), Nielsen and Speyer (1967), Ramsar Convention Bureau (1993), Scott (1976a,b,c, 1978a, in press), Summers *et al.* (1987).

017 Bandar Kiashar Lagoon and Mouth of Sefid Rud (Gilan)

37°20′N 49°55′E
500 ha
Ramsar Site

formerly Bandar Farahnaz Lagoon
Unprotected

Site description

Bandar Kiashahr Lagoon lies immediately east of the mouth of the Sefid Rud (river), c.40 km east of Bandar Anzali, in the south-west Caspian region. In the early 1970s it was a shallow, brackish coastal lagoon with fringing *Juncus* marshes in an area of coastal sand-dunes and grassland; it was fed by local run-off, and drained north-east through a narrow channel into the Caspian, having formed in 1960 as a result of the falling level of the Caspian and development of coastal sand spits. The 1.8 m rise in the level of the Caspian since 1978 has converted the wetland into a bay with broad entrance to the sea, similar to the situation in the 1950s. The marshy grassland and sand-dune areas at the mouth of the Sefid Rud have, however, remained more or less unchanged, while new wetland habitats have been created to the west of the river mouth. The lagoon supports relatively little vegetation other than algae. Freshwater marshes at the extreme west end of the lagoon support some beds of *Phragmites* and *Typha*, while the southern and eastern shores are dominated by *Juncus* and grasses. Sandy areas to the west and north-west are covered in scrub and grassland which give way to sand-dune vegetation near the Caspian shore. Grassland along the banks of the Sefid Rud floods seasonally. Land to the south of the wetland is mostly under cultivation, although there are some relict patches of *Alnus* woodland near the wetland. The lagoon is an important centre for commercial fishing, and there is a large fisheries station on the south shore. Grazing of livestock, reed-cutting and wildfowl hunting also occur. Land ownership is public.

Birds

See boxes for key species. The area is an important staging and wintering area for a wide variety of migratory waterfowl, notably grebes, *Phalacrocorax pygmeus*, ducks, shorebirds, gulls and terns, and for *Circus aeruginosus* and *Falco columbarius*. The open

Globally threatened species

Phalacrocorax pygmeus	Up to 300 winter.
Pelecanus crispus	A flock (usually 30–40 birds) wintered during the 1970s but apparently disappeared by about 1980, probably because of increased disturbance.
Anser erythropus	Wintered in the 1970s (max. 10), but no recent records.
Branta ruficollis	One, January 1973; no recent records.
Oxyura leucocephala	Three, February 1972.
Haliaeetus albicilla	Present all year (max. 5 in winter). Breeds locally.

grassy areas and dunes near the river mouth provide breeding habitat for *Glareola pratincola*, while a small patch of woodland to the south of the lagoon supports a large colony of *Phalacrocorax carbo*, *Nycticorax nycticorax* and other herons and egrets. *Ixobrychus minutus* is a passage migrant or summer visitor.

1% or more of population

	Breeding (pairs)	Wintering	Passage
Podiceps cristatus	—	340	—
Podiceps nigricollis	—	340	—
Phalacrocorax carbo	1,000	1,250	—
Phalacrocorax pygmeus	—	300	—
Pelecanus crispus	—	41	—
Nycticorax nycticorax	200	—	—
Egretta garzetta	30	—	875 (Jul)
Casmerodius albus	—	644	—
Ardea cinerea	may breed	120	—
Cygnus olor	—	271 [210]	—
Cygnus columbianus	—	24	—
Cygnus cygnus	—	130 [36]	—
Anas platyrhynchos	—	12,400	—
Bucephala clangula	—	112	—
Oxyura leucocephala	—	3	—
Glareola pratincola	20–30	—	150 (Aug)
Vanellus vanellus	—	3,500 [500]	—
Tringa erythropus	—	—	100 (Oct)
Tringa totanus	—	—	300 (Dec)
Larus ridibundus	—	3,500 [1,800]	—
Larus cachinnans	—	1,000	—

Species restricted wholly or largely to the Middle East

Sylvia mystacea Summer visitor.

■ Other threatened/endemic wildlife

None known to BirdLife International.

■ Conservation issues

There is no legal protection, though Bandar Kiashahr Lagoon and the mouth of Sefid Rud were designated a Ramsar Site in 1975, including the whole of the lagoon area, its associated marshes and the marshes and sand flats at the mouth of the Sefid Rud to the west. The number of wintering waterfowl has decreased considerably since the 1970s because of increased disturbance from fishing activities. Further investigations are required to assess the ecological changes which have occurred at the wetland, and to identify ways of reducing the disturbance to waterfowl from fishing activities.

■ Further reading

Carp (1980), Ramsar Convention Bureau (1993), Scott (1976a,c, 1978a), Summers *et al.* (1987).

018 Amirkelayeh Lake (Gilan)

Wildlife Refuge

37°18′N 50°10′E
1,230 ha
Ramsar Site

■ Site description

The lake lies on the coastal plain of the Caspian Sea, c.12 km north of Langarud, fed by springs and local run-off; at high water levels, it drains north through a small stream into the Caspian. It is a rather deep, permanent, freshwater lake with rich growth of floating and submergent vegetation, extensive beds of *Typha* and *Phragmites* and some *Salix* thickets. The open areas of the lake support abundant submerged and floating vegetation including *Nelumbium*, *Lemna*, *Potamogeton*, *Hydrilla*, *Myriophyllum* and *Ceratophyllum*. Surrounding areas are largely cultivated with rice. The lake is important for duck hunting and provides water for irrigation. Land ownership is public.

Globally threatened species

Phalacrocorax pygmeus	Winter visitor (see below).
Marmaronetta angustirostris	One, November 1969.
Haliaeetus albicilla	Present all year; one pair breeds.

1% or more of population

	Breeding (pairs)	Wintering	Passage
Phalacrocorax pygmeus	—	100	—
Casmerodius albus	—	—	140 (Dec)
Cygnus columbianus	—	16	—
Anas strepera	—	1,300 [165]	—
Netta rufina	—	2,500	—
Aythya ferina	—	4,200 [3,000]	—
Fulica atra	—	45,000	—

Regionally threatened or declining species

Aythya nyroca Winter visitor (max. 5).

■ Birds

See box for key species. A very important wintering area for diving ducks, notably *Netta rufina*, and for *Fulica atra* and *Phalacrocorax pygmeus*. Up to 20 *Circus aeruginosus* are present in winter. *Rallus aquaticus* and *Carduelis spinus* also winter. A pair of *Haliaeetus albicilla* nested close to the lake in the 1970s and may still do so. At least 101 species have been recorded in the reserve.

Other threatened/endemic wildlife

None known to BirdLife International.

Conservation issues

The lake and marshes were designated a Protected Region in 1970 and upgraded to Wildlife Refuge (1,230 ha) in 1971. This area was designated a Ramsar Site in 1975. Prior to its designation as a Wildlife Refuge, the lake had been an important waterfowl hunting area for local villagers, who employed a traditional clap-netting technique to trap ducks and coots for the market. During the revolution, local villagers burned down the Department of the Environment's Game Guard Station and Watch Tower, and re-assumed control of the lake. Duck-trapping has re-commenced, and it is reported that there are currently c.60 teams of netters operating at the lake. Thus, although Amirkelayeh Lake remains a Wildlife Refuge and Ramsar Site on paper, it is no longer under the control of the Department of the Environment. However, it appears that the ecological character of the site has remained unchanged. The lake is sufficiently high above the level of the Caspian Sea to have have been unaffected by the recent rise in sea-level.

The Department of the Environment should seek to re-establish its authority at the site. The best solution might be for the Department to downgrade the reserve to Protected Area, thereby allowing hunting to take place, and to enter into a management agreement with the local people whereby they are permitted to continue their hunting activities on a rational basis.

Further reading

Carp (1980), Ramsar Convention Bureau (1993), Scott (1976a,b,c).

019 Fereidoonkenar Marshes (Mazandaran)

36°35′N 52°31′E
1,000 ha

also known as Fereydun Kenar
Protected Area (148 ha)

Site description

Fereidoonkenar is an artificial wetland (damgah) on the coastal plain of the South Caspian, 5 km south of the village of Fereidoonkenar and 13 km south-west of Babolsar. It was created and is maintained primarily as a privately-owned duck-hunting area, but also serves to supply irrigation water in summer. The core of the damgah comprises a series of shallow freshwater impoundments with a rich submerged and floating aquatic vegetation, including *Nalumio nucifera* and extensive beds of *Phragmites* and *Typha*. The impoundments are almost entirely surrounded by an embankment and narrow belt of tall trees in which there are c.100 duck-trapping stations. The wetland is situated in the middle of a large expanse of rice paddies which provide excellent feeding habitat for ducks, geese, shorebirds and cranes. Live decoys are used to lure ducks into flight nets. The duck netting is licensed by the Department of the Environment, each trapping station of two men being permitted to capture five birds per day.

Globally threatened species

Anser erythropus	Winter visitor (max. 11).
Haliaeetus albicilla	Regular winter visitor (max. 4).
Aquila heliaca	Winter visitor.
Grus leucogeranus	A small group winters regularly (see text).

1% or more of population

	Breeding (pairs)	Wintering	Passage
Phalacrocorax carbo	—	1,560 [620]	—
Anser albifrons	—	1,700 [—]	—
Anser anser	—	6,000 [—]	—
Anas penelope	—	14,500 [—]	—
Anas strepera	—	20,000 [—]	—
Anas crecca	—	80,000 [—]	—
Anas platyrhynchos	—	80,000 [—]	—
Anas acuta	—	60,000 [—]	—
Anas clypeata	—	12,000 [—]	—
Grus leucogeranus	—	11	—
Vanellus vanellus	—	16,000 [5,000]	—
Philomachus pugnax	—	—	2,800 (Mar)
Limosa limosa	—	5,000	—

Regionally threatened or declining species

Gallinago media	Occurs, presumably as a scarce passage migrant.

Birds

See box for key species. The artificially maintained shallow impoundments and extensive rice fields at Fereidoonkenar provide excellent feeding and roosting habitat for large numbers of wintering waterfowl, notably dabbling ducks (up to 200,000), *Anser anser*, *Vanellus vanellus* and *Limosa limosa*. These concentrations attract a variety of wintering raptors including *Haliaeetus albicilla* and *Aquila heliaca*. Large concentrations of *Philomachus pugnax* have been recorded on spring migration. In 1978 ornithologists from the Department of the Environment discovered a tiny wintering population of *Grus leucogeranus* at the site. The local duck-hunters were very familiar with the cranes, and reported that they had been coming to this area for many years. Since their discovery, 7–11 birds have wintered each year. At least 11 were present in January 1992, including two juveniles, and thus the alarming rumours in early 1991 that 4–5 cranes had been shot or captured for zoos were clearly erroneous, as nine of the ten birds present in the winter of 1990/91 could still be accounted for. Other winter visitors include *Cygnus olor*, *Gallinago gallinago*, *Scolopax rusticola*, *Tringa totanus* and *Emberiza schoeniclus*.

■ Other threatened/endemic wildlife

None known to BirdLife International.

■ Conservation issues

Part of the area (148 ha) is under protection as the Fereidoonkenar Protected Area, originally established in the late 1970s as a Wildlife Refuge but since downgraded. To ensure that the waterfowl are not disturbed, the duck trappers enforce a very strict ban not only on shooting in the area, but also on all other unnecessary human activity. As a result, the damgah wetland and surrounding paddies constitute one of the best protected and least disturbed wetlands in the South Caspian lowlands. Few birds other than *A. platyrhynchos* and *A. crecca* are trapped, and thus for the many thousands of other ducks, geese and shorebirds, and for the cranes, conditions are ideal. Towards the end of each season, when duck-netting becomes unprofitable, the area is opened up to hunting with guns in a massive 'shoot-out'. Large numbers of waterfowl of many species are shot at this time, and there is a danger that *Grus leucogeranus* could be killed accidentally.

■ Further reading

Scott (1976a).

020 Seyed Mohalli, Zarin Kola and Larim Sara (Mazandaran)

36°45′N 53°00′E
1,600 ha

Seyed Mohalli also known as Saidmahaleh
Unprotected

■ Site description

Located c.20 km north of Sari and 10 km from the Caspian shore at 36°44′N 53°00′E, the Seyed Mohalli and Zarin Kola comprise a 600–hectare complex of shallow, freshwater irrigation ponds (ab-bandans) surrounded by rice fields and maintained through the winter as private duck-hunting reserves. Much of the nearby Larim Sara plains (36°45′N 53°03′E, 1,000 ha) are now converted to agriculture but were formerly open and grassy with a central area of *Salicornia* flats subject to winter flooding. Freshwater areas have rich submerged, floating and emergent vegetation, including extensive *Typha* and *Phragmites*; there are also *Salix* thickets. Duck-trapping by dazzling in the 1970s reportedly accounted for up to a thousand ducks in a night.

■ Birds

See boxes for key species. The marshes are a very important wintering area for a wide variety of waterfowl, especially dabbling ducks (regularly over 100,000 in the 1970s), swans, *Fulica atra* and some shorebirds, as well as *Circus aeruginosus* (up to 60). It is a breeding area for five species of herons and

1% or more of population

	Breeding (pairs)	Wintering	Passage
Phalacrocorax pygmeus	—	100	—
Ardeola ralloides	250	—	—
Bubulcus ibis	20	—	120 (Sep)
Egretta garzetta	40	—	300 (Sep)
Anser erythropus	—	359	—
Anas penelope	—	32,300	—
Anas strepera	—	16,200	—
Anas crecca	—	86,000	—
Anas platyrhynchos	—	12,850	—
Anas acuta	—	20,400	—
Anas clypeata	—	25,000	—
Netta rufina	—	4,435	—
Aythya ferina	—	4,840 [3,000]	—
Aythya fuligula	—	2,000	—
Aythya nyroca	—	6	185 (Nov)
Oxyura leucocephala	—	27 [2]	—
Fulica atra	—	34,550	—
Glareola pratincola	30–40	—	—
Vanellus vanellus	—	1,000	—
Limosa limosa	—	150	500 (Mar)
Chlidonias hybridus	150–200	—	—

Regionally threatened or declining species

Aythya nyroca	Passage migrant and winter visitor (see above).

Globally threatened species

Phalacrocorax pygmeus	Regular winter visitor (generally 10–30).
Anser erythropus	Winter visitor (formerly in large numbers—see text).
Branta ruficollis	Reported formerly to have wintered in small numbers (see text).
Oxyura leucocephala	Winter visitor (see below).
Milvus milvus	Vagrant (1, February 1971).
Haliaeetus albicilla	Pair nesting at Seyed Mohalli in 1970s; regular winter visitor (max. 3).
Aquila heliaca	Regular winter visitor (max. 2).

egrets and for *Chlidonias hybridus*; *Haliaeetus albicilla* has also nested (see below) and *Remiz pendulinus* probably breeds. In the 1970s, the Larim Sara plains were an important wintering area for *Phoenicopterus ruber*, *Anser erythropus* and *A. anser*, and also supported a small breeding colony of *Glareola pratincola*, but much of the area has since been reclaimed for agriculture and most of these birds have disappeared. (Huge flocks of *Anser erythropus* are reported to have wintered in this area in the 1950s and early 1960s, along with much smaller numbers of *Branta ruficollis*.)

Other threatened/endemic wildlife
None known to BirdLife International.

Conservation issues
There is no formal protection, but the duck hunters protect the waterfowl from disturbance by day and prohibit all shooting in the area during the main duck-hunting season.

Further reading
Scott (1976a,c, 1978a).

021 Dasht-e Naz (Mazandaran)
Wildlife Refuge

36°42′N 53°12′E
55 ha

Site description
The Dasht-e Naz Wildlife Refuge, c.25 km north-north-east of Sari on the coastal plain of the South Caspian, protects an 'island' of dense scrub-forest of *Quercus* (dominant), *Alnus*, *Parrotia* and *Crataegus*, with an intermingling of large trees and surrounded by cultivation. This is the last remnant of native lowland forest on the plains of Mazandaran. Land ownership is public.

Birds
See box for key species. The resident forest bird fauna is impoverished, because of the small size and isolation of the reserve, but a number of woodland species occur in large numbers on passage, including some raptors and *Phylloscopus trochiloides nitidus* (up to 50 in autumn). Large concentrations of *Columba oenas* (several thousands) and *C. palumbus* occur in winter, along with high densities of *Scolopax rusticola*. *Haliaeetus albicilla* is regular in winter and *Phasianus colchicus* is present. At least 92 species have been recorded in the reserve.

Globally threatened species

Haliaeetus albicilla	Regular winter visitor (max. 2).
Aquila heliaca	Occasional winter visitor.
Falco naumanni	Autumn passage migrant (max. 55).

Regionally threatened or declining species

Pernis apivorus	Single migrants recorded in spring and autumn.
Falco cherrug	One record in October.

Species restricted wholly or largely to the Middle East

Sylvia mystacea	Passage migrant; a few pairs probably breed.

Other threatened/endemic wildlife
None known to BirdLife International.

Conservation issues
The area was originally set aside as a private reserve. The Department of the Environment gained control of the area in 1964, and immediately introduced wild-caught *Dama mesopotamica* from the dwindling native population in the riparian forests along the Karkheh river in Khuzestan. The entire refuge is fenced with deer-proof fencing, and is intensively managed as a captive-breeding facility; *Axis axis* were also introduced into the reserve in 1966. There has been some replanting of native species to improve forage for the deer.

Further reading
Firouz *et al.* (1970), Scott (1976b).

022 Lapoo-Zargmarz Ab-bandans (Mazandaran)

Unprotected

36°50′N 53°17′E
950 ha
Ramsar Site

■ Site description

Two long narrow freshwater lagoons near the Caspian shore, 5–10 km west of Miankaleh Wildlife Refuge, c.10 km west of the extreme west end of the Gorgan Bay marshes, and c.25 km north-west of Behshahr. They are fed by irrigation ditches and local run-off, and drain east into the Gorgan Bay marshes. The water level fluctuates considerably, and extensive mudflats can be exposed, but the ab-bandans do not appear to have been affected by the recent rise in level of the Caspian Sea. Open-water areas support a rich growth of submerged and floating aquatic vegetation, mainly *Ceratophyllum* with some *Potamogeton*. The fringing marshes are dominated by *Phragmites* beds with some *Typha*, but there are scrubby areas of *Salix*, *Ribes*, *Rubus* and *Punica*. The wetlands are bounded to the north by dune vegetation and to the south by cotton and wheat fields. Wildfowl hunting and reed-cutting occur. Land ownership is private.

■ Birds

See box for key species. The wetland is used by a wide variety of waterfowl during the migration seasons and in winter, but few species except *Fulica atra* (18,600 recorded) occur in large numbers. There is a large colony of *Chlidonias hybridus* and *Haliaeetus albicilla* breeds locally. A small flock of *Oxyura leucocephala* wintered in the area in the 1970s, feeding by night on the ab-bandans and roosting by day on the adjacent Caspian Sea; none have been recorded since 1978, but it may be that the birds have simply moved a few kilometres east to Gorgan Bay, where the increased water depth has created more favourable conditions. The numbers of other ducks using the site have increased in recent years, presumably because of the better protection from disturbance now being afforded by the local hunters. *Phylloscopus trochiloides nitidus* is fairly common on passage, and *Tadorna tadorna* and *Falco pelegrinoides* are occasional visitors.

Globally threatened species

Phalacrocorax pygmeus	Regular winter visitor (max. 15).
Oxyura leucocephala	Winters in the area or nearby (see text and below).
Haliaeetus albicilla	Regular winter visitor (max. 3), breeding nearby.

1% or more of population

	Breeding (pairs)	Wintering	Passage
Ardeola ralloides	—	—	150 (Aug)
Cygnus columbianus	—	5	—
Anas strepera	—	1,500 [150]	—
Oxyura leucocephala	—	28	—
Vanellus vanellus	—	—	500 (Sep)
Chlidonias hybridus	100–150	—	—

Regionally threatened or declining species

Botaurus stellaris	One November record.
Aythya nyroca	Winter visitor (max. 5).

Species restricted wholly or largely to the Middle East

Sylvia mystacea	Common summer visitor in coastal scrub.

■ Other threatened/endemic wildlife

None known to BirdLife International.

■ Conservation issues

The ab-bandans are included together with Miankaleh Peninsula and Gorgan Bay (site 023) in a Ramsar Site of 100,000 ha. They have no legal protection, but are well managed and protected by the owners in the nearby village of Zargmarz who use the wetland for waterfowl hunting in winter and as a source of water for irrigation in summer. Under an agreement with the Department of the Environment, the owners are permitted to hunt on up to three days per month during the hunting season. To protect their interests, the owners pay a warden to prevent poaching, and in fact hunt at the site on only three or four occasions per season.

■ Further reading

Carp (1980), Ramsar Convention Bureau (1993), Scott (1976a,c).

023 Miankaleh Peninsula and Gorgan Bay (Mazandaran)

Wildlife Refuge (68,800 ha)

36°50′N 53°45′E
97,200 ha
Ramsar Site, Biosphere Reserve (68,800 ha)

Site description

Gorgan Bay is a large, shallow inlet (23,800 ha) at the extreme south-east corner of the Caspian Sea, north and east of the town of Behshahr, almost totally cut off from the open sea by the Miankaleh Peninsula (24,200 ha), which is 60 km long and averages c.2 km wide. It is low and sandy with a chain of dunes 50 m wide paralleling the Caspian Sea coast. Gorgan Bay is brackish and receives freshwater inflow from a number of small rivers and streams rising on the humid north slope of the Alborz Mountains to the south. Some freshwater marshes occur at the west end of the bay, where inflow is greatest. The rise in the level of the Caspian during the 1980s has resulted in a marked increase in the level of Gorgan Bay and re-flooding of all those bare flats at the west end of the bay which had been exposed by previous falling sea-levels. On the seaward side of the peninsula, the sandy beach has virtually disappeared and no longer provides easy vehicular access to the fishing village of Ashuradeh at the eastern tip of the peninsula. Most of the peninsula is covered with herbs and grasses, and the western half also supports scrub of scattered *Punica*, *Crataegus*, *Rhamnus* and *Rubus*. There are a few large *Salix* planted around some of the houses. Much of the shoreline of the bay is fringed with a broad belt of *Juncus* and there are some large areas of *Salicornia* flats. The extensive seasonally flooded marshes at the west end of the bay are dominated by *Carex* with clumps of *Juncus* and a large stand of *Tamarix* which spread greatly as water levels fell during the early 1970s but has since started to die back as the Caspian has risen again. Much of the peninsula is heavily grazed by sheep, goats and water buffalo.

Birds

See boxes for key species. Miankaleh Wildlife Refuge is undoubtedly one of the finest bird reserves in the Palearctic. At least 288 species have been recorded, including 15 species currently listed in the *IUCN Red Data Book of Threatened Animals*. Of the 126 species of waterfowl which have occurred, no less than 63 have been present in internationally significant numbers. The reserve is extremely important throughout the year, supporting perhaps 250,000 waterfowl in winter and large colonies of herons, egrets, pratincoles and terns in summer. It also serves as a major staging area for migrant water- and landbirds in spring and autumn, and is the most important staging area for many species of shorebirds in the South Caspian region. The reserve is especially noted for its large wintering populations of grebes, *Pelecanus crispus*, *Phalacrocorax carbo*, herons, *Phoenicopterus ruber*, swans, geese, surface-feeding and diving ducks, raptors (*Haliaeetus albicilla*, harriers, eagles and falcons), shorebirds and gulls, and for its breeding colonies of herons and egrets, *Glareola pratincola* and *Sterna albifrons*. A wide variety of landbirds occurs on passage, and

Globally threatened species

Phalacrocorax pygmeus	Regular winter visitor (max. 28) to western marshes.
Pelecanus crispus	Common winter visitor to Gorgan Bay and adjacent Caspian Sea.
Anser erythropus	Regular winter visitor in the 1970s (up to 4,900). Numbers fell rapidly in the late 1970s, and the flocks disappeared in the early 1980s.
Branta ruficollis	One flock of 19, winter 1975/76.
Marmaronetta angustirostris	An occasional passage migrant (max. 29).
Oxyura leucocephala	Regular winter visitor in small numbers, usually less than 20.
Haliaeetus albicilla	Present all year (max. 50–100 in winter).
Haliaeetus leucoryphus	One immature in 1975.
Aquila heliaca	Regular winter visitor (max. 6).
Falco naumanni	Two autumn records.
Tetrax tetrax	Common winter visitor in the early 1970s in flocks of over 100 (max. 602). A few pairs were present in summer and presumably bred. Small flocks were reported until the late 1980s, but none has been seen since.
Chlamydotis undulata	Two records of migrants.
Otis tarda	A female in January 1971 is the only record.
Vanellus gregarius	One in October 1971, 2 in November 1971.
Numenius tenuirostris	One bird on two dates in August 1963 (Feeny *et al.* 1968).

Regionally threatened or declining species

Botaurus stellaris	Occasional in winter. May breed.
Aythya nyroca	Recorded as non-breeder (max. 9).
Pernis apivorus	One passage record.
Neophron percnopterus	One passage record.
Aquila pomarina	Passage migrant in autumn; max. 8 at the site, but much larger numbers (115 in two hours, October) pass down the east coast of Gorgan Bay, opposite the tip of the peninsula.
Falco cherrug	Regular winter visitor (max. 4).
Francolinus francolinus	Common resident.

Species restricted wholly or largely to the Middle East

Oenanthe finschii	One February record.
Hippolais languida	Two passage records.
Sylvia mystacea	Very common summer visitor.

1% or more of population

	Breeding (pairs)	Wintering	Passage
Podiceps cristatus	—	3,000	—
Podiceps nigricollis	—	2,000+	—
Phalacrocorax carbo	—	15,000	—
Pelecanus crispus	—	690 [350]	—
Ardeola ralloides	200	—	—
Bubulcus ibis	15	—	150 (Sep)
Egretta garzetta	100	15	450 (Sep)
Casmerodius albus	—	2,685	—
Ardea cinerea	2	630	1,860 (Sep)
Platalea leucorodia	—	—	423 (Mar)
Phoenicopterus ruber	—	25,080 [4,250]	—
Cygnus olor	—	2,174	—
Cygnus columbianus	—	16	—
Anser erythropus	—	4,900	—
Anser anser	—	10,020	—
Tadorna ferruginea	—	328	—
Tadorna tadorna	—	1,605 [1,200]	—
Anas penelope	—	61,100	—
Anas strepera	—	20,300	—
Anas crecca	—	57,000	—
Anas platyrhynchos	—	56,600 [9,800]	—
Anas acuta	—	30,400 [3,400]	—
Anas querquedula	—	—	3,640 (Aug)
Anas clypeata	—	18,200	—
Aythya ferina	—	22,500 [2,680]	—
Aythya fuligula	—	8,000 [7,750]	—
Bucephala clangula	—	1,110	—
Mergus serrator	—	703	—
Oxyura leucocephala	—	453	—
Fulica atra	—	50,000 [19,100]	—
Himantopus himantopus	—	140	938 (Apr)
Recurvirostra avosetta	—	816	—
Glareola pratincola	500+	—	—
Charadrius alexandrinus	150–200	200	1,350 (Aug)
Charadrius leschenaultii	—	10	190 (Jul)
Pluvialis squatarola	—	155	500 (Oct)
Vanellus vanellus	—	1,500	—
Calidris alba	—	150	4,820 (May)
Calidris minuta	—	5	2,450 (Aug)
Calidris ferruginea	—	—	2,650 (Aug)
Calidris alpina	—	5,000	—
Limicola falcinellus	—	—	189 (Aug)
Philomachus pugnax	—	—	1,470 (Mar)
Limosa limosa	—	800	3,770 (Feb)
Numenius phaeopus	—	—	880 (Aug)
Numenius tenuirostris	—	—	1 (Aug)
Numenius arquata	—	157	530 (Sep)
Tringa totanus	—	650	1,810 (Oct)
Tringa stagnatilis	—	—	563 (Jul)
Tringa nebularia	—	44	270 (Oct)
Arenaria interpres	—	5	562 (Aug)
Larus ichthyaetus	—	2,250	—
Larus minutus	—	750	—
Larus ridibundus	—	5,000	—
Larus genei	—	1,330	2,950 (Nov)
Larus cachinnans	—	865	1,850 (Sep)
Sterna sandvicensis	—	38	1,450 (Mar)
Sterna hirundo	10–20	—	955 (Sep)
Sterna albifrons	300–400	—	1,370 (Sep)
Chlidonias hybridus	—	—	820 (Jul)

large numbers of larks, thrushes, finches and buntings remain to winter. Notable species recorded include *Podiceps grisegena*, *Cygnus cygnus*, *Mergus serrator*, *Mergellus albellus*, *Aquila clanga*, *Pandion haliaetus* (breeds), *Charadrius asiaticus*, *Larus ichthyaetus*, *Sterna caspia*, *Caprimulgus aegyptius*, *Melanocorypha leucoptera*, *Acrocephalus agricola*, *Phylloscopus trochiloides nitidus* (common passage migrant), *Remiz pendulinus* and *Sturnus roseus*.

The 1.8 m rise in the level of the Caspian since 1978 has had a profound influence on waterfowl populations in the marshes at the west end of Gorgan Bay, which are now permanently flooded. These marshes formerly held 3,000–10,000 *Anser anser*, 4,000–5,000 *A. erythropus* and huge numbers of surface-feeding ducks. Large numbers of waterfowl continue to winter in the marshes, but now the great majority are *Fulica atra*, which was relatively uncommon in the 1970s (then usually 500–2,500). Only small numbers of *Anser anser* have been observed in recent years, and no *A. erythropus* since 1989. These changes in populations are clearly related to the increased water depth in the western marshes.

Other threatened/endemic wildlife

Mammals: *Phoca caspica* (V) occasionally haul out on the Caspian beach.

Conservation issues

The entire area was designated a Protected Region in 1970. Cultivated land along the southern edge of the bay was subsequently excised from the reserve, reducing the area to 68,800 ha, and the reserve was upgraded to Wildlife Refuge. This refuge includes Miankaleh Peninsula, the open waters of Gorgan Bay and the marshes at the west end of the bay. Miankaleh Peninsula, Gorgan Bay and the nearby Lapoo-Zargmarz Ab-bandans (site 022) were designated a Ramsar Site of 100,000 ha in 1975. The entire Wildlife Refuge was designated a Biosphere Reserve in 1976. Some poaching occurs along the south-west boundary of the reserve, but this is probably not a serious problem. The major threat is the proposed construction of an asphalt highway down the centre of the peninsula to provide easy access to the fishery stations along the beach and at Ashuradeh. A highway has already been constructed up to the western boundary of the reserve, but work was halted following intervention by the Department of the Environment. The greatly improved access to the reserve would inevitably lead to increased pressure for settlement, increased farming activities and increased poaching.

Further reading

van Beuningen *et al.* (1975), Carp (1980), Feeny *et al.* (1968), Harrington and Scott (1972), Matthews (1973), Ramsar Convention Bureau (1993), Scott (1976a,b,c, 1978a, in press), Summers *et al.* (1987).

024 Gomishan Marshes and Turkoman Steppes (Mazandaran) 37°15'N 53°55'E
No-hunting Area (partly) c.20,000 ha

Site description
In the 1970s, the Gomishan wetlands consisted of a chain of narrow, brackish lagoons behind the Caspian Sea beach, stretching from 2 km north of the town of Gomishan north to the Turkmenistan border (and beyond). In the east, the wetland bordered on a vast area of low-lying plains with salt-tolerant vegetation. The recent 1.8 m rise in the level of the Caspian has resulted in extensive flooding of these plains, so that the Gomishan Marshes now comprise a large area of shallow, brackish lagoons and marshes covering c.4,850 ha. The wetland lies at the western edge of the Turkoman Steppes, a vast region of grass-covered plains and rolling hills extending for over 100 km to the east in Iran and even further to the north in Turkmenistan; much of the natural grassland near Gomishan Marshes has been converted to arable land. The main wetland area contains saltmarsh vegetation and seasonally-inundated flats of *Salicornia* mixed with *Halostachys* and *Halocnemum* grasses. The site is bounded in the west by low coastal dunes with typical sand-dune vegetation, and in the east extends onto the short-grass plains of the Turkoman Steppes, large areas of which are under cultivation for wheat and cotton. Land ownership is public. Livestock grazing (mainly sheep and goats) and waterfowl hunting occur.

Birds
See box for key species. In the 1970s, when the permanent wetland area was restricted to a chain of narrow, brackish lagoons behind the Caspian beach, the area was primarily important for breeding *Himantopus himantopus* and terns (c.500 pairs of four species), and wintering geese (including *Anser erythropus*), *Vanellus vanellus* and *Pterocles alchata* (up to 50,000). *Syrrhaptes paradoxus* may be a regular winter visitor, as small numbers were found amongst the large flocks of *P. alchata* in December 1970. In recent years, the rise in level of the Caspian has flooded large areas of former *Salicornia* flats, creating large lagoons which have rapidly become of great importance for wintering waterfowl of many species, notably *Pelecanus crispus*, *Phoenicopterus ruber*, *Anser anser*, dabbling ducks (regularly over 50,000), *Fulica atra* and *Himantopus himantopus*.

Globally threatened species

Pelecanus crispus	Winter visitor (max. 334 in recent years).
Anser erythropus	Perhaps a regular winter visitor in the 1970s (see below).
Haliaeetus albicilla	Regular winter visitor (max. 4).
Aquila heliaca	Regular winter visitor (max. 3).
Falco naumanni	Summer visitor: colony of 20 pairs in town of Bandar-e Shah at south edge of Turkoman Steppes.
Tetrax tetrax	One winter record (January 1969).

1% or more of population

	Breeding (pairs)	Wintering	Passage
Podiceps cristatus	—	800 [—]	—
Phalacrocorax carbo	—	2,330 [—]	—
Pelecanus crispus	—	334 [—]	—
Casmerodius albus	—	1,120 [—]	—
Ardea cinerea	—	1,120 [—]	—
Phoenicopterus ruber	—	55,000 [—]	—
Cygnus cygnus	—	256 [—]	—
Anser erythropus	—	1,773	—
Anser anser	—	3,200 [453]	—
Anas penelope	—	16,000 [—]	—
Anas strepera	—	13,000 [—]	—
Anas crecca	—	30,000 [—]	—
Anas platyrhynchos	—	40,000 [—]	—
Anas acuta	—	14,200 [—]	—
Anas clypeata	—	12,000 [—]	—
Aythya ferina	—	17,000 [—]	—
Mergus serrator	—	204 [—]	—
Fulica atra	—	65,200 [—]	—
Himantopus himantopus	250	1,700 [—]	—
Vanellus vanellus	—	5,000	—
Limosa limosa	—	400 [—]	—
Tringa totanus	—	1,500 [—]	—
Larus ichthyaetus	—	529 [—]	—
Sterna albifrons	200–300	—	—
Chlidonias hybridus	100	—	—

Other threatened/endemic wildlife
None known to BirdLife International.

Conservation issues
Part of the wetland has recently been designated a No-hunting Area, and there are plans to upgrade this to Protected Area within five years. In recent years there has been intensive shooting in winter. Large areas of natural grassland in the east have been converted to agricultural land. It has been proposed that Gomishan Marshes be designated a Ramsar Site.

Further reading
Scott (1976a,c).

025 Lake Alagol, Lake Ulmagol and Lake Ajigol (Mazandaran) 37°23′N 54°38′E

Unprotected

1,540 ha

Ramsar Site (1,400 ha)

Site description

The site comprises three small lakes, with associated marshes and intervening grassy steppe, on the Turkoman Steppes near the border with Turkmenistan, c.60 km north-north-east of Gorgan. Lake Alagol (37°21′N 54°35′E, 900 ha) lies c.6 km south-west of Lakes Ulmagol (37°25′N 54°38′E, 280 ha) and Ajigol (37°24′N 54°40′E, 360 ha); it is slightly saline and fed by seepage, springs and local run-off, flooding in winter and sometimes drying out completely in summer. When full, it overflows westwards. The lake is oligotrophic, supporting little vegetation. Lake Ulmagol and Lake Ajigol are eutrophic freshwater lakes fed by local rainfall in autumn and winter. Both are subject to wide fluctuations in water level, and occasionally dry out completely. The lakes rarely, if ever, freeze over in winter. Lake Alagol supports little aquatic vegetation except for some *Juncus*, *Carex* and grasses, mainly in the north-east, and a few small patches of *Phragmites*. Ulmagol and Ajigol support a more varied vegetation of *Juncus*, *Lemna*, *Phragmites*, *Alhagi* and algae. Much of Ajigol is overgrown with *Phragmites*, and the lake has some adjacent stands of *Tamarix*. The surrounding steppes are a vast gently undulating grassland with low sandy hills. There are several small settlements near the lake complex, and reed-cutting, grazing, wildfowl hunting and some fishing occur. Land ownership is public.

Birds

See box for key species. The lakes are utilized by a wide variety of waterfowl during the migration seasons and in winter, and are especially important for *Phoenicopterus ruber*, *Anser anser*, dabbling ducks, *Netta rufina*, *Mergellus albellus* and *Fulica atra*. Breeding species include *Himantopus himantopus*, *Charadrius alexandrinus*, *Larus genei* and *Remiz pendulinus*. *Ciconia nigra* has been recorded in summer and may breed.

Other threatened/endemic wildlife

None known to BirdLife International.

Globally threatened species

Pelecanus crispus	One winter record of a single bird.
Anser erythropus	A flock of 150 in winter 1974.
Oxyura leucocephala	A flock of 19 in January 1975.
Haliaeetus albicilla	Regular winter visitor (max. 9).
Aegypius monachus	Occasional visitor (max. 5).
Aquila heliaca	Regular winter visitor (max. 3).

1% or more of population

	Breeding (pairs)	Wintering	Passage
Casmerodius albus	—	278	—
Ciconia nigra	may breed in area	—	10 (Jul)
Cygnus olor	—	260 [25]	—
Anas strepera	—	2,480	—
Anas clypeata	—	1,600	—
Aythya fuligula	—	4,000 [510]	—
Oxyura leucocephala	—	19	—
Fulica atra	—	50,750	—
Himantopus himantopus	60	—	—
Charadrius alexandrinus	100	—	—
Larus ridibundus	—	2,500 [—]	—
Larus cachinnans	—	1,000 [—]	—

Regionally threatened or declining species

Falco cherrug	Single birds occur in winter.
Francolinus francolinus	Fairly common resident.

Species restricted wholly or largely to the Middle East

Oenanthe finschii	Common winter visitor.
Sylvia mystacea	Summer visitor; probably breeds.

Conservation issues

The lakes were designated a Ramsar Site in 1975, but there is no legal protection and no conservation measures are known to have been proposed. Ulmagol and Ajigol have long been subjected to high levels of disturbance from wildfowl hunters, and Alagol (the least accessible of the three) is also now affected by disturbance from hunters. Thorough investigation of these lakes has been recommended by the Department of the Environment.

Further reading

Carp (1980), Ramsar Convention Bureau (1993), Scott (1976a,c).

026 Incheh Borun Lake and Marshes (Mazandaran)

Unprotected

37°13´N 54°30´E
50 ha

■ Site description

Lying c.40 km north of Gorgan, the site comprises a small freshwater lake with some emergent marsh vegetation. It is surrounded by grassy steppe and arable land.

■ Birds

See box for key species. A wintering area for a wide variety of waterfowl including good numbers of *Cygnus olor* and *Mergellus albellus*. The surrounding plains are probably an important staging area for *Charadrius asiaticus*.

■ Other threatened/endemic wildlife

None known to BirdLife International.

■ Conservation issues

No conservation measures are known to have been proposed and there is no information on threats to the site.

Globally threatened species

Anser erythropus	A flock of 36 in February 1973.
Branta ruficollis	One in February 1973.
Oxyura leucocephala	Four in January 1972.
Haliaeetus albicilla	Winter visitor (max. 2).
Aegypius monachus	One record in winter.
Aquila heliaca	Winter visitor (max. 2).

1% or more of population

	Breeding (pairs)	Wintering	Passage
Casmerodius albus	—	135	—
Ardea cinerea	—	123 [—]	—
Oxyura leucocephala	—	4	—
Charadrius asiaticus	—	—	110 (Jul)

Species restricted wholly or largely to the Middle East

Oenanthe finschii	Fairly common in winter.

■ Further reading

Scott (1976a).

027 Voshmigir Dam (Mazandaran)

Unprotected

37°12´N 54°45´E
500 ha

■ Site description

A small irrigation storage reservoir on the Gorgan river, c.50 km north-north-east of Gorgan and 35 km west of Gonbad-e Qaboos, in a region of steppe and arable land. The water level fluctuates widely, and extensive mudflats can be exposed, but in most places the banks shelve steeply and there is little emergent vegetation.

■ Birds

See box for key species. A wintering area for ducks and grebes, notably *Netta rufina* (up to 340 birds) and *Mergellus albellus*, and a staging area for shorebirds. *Sterna albifrons* breeds.

Globally threatened species

Pelecanus crispus	One record of 2 birds in winter.

1% or more of population

	Breeding (pairs)	Wintering	Passage
Aythya nyroca	—	15	—
Mergellus albellus	—	340	—
Recurvirostra avosetta	—	430 [—]	—
Charadrius alexandrinus	—	—	350 (Aug)
Sterna albifrons	40	—	—

Regionally threatened or declining species

Aythya nyroca	Winter visitor (see above).

■ Other threatened/endemic wildlife

None known to BirdLife International.

■ Conservation issues

No conservation measures are known to have been proposed and there is no information on threats to the site.

■ Further reading

Scott (1976a).

028 Lake Bibishervan and Lake Eymar (Mazandaran)

37°09′N 54°52′E
550 ha

Lake Bibishervan also known as Lake Byby Shirvan
Unprotected

Site description

The site comprises two shallow freshwater lakes, Lake Bibishervan (37°09′N 54°52′E, 300 ha) and Lake Eymar (37°08′N 54°52′E, 250 ha), with fringing *Phragmites* and *Carex* on the southern edge of the Turkoman Steppes 30 km west-south-west of Gonbad-e Qaboos. The surrounding area is cultivated.

Birds

See box for key species. A wintering area for a wide variety of waterfowl including good numbers of *Netta rufina* (up to 740) and *Vanellus vanellus*. Breeding birds include *Glareola pratincola* and *Chlidonias hybridus*, and up to ten *Aquila clanga* have occurred on passage.

Globally threatened species

Oxyura leucocephala	One winter record of 6 birds.
Tetrax tetrax	Flock of 430 in February 1972.

1% or more of population

	Breeding (pairs)	Wintering	Passage
Oxyura leucocephala	—	6	—
Glareola pratincola	75	—	—
Vanellus vanellus	—	3,000	—
Chlidonias hybridus	150	—	—

Regionally threatened or declining species

Neophron percnopterus	One record of 4 migrants.
Aquila pomarina	Four recorded in July 1972.
Francolinus francolinus	Fairly common.

Other threatened/endemic wildlife

None known to BirdLife International.

Conservation issues

No conservation measures are known to have been proposed and there is no information on threats to the site.

Further reading

Scott (1976a,c).

029 Central Alborz Region (Mazandaran)

36°10′N 51°30′E
399,000 ha

also known as Alborz-e Markazi
Protected Area

Site description

The central Alborz (Elburz) region extends from the forested foothills near the Caspian Sea east of Chalus to the summits north of Tehran (4,540 m), some of the highest peaks in the Alborz range. The site is bounded in the west by the main Karadj to Chalus road across the Alborz. It includes the full spectrum of habitat types on the northern slope of the Alborz, including the various types of Caspian forest from sea-level to the treeline, cleared areas on the lower slopes with grassland, cultivated plots and hedgerow communities, stands of *Cupressus* forest in rain-shadow areas at mid-elevations, *Juniperus* forest and alpine meadows on the upper slopes, spectacular cliffs and crags at high elevation, and alpine tundra and permanent snow fields on the mountain tops. The region is rather densely populated, especially at lower elevations in the north, with numerous small villages and many roads. Land ownership is public.

Birds

See box for key species. The reserve supports a very good variety of high Alborz species, including a

Globally threatened species

Aquila heliaca	Pair seen in forest in April; may breed.
Falco naumanni	Common autumn passage migrant.
Crex crex	One on spring passage.

Regionally threatened or declining species

Pernis apivorus	Presumed to breed (pair seen displaying in April). Up to 9 on autumn passage.
Gypaetus barbatus	Resident.
Neophron percnopterus	Summer visitor; max. count 6.
Gyps fulvus	Fairly common resident; max. 21.
Accipiter brevipes	Three spring records.
Aquila pomarina	Presumed to breed.

Species restricted wholly or largely to the Middle East

Tetraogallus caspius	Common on high ridges above 3,750 m; several spring counts of over 30.
Ammoperdix griseogularis	Fairly common on lower, southern slopes.
Prunella ocularis	Fairly common summer visitor.
Irania gutturalis	Fairly common summer visitor.
Oenanthe finschii	Fairly common summer visitor.
Oenanthe xanthoprymna	Common summer visitor.
Sylvia mystacea	Common summer visitor in north.
Phylloscopus neglectus	Common summer visitor.
Rhodopechys sanguinea	Common breeder at high altitudes; fairly common in winter on lower southern slopes.

large population of *Tetraogallus caspius*, and probably the full complement of Caspian forest species, including high densities of *Phasianus colchicus*. The region is rich in birds of prey (see box). Other notable species are *Phoenicurus erythronotus*, *Phylloscopus trochiloides nitidus*, *Ficedula semitorquata*, *F. parva*, *Tichodroma muraria*, *Pyrrhocorax graculus*, *Montifringilla nivalis*, *Serinus pusillus*, *Emberiza leucocephalos* and *E. buchanani*. At least 174 species have been recorded in the reserve.

■ Other threatened/endemic wildlife

Mammals: *Canis lupus* (V), *Ursus arctos* (rare), *Lynx lynx* (rare), *Panthera pardus* (rare), *Capra hircus aegagrus* (rare) and *Ovis ammon* (rare).

■ Conservation issues

Small Protected Regions were established in the central Alborz in 1961 and 1962 and these were included in a much larger Protected Region of 423,250 ha established in 1964 (Alborz-e–Markazi). In the early 1970s, this large reserve was zoned into a National Park of 203,000 ha, a Protected Area of 215,450 ha, a Wildlife Refuge of 50 ha and a National Nature Monument of 4,750 ha. In the 1980s, these four components were combined as a single Protected Area, and the total area was reduced to 399,000 ha. No conservation measures are known to have been proposed. Threats comprise overgrazing by domestic livestock, particularly at high elevations, forest clearance for human settlement and agriculture, and logging.

■ Further reading

Firouz *et al.* (1970), Scott (1976b), Scott and Howell (1976).

030 Upper Lar Valley (Tehran)

Protected Area

35°57′N 51°36′E
28,000 ha

■ Site description

The site comprises 20 km of the upper Lar valley in the high Alborz Mountains, from 2,450 m to peaks at 4,540 m. It lies above the Lar Dam, c.10–30 km upstream from the small town of Polur and c.40 km north-east of Tehran. The Lar is in the Caspian watershed, but at this point lies in a rain shadow and the area is relatively arid. For much of its length, the river meanders across a broad, flat-bottomed valley c.500–1,000 m wide. Habitats include a fast-flowing river with extensive shingle banks, patches of dense riverine *Salix* and *Tamarix* scrub (with a few trees up to 7–8 m high), small areas of natural wet meadow, open hillsides with steppic vegetation, a number of small, spring-fed alpine meadows in side valleys, and the high crags and summits of neighbouring peaks. There is grazing by sheep, goats and horses. The area was a regular bird-ringing site of the Department of the Environment's Ornithology Unit in the 1970s.

■ Birds

See box for key species. The area supports a typical high Alborz avifauna, including a good population of *Tetraogallus caspius*, and also appears to be of considerable importance as a staging area for migrant passerines (e.g. *Phylloscopus trochiloides nitidus*), especially in autumn, when the dense shrubbery and wet meadows along the river provide rich feeding habitat. At least 97 species have been recorded in the valley.

Globally threatened species	
Aegypius monachus	One in September 1976.
Falco naumanni	Autumn passage migrant.
Regionally threatened or declining species	
Gypaetus barbatus	Resident.
Neophron percnopterus	One autumn passage record.
Gyps fulvus	Resident (max. count 3).
Gallinago media	One autumn passage record.
Species restricted wholly or largely to the Middle East	
Tetraogallus caspius	Fairly common resident at high altitudes.
Prunella ocularis	Fairly common summer visitor.
Irania gutturalis	Passage migrant (October); may breed.
Oenanthe xanthoprymna	Fairly common summer visitor.
Rhodopechys sanguinea	Fairly common resident.

■ Other threatened/endemic wildlife

None known to BirdLife International.

■ Conservation issues

A National Park of 73,500 ha was established in the upper drainage of the Lar river in 1976, but this reserve has since been reduced in size to 28,000 ha and downgraded to Protected Area. No conservation measures are known to have been proposed and there are no known threats to the site.

■ Further reading

Argyle (1976b).

031 Lashgarak and Latian Dam (Tehran)

35°47′N 51°40′E
110 ha

Unprotected

Site description

The site lies c.20 km north-east of Tehran at c.1,350 m in a steep-sided valley in the foothills of the Alborz Mountains, with the main massif rising abruptly to the north and the deserts of the Central Plateau stretching away to the south. The site comprises a short stretch of the Jajerud (a fast-flowing river with rocky and boulder bed), a small storage reservoir (Latian Dam) and a complex of gravel banks, small marshy creeks and mudflats where the river enters the reservoir, as well as adjacent small fields, orchards, *Populus* groves, rough pasture and rocky hillsides with steppic vegetation. Low cliffs border the south-west bank of the river. The area is used intensively for picnicing at weekends. Limited grazing, chiefly by cattle, occurs in the marshy areas, but the only large-scale exploitation is the extraction of sand and gravel from the river-bed. The area was a regular bird-ringing site of the Department of the Environment's Ornithology Unit in the 1970s.

Birds

See box for key species. The well-watered valleys in the southern foothills of the Alborz Mountains, with their numerous small fields, gardens, orchards and poplar groves, constitute an important resting and feeding area for migrant birds in spring and autumn. These areas are particularly important during the spring migration, when periods of bad weather in the high Alborz may halt migration. The Lashgarak area, in the valley of the Jajerud, is a good example of such a site, with the added attraction of a small reservoir and some wetland habitat. Although rather few species breed or winter in the area, no less than 267 species have been recorded at the site, including several scarce passage migrants which have seldom been recorded elsewhere in Iran. *Phylloscopus trochiloides nitidus* is a common autumn passage migrant. A very wide variety of waterfowl has been recorded, mostly in rather small numbers. The site seems to be especially important for *Gallinago media*, which occurs regularly in spring.

Other threatened/endemic wildlife

None known to BirdLife International.

Globally threatened species

Marmaronetta angustirostris	Two in March 1973.
Aegypius monachus	Occasional visitor (3 records).
Aquila heliaca	Three records of singles in March.
Falco naumanni	Summer visitor: colony of 15 pairs on hillside above Lashgarak; 150 on passage in October 1974.
Crex crex	Regular spring and autumn passage migrant.

1% or more of population

	Breeding (pairs)	Wintering	Passage
Larus cachinnans/L. argentatus	—	—	165 (Apr)
Sterna albifrons	—	—	120 (May)

Regionally threatened or declining species

Botaurus stellaris	One spring record.
Pernis apivorus	Singles recorded in spring and autumn.
Gypaetus barbatus	One record, February.
Neophron percnopterus	Recorded April and May.
Gyps fulvus	Occasional visitor (max. 6).
Accipiter brevipes	One in October.
Falco cherrug	Occasional in winter.
Gallinago media	Regular on spring and autumn passage (max. 10).

Species restricted wholly or largely to the Middle East

Ammoperdix griseogularis	One record.
Prunella ocularis	Spring and autumn passage migrant.
Oenanthe finschii	Recorded February–April.
Oenanthe xanthoprymna	Spring passage migrant.
Hippolais languida	Autumn passage migrant.
Sylvia mystacea	Spring passage migrant.
Sylvia minula	Four autumn records.
Carpospiza brachydactyla	One record, May.
Rhodopechys sanguinea	Common spring passage migrant.

Conservation issues

The extraction of sand and gravel from the river bed, which began about 1972, has destroyed much of the marsh vegetation and causes considerable disturbance to birds. It has been proposed that a small bird sanctuary be created. The area is within a one-hour drive of Tehran; it offers the public a convenient and attractive place to study nature, and would provide an ideal outdoor educational laboratory.

Further reading

Scott (1973e, 1976f), Summers *et al.* (1987).

032 Kavir Region (Tehran)
National Park and Protected Area

34°45'N 52°10'E
670,000 ha
Biosphere Reserve

Site description

The Kavir region lies near the north-west corner of Iran's vast, arid central basin and between the Dasht-i Kavir (Salt Desert) and Daryacheh Namak (Salt Lake). The centre of the Protected Area is c.110 km south-east of Tehran. A chain of low rocky mountains (rising to 2,015 m at Siah-Kuh) runs through the alluvial plains (700–1,000 m) which form the remainder of this region. During prolonged drought virtually the entire area appears to be barren, shrubs and perennial herbs being confined to wadis or other drainage features. However, winter rains and snow may trigger a profuse growth of grasses and flowering plants which carpet much of the area in spring. Open associations of 'tragacanthic' or other *Astragalus* species, together with some spiny *Cousinia* and *Artemisia* (mostly *A. herb-alba*), are prevalent above 1,500 m. At lower elevations, *Artemisia* species are the commonest shrubs, while salt-tolerant plants such as *Alhagi*, *Salsola*, *Haloxylon*, *Suaeda*, *Zygophyllum* and *Seidlitzia* dominate in the more saline valley basins. The region is within easy access of Tehran, and is ideally situated for the promotion of eco-tourism. An old caravanserai in the west-central portion of the National Park has been restored as a guest house and visitor centre. Land ownership is public.

Birds

See box for key species. The reserve supports the characteristic desert avifauna of Iran's central plateau, and is an important breeding area for *Chlamydotis undulata*. It is also one of the best areas in the country for *Pterocles coronatus*, with up to 600 gathering to drink at a spring in the centre of the reserve. Other notable breeding species include *Buteo rufinus*, *Falco tinnunculus*, *Cursorius cursor*, *Ammomanes cincturus*, *Hirundo obsoleta*, *Scotocerca inquieta* and *Rhodopechys githaginea*. *Rhodopechys mongolica* occurs in large flocks in winter, and *Accipiter nisus* and *Circus cyaneus* also winter. *Aquila nipalensis* is regular on passage, and many passerine night-migrants stop over briefly at the small springs in spring and autumn; other passage migrants include *Ciconia ciconia*, *Circus aeruginosus*, *Coturnix coturnix* and *Grus grus*. At least 121 species have been recorded in the reserve.

Globally threatened species

Aquila heliaca	Winter visitor.
Chlamydotis undulata	Summer visitor (max. count 6 birds).

Regionally threatened or declining species

Gypaetus barbatus	Resident.
Neophron percnopterus	Recorded on passage in spring.
Aquila pomarina	Passage migrant (one autumn record).
Falco cherrug	Passage migrant (two records, September).

Species restricted wholly or largely to the Middle East

Ammoperdix griseogularis	Very common resident.
Prunella ocularis	Common winter visitor.
Oenanthe finschii	Common winter visitor.
Oenanthe xanthoprymna	Fairly common winter visitor.
Oenanthe monacha	Scarce resident.
Oenanthe alboniger	Common resident.
Sylvia mystacea	Recorded on passage in spring and autumn.
Carpospiza brachydactyla	Possibly only a scarce passage migrant.

Other threatened/endemic wildlife

Mammals: *Gazella dorcas fuscifrons* (V), *Ovis ammon* (rare), *Capra hircus aegagrus* (rare), *Caracal caracal* (rare), *Lynx lynx* (rare), *Canis lupus* (V). *Equus hemionus* (V) was fairly common in the 1970s, and *Acinonyx jubatus* (V) was occasionally reported, but these both seem to have disappeared.

Conservation issues

The Kavir Protected Region (609,438 ha) was established in 1964 and given National Park status in the early 1970s. The reserve has since been enlarged to 670,000 ha, but the National Park has been reduced to 420,000 ha and the remainder designated as a Protected Area (250,000 ha). The National Park, Protected Area and some adjacent land (totalling 700,000 ha) were designated a Biosphere Reserve in 1976. There is reported to have been a considerable amount of poaching in the reserve since the revolution, and the populations of large mammals are much depleted.

Further reading

Firouz (1974), Firouz *et al.* (1970), Scott (1976b).

033 Parvar Protected Area (Semnan)

Protected Area

35°57′N 53°35′E
59,840 ha

■ Site description

A portion of the east-central Alborz Mountains c.35 km north of Semnan, spanning the divide from semi-arid steppe at c.1,800 m on the southern slopes to the upper levels of the humid Caspian forest in the north, peaking at 3,888 m. A deep, rain-shadow valley runs east-west through the centre of the reserve, with spectacular cliffs and scree slopes and some of the finest *Juniperus* forest in the Alborz. Other habitats include humid and dry high alpine zones, and rolling semi-arid *Artemisia* steppe in the south. Land ownership is public.

■ Birds

See box for key species. The reserve contains a very good variety of alpine and *Juniperus* forest species, as well as Caspian forest and montane steppic species. It is one of the few known localities for *Mycerobas carnipes* in Iran. Other notable species include *Melanocorypha bimaculata*, *Phoenicurus erythronotus*, *S. hortensis*, *Phylloscopus trochiloides nitidus*, *Serinus pusillus*, *Rhodopechys mongolica* and *Emberiza buchanani*. At least 101 species have been recorded in the reserve.

■ Other threatened/endemic wildlife

Mammals: *Canis lupus* (V), *Ursus arctos* (rare), *Panthera pardus* (rare), *Capra hircus aegagrus* (rare) and *Ovis ammon* (rare).

Regionally threatened or declining species

Gypaetus barbatus	Resident.
Gyps fulvus	Resident.
Aquila pomarina	Summer visitor; probably breeds.
Falco cherrug	Resident/summer visitor.

Species restricted wholly or largely to the Middle East

Tetraogallus caspius	Common resident on high ridges (max. 51).
Ammoperdix griseogularis	Fairly common on dry, southern slopes.
Prunella ocularis	Summer visitor.
Irania gutturalis	Common summer visitor.
Oenanthe finschii	Common summer visitor.
Oenanthe xanthoprymna	Common summer visitor.
Sylvia althaea	Common summer visitor in *Juniperus*.
Phylloscopus neglectus	Common summer visitor.
Carpospiza brachydactyla	Summer visitor to southern slopes.
Rhodopechys sanguinea	Common summer visitor at high elevations.

■ Conservation issues

Parts of the area were first protected as the Parvar Reserve, established in 1962. A Protected Region of 37,937 ha was established in 1965, re-classified as a Protected Area and enlarged to 59,840 ha in the early 1970s. No threats are known.

■ Further reading

Firouz *et al.* (1970), Scott (1976b).

034 Khosh-Yeilagh (Mazandaran)

Wildlife Refuge

36°50′N 55°35′E
154,400 ha

■ Site description

The reserve lies east of the main Shahrud to Shahpasand highway, c.70 km north-east of Shahrud, spanning the divide of the eastern Alborz Mountains from the upper limits of the humid Caspian forest in the north to the semi-arid *Artemisia* steppes of the Central Plateau in the south. Much of the central portion of the reserve consists of high grass plains and tragacanthic steppe between rocky hill ranges. Several springs support luxuriant herbaceous vegetation and some shrubbery. *Juniperus* forest occurs on some of the higher, south-facing slopes.

■ Birds

See box for key species. Spanning Caspian forest, montane steppe and near-desertic steppe, the reserve

Globally threatened species

Aegypius monachus	Probably resident.
Aquila heliaca	One record in April.
Chlamydotis undulata	Reported to occur on passage.

Regionally threatened or declining species

Gypaetus barbatus	Probably resident.
Neophron percnopterus	One record in May; may breed.
Gyps fulvus	Probably resident (max. 4).
Falco cherrug	Probably breeds (max. 3).

Species restricted wholly or largely to the Middle East

Tetraogallus caspius	Resident on highest ridges.
Ammoperdix griseogularis	Fairly common resident.
Irania gutturalis	Passage migrant; may breed.
Oenanthe xanthoprymna	Common summer visitor.
Oenanthe picata	Common summer visitor.
Sylvia althaea	Very common summer visitor (max. 43).
Rhodopechys sanguinea	Summer visitor.

has a very diverse breeding bird fauna including eight species of lark. Other notable species include *Cursorius cursor*, *Melanocorypha bimaculata*, *Phoenicurus erythronotus*, *Sylvia hortensis*, *S. nana*, *Rhodopechys mongolica*, *Emberiza leucocephalos*, *E. buchanani* and *E. bruniceps*. *Phylloscopus trochiloides nitidus* is fairly common as a passage migrant. At least 114 species have been recorded in the reserve.

Other threatened/endemic wildlife

Mammals: *Canis lupus* (V), *Ursus arctos* (rare), *Caracal caracal* (rare), *Panthera pardus* (rare), *Gazella subgutturosa* (rare), *Capra hircus aegagrus* (rare) and *Ovis ammon* (rare). During the 1970s *Acinonyx jubatus* (V) became fairly common, more frequently observed here than anywhere else in Iran. An attempted re-introduction of *Equus hemionus* (V) took place in 1973–1974.

Conservation issues

A Protected Region of 208,937 ha was established in 1963, reduced to 166,880 ha but upgraded to Wildlife Refuge in the early 1970s. The reserve was further reduced to 154,400 ha in the 1980s. No threats are known and no conservation measures are known to have been proposed.

Further reading

Firouz *et al.* (1970), Scott (1976b).

035 Golestan (Mazandaran)

National Park and Protected Area

37°25´N 55°45´E
125,895 ha
Biosphere Reserve

Site description

Golestan is situated at the eastern end of the Alborz Mountains between the cities of Gonbad-e Qaboos and Bojnurd, and spans the divide from the humid lowlands of the Caspian region to the semi-arid interior of the central plateau. The principal habitats consist of lowland deciduous forest, lowland secondary scrub and meadows, semi-arid steppe, open *Juniperus* woodland and scrub, upland meadows, springs and streams, and cliffs and crags. Mountains in the south-west third of the reserve from the lowest to the highest elevations (380–2,410 m) are covered with largely pristine climax forest. Dominant trees below 1,800 m include *Quercus castanaefolia*, *Parrotia*, *Carpinus*, *Zelkova*, *Alnus*, *Fraxinus* and *Tilia*. Higher up, *Quercus macranthera*, *Sorbus*, *Acer* and *Juniperus* are common. The humid influence of the Caspian dwindles to the east, with forest giving way to scrub and then lush steppe. This montane steppe is characterized by *Artemisia*, spiny vegetation (predominantly *Astragalus*, *Acantholimon* and *Cousinia*), grass, open stands of *Juniperus* and copses of *Acer*. Inter-tribal conflicts which prevailed prior to 1913 virtually precluded any human habitation—even grazing of stock was risky—and for this reason the site was relatively undisturbed. The Asian highway winds north and east through the reserve and provides easy access. Land ownership is public.

Birds

See box for key species. There is a very diverse breeding bird fauna with virtually all the species characteristic of Caspian forest and upper shrub and *Juniperus* zones as well as many species characteristic of the upland steppes of north-east Iran. It is one of the few known breeding areas for *Tetrax tetrax* and *Dryocopus martius* in Iran, and is especially rich in birds of prey. Notable breeding species not listed below include *Hieraaetus pennatus*, *H. fasciatus*, *Phasianus colchicus*, *Melanocorypha bimaculata*, *Phoenicurus erythronotus*, *Sylvia hortensis*,

Globally threatened species	
Haliaeetus albicilla	One record, February.
Aegypius monachus	Resident (at least 2 pairs).
Aquila heliaca	Up to 3 recorded in summer; may breed.
Falco naumanni	Autumn passage migrant (max. 12).
Crex crex	Spring passage migrant.
Tetrax tetrax	A few pairs probably breed in the high grasslands.
Regionally threatened or declining species	
Pernis apivorus	Summer visitor; probably breeds.
Gypaetus barbatus	Resident.
Neophron percnopterus	Summer visitor, probably breeding (max. 4).
Gyps fulvus	Resident (max. 9).
Aquila pomarina	Summer visitor; probably breeds.
Falco cherrug	Winter visitor to steppes in east.
Species restricted wholly or largely to the Middle East	
Tetraogallus caspius	Resident on highest ridges.
Ammoperdix griseogularis	Fairly common in south-east.
Irania gutturalis	Fairly common summer visitor.
Oenanthe finschii	Fairly common summer visitor.
Oenanthe picata	Fairly common summer visitor.
Sylvia mystacea	Summer visitor; probably breeds.
Sylvia althaea	Fairly common summer visitor.
Phylloscopus neglectus	Fairly common summer visitor.
Carpospiza brachydactyla	Fairly common summer visitor.
Rhodopechys sanguinea	Fairly common summer visitor.

Phylloscopus trochiloides nitidus, *Ficedula semitorquata*, *F. parva*, *Lanius isabellinus*, *Emberiza buchanani* and *E. bruniceps*. At least 151 species have been recorded.

■ Other threatened/endemic wildlife

Mammals: the mammal fauna is extremely rich and diverse, including *Ovis ammon* (rare), *Capra hircus aegagrus* (rare), *Gazella subgutturosa* (rare), *Lynx lynx* (rare), *Canis lupus* (V) and *Ursus arctos* (rare). *Panthera tigris virgata* was last reliably recorded in Iran in this area in about 1963.

■ Conservation issues

Parts of the area were first protected as the Almeh and Ishaki Protected Region, established in 1957. A Wildlife Park of 91,890 ha was established in 1964. The reserve was enlarged to 125,895 ha and designated a National Park in the early 1970s. Some 34,000 ha have since been downgraded to Protected Area, leaving a National Park of 91,895 ha. The area of the original National Park (125,895 ha) was designated a Biosphere Reserve in 1976. No threats are known. The avifauna is to be studied further by the Department of the Environment.

■ Further reading

Ashtiani (1974), Firouz (1974), Firouz *et al.* (1970), Scott (1972b, 1976b).

036 Touran (Semnan)

Wildlife Refuge and Protected Area

35°40´N 56°20´E
1,872,750 ha
Biosphere Reserve

■ Site description

The topography of this vast area, c.120 km south-east of Shahrud, includes arid mountains and desert plains with desert, semi-desert and steppe vegetation, and borders on the salt wastes of the great Dasht-i Kavir desert in the south. The climate is very dry, with most precipitation falling as thunderstorms in spring. Summers are extremely hot, and winters cold. There is *Artemisia* and *Artemisia–Zygophyllum* steppe in the north, and mainly sparsely vegetated sandy and stony plains and bare saltflats in the south. According to Spooner (1977), both flora and mammalian fauna generally show great affinity to the Kara Kum desert in Turkmenistan to the north. Land ownership is public.

■ Birds

See box for key species. The reserve has the characteristic desert avifauna of Iran's central plateau, and is an important breeding area for *Chlamydotis undulata*. *Podoces pleskei* is a fairly common resident (max. 8 birds) in areas of *Zygophyllum* steppe in the south and south-east. Other notable species include *Cursorius cursor*, *Pterocles coronatus*, *Ammomanes cincturus*, *Melanocorypha bimaculata*, *Alauda gulgula*, *Hirundo obsoleta*, *Hippolais rama*, *Sylvia nana* and *Rhodopechys githaginea*. A wide variety of passerines has been recorded at the many small oases during spring and autumn migration, including *Phylloscopus trochiloides nitidus* and *Remiz coronatus* (one record, 1975). At least 164 species have been recorded in the reserve.

Globally threatened species	
Aegypius monachus	Probably resident (max. 3 birds).
Falco naumanni	Recorded on spring passage.
Chlamydotis undulata	Relatively common summer visitor, May–November (max. 18 birds).
Regionally threatened or declining species	
Neophron percnopterus	Recorded on spring passage.
Gyps fulvus	Occasional visitor.
Accipiter brevipes	Spring passage migrant (max. 1).
Falco cherrug	One record in April.
Species restricted wholly or largely to the Middle East	
Ammoperdix griseogularis	Common throughout hills (max. 40).
Prunella ocularis	Fairly common winter visitor (max. 6).
Irania gutturalis	Passage migrant.
Oenanthe xanthoprymna	Fairly common summer visitor in hills.
Oenanthe picata	Very common summer visitor.
Hippolais languida	Spring passage migrant.
Sylvia mystacea	Spring passage migrant.
Podoces pleskei	Resident (see text).
Carpospiza brachydactyla	Fairly common summer visitor.
Rhodopechys sanguinea	Winter visitor (max. 4).

■ Other threatened/endemic wildlife

Mammals: 65 species recorded, including *Canis lupus* (V), *Caracal caracal* (rare), *Panthera pardus* (rare), *Acinonyx jubatus* (V), *Gazella subgutturosa* (rare), *Gazella dorcas fuscifrons* (V), *Capra hircus aegagrus* (rare) and *Ovis ammon* (rare). The reserve is particularly important for *Equus hemionus* (V), with c.700 individuals in the mid-1970s. Flora: at least 375 species of plant have been recorded.

■ Conservation issues

A reserve of 1,810,400 ha, comprising a Wildlife

Refuge of 434,200 ha and a surrounding Protected Area of 1,376,200 ha, was established in 1973. The Wildlife Refuge has since been enlarged to 537,500 ha and the Protected Area reduced to 1,335,250 ha, giving the present reserve of 1,872,750 ha. Part of the reserve, 1,000,000 ha, was designated a Biosphere Reserve in 1976. No threats are known.

Further reading

Spooner (1977), Tuck (1979).

037 Rud-i Jowin and Rud-i Kalshur (Khorasan)

Unprotected

36°45′N 57°20′E
c.250,000 ha

Site description

A vast area of cultivated upland plains and gently undulating hills, c.90 km from east to west and 30 km north to south, including the broad valleys of the Rud-i Jowin and Rud-i Kalshur rivers. The rivers flood in winter and spring and are reduced to a series of stagnant brackish pools by late summer. There are some seasonally flooded brackish marshes. Other habitats include cultivated land (mainly cereals), salt-tolerant vegetation in depressions on the valley floors, and *Artemisia* steppe on the rolling hills. There is some livestock grazing.

Birds

See box for key species. A wintering area for *Otis tarda* in the 1970s, with birds present from November until late February; up to 13 have been recorded by Department of the Environment personnel, but local farmers have reported flocks of up to 70. The site is also a wintering area for ducks, mainly *Anas platyrhynchos* and *A. crecca*.

Globally threatened species

Haliaeetus albicilla	One record, November.
Otis tarda	Regular winter visitor (see text).

1% or more of population

	Breeding (pairs)	Wintering	Passage
Tadorna ferruginea	—	310	—

Regionally threatened or declining species

Gyps fulvus	One record.
Falco cherrug	One record, November.

Other threatened/endemic wildlife

None known to BirdLife International.

Conservation issues

No conservation measures are known to have been proposed and there is no information on threats to the site.

Further reading

Adhami (1972b), Eftekhar (1973b), Kharom (1976).

038 Shirvan Area (Khorasan)

Unprotected

37°25′N 57°50′E
c.5,000 ha

Site description

Cultivated upland plains (cereals and sugar beet) at c.1,100 m in the vicinity of Hosseynabad village, 5–15 km west of Shirvan. Land ownership is public and private. Livestock grazing occurs.

Birds

See box for key species. An important staging area for *Otis tarda* in November–December. Flocks of 64 (1972) and 53 (1974) have been observed by Department of the Environment personnel, and flocks of over 100 are reported by local farmers. A few birds remain into January, by which time the plains are usually under snow. *Falco pelegrinoides* is an occasional visitor, and *Sturnus roseus* is a common passage migrant.

Globally threatened species

Otis tarda	Occurs November–December (see text).

Regionally threatened or declining species

Neophron percnopterus	One record in summer.

Species restricted wholly or largely to the Middle East

Carpospiza brachydactyla	Summer visitor.

Other threatened/endemic wildlife

None known to BirdLife International.

Conservation issues
No conservation measures are known to have been proposed and there is no information on threats to the site.

Further reading
Adhami (1972b), Kharom (1976), Mansoori and Fotoohi (1974).

039 Sarani (Khorasan)
Protected Area

37°45′N 58°10′E
17,800 ha

Site description
A portion of the Kopet Dagh Mountains on the Turkmenistan border in northern Khorasan, 40 km north-north-east of Shirvan, extending from the rolling plains and semi-arid foothills in the south to the international boundary running along the crest of the mountains. The climate is extreme continental, with hot dry summers and very cold winters. Principal habitats include rolling plains with *Artemisia* steppe and some dry wheat cultivation (1,800–1,950 m), mixed deciduous scrub with herbaceous ground cover and a scattering of *Juniperus* (c.2,000 m), mature *Juniperus* forest with a mixture of other shrubs on steep limestone mountain-sides (1,800–2,500 m) and mountain summits and high ridges with good montane steppe (2,400–2,987 m). Snow patches linger until at least the end of June. The many springs and streams support small patches of lush grassland. The *Juniperus* forests are among the finest in Iran, with some exceptionally large trees.

Birds
See box for key species. The breeding birds include species characteristic of the montane steppes, *Juniperus* forests and high mountain ranges of north-east Iran. This is one of the few areas where *Mycerobas carnipes* is known in Iran, and the only locality where *Emberiza stewarti* has been recorded (found in song in 1973, and may breed). Other notable species include *Melanocorypha bimaculata*, *Sylvia hortensis*, *Montifringilla nivalis* and *Emberiza buchanani*. At least 87 species have been recorded in the reserve.

Globally threatened species	
Aegypius monachus	Resident; probably 2 pairs.
Regionally threatened or declining species	
Gypaetus barbatus	Resident.
Neophron percnopterus	Recorded in summer; may breed.
Gyps fulvus	Resident (max. 12 birds).
Species restricted wholly or largely to the Middle East	
Tetraogallus caspius	Resident on highest ridges.
Irania gutturalis	Common summer visitor.
Oenanthe finschii	Fairly common summer visitor.
Sylvia althaea	Common summer visitor.
Phylloscopus neglectus	Fairly common summer visitor.
Rhodopechys sanguinea	Summer visitor.

Other threatened/endemic wildlife
Mammals: *Canis lupus* (V), *Ursus arctos* (rare), *Caracal caracal* (rare), *Panthera pardus* (rare), *Capra hircus aegagrus* (rare) and *Ovis ammon* (rare).

Conservation issues
The area was established as a National Park in 1971, downgraded to Protected Area in the 1980s. No threats are known.

Further reading
Scott (1972e).

040 Tandoureh (Khorasan)
National Park and Protected Area

37°25′N 58°40′E
76,900 ha

Site description
These two adjacent reserves (Tandoureh National Park and Protected Area), 40 km north-north-east of Quchan, incorporate a section of the Kopet Dagh Mountains with a spectacular central valley flanked by impressive cliffs and containing a large perennial spring (Chehelmere). Most of the area consists of montane steppe with *Juniperus* woodland on steep slopes and some riverine thickets in the valleys. Principal habitats include *Artemisia* steppe and open scrub with scattered *Juniperus* in the central valley (930–1,500 m), steep rocky hillside with good montane steppe and stunted *Juniperus* (1,200–2,000 m), summit ridges and plateaus with well-watered

montane steppe and some rocky outcrops (2,000–2,612 m), and spectacular cliffs, crags and gorges. There is a dense stand of riparian woodland in the gorge below Chehelmere spring.

Birds

See box for key species. Breeding birds include species characteristic of the montane steppes, *Juniperus* forest and high mountains of north-east Iran. Breeders not listed below include *Melanocorypha bimaculata*, *Sylvia hortensis*, *Emberiza buchanani* and *E. bruniceps*. At least 76 species have been recorded in the reserve.

Globally threatened species	
Aegypius monachus	Resident; probably 2 pairs.
Regionally threatened or declining species	
Gypaetus barbatus	Resident.
Neophron percnopterus	Probably breeds (max. 2 birds).
Gyps fulvus	Probably resident (max. 5 birds).
Species restricted wholly or largely to the Middle East	
Tetraogallus caspius	Resident on highest ridges.
Ammoperdix griseogularis	Fairly common resident on lower slopes.
Oenanthe picata	Very common summer visitor.
Sylvia althaea	Common summer visitor.
Phylloscopus neglectus	Very common summer visitor.
Carpospiza brachydactyla	Summer visitor.
Rhodopechys sanguinea	Summer visitor.

Other threatened/endemic wildlife

Mammals: *Canis lupus* (V), *Ursus arctos* (rare), *Panthera pardus* (rare), *Capra hircus aegagrus* (rare) and *Ovis ammon* (rare).

Conservation issues

A Protected Region of 73,435 ha was established in 1968, and reduced to 53,780 ha but upgraded to National Park in the early 1970s. Later, 23,000 ha of the National Park were downgraded to Protected Area (erroneously given as 2,300 ha in IUCN 1991). Currently, the National Park stands at 35,000 ha and the Protected Area at 41,900 ha. No threats are known.

Further reading

Firouz *et al.* (1970), Scott (1972d, 1976b).

041 Lotfatabad and Darregaz Area (Khorasan)

Unprotected

37°31′N 59°20′E
c.2,500 ha

Site description

A small area of sandy plains on the southern edge of the Kara Kum desert, around the small town of Lotfatabad and village of Shilagan on the Turkmenistan border. This is one of only two places in north-east Iran where the international border extends down from the hills to incorporate a section of the sparsely vegetated sandy plains of the Kara Kum desert. Much of the area is under irrigated cultivation (vegetable gardens, vineyards and wheat fields), and ponds and ditches support dense herbaceous vegetation with some *Salix*.

Birds

See box for key species. One of only two localities in Iran where *Parus bokharensis* has been recorded. Other breeding species include *Accipiter badius*, *Sturnus roseus* and *Emberiza bruniceps*.

Species restricted wholly or largely to the Middle East	
Sylvia mystacea	Summer visitor.

Other threatened/endemic wildlife

None known to BirdLife International.

Conservation issues

No conservation measures are known to have been proposed and there is no information on threats to the site.

042 Hari Rud Valley near Sarrakhs (Khorasan)

Unprotected

36°30′N 61°09′E
c.8,000 ha

Site description

A 40-km strip of land c.2 km wide on the west (Iranian) bank of the Hari Rud river up to the point where it leaves Iranian territory c.10 km north of the town of Sarrakhs. The river meanders down a wide valley in gently undulating sandy steppe at the southern edge of the Kara Kum desert, one of only two places in north-east Iran where the border with Turkmenistan extends down from the hills to incorporate a section of these plains. The river floods in winter and spring, but by late summer surface water may be reduced to a series of large pools in the deepest parts of the bed. A group of fishponds has recently been constructed near Sarrakhs and provides permanent wetland habitat. There are extensive riverine thickets along the Turkmenistan bank, but only one small patch of *Salix* and *Tamarix* woodland (c.4 ha) remains on the Iranian side, c.26 km south of Sarrakhs. There are patches of *Phragmites* along the river, sandy plains with steppic vegetation in the south, and irrigated cultivation (mainly wheat) and *Populus* groves around Sarrakhs in the north. Other plants include *Euphorbia charolepsis* and *Heliotropum khorasanecum*. There is public land ownership.

Birds

See box for key species. The riverine thickets along the Hari Rud are the only known locality for *Phasianus colchicus principalis* in Iran, and one of only two localities for *Parus bokharensis*. This is also the best area in Iran for *Columba eversmanni*: up to 100 have been observed in September and the species probably breeds. There is a breeding colony of *Falco naumanni* (at least 20 pairs) in sandy cliffs in the south of the area. Other notable species include *Cursorius cursor*, *Glareola pratincola*, *Alauda gulgula*, *Saxicola caprata*, *Acrocephalus stentoreus*, *Hippolais rama*, *Emberiza bruniceps* and *Rhodopechys obsoleta*. *Lanius vittatus* and *Sturnus roseus* have been observed in summer, and may breed. *Phylloscopus trochiloides nitidus* has been recorded on autumn passage. Small numbers of ducks have been recorded at the fishponds near Sarrakhs.

Globally threatened species

Falco naumanni	Summer visitor (see text).

1% or more of population

	Breeding (pairs)	Wintering	Passage
Casmerodius albus	—	130	—

Regionally threatened or declining species

Neophron percnopterus	Recorded in summer; may breed in the area.
Columba eversmanni	Probably breeds (see text).

Species restricted wholly or largely to the Middle East

Ammoperdix griseogularis	Resident on low hills in south.
Sylvia mystacea	Fairly common summer visitor.
Sylvia minula	Recorded on autumn passage (max. 7).

Other threatened/endemic wildlife

None known to BirdLife International.

Conservation issues

There is no legal protection and no conservation measures are known to have been proposed. Only one small patch of forest remained by the mid-1970s, and this, if it still exists, is threatened by cutting for timber and fuelwood.

Further reading

Scott (1973c), Scott and Howell (1976).

043 Tayebad Plains at Ghoomi and Sarhad (Khorasan)

34°45´N 60°55´E
c.40,000 ha
Unprotected

Site description

Plains around the villages of Ghoomi and Sarhad near the Afghanistan border north-east of Tayebad. The site is cultivated land (mainly cereals) and fallow land adjacent to sparsely vegetated semi-arid steppic plains and rolling hills. Land ownership is public. Livestock are grazed.

Birds

See box for key species. A very important wintering area for *Otis tarda* in the 1970s, with birds present from November or December to February. Only small flocks (maximum 26) were observed by Department of the Environment personnel, but local farmers reported concentrations of 500 to 1,000 in mid-winter. *Pterocles orientalis* is a common resident, and *P. alchata* occurs (probably as a winter visitor). *Cursorius cursor* probably breeds on the adjacent semi-desertic plains.

Globally threatened species

Chlamydotis undulata	Occurs; probably a passage migrant.
Otis tarda	Winter visitor (see text).

1% or more of population

	Breeding (pairs)	Wintering	Passage
Grus grus	—	274	—

Other threatened/endemic wildlife

None known to BirdLife International.

Conservation issues

No conservation measures are known to have been proposed and there is no information on threats to the site.

Further reading

Eftekhar (1973b), Kahrom (1976), Mansoori and Fotoohi (1974), Scott (1980).

044 Namakazar Basin (Khorasan)

Unprotected

34°00′N 60°30′E
c.80,000 ha

Site description

The Iranian portion of a large internal drainage basin, c.40 km from north to south and 20 km east to west, straddling the border with Afghanistan. The central part of the basin is occupied by bare saltflats which are subject to flooding during exceptional desert storms. This area is surrounded by a broad, sandy outwash plain with large areas of stabilized dunes and excellent desertic vegetation. The region is extremely arid, with no permanent water other than a few small springs at the base of the surrounding hills. The desertic steppe is dominated by *Zygophyllum*, and there is typical dune vegetation with scattered *Tamarix*, and some large patches of *Tamarix* scrub. The nearby stony hillsides are largely without vegetation. There may be some livestock grazing, but the area is very remote, very sparsely populated and far from any substantial supplies of fresh water.

Birds

See box for key species. The extensive *Zygophyllum* steppe probably supports a large population of *Podoces pleskei*; five birds were seen in a brief survey in June 1973. The breeding avifauna is characteristic of Iran's central and eastern deserts, with *Ammomanes cincturus* particularly common.

Species restricted wholly or largely to the Middle East	
Podoces pleskei	Resident (see text).

Other threatened/endemic wildlife

None known to BirdLife International.

Conservation issues

No conservation measures are known to have been proposed and there is no information on threats to the site.

045 Sahlabad Area (Khorasan)

Unprotected

32°05′N 59°55′E
c.30,000 ha

Site description

Desert in the basin of the Lurg-i-Shuturan salt-lake (altitude c.1,350 m) at the eastern edge of Iran's Central Plateau. The site lies south of the village of Sahlabad, c.110 km south-south-east of Birjand. The 'lake' is an extensive bare saltflat, flooding only after exceptional storms, surrounded by a broad, sandy outwash plain with some areas of stabilized dunes. The main Mashad to Zahedan highway passes through the east of the site. There is excellent desertic steppe and sand-dune vegetation dominated by *Zygophyllum*, *Ephedra*, *Artemisia* and *Tamarix*, and adjacent hills support *Artemisia* steppe. There may be some livestock grazing, but the area is very remote, very sparsely populated and far from any substantial supplies of fresh water.

Birds

See box for key species. One of the best areas in Iran for *Podoces pleskei*; 13 birds (including several juveniles) were seen along 16 km of the Mashad–Zahedan highway in June 1973. The breeding avifauna is characteristic of Iran's central and eastern deserts, and includes *Cursorius cursor*, *Pterocles coronatus*, *P. orientalis* and *Sylvia nana*.

Globally threatened species	
Chlamydotis undulata	Occurs, probably as a breeding bird and passage migrant.
Species restricted wholly or largely to the Middle East	
Podoces pleskei	Fairly common resident (see text).

Other threatened/endemic wildlife

None known to BirdLife International.

Conservation issues

No conservation measures are known to have been proposed and there is no information on threats to the site.

046 Divandareh/Zarrineh Owbatu (Kurdistan)

Unprotected

35°53´N 47°07´E
c.5,000 ha

Site description

Rolling plains, deeply dissected by a number of intermittent streams, at 1,800 m in northern Kurdistan, c.65 km north of Sanandaj. Most of the area is cultivated with wheat, and there is *Artemisia* steppe on the adjacent hills. There are few villages and virtually no roads. Land ownership is private.

Birds

See box for key species. *Otis tarda* is a regular visitor from August to November and may breed; up to 16 were observed by Department of the Environment personnel in the early 1970s, and local farmers reported concentrations of 30–40. Breeding species include *Buteo rufinus*, *Falco tinnunculus*, *Pterocles orientalis*, *Columba livia* and *Athene noctua*. Winter visitors include *Accipiter nisus* and *Montifringilla nivalis*, and passage migrants include *Aquila nipalensis* and *Grus grus*.

Globally threatened species

Aquila heliaca	Occasional passage migrant.
Otis tarda	May breed (see text).

Regionally threatened or declining species

Gyps fulvus	Occasional non-breeding visitor.

Species restricted wholly or largely to the Middle East

Ammoperdix griseogularis	Resident (at extreme edge of range in Iran).

Other threatened/endemic wildlife

None known to BirdLife International.

Conservation issues

No conservation measures are known to have been proposed and there is no information on threats to the site.

Further reading

Adhami (1972a), Eftekhar (1972b, 1973a), Fotoohi and Mansoori (1974), Kahrom (1975), Scott (1971b).

047 Lake Zaribar (Kurdistan)

Unprotected

35°32´N 46°07´E
1,550+ ha

Site description

The site lies at 1,280 m in the foothills of the north-west Zagros Mountains near the Iraq border, a few kilometres west of Marivan, and comprises Lake Zaribar (1,150 ha) and the surrounding broad valley and hillsides. The lake is deep, fresh water, with extensive marshes at northern and southern ends, and is fed by several small streams and a large spring at the north-east corner, overflowing into a small river at the south end. It is often frozen in mid-winter. Habitats include extensive *Phragmites* and *Typha* beds, *Carex* marshes with scattered clumps of *Salix* and *Populus*, wet meadows, arable land (mainly wheat) with orchards and *Populus* groves, and stony hillsides with heavily grazed *Quercus* scrub on the lower slopes and taller, less disturbed *Quercus* forest higher up. Land ownership is public. There is fishing and waterfowl hunting at the lake, and a small resort area.

Birds

See boxes for key species. The extensive marshes are important for breeding waterfowl (notably *Podiceps cristatus*, *Anser anser*, *Aythya nyroca* and *Oxyura leucocephala*) and *Circus aeruginosus* (c.5 pairs), and provide feeding habitat for the large numbers of *Ciconia ciconia* which nest nearby. The lake is also of some importance for wintering waterfowl, especially diving ducks, and is the most important wintering site for *Mergus merganser* in Iran (up to

Globally threatened species

Marmaronetta angustirostris	Three in January 1975.
Oxyura leucocephala	Summer visitor; at least 8 adults and 6 chicks in July 1974.

1% or more of population

	Breeding (pairs)	Wintering	Passage
Podiceps cristatus	50–100	—	—
Ciconia ciconia	120	—	—
Aythya fuligula	—	4,000	—
Aythya nyroca	20–50	2	250 (Jul)
Oxyura leucocephala	several	—	—
Vanellus vanellus	50	450	—

Regionally threatened or declining species

Aythya nyroca	Relatively common summer visitor (see above).
Neophron percnopterus	Recorded in summer; may breed in the area.
Gyps fulvus	Occasional visitor (max. 3).
Accipiter brevipes	One in July 1974; probably breeds in the area.

Species restricted wholly or largely to the Middle East	
Oenanthe finschii	Summer visitor to surrounding hills.
Hippolais languida	Common summer visitor to surrounding *Quercus* forest.
Sylvia althaea	Summer visitor to surrounding *Quercus* forest.
Emberiza cineracea	Scarce summer visitor to adjacent scrub-covered hills.

35 birds). The nearby *Quercus* forest supports a characteristic Zagros bird fauna. There is an exceptionally large breeding colony of *Ciconia ciconia* in a patch of forest north of the lake. *Clamator glandarius* apparently bred in 1974 (the only recent record of this species in Iran). Other notable breeding or probably breeding species are *Hieraaetus pennatus*, *Dendrocopos medius*, *Ficedula semitorquata*, *Parus lugubris*, *Remiz pendulinus* and *Lanius nubicus*.

Other threatened/endemic wildlife

None known to BirdLife International.

Conservation issues

There is no legal protection. *Quercus* forest on the lower slopes around the lake had been badly degraded by overgrazing and cutting for fuel in the 1970s. The area has experienced major changes in recent years and as such should be thoroughly studied.

Further reading

Fotoohi and Scott (1975), Scott (1976a,c).

048 Western Zagros North of Nowsud (Kurdistan)

Unprotected

35°13′N 46°14′E
Area undefined

Site description

An extensive region of high mountain ridges and steep-sided valleys with spectacular limestone crags and pinnacles at the extreme north-west end of the Zagros chain, north of the small town of Nowsud and c.30 km south-south-east of Marivan. No site boundaries are yet determined. The region contains a broad spectrum of Zagros habitats: luxuriant riverine forest of *Quercus*, *Juglans* and *Populus* in the valley bottoms; mature *Quercus* forest, scrubby *Quercus* woodland and terraced wheat cultivation on the lower slopes; rocky hillsides with tragacanthic steppe and scattered *Pistacia* trees on the higher slopes; and rocky outcrops and alpine tundra at the summits, peaking at 2,984 m. Snow patches linger on the highest ridge until at least mid–July.

Birds

See box for key species. The region has a characteristic Zagros avifauna, including most species typical of the Zagros *Quercus* forest as well as most of the high montane species. Other notable breeding species include *Dendrocopos medius*, *Lanius nubicus*, *Pyrrhocorax graculus*, *Montifringilla nivalis* and *Emberiza buchanani*.

Regionally threatened or declining species	
Gypaetus barbatus	Probably resident.
Gyps fulvus	Probably resident (max. 3).
Accipiter brevipes	Summer visitor; 2 pairs in 1975.

Species restricted wholly or largely to the Middle East	
Irania gutturalis	Common summer visitor.
Oenanthe finschii	Fairly common summer visitor.
Oenanthe xanthoprymna	The black-throated *O. x. xanthoprymna* is a common summer visitor at 1,800–2,650 m (elsewhere in Iran, this form is replaced by the grey-throated *O. x. chrysopygia*).
Hippolais languida	Common summer visitor.
Phylloscopus neglectus	Fairly common summer visitor.
Carpospiza brachydactyla	Summer visitor.
Rhodopechys sanguinea	Fairly common summer visitor.
Emberiza cineracea	Scarce summer visitor.

Other threatened/endemic wildlife

None known to BirdLife International.

Conservation issues

No threats are known and no conservation measures are known to have been proposed.

049 **Dasht-i Gaz** (Kurdistan)

Unprotected

35°16´N 47°20´E
c.5,000 ha

Site description
Gently rolling plains at 1,820 m, bordered to the north by the Sanandaj–Hamadan road, to west and south by hill ranges, and to the east by the Cham-e-Golan river. The area is entirely under cultivation for cereals or fallow land, except for several marshy streams. There is a small village at the edge of the hills and several villages along the Cham-e-Golan, but the area is very sparsely populated.

Birds
See box for key species. An important breeding area for *Otis tarda* in the 1970s; 5–10 females were thought to nest, the birds being present May–September. Flocks of *Anas querquedula* and *Philomachus pugnax* have been observed in the marshy areas in autumn.

Other threatened/endemic wildlife
None known to BirdLife International.

Globally threatened species	
Aegypius monachus	One record.
Otis tarda	Summer visitor (see text).
Regionally threatened or declining species	
Neophron percnopterus	One record, August.
Gyps fulvus	One record of 11 birds.
Falco cherrug	One record, August.
Species restricted wholly or largely to the Middle East	
Oenanthe finschii	Summer visitor to adjacent hills.

Conservation issues
No threats are known and no conservation measures are known to have been proposed.

Further reading
Adhami (1972a), Baheri (1971), Scott (1971a).

050 **Plains near Ghorveh** (Hamadan)

Unprotected

35°05´N 47°54´E
c.5,000 ha

Site description
Gently rolling plains at 1,820 m, c.15 km south-east of the town of Ghorveh and south of the Ghorveh–Hamadan road. The area is entirely agricultural (cereals or fallow), except in the north-east where there is a small seasonal marsh. The site is sparsely populated, with only a few small villages. Land ownership is public.

Birds
See box for key species. *Otis tarda* was a summer visitor to the area in the 1970s, with birds present April–November. As many as 25 birds have been recorded, and c.10 females were thought to nest. Other breeding species include *Falco tinnunculus*, *Coracias garrulus*, *Athene noctua* and *Corvus corax*. Winter visitors and/or passage migrants include *Circus aeruginosus*, *Falco peregrinus*, *F. pelegrinoides*, *Rallus aquaticus* and *Corvus frugilegus*.

Globally threatened species	
Otis tarda	Summer visitor (see text).
Species restricted wholly or largely to the Middle East	
Ammoperdix griseogularis	Resident (near the edge of its range).

Other threatened/endemic wildlife
None known to BirdLife International.

Conservation issues
No threats are known and no conservation measures are known to have been proposed.

Further reading
Adhami (1972a), Eftekhar (1972a), Fotoohi and Mansoori (1974), Kahrom (1975), Scott (1971a).

051 Assadabad Plain (Hamadan)

Unprotected

34°42´N 48°02´E
20,000 ha

Site description

Lying c.45 km west-south-west of Hamadan, the site is a shallow basin 21 km long by up to 12–14 km wide, almost completely surrounded by a ring of hills 1,800–2,100 m high. The central area remains grassland, but is heavily grazed by domestic livestock and *Euphorbia* is common, while the gently sloping perimeter is cultivated with cereals. The small towns of Assadabad and Kharkiz are situated on the northern margin, and there are about nine small villages scattered across the plain. The main Hamadan to Kermanshah road crosses the eastern edge of the plain. The surrounding hills are *Artemisia* steppe. The plain is relatively densely populated. Land ownership is private.

Birds

See box for key species. The best breeding area for *Otis tarda* in western Iran in the 1970s. Birds were present March–September, and it was believed that c.20 females were nesting; up to 30 birds (8 males, 22 females) were recorded in the early 1970s, but local farmers reported that numbers in autumn had been as high as 80–100 c.15 years previously. Winter visitors include *Aquila chrysaetos* and *Accipiter nisus*, and passage migrants include *Aquila nipalensis*, *Circus pygargus* and *C. macrourus*.

Globally threatened species

Otis tarda	Summer visitor (see text).

Regionally threatened or declining species

Neophron percnopterus	Summer visitor (max. 3); probably breeds in the area.
Falco cherrug	One record, August.

Other threatened/endemic wildlife

None known to BirdLife International.

Conservation issues

A maze of small roads provides easy access to much of the area, and disturbance is high. There was some illegal hunting of bustards in the early 1970s. It has been proposed that a bustard sanctuary of c.600 ha be established in the central, uncultivated part of the plain to create a disturbance-free refuge (Kahrom 1975).

Further reading

Adhami (1972a), Baheri (1971), Eftekhar (1972a,b, 1973a), Fotoohi and Mansoori (1974), Kahrom (1975), Scott (1971a,b), Vaziri and Kahrom (1975).

052 Hashelan Marsh and Doh Tappeh Plains (Kermanshah)

Unprotected

34°33´N 46°55´E
c.10,400 ha

Site description

The site lies at c.1,500 m in a broad intermontane basin in the north-west Zagros Mountains, c.20–30 km north-west of Kermanshah, and comprises a small area of permanent freshwater pools and marshes fed by a group of large springs (Hashelan Marsh, 400 ha) and the adjacent flat cultivated plains (c.10,000 ha) which extend to the region of Doh Tappeh c.10 km to the south. The site is bordered to north, east and west by mountains, and is contiguous with the densely populated plains around Kermanshah. The principal area for bustards comprises c.5,000 ha of wheat cultivation, fallow land and rough pasture between the Ab-e-Razavar and Ghara-Su rivers. There are several small villages in the area, and high-tension power lines cross the southern edge. The pools have abundant submerged and floating vegetation, and the marshes are dominated by sedges and rushes. Land ownership is public.

Birds

See box for key species. Hashelan Marsh supports small breeding populations of *Ardea purpurea* and *Aythya nyroca*, and is of some importance for wintering waterfowl (notably *A. nyroca*). *Ciconia ciconia*

Globally threatened species

Otis tarda	Summer visitor (see text).

1% or more of population

	Breeding (pairs)	Wintering	Passage
Aythya nyroca	several	130	—

Regionally threatened or declining species

Aythya nyroca	Resident and winter visitor (see above).
Neophron percnopterus	Regular in summer (max. 2); probably breeds in the area.
Gyps fulvus	Occasional visitor (max. 4).

Species restricted wholly or largely to the Middle East

Hippolais languida	One in song, May 1971.

is a common summer visitor. *Otis tarda* was a summer visitor in the 1970s; 5–10 females were thought to nest.

Other threatened/endemic wildlife
None known to BirdLife International.

Conservation issues
There is a considerable amount of duck hunting at Hashelan Marsh. The plains are densely populated and disturbance is high. A reserve encompassing the wetlands and main bustard area was proposed in the 1970s, but was never implemented. This area is currently under study by the Department of the Environment.

Further reading
Fotoohi and Mansoori (1974), Fotoohi and Scott (1975), Kahrom (1975), Scott (1971a, 1976a).

053 Telesm Plain (Kermanshah)
Unprotected

34°08´N 46°22´E
4,500 ha

Site description
Gently rolling, cultivated plains set in a valley between folds of the north-west Zagros Mountains and almost completely surrounded by low stony hills. The site is 5–10 km south-south-east of the village of Kerend and 70 km west-south-west of Kermanshah. The land is cultivated (mostly cereals) or fallow, with *Artemisia* steppe on the surrounding hills. The area is sparsely populated, with only one small village in the extreme south-east. There is some livestock grazing. Land ownership is public and private.

Birds
See box for key species. An important breeding area for *Otis tarda* in the 1970s, with probably at least 10 nesting females; the birds were present May–September, local farmers reporting concentrations of up to 50–60. *Buteo rufinus* also breeds, and *Aquila chrysaetos* is an occasional visitor. Winter visitors include *Accipiter gentilis* (scarce), and passage migrants include *Buteo buteo* and *Grus grus*.

Other threatened/endemic wildlife
None known to BirdLife International.

Globally threatened species	
Aegypius monachus	Occasional visitor.
Aquila heliaca	Passage migrant and possibly a winter visitor.
Otis tarda	Summer visitor (see text).
Regionally threatened or declining species	
Gyps fulvus	Occasional visitor (max. 1).
Species restricted wholly or largely to the Middle East	
Ammoperdix griseogularis	Resident.
Carpospiza brachydactyla	Very common summer visitor to surrounding stony hills.

Conservation issues
The area was very little disturbed in the 1970s and no other threats are known. No conservation measures are known to have been proposed.

Further reading
Adhami (1972a), Eftekhar (1972a,b, 1973a), Fotoohi and Mansoori (1974), Scott (1971a,b).

054 Ilam Area (Ilam)
Unprotected

33°40´N 46°30´E
Area undefined

Site description
Rugged limestone ridges and broad valleys in the north-west Zagros Mountains c.10 km north of Ilam (38 km by road). No site boundaries are yet determined for this extensive region. The principal habitats are large tracts of mature forest with *Quercus*, *Pistacia* and *Acer* in the valleys, scrubby *Quercus* woodland on rocky hillsides, and spectacular limestone ridges and outcrops peaking at 2,650 m. The *Quercus* forest, very open and park-like in some

areas, is among the finest in the northern Zagros, with many very large trees. There is some wheat cultivation.

Birds

See box for key species. The region possesses a characteristic Zagros *Quercus* forest avifauna, and is one of the few localities in Iran where *Emberiza cineracea* is known to breed. Other notable breeding species are *Dendrocopos medius*, *Hirundo obsoleta*, *Parus lugubris*, *Lanius nubicus* and *Petronia xanthocollis*. The site is important for *Grus grus* in winter.

1% or more of population

	Breeding (pairs)	Wintering	Passage
Grus grus	—	250	—

Species restricted wholly or largely to the Middle East

Carpospiza brachydactyla	Summer visitor.
Emberiza cineracea	Scarce summer visitor; recorded in June 1975.

Other threatened/endemic wildlife

None known to BirdLife International.

Conservation issues

No threats are known. The area is recommended for further study by the Department of the Environment.

Further reading

Fotoohi and Scott (1975), Scott (1980).

055 Oshtrankuh (Kermanshah)

Protected Area

33°20′N 49°15′E
93,950 ha

Site description

The mountain of Oshtrankuh (4,330 m) in the high central Zagros c.80 km south-west of Borujerd. Gaharl lake, of glacial origin, c.1.75 km long and 600 m wide, lies at 2,350 m in the central valley, with a dense stand of very old *Salix* trees. Other habitats include some *Quercus* forest and *Pistacia–Amygdalus* forest on the lower slopes, several fast-flowing perennial mountain streams, montane steppe, alpine meadows, rocky mountain slopes and high crags. Plants include *Daphne angustifolia*, *Euphorbia* species and *Circium congestum*. Land ownership is public.

Birds

See box for key species. The breeding bird fauna is characteristic of the high Zagros and includes some woodland species typical of lower elevations. Other notable species include *Dendrocopos medius*, *Melanocorypha bimaculata*, *Hirundo rupestris*, *Ficedula semitorquata*, *Parus lugubris*, *Pyrrhocorax graculus*, *Montifringilla nivalis* and *Emberiza buchanani*. *Hippolais icterina* was thought to have bred in 1974. At least 81 species have been recorded in the reserve.

Regionally threatened or declining species

Gypaetus barbatus	Resident.
Gyps fulvus	Resident (max. 23 birds).

Species restricted wholly or largely to the Middle East

Tetraogallus caspius	Resident on highest ridges.
Irania gutturalis	Common summer visitor.
Oenanthe finschii	Common summer visitor.
Oenanthe xanthoprymna	Common summer visitor.
Hippolais languida	Very common summer visitor.
Sylvia althaea	Very common summer visitor.
Phylloscopus neglectus	Very common summer visitor.
Carpospiza brachydactyla	Common summer visitor.
Rhodopechys sanguinea	Summer visitor.

Other threatened/endemic wildlife

Mammals: *Canis lupus* (V), *Ursus arctos* (rare), *Panthera pardus* (rare), *Capra hircus aegagrus* (rare) and *Ovis ammon* (rare).

Conservation issues

The whole site was designated a Protected Area in 1970. No threats are known.

Further reading

Scott (1976b).

056 Mooteh (Isfahan)

Protected Area

33°40′N 50°50′E
200,000 ha

Site description

The site lies in an intermontane basin on the western edge of the Central Plateau, c.135 km north-west of Isfahan. About half is mountainous (peaks rising to 2,930 m) or rolling foothills (2,000–2,225 m), and the remainder comprises open plains in four valley regions (1,770–2,000 m). The dominant plant community throughout most of the site is tragacanthic steppe with *Artemisia*. Land ownership is public. Livestock are grazed.

Birds

See box for key species. The avifauna of the reserve is characteristic of the extensive semi-arid steppic plains which fringe the central desert basin of Iran. Other breeding species include *Aquila chrysaetos*, *Falco tinnunculus*, *Pterocles orientalis* (particularly common), *Columba livia*, *Streptopelia decaocto*, *Athene noctua*, *Coracias garrulus*, *Upupa epops* and *Lanius excubitor* (presumed). Passage migrants include *Falco peregrinus*, and *F. pelegrinoides* is an occasional visitor.

Globally threatened species

Aegypius monachus	Resident (probably at least one pair).
Aquila heliaca	Passage migrant and winter visitor.
Tetrax tetrax	One record, winter 1970.
Chlamydotis undulata	Regular on migration (max. 9) and probably bred in the 1970s.

Regionally threatened or declining species

Neophron percnopterus	Recorded in summer; may breed.
Gyps fulvus	Occasional visitor (max. 3).
Aquila pomarina	Passage migrant.
Falco cherrug	Probably regular in winter.

Species restricted wholly or largely to the Middle East

Ammoperdix griseogularis	Common resident.
Oenanthe finschii	Fairly common winter visitor.
Rhodopechys sanguinea	Fairly common winter visitor.

Other threatened/endemic wildlife

Mammals: *Capra hircus aegagrus* (rare), *Ovis ammon* (rare, estimated 700–800 in 1970), *Gazella subgutturosa* (rare, c.5,000), *Lynx lynx* (rare), *Canis lupus* (V), *Acinonyx jubatus* (V; an occasional visitor in the mid- and late 1970s, but has not been observed in recent years).

Conservation issues

A Protected Region of 343,940 ha was established in 1964, primarily for the protection of the gazelle. This was reduced to 291,920 ha in the early 1970s, and re-notified partly as a Wildlife Refuge (132,720 ha) and partly as a Protected Area (159,200 ha). The reserve was further reduced to 200,000 ha in the 1980s, and the Wildlife Refuge was downgraded to Protected Area. There is very heavy grazing by domestic sheep and goats throughout the well-watered parts of the reserve. Sheet erosion has been very damaging to mountain slopes in a number of parts of the reserve.

Further reading

Firouz (1974), Firouz *et al.* (1970), Noll and Noll (1970), Scott (1976b).

057 Dez Dam (Khuzestan)

Unprotected

32°38′N 48°28′E
1,500 ha

Site description

A large storage reservoir on the Dez river in the arid Zagros foothills c.15 km north-east of Dezful.

Birds

See box for key species. An important site for wintering waterfowl, notably herons and egrets, *Anser anser* and *Grus grus*.

Globally threatened species

Marmaronetta angustirostris	Good numbers have been recorded in mid-winter (70, 1992.

1% or more of population

	Breeding (pairs)	Wintering	Passage
Egretta garzetta	—	300 [–]	—
Casmerodius albus	—	300 [–]	—
Ardea cinerea	—	190 [–]	—
Anser anser	—	4,500 [–]	—
Grus grus	—	1,125 [–]	—

Other threatened/endemic wildlife

None known to BirdLife International.

Conservation issues

No conservation measures are known to have been proposed and there is no information on threats to the site.

058 Karkheh River Marshes (Khuzestan)

Wildlife Refuge (3,600 ha) and Protected Area (9,427 ha)

31°45′N 48°25′E
c.15,000 ha

Site description

A 55-km stretch of the Karkheh river and adjacent marshy plains (3,500 ha of wetlands), c.35–90 km north-north-west of Ahwaz. The river flows in a deep channel with steep earth banks. Dense riverine forest of *Tamarix* and *Populus euphraticus*, up to several hundred metres wide, lines the river banks. The adjacent plains, largely cultivated with wheat, are dotted with shallow marshy depressions and meandering creeks which flood in winter.

Birds

See box for key species. The riverine forest supports a typical Mesopotamian bird fauna including large breeding populations of *Hypocolius ampelinus* and *Passer moabiticus*. The river and adjacent floodplain are of some importance for wintering *Pelecanus crispus* and surface-feeding ducks. Other notable species are *Ceryle rudis*, *Halcyon smyrnensis* and *Petronia xanthocollis*.

Globally threatened species

Pelecanus crispus	Regular winter visitor (max. 62).
Marmaronetta angustirostris	Common winter visitor (max. 250); a few pairs breed.

1% or more of population

	Breeding (pairs)	Wintering	Passage
Pelecanus crispus	—	62	—
Marmaronetta angustirostris	breeds	250	—

Regionally threatened or declining species

Aythya nyroca	Winter visitor (max. 3).
Francolinus francolinus	Common resident.

Species restricted wholly or largely to the Middle East

Hypocolius ampelinus	Common summer visitor (max. 30).
Sylvia mystacea	Common summer visitor.
Passer moabiticus	Fairly common resident (max. 12).

Other threatened/endemic wildlife

Mammals: a tiny population of *Dama mesopotamica* (E) still survived along the Karkheh river until the early 1970s, but apparently became extinct in the mid- or late 1970s, leaving the population along the Dez river to the east as the only one known in the wild. Other species include *Gazella subgutturosa* (rare).

Conservation issues

A Protected Region of 18,125 ha was established in 1960 to protect the dwindling habitat of the deer. The reserve was reduced to 13,027 ha in the early 1970s, and re-notified partly as a Wildlife Refuge (3,600 ha) and partly as a Protected Area (9,427 ha). Much of the riparian forest has been degraded as a result of grazing by domestic livestock and cutting for fuel. The cultivated plains are subject to much disturbance from farming and hunting.

Further reading

Firouz *et al.* (1970), Scott (1976a,b,c, 1980), Summers *et al.* (1987).

059 Dez River Marshes and Plains (Khuzestan)

Wildlife Refuge (5,240 ha) and Protected Area (10,633 ha)

31°50′N 48°38′E
c.20,000 ha

Site description

A 55-km stretch of the Dez river, several associated oxbow lakes, and the adjacent marshy plains of Deh Noh and Ahu Dasht (8,000 ha of wetlands), c.35–90 km north of Ahwaz. The river forms a deep channel with steep earth banks. Dense riparian forest (*Tamarix* and *Populus euphraticus*) up to several hundred metres wide lines the river and surrounds the lakes which also have some *Phragmites* beds. The adjacent plains, largely under wheat and other crops, are dotted with shallow marshy depressions and meandering creeks which flood in winter.

Birds

See boxes for key species. The wetlands are very important for wintering surface-feeding ducks, geese (including *Anser erythropus*), *Pelecanus crispus* and *Threskiornis aethiopicus*. This stretch of river is the only known haunt of *Anhinga rufa* in Iran while the reeds around the oxbow lakes form one of the very few sites in Iran where *Turdoides altirostris* is known. The riverine thickets support a typical Mesopotamian bird fauna, with large breeding populations of *Hypocolius ampelinus* and *Passer moabiticus*, but also several species (e.g. *Columba palumbus*, *Turdus*

Globally threatened species

Pelecanus crispus	Regular winter visitor; usually c.30 (max. 162).
Anser erythropus	Present in winters of 1970/71 and 1973/74 (max. 190).
Branta ruficollis	One in February 1971.
Marmaronetta angustirostris	Breeds around the oxbow lakes (c.10–20 pairs).
Aquila heliaca	Regular winter visitor (max. 3).
Tetrax tetrax	Party of 4, January 1974.
Chlamydotis undulata	Winter visitor.

1% or more of population

	Breeding (pairs)	Wintering	Passage
Anhinga rufa	—	3	—
Pelecanus crispus	—	162	—
Nycticorax nycticorax	—	170	—
Threskiornis aethiopicus	—	41	—
Anser albifrons	—	420	—
Anser erythropus	—	190	—
Anas platyrhynchos	—	11,000	—
Aythya nyroca	—	11	—
Vanellus indicus	5–10	65	—

Regionally threatened or declining species

Anhinga rufa	Very scarce winter visitor; see text.
Botaurus stellaris	One record, January.
Threskiornis aethiopicus	Regular winter visitor to marshy plains (see above).
Aythya nyroca	Winter visitor (see above).
Neophron percnopterus	One record, February.
Gyps fulvus	Occasional visitor (max. 7).
Francolinus francolinus	Very common resident.

merula, *Parus major*) more typical of Zagros oak forest. Other notable species include *Eudromias morinellus*, *Ceryle rudis*, *Halcyon smyrnensis* and *Petronia xanthocollis*. At least 133 species have been recorded in the area.

Species restricted wholly or largely to the Middle East

Ammoperdix griseogularis	Resident on low hills.
Hypocolius ampelinus	Common summer visitor (max. 40).
Prunella ocularis	Fairly common winter visitor (max. 6).
Oenanthe finschii	Fairly common winter visitor.
Sylvia mystacea	Common summer visitor.
Turdoides altirostris	Resident in reedbeds (max. 15 birds); see text.
Passer moabiticus	Very common resident (max. 100 birds).

■ Other threatened/endemic wildlife

Mammals: a few tens of *Dama mesopotamica* (E) still survive in the forest along the river; this is the only known truly wild population in the world. Other species include *Gazella subgutturosa* (rare).

■ Conservation issues

A Protected Region of 18,812 ha was established in 1960 to protect the dwindling habitat of the deer. Some 3,837 ha of this reserve were re-notified as a Wildlife Park in 1970. The reserve was reduced to 15,873 ha in the early 1970s, and re-notified partly as a Wildlife Refuge (5,240 ha) and partly as a Protected Area (10,633 ha). Parts of the riparian forest have been degraded by the grazing of livestock and cutting for fuel. The cultivated plains are much disturbed by farming and hunting, and the wetlands are reported to have become very polluted in recent years.

■ Further reading

Firouz *et al.* (1970), Scott (1976a,b,c, 1980), Scott and Carp (1972), Summers *et al.* (1987).

060 Karun River Marshes (Khuzestan)

31°45′N 48°54′E
2,500 ha

Unprotected

■ Site description

Seasonally flooded arable land (mainly wheat), with scattered ponds and permanent marshy areas, on the east bank of the Karun river 55 km north-north-east of Ahwaz. Most of the area dries out completely in summer, but a few of the deeper pools and meandering watercourses remain wet and provide some breeding habitat for waterfowl.

■ Birds

See boxes for key species. A very important wintering area for geese, *Tadorna ferruginea*, surface-feeding ducks, *Grus grus*, several shorebirds and *Pterocles alchata*. *Motacilla citreola* is also fairly common in winter.

Globally threatened species

Pelecanus crispus	Occasional in winter (max. 6).
Anser erythropus	Regular winter visitor (max. 590).
Branta ruficollis	Two in February 1971.
Marmaronetta angustirostris	Present in breeding season (max. 34) and presumably breeds; small numbers in winter.
Aquila heliaca	Regular winter visitor (max. 2).

Regionally threatened or declining species

Botaurus stellaris	One record, January.
Threskiornis aethiopicus	Occasional winter visitor.
Aythya nyroca	Winter visitor (max. 4).
Falco cherrug	One record, January.
Francolinus francolinus	Common resident.

Species restricted wholly or largely to the Middle East

Oenanthe finschii	Fairly common winter visitor.
Oenanthe xanthoprymna	Recorded in winter (max. 2).

1% or more of population

	Breeding (pairs)	Wintering	Passage
Threskiornis aethiopicus	—	12	—
Anser albifrons	—	1,730	3,500 (Nov)
Anser erythropus	—	590	—
Anser anser	—	10,050	—
Tadorna ferruginea	—	400	1,510 (Nov)
Anas crecca	—	15,300	—
Anas platyrhynchos	—	6,170	—
Anas clypeata	—	3,000	—
Grus grus	—	1,350	—
Vanellus leucurus	—	150	—
Limosa limosa	—	2,000	—

Other threatened/endemic wildlife
None known to BirdLife International.

Conservation issues
There is no legal protection. The area is highly disturbed by farming activity and by hunting.

Further reading
Fotoohi and Scott (1975), Scott (1976a,c, 1980), Scott and Carp (1972), Summers *et al.* (1987).

061 Horeh Bamdej (Khuzestan)
also known as Sadi Shavour Marshes
Unprotected

31°45′N 48°36′E
12,000 ha

Site description
A large permanent freshwater marsh with relatively little open water, in an inter-fluvial depression between the Dez and Karkheh rivers 45 km north-north-west of Ahwaz. Open water supports abundant floating and submerged aquatic vegetation, and the marsh is dominated by extensive *Phragmites* and *Typha* with a surrounding belt of seasonally inundated sedge marsh and arable land.

Birds
See boxes for key species. Horeh Bamdej is an important breeding area for herons and egrets (including *Ardea purpurea*), *Marmaronetta angustirostris*, *Circus aeruginosus*, *Porphyrio porphyrio*, *Himantopus himantopus*, *Glareola pratincola* and *Vanellus leucurus*. *Acrocephalus melanopogon* and *A. stentoreus* breed in the reedbeds. The site is also very important for wintering *Pelecanus crispus*, herons and egrets, *Platalea leucorodia*, *Anser anser*, surface-feeding ducks (regularly over 20,000), *Fulica atra*, *Himantopus himantopus*, *Vanellus leucurus* and *Limosa limosa*. *Threskiornis aethiopicus* occurs in winter, and small numbers (apparently non-breeders) have been observed in summer, as also *Ciconia ciconia*.

Other threatened/endemic wildlife
None known to BirdLife International.

Globally threatened species

Phalacrocorax pygmeus	One, January 1975.
Pelecanus crispus	Regular winter visitor (max. 51).
Marmaronetta angustirostris	Fairly common breeder. Common in winter, occasionally in large numbers (see below).
Haliaeetus albicilla	One January record.

1% or more of population

	Breeding (pairs)	Wintering	Passage
Pelecanus crispus	—	51	—
Nycticorax nycticorax	30	—	—
Ardeola ralloides	60	—	—
Bubulcus ibis	40	32	—
Egretta garzetta	50	335	—
Casmerodius albus	—	128	—
Ardea cinerea	—	267	—
Threskiornis aethiopicus	—	50	—
Platalea leucorodia	—	120	—
Anser anser	—	2,500 [350]	—
Anas penelope	—	5,300	—
Anas strepera	—	6,500	—
Anas crecca	—	15,850	—
Anas platyrhynchos	—	15,500	—
Anas clypeata	—	4,960	—
Marmaronetta angustirostris	20+	1,100	—
Fulica atra	—	23,000 [9,130]	—
Grus grus	—	3,000 [33]	—
Himantopus himantopus	100–150	620	—
Glareola pratincola	150–200	—	—
Vanellus indicus	—	65	—
Vanellus leucurus	100+	390	—
Vanellus vanellus	—	400	—
Limosa limosa	—	980	—
Tringa totanus	—	500	—

Regionally threatened or declining species

Threskiornis aethiopicus	Regular in winter. Nine in June 1974 were probably non-breeders.
Falco cherrug	One January record.
Francolinus francolinus	Common resident.

Species restricted wholly or largely to the Middle East

Hippolais languida	One spring record.
Sylvia mystacea	One summer record; probably breeds in the area.

Conservation issues
There is no legal protection. Parts of the wetland are currently being drained for agriculture.

Further reading
Scott (1976a,c, 1978a), Scott and Carp (1972).

062 **Hamidieh (Omidiyeh) Plains** (Khuzestan)

31°20′N 48°20′E
20,000 ha

Unprotected

Site description
Semi-desertic steppe and irrigated arable land subject to winter flooding on the plain of the Karkheh river c.30 km west-north-west of Ahwaz. The site includes Hamidieh lake, an oxbow lake of c.3 ha with extensive *Phragmites* and *Typha*.

Birds
See box for key species. The flood-plain wetlands are an important wintering area for herons and egrets, *Anser anser*, *Tadorna tadorna*, surface-feeding ducks, *Himantopus himantopus* and *Recurvirostra avosetta*. *Marmaronetta angustirostris* breeds at Hamidieh lake, and small numbers have been recorded on the flood-plain wetlands in winter. Small numbers of *Grus grus* winter (100). *Turdoides altirostris* is resident in the reeds; *Hypocolius ampelinus* is a fairly common summer visitor to the scrub around the lake, and *Passer moabiticus* is probably resident. Other notable breeding species are *Pterocles alchata*, *Ceryle rudis*, *Acrocephalus stentoreus* and *Rhodopechys obsoleta*.

Globally threatened species

Marmaronetta angustirostris Breeds (15–20 pairs) at Hamidieh lake, and up to 20 have been recorded on the flood-plain in winter.
Aquila heliaca One record in winter.

1% or more of population

	Breeding (pairs)	Wintering	Passage
Casmerodius albus	—	110 [—]	—
Ardea cinerea	—	110 [—]	—
Anser anser	—	9,700 [—]	—
Tadorna tadorna	—	1,320 [—]	—
Anas penelope	—	3,835 [—]	—
Anas strepera	—	6,440 [—]	—
Anas clypeata	—	4,900 [—]	—
Himantopus himantopus	—	650 [—]	—

Regionally threatened or declining species

Neophron percnopterus One record, May.

Species restricted wholly or largely to the Middle East

Hypocolius ampelinus Fairly common summer visitor (max. 7).
Turdoides altirostris Several pairs resident in reeds at Hamidieh lake.
Passer moabiticus Pair observed in May; probably resident.

Other threatened/endemic wildlife
None known to BirdLife International.

Conservation issues
No conservation measures are known to have been proposed and there is no information on threats.

Further reading
Scott (1976a).

063 **Susangerd Marshes** (Khuzestan)

31°45′N 47°55′E
c.30,000 ha

also known as Horeh Sosangerd
Unprotected

Site description
A complex of permanent and seasonal, freshwater to brackish marshes and seasonally flooded arable land on the flood-plain of the Karkheh river, 60–90 km west-north-west of Ahwaz near the Iraqi border. The site comprises the north-east extremity of the vast Hoor Al Azim (Haur Hawizeh) marshes, the bulk of which lies in Iraq. The adjacent semi-desertic plains have sparse steppic vegetation.

Birds
See boxes for key species. An important wintering area for geese, surface-feeding ducks and shorebirds, notably *Anser anser*, *Anas strepera* and *Himantopus himantopus*.

Other threatened/endemic wildlife
None known to BirdLife International.

Globally threatened species

Marmaronetta angustirostris	Winter visitor (60 in November 1973).
Haliaeetus albicilla	One, January.

1% or more of population

	Breeding (pairs)	Wintering	Passage
Anser anser	—	1,995 [—]	—
Anas strepera	—	1,755 [—]	—
Himantopus himantopus	—	140	—
Vanellus indicus	—	72	—
Limosa limosa	—	—	250 (Nov)

Regionally threatened or declining species

Botaurus stellaris	Singles recorded January and March.
Francolinus francolinus	Resident.

Species restricted wholly or largely to the Middle East

Hypocolius ampelinus	One, November.
Sylvia mystacea	Two, November.

Conservation issues

There is no legal protection. Parts of the wetland are reported to have been damaged during the Iran–Iraq war.

Further reading

Scott (1976a).

064 Shadegan Marshes and Tidal Mudflats of Khor-al Amaya and Khor Musa (Khuzestan)

Wildlife Refuge (296,000 ha)

30°10′N 48°40′E
425,140 ha
Ramsar Site (400,000 ha)

Site description

Lying at the head of the Persian Gulf near Abadan, the site comprises the southern portion of the extensive flood-plain and delta system of the Karun, Dez and several other major rivers which rise in the north-west Zagros Mountains. The better-drained areas in the north support fresh to brackish sedge marshes dominated by *Scirpus* which give way to salt-tolerant vegetation in the central flood-plain and bare, dry mudflats in the south, dominated by *Tamarix* (Shadegan Marshes, 30°20′N 48°20′E, 282,500 ha). The coastal zone comprises extensive intertidal mudflats, creeks, sandbanks and low muddy islands (Khor-al Amaya, 30°00′N 48°40′E, 19,200 ha; Khor Musa, 30°10′N 49°00′E, 123,440 ha). Autumn and winter rains in the high Zagros cause extensive flooding, creating a vast complex of shallow lagoons which may dry out completely by the end of the summer. The Ahwaz–Abadan road passes along the west side of the site, while the main highway from Abadan to the port of Bandar-e Shahpur runs west to east across the southern edge of the marshes. Summer temperatures are extremely high, with means of over 45°C in July and over 7°C in January; frosts are rare. Precipitation is largely in winter, with an abrupt onset in November and terminating more gradually in April–May. Run-off peaks in late winter, when discharge from the Karun river may be ten times greater than in late summer. The wetland is bordered by barren flats to the north, east and north-west, but there is a large area of rice fields, date gardens and human settlement to the north-east. The land is publicly owned.

Birds

See boxes for key species. The area is extremely important for a wide variety of wintering waterfowl, especially dabbling ducks, and also a very important breeding and migration staging area. Shadegan Marshes are the most important site in the world for *Marmaronetta angustirostris*, regularly supporting 30–60% of the world population in winter. There are also notable wintering concentrations of *Pelecanus crispus*, *Ciconia ciconia*, *Anser anser*, dabbling ducks

Globally threatened species

Pelecanus crispus	Regular winter visitor; one pair bred near Bandar-e Shapur in 1975.
Marmaronetta angustirostris	Abundant winter visitor, probably 15,000–20,000 in most years (see text). A few pairs probably breed (e.g. 10 birds in June 1974).
Haliaeetus albicilla	Regular in winter (max. 4).
Aquila heliaca	Fairly common in winter, often over 10 (max. 19).

Regionally threatened or declining species

Botaurus stellaris	Presumably breeds; up to 6 booming in spring.
Threskiornis aethiopicus	Occasional in winter and spring (max. 8, May).
Aythya nyroca	Breeds and winters (see above).
Neophron percnopterus	Recorded May and August (max. 2).
Falco cherrug	Regular winter visitor.

Species restricted wholly or largely to the Middle East

Hypocolius ampelinus	One record of 3 birds in March; probably breeds in the area.
Oenanthe finschii	Fairly common in winter.
Sylvia mystacea	One, November.

1% or more of population	Breeding (pairs)	Wintering	Passage
Pelecanus crispus	1+	75	—
Nycticorax nycticorax	1+	140	—
Ardeola ralloides	100	—	—
Egretta garzetta	100	350 [—]	—
Casmerodius albus	—	200 [172]	—
Ardea cinerea	—	670	—
Ciconia ciconia	—	1,340	—
Threskiornis aethiopicus	—	1	8 (May)
Anser anser	—	3,500 [2,080]	—
Tadorna tadorna	—	3,720 [80]	—
Anas penelope	—	9,050	—
Anas strepera	—	10,000 [9,050]	—
Anas crecca	—	348,000	—
Anas platyrhynchos	—	9,500 [4,800]	—
Anas acuta	—	237,000	—
Anas querquedula	—	61	12,500 (Mar)
Anas clypeata	—	16,980	—
Marmaronetta angustirostris	several	20,000	—
Aythya ferina	—	10,050 [110]	—
Aythya nyroca	several	10	—
Haematopus ostralegus	—	1,820	—
Himantopus himantopus	60	800	—
Recurvirostra avosetta	several	883 [172]	—
Vanellus leucurus	60+	320	—
Vanellus vanellus	—	600	—
Limosa limosa	—	750	—
Limosa lapponica	—	2,120	—
Numenius arquata	—	950	—
Tringa totanus	—	1,260	—
Larus ridibundus	—	12,000	—
Larus genei	400–800	5,000	—
Larus cachinnans/argentatus	—	3,000+	—
Sterna nilotica	100–200	1,820	—
Sterna hirundo	60–100	—	—
Sterna albifrons	150–250	—	—

(over 500,000, mainly *Anas crecca* and *A. acuta*) and gulls (over 15,000, mainly *Larus ridibundus* and *L. genei*). The mudflats at the head of the Persian Gulf hold many thousands of shorebirds, including large numbers of *Haematopus ostralegus*, *Limosa lapponica*, *Numenius arquata* and *Tringa totanus*. *Aquila heliaca* winters more commonly here than anywhere else in Iran, and *Circus aeruginosus* (up to 70) and *Aquila clanga* (up to nine) also winter in good numbers. Breeding birds include various herons and egrets, *Marmaronetta angustirostris*, *Aythya nyroca*, *Circus aeruginosus* (25–50 pairs), various shorebirds, *Larus genei* and five species of terns. A variety of landbirds typical of the Persian Gulf coastal plain occur in the surrounding scrub and date gardens, including *Hypocolius ampelinus*, while the sedge marshes are the stronghold of *Cisticola juncidis* in Iran. At least 149 species have been recorded in the reserve.

■ Other threatened/endemic wildlife

None known to BirdLife International.

■ Conservation issues

A Wildlife Refuge of 296,000 ha, encompassing all the main wetland areas and the coastal mudflats in the south, was established in 1972. The central and southern portions of Shadegan Marshes and the mudflats of Khor-al Amaya and Khor Musa (a total of 190,000 ha) were designated a Ramsar Site in 1975. The principal long-term threat is diminished water supply following its diversion for irrigation schemes further north. Parts of the marshes are reported to have been damaged during the Iran–Iraq war, and may have suffered some damage as a result of 'acid rainfall' during the Gulf War.

■ Further reading

Carp (1980), IUCN (1991), Ramsar Convention Bureau (1993), Scott (1972c, 1975b, 1976a,c, 1978a, 1991, in press), Scott and Carp (1972), Summers *et al.* (1987).

065 Izeh and Sheikho Lakes (Khuzestan)

31°52′N 49°54′E
1,400 ha

Unprotected

■ Site description

Two small freshwater lakes in a broad valley in the foothills of the western Zagros Mountains near the small town of Izeh, 125 km east-north-east of Ahwaz. Sheikho, the larger lake (c.300 ha), lies north-west of the town. It is shallow and almost entirely overgrown with emergent vegetation except around the edges where heavy grazing and trampling by cattle maintain some open water. Izeh lake (c.250 ha), east of the town, is somewhat deeper with much more open water. Both lakes are fed by local run-off and large springs at the base of nearby hills. The plains around the lake and to the south are cultivated, mainly for wheat, and there are several small villages and seasonal encampments in the vicinity. Sparsely vegetated stony hillsides rise abruptly to the north. Land ownership is public.

Birds

See box for key species. An important wintering area for *Tachybaptus ruficollis* (3,500), herons, egrets, *Anser anser*, *Tadorna ferruginea*, surface-feeding and diving ducks, *Fulica atra* and *Grus grus*. Several species of waterfowl breed in small numbers, and many *Ciconia ciconia* nest in the general area, including over 20 pairs on telegraph poles in Izeh town. Mid-winter waterfowl counts in the 1970s seldom exceeded 5,000, but numbers have been much higher in recent years. The numbers of *Grus grus* appear to have remained stable since the 1970s.

Other threatened/endemic wildlife

None known to BirdLife International.

Conservation issues

There is no legal protection. The emergent marsh vegetation is heavily grazed, but no other threats are known.

Further reading

Scott (1976a, 1980).

1% or more of population

	Breeding (pairs)	Wintering	Passage
Egretta garzetta	—	400 [—]	—
Casmerodius albus	—	330 [—]	—
Ardea cinerea	—	260 [—]	—
Anser anser	—	3,500 [—]	—
Tadorna ferruginea	—	750 [175]	—
Anas strepera	—	4,150 [230]	—
Anas crecca	—	13,150 [3,350]	—
Anas acuta	—	12,100 [2,425]	—
Anas clypeata	—	5,860 [250]	—
Aythya ferina	—	9,360 [—]	—
Aythya fuligula	—	6,400 [—]	—
Fulica atra	—	86,550 [—]	—
Grus grus	—	390 [400]	—
Recurvirostra avosetta	—	400 [—]	—
Vanellus vanellus	—	3,000 [—]	—

Regionally threatened or declining species

Falco cherrug One record, January.

Species restricted wholly or largely to the Middle East

Oenanthe alboniger Fairly common resident in surrounding hills.

066 Cheghakor Marsh (Chaharmahal, Bakhtiari)

Unprotected

31°50′N 50°50′E
1,600 ha

Site description

Cheghakhor (Chogakhor) Marsh lies in the upper drainage of the Karun river on a broad grassy plain at c.2,100 m in the central Zagros Mountains, c.95 km west of Shahreza. It is a permanent freshwater marsh which floods in winter and spring, but by late summer much of it is dry and the remainder is almost entirely overgrown with emergent vegetation. The vegetation is *Phragmites* and *Typha* beds surrounded by sedge. Large portions of the adjacent grassy plains are cultivated with wheat. Land ownership is public.

Birds

See box for key species. An important wintering area for *Casmerodius albus*, *Anas platyrhynchos* (up to 6,700) and *Aythya nyroca*. *Marmaronetta angustirostris* has been recorded recently.

Other threatened/endemic wildlife

None known to BirdLife International.

Conservation issues

There is no information on threats. The site has been proposed for Protected Area status, and has been recommended for designation as a Ramsar Site.

Further reading

Scott (1976a).

Globally threatened species

Marmaronetta angustirostris Winter visitor (57 in January 1992).
Oxyura leucocephala Occurs; status uncertain.

1% or more of population

	Breeding (pairs)	Wintering	Passage
Casmerodius albus	—	100 [—]	—
Aythya nyroca	—	103 [—]	—

Regionally threatened or declining species

Aythya nyroca Winter visitor (see above).

Species restricted wholly or largely to the Middle East

Oenanthe finschii Recorded on autumn passage.

067 Gandoman Marsh (Chaharmahal, Bakhtiari)

31°50′N 51°06′E
1,500 ha

Unprotected

Site description

A largely seasonal freshwater marsh on a vast grassy plain at 2,250 m in the central Zagros Mountains, c.25 km south-west of Borujen and 75 km west-south-west of Shahreza. The wetland, dominated by sedges, floods in winter and spring, but by late summer is almost completely dry. There is some rice cultivation along the central main stream and some wheat on the surrounding grassy plains. Land ownership is public and private.

Birds

See box for key species. An important wintering area for *Casmerodius albus*, *Ardea cinerea*, *Tadorna ferruginea*, *Anas platyrhynchos* (up to 5,000) and *Aythya nyroca*. *Haliaeetus albicilla* and *Aquila clanga* have occurred in winter. Breeding species include *Ciconia ciconia* (summer visitor locally) and *Buteo rufinus*. *Ciconia nigra* occurs (status unknown) and *Buteo buteo* is a passage migrant.

Other threatened/endemic wildlife

None known to BirdLife International.

Globally threatened species

Haliaeetus albicilla	Winter visitor (max. 2).

1% or more of population

	Breeding (pairs)	Wintering	Passage
Tadorna ferruginea	—	750	—
Anas crecca	—	300	—
Aythya nyroca	—	140 [—]	—

Regionally threatened or declining species

Aythya nyroca	Winter visitor (see above).
Neophron percnopterus	Recorded in August.
Gyps fulvus	Occasional visitor (max. 1).

Conservation issues

There is no information on threats. The site has been proposed for Protected Area status, and has been recommended for designation as a Ramsar Site.

Further reading

Scott (1976a,c).

068 Gavekhoni Lake, and Marshes of the Lower Zaindeh Rud (Isfahan)

32°20′N 52°47′E
63,300 ha
Ramsar Site (43,000 ha)

also known as Gavkhouni Lake

Unprotected

Site description

Gavekhoni lake is a large (c.13,000 ha), shallow, saline lake in an enclosed drainage basin at 1,470 m on the western edge of the deserts of Iran's Central Plateau, c.40–100 km east-south-east of the city of Isfahan. The lake is fed almost entirely by the Zaindeh Rud, a large river rising in the Zagros. Flooding occurs in winter and spring, but the extent varies widely and the lake is often almost completely dry by the end of summer. There are *Phragmites* marshes with some *Tamarix* scrub at the mouth of the river, but the lake is otherwise largely devoid of vegetation except algae; plant growth elsewhere around the lake is very sparse and halophytic. The marshes of the lower Zaindeh Rud, fed by flooding from the river itself and by several irrigation canals, comprise a c.60 km chain of freshwater marshes and flood-plain wetlands ending at Gavekhoni lake, covering c.30,000 ha or more. Very little natural marsh vegetation remains (now mainly *Phragmites* and *Typha*), the main flooding now occurring over degraded steppe and land under wheat and rice. The lake is relatively inaccessible and undisturbed, although there is some grazing, hunting and cutting of wood for fuel in the marshes at the river mouth. Land ownership is public.

Birds

See boxes for key species. An important wintering area for a variety of waterfowl, notably *Phoenicopterus ruber* (1,720 recorded), *Anser anser*, *Tadorna ferruginea*, *T. tadorna*, surface-feeding ducks and some shorebirds. Mid-winter waterfowl counts in the 1970s seldom exceeded 10,000 birds in total, but numbers have been much higher in recent years.

Globally threatened species

Haliaeetus albicilla	Regular winter visitor (max. 5).
Aegypius monachus	Occasional visitor (max. 1).
Aquila heliaca	Regular winter visitor (max. 1).

1% or more of population

	Breeding (pairs)	Wintering	Passage
Anser anser	—	1,740 [—]	—
Tadorna ferruginea	—	3,280 [530]	—
Tadorna tadorna	—	11,300 [1,090]	—
Anas penelope	—	4,560 [—]	—
Anas strepera	—	6,600 [—]	—
Anas crecca	—	41,500 [7,600]	—
Anas acuta	—	13,250 [110]	—
Anas clypeata	—	8,370 [—]	—
Himantopus himantopus	—	286 [—]	—
Tringa totanus	—	1,214 [35]	—

Regionally threatened or declining species

Gyps fulvus	Occasional visitor (max. 2).
Falco cherrug	Occasional winter visitor.

Other threatened/endemic wildlife

None known to BirdLife International.

Conservation issues

There is no legal protection, though the whole area was designated a Ramsar Site in 1975. The principal threat is water-borne pollution from the city of Isfahan and other urban centres upstream along the Zaindeh Rud.

Further reading

Carp (1980), Ramsar Convention Bureau (1993), Scott (1976a,c, 1980).

069 Kalmand (Yazd)

Protected Area

31°30′N 54°40′E
241,900 ha

Site description

This desert site lies at c.900–1,200 m on the south-west edge of the Central Plateau near the city of Yazd. No detailed information is available on the habitat, etc. Land ownership is public.

Birds

See box for key species. An important breeding area for *Chlamydotis undulata*. Other breeding species include *Buteo rufinus*, *Aquila chrysaetos*, *Falco tinnunculus*, *Alectoris chukar*, *Cursorius cursor*, *Pterocles orientalis*, *Columba livia* and *Athene noctua*. Passage migrants include *Buteo buteo*, *Aquila nipalensis*, *Accipiter nisus* and *Asio flammeus* (rare).

Other threatened/endemic wildlife

None known to BirdLife International.

Globally threatened species

Aquila heliaca	Passage migrant and possibly also a winter visitor.
Chlamydotis undulata	Summer visitor.

Regionally threatened or declining species

Gyps fulvus	Resident or occasional visitor.
Falco cherrug	Winter visitor, and may breed in the area.

Species restricted wholly or largely to the Middle East

Ammoperdix griseogularis	Common resident.

Conservation issues

Established as a Protected Area in 1991 to protect the large population of *Chlamydotis undulata*. There is no information on threats.

070 Kuh-i Dena, and Yasuj and Sisakht Area (Fars)

also known as Kuh-i Dinar
Unprotected

31°00′N 51°25′E
90,200 ha

Site description

Lying c.180 km north-west of Shiraz, the site comprises the Kuh-i Dena massif in the central Zagros Mountains. The region extends from the forested valleys and foothills at c.1,450 m in the region of Yasuj and Sisakht in the south to the summit of Kuh-i Dena, at 4,404 m the highest peak in the Zagros. The topography is very dissected, with rugged limestone ridges separating steep-sided valleys, and many perennial springs, streams and rivers. The lower slopes and valleys have mature *Quercus* forest and some wheat cultivation; there is *Pistacia–Amygdalus* scrub and some *Juniperus* on the upper slopes, and alpine tundra and permanent snow fields on the highest summits. Around springs and along river banks are stands of *Salix* and *Populus* with some dense herbaceous vegetation. There are several small villages in the valleys, and livestock grazing occurs. Land ownership is public.

■ Birds

See box for key species. The region supports the typical avifauna of the Zagros oak forest and montane habitats. Other breeding species include *Dendrocopos medius*, *Sylvia hortensis*, *Parus lugubris*, *Lanius nubicus*, *Petronia xanthocollis*, *Montifringilla nivalis*, *Serinus pusillus* and *Emberiza buchanani*.

■ Other threatened/endemic wildlife

None known to BirdLife International.

Regionally threatened or declining species

Gyps fulvus	Resident.
Accipiter brevipes	One August record; may breed.

Species restricted wholly or largely to the Middle East

Tetraogallus caspius	Resident on highest ridges.
Irania gutturalis	Common summer visitor.
Oenanthe xanthoprymna	Fairly common summer visitor.
Hippolais languida	Fairly common summer visitor.
Sylvia althaea	Fairly common summer visitor.
Phylloscopus neglectus	Common summer visitor.
Carpospiza brachydactyla	Fairly common summer visitor.
Rhodopechys sanguinea	Breeds at high elevations.

■ Conservation issues

No conservation measures are known to have been proposed and there is no information on threats to the site.

071 Dorudsan Dam (Fars)

also known as Dorodzan Dam
Unprotected

30°15′N 52°20′E
Area undefined

■ Site description

Dorudsan Dam maintains a large storage reservoir in a broad valley on the Kur river, at c.1,800 m in the southern Zagros Mountains c.70 km north-north-west north of Shiraz. No information is available on the habitats, etc.

■ Birds

See box for key species. An important wintering area for ducks.

■ Other threatened/endemic wildlife

None known to BirdLife International.

■ Conservation issues

No conservation measures are known to have been proposed and there is no information on threats to the site.

1% or more of population

	Breeding (pairs)	Wintering	Passage
Podiceps cristatus	—	1,200 [62]	—
Anas platyrhynchos	—	5,550 [7,400]	—
Anas acuta	—	10,000	—

Regionally threatened or declining species

Gyps fulvus	Occasional visitor (max. 5).

Species restricted wholly or largely to the Middle East

Ammoperdix griseogularis	Common on adjacent hills.
Oenanthe finschii	Fairly common in winter.
Oenanthe xanthoprymna	Fairly common in winter.
Oenanthe alboniger	Fairly common resident on adjacent hills.

072 Kaftar Lake (Fars)

Unprotected

30°34′N 52°47′E
4,700 ha

■ Site description

A freshwater lake of at least 500 ha lying at c.2,300 m on the north slope of the southern Zagros, c.105 km north-north-east of Shiraz. Situated in a region of rolling *Artemisia* steppe and wheat cultivation, the lake and marsh are generally frozen all winter and can dry out completely in summer. The dominant vegetation in the eastern part is *Butomus umbellatus* and *Sparganium*, and in the western part mainly grassy plants.

■ Birds

See box for key species. A very important staging area for *Phoenicopterus ruber*, geese, ducks and

Grus grus, and occasionally (if not frozen) also a very important wintering area. In spring and autumn the lake can hold as many as 120,000 migratory waterfowl (including *P. ruber* and *G. grus*). Other passage migrants include *Pelecanus onocrotalus*, *Anser anser* and *Tadorna ferruginea*.

Globally threatened species

Haliaeetus albicilla	Winter visitor (max. 1), presumably regularly and in small numbers.
Chlamydotis undulata	Five in August 1972.

1% or more of population

	Breeding (pairs)	Wintering	Passage
Phoenicopterus ruber	—	—	12,000 (Aug)
Anas platyrhynchos	—	7,500 [8,000]	—
Anas acuta	—	15,000	—
Anas clypeata	—	2,000 [30,000]	—
Aythya fuligula	—	6,000	—
Grus grus	—	2,928 [—]	—

Other threatened/endemic wildlife
None known to BirdLife International.

Conservation issues
There is no legal protection, though the lake has been proposed as a Ramsar Site. A proposal by the Ministry of Jihad to utilize the water for irrigation purposes has recently been blocked by the Department of the Environment because of the site's ornithological importance, but this could resurface. In recent years, large-scale die-offs of waterfowl, possibly due to botulism, have been reported during the breeding and migration seasons, and the mortality can be as high as 10,000 birds.

Further reading
Scott (1976a).

073 Haft Barm (Fars)
Unprotected

29°40′N 52°10′E
70 ha

Site description
The Haft Barm (Seven Lakes) are a group of small, slightly saline lakes lying at 2,200 m in hollows in broken undulating country east of Kuh-i Anar and c.65 km west-north-west of Shiraz. Fed by local run-off, principally spring snow-melt, they are generally frozen in mid-winter. The southernmost five lakes generally dry out completely in summer. The two largest (in the north) are surrounded by belts of *Phragmites* with patches of *Butomus*, but the other smaller lakes are almost barren except for algae and some small patches of *Butomus*. The surrounding uplands support tragacanthic steppe communities and some wheat farming. The lakes are used by the local nomadic tribes for watering livestock, washing and reed-cutting. Land ownership is public.

Birds
See box for key species. *Marmaronetta angustirostris* has been recorded in summer and probably breeds. *Tringa totanus* probably breeds. Notable on autumn passage are *Tadorna ferruginea* and *Fulica atra*; *Anas strepera* and *A. penelope* are also passage migrants.

Globally threatened species

Marmaronetta angustirostris	Probably breeds; 200 present in June 1971.
Oxyura leucocephala	Occurs; presumably an occasional passage migrant or non-breeding summer visitor.
Haliaeetus albicilla	Occurs; presumably a regular winter visitor in small numbers.

1% or more of population

	Breeding (pairs)	Wintering	Passage
Tadorna ferruginea	—	—	630

Other threatened/endemic wildlife
None known to BirdLife International.

Conservation issues
No threats are known and no conservation measures are known to have been proposed.

Further reading
Cornwallis (1968), Scott (1976a).

074 Dasht-e Arjan and Lake Parishan (Fars)

29°34´N 51°53´E
52,800 ha
Protected Area
Ramsar Site (6,600 ha), Biosphere Reserve

■ Site description

The site comprises the Arjan Protected Area lying 40–80 km west of Shiraz and incorporating a wide spectrum of Zagros habitats from spectacular high peaks at over 3,000 m, through rolling uplands, and down through the *Quercus* forest zone to the *Acacia* woodlands and date gardens of Iran's southern coastal zone. Two very important wetlands are included, Dasht-e Arjan (29°37´N 51°59´E) at 2,000 m and Lake Parishan (29°31´N 51°48´E) at 850 m, only c.15 km apart. The physiography of the region is of great interest. Oligo-miocene ('Asmari') limestones form spectacular escarpments, generally aligned as parallel ridges enclosing broad valleys with open *Quercus brantii* woodland. The lower slopes are partially covered with steppic forest of *Amygdalus*, *Crataegus*, *Celtis*, etc. In much of the area, the shrub-like tree *Amygdalus erioclada* is conspicuous.

Dasht-e Arjan is a shallow freshwater lake with extensive *Phragmites* and *Typha*. The lake lies in an enclosed basin and drains through swallow-holes at its south-east corner. It reaches c.2,200 ha after wet winters but may shrink to several hundred hectares in drought years. Most of the basin dries out in summer, but two large springs on the west side maintain some permanent marsh. Much of the wetland freezes in winter, and deep snow is not unusual. Good rainfall in recent years has considerably expanded the area covered by tall reeds. Much of the surrounding plain has been overgrazed.

Lake Parishan, fed by permanent springs and seasonal watercourses, lies in an enclosed drainage basin in a broad valley and is brackish to saline, the salinity varying widely with the size of the lake. At maximum extent (c.4,000 ha), the lake is almost fresh. During the early 1970s, water levels were low, the lake was brackish to saline, marsh vegetation was confined to the western and eastern ends near freshwater inflow, and there were large areas of bare saltflats in the south-west bay. In recent years, however, water has remained high and is now almost fresh, and there is very extensive *Phragmites* and *Typha* in many parts. Salt-tolerant vegetation (principally Chenopodiaceae) is predominant around the lake and large areas of grassland are now under wheat. There is some reed-cutting at both wetlands, and the Department of the Environment plans to establish a Guest House and Visitor Centre overlooking Lake Parishan. Land ownership is public.

■ Birds

See boxes for key species. The great range of habitats supports almost the full range of species typical of the montane steppe, *Pistacia–Amygdalus* forest, *Quercus* forest and wetland systems of the central and southern Zagros, as well as some species more typical of the Persian Gulf coastal lowlands. At least 263 species have been recorded in the reserve. The region is one of the best in the country for *Hippolais languida*.

Both Lake Parishan and Dasht-e Arjan are extremely important for a wide variety of wintering waterfowl and also for breeding waterfowl (notably *Pelecanus crispus* and *Oxyura leucocephala*), especially in wet years. The numbers of ducks and *Fulica atra* at Lake Parishan in recent years have been well below the numbers in the 1970s (an average of 25,000 ducks and 120,000 *F. atra* in the four winters 1972/73–1975/76). This decline may be due to the greatly increased disturbance from fishermen in high-speed motor boats. Numbers of *Oxyura leucocephala* also appear to have fallen, with a maximum of 25 in recent years compared with as many as 90 in the 1970s. However, improved agriculture to the south of the lake now provides better feeding habitat for *Anser anser* and *Grus grus*, and numbers of both have recently been much higher than in the 1970s. There are high winter counts of *Circus aeruginosus* (up to 40) and *Aquila clanga* (up to five). The extensive reedbeds now support large colonies of herons, egrets, *Plegadis falcinellus* and *Platalea leucorodia*, and the small resident population of *Pelecanus crispus* has shown a slight increase. *Porphyrio porphyrio* colonized the area in the 1980s and is now common.

■ Other threatened/endemic wildlife

Mammals: *Canis lupus* (V), *Ursus arctos* (rare), *Caracal caracal* (rare), *Panthera pardus* (rare), *Gazella subgutturosa* (rare), *Capra hircus aegagrus* (rare) and *Ovis ammon* (rare). *Panthera leo persica* is known to have survived until c.1940.

■ Conservation issues

A National Park of 65,750 ha was created in 1972. The original plans to establish the reserve under the control of an international committee were never implemented, and following the revolution the reserve was downgraded to Protected Area and reduced in size to 52,800 ha. In 1975 Lake Parishan and Dasht-e Arjan were designated a Ramsar Site in two parts, comprising only the wetland areas

Globally threatened species

Pelecanus crispus	Present all year; 5–10 pairs breed at Lake Parishan and has bred at Dasht-e Arjan; usually about 60 in winter, but max. of 100 in 1970s and 185 in recent years.
Anser erythropus	Two in October 1974.
Marmaronetta angustirostris	Large breeding population at Lake Parishan when conditions suitable; probably 200–300 pairs in 1976–1977. Also breeds in small numbers at Dasht-e Arjan in wet years. In 1970s up to 2,000 wintered at Lake Parishan and 40 at Dasht-e Arjan. Recently up to 5,500 at Lake Parishan.
Oxyura leucocephala	Several pairs breed at Lake Parishan. Up to 455 reported wintering, but maximum in recent years only 17.
Haliaeetus albicilla	Regular in winter, mainly at Dasht-e Arjan (max. 4).
Aegypius monachus	Occasional visitor or scarce resident.
Aquila heliaca	Regular in winter; up to 3 at Dasht-e Arjan and 4 at Lake Parishan.
Falco naumanni	Summer visitor: colony of 10–15 pairs at Dasht-e Arjan.
Chlamydotis undulata	Occasional non-breeding visitor, recorded June, July and December (max. 2).

1% or more of population

	Breeding (pairs)	Wintering	Passage
Podiceps cristatus	50–100	300	430 (Oct)
Podiceps nigricollis	has bred (20)	—	500 (Nov)
Pelecanus onocrotalus	—	800	—
Pelecanus crispus	5–10	185 [100]	—
Nycticorax nycticorax	100	300	—
Ardeola ralloides	200	—	—
Egretta garzetta	100	350	—
Casmerodius albus	—	370	—
Ardea cinerea	—	255	—
Plegadis falcinellus	30–100	930 [200]	—
Platalea leucorodia	50–400	200 [50]	—
Phoenicopterus ruber	—	7,080	9,800 (Oct)
Anser albifrons	—	180 [–]	—
Anser anser	—	5,760 [1,845]	—
Tadorna ferruginea	—	4,180 [3,820]	—
Anas penelope	—	5,000 [5,610]	—
Anas strepera	—	2,200 [990]	—
Anas crecca	—	45,000	—
Anas platyrhynchos	—	14,000	—
Anas acuta	—	25,000	—
Anas clypeata	—	3,500	—
M. angustirostris	200–300	5,500 [2,000]	—
Aythya ferina	—	20,000	—
Aythya fuligula	—	2,520 [200]	—
Aythya nyroca	several	150	—
Oxyura leucocephala	several	455 [93]	—
Porphyrio porphyrio	breeds	140 [–]	—
Fulica atra	—	24,300 [172,500]	—
Grus grus	—	2,204 [1,000]	—
Himantopus himantopus	10+	100	210 (Nov)
Glareola pratincola	30	—	—
Vanellus indicus	20	46	150 (Nov)
Vanellus leucurus	20+	150	—
Vanellus vanellus	—	4,000	—
Limosa limosa	—	900	—
Tringa totanus	—	290	—
Larus ridibundus	—	4,300 [3,400]	—
Larus cachinnans/argentatus	—	—	120 (Nov)

Regionally threatened or declining species

Botaurus stellaris	Regular winter visitor (max. 1). May have bred at Dasht-e Arjan.
Aythya nyroca	Breeds and winters (see above).
Neophron percnopterus	Recorded in summer; may breed.
Gyps fulvus	Resident (max. 6 birds).
Falco cherrug	One record, May.
Gallinago media	Recorded on passage, May.
Francolinus francolinus	Fairly common resident around Lake Parishan.

Species restricted wholly or largely to the Middle East

Ammoperdix griseogularis	Common resident.
Prunella ocularis	Fairly common winter visitor.
Irania gutturalis	Fairly common summer visitor.
Oenanthe finschii	Common winter visitor.
Oenanthe xanthoprymna	Very common winter visitor.
Oenanthe alboniger	Fairly common resident, especially in south.
Hippolais languida	Common summer visitor to *Quercus* forest.
Sylvia mystacea	Recorded at Lake Parishan in July; may breed.
Phylloscopus neglectus	Common summer visitor at higher elevations.
Carpospiza brachydactyla	Very common summer visitor.

(6,600 ha). The area of the original National Park was designated a Biosphere Reserve in 1976. There has been a considerable increase in fishing, and the widespread use of motor boats (instead of the traditional reed boats) has resulted in much disturbance to waterfowl. Consideration should be given to the establishment of one or more no-fishing zones at Lake Parishan to resolve this problem. An estimated 500–1,000 birds are poached annually, despite the presence of a small Game Guard Station in the village of Dasht-e Arjan, and there are reports that significant numbers of waterfowl are accidentally killed in fishing nets. The possibility of re-routing the power lines at Dasht-e Arjan should be investigated, as they severely compromise the great beauty of the area and may cause considerably mortality to waterfowl. Some 20 ha of marsh at the extreme north-west corner of Lake Parishan were drained for agriculture by the Ministry of Jihad shortly after the revolution. There has been some development of aquaculture on the plains west of the lake, and it is reported that three species of carp *Cyprinus* have been introduced to the lake itself. It has been recommended that both parts of the Ramsar Site and other appropriate sections of the Protected Area be upgraded to Wildlife Refuge status.

■ Further reading

Argyle (1975), Carp (1980), Cornwallis (1968), Firouz (1974), Ramsar Convention Bureau (1993), Scott (1973d, 1976a,c, 1978a, 1980), Summers *et al.* (1987).

075 **Bamou** (Fars)
National Park

29°40′N 52°40′E
48,075 ha

Site description
A rugged area of the Zagros Mountains (c.1,500 m to 2,655 m) immediately north-east of the city of Shiraz. The massif has spectacular cliffs and crags and is surrounded by broad steppic outwash plains. The dominant vegetation throughout is *Artemisia* steppe.

Birds
See box for key species. The breeding avifauna is typical of the rather barren steppic mountain ranges of the southern Zagros. Other notable breeding species include *Apus affinis*, *Melanocorypha bimaculata* and *Scotocerca inquieta*. At least 54 species have been recorded in the reserve.

Globally threatened species

Aegypius monachus	Probably resident; several records.

Regionally threatened or declining species

Gypaetus barbatus	Probably resident; several records.
Neophron percnopterus	Recorded in April; may breed.
Gyps fulvus	Resident, with colony on cliffs (max. count 20 birds).
Falco cherrug	One record, April.

Species restricted wholly or largely to the Middle East

Ammoperdix griseogularis	Common resident.
Oenanthe finschii	Common winter visitor.
Oenanthe xanthoprymna	Very common winter visitor.
Oenanthe alboniger	Fairly common resident.
Carpospiza brachydactyla	Fairly common summer visitor.

Other threatened/endemic wildlife
Mammals: *Panthera pardus* (rare), *Gazella subgutturosa* (rare), *Capra hircus aegagrus* (rare) and *Ovis ammon* (rare).

Conservation issues
The area was first protected as the Bamou Protected Region (67,188 ha), established in 1962. This was reduced in size 48,075 ha and given National Park status in the early 1970s. No threats are known.

Further reading
Firouz *et al.* (1970), Scott (1976b).

076 **Lake Maharlu** (Fars)
Unprotected

29°30′N 52°48′E
21,600 ha

Site description
A large, shallow, saline lake at 1,480 m in the Shiraz basin of the southern Zagros. The lake is fed by the run-off from numerous small ephemeral wadis, by the Pul-i-Fasa stream in the west, and by numerous small springs around the shore, and covers 21,600 ha at maximum extent of flooding. Much the largest perennial springs are at Barmishur at the north-west corner and at Ab-e Paravan in the north, both creating pools c.2 m deep which overflow into extensive permanent marshes with *Phragmites* and *Typha* as well as feeding open marsh communities dominated by sedges, rushes and *Chara*. At maximum extent, the Barmishur marshes cover c.150 ha and Ab-e Paravan 250 ha. Water level varies widely with rainfall, and in prolonged droughts the entire lake dries out except for the pools at Barmishur and Ab-e Paravan. The lake shores support salt-tolerant plant communities dominated by *Tamarix*, *Suaeda* and *Salicornia*. The lake is bounded by limestone hills to the north and dry steppe to east and south. Land to the west (towards Shiraz) is largely under irrigated cultivation for rice, wheat, barley, melons, cotton and sugar beet. The lake is used for salt production and there are numerous large salt pans, particularly in the eastern portion. There is some livestock grazing and reed-cutting in the Barmishur and Ab-e Paravan marshes.

Birds
See boxes for key species. Lake Maharlu is important for a wide variety of resident and migratory waterfowl, notably surface-feeding ducks, geese, fla-

Globally threatened species

Pelecanus crispus	Occasional winter visitor (max. 7).
Anser erythropus	Regular winter visitor 1971–1975; usually 40–80, max. 102.
Marmaronetta angustirostris	Bred (10 pairs) and wintered (max. 37) in early 1970s.
Oxyura leucocephala	Nine in January 1987.
Haliaeetus albicilla	Regular winter visitor (max. 3).
Aquila heliaca	Regular winter visitor (max. 2).
Falco naumanni	Summer visitor: colony of 20 birds on cliffs north of lake; up to 100 on passage in May.

1% or more of population

	Breeding (pairs)	Wintering	Passage
Tadorna ferruginea	—	6,255 [570]	2,200 (Oct)
Tadorna tadorna	—	950 [460]	—
Anas strepera	—	1,405 [50]	—
Anas crecca	—	6,500	16,500 (Nov)
Anas platyrhynchos	—	8,000 [2,150]	—
Oxyura leucocephala	—	9 [—]	—
Grus grus	—	2,134 [231]	350 (Oct)
Himantopus himantopus	25	260 [110]	—
Vanellus leucurus	25	160	—
Vanellus vanellus	—	250	—
Larus ridibundus	—	5,400 [900]	—

Regionally threatened or declining species

Botaurus stellaris	One in winter.
Neophron percnopterus	One in June.
Falco cherrug	Occasional in winter.

Species restricted wholly or largely to the Middle East

Ammoperdix griseogularis	Common resident on adjacent hills.
Prunella ocularis	Fairly common winter visitor (max. 6).
Oenanthe finschii	Fairly common winter visitor.
Oenanthe xanthoprymna	Very common winter visitor.
Oenanthe alboniger	Common resident on adjacent hills.
Carpospiza brachydactyla	Fairly common summer visitor.

mingos, cranes and some shorebirds. Other breeding species include *Porzana pusilla*, *Himantopus himantopus*, *Vanellus leucurus* and *Sterna albifrons*.

Wintering waterfowl have included especially *Pelecanus onocrotalus*, *Anser anser*, *Tadorna ferruginea*, *T. tadorna*, *Anas crecca*, *M. angustirostris*, *Grus grus*, *Himantopus himantopus*, *Recurvirostra avosetta* and *Vanellus leucurus*. In good numbers on passage are *Phoenicopterus ruber*, *T. ferruginea* and *A. crecca*, and several *Aquila clanga* winter.

Other threatened/endemic wildlife

None known to BirdLife International.

Conservation issues

There is no legal protection. Pollution is reported to be a problem. The Soltanabad Marshes, c.15 km west of Lake Maharlu, formerly covered c.700 ha and provided important feeding habitat for wintering wildfowl which used Lake Maharlu as a day roost. The marshes also supported a small breeding population of *Marmaronetta angustirostris*. However, these marshes were completely drained for agricultural purposes in the 1980s. No conservation measures are known to have been proposed.

Further reading

Cornwallis (1968), Fotoohi and Scott (1975), Scott (1976a,c), Summers *et al.* (1987).

077 Lake Bakhtegan, Lake Tashk and Kamjan Marshes (Fars)

29°40′N 53°30′E
338,000 ha

Wildlife Refuge (327,820 ha)
Ramsar Site (108,000 ha)

Site description

The site lies in the eastern Zagros Mountains, 50–160 km east of Shiraz, and includes two very large salt-lakes, Tashk and Bakhtegan, in an internal drainage basin at 1,525 m, the intervening steppic plains and hills (to 2,597 m), and a large area of permanent freshwater marshes and seasonally flooded plains along the lower Kur river to the west (Kamjan Marshes). Lake Tashk is fed by overflow from the Kamjan Marshes at its west end and by a large permanent spring at Gumoon in the north-west. Lake Bakhtegan receives the bulk of its water from the main channel of the Kur which enters at the west. The two lakes are normally separated by narrow strips of land but may be joined during very wet winters to form a single expanse of water covering up to 136,500 ha. After several years of low rainfall, on the other hand, both lakes may dry out completely except in the vicinity of the main springs (e.g. Gumoon Spring at the north-west corner of Lake Tashk and Sahlabad Spring on the south shore of Lake Bakhtegan). Both lakes have an extraordinary range of salinities. In January 1992, the lakes were almost fully flooded, following several years of above-average rainfall. The lakes are oligotrophic and support a submerged vegetation of various algae, *Chara*, *Ruppia* and *Althenia*. Fringing vegetation consists of *Tamarix*, *Suaeda*, *Cressa* and *Salicornia*, and the area between the lakes comprises sparsely vegetated mountain ranges with some *Pistacia* woodland and steppic *Artemisia* plains.

Kamjan Marshes (29°40′N 53°05′E) formerly comprised c.10,000 ha of permanent and seasonal freshwater marshes, mainly reedbeds. Drainage of the wetland for rice farming began in 1967, and much has now been converted to agriculture. However, although the marshes have been extensively modified by the drainage canals, 5,250 ha of wetland remains, including expanses of wet mudflats, *Phragmites* and other emergent aquatic vegetation along canals, and large areas of rice fields. Furthermore, a large portion of the reclaimed land remains uncultivated because of a shortage of water for irrigation and because of the high salt content of the soils. Some irrigation canals are already silting up, and parts of the drained land are reverting to marsh. In addition, new marshes have developed at the mouths of the three main drainage canals where they enter the western ends of Lake Tashk and Lake Bakhtegan. The marshes are dominated by *Carex*, *Phragmites*, Chenopodiaceae and grasses. Livestock are grazed in the marshes and around the lake margins.

Birds

See box for key species. The hills and plains support a breeding bird fauna typical of the semi-arid eastern Zagros, while Lake Tashk and Lake Bakhtegan regularly hold huge numbers of waterfowl in winter (e.g. 120,000–140,000 surface-feeding ducks and 50,000 *Phoenicopterus ruber* in January 1992). The large wintering population of *P. ruber* apparently constitutes the bulk of the Lake Uromiyeh breeding population. Several *Aquila clanga* are present in winter. A wide variety of waterfowl occur on migration, and several species breed, including *Marmaronetta angustirostris*. *Pelecanus onocrotalus* occasionally appears in large flocks, and is known to have bred in the 1960s.

Despite the changes which have occurred at Kamjan Marshes, the area continues to provide ideal feeding habitat for a variety of waterfowl, notably *Ciconia ciconia*, *Plegadis falcinellus* and *Limosa limosa*. These marshes also constitute an important feeding area for large numbers of ducks which roost by day on Lake Bakhtegan and Lake Tashk.

Other notable landbirds include *Apus affinis*, *Melanocorypha bimaculata*, *Anthus similis*, *Phoenicurus erythronotus*, *Sylvia nana*, *Lanius isabellinus*, *Rhodopechys githaginea* and *R. obsoleta*. At least 220 species have been recorded in the Bakhtegan Wildlife Refuge, which comprises almost the whole of the site except for Kamjan Marshes.

Globally threatened species

Pelecanus crispus	Only occasional in 1970s, but up to 67 wintering in recent years.
Anser erythropus	Regular winter visitor (max. 90) in early 1970s.
Marmaronetta angustirostris	At least 100 breeding pairs in 1970. Up to 1,500 in mid-winter in 1970s, and up to 5,000 in recent years.
Haliaeetus albicilla	Regular in winter (max. 15).
Aquila heliaca	Regular in winter (max. 2).
Chlamydotis undulata	Regular non-breeding visitor in late summer (max. 30 in July 1974).

1% or more of population

	Breeding (pairs)	Wintering	Passage
Pelecanus onocrotalus	bred 1960s	—	300 (Jun)
Pelecanus crispus	—	67 [3]	—
Casmerodius albus	—	340 [111]	—
Ardea cinerea	—	193 [129]	—
Ciconia ciconia	—	550	—
Plegadis falcinellus	—	445	—
Phoenicopterus ruber	—	73,430 [50,000]	—
Anser albifrons	—	154	—
Anser anser	—	8,245 [740]	—
Tadorna ferruginea	—	13,400 [2,130]	4,200 (Nov)
Tadorna tadorna	—	5,700 [10,700]	—
Anas penelope	—	14,300 [4,800]	—
Anas strepera	—	8,300 [2,000]	—
Anas crecca	—	48,800 [58,800]	—
Anas platyrhynchos	—	127,500 [13,500]	—
Anas acuta	—	14,550 [104,000]	—
Anas clypeata	—	14,400 [3,500]	—
Marmaronetta angustirostris	100+	5,000 [1,500]	—
Fulica atra	—	29,300	—
Grus grus	—	3,427 [750]	—
Himantopus himantopus	35	450 [220]	350 (Aug)
Recurvirostra avosetta	20	777 [500]	1,000 (Aug)
Charadrius alexandrinus	—	—	1,000 (Nov)
Vanellus leucurus	40+	29	—
Vanellus vanellus	—	800 [540]	—
Calidris alpina	—	—	6,000 (Nov)
Limosa limosa	—	4,500	—
Tringa totanus	—	800	—
Larus genei	—	2,500 [750]	—

Regionally threatened or declining species

Botaurus stellaris	Winter visitor (max. 2).
Neophron percnopterus	Summer visitor, probably breeds (max. 4).
Gallinago media	Recorded on spring and autumn passage.

Species restricted wholly or largely to the Middle East

Ammoperdix griseogularis	Common resident.
Prunella ocularis	Fairly common winter visitor.
Oenanthe finschii	Very common winter visitor.
Oenanthe xanthoprymna	Common winter visitor.
Oenanthe alboniger	Fairly common resident.
Hippolais languida	Summer visitor; probably breeds.
Sylvia minula	Recorded on passage in November.
Carpospiza brachydactyla	Fairly common summer visitor.

Other threatened/endemic wildlife

Mammals: *Canis lupus* (V), *Ursus arctos* (rare), *Caracal caracal* (rare), *Panthera pardus* (rare), *Gazella subgutturosa* (rare), *Capra hircus aegagrus* (rare) and *Ovis ammon* (rare).

Conservation issues

Lake Bakhtegan, Lake Tashk and the intervening hill ranges were first protected as the Bakhtegan Protected Region (310,438 ha) established in 1968. This status was upgraded to Wildlife Refuge in the early 1970s, and the size increased to 327,820 ha. However, the reserve does not include either the Gumoon springs area or most of the marshes at the mouth of the Kur. Kamjan Marshes are also unprotected. In 1975 both lakes and the Kamjan Marshes were designated a Ramsar Site (108,000 ha), including also the Gumoon area and all the marshes at the delta of the Kur but excluding the terrestrial portion of Bakhtegan Wildlife Refuge between the lakes. A proposal to upgrade part of the Wildlife Refuge to National Park has recently been approved by the relevant ministries and is likely to be implemented in the near future. The National Park would include the greater portion of the two lakes and a range of hills to the north of Lake Bakhtegan.

It has been recommended that Kamjan Marshes be designated a buffer zone for the Wildlife Refuge. The use of fertilizers and pesticides should be carefully controlled, and all or part of the area closed to hunting. Parts of the marsh which prove unsuitable for agriculture, such as the large saline areas in the east, should as far as possible be restored to their former condition and might be given special protection, e.g. as part of an enlarged Bakhtegan Wildlife Refuge. Negotiation with the Ministry of Power and local authorities may be necessary to ensure that an adequate supply of water is available to maintain the most important areas of marsh during dry years.

The construction of a large storage reservoir on the Kur (Dorudsan Dam) in the 1970s, and various other irrigation projects in the upper reaches of the river, have reduced water inflow to the lakes. In 1981, the Ministry of Jihad started a major programme of drainage in the Kamjan Marshes to provide land for agriculture (principally rice, wheat and cotton). Three large canals were constructed through the marshes, two to the north of the Kur river, emptying into Lake Tashk, and one to the south, emptying into Lake Bakhtegan. The entire marsh is now criss-crossed with canals and ditches, and much of the vegetation has been destroyed. As much of the water entering Lake Tashk and Lake Bakhtegan passes through Kamjan Marshes, agricultural activities in these marshes could have a profound effect on the quality of the water entering the lakes. Most of the spring-fed marshes at Gumoon have also now been drained for agriculture or converted into fishponds.

There are plans to construct an all-weather road through the centre of the Refuge linking villages to the east of Lake Tashk with the asphalt highway to Shiraz from the west end of Lake Bakhtegan. This would include a causeway across the low-lying flats between the lakes, and could have a significant effect on the overall hydrology. It would also greatly facilitate access to the central hilly portion of the Refuge, an area which has been remote and relatively undisturbed. Some poaching occurs at the west end of Lake Bakhtegan, and improved access to the interior of the Refuge could make this problem serious.

Further reading

Carp (1980), Cornwallis (1968a,b), Firouz *et al.* (1970), Ramsar Convention Bureau (1993), Scott (1973a, 1976a,b,c, 1980, in press), Summers *et al.* (1987).

078 Harm Lake (Fars)

Unprotected

28°10′N 53°30′E
Area undefined

Site description

A small lake surrounded by cultivated plains, c.35 km south-south-east of Jahrom, in an intermontane basin at c.900 m in the southern Zagros Mountains. No information is available on the habitats, etc. Land ownership is public.

Birds

See box for key species. An important wintering area for *Tadorna ferruginea*, *Oxyura leucocephala* and *Grus grus*.

Other threatened/endemic wildlife

None known to BirdLife International.

Globally threatened species

Oxyura leucocephala Winter visitor (max. 230).

1% or more of population

	Breeding (pairs)	Wintering	Passage
Tadorna ferruginea	—	1,800 [–]	—
Oxyura leucocephala	—	230 [–]	—
Grus grus	—	3,246 [–]	—

Conservation issues

No conservation measures are known to have been proposed and there is no information on threats to the site.

079 **Hormod** (Fars)

also known as Hormud
Protected Area

27°40´N 54°50´E
151,284 ha

■ Site description

The Hormod Protected Area encompasses a region of semi-desertic plains and volcanic hills (peaking at 1,630 m) in the south-east Zagros mountains 50–100 km east of Lar. The reserve is bounded to the north by the Rud-i Shur river and in the south-west by the Lar to Bandar Abbas road. Habitats include: dissected stony outwash plains with scattered trees and bushes of *Ziziphus*, *Berberus*, *Euphorbia* and *Acacia*, and patches of grass *Poa* in the gullies; sandy areas with *Zygophyllum* steppe; small springs with *Phoenix* and *Tamarix* scrub; barren, rocky volcanic hills; and the rocky river bed of the Rud-i Shur, with little surface flow but many deep pools. There is some livestock grazing, also a small area of wheat cultivation on a plain in the centre of the reserve. The village of Hormod lies at the southern extremity of the reserve.

■ Birds

See box for key species. The avifauna is typical of Iran's southern deserts and barren hill ranges. Breeding species not listed below include *Pterocles coronatus*, *Ammomanes cincturus* and *Hirundo obsoleta*. *Chlamydotis undulata* is regular in winter. The Rud-i Shur valley is an important wintering area for *Ciconia nigra*, with up to 15 recorded on this stretch in January. At least 42 species have been recorded in the reserve.

Globally threatened species	
Chlamydotis undulata	Regular winter visitor (max. 28, January 1975).
Species restricted wholly or largely to the Middle East	
Ammoperdix griseogularis	Common resident.
Hypocolius ampelinus	One, January.
Oenanthe finschii	Fairly common winter visitor.
Oenanthe xanthoprymna	Common winter visitor.
Oenanthe picata	Fairly common winter visitor.
Oenanthe monacha	Resident.
Oenanthe alboniger	Fairly common resident.
Phylloscopus neglectus	Fairly common winter visitor.

■ Other threatened/endemic wildlife

Mammals: *Capra hircus aegagrus* (rare) and *Ovis ammon* (rare).

■ Conservation issues

The entire area was designated a Protected Area in 1976. No threats are known.

080 **Bahram-e-Gour** (Fars)

Protected Area

29°00´N 55°00´E
385,000 ha

■ Site description

The site encompasses a region of salt basins, desertic plains and barren rocky hills rising to c.2,750 m in the south-east Zagros Mountains c.90 km south-west of Sirjan. Habitats include bare saline flats subject to flooding during exceptional rains, sandy plains with *Zygophyllum* steppe, dissected stony outwash plains with sparse *Artemisia* steppe, and sparsely vegetated rocky hills. Land ownership is public.

■ Birds

See box for key species. The avifauna is typical of Iran's southern deserts and barren hill ranges. *Podoces pleskei* is a fairly common resident in *Zygophyllum* steppe near Beshneh in the east. Other breeding species include *Aquila chrysaetos*, *Falco pelegrinoides* (probable), *Alectoris chukar*, *Pterocles orientalis*, *Athene noctua*, *Coracias garrulus*, *C. benghalensis*, *Alaemon alaudipes* and *Lanius excubitor*. Rare winter visitors include *Falco columbarius*, *Asio otus* and *A. flammeus*. Passage migrants include *Aquila nipalensis*, *Falco peregrinus* and *Emberiza melanocephala* (abundant). At least 65 species have been recorded in the reserve.

Globally threatened species	
Aquila heliaca	Scarce passage migrant or winter visitor.
Chlamydotis undulata	Present all year and presumably breeds (up to 24 have been recorded in summer, and up to 30 in winter).
Regionally threatened or declining species	
Falco cherrug	Winter visitor or resident.
Species restricted wholly or largely to the Middle East	
Ammoperdix griseogularis	Common resident.
Podoces pleskei	Resident (see text).

Other threatened/endemic wildlife

Mammals: *Canis lupus* (V), *Caracal caracal* (rare), *Panthera pardus* (rare), *Gazella subgutturosa* (rare), *Gazella dorcas fuscifrons* (V), *Capra hircus aegagrus* (rare) and *Ovis ammon* (rare). *Equus hemionus* (V) was present until at least the late 1970s.

Conservation issues

The entire area was designated a Protected Area in 1973. There is no information on any threats.

Further reading

Farnsworth (1992).

081 Khabr-va-Rouchoon (Kirman)

Wildlife Refuge

28°51′N 56°28′E
173,750 ha

Site description

The site lies in the eastern Zagros Mountains c.180 km north of Bandar Abbas and encompasses the somewhat isolated Kuh-i Khabr massif with the twin peaks of Khabr and Rouchoon, and extends from the sandy plains at the base of the foothills (at c.1,800 m) to the highest peaks at 3,862 m. The mountains are extremely rugged, with precipitous cliffs and crags, and volcanic outcrops. Snow fields near the summits linger well into summer. Habitats include: sandy plains and stony outwash plains at low elevations, with steppic vegetation dominated by *Artemisia* and some areas of wheat cultivation; open park-like woodland of *Pistacia*, *Amygdalus*, *Acer* and *Ephedra* on the lower slopes and in the central valley; mixed *Juniperus* and *Amygdalus* woodland on the higher slopes and crags; and montane steppe with low cushion-like vegetation on the highest ridges and summits. Large springs in the central valley support stands of *Populus* and *Juglans* and are used to irrigate orchards and small areas of wheat. There are several small villages.

Birds

See box for key species. The breeding avifauna is typical of the high mountains of south-east Iran, with a good variety of woodland and high montane species, and some desert species at the lowest elevations. *Ciconia nigra* was suspected of breeding in 1975. Other notable breeding species not listed below include *Hirundo obsoleta*, *Anthus similis*, *Turdoides caudatus*, *Parus lugubris*, *Lanius isabellinus*, *Pyrrhocorax graculus*, *Petronia xanthocollis* and *Emberiza buchanani*. At least 92 species have been recorded.

Globally threatened species	
Chlamydotis undulata	Reported to occur on passage and in winter.
Regionally threatened or declining species	
Gypaetus barbatus	Probably resident.
Neophron percnopterus	Observed in May; may breed.
Gyps fulvus	Probably resident (max. 2 birds).
Francolinus francolinus	Fairly common resident.
Species restricted wholly or largely to the Middle East	
Ammoperdix griseogularis	Common resident.
Otus brucei	Resident or summer visitor.
Prunella ocularis	Summer visitor, breeding at 3,200–3,500 m.
Irania gutturalis	Common summer visitor.
Oenanthe xanthoprymna	Fairly common summer visitor at high elevations.
Oenanthe picata	Fairly common breeder.
Oenanthe monacha	Scarce resident at low elevations.
Oenanthe alboniger	Fairly common resident.
Hippolais languida	Fairly common summer visitor.
Sylvia althaea	Fairly common summer visitor.
Phylloscopus neglectus	Common summer visitor at high elevations.
Carpospiza brachydactyla	Fairly common summer visitor.

Other threatened/endemic wildlife

Mammals: *Canis lupus* (V), *Caracal caracal* (rare), *Panthera pardus* (rare), *Gazella dorcas fuscifrons* (V), *Capra hircus aegagrus* (rare) and *Ovis ammon* (rare). *Selenarctos thibetanus* (V) may occur.

Conservation issues

The entire area has been protected as a Wildlife Refuge since 1971. No threats are known.

082 Deh Bakhri Area (Kirman)

Unprotected

28°57′N 57°55′E
Area undefined

Site description

A region of forested valleys and hillsides with rocky peaks rising to 2,500 m near the south-east extremity of the Zagros Mountains. The site lies south of the village of Deh Bakhri, c.45 km west-south-west of Bam, but its boundaries have yet to be determined. Between c.2,000 and 2,400 m, there is an extensive zone of excellent *Pistacia–Amygdalus* woodland, some of the finest in south-east Iran, with a canopy approaching 80% cover in places; conspicuous shrubs and trees include *Pistacia mutica*, *P. kinjuk*, *Acer cinerescens*, *Amygdalus scirparia* and *A. reuteri*. Elsewhere, the dominant plant community is a steppic vegetation with *Artemisia* averaging c.30 cm high. Oleander *Nerium* grows widely in stream beds and along irrigation channels, and there are a few very big *Juniperus* on the higher rocky slopes. Small patches of irrigated cultivation in the valleys comprise vegetable gardens, orchards, wheat fields and *Populus* groves. There is grazing by sheep and goats.

Birds

See box for key species. The area supports a breeding avifauna typical of the montane woodlands of south-east Iran, with a few montane species at higher elevations. Other notable breeding species include *Hieraaetus fasciatus*, *Anthus similis*, *Sylvia hortensis*, *Parus lugubris*, *Lanius isabellinus*, *Petronia xanthocollis*, *Serinus pusillus* and *Emberiza buchanani*. *Phylloscopus trochiloides nitidus* has been recorded on spring passage.

Species restricted wholly or largely to the Middle East	
Ammoperdix griseogularis	Fairly common resident.
Otus brucei	Summer visitor or resident (at least 2 calling, April–May).
Irania gutturalis	Fairly common summer visitor.
Oenanthe xanthoprymna	Common breeder at high elevations; winters on lower slopes.
Oenanthe picata	Fairly common breeder.
Hippolais languida	Recorded in spring; may breed.
Sylvia minula	Recorded on spring passage.
Sylvia althaea	Common summer visitor above 2,200 m.
Phylloscopus neglectus	Common summer visitor above 2,400 m.
Carpospiza brachydactyla	Fairly common summer visitor.

Other threatened/endemic wildlife

None known to BirdLife International.

Conservation issues

There is no legal protection. At lower elevations, the forest understorey has been badly overgrazed.

Further reading

Desfayes and Praz (1978).

083 Mehrouyeh (Bandar Abbas)

Wildlife Refuge

28°06′N 57°25′E
7,468 ha

Site description

Semi-desertic and wooded plains at the base of the eastern Zagros Mountains, c.65 km south-south-west of Jiroft. Much of the centre and south of the reserve is occupied by a broad belt of excellent *Prosopis* woodland with scattered *Tamarix*. This gives way to open *Tamarix* woodland with a grassy understorey in the north, and sandy plains with *Salsola*, *Haloxylon* and scattered *Tamarix* shrubs along the northern boundary. To the south is a boulder-strewn outwash plain and a range of barren, rocky hills. There are several small villages in the reserve, with some irrigated cultivation. The Bandar Abbas to Jiroft road passes along the north-west boundary of the reserve. Cultivated areas (mostly in the south of the reserve) comprise date gardens and irrigated wheat fields.

Birds

See box for key species. The avifauna is characteristic of the coastal lowlands of south-east Iran, with common breeders including *Francolinus pondicerianus*, *Hypocolius ampelinus*, *Hippolais rama*, *Turdoides caudatus*, *Lanius vittatus* and *Petronia xanthocollis*. The reserve lies in the zone of hybridi-

Globally threatened species	
Chlamydotis undulata	Regular winter visitor (18 in 1974).
Regionally threatened or declining species	
Francolinus francolinus	Common resident.
Species restricted wholly or largely to the Middle East	
Dendrocopos assimilis	Resident (see text).
Hypocolius ampelinus	Fairly common summer visitor (max. 12).
Hippolais languida	Recorded on spring passage.

zation between *Dendrocopos syriacus* and *D. assimilis*, with hybrid types predominating. A brief survey in May 1975 recorded 32 species in the reserve.

■ Other threatened/endemic wildlife

Mammals: the very rare Baluchistan race of *Selenarctos thibetanus* (V) is known to have occurred in the 1970s. Other mammals include *Vulpes rueppellii* (K) and *Gazella dorcas fuscifrons* (V).

■ Conservation issues

The entire area has been protected as a Wildlife Refuge since 1971. No threats are known.

084 Kuh-i Bazman (Sistan/Baluchistan)

28°05′N 60°00′E
324,688 ha

also known as Kuh-i Khesr
Unprotected

■ Site description

The site comprises the Kuh-i Bazman massif, a very isolated, volcanic peak (3,489 m) between the great Dasht-i Lut desert to the north and the Hamoun-i Jaz Murian basin to the south. The mountain, situated c.180 km south-south-west of Zahedan, rises as an almost perfect volcanic cone from a vast desertic plain. The sandy desert, stony outwash plains and rocky slopes from the base of the mountain at c.600 m up to c.1,500 m support a sparse shrub-steppic vegetation of *Haloxylon*, *Zygophyllum* and *Artemisia* with scattered bushes of *Prosopis*, *Ziziphus*, *Tamarix*, *Euphorbia* and *Nerium*, especially in the gullies. From 1,500 to c.2,700 m, the dominant cover is *Artemisia* steppe with some *Zygophyllum* and scattered *Pistacia* and *Amygdalus* shrubs. Small patches of *Pistacia–Amygdalus* woodland are present in some of the higher gullies, but above c.2,700 m the rocky scree is almost bare. The area is very remote and sparsely populated, but small springs at the base of the mountain support orchards, date gardens and patches of wheat and livestock are grazed on the lower slopes.

■ Birds

See box for key species. The area supports a breeding avifauna typical of the arid mountain ranges of south-east Iran, with a strong Indo-Malayan influence. *Alectoris chukar* occurs at unusually high densities. Other notable breeding species are *Pterocles coronatus*, *Athene brama*, *Hirundo obsoleta*, *Turdoides caudatus*, *Lanius vittatus*, *Petronia xanthocollis* and *Emberiza buchanani*. At least 61 species have been recorded in the area.

Globally threatened species	
Chlamydotis undulata	Reported to occur on the lower slopes in winter.
Regionally threatened or declining species	
Gyps fulvus	Probably resident (max. 3 birds).
Species restricted wholly or largely to the Middle East	
Ammoperdix griseogularis	Very common resident.
Oenanthe picata	Very common summer visitor.
Oenanthe alboniger	Fairly common resident.
Hippolais languida	Recorded in May (4+); may breed.
Sylvia mystacea	Recorded on autumn passage.
Sylvia minula	Common autumn passage migrant.
Phylloscopus neglectus	Recorded on autumn passage; may breed.
Carpospiza brachydactyla	Common summer visitor.

■ Other threatened/endemic wildlife

Mammals: *Canis lupus* (V), *Caracal caracal* (rare), *Panthera pardus* (rare), *Gazella dorcas fuscifrons* (V), *Capra hircus aegagrus* (rare) and *Ovis ammon* (rare). The rare Baluchistan race of *Selenarctos thibetanus* (V) is believed to have occurred at least until the late 1970s.

■ Conservation issues

A Protected Region covering the whole area was established in 1969. This was reclassified as a Protected Area in the early 1970s, but de-notified in the 1980s. The Department of the Environment is currently investigating the possibility of re-establishing a reserve. There is no information on threats.

■ Further reading

Firouz *et al.* (1970), Scott (1976b).

085 **Hamoun-i Gabi** (Sistan/Baluchistan)

Unprotected

28°07′N 60°50′E
c.60,000 ha

Site description

A large inland drainage basin at c.1,500 m with a central area of bare saltflats surrounded by a very gently sloping sandy plain. The saltflats are flooded at irregular intervals, following exceptionally heavy rains. The small town of Khash lies 30 km north-east of the basin, and the main Zahedan–Chahbahar road passes along its eastern edge. Almost the entire area, except for the central salt waste, consists of a sandy plain with excellent desertic steppe vegetation dominated by *Zygophyllum* and a species of Umbelliferae. There is a narrow belt of stunted *Tamarix* around the edge of the saltflats. Because of its remoteness from any reliable fresh water, the area is not utilized to any great extent by domestic livestock, and the vegetation remains in excellent condition, with *Zygophyllum* bushes over 1.5 m high.

Birds

See box for key species. The site supports the typical avifauna of Iran's central and eastern deserts, and is one of the country's best localities for *Podoces pleskei*. Other notable breeding species are *Ammomanes cincturus*, *Oenanthe deserti* and *Carpospiza brachydactyla*.

Globally threatened species

Chlamydotis undulata	Probably breeds (display observed in 1972) and winters.

Species restricted wholly or largely to the Middle East

Hippolais languida	Common on spring passage.
Sylvia mystacea	Recorded on autumn passage.
Sylvia minula	Recorded on spring passage.
Podoces pleskei	Fairly common resident (see text).
Carpospiza brachydactyla	Very common summer visitor.

Other threatened/endemic wildlife

None known to BirdLife International.

Conservation issues

There is no legal protection and no threats are known.

086 **Kuh-i Taftan** (Sistan/Baluchistan)

Unprotected

28°36′N 61°08′E
c.180,000 ha

Site description

The Kuh-i Taftan massif, a dormant volcano, is the highest mountain range in northern Baluchistan, situated near the Pakistan border, c.100 km south-south-east of Zahedan. The site extends from the deeply dissected stony outwash plains, at c.900 m in the east and 1,800 m in the west, to the summit at over 4,042 m. The dominant plant community at all altitudes is a steppic vegetation with *Artemisia* averaging c.30 cm high. Other associations, such as those formed by the thorny cushions of *Astragalus* or by a species of Umbelliferae, occur locally. No grassy areas exist except for a small patch near the top of the east slope. A belt of very open woodland with *Pistacia* and *Amygdalus* trees occurs at elevations varying from c.2,200 m on the eastern slope to 2,600 m on the west. Here the *Artemisia* association is mixed with taller species, sometimes reaching 1 m high. There are a few scattered *Juniperus* trees on the upper slopes. Snow fields near the summit linger well into summer and feed a number of perennial mountain streams which support small areas of irrigated agriculture and *Populus* groves in the valleys below c.2,000 m. There is some grazing by sheep and goats on the lower slopes. The Zahedan–Chahbahar road passes over the western flank of the mountain.

Birds

See box for key species. The avifauna is typical of the high mountain ranges and *Pistacia–Amygdalus* woodland of south-east Iran. Other notable breeding species include *Anthus similis*, *Hippolais rama*, *S.*

Globally threatened species

Chlamydotis undulata	Recorded in suitable habitat in April, and may breed.

Species restricted wholly or largely to the Middle East

Ammoperdix griseogularis	Common resident.
Prunella ocularis	Common breeder at high elevation.
Oenanthe xanthoprymna	Common breeder at high elevation.
Oenanthe picata	Very common breeder at 2,100–2,400 m.
Oenanthe alboniger	Rather scarce resident on lower slopes.
Sylvia althaea	Common summer visitor to shrubby areas at 2,400–2,700 m (max. 10).
Phylloscopus neglectus	Very common in summer, breeding at 2,400–3,200 m (max. 20).
Carpospiza brachydactyla	Fairly common summer visitor.

hortensis, *Lanius isabellinus*, *L. vittatus*, *Petronia xanthocollis*, *Serinus pusillus* and *Emberiza buchanani*. *Phylloscopus inornatus humei* is a fairly common passage migrant and/or winter visitor.

Other threatened/endemic wildlife
None known to BirdLife International.

Conservation issues
There is no legal protection and no threats are known.

Further reading
Desfayes and Praz (1978).

087 Hamoun-i Sabari and Hamoun-i Hirmand (Sistan/Baluchistan)

Hamoun-i Hirmand also known as Hamoun-i Helmand
Protected Area (193,500 ha)

31°10´N 61°10´E
c.250,000 ha
Ramsar Site (50,000 ha)

Site description
The Sistan basin, at c.470 m on the border between Iran and Afghanistan, contains a complex of freshwater lakes with extensive reedbeds which at times of peak flooding can cover over 200,000 ha. These wetlands are unusual in that the three main lakes, Hamoun-i Puzak (see site 088), Hamoun-i Sabari and Hamoun-i Hirmand, are predominantly freshwater despite lying within an internal drainage basin. The system lies in an extremely arid region, and receives the great bulk of its water from the Hirmand (Helmand), Fara and several other smaller rivers rising in the highlands of central and northern Afghanistan. During long droughts, as in the late 1960s and mid-1980s, these rivers supply sufficient water to flood only the uppermost of the lakes, Hamoun-i Puzak, which lies almost entirely within Afghanistan. However, during years of unusually heavy rain, as in the late 1970s and 1989–1991, the floodwaters sweep through all three lakes and overflow into a vast salt waste to the south-east, flushing the salts out of the system in the process. The Hamoun-i Sabari (31°20´N 61°20´E; up to 101,300 ha), about half of which lies in Iran, receives water from the Fara Rud, which enters in the north-east (in Afghanistan), and overflow from the Hamoun-i Puzak to the east. The Hamoun-i Hirmand (30°50´N 61°15´E; up to 65,600 ha) receives water from the southern (Sistan) branch of the Hirmand and overflow from the Hamoun-i Sabari to the north. During flooding, both lakes support extensive growths of *Phragmites*, *Typha*, *Carex* and *Tamarix*, as well as abundant submerged aquatic vegetation, but very little emergent growth has re-appeared since the drought of the early and mid-1980s. Other habitats include extensive mudflats, saltmarshes and bare saltflats. The wetlands are bordered to the east and south by vast desertic plains, those to the south consisting of extensive bare saltflats and sparsely vegetated sandy plains with dune areas and some *Tamarix* scrub. In the west, the hamouns are bounded by a line of low earth cliffs at the edge of a vast undulating desert plain. An isolated flat-topped volcanic plug (Kuh Khvajeh) rises abruptly out of the marshes to 609 m on the east side of Hamoun-i Hirmand and has a ruined settlement of considerable archaeological interest. Much of the land around Zabol and its many satellite villages east of the hamouns is under irrigated cultivation. Livestock grazing, reed-cutting and fishing occur in the wetlands, and in recent years the lakes have been stocked with grass carp *Ctenopharyngodon idella*. The land is publicly owned.

Birds
See box for key species. The wetlands are extremely important as a staging and wintering area for a wide variety of waterbirds, notably pelicans, herons, dabbling ducks and shorebirds, and in years of high water level are also important for many breeding species. Comprehensive ground and aerial censuses between 1969/70 and 1975/76 indicated that numbers of ducks and geese wintering in the Iranian portion of the Sistan wetlands varied from almost nil in exceptionally dry years (e.g. 1970/71) to over 700,000 in wet years (e.g. 1972/73). There has been a dramatic decline in numbers since then, and this has been attributed to the prolonged drought of the early and mid-1980s and large-scale degradation of the aquatic vegetation. The lush vegetation around the wetlands provides a staging area for large numbers of migratory landbirds, while the surrounding deserts support a typical desert avifauna. Other notable species include *Circus aeruginosus* (over 15 pairs breeding), *Aquila clanga*, *Falco pelegrinoides*, *Porphyrio porphyrio*, *Pterocles senegallus*, *Bubo bubo*, *Caprimulgus aegyptius*, *Melanocorypha bimaculata*, *Ammomanes cincturus*, *Alauda gulgula*, *Motacilla citreola* and *Sylvia nana*. *Phylloscopus trochiloides nitidus* has occurred on autumn passage. At least 170 species have been noted at the site.

Globally threatened species

Pelecanus crispus	Regular winter visitor (max. 88).
Marmaronetta angustirostris	Probably a scarce resident; one recorded in June 1973 (probably breeding). Max. 7 in mid-winter.
Haliaeetus albicilla	Fairly common in winter (max. 13).
Aegypius monachus	Resident (max. 10, at a carcass).
Aquila heliaca	Regular winter visitor (max. 4).
Chlamydotis undulata	Regular winter visitor (max. 6).

1% or more of population

	Breeding (pairs)	Wintering	Passage
Pelecanus onocrotalus	—	1,300	484 (Jun)
Pelecanus crispus	—	75 [88]	—
Casmerodius albus	—	2,150	—
Ardea cinerea	40	208	—
Platalea leucorodia	120	55	—
Anser anser	—	2,600 [2,200]	—
Tadorna ferruginea	—	666 [45]	—
Tadorna tadorna	—	1,600	—
Anas penelope	—	5,000	—
Anas strepera	—	13,000	—
Anas crecca	—	222,500	—
Anas platyrhynchos	—	36,000	—
Anas acuta	—	300,000	—
Anas clypeata	—	10,000	—
Aythya ferina	—	4,110	—
Aythya nyroca	5–10	2	—
Himantopus himantopus	100	—	790 (Apr)
Vanellus leucurus	5–10	—	126 (Mar)
Vanellus vanellus	—	760	—
Limosa limosa	—	300	550 (Jun)
Tringa totanus	—	350	—
Larus ridibundus	—	2,860	—
Larus cachinnans/L. argentatus	—	365	—
Sterna albifrons	40–60	—	—
Chlidonias hybridus	300–400	—	—

Regionally threatened or declining species

Botaurus stellaris	20–30 booming at Hamoun-i Sabari in June 1973.
Aythya nyroca	Breeds and winters (see above).
Falco cherrug	Probably regular winter visitor (max. 1).
Francolinus francolinus	Fairly common resident.

Species restricted wholly or largely to the Middle East

Ammoperdix griseogularis	Several pairs resident on Kuh Khvajeh.
Hypocolius ampelinus	Probably summer visitor; fairly common in cultivated areas around Zabol.
Oenanthe finschii	Fairly common in winter.
Oenanthe xanthoprymna	Up to 4 wintering on Kuh Khvajeh.
Oenanthe picata	Fairly common in winter.
Oenanthe alboniger	Several pairs resident on Kuh Khvajeh.
Sylvia mystacea	Fairly common summer visitor.
Sylvia minula	Fairly common in winter and common passage migrant.
Passer moabiticus	Scarce resident, nesting in *Tamarix* scrub.

■ Other threatened/endemic wildlife

Mammals: *Canis lupus* (V), *Caracal caracal* (rare), *Gazella subgutturosa* (rare) and *Gazella dorcas fuscifrons* (V).

■ Conservation issues

The western half of the Hamoun-i Sabari and Hamoun-i Hirmand and a large area of desert to the west were designated the Hamoun Protected Region in 1967, and the boundaries were revised in 1969 to give an area of 201,062 ha. The reserve was reduced to 193,500 ha in the early 1970s, and upgraded to Wildlife Refuge. It has since been downgraded to Protected Area, and this includes only the main open water areas of the two lakes and their western shorelines, and excludes the important marshes in the east. The Iranian portion of the Hamoun-i Sabari and the northern section of the Hamoun-i Hirmand were designated a Ramsar Site of c.50,000 ha in 1975, c.37,000 ha of which lies within the Hamoun Protected Area. In the mid-1970s, considerable progress was made with a proposal to extend the boundaries of the Hamoun Wildlife Refuge eastwards to incorporate the whole of the Hamoun-i Sabari and Hamoun-i Hirmand wetlands (including Kuh Khvajeh), as well as the Iranian portion of the Hamoun-i Puzak, and indeed the proposed boundaries have appeared on Department of the Environment maps. However, the new boundaries were never formally gazetted, and the Hamoun Protected Area remains in its original form (apart from a minor boundary change in 1969). Extension of the reserve to incorporate the whole of the wetland area (and Ramsar Site) remains highly desirable.

Irrigation schemes on the Hirmand river in both Afghanistan and Iran have reduced the flow into the hamouns, and consequently the wetlands fill completely only in very wet years and are more prone to drying out in summer. Many of the problems of drought in the Sistan basin have been attributed to dam construction and water diversion on the Hirmand in Afghanistan. The Kajaki Dam, built c.40 years ago, was increased in capacity c.20 years ago and undoubtedly caused a considerable reduction in water reaching the hamouns, especially during dry years. However, according to recent reports from FAO in Islamabad, the exceptional floods of early 1991 destroyed the Kajaki Dam and damaged other irrigation systems on the Hirmand in Afghanistan, so for the present there seems to be no problems of water supply in the Hirmand river—though there is apparently a proposal to build a new dam in Afghanistan (the Kamal Khan Dam).

Despite high water levels and prolonged flooding in the Hamoun-i Sabari and much of the Hamoun-i Hirmand each year since 1989, there was still an almost complete absence of emergent aquatic vegetation by early 1992. This contrasts markedly with the early 1970s, when the aquatic vegetation recovered almost immediately after the severe drought of 1970/71 (when all of the wetlands on the Iranian side of the border were completely dry). The reasons for the present lack of vegetation are unclear. It has been argued that the length of the drought in the early

1980s is the principal cause (some parts of the Hamoun-i Hirmand remained dry for six years), and the digging up of tubers for fuel may also have contributed. Another possible cause is the massive stocking of the lakes in recent years with herbivorous fish. The voracious *Ctenopharyngodon idella* (grass carp) was introduced about 1988, and now supports a major fishery. Introductions continue, with some two million fish released into the Hamoun-i Hirmand in 1992. The lack of emergent vegetation is of considerable concern to local people, who depend on the marsh for grazing cattle and water buffalo. Very few livestock are now present around the Hamoun-i Hirmand and Hamoun-i Sabari, most having been moved to the Hamoun-i Puzak marshes on the Afghan border.

An asphalt highway is currently being constructed across the low-lying flats between the north end of the Hamoun-i Hirmand and the south end of the Hamoun-i Sabari, passing through the middle of the Ramsar Site and the Hamoun Protected Area. The road incorporates several bridges, but water flow between the two hamouns has been impeded to some extent, with unknown effects on their hydrology and ecology. A canal recently constructed between the south end of the Hamoun-i Puzak and the Hamoun-i Sabari, to accelerate the flow of water into the Sabari, will also have a major impact on the hydrology.

Further reading

Carp (1980), Firouz *et al.* (1970), IUCN (1991), Ramsar Convention Bureau (1993), Scott (1975a, 1976a,b,c, 1978a,b, 1991, in press), Summers *et al.* (1987).

088 South end of the Hamoun-i Puzak (Sistan/Baluchistan)

31°20′N 61°45′E
14,900 ha
Unprotected
Ramsar Site (10,000 ha)

Site description

The Hamoun-i Puzak is a freshwater lake of c.35,000 ha, with extensive reedbeds, in the Sistan basin. Most of the lake lies in Afghanistan, but c.10,000 ha in the south-west is within Iran. The entire lake is very shallow, probably not exceeding 1 m deep. The Iranian portion consists of a complex of open-water areas with rich submerged vegetation (principally *Ceratophyllum*) and extensive *Typha* and *Phragmites*. The Hamoun-i Puzak receives most of its water from the Parian branch of the Hirmand river which enters the lake in the north and east. The Puzak is the first of the three hamouns to fill during wet periods and probably never dries out completely, even in the severest droughts. In early 1992, following a series of wet years, the wetlands were in excellent condition, with clear water, rich submerged vegetation and extensive reedbeds. The site includes the marshes around Takht-e Edalat (formerly Takht-e Shah) and Mahmoodi. Vast beds of *Phragmites* cover much of the Hamoun-i Puzak, and there is relatively little open water. On the Iranian side of the border, *Typha* now dominates, having replaced *Phragmites* since the 1970s, apparently as a result of heavy grazing. The wetland is fringed with *Tamarix* thickets and the adjacent land is degraded steppe and irrigated cultivation. There are several small villages on the edge of the marsh, and, though primarily dependent on livestock breeding, the local people are increasingly taking advantage of the lake's rich fishery. Reeds are cut and used locally as forage for livestock, for constructing boats, for fabricating wind-breaks and as fuel.

Birds

See boxes for key species. An important wintering area for ducks and *Fulica atra* and a staging area for a wide variety of species, including many shorebirds. In wet years, the wetlands may also be important for breeding waterfowl. *Circus aeruginosus* is present all year, with up to 45 in winter.

Other threatened/endemic wildlife

None known to BirdLife International.

Conservation issues

The site is not legally protected, although personnel of the Department of the Environment try to maintain some control in the region and have a small

Globally threatened species	
Pelecanus crispus	Regular winter visitor (max. 82).
Marmaronetta angustirostris	One in January 1977.
Oxyura leucocephala	A record of 42 in January 1970.
Haliaeetus albicilla	Regular winter visitor (max. 7).
Aegypius monachus	Occasional visitor (max. 5).
Aquila heliaca	Regular winter visitor (max. 5).
Chlamydotis undulata	One in October 1975.

Regionally threatened or declining species	
Botaurus stellaris	At least three booming in June 1973.
Aythya nyroca	Winter visitor (see above).

Species restricted wholly or largely to the Middle East	
Passer moabiticus	Scarce resident, nesting in *Tamarix*.

1% or more of population

	Breeding (pairs)	Wintering	Passage
Pelecanus onocrotalus	—	118 [115]	240 (Nov)
Pelecanus crispus	—	75 [82]	—
Casmerodius albus	—	1,200	—
Ardea cinerea	—	200	—
Phoenicopterus ruber	—	192	—
Anser anser	—	2,450	—
Anas penelope	—	2,500	—
Anas strepera	—	4,500	—
Anas crecca	—	58,000	—
Anas platyrhynchos	—	12,100	—
Anas clypeata	—	18,100	—
Aythya ferina	—	8,000	—
Aythya nyroca	—	30	—
Oxyura leucocephala	—	42	—
Fulica atra	—	37,000	—
Grus grus	—	450	—
Himantopus himantopus	—	50	650 (Oct)
Vanellus vanellus	—	300	—
Limosa limosa	—	5,500	—
Tringa totanus	—	60	300 (Oct)

office at Gorgori near the wetland. The entire wetland area was designated a Ramsar Site in 1975. It has been recommended that the Hamoun Protected Area (see site 087) be extended eastwards to incorporate the Iranian portion of the Hamoun-i Puzak; ideally, the new boundaries should follow those of the Ramsar Site. Irrigation schemes on the Hirmand river, in both Afghanistan and Iran, have caused some reduction in the flow into the Hamoun-i Puzak. Recent developments likely to affect the Hamoun-i Puzak wetlands include the construction of a number of major irrigation canals taking water directly from the Hirmand river, and the construction of a large reservoir (Chahnimeh) in the desert east of Zabol, supplied by a feeder canal from the Parian branch of the Hirmand.

During the last decade, there has been a major change in the dominant vegetation of the reedbeds, with *Typha* having almost completely replaced *Phragmites*. It is supposed that the severe drought of the 1980s and extremely heavy grazing of *Phragmites* are responsible for this. Large numbers of livestock have been brought from the Hamoun-i Hirmand and Hamoun-i Sabari marshes, and the numbers are said to have increased from c.10,000 to 26,000. This intensive grazing and large-scale cutting of reeds for fodder may cause permanent damage to the marsh vegetation.

■ Further reading

Carp (1980), Petocz *et al.* (1976), Ramsar Convention Bureau (1993), Scott (1975a, 1976a,c, 1978b, 1980, 1991, in press), Summers *et al.* (1987).

089 Kharku Island (Persian Gulf Coast)

29°19′N 50°21′E
312 ha

also known as Kharko Island
Unprotected

■ Site description

Kharku is a low, sandy, coral island with fringing reefs in the northern Persian Gulf, c.30 km off the mainland coast and 60 km north-west of Bushire. Surface water is lacking, but there is a freshwater well. Most of the island is covered in dune vegetation of grasses and low shrubs. It is fringed by a sandy beach with low vegetation. There are a few banyan trees near the south end of the island. The island was uninhabited until the late 1970s, when an airforce camp with a substantial landing stage and a number of permanent buildings was built at the north end. The nearby island of Khark (Kharg) is a major oil terminal.

■ Birds

See box for key species. An important site for breeding terns. Surveys in 1974 and 1977 indicated that c.5 pairs of *Sterna bergii*, 600 pairs of *S. bengalensis*, 2,500 pairs of *S. repressa* and 250–300 pairs of *S. anaethetus* were frequenting the island, but breeding success was minimal in both years because of egg-collecting by local fishermen.

1% or more of population

	Breeding (pairs)	Wintering	Passage
Sterna bengalensis	600	—	—
Sterna repressa	2,500	—	—

Species restricted wholly or largely to the Middle East

Sterna repressa Common summer visitor (see above).

■ Other threatened/endemic wildlife

None known to BirdLife International.

■ Conservation issues

Kharku and the nearby much larger island of Khark were designated as a Protected Region in 1960 with a total area of 2,438 ha. The reserve was upgraded to

Wildlife Refuge in the early 1970s, but the Khark portion was de-notified a few years later leaving only Kharku protected in the Kharko Wildlife Refuge (312 ha). The island was visited by egg-collectors every year during the 1970s, and the terns' breeding success was extremely low. There is an ever-present threat of oil pollution from the major terminal on the nearby island of Khark.

Further reading

Argyle (1977a), Firouz *et al.* (1970), Gallagher *et al.* (1984), Scott (1975b, 1976a,b).

090 Hilleh River Delta (Persian Gulf Coast)

Protected Area

29°10′N 50°50′E
42,600 ha

Site description

The site comprises the Hilleh Protected Area, 35 km north-west of Bushire, established to protect the only major freshwater wetland on the south coast of Iran east of Khuzestan—a complex of permanent freshwater lagoons with extensive sedge marshes on seasonally flooded plains near the mouth of the Hilleh (Helleh, Halileh) Rud. The site also includes a large area of the adjacent sparsely vegetated desert plains and extensive intertidal mudflats. Overall there are c.35,600 ha of wetland. Land ownership is public.

Birds

See box for key species. The wetland supports large numbers of breeding, passage and wintering waterfowl of a wide variety of species, and is especially important for wintering *Phalacrocorax carbo*, herons and egrets, *Platalea leucorodia*, *Phoenicopterus ruber*, *Anser anser*, surface-feeding ducks, *Circus aeruginosus*, *Grus grus* (120) and shorebirds. *Pterocles alchata* breeds fairly commonly on the adjacent plains, and *Coracias benghalensis* is a fairly common resident. *Plegadis falcinellus* is an occasional passage migrant or winter visitor. At least 111 species have been recorded in the reserve.

Other threatened/endemic wildlife

None known to BirdLife International.

Conservation issues

The wetlands and a large area of surrounding desert (totalling 42,600 ha) were designated as a Wildlife Refuge in 1977, downgraded to Protected Area in the 1980s (this Protected Area is not listed in IUCN 1991). There are no threats known; the wetland is in a sparsely populated area and remains in excellent condition. It has been proposed that the Hilleh Delta Marshes be designated a Ramsar Site.

Globally threatened species

Pelecanus crispus	Winter visitor in small numbers (max. 10).
Anser erythropus	Winter visitor (21, 1974; 37, 1975).
Marmaronetta angustirostris	Particularly important for both wintering and breeding birds (see below; breeding figures from 1974).
Oxyura leucocephala	Not recorded in 1970s, but 173 in January 1988.
Haliaeetus albicilla	One immature recorded, January.
Aquila heliaca	One record, January.

1% or more of population

	Breeding (pairs)	Wintering	Passage
Phalacrocorax carbo	—	3,060	—
Nycticorax nycticorax	10	—	—
Casmerodius albus	—	351	—
Ardea cinerea	—	582	—
Platalea leucorodia	—	278	—
Anser anser	—	7,859 [950]	—
Tadorna ferruginea	—	750 [26]	—
Tadorna tadorna	—	1,388 [400]	—
Anas penelope	—	8,070 [2,300]	—
Anas strepera	—	1,915 [350]	—
Anas platyrhynchos	—	8,000 [1,260]	—
Anas acuta	—	12,000 [3,750]	—
Anas clypeata	—	3,914 [1,400]	—
Marmaronetta angustirostris	15–20	1,000	—
Oxyura leucocephala	—	173 [–]	—
Recurvirostra avosetta	7	300	—
Limosa limosa	—	250	—
Tringa totanus	—	250	—
Larus cachinnans/L. argentatus	—	2,500 [–]	—
Sterna albifrons	40	—	—

Regionally threatened or declining species

Francolinus francolinus	Fairly common resident.

Further reading

Scott (1975b, 1976a,c, 1978a, 1980).

091 Bushire Bay (Persian Gulf Coast)

Unprotected

29°00′N 50°53′E
27,000 ha

Site description

Extensive intertidal mudflats, sand spits and low muddy and sandy islets on the Persian Gulf coast, extending from the town of Bushire on a rocky peninsula in the south to the southern limits of the Hilleh Rud Delta 20 km to the north-west. The largest island, near the south end of the bay, is mainly bare mudflats with low dunes at the north and south ends, and a small fishing village at the north end. Inland are bare mudflats and sparsely vegetated desertic plains.

Birds

See box for key species. An important wintering area for shorebirds and gulls, especially *Dromas ardeola*, *Larus ichthyaetus* and *Larus cachinnans/L. argentatus*. Small numbers of terns, including *Sterna nilotica*, breed on islets in the bay. *Pterocles alchata* breeds commonly on the adjacent sandy flats.

1% or more of population

	Breeding (pairs)	Wintering	Passage
Larus ichthyaetus	—	250 [55]	—
Larus cachinnans/L. argentatus	—	7,500 [4,000]	—

Species restricted wholly or largely to the Middle East

Dromas ardeola	Winter visitor (max. 84).
Sterna repressa	Summer visitor (50 pairs).
Sterna saundersi	Summer visitor (10–15 pairs).

Other threatened/endemic wildlife

None known to BirdLife International.

Conservation issues

There is no legal protection and no information on threats.

092 Monde River Delta (Persian Gulf Coast)

Protected Area

28°10′N 51°18′E
46,700 ha

Site description

Lying on the Persian Gulf coast 100 km south-south-east of Bushire, the site comprises the Monde Protected Area which encompasses the lower reaches and delta of the Monde river, the adjacent sandy plains and low rocky hills, and a large creek system and extensive area of well-vegetated coastal dunes to the south. In its lower reaches, the river meanders across a broad sandy plain with steppic vegetation and has created a number of long, thin oxbow lakes with some marsh vegetation and *Tamarix* scrub. Other habitats include wide sandy beaches, intertidal mudflats with sand spits and low sandy islets, small areas of irrigated wheat cultivation, and low rocky hills almost unvegetated except in gullies. Wetland covers c.26,870 ha. The region is very sparsely populated and little disturbed. The land is publicly owned.

Birds

See box for key species. An important wintering area for *Phalacrocorax carbo*, *Phoenicopterus ruber*, *Grus grus* (112), shorebirds, gulls and terns. *Pterocles alchata* breeds. Winter visitors include *Tadorna tadorna*, *Buteo rufinus*, *Pandion haliaetus* and *Falco peregrinus*. Uncommon passage migrants include *Bubulcus ibis* and *Buteo buteo*.

Globally threatened species

Pelecanus crispus	Occasional winter visitor (max. 4).
Haliaeetus albicilla	Regular winter visitor (max 3).
Chlamydotis undulata	Regular winter visitor (max. 40, January 1975).

1% or more of population

	Breeding (pairs)	Wintering	Passage
Phalacrocorax carbo	—	3,600	—
Larus ichthyaetus	—	1,000 [250]	—

Regionally threatened or declining species

Falco cherrug	Probably a regular winter visitor in small numbers.

Species restricted wholly or largely to the Middle East

Ammoperdix griseogularis	Resident in adjacent hills.
Hypocolius ampelinus	Recorded in June 1975; probably breeds in the area.
Oenanthe xanthoprymna	Fairly common winter visitor.
Oenanthe picata	Fairly common winter visitor.
Oenanthe alboniger	Fairly common resident.
Sylvia mystacea	Recorded on autumn passage.
Sylvia minula	Recorded on autumn passage.

Other threatened/endemic wildlife

Mammals: *Gazella subgutturosa* (rare).

Conservation issues

The site was designated a Wildlife Refuge in 1976, downgraded to Protected Area in the 1980s. There is no information on threats.

Further reading

Scott (1975b, 1980).

093 Nakhilu, Morghu and Ummal Karam Islands (Persian Gulf Coast)

Unprotected

27°50′N 51°30′E
2,045 ha

Site description

Three small, low-lying Persian Gulf islands a few kilometres offshore c.40 km south-east of the Monde river delta. Nakhilu, the westernmost island and furthest offshore, is c.15 ha, almost circular, and composed mainly of sand with some rocky shores in the south and west. It is fringed with low dunes which encircle a central basin almost completely covered in dense, low scrub. There are two small brackish pools near the south end. Morghu is c.10 km from north to south and c.2 km across (c.2,000 ha), consisting of a broad expanse of bare mudflats with a chain of low vegetated dunes along its south-west margin and round the southern end. The dunes are separated by narrow tidal channels which open up into a chain of shallow lagoons on the mudflats on the landward side of the dunes. Ummal Karam, the easternmost island, lies less than 1 km off the mainland and is c.1.5 km long and 200 m wide (c.30 ha), with rocky shores in the south, sand beaches in the north, and extensive dunes particularly in the west. There are extensive bare mudflats flooded only at the highest tides, and a system of tidal creeks drains a small *Salicornia* marsh near the east end of the island. Elsewhere in the interior, the vegetation consists of low scrub with one small patch of thorn bushes and a few stunted *Phoenix* palms. All three islands are devoid of fresh water and uninhabited.

Birds

See box for key species. A large colony of *Dromas ardeola* was discovered in the dunes on Ummal Karam during a survey of all three islands in June 1975. Other terns nesting on the islands at that time were *Sterna nilotica* (2+ pairs), *S. caspia* (5–10 pairs) and *S. bergii* (at least 40 pairs). There was also a colony of *Egretta gularis* (26 pairs) on Ummal Karam. Small numbers of *Platalea leucorodia* have been recorded on Morghu mudflats in winter.

1% or more of population

	Breeding (pairs)	Wintering	Passage
Dromas ardeola	1,500	—	—
Sterna bengalensis	1,000	—	—
Sterna anaethetus	21,500	—	—

Regionally threatened or declining species

Neophron percnopterus	A single bird in June.

Species restricted wholly or largely to the Middle East

Dromas ardeola	Breeds (see above).
Sterna repressa	Summer visitor (535 pairs).
Sterna saundersi	Summer visitor (9 pairs).

Other threatened/endemic wildlife

Reptiles: Nakhilu and Ummal Karam are important breeding sites for sea-turtles including *Eretmochelys imbricata* (E).

Conservation issues

The islands are unprotected but remote and have few known threats. In June 1975 there was a plague of small mice on Nakhilu Island, which could have compromised breeding success of terns.

Further reading

Gallagher *et al.* (1984), Scott (1975b).

094 Sheedvar Island (Persian Gulf Coast)

also known as Maru Island

Wildlife Refuge

26°48′N 53°24′E
160 ha

Site description

A small island c.2 km due east of the eastern tip of Lavan island and c.9 km off the mainland coast in the central Persian Gulf. The island is relatively flat (maximum elevation c.6 m), composed of a coral conglomerate covered by dunes and sandy soils. There are no springs or surface water. Rainfall is very low, and the summer temperatures frequently exceed 40°C. Along the southern, western and north-west shores the rock is exposed as cliffs up to c.2 m high. In the south-east corner the rocks form a jumbled heap of boulders just above high water. The remainder of the shoreline is a narrow sand beach which widens at the north-east corner to form a sandy promontory. There are two main areas of sparsely vegetated dunes, stretching across the north and south of the island. The flat area across the centre of the island is densely clad with arid steppic vegetation dominated by *Atriplex*, in places forming an impenetrable shrub layer up to 60 cm high. Land ownership is public. The island is uninhabited, although a ruined building indicates former occupation.

Birds

See box for key species. The island supports the largest known colony of terns in Iran, believed to contain c.300,000 pairs of *Sterna repressa* and 3,000–5,000 pairs of *S. anaethetus* in 1972, along with much smaller numbers of *S. bergii* and *S. bengalensis*. However, by 1976 and 1977, *S. repressa* had declined dramatically to only 25,000–50,000 pairs, almost certainly due to massive egg-collecting by the Lavan islanders. There is a colony of *Egretta gularis* (8–12 pairs) as well as 3–4 pairs of *Butorides striatus*.

1% or more of population

	Breeding (pairs)	Wintering	Passage
Sterna repressa	300,000	—	—
Sterna anaethetus	3,000–5,000	—	—

Species restricted wholly or largely to the Middle East

Phalacrocorax nigrogularis	Breeds (50–100 pairs); Iran's only known colony.
Sterna repressa	Abundant summer visitor (see text).

Other threatened/endemic wildlife

Reptiles: the island is a very important nesting site for sea-turtles, mainly *Chelonia mydas* (E), with smaller numbers of *Eretmochelys imbricata* (E) and possibly one other species. A small poisonous snake (Viperidae) is abundant and has given the island its alternative name of Maru (Snake) Island.

Conservation issues

The island was designated a Protected Region in 1971 and later upgraded to Wildlife Refuge. Egg-collecting for human consumption was a major problem in the 1970s. In 1972, it seemed that only the larger terns (*Sterna bergii* and *S. bengalensis*) were being targeted and *Sterna repressa* was scarcely disturbed. However, collecting increased enormously over the next few years, and by 1976 the *S. repressa* colony had been reduced to c.10% of its former size. *S. anaethetus*, which breeds under rocks or beneath the dense vegetation, did not appear to have been affected. There is an ever-present threat of oil pollution from the oil terminal on Lavan Island and from the many oil tankers passing nearby. Various recommendations were made in the 1970s concerning improved protection for the tern colonies, including the erection of notices and the stationing of Department of the Environment personnel on the island during the breeding season. Surveys of the seabird breeding colonies are recommended by the Department of the Environment, in autumn and in winter, in order to assess their current status.

Further reading

Argyle (1976a), Cornwallis (1977), Gallagher *et al.* (1984), Scott (1972b, 1975b).

095 Faror Islands (Persian Gulf Coast)

Protected Area

26°15′N 54°31′E
2,620 ha

Site description

Faror Island is 24 km offshore in the southern Persian Gulf, 45 km south-west of Bandar Lengeh, at 26°17′N 54°30′E. The tiny islet of Bani Faror (26°07′N 54°27′E) is a further 16 km south-southwest of Faror. Faror is c.6.5 km long and 4 km wide, and rises in dark volcanic hills to a peak at 142 m. There is no information on the habitats, etc. Land ownership is public.

Birds

No ornithologist appears to have been to the island since the visit by La Personne in July 1923 when *Sterna repressa* and *S. anaethetus* were breeding in large numbers, and *Puffinus persicus* was offshore in flocks of 20–30. *Pandion haliaetus* was breeding.

Other threatened/endemic wildlife

None known to BirdLife International.

Conservation issues

The islands have recently been designated a Protected Area. No threats are known other than the ever-present one of a major oil spill.

Further reading

Gallagher *et al.* (1984), Ticehurst *et al.* (1925).

096 Khouran Straits (Bandar Abbas)

formerly known as Clarence Straits
Protected Area (85,686 ha)

26°50′N 55°40′E
100,000 ha
Ramsar Site, Biosphere Reserve

Site description

The Khouran Straits lie in the southern Persian Gulf between the region of the Mehran and Kul/Rasul (Gol) deltas and the island of Gheshm (110 km from east to west and up to 20 km across). Within the straits, there are c.100,000 ha of low-lying islands, mangrove, mudflats and creeks which constitute much the largest of the mangrove/mudflat ecosystems in Iran. The mangrove forests reach their greatest development around a group of low-lying muddy islands in a large bay on the north shore of Gheshm Island, but there are also significant stands along the outer margins of the Mehran delta. In these areas and in the Kul/Rasul delta to the east, there are vast intertidal mudflats. Elsewhere along the Gheshm and mainland coasts, the shoreline consists of wide sandy beaches and sandflats. The mangrove forests are monospecific stands of *Avicennia marina*, here at the north-west limit of its distribution. Red and brown algae (Rhodophyceae, Phaeophyceae) are the other dominant vegetation in the shallow coastal waters. The adjacent coastal plains are mainly barren sandflats with scattered *Acacia*, *Prosopis* and other thorn trees. A few small settlements are scattered along the shore, with some small date gardens. Fishing (commercial and subsistence) is an important activity. Land ownership is public.

Birds

See box for key species. The mangrove supports substantial breeding populations of egrets and herons as well as some shorebirds (notably *Dromas ardeola* and *Burhinus recurvirostris*) and terns. *Ardea goliath* has its only confirmed breeding site in Iran here, and there is a small colony of *Casmerodius albus modestus* (South Asian race), which probably reaches its western limit in this region. The site holds Iran's largest colony of *Ardeola grayii* (at least 30 pairs), and *Butorides striatus* may breed. The extensive mudflats are an extremely important staging and wintering area for shorebirds and gulls, along with smaller numbers of *Pelecanus crispus*, *Platalea leucorodia*, *Phoenicopterus ruber* and many other species. The adjacent desertic plains with scattered thorn trees and date gardens support a typical Baluchi avifauna with several primarily Indo-Malayan species. At least 93 species have been recorded in the reserve.

Other threatened/endemic wildlife

None known to BirdLife International.

Globally threatened species

Pelecanus crispus	Fairly common in winter (generally c.100 but 210 in January 1975).
Haliaeetus albicilla	One record of an immature in January.

1% or more of population

	Breeding (pairs)	Wintering	Passage
Pelecanus crispus	—	210	—
Egretta gularis	50+	458	—
Casmerodius albus	25–30	445	—
Ardea cinerea	—	400	—
Ardea goliath	1+	7	—
Platalea leucorodia	—	442	—
Haematopus ostralegus	—	331	—
Dromas ardeola	20+	940	—
Charadrius leschenaultii	—	200	—
Limosa lapponica	—	2,410	—
Numenius arquata	—	5,850	—
Tringa totanus	—	3,000+	—
Tringa cinerea	—	1,000+	—
Larus ridibundus	—	20,000	—
Larus cachinnans/L. argentatus	—	3,000	—
Sterna nilotica	10–20	355	—

Regionally threatened or declining species

Ardea goliath	Scarce resident (max. 7 birds).
Neophron percnopterus	Up to 15 present in summer; presumably breeds locally. Fairly common in winter (max. 35).

Species restricted wholly or largely to the Middle East

Burhinus recurvirostris	Resident (several pairs).
Dromas ardeola	Breeds and winters (see above).
Oenanthe picata	Common winter visitor.
Sylvia mystacea	Recorded on autumn passage.
Sylvia minula	Fairly common winter visitor.

Conservation issues

The main area of mangrove and mudflat (82,360 ha) was designated a Protected Region in 1972. This was later increased to 85,686 ha and upgraded to National Park (Hara National Park), but downgraded to Protected Area in the 1980s. The entire area of mangrove, mudflats and creeks in the Khouran Straits (100,000 ha) was designated a Ramsar Site in 1975, and the reserve (85,686 ha) was designated a Biosphere Reserve in 1976. Some illegal cutting of mangrove for fuel and grazing by domestic livestock has been reported. The easternmost part of the site is not included within any legally protected area, and has been subject to logging of mangrove for charcoal production. A part of the area is at risk from the proposed development of a free port and tourist facilities on Gheshm. There may be some pollution from the nearby port of Bandar Abbas, and oil pollution is possible.

Further reading

Argyle (1975, 1976c, 1977b), Carp (1980), Gallagher *et al.* (1984), Ramsar Convention Bureau (1993), Scott (1975b, 1976a,c, 1978a, in press), Summers *et al.* (1987).

097 **Geno** (Bandar Abbas)

Protected Area

27°25′N 56°11′E
27,500 ha
Biosphere Reserve

Site description

The Geno Protected Area encompasses Kuh-i Geno (2,372 m), an isolated mountain on the coastal plain of the Persian Gulf c.25 km north-north-west of Bandar Abbas. A road winds up the south side of the mountain to a radio and weather station at the rocky summit. Principal habitats are: stony outwash plains with little vegetation (e.g. *Acacia flava*) except in gullies (150–500 m); rugged boulder-strewn slopes with patches of open *Amygdalus* and *Pistacia* woodland (500–2,000 m); and cliffs, crags and summit ridges with mixed *Juniperus*, *Amygdalus* and *Pistacia* woodland and a ground cover of *Artemisia* shrubs (above c.2,000 m). On the lower slopes there are *Populus* groves, orchards and irrigated fields around settlements by perennial springs.

Birds

See box for key species. The avifauna is typical of the arid mountains of south-east Iran, with a number of Indo-Malayan species. Other notable breeding species are *Francolinus pondicerianus*, *Hirundo obsoleta*, *Anthus similis*, *Sylvia hortensis*, *Turdoides caudatus*, *Lanius isabellinus* and *L. vittatus*. *Phoenicurus erythronotus* is a common winter visitor. At least 42 species have been recorded in the reserve.

Regionally threatened or declining species	
Gypaetus barbatus	Probably resident.
Gyps fulvus	Resident or occasional visitor (max. 2).
Species restricted wholly or largely to the Middle East	
Ammoperdix griseogularis	Common resident.
Prunella ocularis	Fairly common winter visitor.
Oenanthe xanthoprymna	Fairly common winter visitor.
Oenanthe picata	Fairly common winter visitor.
Oenanthe alboniger	Fairly common resident.
Hippolais languida	One record in June; may breed.
Sylvia mystacea	Recorded on autumn passage.
Sylvia minula	Fairly common winter visitor.
Phylloscopus neglectus	Fairly common winter visitor.
Carpospiza brachydactyla	Recorded on passage.

Other threatened/endemic wildlife

Mammals: *Capra hircus aegagrus* (rare) and *Ovis ammon* (rare).

Conservation issues

The entire mountain (81,230 ha) was established as Geno National Park in 1972. A large portion was excised in the 1980s, and the remaining 27,500 ha downgraded to Protected Area. Some 49,000 ha of the original National Park were designated a Biosphere Reserve in 1976. There is no information on any threats.

Further reading

Argyle (1977b).

098 **Hormoz Island** (Bandar Abbas)

Unprotected

27°03′N 56°28′E
c.4,000 ha

Site description

The island, c.7 km offshore in the Straits of Hormoz, is roughly circular and c.7 km across. Most of the shore is sand beach, but there are some rocky shores and low cliffs, and a small tidal creek system with saltmarsh vegetation just east of the main harbour. Inland are sandy plains with little vegetation other than a few scattered thorn trees, and bare volcanic hills rising to 235 m. There is one substantial fishing village and a few small settlements with small patches of irrigated cultivation and date gardens.

Birds

See boxes for key species. No proper surveys have been carried out. The island is probably an important staging and/or wintering area for shorebirds, gulls and terns, and figures are given below for a brief survey in May 1974.

1% or more of population

	Breeding (pairs)	Wintering	Passage
Larus hemprichii	—	—	510
Larus cachinnans/L. argentatus	—	—	400
Sterna saundersi	breeds	—	56

Species restricted wholly or largely to the Middle East

Burhinus recurvirostris	Resident (at least one pair).
Larus hemprichii	Recorded in May—presumably a non-breeding visitor.
Sterna saundersi	Breeds and occurs on passage.
Oenanthe alboniger	Fairly common resident in hills.
Carpospiza brachydactyla	Common spring passage migrant.

Regionally threatened or declining species

Neophron percnopterus	Recorded in May (3 birds); may breed.

Other threatened/endemic wildlife
None known to BirdLife International.

Conservation issues
There is no legal protection and no information on threats.

Further reading
Gallagher *et al.* (1984), Scott (1975b).

099 Rud-i-Shur, Rud-i-Shirin and Rud-i-Minab Deltas (Hormozgan)

Unprotected

27°05′N 56°45′E
11,800 ha
Ramsar Site

Site description
A 55 km stretch of coast along the Straits of Hormoz, c.10–70 km east of Bandar Abbas, incorporating three river deltas. The site includes extensive inter-tidal mudflats (over 1 km wide), significant stands of mangrove at the river mouths and along adjacent creeks, long sand beaches, low sandbars and sand spits, and two large shallow bays, Khor Tiab and Khor Kolahy, near the mouth of the Rud-i Minab in the east. The rivers flow only after erratic rainfall in the interior, usually in winter. The waters of the Rud-i-Shirin and Rud-i-Minab are fresh, but the Rud-i-Shur is somewhat brackish. Mangrove *Avicennia marina* occurs at the river mouths, and fringes the tidal creeks. The adjacent arid plain supports a sparse woodland of *Acacia*, *Prosopis*, *Ziziphus* and *Tamarix* with large areas of bare, sandy flats. Land ownership is public. There are a few small settlements, generally with date gardens. Fishing is important.

Birds
See box for key species. An extremely important wintering area for shorebirds and gulls, notably *Haematopus ostralegus*, *Limosa lapponica*, *Numenius arquata* and *Larus cachinnans/L. argentatus*. The site may also be important for breeding herons and egrets including *Ardea goliath* and *Ardeola grayii*. The adjacent plains and woodland have a typical Baluchi avifauna with several Indo-Malayan species at or near their western limit, notably *Gyps bengalensis*, *Francolinus pondicerianus*, *Athene brama*, *Dendrocopos assimilis* and *Acridotheres tristis*. Common winter visitors include *Phylloscopus inornatus humei*.

Other threatened/endemic wildlife
None known to BirdLife International.

Globally threatened species

Pelecanus crispus	Regular winter visitor (max. 19).
Haliaeetus albicilla	One record of 2 immatures, January.

1% or more of population

	Breeding (pairs)	Wintering	Passage
Casmerodius albus	—	250 [—]	—
Ardea cinerea	—	140 [20]	—
Ardea goliath	—	1	—
Haematopus ostralegus	—	3,500	—
Limosa lapponica	—	5,000	—
Numenius arquata	—	1,500	—
Larus cachinnans/L. argentatus	—	3,000 [—]	—

Regionally threatened or declining species

Ardea goliath	Recorded in winter in mangrove (max. 1).
Neophron percnopterus	Winter visitor (max. 3).
Gyps fulvus	Occasional visitor (max. 6).

Species restricted wholly or largely to the Middle East

Dendrocopos assimilis	Scarce resident in woodland.
Oenanthe xanthoprymna	Fairly common winter visitor.
Oenanthe picata	Common winter visitor.
Sylvia mystacea	Recorded on autumn passage (max. 10).
Sylvia minula	Common winter visitor.
Phylloscopus neglectus	Fairly common winter visitor.

Conservation issues
There is no legal protection, though the area lies within a Ramsar Site (20,000 ha) designated in 1975. There is some cutting of mangrove for fuel and grazing by domestic livestock. There may be some pollution from the nearby port of Bandar Abbas, and oil pollution is a constant threat.

Further reading
Carp (1980), Ramsar Convention Bureau (1993), Scott (1975b, 1976a,c), Summers *et al.* (1987).

100 Rud-i-Gaz and Rud-i-Hara Deltas (Sistan/Baluchistan)

Unprotected

26°40′N 56°50′E
15,000 ha
Ramsar Site

Site description

The site covers c.40 km of shore on the Straits of Hormoz, 120 km south-east of Bandar Abbas: an extensive complex of tidal creeks, mudflats, mangrove swamps, sandbanks and low muddy offshore islands and sandbars at the mouths of the Rud-i-Gaz (26°30′N 57°00′E) and the Rud-i-Hara (26°50′N 56°40′E). The rivers flow only after erratic rainfall in the interior (usually in winter). Extensive stands of mangrove *Avicennia marina* occur at the mouths of the rivers, along tidal creeks and as a broad fringe along the landward side of coastal sandbars. The adjacent arid plain supports a sparse woodland of *Acacia*, *Prosopis*, *Ziziphus* and *Tamarix* with large areas of bare sandy flats. Land ownership is public. The area is remote, with only a few tiny fishing villages nearby.

Birds

See box for key species. An extremely important wintering area for shorebirds, notably *Haematopus ostralegus*, *Limosa lapponica*, *Numenius arquata* and *Tringa totanus*, along with smaller numbers of *Platalea leucorodia* and *Dromas ardeola*. The site may also be important for breeding herons and egrets including *Ardea goliath* and *Ardeola grayii*. The adjacent sandy plains and thorn woodland support a typical Baluchi avifauna including *Dendrocopos assimilis* and *Calandrella raytal*.

Other threatened/endemic wildlife

None known to BirdLife International.

Globally threatened species

Pelecanus crispus	Fairly common winter visitor.
Haliaeetus albicilla	Regular winter visitor (max. 6).

1% or more of population

	Breeding (pairs)	Wintering	Passage
Pelecanus crispus	—	68	—
Ardea goliath	—	2	—
Haematopus ostralegus	—	2,000+	—
Limosa lapponica	—	11,500	—
Numenius arquata	—	5,000	—
Tringa totanus	—	2,000	—

Regionally threatened or declining species

Ardea goliath	Recorded in mangrove in winter (max. 2); may be resident.
Gyps fulvus	Occasional visitor (max. 7).

Species restricted wholly or largely to the Middle East

Burhinus recurvirostris	At least one pair; probably resident.
Dromas ardeola	Winter visitor.
Dendrocopos assimilis	Fairly common resident in woodland.
Sylvia minula	Common winter visitor.

Conservation issues

There is no legal protection, though the area was designated a Ramsar Site in 1975. No threats are known.

Further reading

Carp (1980), Ramsar Convention Bureau (1993), Scott (1975b, 1976a,c), Summers *et al.* (1987).

101 Khor Jask (Sistan/Baluchistan)

Unprotected

25°40′N 57°40′E
11,500 ha

Site description

A large tidal creek (Khor Jask) and adjacent mudflats, beaches, dunes and sparsely vegetated sandy plains on the coast of south-west Iranian Baluchistan, a few kilometres north of the fishing port of Jask. The creek extends several kilometres inland and contains a particularly fine stand (c.100 ha) of mangrove *Avicennia marina* at its far end. Land ownership is public.

Birds

See boxes for key species. An important staging and wintering area for a wide variety of shorebirds, gulls and terns. *Ardeola grayii* and *Burhinus recurvirostris* are probably resident, and *Ardea goliath* has been recorded. *Pterocles exustus* and *Calandrella raytal* occur on the plains.

1% or more of population

	Breeding (pairs)	Wintering	Passage
Pelecanus crispus	—	42	—
Ardea goliath	—	1	—
Numenius arquata	—	250	—
Larus cachinnans/L. argentatus	—	1,200 [—]	350 (Oct)
Sterna hirundo	—	—	880 (Oct)

Globally threatened species

Pelecanus crispus	Regular winter visitor.
Haliaeetus albicilla	Regular winter visitor (max. 3).

Regionally threatened or declining species

Ardea goliath	Probably a non-breeding visitor; singles recorded in mangrove, October and January.

Species restricted wholly or largely to the Middle East

Burhinus recurvirostris	Resident (at least one pair).
Oenanthe xanthoprymna	Winter visitor (max. 2).
Oenanthe picata	Fairly common winter visitor.
Sylvia minula	Fairly common winter visitor.

Other threatened/endemic wildlife
None known to BirdLife International.

Conservation issues
There is no legal protection and no information on threats.

Further reading
Scott (1976a).

102 Rud-i-Jagin and Rud-i-Gabrik Deltas (Sistan/Baluchistan)
Unprotected

25°35′N 58°20′E
c.14,000 ha

Site description
The site covers c.35 km of Arabian Sea coast 45–80 km east of Jask, comprising an extensive complex of tidal creeks, mudflats, mangrove, sandbanks and low muddy offshore islands and sandbars. The rivers flow only after erratic rainfall in the interior, usually in winter. Extensive stands of mangrove *Avicennia marina* occur at the river mouths and along tidal creeks. The adjacent arid plain supports a relatively dense woodland of *Acacia*, *Prosopis* and *Ziziphus* interspersed with bare sandflats. Stands of tall *Tamarix* forest line the river banks. The area is remote, with only a few tiny fishing villages nearby.

Birds
See box for key species. An important wintering area for shorebirds, gulls and terns, with smaller numbers of *Pelecanus crispus*, *Platalea leucorodia* and *Phoenicopterus ruber*. *Ardeola grayii* is probably resident in the mangrove. The sandy plains and woodland support a typical Baluchi avifauna including *Francolinus pondicerianus* and *Dendrocopos assimilis*. *Accipiter badius*, *Streptopelia orientalis*, *Saxicola caprata* and *Sylvia nana* have been recorded in autumn.

Globally threatened species

Pelecanus crispus	Regular winter visitor.
Haliaeetus albicilla	Regular winter visitor (max. 4).
Chlamydotis undulata	Possibly a winter visitor; one in March 1971.

1% or more of population

	Breeding (pairs)	Wintering	Passage
Pelecanus crispus	—	48	—
Numenius arquata	—	350	—

Regionally threatened or declining species

Neophron percnopterus	Passage migrant/winter visitor (max. 6).
Gyps fulvus	Occasional visitor (max. 9).

Species restricted wholly or largely to the Middle East

Dendrocopos assimilis	Fairly common resident in woodlands.
Oenanthe picata	Common winter visitor.
Sylvia mystacea	One record, October.
Sylvia minula	Common passage migrant/winter visitor.

Other threatened/endemic wildlife
None known to BirdLife International.

Conservation issues
There is no legal protection and no threats are known.

Further reading
Scott (1976a).

103 Pozam–Maytab Coast (Sistan/Baluchistan)
Unprotected

25°20′N 60°20′E
9,000 ha

Site description
Long sandy beaches, tidal creeks and mudflats, between Pozam and Maytab in southern Iranian Baluchistan, 150 km west of Chahbahar. Land ownership is public.

Birds

See box for key species. An important wintering area for *Pelecanus crispus*, shorebirds and gulls, including *Larus ichthyaetus* and *Larus cachinnans/L. argentatus*. Other common winter visitors are *Phoenicopterus ruber* and *Pandion haliaetus*. *Egretta gularis* is a common resident and may breed in the area.

Other threatened/endemic wildlife

None known to BirdLife International.

Conservation issues

There is no legal protection and no information on threats.

Globally threatened species

Pelecanus crispus	Regular winter visitor in small numbers (max. 20).
Haliaeetus albicilla	Probably regular in winter (max. 2).

1% or more of population

	Breeding (pairs)	Wintering	Passage
Ardea cinerea	—	151 [—]	—
Larus cachinnans/L. argentatus	—	2,500 [—]	—

Species restricted wholly or largely to the Middle East

Larus hemprichii	Occurs; probably a fairly common non-breeding visitor.

104 Chahbahar Bay and Khor Konarak (Sistan/Baluchistan)

25°25′N 60°30′E
33,500 ha

Unprotected

Site description

Chahbahar Bay, on the coast of south-east Iranian Baluchistan, is an almost circular bay c.22 km across and 18 km from north to south, with an entrance 14 km wide between rocky headlands. The shore is a sand beach backed by a broad belt of low dunes. There is a large creek with extensive intertidal mudflats near the small fishing village of Konarak on the west side of the bay (Khor Konarak, 25°20′N 60°20′E). The much larger harbour town of Chahbahar is situated in the lee of the rocky headland at the east side. The sand beaches and tidal mudflats lack vegetation other than algae. The coastal dunes support typical vegetation, while the inland plain supports an open woodland of *Acacia*, *Prosopis*, *Ziziphus* and *Tamarix*, with large areas of bare sandflats. Land ownership is public.

Birds

See box for key species. The site has little importance for breeding waterbirds, although *Burhinus recurvirostris* is resident. A small flock of *Pelecanus crispus* winters, along with reasonable numbers of shorebirds and large numbers of gulls and terns, notably *Larus genei*, *L. cachinnans/L. argentatus* and *Sterna sandvicensis*. Other wintering waterfowl include many *Podiceps cristatus*. The dunes, open thorn woodland and rocky hills around the bay support a typical Baluchi avifauna including *Francolinus pondicerianus*, *Athene brama*, *Calandrella raytal*, *Hirundo obsoleta* and *Oenanthe alboniger*.

Globally threatened species

Pelecanus crispus	Regular winter visitor.
Haliaeetus albicilla	Regular winter visitor (max. 2).
Larus leucophthalmus	Vagrant: one adult, January 1975.

1% or more of population

	Breeding (pairs)	Wintering	Passage
Pelecanus crispus	—	48	—
Charadrius leschenaultii	—	70	150 (Nov)
Larus cachinnans/L. argentatus	—	3,500	—
Sterna sandvicensis	—	500	—

Regionally threatened or declining species

Neophron percnopterus	Winter visitor (max. 2).
Gyps fulvus	Occasional visitor (max. 6).

Species restricted wholly or largely to the Middle East

Ammoperdix griseogularis	Fairly common resident in adjacent hills.
Burhinus recurvirostris	Resident (at least 2 pairs).
Oenanthe xanthoprymna	Fairly common winter visitor.
Oenanthe picata	Fairly common winter visitor.
Oenanthe alboniger	Fairly common resident in adjacent hills.
Sylvia mystacea	Singles in January, March and October.
Sylvia minula	Common winter visitor (max. 9).

Other threatened/endemic wildlife

None known to BirdLife International.

Conservation issues

There is no legal protection. The principal threat is pollution from the busy harbour town of Chahbahar.

Further reading

Scott (1975b).

105 Lower Sarbaz River and Khor Govater (Sistan/Baluchistan) 25°25′N 61°15′E

Protected Area — 382,430 ha

Site description

The site comprises the Bahu Kalat Protected Area in the extreme south-east corner of Iranian Baluchistan along the Pakistan border. The reserve comprises arid mountain and semi-arid desert habitats straddling the Sarbaz river (25°40′N 61°00′E). Erratic winter rains in the interior of Baluchistan produce some surface flow in most years and occasional torrential floods, but for much of the year the river holds only a series of deep, stagnant pools; there is up to 2,900 ha of 'wetland' habitat. In the south, the reserve includes a stretch of Arabian Sea coast, with high cliffs, long sand beaches and dunes, as well as the estuarine system of the Sarbaz river in Govatar Bay (Khor Govater, 25°10′N 61°30′E, 11,560 ha). A large stand of mangrove *Avicennia marina* at the river mouth has some of the largest mangrove trees in the country. There are extensive intertidal mudflats, and a tiny rocky islet offshore provides a roost for large numbers of seabirds. The climate is extremely hot all year, with very low winter rainfall; the south-west monsoon keeps humidity high in summer but heavy rain is unusual. The fauna and flora are characteristically Indo-Malayan. A high water-table in the main valley supports open woodland of *Acacia*, *Prosopis*, *Ziziphus*, *Tamarix* and *Phoenix*, with stands of oleander *Nerium* and fan-palms along the river bed. Away from the river the vegetation is extremely sparse, and much of the reserve is almost devoid of plant life except after the very infrequent rains. There is a small fishing village near the river mouth and some livestock grazing in the reserve, but the area is remote and very sparsely populated.

Birds

See box for key species. The avifauna of the lower Sarbaz valley is typical of the lowlands of Baluchistan, and has much stronger affinities with the Indo-Malayan fauna than with the Palearctic. Characteristic species include *Butastur teesa*, *Aquila rapax*, *Gyps bengalensis*, *Francolinus pondicerianus*, *Turnix sylvatica*, *Pterocles exustus*, *Athene brama*, *Caprimulgus mahrattensis*, *Dendrocopos assimilis*, *Calandrella raytal*, *Saxicola caprata*, *Lanius vittatus*, *Acridotheres tristis*, *Passer pyrrhonotus* and *Lonchura malabarica*; all except *G. bengalensis* are known or thought to breed. Other notable breeding species include *Hieraaetus fasciatus*, *Pterocles senegallus*, *P. lichtensteinii*, *Anthus similis*, *Hippolais rama*, and *Petronia xanthocollis*. Winter visitors include *Accipiter badius*, *Phoenicurus erythronotus*, *Sylvia nana* and *Phylloscopus inornatus humei*. The habitats at the mouth of the Sarbaz river are an important wintering area for *Phalacrocorax carbo*, *Pelecanus crispus*, *Platalea leucorodia* and a variety of shorebirds and gulls. Large numbers of terns occur on passage, including many *Sterna bergii*. Breeding birds on the coast include *Ardeola grayii*, *Burhinus recurvirostris*, *Dromas ardeola* and *Sterna saundersi*. *Pandion haliaetus* occurs in winter, and is thought to breed. At least 204 species have been recorded in the reserve.

Globally threatened species

Pelecanus crispus	Regular winter visitor (max. 52 in 1970s, 112 in recent years).
Haliaeetus albicilla	One record, January.
Aegypius monachus	Resident (max. 9).
Aquila heliaca	Winter visitor (two winter records).
Chlamydotis undulata	Regular winter visitor to plains of Dasht-i Ari (max. 11, March 1971).

1% or more of population

	Breeding (pairs)	Wintering	Passage
Phalacrocorax carbo	—	3,500	—
Pelecanus crispus	—	112 [52]	—
Vanellus indicus	—	63	—
Limosa lapponica	—	1,000	—
Larus hemprichii	—	—	500 (Apr)
Larus ichthyaetus	—	30	300 (Mar)
Larus genei	—	1,000	1,500 (Mar)
Larus cachinnans/L. argentatus	—	1,000+	—
Sterna caspia	—	—	110 (Apr)
Sterna bergii	—	—	2,000 (Apr)
Sterna sandvicensis	—	—	675 (Apr)

Regionally threatened or declining species

Neophron percnopterus	Present all year and fairly common; breeds; max. 27 in winter.
Gyps fulvus	Probably resident in area; many records (max. 6).
Falco cherrug	One record in January.
Francolinus francolinus	Fairly common resident.

Species restricted wholly or largely to the Middle East

Ammoperdix griseogularis	Common resident.
Burhinus recurvirostris	Resident (at least 2 pairs) near Govater.
Dromas ardeola	Breeds (at least 2 pairs).
Sterna saundersi	Breeds.
Dendrocopos assimilis	Common resident in woodland.
Oenanthe xanthoprymna	Fairly common winter visitor.
Oenanthe picata	Common winter visitor.
Oenanthe monacha	Not-uncommon resident.
Oenanthe alboniger	Fairly common resident.
Hippolais languida	Fairly common spring passage migrant.
Sylvia mystacea	Passage migrant; one October record.
Sylvia minula	Very common winter visitor.
Phylloscopus neglectus	Very common winter visitor.

Other threatened/endemic wildlife

Reptiles: the Sarbaz river has a thriving population of *Crocodylus palustris* (V), at its western limit.

Mammals: *Caracal caracal* (rare), *Lynx lynx*, *Gazella bennetti* (V), *Capra hircus aegagrus* (rare) and *Ovis ammon* (rare), and the rare Baluchistan race of *Selenarctos thibetanus* (V) is believed to occur.

■ Conservation issues

The entire area was designated the Bahu Kalat Protected Area in 1971, later re-named the Gandu (Gando) Protected Area. No threats are known.

■ Further reading

Firouz (1974), Scott (1975b, 1976a).

MAIN REFERENCES

ADHAMI, A. (1972a) Great Bustard studies in western Iran. Internal report. Department of the Environment, Tehran, Iran.

ADHAMI, A. (1972b) Great Bustard *Otis tarda* survey in Eastern Iran, Dey 1351 (December 1972). Internal report. Department of the Environment, Tehran, Iran.

ARGYLE, F. B. (1975) Waterfowl ringing at Hara N.P. (Persian Gulf) and Lake Parishan (Fars); Khordad 1354 (June 1975). Internal report. Department of the Environment, Tehran, Iran.

ARGYLE, F. B. (1976a) Report on the field trip to Lavan and Sheedvar Islands: 1–5 Tir 2535 (22–26 June 1976). Internal report. Department of the Environment, Tehran, Iran.

ARGYLE, F. B. (1976b) Bird-ringing in the Lar Valley: 25/26 Shahrivar 2535, 16/17 September 1976. Internal report. Department of the Environment, Tehran, Iran.

ARGYLE, F. B. (1976c) Hara N.P., Nakhilu Islands and Lake Parishan, 11–22 Tir 2535 (2–13 July 1976). Internal report. Department of the Environment, Tehran, Iran.

ARGYLE, F. B. (1977a) Khark and Kharku W.R., Persian Gulf, avifaunal survey and general survey, 12–14 Tir 2536, 3–5 July 1977. Internal report. Department of the Environment, Tehran, Iran.

ARGYLE, F. B. (1977b) Bird-ringing and avifaunal survey at Hara N.P. and Geno N.P., Coastal Province, 1–6 Tir 2536, 22–27 June 1977. Internal report. Department of the Environment, Tehran, Iran.

ARGYLE, F. B. (1977c) Caucasian Black Grouse (*Lyrurus mlokosiewiczi*) survey, 29 Fravardine–8 Ordibehesht 2536, 18–28 April 1977. Internal report. Department of the Environment, Tehran, Iran.

ASHTIANI, M. A. (1974) An avifaunal survey in Mohammad Reza Shah National Park with particular reference to the Black Woodpecker *Dryocopus martius*. Internal report. Department of the Environment, Tehran, Iran.

BAHERI, A. (1971) Further investigations into the status and distribution of the Great Bustard *Otis tarda* in western Iran. Internal report. Department of the Environment, Tehran, Iran.

CARP, E. (1980) *A directory of western Palaearctic wetlands*. Nairobi: United Nations Environment Programme/Gland (Switzerland): International Union for Conservation of Nature and Natural Resources.

CORNWALLIS, L. (1968a) Some notes on the wetlands of the Niriz Basin in S.W. Iran. Proc. Pp. 152–164 in *Technical Meeting on Wetland Conservation, Ankara–Bursa–-Istanbul, 9 to 16 October 1967*. Gland, Switzerland: International Union for Conservation of Nature and Natural Resources (IUCN Publ. New Series 12).

CORNWALLIS, L. (1968b) A report on the wetlands and waterfowl of Fars, S.W. Iran. Unpublished report.

CORNWALLIS, L. (1976) The impact of the Mahabad Project on Lake Rezaiyeh and its southern satellite wetlands together with proposals for the conservation of the latter. Internal report. Department of the Environment, Tehran, Iran.

CORNWALLIS, L. (1977) Surveys of the birds of Sheedvar and Lavan Islands, Persian Gulf, in 2536 (1977). Internal report. Department of the Environment, Tehran, Iran.

CORNWALLIS, L. (1983) A review of the bustard situation in Iran. Pp. 81–88 in P. A. Goriup and H. Vardhan, eds. *Bustards in decline. Proc. International Symposium on Bustards, Jaipur, India, 1980*. Dehra Dun, India: Natraj Publishers.

DESFAYES, M. AND PRAZ, J. C. (1978) Notes on habitat and distribution of montane birds in southern Iran. *Bonn. zool. Beitr.* 29: 18–37.

EFTEKHAR, A. (1972a) Great Bustard ground survey in western Iran. Internal report. Department of the Environment, Tehran, Iran.

EFTEKHAR, A. (1972b) Great Bustard *Otis tarda* studies in western Iran. Internal report. Department of the Environment, Tehran, Iran.

EFTEKHAR, A. (1973a) Great Bustard survey in western Iran. Internal report. Department of the Environment, Tehran, Iran.

EFTEKHAR, A. (1973b) Great Bustard survey in Khorasan, November 1973. Internal report. Department of the Environment, Tehran, Iran.

EFTEKHAR, A. (1973c) Caucasian Black Grouse survey in Kalibar Restricted Region. Internal report. Department of the Environment, Tehran, Iran.

ERARD, C. AND ETCHÉCOPAR, R. D. (1970) Contribution a l'étude des oiseaux d'Iran. *Mem. Mus. Nat. Hist. Nat.* Serie A: 64: 1–146.

FARNSWORTH, S. J. (1992) Bird observations in southern Iran 1975/76 with particular reference to the Bahram-e-Gour Protected Area. *Orn. Soc. Middle East Bull.* 28: 10–17.

FEENY, P. P., ARNOLD, R. W. AND BAILEY, R. S. (1968) Autumn migration in the south Caspian Region. *Ibis* 110: 35–86.

FERGUSON, D. A. (1972) Waterfowl wintering, resting and breeding areas of the south-west Caspian lowlands. *Wildfowl* 23: 5–24.

FIROUZ, E. (1974) *Environment Iran*. Tehran, Iran: Nat. Soc. Conservation of Natural Resources and Human Environment.

FIROUZ, E. AND HARRINGTON, F. (1976) *Iran: concepts of biotic community conservation*. Morges, Switzerland: International Union for Conservation of Nature and Natural Resources (IUCN Occ. Pap. 15.)

FIROUZ, E., HASSINGER, J. D. AND FERGUSON, D. A. (1970) The wildlife parks and protected regions of Iran. *Biological Conservation* 3: 37–45.

FOTOOHI, H. (1974) Management of Selke Protected Region. Internal report. Department of the Environment, Tehran, Iran.

FOTOOHI, H. AND MANSOORI, J. (1974) Great Bustard ground survey in western Provinces. Internal report. Department of the Environment, Tehran, Iran.

FOTOOHI, H. AND SCOTT, D. A. (1975) The White Stork census in Iran 1353 : 1974. Internal report. Department of the Environment, Tehran, Iran.

GALLAGHER, M. D., SCOTT, D. A., ORMOND, R. F. G., CONNOR, R. J. AND JENNINGS, M. C. (1984) The distribution and conservation of seabirds breeding on the coasts and islands of Iran and Arabia. Pp. 421–456 in J. P. Croxall, P. G. H. Evans and R. W. Schreiber, eds. *Status and conservation of the world's seabirds*. Cambridge, U.K.: International Council for Bird Preservation (Techn. Publ. 2).

GHARAMANI, A. (1971) A survey of the Kalibar Mountains, with particular reference to the Caucasian Black Grouse. Internal report. Department of the Environment, Tehran, Iran.

HARRINGTON, F. A. JR. (1977) *A guide to the mammals of Iran*. Tehran, Iran: Department of the Environment.

HARRINGTON, F. A. JR. AND SCOTT, D. A. (1972) Mian Kaleh development. Internal report. Department of the Environment, Tehran, Iran.

HOWELL, D. (1976) Selke Wildlife Refuge management proposal. Internal report. Department of the Environment, Tehran, Iran.

IUCN (1991) *Protected areas of the world: a review of national systems. 2: Palaearctic*. Compiled by the World Conservation Monitoring Centre. IUCN–The World Conservation Union, Gland, Switzerland and Cambridge, U.K.

KAHROM, E. (1975) Ground survey of Assadabad Plain and aerial survey of Great Bustard habitat in western Iran. Internal report. Department of the Environment, Tehran, Iran.

KAHROM, E. (1976) Great Bustard and Crane ground survey in Khorasan. Internal report. Department of the Environment, Tehran, Iran.

MANSOORI, J. (1974) Caucasian Black Grouse survey, Tir 1353 (July 1974). Internal report. Department of the Environment, Tehran, Iran.

MANSOORI, J. AND FOTOOHI, H. (1974) Great Bustard ground survey in Khorasan. Internal report. Department of the Environment, Tehran, Iran.

MATTHEWS, G. V. T. (1973) The improvement of the Mian Kaleh Protected Region for waterfowl. Internal report. Department of the Environment, Tehran, Iran.

NIELSEN, B. P. (1969) Further spring observations on the birds of Gilan, northern Iran. *Dansk Orn. Foren. Tidsskr.* 63: 50–73.

NIELSEN, B. P. AND SPEYER, H. J. (1967) Some observations of birds in northern Iran. *Dansk Orn. Foren. Tidsskr.* 61: 30–39.

NOLL, W. T. AND NOLL, B. E. (1970) Mooteh Protected Region gazelle population survey. Internal report. Department of the Environment, Tehran, Iran.

PETOCZ, R. G., RODENBURG, W. F. AND HABIBI, K. (1976) The birds of Hamoun-i-Puzak observed from 27 February to 2 March 1976. Unpublished report. Wildlife Conservation Project, AFG/74/016. Kabul, Afghanistan: Food and Agriculture Organization of the United Nations.

RAMSAR CONVENTION BUREAU (1993) Iran. In *Directory of Wetlands of International Importance: Sites designated for the List of Wetlands of International Importance*. Prepared by IWRB for the Ramsar Convention Bureau, Gland, Switzerland.

SAVAGE, C. D. W. (1964) Lake Rezaiyeh: a specialized summer habitat for Shelduck and Flamingos. *Wildfowl Trust 15th Annual Report*: 108–113.

SCOTT, D. A. (1971a) Preliminary survey of status and distribution of Great Bustard *Otis tarda* in western Iran. Internal report. Department of the Environment, Tehran, Iran.

SCOTT, D. A. (1971b) Aerial survey of Great Bustard habitat in western Iran. Internal report. Department of the Environment, Tehran, Iran.

SCOTT, D. A. (1972a) A preliminary check-list of the birds of Mohammad Reza Shah National Park. Internal report. Department of the Environment, Tehran, Iran.

SCOTT, D. A. (1972b) Preliminary survey of the birds of Sheedvar Island Protected Region, Persian Gulf. Internal report. Department of the Environment, Tehran, Iran.

SCOTT, D. A. (1972c) Proposal for the establishment of a Waterfowl Refuge at Shadegan Marshes in Khuzestan. Internal report. Department of the Environment, Tehran, Iran.

SCOTT, D. A. (1972d) A preliminary check list of the birds of Tandoureh Wildlife Park. Internal report. Department of the Environment, Tehran, Iran.

SCOTT, D. A. (1972e) A preliminary check list of the birds of Sarani Protected Region. Internal report. Department of the Environment, Tehran, Iran.

SCOTT, D. A. (1973a) Some notes on the Bakhtegan Protected Region, Fars. Internal report. Department of the Environment, Tehran, Iran.

SCOTT, D. A. (1973b) Pelican and Flamingo ringing, and aerial censusing at Lake Rezaiyeh, Azarbaijan; August 1973. Internal report. Department of the Environment, Tehran, Iran.

SCOTT, D. A. (1973c) Small game management and research in Iran with special reference to the partridges and pheasants. Internal report. Department of the Environment, Tehran, Iran.

SCOTT, D. A. (1973d) Recent wetland surveys and wildfowl counts at Dasht-i Arjan and Lake Parishan; with a preliminary check-list of the birds of the Arjan International Reserve. Internal report. Department of the Environment, Tehran, Iran.

Scott, D. A. (1973e) Proposal for the establishment of a Bird Sanctuary at Lashgarak, District of Shemiran, Tehran. Internal report. Department of the Environment, Tehran, Iran.

Scott, D. A. (1975a) Mid-winter waterfowl counts in the wetlands of the Seistan Basin: 1970–75. Internal report. Department of the Environment, Tehran, Iran.

Scott, D. A. (1975b) The avifauna of the southern coast of Iran. Internal report. Department of the Environment, Tehran, Iran.

Scott, D. A. (1975c) The Greater Flamingo in Iran. Pp. 28–32 in J. Kear and N. Duplaix-Hall, eds. *Flamingos*. Berkhamsted, U.K.: Poyser.

Scott, D. A. (1976a) A list of the wetlands of Iran. Internal report. Department of the Environment, Tehran, Iran.

Scott, D. A. (1976b) The avifauna of the Department's reserves. Internal report. Department of the Environment, Tehran, Iran.

Scott, D. A. (1976c) Iran National Report. Pp. 27-33 in M. Smart, ed. *Proc. International Conference on Conservation of Wetlands and Waterfowl, Heiligenhafen, Germany, 2–6 December 1974*. Slimbridge, U.K.: International Waterfowl and Wetlands Research Bureau.

Scott, D. A. (1976d) The Caucasian Black Grouse *Lyrurus mlokosiewiczi* in Iran. *World Pheasant Ass. J.* (1975–76) 66–68.

Scott, D. A. (1976e) A summary of mid-winter wildfowl counts in Iran 1345 to 1353 (1966/67 to 1974/75) inclusive. Internal report. Department of the Environment, Tehran, Iran.

Scott, D. A. (1976f) The birds of the Latian Dam and Lashgarak area, Tehran: June 1972 to February 1976. Internal report. Department of the Environment, Tehran, Iran.

Scott, D. A. (1978a) Colonial breeding birds in Iran. Unpublished report.

Scott, D. A. (1978b) The birds of the Seistan Basin, Iran. Unpublished report.

Scott, D. A. (1980) Status and distribution of Cranes in Iran and some observations in Iraq. Pp. 70-72 in J. C. Lewis and H. Masatomi, eds. *Crane research around the world*. Baraboo, Wisconsin: International Crane Foundation.

Scott, D. A. (1990) Birds in Iran. Pp. 265–272 in E. Yarshater, ed. *Encyclopaedia Iranica*, 4. London: Routledge and Kegan Paul.

Scott, D. A. (1991) Asia and the Middle East. Pp. 149–178 in M. Finlayson and M. Moser, eds. *Wetlands*. Oxford: Facts On File.

Scott, D. A. (in press) Wetlands of West Asia—a regional overview. Paper presented at the IWRB/AWB International Conference on Wetland and Waterfowl Conservation in South and West Asia, Karachi, Pakistan, 14–20 December 1991.

Scott, D. A. and Carp, E. (1972) A survey in Khuzestan, Iran. Pp. 292-298 in E. Carp, ed. *Proc. International Conference on Conservation of Wetlands and Waterfowl, Ramsar, Iran*. Slimbridge, U.K.: International Waterfowl and Wetlands Research Bureau.

Scott, D. A., Hamadani, H. M. and Mirhosseyni, A. A. (1975) [*The birds of Iran*.] Tehran: Department of the Environment. (In Farsi.)

Scott, D. A. and Howell, D. L. (1976) Pheasant conservation in Iran. *World Pheasant Ass. J.* 1975–76: 82–87.

Spooner, B., ed. (1977) Case study on desertification—Iran: Turan. Internal report. Department of the Environment, Tehran, Iran.

Summers, R. W., Underhill, L. G., Pearson, D. J. and Scott, D. A. (1987) Wader migration systems in southern and eastern Africa and western Asia. *Wader Study Group Bull.* 49/*IWRB Spec. Publ.* 7: 15–34.

Ticehurst, C. B., Cox, P. Z. and Cheesman, R. E. (1925) Birds of the Persian Gulf islands. *J. Bombay Nat. Hist. Soc.* [December 1925]: 1–9.

Tuck, R. G. Jr. (1979) Notes on the Turan Biosphere Reserve herpetofauna, northeastern Iran. *Bull. Maryland Herpetological Soc.* 15: 95–123.

van Beuningen, C. S., de Boer, I. J., de Jocheere, M. A. and van de Velde, Y. M. A. (1975) An analysis of the human use problem in the western part of the Mian Kaleh Protected Region. Internal report. Department of the Environment, Tehran, Iran.

Vaziri, R. and Kahrom, E. (1975) Selection of a site for a Great Bustard refuge, Farvardin 1354 (April 1975). Internal report. Department of the Environment, Tehran, Iran.

■ REPUBLIC OF IRAQ

Iraq Babbler *Turdoides altirostris*

GENERAL INFORMATION

Iraq covers 446,713 km^2 and is bordered by Iran to the east, Saudi Arabia and Kuwait to the south, Syria and Jordan to the west and Turkey to the north. The human population is c.20 million, but large areas of the country are very sparsely populated. About 80% of the country is desert, c.15% is steppe and c.5% is forest and high mountain scrub. The country can be divided into four main biogeographical regions:

Lower Mesopotamia

This region is the flood-plain of the Tigris and Euphrates rivers, comprising most of the irrigated areas of lower Iraq and occupying the floor of a great depression which extends north-east from the Arabian Gulf practically to the foot of Jabal Hamrin. The flood-plain occupies the site of an ancient delta which has been growing out into the Arabian Gulf for centuries—at least since the days when the shore of the Gulf was situated near Balad, c.70 km north of Baghdad. The region is exceedingly flat, and the average slope does not exceed 10 cm/km. In the triangle between Amara, Nasiriyah and Basrah, there are extensive areas of permanent or seasonal shallow lakes or haurs, including the huge permanent lakes of Haur al Hammar, the Central Marshes and Haur al Hawizeh. Patches of temporarily inundated 'ahrash' forest of *Populus* and *Tamarix* occur on more stable islands and banks along the Euphrates and Tigris rivers.

Desert Plateau

This is a vast area of desert south-west of the Euphrates, rising to an elevation of c.1,000 m close to the Syrian border in the west. In the east, this region meets the western, south-western and southern boundary of the alluvial plain. To the north-west of Baghdad, in the area between the two rivers, lies a smaller but nonetheless substantial tract of semi-desert plain, the Jazirah, stretching northwards toward Jabal Sinjar.

Upper Plains and Foothills

This region is separated from Lower Mesopotamia by a low range of hills, Jabal Hamrin (up to c.200 m), which extends across the country in a north-westerly direction from Mansuriya (100 km north-east of Baghdad). This region is dominated by steppic plains and the lower mountain slopes. Altitude varies from 200 to 500 m, and the rainfall (350–500 mm per year) increases towards the northern mountains. Much of the steppe has been converted into agricultural land for growing spring cereals (non-irrigated, rain-fed winter wheat is the principal crop). Uncultivated land is covered by luxuriant grassland in spring, and is used for grazing sheep and other livestock. A few remnants of open, steppe parkland of *Pistacia* trees exist, with occasional *Ficus*, *Prunus* and *Olea* trees/shrubs. There is a large, settled agricultural population, notably on the plain of Arbil where the soil is exceptionally fertile.

Mountains

This region is bounded by the north and north-eastern border of Iraq, and extends roughly from Zakho to Halabja, with rolling plains intersected by many, deep, well-watered valleys and gorges. Altitude varies from 500 m in the lowest valleys to over 3,500 m at the summit of the highest mountains, the Helgurd. There is only c.4% of natural forest left in Iraq, nearly all in this region, and mostly over-exploited and overgrazed; in a few places coppicing of *Quercus* is practised, and tree cover remains relatively good. A belt of *Quercus* and *Pinus* forest occurs at 500–1,800 m, and above this there are about 100 km^2 of rather barren, rocky slopes on the higher summits, harbouring a very low, open, alpine vegetation. Major wetlands include Dukan lake and Darbandikhan lake near Sulaimaniyah, and natural wetlands along the Great Zab, Lesser Zab, Diyala and Tigris rivers in the Kirkuk–Mosul region of northern Iraq are said to be numerous. These were known to have offered good habitat for wintering ducks in the 1960s but some or many may have lost their importance as a result of drainage for agricultural purposes. The people cultivate and grow fruit in the valleys, but the greater part of this region is used for forestry and as summer pasture for grazing sheep. Due to human exploitation and intensive wood-cutting, exacerbated by the present political situation in northern Iraq, the few remaining tracts of natural forest (in the more isolated areas of the northern mountains) are probably threatened. Where the forest has been completely eliminated, secondary steppe vegetation replaces it or it is converted to dry cultivation of cereals.

The two great rivers of Iraq, the Tigris and the Euphrates, both rise in the eastern mountains of Turkey and enter Iraq at its north-western border. After flowing c.1,200 km through the country they join at Qarmat Ali, c.65 km north of Basra, to form the Shatt al Arab waterway, which reaches the Arabian Gulf at Fao, c.160 km south-east of Qurnah. In the past, Iraq's agriculture was dependent on the annual spring flooding along the lower courses of the two rivers which spreads silt over the fields. In recent years dam-building in the upper reaches of the rivers and the creation of huge storage basins in depressions west and north-west of Baghdad has brought the annual flooding (which tended to vary in volume) largely under control. The most important storages are Lakes Tharthar, Habbaniya and Razazah. Since the 1950s, many drainage and irrigation projects have been carried out as well, using the Tigris and Euphrates and their tributaries. Started in 1980, the aim of the government's irrigation projects was to double the area under cultivation, and such ambitious schemes for river control and irrigation are thought to have significantly reduced the extent of the water level in the marshlands of southern Iraq.

ORNITHOLOGICAL IMPORTANCE

Iraq is situated in the south-east corner of the western Palearctic biogeographical realm, although there is a small Indo-Malayan influence to the avifauna in southern Iraq, especially near the coast. There is no recent review of the status of the birds of Iraq, but least 172 species breed or are presumed to breed.

The marshlands of southern Iraq, or Mesopotamia, are one of the principal wintering areas for migratory waterfowl in western Eurasia. Several brief and very incomplete surveys of the wetlands were carried out between 1966 and 1979, covering only a tiny fraction of the enormous wetland area. The survey in 1979 found over 324,000 waterfowl of 79 species, including 3,300 pelicans, 7,850 flamingos, 2,340 geese, 155,000 ducks, 128,000 coots, 16,600 shorebirds and 13,400 gulls and terns, as well as over a thousand raptors of 15 species. These surveys showed that the marshlands of southern Iraq supported internationally important concentrations in winter of at least 22 species of waterfowl (and probably at least 70 species if adequate population estimates were available for most species). Up until modifications to the hydrology of lower Iraq started in a major way in the 1950s, the total number of waterfowl supported by the marshes annually is likely to have run into many millions, and may still have been several million in the winter of 1978/79. Georg and Savage (1970) believed that the marshes of Haur Al Hammar and Haur Al Hawizeh alone probably provided habitat for two-thirds of the wintering wildfowl of the Middle East.

The wetlands of Mesopotamia are particularly important for several globally threatened species. About 10% of the world population and c.30% of the biogeographical population of *Pelecanus crispus* were thought to be present in winter in 1978/79 (247 seen, but probably up to 1,000 actually present), and some if not many were thought likely to remain to breed in the marshes during summer. *Phalacrocorax pygmeus* was common at least up until the 1950s, and is still fairly common, with an estimated total winter population of perhaps 500 birds in 1978/79 (10% of the flyway population); while the species bred in 'vast' numbers in the marshes in the 1920s, there have been no records of nesting since, and its current breeding status is obscure. Southern Iraq is probably the most important breeding area in the world for *Marmaronetta angustirostris*; 4,000–6,000 pairs probably breed, representing some 40–60% of the world population. Very few have been recorded in winter, when it seems that the vast majority moves to neighbouring Khuzestan in Iran. Up to 100 *Aquila heliaca* were wintering in the marshes in 1978/79, a very significant concentration for a species with a world breeding population of only about 1,000–2,000 pairs. There are only three records of *Numenius tenuirostris* in Iraq (all in Mesopotamia: 'many' in December 1917, 6 in January 1979 and 1 in autumn 1979), but in view of the vast extent of suitable habitat and its very poor coverage by ornithologists, there is a distinct possibility that a significant wintering population continues to survive here. *Haliaeetus albicilla* is a winter visitor in small numbers (max. 5, 1968–1972). *Anser erythropus* and *Branta ruficollis* were formerly regular and sometimes numerous winter visitors, especially in central Iraq, but are today probably found only in insignificant numbers or as vagrants, having shifted their centres of winter distribution elsewhere. Similarly *Haliaeetus leucoryphus*, though once a regular visitor to Mesopotamia, has not been recorded in Iraq since the 1940s.

Other globally threatened species which occur in significant numbers in Iraq include *Aegypius monachus* (probably breeding in the mountains of Kurdistan in good numbers, and visiting the lowlands occasionally in winter) and *Falco naumanni* (a passage migrant, until the 1960s in thousands at the head of the Arabian Gulf in spring, now greatly reduced in numbers). *Vanellus gregarius* was a common passage migrant and winter visitor to the cultivated plains of southern and central Iraq in the first two decades of the century, but has not been recorded since the 1950s. *Otis tarda* is no doubt a winter visitor to the northernmost plains of Iraq, and has been recorded breeding there, and *Chlamydotis undulata* is probably a passage migrant and winter visitor to southern desert areas, possibly breeding also.

The lowlands of Mesopotamia also support very small resident populations of three relict Afrotropical species (*Anhinga rufa*, *Ardea goliath* and *Threskiornis aethiopicus*), as well as two passerines with very restricted ranges which breed nowhere else, *Acrocephalus griseldis* and *Turdoides altirostris*. There are also several distinct subspecies endemic to Mesopotamia, e.g. *Corvus corone capellanus*. This unusually high density of endemics means that the Mesopotamian lowlands are a globally important 'hotspot' for bird biodiversity, i.e. an 'Endemic Bird Area' (ICBP 1992), of which there are only three other such areas in the Middle East and only c.10 other such wetland areas in the world. Iraq also holds a significant proportion of the world breeding populations of *Otus brucei*, *Hypocolius ampelinus* and *Passer moabiticus*.

The valleys of the two great rivers are an important migratory route and staging area for many species of long-distance migrant birds, including pelicans, storks, and numerous species of herons and egrets (e.g. *Egretta garzetta*, *Bubulcus ibis* and *Ixobrychus minutus*), and *Anas querquedula*, which breed around the Caspian area and central Asia, and which winter in Africa and Arabia. Shorebirds such as *Charadrius asiaticus*, *C. hiaticula*, *Numenius phaeopus*, various *Tringa* species and *Calidris ferruginea*, which breed in western Siberia and spend the winter in the wetlands or along the coasts of eastern and southern Africa, also occur in large numbers. Vast numbers of migrant passerines can be found on the desert plateaus in spring if the rainfall has been good.

CONSERVATION INFRASTRUCTURE AND PROTECTED-AREA SYSTEM

There is apparently no legislation to protect sites for nature conservation; there are a number of wild animal breeding stations, each of a few hundred hectares, but with little significance for *in situ* conservation of wildlife. Responsibility for management of the natural environment in Iraq lies with the Ministry of Agriculture, although hardly any plans for its conservation have been developed or implemented. In the past, the Ministry of Agriculture has issued temporary bans on hunting, but with minimal enforcement. A National Forests Foundation has been established, partly to protect forests and preserve nature. There are many 'National Parks' which are principally state-owned areas for public recreation, and with no specific management for wildlife.

INTERNATIONAL MEASURES RELEVANT TO THE CONSERVATION OF SITES

Iraq is a contracting party to the World Heritage Convention but has not designated any natural World Heritage Sites, nor has it signed the Ramsar, Biodiversity or Bonn Conventions. It is a party to the Regional Convention for Cooperation on the Protection of the Marine Environment from Pollution, and to the Action Plan for the Protection and Development of the Marine Environment and the Coastal Areas. There is a National Committee of the UNESCO Man and Biosphere Programme.

OVERVIEW OF THE INVENTORY

This inventory contains 42 sites, covering a total area of c.35,000 km^2 or about 8% of the area of the country. Permanent wetland sites are relatively well covered, especially in the south of the country, but the more seasonal or temporary wetlands are under-represented, and other habitats are even more poorly represented, such as the grasslands and woodlands of the northern mountains, the shrub-steppes and dry grasslands of the foothills and adjacent plains, and the deserts which dominate the south and west of the country. This is due mainly to the low level of systematic ornithological survey of these areas during the last 30 years, as well as a lack of knowledge of their current intactness. As such, it has only been possible to select some representative sites covering some of these habitats, based on what little information is available. None of the sites in the inventory receive any form of legal protection aimed at conservation of their biodiversity, and many of the wetlands in particular are under critical threat, due to hydrological changes associated with flood control, irrigation and drainage projects being carried out in Iraq and in neighbouring countries. This is nowhere more apparent than in the marshlands of southern Iraq, particularly the Central Marshes, Haur Al Hammar and Haur Al Hawizeh. Wildfowl hunting exerts a heavy toll on populations, especially during winter months, and may be exceeding sustainable levels; in Kurdistan, hunting is mainly directed at *Alectoris chukar*, and birds are not trapped generally nor are birds of prey persecuted. The majority of the steppes and grasslands which lie between the desert and the foothills have been ploughed up for cultivation of cereals, thus the almost complete lack of sites in the inventory covering this habitat-type is a major gap in coverage.

ACKNOWLEDGEMENTS

The site accounts were compiled from data-sheets and other information supplied by Dr K. Y. Al-Dabbagh, Dr H. Y. Siman, Dr P. Ctyroký, Dr D. A. Scott, S. Marchant and C. King. D. J. Brooks researched the existing literature and produced the first draft of most site accounts. The introduction was compiled mainly from information supplied by Dr H. Y. Siman. Prof. M. K. Bunni commented on the inventory. V. C. Robertson, J. Robson, S. Western, Dr M. F. Mörzer Bruyns and R. Slothouwer provided valuable assistance.

SITE INVENTORY

Site	Site name	Region	Criteria used to select site									
no.			1	2i	2ii	2iii	3	4	5i	5ii	6	0
001	Benavi	DH	—	—	—	—	•	•	—	•	—	—
002	Dori Serguza	DH	—	—	—	—	•	—	—	•	—	—
003	Ser Amadia	DH	—	—	—	—	•	•	•	•	—	—
004	Bakhma, Dukan and Darbandikhan Dams	DH, AB, SL	—	—	—	—	•	—	—	—	—	—
005	Huweija Marshes	TM	•	•	—	—	•	—	—	•	—	—
006	Anah and Rawa	AN	•	—	—	—	•	—	—	—	—	—
007	Mahzam and Lake Tharthar	SD	•	•	—	—	•	•	•	—	—	—
008	Samara Dam	SD	•	•	—	•	—	—	—	—	—	—
009	Abu Dalaf and Shari Lake	SD	•	•	—	—	—	•	•	—	—	—
010	Augla	AN	—	—	—	—	—	•	—	—	—	—
011	Baquba Wetlands	DY	•	•	•	—	•	—	—	—	—	—
012	Gasr Muhaiwir	AN	—	—	—	—	—	—	—	—	—	•
013	Attariya Plains	BD	•	•	—	—	•	—	•	•	—	—
014	Abu Habba	BD	—	—	—	—	—	•	•	—	—	—
015	Al Jadriyah and Umm Al Khanazeer Island	BC	•	—	—	—	•	•	•	—	•	—
016	Haur Al Habbaniya and Ramadi Marshes	AN	•	•	—	—	—	•	—	—	—	—
017	Haur Al Shubaicha	DY, WS	—	—	—	—	—	—	—	—	—	•
018	Al Musayyib–Haswa Area	BB	—	•	•	—	—	—	—	—	—	—
019	Hindiya Barrage	BB	—	—	—	—	—	—	—	—	—	•
020	Haur Al Suwayqiyah	WS	•	•	—	—	•	—	—	—	—	—
021	Bahr Al Milh	KB	•	•	•	—	—	—	—	•	—	—
022	Haur Al Abjiya and Umm Al Baram	WS	—	—	—	—	—	—	—	—	—	•
023	Haur Delmaj	WS	—	—	—	—	—	—	—	—	—	•
024	Haur Sarut	MY	•	—	—	—	—	—	—	—	—	—
025	Haur Al Sa'adiyah	WS	•	•	•	—	—	—	—	—	—	—
026	Haur Ibn Najim	BB	—	—	—	—	—	—	—	—	—	•
027	Haur Al Hachcham and Haur Maraiba	WS	—	—	—	—	—	—	—	—	—	•
028	Haur Al Haushiya	MY	•	•	—	—	—	—	—	—	—	—
029	Shatt Al Gharraf	WS, DQ	•	—	—	—	—	—	—	—	—	—

Site no.	Site name	Region	Criteria used to select site									
			1	2i	2ii	2iii	3	4	5i	5ii	6	0
030	Haur Chubaisah Area	MY	•	•	—	—	•	•	—	—	—	—
031	Haur Sanniya	MY	—	—	—	—	—	—	—	—	—	•
032	Haur Om am Nyaj	MY	•	•	—	—	—	—	—	—	—	—
033	Haur Al Rayan and Umm Osbah	MY	•	•	—	—	•	—	—	—	—	—
034	Haur Auda	MY	—	—	—	—	—	—	—	—	—	•
035	Haur Uwainah	DQ	•	•	—	—	—	—	—	—	—	—
036	Haur Al Hawizeh	MY, BS	•	—	—	—	•	•	—	•	—	—
037	Haur Lafta	MT	—	—	—	—	—	—	—	—	—	•
038	Central Marshes	MY, DQ, BS	•	•	•	—	—	•	—	•	—	—
039	Haur Al Hammar	DQ, BS	•	•	•	—	•	•	—	•	•	—
040	Shatt Al Arab Marshes	BS	•	•	—	—	—	•	—	—	•	—
041	Khawr Al Zubair	BS	—	—	—	—	—	—	—	—	—	•
042	Khawr Abdallah	BS	—	•	—	—	•	•	—	—	—	—

Key to regions

AB	Arbil	BD	Baghdad	DY	Diyala	SD	Salah Al Din
AN	Al Anbar	BS	Al Basrah	KB	Karbala	SL	Al Sulaymaniyah
BB	Babil	DK	Dahuk	MT	Al Muthanna	TM	Al Ta'mim
BC	Baghdad City	DQ	Dhi Qar	MY	Maysan	WS	Wasit

Key to criteria

1 Regularly holds a significant number of a globally threatened species.

2i Regularly holds 1% or more of a species' biogeographical or flyway or Middle Eastern population (waterbirds and seabirds only).

2ii Regularly holds 20,000 or more waterbirds.

2iii Migratory 'bottleneck' site: more than 3,000 raptors or more than 5,000 storks or more than 2,000 cranes pass in a season.

3 Regularly holds a significant number of a species which is threatened or declining within the Middle East. Only the top five sites for each such species in the country are considered to qualify as IBAs.

4 Regularly holds a significant number of a species whose world population is wholly or largely restricted to the Middle East. Only the top five sites for each such species in the country are considered to qualify as IBAs.

5i Representative example of a habitat, associated with a characteristic assemblage of bird species.

5ii Rare/threatened/unique habitat, associated with a characteristic assemblage of bird species.

6 Site important for bird conservation through education/research/tourism.

0 Selected for other reasons. See 'Comments on the inventory'.

Comments on the inventory

1. The site name has been transliterated from the Arabic, and is sometimes followed by an alternative site name in brackets. This is then followed by the name of the region in brackets. The regions given are the governorates (muhafazat).
2. Information on bird populations is comparatively scant, and even the distribution of some species is not known. One result is a bias in favour of better explored areas, therefore the inventory should be regarded as preliminary.
3. Precise areas are given only for some of the sites which have been well documented. Boundaries have not been defined for most sites, and any areas given in these cases are only crude estimates.
4. The great majority of ornithological information quoted in this report derives from fieldwork conducted between 1960 and 1980, in particular the four IWRB wetland surveys carried out during this period. Where older information is included, a year is generally given. The only sites for which there is more recent ornithological information (up to 1990) are 007, 008 and 009.
5. Figures in brackets after species' names, and in the boxes, are the maximum daily counts of individuals recorded (not pairs), unless otherwise stated. All counts of wintering birds are from the month of January, unless otherwise stated.
6. There is an almost total lack of observations at key wetlands during the spring and autumn, which is reflected in the lack of counts of passage birds in the site inventory. However, it is likely that large numbers of migrating waterfowl, often equal in magnitude to winter counts, are supported by many of these wetlands.
7. The majority of sites are believed to meet the criteria. Those sites that have been included for other reasons (column 0 in the above table) include the following.

   • Sites identified as potential Wetlands of International Importance according to the criteria of the Ramsar Convention (Carp 1980) due to their potential importance for waterfowl, but for which there is little or no documented ornithological information from recent years (sites 022, 023, 026, 027, 034, 037 and 041)

   • Wetlands considered by Scott and Carp (1982) to be possibly of great importance to waterfowl, but lacking any recent survey (sites 017 and 034)

   • A wetland that was obviously important to waterfowl in the 1930s, but for which no recent information is available (site 019)

   • A desert site which has never been compre-

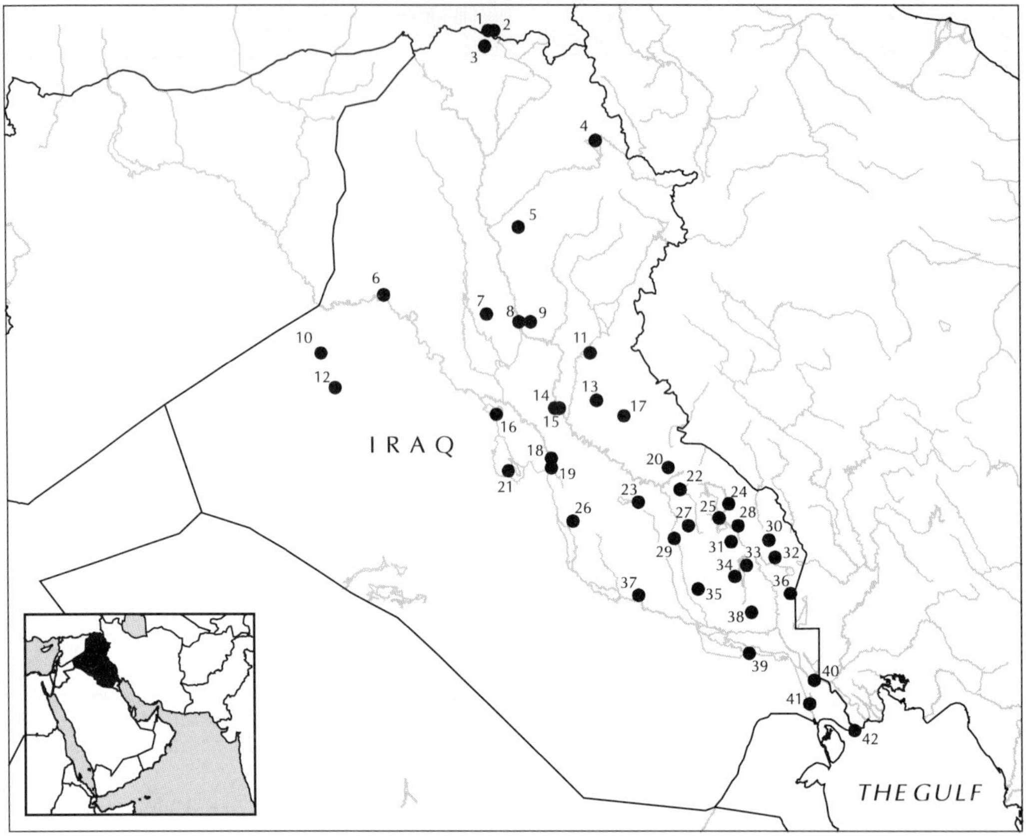

hensively surveyed but which is suspected of being a good representative example of this habitat-type (site 012).

8. The application of the criteria in categories 3 and 4 as depicted in the above table is provisional only, due to scarcity of recent or comprehensive information. Some landbird areas have been chosen to include a representative cross-section of bird habitats.
9. Most sites qualify as either a 'representative bird community' or a 'rare/threatened/unique bird community', but have only been explicitly selected on these criteria when they are weak on the other criteria.
10. Following recent changes in the scientific names of large gulls *Larus*, it has been difficult to retrospectively separate out counts of large gulls in Iraq into the four species currently distinguished: *Larus fuscus*, *L. cachinnans*, *L. argentatus* and *L. armenicus*. Following the balance of probabilities, most counts have thus been assigned to '*Larus cachinnans/L. argentatus*'.
11. In addition to the major wetland areas described below, there are in winter and spring countless small rainwater pools and areas of temporary inundation (with associated flushes of annual grasses and herbs) throughout the 'deserts' of southern and central Iraq which hold good numbers of waterfowl. Although each of these sites may hold only a few tens or hundreds of birds, together they constitute very important staging and wintering habitat for a wide range of species, especially geese, ducks and shorebirds. Similarly, there are numerous small impoundments of between 5 ha and 15 ha in size which are maintained both for irrigation during the summer months and duck-netting during the winter months. Conditions are ideal for dabbling ducks, shorebirds and some herons and egrets, and large concentrations of birds can be found on some of these ponds. The cumulative importance of these numerous artificial wetlands is clearly very great.

Glossary

bahr, large waterbody, sea
haur, permanent or seasonal freshwater lake or pool, or part of one
jabal, mountain
khawr, tidal inlet or coastal lagoon
shatt, waterway or canal
wadi, drainage line or bed of seasonal river

001 **Benavi** (Dahuk)
Unprotected

37°20′N 43°25′E
c.600 ha

Site description
The site lies at 1,500–1,700 m and includes the valley containing Benavi village and the adjacent mountain ridge. The slopes are rocky and grassy, with a rich herb flora and isolated *Quercus* scrub and trees. The local economy depends mainly on sheep grazing.

Birds
A representative assemblage of breeding species characteristic of the northern uplands; see box for key species. Other breeding species include *Coracias garrulus*, *Lullula arborea*, *Motacilla cinerea*, *Parus lugubris*, *Sitta neumayer*, *Lanius minor*, *L. nubicus* and *Serinus pusillus*, probably *Caprimulgus europaeus* and possibly *Neophron percnopterus*. Over 40 species are known or presumed to breed.

Regionally threatened or declining species

Neophron percnopterus	Possibly breeds.

Species restricted wholly or largely to the Middle East

Irania gutturalis	Summer visitor.
Emberiza cineracea	Possible summer visitor.

Other threatened/endemic wildlife
Flora: there are *Anemone* assemblages, including *A. blanda*. The general area is very important for harbouring wild relatives of important cereal crop species.

Conservation issues
No conservation measures are known to have been taken. In the 1970s there was a threat to the habitat from cutting of trees and shrubs for firewood as well as from the very heavy grazing which was occurring locally. Overall, these trends are likely to have intensified in subsequent years. No conservation measures are known to have been proposed.

Further reading
Chapman and McGeoch (1956), Ctyroký (1987), McGeoch (1963).

002 **Dori Serguza** (Dahuk)
Unprotected

37°20′N 43°30′E
c.400 ha

Site description
A valley at 1,500–1,800 m in the eastern Taurus Mountains, running north from the village of Dori (probably now abandoned), below Jabal Shoroniya on the Turkish border. There are many springs, and open woodland of *Quercus*, *Juniperus* and *Pinus* trees along the valley stream, with bushes. The slopes are rocky, with grass and isolated *Quercus* scrub.

Birds
See box for key species. Other breeding species (known or assumed) include *Neophron percnopterus*, *Dendrocopos syriacus*, *Parus lugubris*, *Sitta neumayer*, *Lanius nubicus* and *Serinus pusillus*.

Regionally threatened or declining species

Neophron percnopterus	Probably breeds.

Species restricted wholly or largely to the Middle East

Irania gutturalis	Probable summer visitor.
Emberiza cineracea	Possible summer visitor.

Other threatened/endemic wildlife
Flora: the general area is very important for harbouring wild relatives of important cereal crop species.

Conservation issues
No conservation measures are known to have been taken. There is no information available on current threats to this relatively intact area. Significant human influence may have ceased after abandonment of the village. No conservation measures are known to have been proposed.

Further reading
Chapman and McGeoch (1956), McGeoch (1963).

003 **Ser Amadiya** (Dahuk) — 37°10′N 43°22′E — 6,500 ha

Unprotected

Site description

Ser Amadiya is an east-west mountain ridge rising to c.2,000 m, just north-west of the town of Amadiya in Kurdistan and c.20 km south of the Turkish border. The section of the Amadiya valley to the south lies at 1,450–1,550 m, 3 km west of Amadiya. The site includes rocky cliffs at Sulaf and gorges to the south, e.g. Sulaf, Geli-e-Mazurka. The treeline is at c.1,650 m, and the ridge has a grassy saddle at 1,850 m. The area to the north descends through thin scrub and shrubs to scrub *Quercus* and *Juniperus* forest with a rocky and grassy floor and numerous streams and springs. Along the valley streams in the south there are *Populus* trees with grass and scrub, and the valley slopes are rocky, with grass and *Quercus* bushes. Patches of cultivation, e.g. tobacco fields, surround the small villages. Summers are hot and dry, and winters are cold with snow.

Birds

See box for key species. The breeding bird community is characteristic of the northern uplands and comprises at least 30 species including *Alectoris chukar*, *Caprimulgus europaeus*, *Dendrocopos syriacus*, *Hirundo rupestris*, *Sylvia hortensis*, *Parus lugubris*, *Lanius nubicus*, *Pyrrhocorax graculus*, *P. pyrrhocorax* and *Emberiza hortulana*. Both *Sitta tephronota* and *S. neumayer* occur, the latter at least breeding. *Prunella collaris* and *Montifringilla nivalis* (a flock of c.150) have been noted as non-breeding visitors in March on the snowfields.

Regionally threatened or declining species	
Gypaetus barbatus	Occurred in the area in the 1940s and 1950s and probably still does.
Neophron percnopterus	Occurred in the area in the 1940s and 1950s and probably still does.
Gyps fulvus	Occurred in the area in the 1940s and 1950s and probably still does.
Species restricted wholly or largely to the Middle East	
Irania gutturalis	Summer visitor.
Emberiza cineracea	Possible summer visitor (recorded in August).

Other threatened/endemic wildlife

Flora: the general area is very important for harbouring wild relatives of important cereal crop species.

Conservation issues

No conservation measures are known to have been taken. Deforestation is likely to be a severe problem, but there is no recent information on threats. No conservation measures are known to have been proposed.

Further reading

Chapman and McGeoch (1956), Harrison (1959), McGeoch (1963), Moore and Boswell (1956–1957).

004 **Bakhma, Dukan and Darbandikhan Dams** (Dahuk, Arbil, Al Sulaymaniyah) — 36°10′N 44°55′E — 40,000 ha

Unprotected

Site description

Dukan and Darbandikhan are two dammed lakes, each c.30 km long, lying in the foothills of Kurdistan in north-east Iraq. Dukan (36°10′N 44°55′E, c.25,000 ha) is in the Lesser Zab river valley, and Darbandikhan (35°10′N 45°45′E, c.7,500 ha) is in the Diyala river valley. Contrary to most maps, construction of the Bakhma dam (36°45′N 44°15′E) in the Great Zab river valley has not been completed, having presumably been abandoned in 1991, and there is as yet no lake there. The general aspect is of deep valleys eroded into limestone country, with steep and craggy slopes. There are patches of semi-natural parkland of small oak *Quercus* and juniper *Juniperus* trees on slopes, particularly extensive and undisturbed around Bakhma. There is limited cultivation of tobacco, rice, wheat and vines on the flood-plains in the valleys; the main land-use is as rangeland for goats and sheep. Dukan and Darbandikhan dams are presumably used to generate hydroelectric power.

Birds

See box for key species. The lakes are likely to be important for wintering waterfowl, but no surveys have been carried out. The three river valleys supported large numbers of wintering ducks in the 1960s (Savage 1968). The surrounding hills and crags are likely to support important numbers of breeding raptors, e.g. vultures, eagles and falcons. Other breeding species include *Ciconia ciconia*, *Alectoris chukar* and *Sitta tephronota*.

Regionally threatened or declining species

Gypaetus barbatus	Likely to breed or to visit from higher altitudes.
Neophron percnopterus	Common resident.
Gyps fulvus	Likely to breed or to visit from higher altitudes.

Species restricted wholly or largely to the Middle East

Prunella ocularis	Probably a winter visitor from higher areas.

Other threatened/endemic wildlife

Flora: the general area is very important for harbouring wild relatives of important cereal crop species.

Conservation issues

No conservation measures are known to have been taken. There is little information on current threats to the site; however, the area around Bakhma is relatively remote and sparsely populated, and deforestation is at a relatively low level compared to some other areas of Kurdistan (e.g. the Sulaimaniyah district). No conservation measures are known to have been proposed.

005 Huweija Marshes (Al Ta'mim)

Unprotected

35°15′N 43°50′E
Area not defined

Site description

An area of marshes and lakes c.65 km west-south-west of Kirkuk, along the pipeline road. Wheat is cultivated on the surrounding plains.

Birds

A wide selection of ducks, waders and other waterbirds, mostly in small numbers, occurs in winter and on passage. *Vanellus indicus* and *V. leucurus* are common breeding species.

Globally threatened species

Marmaronetta angustirostris Passage migrant (max. 2).

1% or more of population

	Breeding (pairs)	Wintering	Passage
Anser albifrons	—	—	2,000
Himantopus himantopus	?	75–100	75–100

Regionally threatened or declining species

Botaurus stellaris	Winter visitor and passage migrant.

Other threatened/endemic wildlife

Flora: the general area is very important for harbouring wild relatives of important cereal crop species.

Conservation issues

No conservation measures are known to have been taken. There is no information on current threats to the site, although it may well have been drained for agriculture. No conservation measures are known to have been proposed.

Further reading

Marchant and Macnab (1962).

006 Anah and Rawa (Al Anbar)

Unprotected

34°32′N 41°55′E
c.400 ha

Site description

The site covers the area surrounding the villages of Anah and Rawa, lying in the narrow Euphrates valley c.240 km north-west of Baghdad, and includes the river itself. The region is stony desert on limestones and sandstones with much bare rock, sparsely vegetated with mostly spiny herbs. The river plain is sandy and silty, and there is some cultivation (dense date-palm groves with undergrowth, and cotton fields. There are flat, sandy islands in the river.

Birds

See box for key species. The breeding avifauna also includes *Tadorna ferruginea*, *Cursorius cursor*, *Halcyon smyrnensis*, *Merops superciliosus* and *Pycnonotus leucotis*.

Globally threatened species

Marmaronetta angustirostris Summer visitor (c.10 in 1985).

Regionally threatened or declining species

Francolinus francolinus	Resident.

Other threatened/endemic wildlife

Reptiles: the desert has a rich reptile fauna.

Conservation issues

No conservation measures are known to have been

taken. In recent years dams on the Euphrates in Turkey and Syria have caused considerable fluctuations in the water level, with consequent negative effects on the alluvial habitats. No conservation measures are known to have been proposed.

007 **Mahzam and Lake Tharthar** (Salah Al Din)

34°20′N 43°22′E
Unprotected c.455,000 ha

■ Site description

Lying between the Tigris and the Euphrates rivers, 120 km north of Baghdad in north-central Iraq, the site comprises c.80,000 ha of the north-eastern part of Lake Tharthar (Mileh Tharthar, c.230,000 ha) plus a large adjacent area of semi-desert to the east (c.375,000 ha). The lake is deep and nutrient-poor. The site's northern edge runs just south of the Baiji–Haditha road, and the eastern edge is 10 km from Samara, Tikrit and Baiji. The soil is calcareous with a rather uniform surface: a pavement of small sandy stones in the south and central parts, and mainly sandy in the north (near Baiji). Low hills rise near Lake Tharthar, these being covered with larger stones. A few shallow wadis cross the area, running towards the lake, and the area has a rich supply of underground water. Vegetation is sparse, and mainly small shrubs (*Haloxylon, Achillea, Artemisia, Rhanterium*), though there are patches of denser growth, particularly in depressions, and scattered small *Ziziphus* trees. After the light December–February rains, most of the area develops a thin cover of grasses and annuals. Using water from tube-wells, the area has been farmed since c.1980, and there are now at least 150–200 farms of c.10 ha each, mostly in the south and east of the site. There is some sheep grazing. A strip of land c.20 km wide along the lake shore is not exploited because of the unsuitable soils. Lake Tharthar is connected to the Tigris by an inlet canal via the Samara Dam, and is used for water storage and flood-relief; an outlet canal feeds back into the Tigris further downstream, and a branch from this canal reaches south to feed into the Euphrates as well.

■ Birds

See box for key species. Large numbers of waterbirds are present in winter; other winter visitors or passage migrants include *Charadrius asiaticus* (up to 60 on passage) and *Pterocles alchata* (max. 1,000). Other breeding species include *Cursorius cursor* (20 pairs), *Vanellus indicus* (20 pairs), *V. leucurus* (4 pairs), *Bubo bubo* (1 pair) and *Pycnonotus leucotis*; *Oenanthe isabellina* probably breeds. Lake Tharthar was listed as a wetland of international importance by Carp (1980).

Globally threatened species

Phalacrocorax pygmeus	Winter visitor (max. 10).
Marmaronetta angustirostris	Winter visitor (max. 2); possibly breeds.
Falco naumanni	Passage migrant; possibly breeds.
Chlamydotis undulata	Resident or summer visitor (2 pairs).

1% or more of population

	Breeding (pairs)	Wintering	Passage
Anas platyrhynchos	—	10,000	—
Aythya ferina	—	10,000	—
Aythya nyroca	—	10	—

Regionally threatened or declining species

Neophron percnopterus	Non-breeding visitor (max. 4).

Species restricted wholly or largely to the Middle East

Aythya nyroca	Winter visitor (10).
Ammoperdix griseogularis	Resident.
Oenanthe finschii	Probable summer visitor.

■ Other threatened/endemic wildlife

Mammals: *Canis lupus* (V) and *Gazella subgutturosa* (rare). Reptiles: *Varanus griseus* (rare). Flora: the general area is very important for harbouring wild relatives of important cereal crop species.

■ Conservation issues

No conservation measures are known to have been taken. The establishment of farms in the area has involved considerable damage to topsoil by vehicles, and a road was built through the site from Tikrit to the lake. There is hunting, and the lake is threatened by overfishing. No conservation measures are known to have been proposed.

■ Further reading

Al-Dabbagh (in prep.), Carp (1975a), Koning and Dijksen (1973).

008 Samara Dam (Salah Al Din)

34°15′N 43°50′E

Unprotected

c.20,000 ha

Site description

This lake is c.8 km across and straddles the Tigris, running from the Samara Dam c.25 km north to Al Dor. Soils are mostly alluvial, and in some parts hills reach the river forming cliffs. Elsewhere the river banks are gravel. The lake and marsh above Samara dam extend for more than 5 km, and have large beds of *Phragmites* and *Typha* with a rich growth of submerged vegetation, particularly where the water depth is c.1.5 m. Riverine forest dominated by *Populus euphratica* occurs in patches along the banks and more especially on small islands. Much of the area is cultivated, mainly with date-palm gardens, wheat fields, orchards and some vegetables, and there is grazing by sheep and cattle. Parts of the river bank are used for gravel extraction, some such sites being now filled with water and surrounded by a thick growth of *Populus* and *Tamarix*.

Birds

See boxes for key species. A wide range of species breed, including *Phalacrocorax pygmeus* (possibly: see box), *Marmaronetta angustirostris* (possibly: see box), *Accipiter nisus* (probably), *Falco naumanni* (possibly), *Columba palumbus*, *Halcyon smyrnensis*, *Ceryle rudis* and *Pycnonotus leucotis*. *Tadorna ferruginea* has bred in the area. The site is used by large numbers of waterfowl and other waterbirds outside the breeding season; other wintering species include *Circus aeruginosus* (20) and Ticehurst *et al.* (1921–1922) noted vast flocks of *Eudromias morinellus* and several flocks of *Eremophila bilopha* wintering near Samara. At least 3,000 raptors move through the Tigris valley in this general area on passage. At least 146 species have been recorded at the site.

Globally threatened species

Phalacrocorax pygmeus	May breed. Max. 14 in winter.
Marmaronetta angustirostris	May breed. Max. 6 in winter.
Haliaeetus albicilla	Formerly bred on river cliffs, in the 1960s.
Falco naumanni	Occurs, and may breed.
Chlamydotis undulata	Has bred in the area.
Vanellus gregarius	Has occurred in winter (max.2).

1% or more of population

	Breeding (pairs)	Wintering	Passage
Aythya ferina	—	10,000	—
Aythya nyroca	—	25	—
Vanellus indicus	20	—	—
Vanellus leucurus	50	—	—

Regionally threatened or declining species

Botaurus stellaris	Has occurred in winter.
Ardea goliath	Has occurred.
Aythya nyroca	Winter visitor (see above).
Francolinus francolinus	Common resident.

Species restricted wholly or largely to the Middle East

Ammoperdix griseogularis	Resident.
Hypocolius ampelinus	Summer visitor (50 pairs).

Other threatened/endemic wildlife

Fish: the river and lake hold endemic cyprinid species. Flora: the general area is very important for harbouring wild relatives of important cereal crop species.

Conservation issues

The lake appears to be under the control of one important government official for private use and for conservation. Duck hunting is common away from the dam and there is the possibility of the extension of agriculture and of mineral extraction, but there are no other major threats apparent. No conservation measures are known to have been officially proposed.

Further reading

Al-Dabbagh (in prep.), Koning and Dijksen (1973).

009 Abu Dalaf and Shari Lake (Salah Al Din)

Unprotected

34°15′N 44°00′E
c.127,000 ha

Site description

Shari lake (5,000–8,000 ha) lies east of the Tigris, c.30 km north-east of Samara. It is largely rain-fed and saline, and there are some small *Phragmites* reedbeds. The site includes a large area of semi-desert (c.120,000 ha) on the western side of the lake and extending c.20 km from it, the habitat being of similar type to that at Mahzam (see site 007), though with more bushes and a denser growth of grass in spring, particularly close to the lake. Part of the area is farmed, and sheep graze freely, with extra stock being brought in during spring to graze near the lake. There is commercial salt extraction at the lake.

Birds

See boxes for key species. Other breeding species include *Cursorius cursor*, *Pterocles alchata* (max. 2,000 birds), *Pycnonotus leucotis* and *Oenanthe isabellina* (probably). Small numbers of waterfowl winter, and notable passage migrants include *Charadrius asiaticus* (max. 20).

Globally threatened species

Phalacrocorax pygmeus	Winter visitor (max. 6).
Falco naumanni	Has occurred; possibly breeds.
Chlamydotis undulata	Has occurred; possibly breeds.

1% or more of population

	Breeding (pairs)	Wintering	Passage
Vanellus indicus	20	—	—

Species restricted wholly or largely to the Middle East

Ammoperdix griseogularis	Resident.
Oenanthe finschii	Probably breeds.

Other threatened/endemic wildlife

Mammals: *Canis lupus* (V). Reptiles: the monitor *Varanus griseus* (rare).

Conservation issues

No conservation measures are known to have been taken. Threats to the site are similar to those at Mahzam. No conservation measures are known to have been proposed.

Further reading

Al-Dabbagh (in prep.).

010 Augla (Al Anbar)

Unprotected

33°55′N 41°02′E
c.500 ha

Site description

Part of a limestone and sand desert plateau c.30 km west-south-west of Haditha and c.200 km west-north-west of Baghdad. The area contains large, deep wadis surrounded by shallow depressions which are wet from November to March and carry a rich vegetation of *Haloxylon*, *Artemisia* and *Astragalus*. At least three water wells have been drilled, and since c.1960 part of the area has been farmed (dates, orchards, etc.) and there is some livestock grazing by nomads. Annual rainfall is 100–200 mm, mainly in December–February.

Birds

See box for key species. Other breeding species (known or assumed) include *Cursorius cursor*, *Pterocles alchata*, *Eremophila bilopha*, *Pycnonotus leucotis* and *Oenanthe isabellina*. *Grus virgo* (12 birds) has occurred on spring passage, and the area may lie on a main migration route for it.

Species restricted wholly or largely to the Middle East

Ammoperdix griseogularis	Resident.
Oenanthe finschii	Probably breeds.
Carpospiza brachydactyla	Spring passage migrant.

Other threatened/endemic wildlife

Reptiles: there is a rich reptile fauna.

Conservation issues

No conservation measures are known to have been taken. The site is unprotected and in the early 1980s was apparently not threatened. No conservation measures are known to have been proposed.

Further reading

Siman (in prep.).

011 **Baquba Wetlands** (Diyala)

also known as Shaikh Sayed Marshes

Unprotected

33°55´N 44°50´E

2,000+ ha

■ Site description

A group of marshes in the Diyala valley between Baquba and Shahraban, c.75 km north-east of Baghdad. These include Haur Abu Abbas (33°50´N 44°45´E, a shallow freshwater lake, c.500–1,000 ha), Haur Shaikh Sayed (33°51´N 44°46´E, by 1972 a lake of only 10 ha, almost drained), Haur Al Ahmar (34°00´N 44°55´E, freshwater, c.600 ha), Haur Al Habara, Haur Abdul Warid, Haur Al Ugur (34°00´N 44°55´E) and a rain-flooded area near Shahraban (Al Miqdadiyah). At Haur Al Ahmar the flat shore is covered with dense reedbeds, and mudflats are exposed at low water; the area surrounding the southern shore area is fertile cultivation, with cotton, corn, date-palm groves and orchards, and the lake serves for irrigation of these.

■ Birds

See box for key species. The site is important for wintering waterbirds, e.g. 39,900 wildfowl were present in January 1968. Other wintering species include *Circus aeruginosus* (17), *Remiz pendulinus* (4, Haur Al Ahmar) and *Corvus frugilegus* (5,000, Haur Al Ahmar); *Anthus spinoletta* is common. There is little information from other times of year, but *Coracias garrulus* has bred. The entire area was listed as a wetland of international importance by Carp (1980).

Globally threatened species

Marmaronetta angustirostris Occurs outside breeding season at least (180 in January 1968, 13 in March).

1% or more of population

	Breeding (pairs)	Wintering	Passage
Ciconia ciconia	—	571	—
Plegadis falcinellus	—	255	—
Anas clypeata	—	8,650	—
Aythya nyroca	—	30	—
Vanellus indicus	—	70	—
Vanellus leucurus	abundant	56	—

Regionally threatened or declining species

Aythya nyroca	Winter visitor (30).
Francolinus francolinus	Resident.

■ Other threatened/endemic wildlife

No information available to BirdLife International.

■ Conservation issues

No conservation measures are known to have been taken. Hunting occurs, and commercial duck-netting is frequent. Haur Shaikh Sayed had been subject to drainage in 1972. There is no information on the (likely) current status of this site. No conservation measures are known to have been proposed.

■ Further reading

Ctyroký (1987), Georg and Vielliard (1970), Koning and Dijksen (1973), Marchant and Macnab (1962).

012 **Gasr Muhaiwir** (Al Anbar)

Unprotected

33°33´N 41°14´E

c.600 ha

■ Site description

Gasr Muhaiwir lies c.80 km east-north-east of Rutbah in Wadi Hauran, the main wadi crossing the western desert of Iraq to the Euphrates. The stony desert carries only a sparse herb growth, and only in the wadi where there are temporary pools and springs is there more abundant vegetation. Summers are extremely hot, while winter temperatures can fall below freezing. There is archaeological evidence in the area of its use by man since Neolithic times.

■ Birds

The site's main interest lies in the attraction it holds for spring and autumn migrants crossing a huge area of desert, and large numbers of a wide variety of passerines and other species occur. The desert avifauna includes *Cursorius cursor*, *Ammomanes deserti*, *Alaemon alaudipes*, and *Pterocles senegalensis* and *Eremophila bilopha* may also breed.

■ Other threatened/endemic wildlife

No information available to BirdLife International.

■ Conservation issues

No conservation measures are known to have been taken. No threats are apparent. No conservation measures are known to have been proposed.

■ Further reading

Ctyroký (1988, in press).

013 Attariya Plains (Baghdad)

Unprotected

33°25′N 44°55′E
c.50,000 ha

Site description

An area of semi-desertic plains, arable land, grassland, temporary inundation and small permanent marshes c.40 km east-north-east of Baghdad. The marshes are fed mainly from the Baquba area to the north and are surrounded by *Phragmites* and *Typha* beds. The area is grazed, and adjacent plains are dominated by *Alhaja* and *Acacia*. The local human population is very sparse, and the environment is unusually intact.

Birds

See box for key species. The site is important for wintering waterfowl, and 8,800 ducks and geese and *Fulica atra* were recorded in January 1975. Other breeding species include *Glareola pratincola* (14 pairs). *Charadrius asiaticus* occurs on passage (max. 300). Data shown in box, from Carp (1975a, 1975b) and Scott and Carp (1982), may include some winter counts from the Baghdad area.

Globally threatened species

Phalacrocorax pygmeus	Winter visitor (max. 2).
Chlamydotis undulata	Probably breeds (seen in April).

1% or more of population

	Breeding (pairs)	Wintering	Passage
Tadorna ferruginea	—	412	—
Aythya nyroca	—	13	—
Limosa limosa	—	2,500	—

Regionally threatened or declining species

Botaurus stellaris	Recorded in winter (max. 2).
Aythya nyroca	Winter visitor (see above).

Species restricted wholly or largely to the Middle East

Glareola nordmanni	Summer visitor (20 pairs).

Other threatened/endemic wildlife

Flora: the general area is very important for harbouring wild relatives of important cereal crop species.

Conservation issues

No conservation measures are known to have been taken. The site is threatened by drainage of the wetlands to the north from which it obtains its water. Hunting pressure was heavy in 1975, both through shooting from cars and from netting. No conservation measures are known to have been proposed.

Further reading

Carp (1975a,b), Scott and Carp (1982).

014 Abu Habba (Baghdad)

Unprotected

33°20′N 44°20′E
c.400 ha

Site description

The site lies 12 km west of Mahmudiya and was originally a flat, silt desert with sparse herbs, but much of it has long been under cultivation, irrigated by water from the Mahmudiya channel of the River Tigris. The area is dominated by date-palm groves, with an understorey of orange, plum and pomegranate trees; cotton, corn and vegetables are also grown. Temporary pools form after winter rains.

Birds

See box for key species. Other breeding species include *Ciconia ciconia* (3 pairs), *Vanellus leucurus* (12 pairs), *Caprimulgus aegyptius*, *Halcyon smyrnensis*, *Merops superciliosus* (40 pairs), *Coracias garrulus*, *C. benghalensis*, *Turdoides caudatus* (min. 4) and *Pycnonotus leucotis* (min. 8). The area attracts large numbers of migrant passerines and near-passerines in spring (no autumn data). *Anthus spinoletta* is common in winter.

Species restricted wholly or largely to the Middle East

Otus brucei	Resident or summer visitor (3 pairs).
Turdoides altirostris	Resident (8 pairs).

Other threatened/endemic wildlife

No information available to BirdLife International.

Conservation issues

No conservation measures are known to have been taken. The development of vegetation depends largely on the maintenance of the irrigation system. Degradation of some irrigation channels and palm groves was apparent in 1980, caused probably by the movement of local people to Baghdad. No conservation measures are known to have been proposed.

015 Al Jadriyah and Umm Al Khanazeer Island (Baghdad City)

33°20'N 44°24'E
c.310 ha

also known as Karradah Sharqiyah
Unprotected

Site description

Al Jadriyah (c.200 ha) lies on the bank of the River Tigris within south-west Baghdad, and comprises irrigated cultivation (date palms, orchards, vegetables, cereals, cotton) with scrub and some livestock grazing. A large university campus was built on the site in the late 1970s, but much of the habitat described here was still present in 1981. Umm Al Khanazeer island (c.110 ha), lying in the Tigris and connected to Al Jadriyah by road bridge, is mostly used for recreation by the local population, and a tourist centre has recently been built there; parts of the western side are cultivated for vegetables and there are remnant patches of riverine thickets of *Populus euphratica* with *Tamarix* and other shrubs and scattered mulberry trees, especially along the banks.

Birds

See box for key species. Other breeding species include *Vanellus indicus* (42 pairs), *V. leucurus* (15 pairs), *Psittacula krameri*, *Halcyon smyrnensis*, *Alcedo atthis*, *Ceryle rudis*, *Merops apiaster* (50 pairs), *M. superciliosus*, *Coracias benghalensis*, *Pycnonotus leucotis*, *Turdoides caudatus* and *Petronia xanthocollis*. *Rhodopechys obsoleta* is a winter visitor. Most counts date from before the completion of the university at Al Jadriyah.

Globally threatened species

Marmaronetta angustirostris Summer visitor in small numbers.

Regionally threatened or declining species

Francolinus francolinus	Common resident.

Species restricted wholly or largely to the Middle East

Hypocolius ampelinus	Common summer visitor in groves along river-banks (90 pairs).
Acrocephalus griseldis	Summer visitor (5 pairs).
Turdoides altirostris	Common resident (40 pairs).
Passer moabiticus	Common breeder (80 pairs).

Other threatened/endemic wildlife

None known to BirdLife International.

Conservation issues

No conservation measures are known to have been taken. Al Jadriyah is subject to wood-cutting and built development as well as general human disturbance; hunting is common. The woodland of Umm Al Khanazeer island is threatened by extensive wood collecting, fire and cultivation. No conservation measures are known to have been proposed.

Further reading

Al-Dabbagh and Bunni (1981), Marchant (1961, 1962), Siman (1975), Siman and Bunni (1978).

016 Haur Al Habbaniya and Ramadi Marshes (Al Anbar)

33°16'N 43°30'E
c.20,000 ha

Unprotected

Site description

The site lies just south of the Euphrates between Ramadi and Felluja, 85 km west of Baghdad. Haur Al Habbaniya is a storage reservoir used to control floods on the Euphrates. There is an intake channel at its west end near Ramadi, and water is discharged back into the river during August–October through the Dhibban channel which has vertical sides c.30 m high, cut through the gypsum plateau separating the lake from the river. In addition, a third channel at the south end discharges any excess water into the Bahr Al Milh (see site 021). The lake's water level thus varies annually by c.6 m, being highest from about the end of April to August and lowest in November–March, when extensive mudflats are exposed at the Ramadi end of the lake where there are also marshes. Most of the above information dates from the 1950s.

Birds

See box for key species. *Sterna hirundo* and *S. albifrons* breed on islands formed during periods of high water levels, and *Cursorius cursor*, *Merops superciliosus* and *Pycnonotus leucotis* breed in the surrounding area (see also below). Large numbers of *Platalea leucorodia* (200) have occurred in winter. A wide selection of waders, gulls and terns uses the area on passage. Counts of wintering waterfowl have included 300 *Anser anser*, 84 *Tadorna ferruginea* and 30 *Mergellus albellus*, and *Grus grus* is common. Haur Al Habbaniya was listed as a wetland of international importance by Carp (1980).

Other threatened/endemic wildlife

No information available to BirdLife International.

Globally threatened species

Marmaronetta angustirostris	Breeds (probably 2 pairs).
Oxyura leucocephala	One record (1, November 1956).
Falco naumanni	Flocks of up to c.200 occurred on spring passage along the nearby Euphrates in the 1950s.

1% or more of population

	Breeding (pairs)	Wintering	Passage
Sterna albifrons	15	—	150

Species restricted wholly or largely to the Middle East

Otus brucei	Summer visitor in surrounding area.
Turdoides altirostris	Resident in surrounding area.

Conservation issues

No conservation measures are known to have been taken. In the 1950s it was apparently proposed to raise the level by 2 m, which would have endangered nesting sites of terns. There are no known proposals for conservation measures.

Further reading

Chapman and McGeoch (1956).

017 Haur Al Shubaicha (Diyala, Wasit)

Unprotected

33°15′N 45°18′E
c.75,000 ha

Site description

The site is shown on maps as an extensive marsh, fed by rivers from the north, lying c.40 km north of the Tigris and c.85 km east of Baghdad. No further information is available.

Birds

The site appears never to have been visited by an ornithologist, though it was considered by Scott and Carp (1982) to be possibly of great importance for wintering waterbirds.

Other threatened/endemic wildlife

No information available to BirdLife International.

Conservation issues

No conservation measures are known to have been taken. No conservation measures are known to have been proposed and there is no information on current threats to the site.

018 Al Musayyib–Haswa Area (Babil)

Unprotected

32°48′N 44°17′E
Area undefined

Site description

Georg and Vielliard (1970) gave a number of counts made between Al Musayyib and Haswa in January 1968. The area, evidently a wetland but not further described, lies north of Al Musayyib, between the Tigris and the Euphrates.

Birds

See box for key species. Georg and Vielliard (1970) counted 21,523 ducks and geese as well as a range of other waterbirds. There have been no other surveys.

1% or more of population

	Breeding (pairs)	Wintering	Passage
Anas clypeata	—	6,000	—
Tringa erythropus	—	130	—

Other threatened/endemic wildlife

No information available to BirdLife International.

Conservation issues

No conservation measures are known to have been taken. There is no information on current threats to the site, though its habitats have presumably suffered badly from the decreasing flow of the Euphrates since the 1970s (see site 039). No conservation measures are known to have been proposed.

Further reading

Georg and Vielliard (1970).

019 Hindiya Barrage (Babil)
Unprotected

32°42′N 44°17′E
Area undefined

Site description
A barrage on the River Euphrates c.5 km south of Al Musayyib and c.65 km south of Baghdad. In 1934 there were a few marshy spots and pools near the river, with *Salix* patches, extensive fruit and vegetable gardens and date-palm groves, and further away open irrigated land with corn and scrub.

Birds
See box for key species. There is little information from the site since the 1930s. Other breeding species included *Podiceps nigricollis*, *Circus aeruginosus* (common), *Porphyrio porphyrio* (common), *Glareola pratincola*, *Cursorius cursor*, *Vanellus leucurus* (common), *Larus genei*, *Sterna hirundo* (large colonies) and *Halcyon smyrnensis* (abundant). *Calidris minuta* occurred in large numbers on passage.

Globally threatened species

Marmaronetta angustirostris	The species bred in c.1914–1918 (Ticehurst *et al.* 1921–1922) and was described as 'plentiful', though it seems not to have been noted there in spring and summer 1934 (Moore and Boswell 1956).

Regionally threatened or declining species

Botaurus stellaris	Heard calling in late May; possibly breeding.
Ardea goliath	Has occurred.

Species restricted wholly or largely to the Middle East

Glareola nordmanni	Summer visitor, at least formerly.
Passer moabiticus	A flock recorded in September.

Other threatened/endemic wildlife
No information available to BirdLife International.

Conservation issues
No conservation measures are known to have been taken. There is no information on current threats to the site, though its habitats have presumably suffered badly from the decreasing flow of the Euphrates since the 1970s (see site 039). No conservation measures are known to have been proposed.

Further reading
Moore and Boswell (1956–1957), Ticehurst *et al.* (1921–1922, 1926).

020 Haur Al Suwayqiyah (Wasit)
Unprotected

32°42′N 45°55′E
c.50,000 ha

Site description
A large isolated lake on arid steppic plains c.10 km north of the River Tigris and c.20 km north-east of Kut. This rather shallow and brackish lake formerly covered c.50,000 ha but was partly drained in 1945; it is supplied by numerous streams from the Zagros mountains and by rainfall run-off, as well as by flooding overspill from the Tigris (although this is now rare due to flood control barrages). In 1968 and 1972 there were no reedbeds and little other emergent vegetation, but earlier sources indicate this was not formerly the case. The surrounding steppe becomes thickly vegetated with annual grasses, herbs and *Salicornia* after good winter rains. There is arable land to the south-west. Duck-netting was widespread in 1972.

Birds
See box for key species. Prior to 1945, the haur was known as a traditional wintering area for geese, ducks, shorebirds and other waterfowl, with huge numbers of *Anser anser*, *A. albifrons*, *Branta ruficollis*, *Tadorna ferruginea*, *Anas platyrhynchos*, *A. strepera*, *A. crecca*, *A. penelope*, *A. acuta*, *A. clypeata*, *Phoenicopterus ruber* and *Recurvirostra avosetta* (Georg and Savage 1970a,b, V. Robertson *in litt.*). According to Savage (1968), the area probably held one of the highest concentrations of geese in the Middle East, and was also very important for *Anas querquedula* on passage. Surveys in January 1968, December 1972 and January 1979 revealed that the lake was still important for flamingos and shorebirds, while the surrounding flooded steppe, arable land and *Salicornia* flats remained a very important feeding habitat for geese (e.g. min. 600 *Anser anser*) and *Tadorna ferruginea*. A total of 11,900 ducks and geese were counted in January 1968. The haur was listed as a wetland of international importance by Carp (1980).

Older observations on breeding species, many dating back to c.1914–1918, indicate that current

Globally threatened species

Pelecanus crispus	Winter visitor (max. 3, 1968–1979).
Anser erythropus	Winter visitor (max. 70, 1968–1979). This seems to be a traditional site, since a flock was recorded in December, c.1914–1918, and it was common in the area in the winter of 1954/55.
Branta ruficollis	Formerly a common winter visitor; the last known record is of c.1,000, winter 1954/55.
Marmaronetta angustirostris	Formerly a common resident (100 birds in June, presumably breeding, and 500 in February), but none recorded during 1968–1979 counts.
Haliaeetus albicilla	Winter visitor (max. 1, before 1968–1979).
Aquila heliaca	Winter visitor (max. 3, 1968–1979).
Vanellus gregarius	Huge flocks were recorded west of the site (cultivated plain between Kut and Aziziyah) in February, c.1914–1918. There is no more recent information.

1% or more of population

	Breeding (pairs)	Wintering	Passage
Ardea cinerea	—	133	—
Ardea goliath	—	—	2
Anser albifrons	—	325	—
Tadorna ferruginea	—	1,280	—
Anas penelope	—	2,700	—
Anas clypeata	—	3,000	—
Marmaronetta angustirostris	100 birds	500	—
Recurvirostra avosetta	—	373	—
Charadrius alexandrinus	150	724	—
Philomachus pugnax	—	2,000	—
Larus cachinnans/L. argentatus	—	645	—

Regionally threatened or declining species

Ardea goliath	One record of 2, August.
Grus virgo	Recorded in 'fair numbers' before 1918 (outside the breeding season).

breeding species may still include *Pelecanus onocrotalus* (thousands with 'quite small young' in August), *Ardea purpurea* (possibly breeding), *Plegadis falcinellus* (possibly breeding), *Anser anser* (small numbers in July), *Glareola pratincola* (breeding confirmed), *Larus ichthyaetus* (possibly breeding: recorded in August), *Chlidonias leucopterus* (breeding confirmed) and *C. hybridus* (breeding confirmed).

No information more recent than 1979 is available; the lake is difficult to approach, and surveys have gained only limited access, so actual numbers of birds present were undoubtedly much higher than observed.

Other threatened/endemic wildlife

No information available to BirdLife International.

Conservation issues

No conservation measures are known to have been taken. The current status of the site is not clear, in view of the expansion of irrigated cultivation in central Iraq. Duck-netting may constitute a threat if ongoing at an unsustainable level. No conservation measures are known to have been proposed.

Further reading

Ctyroký (1987), Georg and Savage (1970a,b), Georg and Vielliard (1970), Koning and Dijksen (1973), Moore and Boswell (1956–1957), Scott and Carp (1982).

021 Bahr Al Milh (Karbala)

32°40′N 43°40′E
c.150,000 ha

also known as Haur Abu Dibis or Lake Razazah
Unprotected

Site description

Bahr Al Milh is a very large, deep and brackish lake in a closed, sand/silt basin 95 km south-west of Baghdad, surrounded by desert and with a low cliff shore in many places. It was created in the late 1970s as a second storage reservoir (below Haur Al Habbaniya, site 016) to control floods on the River Euphrates. The salinity of the lake has been increasing since its creation and now stands at about 2.0–2.2%. There are many islands and peninsulas. Lake Usathe (also called Shithathah lake, 32°37′N 43°55′E, c.100 ha) lies a few kilometres from the south-east corner of Bahr Al Milh. It is a small, shallow, freshwater lake with some emergent vegetation. The surrounding area has some sandy cliffs and is sparsely vegetated.

Birds

See box for key species (some counts from the Karbala area are included). The lake is important for breeding *Marmaronetta angustirostris*, and holds huge numbers of wintering waterfowl. In January 1979 107,000 waterfowl were counted on Bahr Al Milh, even though only two points in the vast wetland area were surveyed, including very large concentrations of *Podiceps cristatus*, *P. nigricollis*, *Phalacrocorax carbo*, *Pelecanus onocrotalus*, *Mergellus albellus* and *Fulica atra*, while Lake Usathe held 30,500 waterfowl including good numbers of *Phoenicopterus ruber*, dabbling ducks and *Recurvirostra avosetta*. *Pelecanus crispus* was recorded at both lakes. Bahr Al Milh was listed as a wetland of international importance by Carp (1980).

Other threatened/endemic wildlife
No information available to BirdLife International.

Conservation issues
No conservation measures are known to have been taken. In the winter of 1991–1992, over 40,000 ducks and over 40,000 *Fulica atra* were estimated to have been sold in the markets of Karbala and Najaf, most of these probably having come from Bahr Al Milh and Haur Al Hammar (K. Y. Al-Dabbagh *in litt.*). In the 1970s it appeared that military activities and the use of the area for recreation might pose threats. Shrimp farming and the introduction of tilapia fish have both been proposed for Bahr Al Milh. No conservation measures are known to have been proposed.

Further reading
Carp (1975a,b), Ctyroký (1987), Scott and Carp (1982).

Globally threatened species

Pelecanus crispus	Winter visitor (max. 3, 1979).
Marmaronetta angustirostris	Summer visitor (max. 50 pairs at Bahr Al Milh; min. 20 pairs at Ain Tamr at Lake Usathe) in the late 1970s.

1% or more of population

	Breeding (pairs)	Wintering	Passage
Podiceps cristatus	—	600	—
Podiceps nigricollis	—	1,100	—
Phalacrocorax carbo	—	3,001	—
Anas strepera	—	3,000	—
Anas clypeata	—	5,372	—
Mergellus albellus	—	1,000	—
Fulica atra	—	102,522	—
Himantopus himantopus	100	—	500
Recurvirostra avosetta	?	300	—
Charadrius alexandrinus	300	—	—
Vanellus leucurus	300	100	—

022 Haur Al Abjiya and Haur Umm Al Baram (Wasit)
Unprotected

32°28´N 46°05´E
c.10,000 ha

Site description
Two haurs lying south of the River Tigris: Haur Umm Al Baram (32°32´N 46°07´E, 5,000 ha) is c.25 km east of Kut, whilst Haur Al Abjiya (32°25´N 46°03´E, 5,000 ha) is 20 km south-east of Kut. The two haurs are connected by the Dujaila Canal. Maps indicate that they are seasonal freshwater lakes. There is no further information.

Birds
These two haurs were listed as wetlands of international importance by Carp (1980). No specific ornithological information is available.

Other threatened/endemic wildlife
No information available to BirdLife International.

Conservation issues
No conservation measures are known to have been taken. There is no information on current threats to the site, but the site is likely to have suffered habitat degradation due to flood control measures on the Tigris and expanding irrigation schemes in the area. No conservation measures are known to have been proposed.

Further reading
Carp (1980).

023 Haur Delmaj (Wasit)
also known as Haur Dalmaj
Unprotected

32°20´N 45°30´E
c.100,000 ha

Site description
A large, isolated haur to the west of the River Tigris, about 35 km south-west of Kut town. The haur receives overflow from irrigation canals and floodwater from the Tigris.

Birds
The site was listed as a wetland of international importance by Carp (1980), but no specific ornithological information is available.

Other threatened/endemic wildlife
No information available to BirdLife International.

Conservation issues
No conservation measures are known to have been taken. There is no information on current threats to the site, but the site is likely to have suffered habitat degradation due to flood control measures on the Tigris and expanding irrigation schemes in the area. No conservation measures are known to have been proposed.

024 Haur Sarut (Maysan)
Unprotected

32°19′N 46°46′E
50 km

Site description
A long, narrow haur, largely overgrown with reeds *Phragmites*, stretching for 50 km from north to south (32°07′N–32°31′N) on the east bank of the River Tigris south-east of Ali Al Gharbi. The haur is fed by overflow from the Tigris and seasonal streams from the hill ranges to the north-east.

Birds
See box for key species. The site has not been ornithologically surveyed, and there is no specific information. However, the size of the wetland and its reedbed habitat suggest that it is important for birds.

Globally threatened species
Marmaronetta angustirostris Probably breeds.

Other threatened/endemic wildlife
No information available to BirdLife International.

Conservation issues
No conservation measures are known to have been taken. There is no information on the current status of the site nor whether there are any threats to it, but the site is likely to have suffered habitat degradation due to flood control measures on the Tigris and expanding irrigation schemes in the area. No conservation measures are known to have been proposed.

025 Haur Al Sa'adiyah (Wasit)
Unprotected

32°10′N 46°38′E
140,000 ha

Site description
Haur al Sa'adiyah constitutes the largest in a chain of haurs stretching for 120 km from near Ali Al Gharbi in the north to Haur Al Hammar in the south. The haur is a vast shallow lake of 1,400 km^2 bordered on the east by the River Tigris and on the west by the Dujaila Canal. The small north-western section of the haur is known as Haur Umm Roij (1,500 ha). When visited in January 1979, there was little emergent vegetation at the east end. The Dujaila Canal eventually flows into the haur at its southernmost point and this area is known as Haur Dujaila.

Birds
See box for key species. The only ornithological surveys have been in 1967, 1968 and 1979 (all in January). The surrounding fertile plains provide excellent feeding habitat for geese and cranes. The haur is particularly important for *Anser anser*, *Tadorna ferruginea*, *Anas platyrhynchos*, *A. crecca*, *A. acuta*, *A. clypeata*, *Phoenicopterus ruber* (900 in 1979), *Grus grus*, *Fulica atra* and shorebirds (Georg and Savage 1970a, b). The haur was listed as a wetland of international importance by Carp (1980).

Globally threatened species

Haliaeetus albicilla	Winter visitor (2).
Aquila heliaca	Winter visitor (3).

1% or more of population

	Breeding (pairs)	Wintering	Passage
Anser anser	—	1,000	—
Anas penelope	—	2,850	—
Anas strepera	—	5,000	—
Aythya nyroca	—	30	—
Grus grus	—	2,600	—
Charadrius alexandrinus	—	7,000	—
Calidris minuta	—	4,050	—
Calidris alpina	—	9,500	—

Regionally threatened or declining species
Aythya nyroca Winter visitor (max. 30).

Other threatened/endemic wildlife
No information available to BirdLife International.

Conservation issues
No conservation measures are known to have been taken. There is no information on current threats to the site, but the site is likely to have suffered habitat degradation due to flood control measures on the Tigris and expanding irrigation schemes in the area. No conservation measures are known to have been proposed.

Further reading
Georg and Savage (1970a,b), Georg and Vielliard (1970), Scott and Carp (1982).

026 Haur Ibn Najim (Babil)
also known as Haur Abu Najim
Unprotected

32°08′N 44°35′E
c.10,000 ha

Site description
Shown on maps as a seasonal freshwater lake c.10 km east of the River Euphrates and c.130 km south of Baghdad. No further information is available.

Birds
The site appears never to have been visited by an ornithologist, though it was considered by Scott and Carp (1982) to be possibly of great importance for wintering waterbirds, and Vant Leven (1968) provides good evidence for this (see 'Conservation issues'). The haur was listed as a wetland of international importance by Carp (1980).

Other threatened/endemic wildlife
No information available to BirdLife International.

Conservation issues
No conservation measures are known to have been taken. The site has presumably suffered badly from the decreasing flow of the Euphrates since the 1970s (see site 039); the 'Third River' canal presumably passes at least fairly nearby and there may thus be a threat of drainage. Vant Leven (1968) estimated that hunting accounted for c.31% of the ducks and c.56% of the coots wintering at this site, with 20,000 sold in the markets of Najaf and Shamiya in one winter. No conservation measures are known to have been proposed.

Further reading
Vant Leven (1968).

027 Haur Al Hachcham and Haur Maraiba (Wasit)
Unprotected

32°05′N 46°12′E
8,000 ha

Site description
Two small haurs largely overgrown with reeds *Phragmites*, on the plains south-east of Al Hayy. The haurs are fed by the Shatt Al Gharraf.

Birds
See box for key species. The two haurs were listed as a wetland of international importance by Carp (1980). The area was not visited by IWRB survey teams during 1968–1979.

Globally threatened species
Marmaronetta angustirostris Probably breeds.

Species restricted wholly or largely to the Middle East
Acrocephalus griseldis Probable summer visitor.

Other threatened/endemic wildlife
No information available to BirdLife International.

Conservation issues
No conservation measures are known to have been taken. There is no information on current threats. No conservation measures are known to have been proposed.

Further reading
Carp (1980), Georg and Savage (1970a).

028 Haur Al Haushiya (Maysan)

32°05′N 46°54′E
200 ha

also known as Al Kumait Ponds or Ali Sharqi Ponds
Unprotected

Site description
A group of 14 artificial ponds constructed for wildfowl hunting, in the basin of the former Haur Al Haushiya, on the east bank of the River Tigris, north of the village of Al Kumait.

Birds
See box for key species. Georg and Vielliard (1968) visited eight of the 14 ponds in January 1968, and they were also visited in January 1979. Other notable winter visitors included *Ciconia ciconia* (110) and *Calidris minuta* (500).

Globally threatened species

Pelecanus crispus	Winter visitor (1).
Aquila heliaca	Winter visitor (1).

1% or more of population

	Breeding (pairs)	Wintering	Passage
Anas strepera	—	1,310	—
Anas clypeata	—	2,400	—
Recurvirostra avosetta	—	500	—

Other threatened/endemic wildlife
No information available to BirdLife International.

Conservation issues
No conservation measures are known to have been taken. There is no information on current threats, but the site is likely to have suffered habitat degradation due to flood control measures on the Tigris and expanding irrigation schemes in the area. No conservation measures are known to have been proposed.

Further reading
Georg and Vielliard (1968), Scott and Carp (1982).

029 Shatt Al Gharraf (Wasit, Dhi Qar)

31°57′N 46°00′E
125+ km

Unprotected

Site description
A series of small ponds and seasonal wetlands along the 125+ km of the Shatt Al Gharraf waterway between Kut and Shatra, from 32°30′N 45°50′E to 31°25′N 46°10′E.

Birds
See box for key species. The area has only received one documented survey in recent years, in January 1979 (Scott and Carp 1982).

Globally threatened species

Marmaronetta angustirostris	An important breeding area (Savage 1968).
Aquila heliaca	Winter visitor (6).

1% or more of population

	Breeding (pairs)	Wintering	Passage
Himantopus himantopus	—	177	—
Vanellus leucurus	—	116	—

Other threatened/endemic wildlife
No information available to BirdLife International.

Conservation issues
No conservation measures are known to have been taken. There is no information on the current status of the site, but the 'Third River' canal passes through this area and may pose a threat through facilitating the expansion of irrigated cultivation and attendant drainage schemes. No conservation measures are known to have been proposed.

Further reading
Savage (1968), Scott and Carp (1982).

030 Haur Chubaisah Area (Maysan)
Unprotected

31°56′N 47°20′E
c.27,500 ha

Site description
A complex of large haurs with extensive marshes on the plains to the east of the River Tigris, north of Haur Om Am Nyaj. The three main haurs, Haur Jazrah in the west, Haur Chubaisah in the centre and Haur Sanaf in the east, lie close together and merge into one another at high water levels. They are bordered on the south by the Musharra Canal. Haur Sanaf (between Amara and Al Halfaya) is about 20 km long and consists mainly of open water with a few reeds and extensive fringing grasslands. Haur Chubaisah includes the Bani Lam Marshes described by Savage (1968).

Birds
See box for key species. According to Savage (1968), these wetlands are particularly important for *Anser anser*, *Anser erythropus* and *Tadorna ferruginea*. *Anhinga rufa* is resident, and the reference by Ticehurst *et al.* (1921–1922) to a 'colony' of *Marmaronetta angustirostris* near Amara, and to *Turdoides altirostris* being common in reedbeds there, presumably refers to this site. The most recent surveys were in January 1968 and January 1979. The entire area was listed as a wetland of international importance by Carp (1980).

Globally threatened species

Pelecanus crispus	Winter visitor (6).
Anser erythropus	Has occurred at Amara, November, and said to be an important wintering area in the 1960s.
Marmaronetta angustirostris	A breeding 'colony' near Amara.
Aquila heliaca	Winter visitor (1).
Numenius tenuirostris	There is a record from December 1917 of 'many' *Numenius tenuirostris* (a specimen was taken) at a temporary desert lake c.16 km north of Amara.

1% or more of population

	Breeding (pairs)	Wintering	Passage
Anhinga rufa	?	—	—
Nycticorax nycticorax	—	800	—

Regionally threatened or declining species

Anhinga rufa	Resident.

Species restricted wholly or largely to the Middle East

Turdoides altirostris	Common resident.

Other threatened/endemic wildlife
None known to BirdLife International.

Conservation issues
No conservation measures are known to have been taken. There has been no information on the site since 1979, but it does not seem likely that it has escaped some of the degradation suffered by other marshes in southern Iraq (see site 039). No conservation measures are known to have been proposed.

Further reading
Georg and Vielliard (1970), Savage (1968), Scott (1993), Ticehurst *et al.* (1921–1922).

031 Haur Sanniya (Maysan)
Unprotected

31°55′N 46°48′E
40,000 ha

Site description
The second in the chain of large haurs stretching from Haur Sa'adiyah in the north to Haur Al Hammar in the south. The haur receives overflow from Haur Sa'adiyah to the north and from the River Tigris to the east (Georg and Savage 1968).

Birds
The site has not been ornithologically surveyed, but is likely to be of major importance given its size and proximity to wetlands of known importance.

Other threatened/endemic wildlife
No information available to BirdLife International.

Conservation issues
No conservation measures are known to have been taken. There is no information on the current status of the site or whether it is threatened, but it is likely to have suffered habitat degradation due to flood control measures on the Tigris and expanding irrigation schemes in the area. No conservation measures are known to have been proposed.

032 Haur Om Am Nyaj (Maysan)

31°45´N 47°25´E
15,000 ha

also known as Suweid or Sudan Marshes
Unprotected

Site description

Haur Om Am Nyaj is a large wetland about 20 km south-east of Amara. It comprises extensive *Typha* beds with many areas of open water and fast-running creeks, and is partly permanent and partly seasonal. The haur lies at the north-western extremity of Haur Al Hawizeh and is fed by the Al Kahala (Chahala) river, a distributary of the Tigris. The Qalit Salih ponds (31°30´N 47°20´E, 100 ha) lie at the southern end of Haur Om Am Nyaj, and are a group of fresh to brackish impoundments used for duck-netting, on the east bank of the River Tigris near the town of Qalit Salih, west of the Haur Al Hawizeh marshes.

Globally threatened species

Phalacrocorax pygmeus	Recorded in winter at Haur Om Am Nyaj (100) and Qalit Salih ponds (6).
Pelecanus crispus	Winter visitor at Qalit Salih ponds (12).
Aquila heliaca	Winter visitor at Qalit Salih ponds (1).

1% or more of population

	Breeding (pairs)	Wintering	Passage
Phalacrocorax pygmeus	—	100	—
Nycticorax nycticorax	200 birds	poss. hundreds	—
Threskiornis aethiopicus	—	4	—
Anas clypeata	—	2,000	—

Regionally threatened or declining species

Threskiornis aethiopicus	Recorded in winter at Qalit Salih ponds (4).

Birds

See box for key species. Haur Om Am Nyaj was visited briefly in January 1975, and found to be an important area for *Phalacrocorax pygmeus*. The Qalit Salih ponds were visited in January 1979; species included *Pelecanus onocrotalus* (92), *Phoenicopterus ruber* (500), *Anas crecca* (10,000) and *Recurvirostra avosetta* (250). There was a breeding colony of c.200 *Nycticorax nycticorax* on the Al Kahala river in the 1970s and a 'very big roost' of *N. nycticorax* near Qalit Salih in the 1910s may have been the same site.

Other threatened/endemic wildlife

No information available to BirdLife International.

Conservation issues

No conservation measures are known to have been taken. There has been no information on the site since 1979, but it does not seem likely that it has escaped some of the degradation suffered by other marshes in southern Iraq (see site 039): according to a Landsat satellite image from August 1992, much of the area may have been drained and converted to cultivation. No conservation measures are known to have been proposed.

Further reading

Carp (1975a), Scott and Carp (1982), Ticehurst *et al.* (1921–1922).

033 Haur Al Rayan and Umm Osbah (Maysan)

31°40´N 47°01´E
25,000 ha

also known as Maymund or Salam Marshes
Unprotected

Site description

A complex of shallow lagoons and vast reedbeds with some areas of sedge marsh between the villages of Maymund and Salam, about 20 km south-west of Amara. The southern end of these marshes lies a few kilometres to the north of the Feraigat Marshes at the extreme northern end of the main Haur Al Hammar marshes.

Globally threatened species

Pelecanus crispus	Winter visitor (109).
Haliaeetus albicilla	Winter visitor (2).
Aquila heliaca	Winter visitor (5).

1% or more of population

	Breeding (pairs)	Wintering	Passage
Pelecanus onocrotalus	—	750	—
Ardea cinerea	—	122	—
Threskiornis aethiopicus	—	36	—
Limosa limosa	—	480	—

Regionally threatened or declining species

Threskiornis aethiopicus	A flock of 36 was observed in this area in January 1979.

Birds

See box for key species. This is known to be an important area for herons, egrets and coots. The site has only been surveyed (very incompletely) in January 1968 and January 1979. Other notable winter visitors included *Ciconia ciconia* (183), *Anas crecca* (4,000) and *Circus aeruginosus* (25).

Other threatened/endemic wildlife
No information available to BirdLife International.

Conservation issues
No conservation measures are known to have been taken. There is no information on current threats, but it does not seem likely that it has escaped some of the degradation suffered by other marshes in southern Iraq (see site 039). No conservation measures are known to have been proposed.

Further reading
Georg and Vielliard (1970), Scott and Carp (1982).

034 Haur Auda (Maysan)
also known as Haur Al Awdah
Unprotected

31°33´N 46°51´E
7,500 ha

Site description
One of the chain of haurs stretching from Haur Al Sa'adiyah in the north to Haur Al Hammar in the south, situated about 40 km south-west of Amara town (Georg and Savage 1970a). The haur overflows into the extreme north-western portion of the main marshes north of Haur Al Hammar.

Birds
Haur Auda was listed as a wetland of international importance by Carp (1980). It has not been ornithologically surveyed, but is likely to be of major importance given its size and proximity to wetlands of known importance.

Other threatened/endemic wildlife
No information available to BirdLife International.

Conservation issues
No conservation measures are known to have been taken. There is no information on the current status of the site or whether it is threatened, but it does not seem likely that it has escaped some of the degradation suffered by other marshes in southern Iraq (see site 039). No conservation measures are known to have been proposed.

Further reading
Georg and Savage (1970a).

035 Haur Uwainah (Dhi Qar)
also known as Shatra Marshes
Unprotected

31°25´N 46°20´E
c.32,500 ha

Site description
A complex of large haurs and associated marshes on the plains to the east of the Shatt Al Gharraf waterway, east and south-east of the village of Shatra. The two principal haurs are Haur Abu Ajul (31°29´N 46°20´E, 7,500 ha) in the north, and Haur Chamuqa (Ghamuga) (31°22´N 46°25´E, 25,000 ha) in the south. They are fed mainly by the Shatt Al Gharraf. Both haurs formerly supported extensive *Phragmites* reedbeds, but Abu Ajul had been drained by December 1972. By 1979, the northern haur was completely under cultivation, while Haur Chamuqa had been somewhat reduced in size with the construction of an embankment with a road around the northern perimeter. However, much of this haur remained in excellent condition with extensive *Typha* beds and large areas of open water.

Birds
See box for key species. Over 10,000 waterfowl were present in January 1979, mainly *Fulica atra*. The surrounding wet meadows and rain-fed pools provide excellent habitat for a variety of shorebirds. The haur was listed as a wetland of international importance by Carp (1980).

Other threatened/endemic wildlife
No information available to BirdLife International.

Globally threatened species

Pelecanus crispus	Winter visitor (20).

1% or more of population

	Breeding (pairs)	Wintering	Passage
Pelecanus onocrotalus	—	140	—
Ardea cinerea	—	145	—
Himantopus himantopus	—	187	—
Recurvirostra avosetta	—	380	—
Vanellus leucurus	—	111	—
Limosa limosa	—	320	—

Conservation issues

No conservation measures are known to have been taken. There is no recent information on threats to the wetland, although further, major habitat destruction or degradation is a strong probability (see site 039). No conservation measures are known to have been proposed.

Further reading

Savage (1968), Georg and Savage (1970a), Koning and Dijksen (1973), Scott and Carp (1982).

036 Haur Al Hawizeh (Maysan, Al Basrah)

Unprotected

31°22´N 47°38´E
220,000 ha

Site description

Situated to the east of the River Tigris, Haur Al Hawizeh (Hawaizah) and its associated marshes cover an area of approximately 2,200 km^2 between Amara and Basrah (31°00´N–31°45´N, 47°25´E–47°50´E). A small portion of the haur extends over the border into Iranian territory, where it is known as the Hoor Al Azim. The wetland is fed by floodwaters from the River Tigris and from the Karkheh river in the east (in Iran); it is bordered in the north by the Musharra Canal and in the south by the Shatt Al Arab. The marsh is partly seasonal and partly permanent. The latter area has extensive *Phragmites* reedbeds alternating with open sheets of water. The Nahrsabla Marshes (31°30´N 47°35´E) are an area of predominantly seasonal marsh in the north-eastern portion of the haur, near the Iranian border.

Birds

See box for key species. According to Savage (1968), Haur Al Hawizeh provides wintering habitat for some of the largest concentrations of wildfowl in the world. Large numbers of *Anser anser*, *Anas platyrhynchos*, *A. strepera*, *A. crecca*, *A. penelope*, *A. acuta*, *A. clypeata*, *Netta rufina*, *Aythya ferina*, *A. fuligula*, *Phoenicopterus ruber* and *Fulica atra* are believed to occur in winter, while *A. querquedula* is common on passage (Georg and Savage 1970b). However, no systematic ornithological surveys or waterfowl counts have ever been undertaken in the Iraqi portion of these marshes. Haur Al Hawizeh was listed as a wetland of international importance by Carp (1980).

Globally threatened species

Anser erythropus	The Nahrsabla Marshes were reported to be a wintering area in the 1960s.
Haliaeetus albicilla	Probable winter visitor.

Regionally threatened or declining species

Anhinga rufa	Common east of Al Azair in the 1910s; current status unknown.
Botaurus stellaris	Probable winter visitor.
Francolinus francolinus	Common resident.

Species restricted wholly or largely to the Middle East

Hypocolius ampelinus	Probable summer visitor.
Acrocephalus griseldis	Probably an abundant summer visitor.

Other threatened/endemic wildlife

Mammals: *Canis lupus* (V), *Lutra perspicillata* (K; the subspecies *L. p. maxwelli* is endemic to the marshes and endangered), *Gerbillus mesopotamiae* (endemic).

Conservation issues

No nature conservation measures are known to have been taken. An August 1992 Landsat image shows that large areas of the north-western, western and southern shores have been drained, using river control and dyke-building, apparently for security reasons. However, the haur is not under immediate threat of widespread drainage on the vast scale which has affected the Central Marshes and Haur Al Hammar, since it receives much of its water from Iranian rivers which are not currently subject to major flood control, drainage and irrigation projects. Reports from sources in Iraq and Iraq suggest that the marsh vegetation on both sides of the border was badly damaged during the Iran/Iraq war, and there may have been significant wildlife mortality. Several of the largest battles occurred in and around these marshes, involving heavy bombing and shelling, extensive burning and the use of chemical weapons. Large areas of reedbed were cut or burnt in the search for rebels after the 1980–1988 and 1990–1991 Gulf Wars. According to the Landsat image from August 1992, the southern quarter of the marshes is probably now saline, since it appears to be shallow (less than 1 m deep) yet does not support any emergent vegetation. Furthermore, compared to a Landsat image from 1984, it appears that the southern edge of emergent vegetation (*Phragmites*) has retreated northwards by 20 km, implying that any such salinization is a recent development. Although there is little information available, the area must be considered highly threatened if not already severely damaged. Persistent pesticides are reported to have been used to kill and catch fish. No conservation measures are known to have been proposed.

Further reading

Carp (1980), Georg and Savage (1970b), North (1993), Pearce (1993), Prentice (1993), Savage (1968), Ticehurst *et al.* (1921–1922).

037 Haur Lafta (Al Muthanna)

Unprotected

31°21′N 45°30′E
c.20,000 ha

Site description

An isolated haur c.5 km north of the River Euphrates and c.80 km west-north-west of Nasiriya, fed by floodwater from the Euphrates.

Birds

The site was listed as a wetland of international importance by Carp (1980), and was considered by Scott and Carp (1982) to be possibly of great importance for wintering waterbirds, but there is no specific ornithological information available.

Other threatened/endemic wildlife

No information available to BirdLife International.

Conservation issues

No conservation measures are known to have been taken. The site may have suffered major habitat degradation or destruction following the decline in the flow of the Euphrates since the 1970s (see site 039) but there is no other information on current threats and no conservation measures are known to have been proposed.

Further reading

Carp (1980), Georg and Savage (1970a), Scott and Carp (1982).

038 Central Marshes (Maysan, Dhi Qar, Al Basrah)

also known as Amara Marshes
Unprotected

31°10′N 47°05′E
300,000 ha

Site description

The Central Marshes comprise a vast complex of mostly permanent freshwater marshes with scattered areas of open water, to the west of the River Tigris and to the north of the River Euphrates (30°50′N–31°30′N, 46°45′E–47°25′E). The marshes are fed by both rivers, and at maximum flooding in late spring they cover an area of about 3,000 km^2. Almost the entire area is covered in tall reedbeds of *Phragmites* and *Typha*. Large portions of the marshes are difficult of access, and have seldom been visited by biologists. To the north, between the marshes and the Tigris, lies extensive cultivation, including rice fields and huge sugar-cane polders. The Ma'dan or Marsh Arabs have lived in these marshes for at least 5,000 years, but the majority have now been displaced by massive habitat destruction (see 'Conservation issues').

Birds

See box for key species. No comprehensive surveys of birds or wildlife have ever been undertaken. Georg and Vielliard visited the Al Azair area (in the north-east) in January 1967; Koning and Dijksen visited the Chabaish Marshes (in the south-east) in December 1972; Carp and Scott visited the Feraigat Marshes (in the north) and the Chabaish Marshes in January 1979. Other notable wintering species included *Ciconia ciconia* (103), *Plegadis falcinellus* (150)

Globally threatened species

Pelecanus crispus	Winter visitor (72).
Phalacrocorax pygmeus	Winter visitor (31).
Aquila heliaca	Winter visitor (3).

1% or more of population

	Breeding (pairs)	Wintering	Passage
Pelecanus onocrotalus	—	413	—
Ardea cinerea	—	191	—
Larus cachinnans/L. argentatus	—	503	—

and *Circus aeruginosus* (73). The entire area was listed as a wetland of international importance by Carp (1980). Portions of this vast wetland which are, or were, known or thought to be of special importance for waterfowl include the following (comments on current status are based on study of a Landsat image from August 1992).

Feraigat Marshes (31°30′N 47°10′E) The north-easternmost section of the marshes, fed by flood waters from the Tigris. Known to support huge concentrations of wildfowl in winter (Savage 1968). In the 1950s *Anser anser* occasionally remained to breed. Much of this area has now been drained.

Al Azair Marshes (31°17′N 47°23′E) The north-easternmost section of the marshes, just west of the River Tigris. According to Savage (1968), this area of seasonal and permanent marshes was the principal known haunt of *Oxyura leucocephala* in Iraq. The village of Al Azair is also known as 'Ezra's Tomb' in earlier literature. These marshes have now been drained.

Haur Umm Al Binni Marshes (31°15′N 47°05′E) A large area of predominantly permanent marshes around Haur Umm Al Binni lake in the west-central part of the marshes. According to Savage (1968), these marshes were important habitat for wintering *Aythya ferina*. *Marmaronetta angustirostris* was reported to breed. Some of this area may now have been drained.

Fartus Marshes (31°10′N 46°55′E) Along the western edge of the Central Marshes. According to Savage (1968), this area, which includes the Sabil Al Awaidiya, was the habitat of large numbers of wintering *Aythya ferina* and *Anser* sp. *Marmaronetta angustirostris* was said to breed. This area may not yet have been affected by drainage.

Haur Az Zikri (31°10′N 47°10′E) The very large open-water lake in the centre of the marshes, said to be very important for wintering waterfowl (Savage 1968). This area may now have been drained.

Chabaish Marshes (31°00′N 47°00′E) A large area of permanent and temporary marshes in the south, including Haur Birkat (Birkat Baghdad), flooded both from the Tigris and the Euphrates (Savage 1968). This area may not yet have been affected by drainage.

Al Jazair Marshes (31°00′N 47°15′E) The extensive marshes on the north bank of the Euphrates before its confluence with the Tigris (Savage 1968). At least the eastern sector of these marshes has now been drained.

Other threatened/endemic wildlife

Mammals: *Lutra perspicillata* (K; the subspecies *L. p. maxwelli* is endemic to the marshes and endangered), *Gerbillus mesopotamiae* (endemic), *Erythronesokia bunnii* (endemic).

Conservation issues

No nature conservation measures are known to have been taken. Since 1991 intensive hydrological engineering activity has been occurring in the Central Marshes, leading to massive habitat destruction. According to reports in July 1993 and an unsourced satellite image made public in late 1993, a 35-km-long double embankment was built (and completed in July 1992) from the village of Al Jandallah (Maysan Governorate) south-eastwards to Abu Ajil (near the Qal'at Salih airfield), crossing most of the northern and north-eastern end of the Central Marshes, and thus blocking and diverting more than 40 distributary streams and rivers which formerly flowed into the marshes from the Tigris. This double levée joins the 'Al Amarah Canal' or 'Anfal 3' canal, which is another double embankment built for defensive purposes during the Iran–Iraq war (now converted into a drainage canal) and which runs southwards, just west of the Tigris, for 50 km before discharging into the Euphrates at Qurna. In addition, dykes were said to have been constructed up to 30 km into the marshes west of the Al Amarah Canal in 1992–1993, to compartmentalize areas of marsh and facilitate drainage, and it is also claimed that locks, sluice gates and flanking embankments 6–8 m high have been placed at the heads of many of the Tigris distributaries in order to regulate water flow into the marshes. Collectively these measures are said to have prevented water from entering up to two-thirds of the Central Marshes during 1992–1993; a Landsat satellite image from August 1992 showed more than one third of the marsh was dry, and in July 1993 it was claimed that this proportion had increased to two-thirds. The westernmost distributaries of the Tigris still appeared to be unimpeded and flowing into the surviving western sector of the Central Marshes on the August 1992 Landsat image, and this corridor is thus extremely important in sustaining what remains of the Central Marshes, and possibly also in supplying water from the Tigris to the Haur Al Hammar (site 039) further south.

Further reading

Georg and Vielliard (1968, 1970), Koning and Dijksen (1954), North (1993), Pearce (1993), Prentice (1993), Savage (1968), Scott and Carp (1982), Thesiger (1954).

039 Haur Al Hammar (Dhi Qar, Al Basrah)
Unprotected

30°44'N 47°03'E
350,000 ha

Site description
The Haur Al Hammar, its surrounding marshes and neighbouring haurs and areas of temporary inundation comprise some 3,500 km² of almost contiguous wetland habitat. The haur itself is the largest lake in the lower Euphrates, approximately 120 km long by up to 25 km wide. It is bordered in the north by the River Euphrates, in the west by the Southern Desert and in the east by the Shatt Al Arab. The lake is eutrophic, and generally shallow with a maximum depth of about 1.8 m at low-water levels in early winter and about 3.0 m at high-water levels in late spring. Large parts of the littoral zone dry out during periods of low water and banks and islands appear in many places. The hydrology of the lake is not clear: its main source of water re-charge appears to be the Euphrates, but it may also receive a very substantial amount of water from the Tigris via the Central Marshes (see site 038), and there is presumably also some re-charge from groundwater. The Euphrates flows through the marshes and joins the Tigris at Qarmat Ali, where the combined flow becomes the Shatt Al Arab. Habitats include open, fairly shallow water, vast reedbeds, broad muddy shores, sedge marsh and marsh-edge vegetation, moist arable land, irrigation ponds, rainwater pools, communication dams, artificial islands with villages, rice and sugar-cane polders and date-palm groves. Emergent vegetation is dominated by beds of *Phragmites* and *Typha* with some *Cyperus papyrus* and *Arundo*, as well as many other aquatics, both floating (*Nymphoides*, *Nymphaea*, *Nuphar*, *Pistia*, *Lemna*) and submerged (*Vallisneria*, *Potamogeton*, *Myriophyllum*, *Ceratophyllum*, *Chara*, *Najas*, *Salvinia*). The marshes are rich in fish, and an estimate of the annual catch, published in 1966, was 30,000 tonnes, of which 70% were Cyprinidae. The local people, the Ma'dan (Marsh Arabs), are ethnologically and culturally distinct, and have lived in the area for at least 5,000 years. Fishing and wildfowl hunting are a major part of the local economy, and there is considerable dependence on reeds for forage for domestic buffalo, for house building and for the construction of floating islands for villages.

Birds
See box for key species. Haur Al Hammar and its associated marshes comprise one of the most important areas for waterfowl in the Middle East, both in terms of numbers of birds and diversity of species. The vast reedbeds provide breeding habitat for a wide variety of resident species, while in winter the haur attracts huge numbers of migratory waterfowl. Koning and Dijksen (1973) visited the wetland at various points in December 1972—near the villages of Hammar and Fuhud and at three localities east of Nasiriya—and confirmed that this was the most important wintering area for waterfowl in Iraq. Carp visited the east end of the haur and Haur Aluwez in January 1972, while Carp and Scott visited the east end, the south-western shore, Haur Aluwez, the west end near Nasiriya and the Fuhud and Hammar areas in January 1979. P. Ctyroký made some waterfowl counts in the area in 1979. The entire area was listed by Carp (1980) as a wetland of international importance.

Globally threatened species

Phalacrocorax pygmeus	Winter visitor (min. 48).
Pelecanus crispus	Winter visitor (min. 243); may breed.
Oxyura leucocephala	Winter visitor (min. 1); possibly overlooked.
Aquila heliaca	Winter visitor (min. 3).
Numenius tenuirostris	Winter visitor (min. 6 in 1979).

1% or more of population

	Breeding (pairs)	Wintering	Passage
Phalacrocorax pygmeus	?	48	—
Anhinga rufa	?	—	—
Pelecanus onocrotalus	—	1,741	—
Pelecanus crispus	?	243	—
Nycticorax nycticorax	—	1,000	—
Ardea cinerea	—	272	—
Anas penelope	—	6,000	—
Anas strepera	—	10,830	—
Anas crecca	—	59,600	—
Anas platyrhynchos	—	12,300	—
Anas acuta	—	12,200	—
Anas clypeata	—	2,130	—
Aythya fuligula	—	42,280	—
Fulica atra	—	121,455	—
Himantopus himantopus	—	277	—
Charadrius alexandrinus	abundant	6,383	—
Vanellus leucurus	—	145	—
Calidris minuta	—	1,900	—
Calidris alpina	—	2,125	—
Limosa limosa	—	355	—
Numenius tenuirostris	—	6	—
Tringa erythropus	—	181	—
Larus cachinnans/L. argentatus	—	878	—
Sterna caspia	—	104	—
Chlidonias hybridus	—	356	—

Regionally threatened or declining species

Botaurus stellaris	Recorded in winter (min. 1); may breed.
Ardea goliath	Rare resident.

Species restricted wholly or largely to the Middle East

Acrocephalus griseldis	Common summer visitor.
Turdoides altirostris	Common resident.
Passer moabiticus	Summer visitor.

In general, the large open areas of water are too deep for most species of wintering waterfowl other than pelicans, diving ducks, *Fulica atra*, gulls and terns. The vast and almost unbroken reedbeds of *Typha* and *Phragmites* probably support large breeding populations of species such as *Nycticorax nycticorax*, *Ardeola ralloides*, *Ardea purpurea*, *Gallinula chloropus*, *Porphyrio porphyrio* and *Fulica atra*, as well as smaller numbers of *Anser anser*, but there is very little information on breeding species, and that which exists dates mostly from the 1920s or before. The broad, muddy shoreline along the southern edge of the main Haur Al Hammar provides excellent habitat for shorebirds, while sedge marshes and marsh-edge habitat to the east and west of the main haur are particularly suitable for herons, egrets, *Platalea leucorodia*, *Plegadis falcinellus*, dabbling ducks and some shorebirds. Moist arable land, irrigation ponds and rain-water pools on the surrounding plains provide excellent feeding areas for geese, dabbling ducks, *Grus grus* and many shorebirds. The site supports large numbers of wintering birds of prey, including *Circus aeruginosus* (185) and *Aquila clanga* (8). Passerines wintering in large numbers include *Anthus spinoletta*, *Luscinia svecica*, *Lanius isabellinus* and *Passer hispaniolensis*. There is almost no ornithological information from spring and autumn, but the site is likely to be equally as important for migratory waterfowl in these seasons as in winter. Flocks of up to 800 *Phalaropus lobatus* have been seen on Haur Al Hammar in late spring.

Portions of this vast wetland which are or were of special importance for waterfowl include the following (comments on present status are based on study of a Landsat image from August 1992).

Eastern end of Haur Al Hammar (30°35´N 47°45´E) The eastern end of Haur Al Hammar near its outlet comprised a vast expanse of shallow, open water with fringing reedbeds and reed islands. This area was especially important for ducks and *Fulica atra*: over 30,000 were present in January 1979. Much of this area has now been drained.

Haur Aluwez (30°30´N 47°35´E) This comprised the vast marshlands and open water areas in the south-east. Haur Aluwez was especially important for pelicans, diving ducks and coots. The 1975 survey recorded 1,300 pelicans in this area; the 1979 survey found over 40,000 ducks, mainly *Aythya fuligula*, and 73,000 *Fulica atra*, as well as large numbers of shorebirds and gulls. Much of this area has now been drained.

South-west shore of Haur Al Hammar (30°40´N 46°55´E) The extensive mudflats which stretch for over 50 km along the south-western shore of the haur provide excellent habitat for shorebirds. Over 8,000 shorebirds, mainly *Charadrius alexandrinus*, *Calidris minuta* and *C. alpina*, were recorded along a short stretch of this habitat in January 1979. Of particular interest were six *Numenius tenuirostris*. Some of this area has now been drained.

Fuhud and Hammar area (30°57´N 46°46´E) The extensive reedbeds and open water areas in the region of Fuhud and Hammar villages in the north-west are especially important for pelicans and dabbling ducks. The 1979 survey recorded over 1,500 pelicans and 30,000 dabbling duck in this area, along with a day roost of about 1,000 *Nycticorax nycticorax*.

Nasiriya Marshes (31°00´N 46°25´E) These permanent and temporary marshes in dead branches of the Euphrates near Nasiriya are a continuation of the main Haur Al Hammar marshes to the east. They are important for a wide variety of waterfowl, notably herons, egrets and dabbling ducks.

■ Other threatened/endemic wildlife

Mammals: *Canis lupus* (V), *Lutra perspicillata* (K; the subspecies *L. p. maxwelli* is endemic to the marshes and endangered), *Gerbillus mesopotamiae* (endemic), *Erythronesokia bunnii* (endemic).

■ Conservation issues

No nature conservation measures are known to have been taken. Flood control, drainage and irrigation projects upstream on the Euphrates in central Iraq, Turkey and Syria have been progressively reducing the amount of water flowing in the Euphrates and thus into the marshes, especially from the 1970s onwards, and the extent of permanent wetland is likely to have contracted—according to one report, by 10% between 1985 and 1990. In January 1975 a large part of Haur Aluwez had been cut off from the main wetland by a 10-km-long embankment and was being drained to facilitate oil exploration. By 1985, more than 80,000 ha of marsh at the north-eastern end of Haur Al Hammar had been drained in order to exploit the West Qurnah oilfield. Haur Aluwez is one of the parts of Haur Al Hammar most affected by drainage schemes in recent years, and satellite images from 1984 and August 1992 show that much of this area has now been drained, as has much of the extreme eastern end of Haur Al Hammar near its outflow in to the Shatt Al Arab, as well as extensive areas of the southern shores of Haur Al Hammar.

In addition, a huge canal (the 'Third River') was completed in December 1992, extending c.560 km from Mahmudiya (near Baghdad) south-east down the right bank of the Shatt Al Gharraf, crossing the

Euphrates downstream of Nasiriya, skirting round the south-western boundary of Haur Al Hammar before bisecting the south-eastern corner (flanked by raised embankments), and finally discharging into the man-made Shatt Al Basrah canal, which itself links Haur Al Hammar to the sea via Khawr Al Zubair. Much of the drainage of the southern and south-eastern shores of Haur Al Hammar appears to have followed, and/or to have been facilitated by, the isolation of these areas from the rest of the Haur by the embanked Third River. Since 1991 a large earth dam has been built across the Euphrates near the canal's intersection point near Suq Al Shuyukh, as well as another dam c.70 km downstream near Al Madinah; their exact function is not clear. The Third River is intended to drain saline water resulting from the planned washing of 1.5 million hectares of salt-encrusted soil (potential farmland) in the area between the two rivers in central Iraq, and may have already started taking saline water away from smaller, previously functioning irrigation waste-water canals that were formerly discharging directly into Haur Al Hammar. However, it has been claimed that almost the entire flow of the Euphrates has been diverted into the canal and hence into the Gulf (thus completely depriving the marshes of one of their major water sources), either at the point where the canal intersects the river, or at the recently built earth dam nearby. Aerial photos from 1990 indicate that the canal, at that time, was being engineered to pass under the river via an inverted siphon, hence avoiding discharge of saline water into the Euphrates and thence into Haur Al Hammar, but the role of the associated earth dam in any river diversion is still unclear.

A smaller canal, the 'Fourth River', was completed at around the same time as the Third River; this abstracts some of the Euphrates' flow from upstream of Nasiriya, reducing pressure on the new earth dam downstream, and empties it into Khawr Al Zubair, thus depriving Haur Al Hammar of some of its water supply. In addition, according to reports in 1993, a continuous embankment has been built along at least the right bank of the Euphrates (possibly both banks) along much of the northern border of Haur Al Hammar (between the two, new earth dams mentioned above) sometime since 1991, thus greatly hindering any annual re-charge of floodwater into the haur which normally occurs in late spring.

The salinity of Haur Al Hammar has apparently increased in recent years, especially near its outflow into the Shatt Al Arab. Hunting occurs on a massive scale; for example in the winter of 1991–1992, over 40,000 ducks and over 40,000 *Fulica atra* were estimated to have been sold in the markets of Karbala and Najaf, most of these probably having come from Haur al Hammar and Bahr Al Milh. However, at least in the 1970s, this did not clearly pose a serious threat to waterfowl populations because of the vastness of the area. Hunting was said to have been banned completely in Iraq in 1974, although this has not been effective. There is a possibility of major pollution from oil production, and small-scale oil pollution from the motor boats used between the main villages is common.

At the suggestion of the Vice President of the University of Basra, the IWRB/Basra University Expedition of 1979 recommended the establishment of a protected area at Haur Al Hammar; no measures are known to have been proposed by government agencies.

Further reading

Allouse (1953), Carp (1980), Georg and Savage (1970a,b), North (1993), Pearce (1993), Prentice (1993), Scott and Carp (1982), Thesiger (1954, 1964), Ticehurst *et al.* (1921–1922).

040 Shatt Al Arab Marshes (Al Basrah)

Unprotected

30°27′N 47°58′E
c.165 km

Site description

These marshes lie along the c.165 km of the Shatt Al Arab waterway from 31°00′N 47°25′E to 29°55′N 48°30′E, mainly between Qurnah and Basrah (c.65 km), and include Haur Al Shaibah (15 km north of Basrah), Qarmat Ali, Khamisiyah and Shafi. Shafi wetland (30°53′N 47°31′E) is a small reed-marsh near the town of Shafi on the Basrah to Amara road, 30 km from Basrah.

Birds

See box for key species. According to Savage (1968), the marshes are important for wintering *Anser anser* and dabbling ducks, mainly *Anas platyrhynchos* and *A. crecca*, and breeding *Marmaronetta angustirostris*. The muddy shores of the Shatt Al Arab are an important feeding area for passage and wintering shorebirds. The area was most recently surveyed in 1968, 1975 and 1979; all visits were in January, and

Globally threatened species

Pelecanus crispus	Winter visitor (1).
Marmaronetta angustirostris	An important breeding area (Savage 1968).
Aquila heliaca	Winter visitor (1).

1% or more of population

	Breeding (pairs)	Wintering	Passage
Larus ridibundus	—	4,000	—

Species restricted wholly or largely to the Middle East

Acrocephalus griseldis	Summer visitor.

were brief and incomplete; notable winter visitors included *Ciconia ciconia* (105), *Milvus migrans* (305) and *Vanellus leucurus* (50).

Other threatened/endemic wildlife

None known to BirdLife International.

Conservation issues

In 1975 the Museum of Natural History of the University of Basrah established a research station at Shafi wetland. Otherwise no conservation measures are known to have been taken. The lower marshes below Basrah are presumably changing their character as less fresh water is reaching the sea and there is increasing encroachment of sea water. However, the current status of these marshes is completely unknown. No conservation measures are known to have been proposed.

Further reading

Carp (1975a), Georg and Vielliard (1970), Savage (1968), Scott and Carp (1982).

041 Khawr Al Zubair (Al Basrah)

Unprotected

30°12′N 47°54′E
c.20,000 ha

Site description

A huge tidal inlet with associated intertidal mudflats at the head of the Arabian Gulf, c.40 km south-east of Basra. Tidal amplitude is likely to be high (more than 3 m).

Birds

The site appears never to have been visited by an ornithologist, though it was considered by Scott and Carp (1982) to be possibly of great importance for wintering waterbirds. The khawr was listed as a wetland of international importance by Carp (1980).

Other threatened/endemic wildlife

No information available to BirdLife International.

Conservation issues

No conservation measures are known to have been taken. There is no information on current threats. During the Iran–Iraq war, the Shatt Al Basrah canal was constructed as a safer shipping route to Basrah, leading northwards from the Gulf directly through the site to connect with the extreme eastern end of Haur Al Hammar near its discharge into the Shatt Al Arab. This is likely to have led to a major and permanent flooding of the inlet-basin with fresh to brackish water. In addition since December 1992 the 'Third River' canal has been discharging saline water into the Shatt Al Basrah and hence into this site (see site 039); the volume of this discharge may increase substantially in future. It is not known what impact all of these developments have had on the khawr and its wildlife. No conservation measures are known to have been proposed.

042 Khawr Abdallah (Al Basrah)

Unprotected

29°55′N 48°32′E
c.126,00 ha

Site description

Enormous areas of swampy grassflats (c.90,000 ha) and intertidal mudflats (c.36,000 ha) backed by a belt of date palms and then by silt desert, immediately west of the point where the Shatt Al Arab enters the Gulf, and of the town of Fao. Tidal amplitude is large (3 m or more). There is a major oil terminal.

Birds

See box for key species. Except for scattered records from the 1920s and before, the site has been surveyed only once, in January 1968, and then only very incompletely. Counts then included 2,050 ducks, but the area appeared more important for wintering gulls and terns; 2,015 waders were also counted. *Larus genei* and *Coracias benghalensis* were breed-

1% or more of population

	Breeding (pairs)	Wintering	Passage
Threskiornis aethiopicus	—	'plentiful'	—
Numenius arquata	—	500	—
Larus cachinnans/L. argentatus	—	720	—
Sterna nilotica	breeds	200	—

Regionally threatened or declining species

Threskiornis aethiopicus Common in winter in the 1920s.

Species restricted wholly or largely to the Middle East

Dromas ardeola Non-breeding resident.
Hypocolius ampelinus Summer visitor.
Hippolais languida Summer visitor.
Turdoides altirostris Resident.

ing in the 1920s, and *Passer hispaniolensis* occurs in winter. The entire area was listed as a wetland of international importance by Carp (1980).

Other threatened/endemic wildlife

No information available to BirdLife International.

Conservation issues

No conservation measures are known to have been taken. There is no information on current threats, but the area may have undergone land-claim (in common with many other Arabian Gulf shorelines associated with centres of industry and population), and oil pollution is presumably a constant threat. The huge oil spills in 1991 caused by bombing of tankers and the Mina al-Bakr offshore oil terminal apparently did not impact this coast significantly, presumably due to prevailing winds and currents carrying the slicks away from the shore. No conservation measures are known to have been proposed.

Further reading

Cumming (1899, 1918), Georg and Vielliard (1970), Moore and Boswell (1956–1957), Ticehurst *et al.* (1921–1922, 1926).

MAIN REFERENCES

AL-DABBAGH, K. Y. AND BUNNI, M. K. (1981) *Breeding habits of the Iraqi Babbler,* Turdoides altirostris *(Hartert).* Baghdad: Iraq Nat. Hist. Mus. (Publ. 34).

AL-DABBAGH, K. Y. (in prep.) The bird fauna of semi-desert areas of central Iraq. *Sandgrouse.*

ALLOUSE, B. E. (1953) *The avifauna of Iraq.* Baghdad: Iraq Natural History Museum (Publ. 3).

CARP, E. (1975a) Waterfowl counts in Iraq. *IWRB Bull.* 39/40: 51–55.

CARP, E. (1975b) Report on a mission to Iraq: January/February 1975. Unpublished report in IWRB files.

CARP, E. (1980) *A directory of western Palaearctic wetlands.* Nairobi: United Nations Environment Programme/Gland (Switzerland): International Union for Conservation of Nature and Natural Resources.

CHAPMAN, E. A. AND MCGEOCH, J. A. (1956) Recent field observations from Iraq. *Ibis* 98: 577–594.

CTYROKÝ, P (1987) Ornithological observations in Iraq. *Beitr. Vogelkunde* 33: 141–204.

CTYROKÝ, P. (1988) Autumn migration of birds in the western desert of Iraq. *Beitr. Vogelkunde* 34: 230–236.

CTYROKÝ, P. (in press) Spring migration of birds in the western desert of Iraq.

CUMMING, W. D. (1899) Letter on the nesting of *Hypocolius ampelinus. J. Bombay Nat. Hist. Soc.* 12: 760–765.

CUMMING, W. D. (1918) Natural history notes from Fao. *J. Bombay Nat. Hist. Soc.* 26: 292–295.

GEORG, P. V. AND SAVAGE, C. D. W. (1970a) Status of the main waterfowl resorts in Iraq. Pp. 328–332 in Y. A. Isakov, ed. *Proc. Int. Regional Meeting on Conservation of Wildfowl Resources, Leningrad 1968.* Moscow.

GEORG, P. V. AND SAVAGE, C. D. W. (1970b) Status of the species of wildfowl occurring in Iraq. Pp. 177–181 in Y. A. Isakov, ed. *Proc. Int. Regional Meeting on Conservation of Wildfowl Resources, Leningrad 1968.* Moscow.

GEORG, P. V. AND VIELLIARD, J. (1968) Waterfowl counts in Iraq: 21 December 1967–18 January 1968. Unpublished notes in IWRB files.

GEORG, P. V. AND VIELLIARD, J. (1970) Midwinter observations on birds of central and south Iraq. *Bull. Iraq Nat. Hist. Mus.* 4: 61–85.

GREEN, A. J. (1993) *The status and conservation of the Marbled Teal Marmaronetta angustirostris.* Slimbridge, U.K.: International Waterfowl and Wetlands Research Bureau (Spec. Publ. 23).

HARRISON, J. M. (1959) Notes on a collection of birds made in Iraq by Flight Lieutenant David L. Harrison. *Bull. Brit. Orn. Club* 79: 9–13, 31–36, 49–50.

ICBP (1992) *Putting biodiversity on the map: priority areas for global conservation.* Cambridge, U.K.: International Council for Bird Preservation.

JOHNSON, L. R. (1958) *Field notes on some of the birds of Iraq.* Baghdad: Iraq Natural History Museum (Publ. 16).

KONING, F. J. AND DIJKSEN, L. J. (1973) IWRB mission to Iraq and Syria, December 1972. *IWRB Bull.* 35: 57–62.

MARCHANT, S. (1961) Iraq bird notes—1960. *Bull. Iraq Nat. Hist. Mus.* 1 (4): 1–37.

MARCHANT, S. (1962) Iraq bird notes—1961. *Bull. Iraq Nat. Hist. Mus.* 2 (1): 1–40.

MARCHANT, S. AND MACNAB, J. W. (1962) Iraq bird notes—1962. *Bull. Iraq Nat. Hist. Inst.* 2 (3): 1–48.

MCGEOCH, J. A. (1963) Observations from Ser Amadia, Kurdistan, Iraq (17–30 June 1954). *Ardea* 51: 244–250.

MOORE, H. J. AND BOSWELL, C. (1956–1957) *Field observations on the birds of Iraq.* Baghdad: Iraq Natural History Museum (Publ. 9, 10, 12).

NORTH, A. (1993) Saddam's water war. *Geogr. Mag.* July: 10–14.

PEARCE, F. (1993) Draining life from Iraq's marshes. *New Scientist* 17 April: 11–12.

PRENTICE, C. (1993) Degradation of the Mesopotamian marshes, Iraq. *IWRB News* 10: 10–11.

SAVAGE, C. D. W. (1968). The wildfowl and wetland situation in Iraq. Pp.128–133 in H. F. J. Elliott, ed. *Proc. Technical Meeting on Wetland Conservation, Ankara-Bursa-Istanbul, October 1967*. Morges, Switzerland: International Union for Conservation of Nature and Natural Resources (Publ. New Series 12).

SCOTT, D. A. (1993) *Environmental and ecological study of the marshlands of southern Iraq. Chapter III. Wildlife.* Unpublished, draft report to Wetland Ecosystems Research Group, University of Exeter, U.K.

SIMAN, H. Y. (1975) Breeding biology of the Grey Hypocolius on Umm Al-Khanazeer island. M.Sc. thesis, University of Baghdad.

SIMAN, H. Y. (in prep.) Survey of Iraq avifauna (1975–1980). Unpublished report to Iraq Natural History Museum, Baghdad.

SIMAN, H. Y. AND BUNNI, M. K. (1978) Nesting of the Grey Hypocolius *Hypocolius ampelinus* Bonaparte in the Umm Al-Khanazeer Island, Baghdad. *Bull. Nat. Hist. Res. Centre Baghdad* 7(2): 69–83.

THESIGER, W. (1954) The marshmen of southern Iraq. *Geogr. J.* 120: 272–281.

THESIGER, W. (1964) *The marsh arabs.* Harmondsworth, U.K.: Penguin.

TICEHURST, C. B., BUXTON, P. A. AND CHEESMAN, R. E. (1921–1922) The birds of Mesopotamia. *J. Bombay Nat. Hist. Soc.* 28: 210–250, 381–427, 650–674, 937–956.

TICEHURST, C. B., COX, P. AND CHEESMAN, R. E. (1926) Additional notes on the avifauna of Iraq. *J. Bombay Nat. Hist. Soc.* 31: 91–119.

VANT LEVEN, L. (1968) The wildfowl situation of the Euphrates delta. Unpubl. report in IWRB files.

▪ STATE OF ISRAEL, WEST BANK, GAZA, GOLAN HEIGHTS

Sociable Plover *Vanellus gregarius*

GENERAL INFORMATION

Israel is one of the smallest countries in the Middle East; together with the occupied territories of West Bank, Gaza and the Golan Heights it covers some 32,100 km^2. It is bounded by the Mediterranean Sea and Sinai Desert in the west, the Red Sea in the south, the Rift Valley and the Golan Heights in the east and the Upper Galilee Mountains in the north.

This area is inhabited by 6.8 million people (212 persons per km^2), including 5.3 million people in Israel (including the Golan Heights, 240 persons per km^2) and 1.5 million people in the West Bank and Gaza (153 persons per km^2), but there is considerable variation regionally. For example, 28% of the population concentrate in the Tel Aviv area (6,000 persons per km^2), and about 40% in the rest of the Coastal Plain, between Haifa sub-district in the north and Ashqelon sub-district in the south (1,000–1,500 persons per km^2). In the Arava Valley and in the Negev Desert population densities are less then 25 and 10 persons per km^2 respectively.

Over half of Israel's territory is desert, 28% are cultivated or irrigated, 5% are forests (including planted woodland) and maquis scrub, and the rest are scrubland, wetlands and settlements.

Israel, in its relatively small area, has a variety of climatic regions (desert, steppe, Mediterranean) and different habitats (i.e. rocky and sandy deserts, oases, coasts, wetlands, woodlands, high mountains and cultivated land). Average annual rainfall ranges from 20 mm in the southern Negev to over 1,000 mm in the northern mountains.

Over 2,400 plant species are found in Israel, of which 46 are endemic. The vegetation can be divided into four main phytogeographical zones, as follows.

Mediterranean zone (includes forests, maquis and scrubland)

This occupies most of northern Israel. It continues southwards along the Coastal Plain to Ashqelon sub-district, and along the Samaria and Judea Mountains.

Irano-Turanian zone (Oriental steppe)

This is located east and south of the Mediterranean zone along the Jordan Valley, the western part of the Judean Desert and the northern Negev. It also occupies a large area in Mount Hermon and in the Central Negev Mountains.

Saharo-Arabian zone

This is located east and south of the Irano-Turanian zone, including the Judean Desert and the Negev.

Sudanian-Zambesian zone

Elements from this zone penetrates northward along the Arava Valley and the Jordan Valley where they occupy oases and river beds.

ORNITHOLOGICAL IMPORTANCE

Israel is amongst the richest countries in the Middle East for birds, because of its geographical position between Europe, Asia and Africa and its diversity of habitats.

Over 180 species of birds breed in Israel, with 350 or so species regularly occurring. Nearly 500 species have been recorded in Israel, including 110 vagrants.

Israel is very important for its migrating birds. The total number of Palearctic nocturnal migrants through Israel has been estimated at about 400 million birds, in addition to about 100 million diurnal migrants, including 2 million soaring birds (raptors, storks and pelicans). Migration flyways are generally broad (5–60 km wide) and the exact route may drift according to weather conditions. Non-soaring birds tend to migrate on a broad front, all over Israel, with an estimated average density of 5 million birds passing in a season per 1 km front. Thus, theoretically, the whole of the country may be considered as one bottleneck for migrating birds. However, several areas have special importance as stopover sites (Hula Valley, Bet She'an Valley, Carmel Coast and the Arava Valley). In these sites, and especially in cultivated desert areas, special care should be taken in the use of pesticides.

The Hula Valley and the Hula Lake are of importance as a nesting area for the globally threatened *Marmaronetta angustirostris*, and as a stopover site for migrating *Pelecanus onocrotalus*, where most of the Palearctic population (c.70,000) go through, and a few hundred stay for the winter. However, this population, and 1,000–2,000 wintering *P. onocrotalus* in the valleys of Jezre'el, Bet She'an and Zevulun, are under threat from fish-farmers who prevent them from landing at their fish-ponds, and sometimes even shoot them (illegally). The Northern Valleys (mainly Zevulun, Bet She'an and Hula) are an important wintering area for the globally threatened *Phalacrocorax pygmeus* (100–270 birds) which feed mainly in fish-ponds. This population is threatened by fish-farmers, who persecute *Phalacrocorax carbo* and may accidentally shoot *P. pygmeus*.

The Western Negev is the main breeding area in Israel of the globally threatened *Chlamydotis undulata* (270–380 birds). The area of Elat and its mountains is located under a major migration route of raptors, with up to 1.2 million passing over the area during spring. It is also important in spring as the first major stopover site (as an artificial oasis) after birds cross some 2,000 km of desert on their way from Africa.

The Arava Valley and the southern Negev used to be the major habitat of *Torgos tracheliotus negevensis*, with up to 40 pairs breeding on *Acacia* trees 45 years ago. Today, no breeding pairs are found, and 1–2 birds are irregularly seen in different parts of the Israeli desert, including the southern part of the Judean Desert, the Negev Highlands and the Northern Arava. A captive-breeding program has been set up at Tel Aviv University, currently with 13 birds. However, it seems unlikely that birds will be released in their natural habitat in the near future, due to lack of suitable ecological conditions.

For many species of breeding birds of prey, cliffs are the most important nesting sites, especially in the Judean Desert, the Cliffs of Zin, eastern Galilee (at the western border of the Hula Valley and Kinerot) and the Golan Heights. The main threat for these birds (*Gyps fulvus*, *Neophron percnopterus*, *Falco naumanni*, *F. biarmicus* and *F. concolor*, as well as *Buteo rufinus*, *Hieraaetus fasciatus* and *Falco pelegrinoides*), is excessive disturbance by travellers and rock climbers.

CONSERVATION INFRASTRUCTURE AND PROTECTED-AREA SYSTEM

Protected areas are set up and managed by the Nature Reserves Authority and the National Parks Authority of the government, according to the National Parks and Nature Reserves Law of 1963.

Nature Reserve There are 375 Nature Reserves in Israel with a total area of 5,318 km^2 (159 of them, with a total area of 2,402 km^2, are still in the process of declaration). Most Nature Reserves are small and protect ecologically important habitats, or sites with unique flora or fauna. Some of the large and important reserves include Mount Hermon, Yahudia Wood (Golan Heights), Mount Meron, Huleh Lake, Mount Carmel, Ma'agan Mikhael, Judean Desert, Agur (Western Negev), The Craters (Northern Negev), Cliffs of Zin, Negev Mountain, Znifim (Central Negev) and Elat Mountains.

National Park These tend to be large areas set up primarily for the enjoyment of the visiting public, but may have a strong element of nature conservation, such as designated Nature Reserves inside the park bounds.

The land of the Nature Reserves and National Parks, like most of the land in Israel, is state-owned. Wild animals are protected according to the Wild Animals Protection Law of 1955. This law protect all animals including birds, except for pest species and several game species, and it is enforced by the Nature Reserves Authority.

INTERNATIONAL MEASURES RELEVANT TO CONSERVATION OF SITES

Israel has ratified the Barcelona Convention's Protocol concerning Mediterranean Specially Protected Areas (since 1986) as well as the Bonn Convention, and has signed (but not yet ratified) the Ramsar and Biodiversity Conventions. Israel has designated seven Mediterranean Specially Protected Areas, of which three are included in this site inventory. Israel is involved in the UNESCO Man and Biosphere Programme, but has not designated any Biosphere Reserves.

OVERVIEW OF THE INVENTORY

Eighteen sites are contained in the following inventory. The sites are distributed throughout the country and cover a total area of c.5,500 km^2, nearly half of which is within the desert region. Other sites include wetlands, coasts and fish-ponds, cultivated fields, open landscape, and Mediterranean mountains.

The sites listed fall into four main categories: (1) migration bottlenecks; (2) cliffs for nesting raptors; (3) freshwater wetlands, reservoirs and fish-ponds for wintering and nesting waterbirds; (4) large areas of open desert with characteristic and unique associated bird communities.

Many of the sites described are partly protected by the Nature Reserves Authority. However, only c.30% of the total area is fully protected (including proposed nature reserves). Birds in the rest of the area are protected by law from hunting or persecution, but enforcement is limited.

ACKNOWLEDGEMENTS

The site accounts were compiled from data-sheets supplied by S. Blitzblau, Dr R. Frumkin, Dr R. Yosef, M. Adar, D. Alon, R. Inbar, J. H. Morgan, G. and Y. Pearlman, H. Shirihai and A. Tzairi, coordinated by the Society for the Protection of Nature in Israel (including the Israel Ornithological Centre and the Israel Wader Research Group) with major assistance from the International Birding Center Eilat. The first draft of most of the data-sheets was supplied by S. Blitzblau. The site accounts were reviewed and revised by Dr R. Frumkin and Dr R. Yosef, and Dr R. Frumkin coordinated the final stages of the project. The introduction was written by Dr R. Frumkin. Dr E. Shy of the Nature Reserves Authority (NRA) commented on a draft of the site accounts, and Dr E. Frankenberg (NRA) and Prof. H. Mendelssohn helped with some information. Dr B. Shalmon and Dr A. Shmida supplied data on the threatened/endemic flora and non-bird fauna respectively. D. J. Brooks assisted with the compilation of data. Dr B. Pinshow assisted with communications.

SITE INVENTORY

Site no.	Site name	Criteria used to select site									
		1	2i	2ii	2iii	3	4	5i	5ii	6	0
001	Mount Hermon	—	—	—	—	—	•	•	—	•	—
002	Hula Valley	•	•	•	•	•	•	—	•	•	—
003	Golan Heights	•	•	—	•	•	—	—	•	—	—
004	Zevulun Valley	•	•	—	•	•	•	—	—	—	—
005	Lake Kinneret and Kinerot	•	•	—	—	•	—	—	•	—	—
006	Ramot Menashe	•	—	—	—	—	—	—	—	—	—
007	Carmel Coast	•	•	—	•	•	•	—	—	—	—
008	Jezre'el, Harod and Bet She'an Valleys	•	•	•	•	•	•	—	—	—	—
009	Hefer Valley	•	•	—	•	—	—	—	—	—	—
010	Northern Lower Jordan Valley	—	•	—	•	•	•	—	—	—	—
011	Jericho	•	—	—	•	•	•	—	—	—	—
012	Judean Foothills	•	•	—	•	•	•	•	—	—	—
013	Jerusalem	•	—	—	—	—	—	—	—	—	—
014	Judean Desert	•	•	—	•	•	•	•	—	—	—
015	Western Negev	•	•	—	•	•	•	•	—	—	—
016	Northern Arava Valley	•	•	—	•	•	•	—	—	—	—
017	Cliffs of Zin and the Negev Highlands	•	•	—	•	•	•	—	•	•	—
018	Southern Arava Valley and Elat Mountains	•	•	—	•	•	•	•	—	•	—

Key to criteria

1 Regularly holds a significant number of a globally threatened species.

2i Regularly holds 1% or more of a species' biogeographical or flyway or Middle Eastern population (waterbirds and seabirds only).

2ii Regularly holds 20,000 or more waterbirds.

2iii Migratory 'bottleneck' site: more than 3,000 raptors or more than 5,000 storks or more than 2,000 cranes pass in a season.

3 Regularly holds a significant number of a species which is threatened or declining within the Middle East. Only the top five sites for each such species in the country are considered to qualify as IBAs.

4 Regularly holds a significant number of a species whose world population is wholly or largely restricted to the Middle East. Only the top five sites for each such species in the country are considered to qualify as IBAs.

5i Representative example of a habitat, associated with a characteristic assemblage of bird species.

5ii Rare/threatened/unique habitat, associated with a characteristic assemblage of bird species.

6 Site important for bird conservation through education/research/tourism.

0 Selected for other reasons. See 'Comments on the inventory'.

Comments on the inventory

1. Precise areas are given only for protected areas and some of the sites which have been well documented. Boundaries have not been defined for the non-protected sites, and any areas given in these cases are only crude estimates.
2. Ornithological data used for site the accounts generally derives from the late 1980s onwards.
3. Figures in brackets after species' names, and in the boxes, are the maximum daily counts of individuals recorded (not pairs), unless otherwise stated. A minority of counts given for migrating birds in the '1% or more of population' section of the boxes are marked with an asterisk (*), indicating that these counts refer to seasonal totals, not maximum daily counts; in either case a range is sometimes given to indicate the scale of annual variation over the last 10 years or so. All counts of wintering birds are from January, unless otherwise stated; a range is given to illustrate variation over the last 10 years or so.
4. The application of the 'Top 5 site' criteria of categories 3 and 4 (as in the above table) is provisional. It has not been possible to apply the 'Top 5 site' criterion in category 4 for *Pycnonotus xanthopygos* and *Oenanthe finschii*. These species are common and widespread over much of Israel, and occur commonly in many of the listed sites. However, their presence is generally listed, where known, due to their interest in a Middle Eastern context.
5. In the case of Israel, it is unrealistic to designate as Important Bird Areas all sites qualifying according to the migratory 'bottleneck' criterion applicable to category 2 sites (see the above table), due to the huge numbers of soaring birds that pass through the country. Sometimes they concentrate at relatively narrow passes (e.g. Elat Mountains), or along narrow corridors (e.g. Judean Desert) but in other areas the same birds migrate along a broader front (e.g. *Ciconia ciconia* in the Western Negev and raptors in the Northern Valleys). Sites have only been accepted under this criterion when they already qualify according to other criteria (see above table).
6. Some of the geographical names used in the site inventory (including site names) are not official, and cannot be found on maps (e.g. Judean Foothills). In these cases, the area referred to is defined more explicitly in the relevant site account.

Glossary

IBCE, International Birding Center Eilat

MSPA, Mediterranean Specially Protected Area

NRA, Nature Reserves Authority

SPNI, Society for the Protection of Nature in Israel

001 Mount Hermon

Nature Reserve (c.7,000 ha)

33°15′N 35°45′E
c.10,400 ha

Site description

From the area of Majdal Shams, north to the Syrian border. Much of the area is under military control, but a road to a ski resort allows easy access to 2,000 m and the rocky summit lies at 2,814 m. Woodland from 800 m to the treeline at 1,800–1,900 m is dominated by *Quercus calliprinos*, *Q. cerris*, *Colutea cilicica* and *Spartium juneum*, above this by a scrubland of *Phlomis chrysophylla*, *Prunus ursina*, *Astragalus hermoneus*, *Acantholimon libanoticus* and *Onobrychis* species. There are orchards on the lower slopes.

Species restricted wholly or largely to the Middle East	
Hippolais languida	Summer visitor to lower elevations.
Irania gutturalis	Summer visitor, but almost extinct.
Oenanthe finschii	Winter visitor and passage migrant.
Carpospiza brachydactyla	Summer visitor (10–30 pairs).
Serinus syriacus	Summer visitor (50–70 pairs).
Rhodopechys sanguinea	Resident (15–20 pairs).

Birds

See box for key species. Other breeding species include *Lullula arborea*, *Eremophila alpestris*, *Oenanthe oenanthe libanotica*, *Sylvia hortensis*, *Parus lugubris*, *Sitta neumayer* and *Emberiza caesia*.

Other threatened/endemic wildlife

Mammals: *Sciurus anomalus* (rare), *Apodemus hermonensis* (endemic). Reptiles: *Cyrtodactylus amictopholis* (endemic), *Elaphe hohenackeri*, *Vipera bornmuelleri* (I; endemic). Flora: *Alcea dissecta*.

Conservation issues

All the non-military area is a Nature Reserve. Ski-lifts lead to heavy recreational activity and disturbance at the highest elevations in summer, and there is considerable military traffic. Overgrazing, tree-felling and diversion of water are potential threats.

Further reading

Hoter and Ezov (1991), Zuaretz (1983).

002 Hula Valley

also known as Huleh Valley
Nature Reserve (775 ha)

33°05′N 35°37′E
c.24,000 ha

Site description

Part of the northern Jordan Valley and formerly an extensive marshland area, but now drained except for the Hula Nature Reserve near Yesod Hama'ala. The reserve's water level is maintained at c.6 m above that of the surrounding valley, and the main habitats are open water, *Cyperus papyrus* thickets, swamp-meadow with *Cyperus*, *Typha*, *Juncus* and *Scirpus*, and *Phragmites* beds. There are fish-ponds and reservoirs in the area adjacent to the reserve and to the north.

Birds

The Hula valley, and particularly the Hula Nature Reserve, is the most important wetland area in Israel for breeding waterbirds. See boxes for key species; other breeding species include *Halcyon smyrnensis* and *Ceryle rudis*. The reserve provides a roost site for large migrant flocks of *Pelecanus onocrotalus*, and there are high passage numbers of *Ciconia ciconia*, *Anas clypeata*, several raptor species and *Grus grus* (see box). Wintering species include notable numbers of *Circus aeruginosus* (60) and *Aquila*

Globally threatened species	
Phalacrocorax pygmeus	Winter visitor (10–25).
Marmaronetta angustirostris	Resident (3–10 pairs).
Branta ruficollis	Winter visitor (4).
Haliaeetus albicilla	Winter visitor.
Aquila heliaca	Winter visitor (3–5) and passage migrant (up to 10–15 per season).
Falco naumanni	Summer visitor: there is a small colony in Rosh Pina at the southern end of the valley.
Crex crex	Passage migrant (up to 50–150 in a season).
Tetrax tetrax	Winter visitor (3) and passage migrant (daily max. 5).
Vanellus gregarius	Winter visitor (3–10).

Regionally threatened or declining species	
Pernis apivorus	Abundant on passage (15,000–35,000 in a season).
Accipiter brevipes	Abundant on passage (15,000–20,000 in a season).
Aquila pomarina	Abundant on passage (10,000–35,000 in a season).

Species restricted wholly or largely to the Middle East	
Passer moabiticus	Breeds (5–15 pairs).

1% or more of population

	Breeding (pairs)	Wintering	Passage
Phalacrocorax carbo	—	3,500	—
Pelecanus onocrotalus	—	350–500	60,000–70,000*
Nycticorax nycticorax	350–500	900	—
Ardeola ralloides	10–20	—	50–150
Bubulcus ibis	250–550	100–150	—
Egretta garzetta	400–500	300–600	—
Casmerodius albus	—	1300–2100	—
Ardea cinerea	—	1,200–1,650	500–7,500
Ciconia nigra	—	100–350	2,000–4,000*
Ciconia ciconia	—	40–100	65,000–100,000*
Plegadis falcinellus	25–30	50–125	200–350
Platalea leucorodia	—	25–150	—
Anas platyrhynchos	5–25	20,000–25,000	—
Anas clypeata	—	8,000–10,000	8,500–15,000
Marmaronetta angustirostris	3–10	10–18	—
Grus grus	—	3,000–5,000	2,500–6,000
Vanellus vanellus	—	3,600–4,500	—

clanga (23). The site was listed as a wetland of international importance by Carp (1980).

■ Other threatened/endemic wildlife
None known to BirdLife International.

■ Conservation issues
The Hula Nature Reserve (450 ha) was established in 1956, and much hydrological management has been carried out to maintain the quality of the habitat. Potential threats to the birds in the reserve and in the Hula valley are pollution by pesticides and fertilizers from adjacent farmland, and disturbance from visitors.

■ Further reading
Carp (1980), Gorney (1980, 1983), Levy and Yom-Tov (1991).

003 Golan Heights
Nature Reserves (c.16,200 ha)

33°00´N 35°45´E
c.60,000 ha

■ Site description
An upland region east of the Hula Valley and Lake Kinneret (Sea of Galilee), ascending to 1,500 m and roughly bounded by Hamat-Gader, Ramat Magshimim, Alonei Habashan, Kuneitra, El Rom and Kazrin. The area is typified by rolling grassland with scattered trees and bushes of *Quercus*, *Styrax*, *Pistacia*, *Rubus* and *Ziziphus*, and there are some small pools and reservoirs. Much of the area is cultivated or grazed by cattle, and there is considerable military activity.

■ Birds
See box for key species. The region holds good numbers of breeding raptors, with the plateau area around Nahal Gamla, Zavitan and Yehudiya being especially important. Ducks often winter in good numbers, mainly *Anas penelope*, *Aythya ferina* and *A. fuligula*. Stream valleys flowing from the southern Golan into Lake Kinneret were the last refuge of *Ketupa zeylonensis* in this area, now apparently extinct.

■ Other threatened/endemic wildlife
Mammals: *Spalax ehrenbergi* (2n=54), *Canis lupus* (V), *Gazella gazella* (V). Reptiles: *Elaphe quatuorlineata* (endemic). Flora: *Phlomis syriaca*, *Colchicum brachyllum*.

Globally threatened species

Marmaronetta angustirostris	Resident (2–5 pairs).
Aegypius monachus	Winter visitor (2–10).
Tetrax tetrax	Winter visitor (2–10).
Otis tarda	Winter visitor (2–3).
Vanellus gregarius	Winter visitor (5–10).

1% or more of population

	Breeding (pairs)	Wintering	Passage
Grus grus	—	2,000–3,000	—
Ciconia ciconia	10	few	>20,000
Vanellus vanellus	—	950–1,500	—

Regionally threatened or declining species

Neophron percnopterus	Resident (10–20 pairs).
Gyps fulvus	Resident (50 pairs).

■ Conservation issues
All the important sites are Nature Reserves. The military administration cooperates with nature conservation agencies to prevent damage to bird populations, especially of raptors.

■ Further reading
Bahat (1986), Geller (1983), Schluter (1987).

004 Zevulun Valley

Nature Reserves (c.72 ha)

32°53′N 35°06′E
c.5,000 ha

Site description

An area of the coastal plain north of Haifa, largely developed or agricultural, with fish-ponds and some other small wetlands including the marsh at Ein Afeq (66 ha) c.8 km south of Akko.

Birds

See box for key species. Ein Afeq is an important winter roosting site for *Phalacrocorax pygmeus* and holds some breeding herons and egrets. Mishmar Hayam (12 ha), just south of Akko, is a small site with a grove of trees important for many breeding herons and egrets and the largest colony of *Plegadis falcinellus* in Israel. Up to 65 *Circus aeruginosus* and 22 *Aquila clanga* have been present in winter.

Other threatened/endemic wildlife

Reptiles: *Chalcides guentheri*. Flora: *Salsola soda*.

Conservation issues

Ein Afeq (66 ha) is a Nature Reserve, and the Nature Reserves Authority has proposed the same status for Karei-Na'aman (50 ha, swamp and marsh) and Mishmar Hayam (12 ha), which are both threatened by industrial development. Additionally there is a small Nature Reserve (6 ha) with a spring and rare plant species.

Further reading

Blitzblau (1990b, 1991).

Globally threatened species

Phalacrocorax pygmeus	Winter visitor (max. 92) and passage migrant.
Oxyura leucocephala	Winter visitor (max. 80–150).
Crex crex	Passage migrant, up to 20–75 in a season.
Tetrax tetrax	Winter visitor (max. 2–4).
Vanellus gregarius	Winter visitor (max. 21).

1% or more of population

	Breeding (pairs)	Wintering	Passage
Pelecanus onocrotalus	—	—	37,000*
Nycticorax nycticorax	275–300	—	—
Bubulcus ibis	280–325	—	—
Egretta garzetta	250–275	—	—
Casmerodius albus	—	650–850	—
Ciconia nigra	—	125–150	350–500*
Ciconia ciconia	—	—	18,500*
Plegadis falcinellus	35–50	150–250	1,500–2,000*
Anas clypeata	—	5,500	—
Recurvirostra avosetta	—	—	200–300*
Glareola nordmanni	—	—	50–350*
Vanellus vanellus	—	1,434	—
Larus ichthyaetus	—	175–250	—
Larus cachinnans	—	3,500–5,000	—

Regionally threatened or declining species

Pernis apivorus	Passage migrant, up to 500–1,850 in a season.

Species restricted wholly or largely to the Middle East

Glareola nordmanni	Passage migrant (see above).

005 Lake Kinneret and Kinerot

also known as Lake Tiberias or Sea of Galilee
Nature Reserve (500 ha)

32°48′N 35°35′E
32,800 ha

Site description

Lake Kinneret (16,500 ha) is the largest and only natural freshwater lake in Israel. It is 209 m below sea-level.

Birds

See box for key species. The lake holds many wintering waterbirds, and was listed as a wetland of international importance by Carp (1980). The surrounding hills, particularly to the north (e.g. Nahal Amud), hold good numbers of landbirds, including *Anthus similis*.

Other threatened/endemic wildlife

None known to BirdLife International.

Globally threatened species

Marmaronetta angustirostris	Winter visitor (max. 5–8).

1% or more of population

	Breeding (pairs)	Wintering	Passage
Podiceps cristatus	—	1,150	—
Phalacrocorax carbo	—	4,100	—
Egretta garzetta	—	141	—
Casmerodius albus	—	153	—
Ardea cinerea	—	307	—
Ciconia nigra	—	19	—
Aythya fuligula	—	3,813	—
Larus ridibundus	—	4,758	—
Larus cachinnans	—	639	—

Regionally threatened or declining species

Neophron percnopterus	Present.
Gyps fulvus	Present.
Francolinus francolinus	Resident.

Conservation issues

Bet Zaida Nature Reserve forms a 4-km strip on the north-east shore of the lake. The lake is among the main recreational areas in northern Israel, and disturbance from this source constitutes the main threat to the site, though this is not a major problem in winter.

Further reading

Carp (1980), Geller (1983).

006 Ramot Menashe

Unprotected

32°35′N 35°05′E
2,500 ha

Site description

Hilly agricultural country with *Quercus* trees, on the western slopes of Mount Carmel, 5 km east of the Carmel coast. The area of interest lie in, between and around the two villages of Amiqam and Bat Shlomo (4 km apart).

Birds

See box for key species. This is an important site for *Falco naumanni*, which breeds in old buildings at Amiqam (c.30 pairs) and Bat Shlomo (up to 10 pairs); their foraging area covers c.2,500 ha in surrounding fields. *Hippolais olivetorum* also breeds.

Globally threatened species

Falco naumanni	Summer visitor (up to c.40 pairs).

Other threatened/endemic wildlife

None known to BirdLife International.

Conservation issues

The main potential threats are destruction of the old buildings where *F. naumanni* nest, and agricultural intensification involving pesticides in the surrounding fields.

007 Carmel Coast

Nature Reserves (c.490 ha)

32°33′N 34°55′E
c.2,400 ha MSPAs (c.120 ha)

Site description

A 20-km-strip along the Mediterranean coast, from Atlit south to the Taninim River Nature Reserve. The site includes the Atlit saltpans (8 km south of Haifa) and a large complex of fish-ponds at Ma'agan Mikhael and Ma'ayan Zvi, c.25 km north of Netanya, as well as some small islands off Ma'agan Mikhael.

Birds

See boxes for key species. Breeding birds include five species of heron and egret and *Plegadis falcinellus*. The Atlit saltpans hold the only colony of *Sterna albifrons* in Israel. Good numbers of many waterbird species winter, when up to 55 *Circus aeruginosus* are also present. Large flocks of *Pelecanus onocrotalus* occur on passage.

Other threatened/endemic wildlife

Mammals: *Meriones sacramenti* (endemic). Reptiles:

Regionally threatened or declining species

Botaurus stellaris	Winter visitor (10).

Species restricted wholly or largely to the Middle East

Glareola nordmanni	Passage migrant (tens in a season).

Globally threatened species

Phalacrocorax pygmeus	Winter visitor (max. 5).
Marmaronetta angustirostris	Winter visitor (max. 10).
Crex crex	Passage migrant, with up to 100–150 in a season.

1% or more of population

	Breeding (pairs)	Wintering	Passage
Pelecanus onocrotalus	—	30–200	25,000–30,000*
Nycticorax nycticorax	100–250	100–300	—
Ardeola ralloides	2–3	—	100–150*
Bubulcus ibis	500–700	250–1,000	—
Egretta garzetta	50–100	100–300	—
Casmerodius albus	—	100–300	—
Ardea cinerea	10	700–1,000	200–1,000*
Ciconia ciconia	—	50–150	500–50,000*
Plegadis falcinellus	2–3?	35	200
Platalea leucorodia	—	50–100	155–200
Himantopus himantopus	80	100	250
Recurvirostra avosetta	5	300	300–400
Limosa limosa	—	200–300	—
Tringa erythropus	—	—	50–120
Larus ichthyaetus	—	150	—
Larus ridibundus	—	>20,000	>10,000*
Larus cachinnans	10	15,000–17,000	8,000–10,000*
Sterna albifrons	240–250	—	hundreds
Chlidonias hybridus	—	—	1,000–2,500*
Chlidonias leucopterus	—	—	1,000–3,500*

Chalcides guentheri. Flora: *Aegialophila pumilio*, *Salsola soda*.

Conservation issues

Most ornithological sites within the area are protected as Nature Reserves, e.g. the fish-ponds at Ma'agan Mikhael and Ma'ayan Zvi, and three areas are designated as Mediterranean Specially Protected Areas (Taninim River, 5.5 ha; Dor–HaBonim, 113 km; Ma'agan Mikhael Islands, 2 ha). Breeding birds at the Atlit saltpans (c.250 ha) are protected by the owner. Part of the protected area includes a proposed marine reserve (450 ha) with a few small islets and rocky shores, used by breeding terns and gulls.

Further reading

Blitzblau (1990a).

008 Jezre'el, Harod and Bet She'an Valleys

Unprotected

32°32'N 35°20'E
c.40,000 ha

Site description

A valley system stretching north-west from Bet She'an in eastern Israel across most of the width of the country to Kiryat Tiv'on. The area is largely agricultural (orchards, wheat, legumes, cotton), with many fish-ponds and reservoirs.

Birds

An important area for waterbirds throughout the year; see boxes for key species. The fields of the Jezre'el valley supported a wintering population of up to 1,700 *Grus grus* during the 1980s, though this had dropped to 500 by 1991/92. Other wintering species include *Circus aeruginosus* (65), *Aquila clanga* (19) and *Larus ichthyaetus* (150).

Other threatened/endemic wildlife

None known to BirdLife International.

Conservation issues

There are small Nature Reserves within the site, but they do not have any special ornithological importance, and there are no other measures being taken to conserve the region. Human disturbance and agricultural intensification constitute threats to the birds using the area.

Further reading

Allon *et al.* (1992), Levy and Yom-Tov (1991), Tsovel and Allon (1991).

Globally threatened species

Phalacrocorax pygmeus	Resident; winter counts range from 2 to 155.
Marmaronetta angustirostris	Resident (January max. 4)
Oxyura leucocephala	Winter visitor (500–600), mostly at Ma'aleh Kishon reservoirs, 7 km south-west of Gvat.
Haliaeetus albicilla	Winter visitor (fewer than 10).
Aegypius monachus	Winter visitor (1–2).
Aquila heliaca	Winter visitor (2–5) and passage migrant (2–15 in a season).
Falco naumanni	Passage migrant (some tens of birds in a season).
Crex crex	Passage migrant (75–85 in a season).
Vanellus gregarius	Winter visitor (3–8 birds).

Regionally threatened or declining species

Aythya nyroca	Resident (see other box).
Pernis apivorus	Abundant passage migrant (seasonal total 50,000–75,000).
Accipiter brevipes	Abundant passage migrant (seasonal total 15,000–28,000).
Aquila pomarina	Abundant passage migrant (seasonal total 35,000–70,000).
Francolinus francolinus	Resident.

1% or more of population

	Breeding (pairs)	Wintering	Passage
Podiceps nigricollis	—	hundreds	—
Phalacrocorax carbo	—	1,600–1,750	—
Pelecanus onocrotalus	—	1,000–1,500	35,000–40,000*
Nycticorax nycticorax	450–550	thousands	—
Bubulcus ibis	400–500	thousands	—
Egretta garzetta	350–500	thousands	—
Casmerodius albus	—	500–600	250–300*
Ardea cinerea	—	1,000–1,200	800–1,000*
Ciconia nigra	—	150–600	2,000–3,500*
Ciconia ciconia	—	150–200	120,000–150,000*
Plegadis falcinellus	2–5	hundreds	150–300*
Platalea leucorodia	—	150–200	250–400*
Anas clypeata	—	3,000–5,000	8,000–12,000*
Aythya nyroca	<10	tens	—
Oxyura leucocephala	—	500–600	—
Grus grus	—	1,700	1,000–1,250*
Glareola nordmanni	—	—	200–300*
Charadrius hiaticula	—	50–75	1,000–1,250
Vanellus vanellus	—	3,000–4,000	500–600*

Species restricted wholly or largely to the Middle East

Glareola nordmanni	Passage migrant (see above).
Passer moabiticus	Resident (20–45 pairs; 250–300 in winter).

009 Hefer Valley

National Park (600 ha)

32°27′N 34°56′E
c.35,000 ha

■ Site description

A largely agricultural area (orchards, wheat, legumes, cotton), stretching from Karkur to Tira, c.10 km inland from Netanya near the Mediterranean coast. There are some fish-ponds and reservoirs scattered within the valley.

■ Birds

See box for key species. Three species of heron and egret breed, and non-breeding summer visitors include *Casmerodius albus*, *Ardea cinerea*, *A. purpurea*, *Ardeola ralloides*, *Ciconia ciconia*, *Platalea leucorodia*, *Plegadis falcinellus* and *Fulica atra*. Wintering numbers of *Grus grus* have fluctuated but have not been less than 100 since 1980. Other notable wintering species include *Circus aeruginosus* (25). Large flocks of *Pelecanus onocrotalus* occur on passage.

■ Other threatened/endemic wildlife

Flora: *Linaria pelisseriana*, *Verbascum berytheum*.

■ Conservation issues

Most of the area is not protected. A new National Park (Hasharon, c.600 ha) is being developed, which will include Brehat Ya'ar (Birket Ata), a small wetland and proposed Nature Reserve (c.20 ha) holding the breeding waterbirds and non-breeding summer visitors mentioned above. There are local threats from urbanization, human disturbance, agricultural intensification and pollution.

■ Further reading

Levy and Yom-Tov (1991).

Globally threatened species

Crex crex	Passage migrant, up to 50–100 in a season.
Tetrax tetrax	Winter visitor (2–3).

1% or more of population

	Breeding (pairs)	Wintering	Passage
Phalacrocorax carbo	—	1,000–1,500	—
Pelecanus onocrotalus	—	150–300	15,000–20,000*
Nycticorax nycticorax	100–120	75–100	300–400*
Bubulcus ibis	100–350	200–500	—
Casmerodius albus	—	150–1,000	—
Egretta garzetta	50–150	200–500	—
Ardea cinerea	—	300–1,000	—
Platalea leucorodia	—	100–125	150–300
Grus grus	—	600–1,500	—

010 Northern Lower Jordan Valley

Nature Reserves (280 ha)

32°25′N 35°35′E
c.7,000 ha

■ Site description

The Jordan valley from Lake Kinneret to Tirat Zvi, west of the Jordan river. The lowest point of the site is 209 m below sea-level. Most of the area is cultivated fields, date-palm plantations and fish-ponds. Fish-ponds are mainly located near Kefar Ruppin (c.3 km north-east of Tirat Zvi), Afikim and Bet Zera.

■ Birds

See box for key species. Kefar Ruppin is an important breeding site for herons and egrets. Other notable wintering species include *Circus aeruginosus* (10–13) and during migration this species is also common (daily max. 75).

■ Other threatened/endemic wildlife

Mammals: *Caracal caracal* (rare).

■ Conservation issues

A few of the sites of ornithological interest are protected as Nature Reserves. The Kefar Ruppin fish-ponds (c.260 ha) are protected partly by the Nature Reserves Authority but mainly by cooperation between the operators and the Israel Ornithological Center. There are local threats from agricultural intensification, grazing and military activity.

1% or more of population

	Breeding (pairs)	Wintering	Passage
Nycticorax nycticorax	380–400	—	—
Bubulcus ibis	500–600	—	—
Egretta garzetta	480–510	—	—
Ciconia nigra	—	50–100	5,000*
Ciconia ciconia	—	—	200,000*
Glareola pratincola	—	—	250
Glareola nordmanni	—	—	200*
Vanellus vanellus	—	300–500	—

Regionally threatened or declining species

Pernis apivorus	Common passage migrant (up to 12,000 recorded in a season).
Accipiter brevipes	Common passage migrant (up to 15,000 recorded in a season).

Species restricted wholly or largely to the Middle East

Glareola nordmanni	Passage migrant (see above).
Pycnonotus xanthopygos	Common resident.
Passer moabiticus	Breeds (100–125 pairs).

011 Jericho
Unprotected

31°51′N 35°27′E
c.1,000 ha

Site description
The town of Jericho is located in the southern part of the Jordan valley. It is surrounded by cultivated fields and *Citrus* plantations which get their water from several springs flowing from the Judean desert to the west of the town.

Birds
The cliffs of the Rift Valley, north-west of Jericho, hold a small colony of *Falco naumanni*. See box for key species; other breeding species in the area include *Falco pelegrinoides* (1–2 pairs). A major passage route for soaring birds passes above the cliffs of the Rift Valley.

Other threatened/endemic wildlife
None known to BirdLife International.

Globally threatened species

Falco naumanni	Summer visitor (10–25 pairs).
Tetrax tetrax	Winter visitor (min. 2).

Regionally threatened or declining species

Falco biarmicus	Breeds (1–2 pairs).
Francolinus francolinus	Resident.

Species restricted wholly or largely to the Middle East

Ammoperdix heyi	Resident.
Onychognathus tristramii	Resident (10–20 pairs).
Turdoides squamiceps	Resident.
Passer moabiticus	Breeds (tens of pairs).

Conservation issues
Pesticide use in fields where *Falco naumanni* feeds is a potential threat.

012 Judean Foothills
Unprotected

31°45′N 34°55′E
c.60,000 ha

Site description
Low hills and cultivated land on the western slopes of the Judean mountains, 100–300 m above sea-level. The largest towns within this area are Kiryat Gat, Rehovot and Bet Shemesh. There are water reservoirs and sewage ponds.

Birds
See boxes for key species. The wetlands attract wintering waterfowl. A raptor migration route passes over the area.

Other threatened/endemic wildlife
Mammals: *Canis lupus* (V) and *Gazella gazella* (V).

Conservation issues
None known to BirdLife International.

Globally threatened species

Marmaronetta angustirostris	Up to 10 recorded in winter.
Oxyura leucocephala	Up to 100 recorded in winter.
Haliaeetus albicilla	Accidental in winter.
Aquila heliaca	Winter visitor (5) and passage migrant (up to 30 in a season).
Falco naumanni	Summer visitor (10–15 pairs) and passage migrant (up to 30 in a season).
Crex crex	Passage migrant (a few tens of birds in a season).
Tetrax tetrax	Accidental in winter (1–2).

1% or more of population

	Breeding (pairs)	Wintering	Passage
Podiceps nigricollis	—	500	—
Pelecanus onocrotalus	—	—	thousands
Bubulcus ibis	c.300	thousands	—
Ardea cinerea	—	100	—
Ciconia nigra	—	—	hundreds
Aythya nyroca	—	20	—
Grus grus	—	30	hundreds
Himantopus himantopus	250	200	hundreds
Vanellus vanellus	—	1,000	—
Tringa erythropus	—	50	150

Regionally threatened or declining species

Aythya nyroca	Winter visitor (see above).
Pernis apivorus	Passage migrant (thousands in a season).
Accipiter brevipes	Passage migrant (hundreds in a season).
Aquila pomarina	Passage migrant (up to 10,000 in a season).
Falco biarmicus	Winter visitor (single birds) and passage migrant (up to 5 in a season).
Falco cherrug	Scarce migrant.

Species restricted wholly or largely to the Middle East

Glareola nordmanni	Passage migrant (up to 20 in a season).

013 Jerusalem
Unprotected

31°45′N 35°10′E
c.1,000 ha

Site description
The site lies within the city of Jerusalem.

Birds
See box for key species. An important site for *Falco naumanni*.

Globally threatened species

Falco naumanni	Summer visitor; a colony of 70–80 pairs nests under roofs of old buildings and in the walls of the Old City, feeding in the city's parks.

Other threatened/endemic wildlife
None known to BirdLife International.

Conservation issues
The site is unprotected, and the agreement of the municipal authorities is required to leave the vicinity of the colony undeveloped—or to build alternative breeding sites.

Further reading
Hatzofe (1988).

014 Judean Desert
Nature Reserves (58,300 ha)

31°30′N 35°20′E
c.75,000 ha

Site description
Desert to the west of the Dead Sea, from 400 m below to 500 m above sea-level, extending 95 km from Jericho in the north to Mount Sedom in the south. Steep canyons run down to the Dead Sea and cliffs overlook the Rift Valley. There are several oases (e.g. En Gedi, Einot Samar, Einot Kaneh, Einot Zukim), some rocky, steppe and scrubby areas, and a little agriculture (mainly date-palm and *Citrus* plantations, and melons). Einot Zukim (Ein Feshka, 31°45′N 35°25′E, 500 ha) is of particular interest orithologically as a marsh within an arid area on the north-west shore of the Dead Sea: there are many perennial springs, reedbeds *Phragmites* grow where the water-table permits, and vegetation of the arid parts is dominated by *Tamarix nilotica* and *Atriplex halimus*. Einot Zukim was listed as a wetland of international importance by Carp (1980).

Birds
See boxes for key species. The area supports a wide range of species throughout the year. A major raptor and stork migration route passes along the 300–500-m-high cliffs of the Rift Valley, west of the Dead Sea. Large numbers of storks, *Pernis apivorus* and *Accipiter brevipes* pass through on migration. Other breeding species at En Gedi include *Falco*

Globally threatened species

Falco naumanni	Summer visitor (5 pairs in the northern part of the site) and passage migrant (less than 30 in a season).
Crex crex	Passage migrant (a few tens of birds in a season).

1% or more of population

	Breeding (pairs)	Wintering	Passage
Grus grus	—	—	hundreds

Regionally threatened or declining species

Botaurus stellaris	Winter visitor to Einot Zukim (1–2).
Pernis apivorus	Passage migrant, with thousands in a season.
Gypaetus barbatus	A pair last nested in 1980. Present status unclear (1 seen occasionally).
Neophron percnopterus	Resident (9–17 pairs). A few tens of birds occur on passage.
Gyps fulvus	Resident (10–22 pairs).
Torgos tracheliotus	Non-breeding visitor (*T. t. negevensis*); occurs in winter and spring (max. 2).
Accipiter brevipes	Passage migrant (more than 7,000 in a spring season).
Aquila pomarina	Passage migrant (5,000–10,000 in a season).
Falco biarmicus	Breeds (c.5 pairs). Single birds occur in winter and on passage (fewer than 10 in a season).
Falco cherrug	Single birds occur on passage.

Species restricted wholly or largely to the Middle East

Ammoperdix heyi	Resident.
Strix butleri	Resident (c.10 pairs).
Falco concolor	Summer visitor (3–5 pairs in the south of the Judean desert).
Pycnonotus xanthopygos	Resident.
Turdoides squamiceps	Resident.
Oenanthe monacha	Resident (max. 10 pairs, in the south of the site).
Onychognathus tristramii	Common resident (hundreds of pairs).
Passer moabiticus	Breeds at Einot Zukim, where also an abundant winter visitor (thousands) and passage migrant.
Serinus syriacus	Winter visitor to Einot Zukim (fewer than 10).
Emberiza cineracea	Winter visitor to Einot Zukim (fewer than 5).

pelegrinoides, *Halcyon smyrnensis*, *Merops orientalis*, *Ammomanes deserti*, *Hirundo obsoleta*, *Cercomela melanura*, *Oenanthe leucopyga*, *Nectarinia osea*, *Corvus ruficollis* and *C. rhipidurus*.

Other threatened/endemic wildlife

Mammals: *Pipistrellus ariel* (very rare), *Vulpes cana* (K), *Canis lupus* (V), *Caracal caracal* (rare), *Panthera pardus* (rare), *Capra nubiana* (I) and *Gazella gazella* (V). Reptiles: *Atractaspis engaddensis* (endemic). Flora: *Lisaea strigosa*.

Conservation issues

Most sites of ornithological interest in the area are protected as Nature Reserves (e.g. En Gedi, c.2,800 ha; Einot Zukim, 500 ha), and good cooperation exists with the Israel Air Force to prevent low flying which may disturb breeding raptors. Part of Einot Zukim (100 ha) is a National Park but attracts few birds due to disturbance from recreational activities; however, there are no serious problems at present. The main potential threat at Einot Zukim is fire, which sometimes occurs and spreads rapidly, and hunting is also a potential threat.

Further reading

Bahat (1986), Bahat and Leshem (1991), Carp (1980), Frumkin (1986), Frumkin and Man (1984).

015 Western Negev

Nature Reserves (c.1,000 ha)

31°10′N 34°40′E
c.90,000 ha

Site description

A mainly desert area extending as far as Be'er Sheva, Ofakim and Nir Oz in the north and to Mash'abim Sands (1,300 ha), Shunra Sands (2,400 ha), Agur Sands (30°53′N 34°26′E, 24,800 ha) and the Nahal Be'erotayim area (c.5,000 ha, close to Nizzana and the Egyptian border) in the south. The region includes low rocky hills, dry riverbeds, steppe, dunes and scrub, and there is some agriculture, mainly in the Ze'elim and Agur Sands area.

Birds

See box for key species. Other breeders include *Burhinus oedicnemus*, *Cursorius cursor*, four species of sandgrouse and *Eremophila bilopha*. In winter the area supports notable numbers of *Circus aeruginosus* (50), *Aquila clanga* (21), *Grus grus*, *Vanellus vanellus* and *Pterocles alchata* (8,000).

Globally threatened species

Aquila heliaca	Winter visitor (c.30), and a few occur on passage.
Crex crex	Passage migrant (75–100 in a season).
Tetrax tetrax	Winter visitor (2–3).
Chlamydotis undulata	This is the main Israeli breeding area: up to 50 pairs, chiefly within the Ze'elim and Agur Sands area.
Vanellus gregarius	Winter visitor (21).

1% or more of population

	Breeding (pairs)	Wintering	Passage
Ciconia ciconia	—	15–50	35,000–50,000*
Ciconia nigra	—	—	1,000–1,500*
Grus grus	—	2,800	—
Glareola pratincola	—	—	hundreds
Eudromias morinellus	—	hundreds	—
Vanellus vanellus	—	1,000	—

Regionally threatened or declining species

Pernis apivorus	Passage migrant (12,000 in a season).
Aquila pomarina	Passage migrant (12,000 in a season).
Falco biarmicus	A pair breeds in the Nahal Be'erotayim area.

Species restricted wholly or largely to the Middle East

Oenanthe finschii	Winter visitor (hundreds).

Other threatened/endemic wildlife

Mammals: *Meriones sacramenti* (endemic) and *Gazella gazella* (V). Reptiles: *Testudo kleinmanni* (V). Flora: *Allium papillare*, *Garhadiolus angulosus*.

Conservation issues

Some parts of the area are Nature Reserves and a further c.29,000 ha has been proposed. A small part of the Ze'elim and Agur Sands area (600 ha) is protected by the Nature Reserves Authority. Nahal Be'erotayim lies on a traditional major thoroughfare between Israel and Egypt, and there is considerable military activity, with resulting pressure on the desert crust. There is a possibility of the expansion of agriculture.

Further reading

Allon and Shirihai (1991), Baset (1986), Horin (1983), Levy and Yom-Tov (1991).

016 Northern Arava Valley

Nature Reserves (2,045 ha)

30°53′N 35°19′E
c.15,000 ha

Site description

The area along the Rift Valley south of the Dead Sea from the Ne'ot Hakikar Nature Reserve (10 km south of Sedom, 645 ha) south to the Hazeva and Shezaf Nature Reserve (34 km south of Sedom, 1,400 ha). A flat desert area with saltflats (in the north) and low hills, dissected by wide wadis. Vegetation comprises scattered open woodland of *Acacia raddiana* and *A. tortilis* in the wadis, and scrub of *Tamarix*, *Prosopis*, *Atriplex halimus*, *Suaeda monoecia* and *Alhagi maurorum*. There is a little agriculture.

Birds

See box for key species. Large numbers of storks, raptors and *Grus grus* occur on passage, especially in the northern part of the site.

Other threatened/endemic wildlife

Mammals: *Pipistrellus bodenheimeri* (rare endemic), *Canis lupus* (V), *Felis margarita* (rare), *Caracal caracal* (rare), *Panthera pardus* (rare), *Gazella gazella* (V) and *G. dorcas* (V). Reptiles: *Varanus griseus* (rare) and *Uromastyx aegyptius* (rare). Flora: *Isatis microcarpa*, *Convolvulus fatmensis* and *Hippocrepis constricta*.

Conservation issues

Two established Nature Reserves account for 2,045 ha of the site. Parts of the area are threatened by conversion to agriculture and saltpans, and the desert crust has recently become subject to damage by all-terrain vehicles.

Globally threatened species

Aquila heliaca	Scarce passage migrant.
Falco naumanni	Scarce passage migrant.
Crex crex	Scarce passage migrant.

1% or more of population

	Breeding (pairs)	Wintering	Passage
Ciconia nigra	—	1	350–1,000*
Ciconia ciconia	—	—	12,000–18,000*
Plegadis falcinellus	—	—	102*
Platalea leucorodia	—	—	143*
Anas querquedula	—	—	thousands
Grus grus	—	—	2,600*
Circus aeruginosus	—	—	23*
Himantopus himantopus	10–15	c.150	hundreds

Regionally threatened or declining species

Botaurus stellaris	Winter visitor (1).
Pernis apivorus	Passage migrant (11,000 in a season).
Neophron percnopterus	Passage migrant (a few tens in a season).
Torgos tracheliotus	Non-breeding visitor.
Accipiter brevipes	Passage migrant (15,000 in a season).
Aquila pomarina	Passage migrant (thousands in a season).
Falco concolor	Summer visitor (1 pair).

Species restricted wholly or largely to the Middle East

Ammoperdix heyi	Resident.
Strix butleri	Resident (1–2 pairs).
Oenanthe finschii	Winter visitor.
Oenanthe monacha	Resident (2–15 pairs).
Sylvia leucomelaena	Resident (20–40 pairs).
Turdus squamiceps	Resident (c.200 pairs).
Onychognathus tristramii	Resident.
Passer moabiticus	Breeds (15–35 pairs).

Further reading

Afik (1984), Bahat and Leshem (1991), Frumkin and Man (1984).

017 Cliffs of Zin and the Negev Highlands

Nature Reserve (13,000 ha) and National Park (c.500 ha)

30°50′N 34°48′E
c.25,000 ha

Site description

A region of desert near Sede Boqer, 50 km south of Be'er Sheva, 300–600 m above sea-level. It is a mountainous area of sedimentary rock capped with fossil loess and contains some perennial streams and waterholes. The plateau, north of Wadi Zin, is partly settled by Kibbutz Sede-Boqer (mainly agriculture and livestock) and the Sede-Boqer educational campus. The climate is arid. Rainfall occurs in winter, averaging 85 mm, with large annual variation in amount, timing and spatial distribution. The major pulse of plant growth occurs about mid-January to mid-April. A few oases with springs and large rock pools hold water all year. Most of the vegetation on the highest plateau (over 470 m) is of Irano-Turanian origin, dominated mainly by *Artemisia*. The lowest part of the Zin valley (300 m) is vegetated mainly with Saharo-Arabian forms, characterized by *Anabasis*, with sparse and patchy vegetation, being mainly limited to seasonal stream beds. Military activity is considerable and there is a little cultivation.

Birds

See box for key species. An unusually large number of raptors and owls breeds on the cliffs of Wadi Zin: *Neophron percnopterus*, *Gyps fulvus*, *Circaetus gallicus*, *Buteo rufinus*, *Aquila chrysaetos*, *Falco tinnunculus*, *F. concolor*, *F. biarmicus*, *F. pelegrinoides*, *Tyto alba*, *Bubo ascalaphus*, *Athene noctua*, *Strix butleri*, and *Asio otus*. At least 230 bird species have been recorded in the area, including at least 54 confirmed or presumed to breed, and at least 170 migrants. The area lies on a major migratory flyway and there is a passage of over 3,000 raptors in spring.

Other threatened/endemic wildlife

Mammals: *Canis lupus* (V), *Caracal caracal* (rare), *Panthera pardus* (rare), *Capra nubiana* (I), *Gazella gazella* (V) and *G. dorcas* (V). Reptiles: *Varanus griseus* (rare) and *Uromastyx aegyptius* (rare). Flora: *Hammada negevensis* (endemic) and *Origanum dayi*.

Conservation issues

The area with the most breeding raptors is included within the Nature Reserve or within the part of Ein Avdat National Park which lies within this site. The rest of the area (11,500 ha) is also protected by the Nature Reserves Authority (NRA) as an unofficial nature reserve, and the NRA also helps to protect the National Park. The area is open to visitors all year and travellers can reach nest-sites and disturb breeding raptors without knowing. Despite the efforts of the NRA to reduce the disturbance, insufficient manpower is available to cover the area properly. Military helicopters sometimes train in the area, flying low along cliffs and inside canyons, disturbing nesting or roosting raptors. A plan to improve an existing track along Wadi Zin may bring hundreds of private cars closer to the cliffs and risk disturbing breeding raptors. Human land-use may adversely affect the loess plain around Sede Boqer. The introduction of alien or non-local tree species could become more extensive than at present. More supervision is needed, and more educational work with the Israeli Air Force.

Globally threatened species

Aegypius monachus	Winter visitor (1).
Aquila heliaca	Scarce passage migrant.
Falco naumanni	Scarce passage migrant.
Crex crex	Passage migrant (probably some tens in a season).
Chlamydotis undulata	Breeds (max. 3 pairs) and winters (max. 10 birds).

1% or more of population

	Breeding (pairs)	Wintering	Passage
Ciconia nigra	—	—	hundreds
Ciconia ciconia	—	—	33,400*
Grus grus	—	—	250–400*

Regionally threatened or declining species

Pernis apivorus	Passage migrant (more than 2,000 in a season).
Neophron percnopterus	Resident (max. 25 pairs).
Gyps fulvus	Resident (max. 3 pairs); strong decline after 20–25 pairs 15 years ago, now 60–100 birds present throughout the year.
Torgos tracheliotus	Non-breeding visitor in spring and winter (max. 2).
Accipiter brevipes	Passage migrant (thousands in a season).
Aquila pomarina	Passage migrant (thousands in a season).
Falco concolor	Summer visitor (c.20 pairs).
Falco biarmicus	Breeds (3–7 pairs).
Hippolais languida	Scarce passage migrant (daily max. 2).
Carpodacus synoicus	Resident (at least 10 pairs).

Species restricted wholly or largely to the Middle East

Ammoperdix heyi	Resident (at least 50 pairs).
Otus brucei	Summer visitor (1–5 pairs).
Strix butleri	Resident (at least 5 pairs).
Oenanthe monacha	Resident (1–2 pairs).
Turdoides squamiceps	Resident (10–12 pairs).
Pycnonotus xanthopygos	Common resident.

Further reading

Frumkin (1986), Frumkin (1993), Frumkin and Man (1984), Shirihai and Bahat (1993), Yosef (1991).

018 Southern Arava Valley and Elat Mountains

Nature Reserves (c.43,200 ha)

29°40′N 35°00′E
c.60,000 ha

Site description

The tourist resort of Elat lies in the Rift Valley at the head of the Gulf of Elat (Gulf of Aqaba) flanked by mountains, with the Moon Valley and the plateau of the Negev to the west and the Arava valley running off to the north-north-west. The site comprises the region of the Arava valley from Elat to the area of Yotvata c.40 km to the north, and includes the western (Israeli) half of the valley floor and the ridge of the 'Elat Mountains'. The climate is arid (less than 50 mm rainfall per year), and rocky areas and gravel plains may be almost without vegetation, but sandy areas, especially wadis, support large bushes and, after rain, grasses and annual herbs. Large wadis and their alluvial fans support open woodland of *Acacia tortilis* and *A. raddiana*, notably just south of Yotvata, and here a few presumably native *Phoenix dactylifera* also grow where water is close to the surface. There is a tiny relict group of *Hyphaene thebaica* at En Evrona. Other habitats include beaches, agricultural fields, saltpans, sewage ponds and *Phragmites*; a saltmarsh with large *Suaeda* bushes has now almost disappeared.

■ Birds

See box for key species. Elat is a key site for migration through the Middle East, and very large numbers of all types of bird pass through the area in both spring and autumn. Over 420 species have been recorded. Of prime importance are raptors: 1.2 million have been counted in a single spring season and 26,000 in autumn, and the flyway is especially concentrated for *Pernis apivorus* (see box), *Milvus migrans* (max. seasonal total 31,774), *Accipiter brevipes* (see box), *Buteo buteo vulpinus* (max. seasonal total 465,827) and *Aquila nipalensis* (max. seasonal total 75,053). Migrant *Chlidonias leucopterus* also occur in especially high numbers. Numbers of migrating *Pelecanus onocrotalus* and *Ciconia nigra* are highest in spring, and seasonal totals from the Moon Valley are given (see box). Other breeding species include *Aquila verreauxii* (not proven: records of 1–2 birds), *Falco pelegrinoides* (1–2 pairs), *Pterocles lichtensteinii* and *Eremalauda dunni* (0–20 pairs, last bred 1989).

■ Other threatened/endemic wildlife

Mammals: *Pipistrellus bodenheimeri* (rare endemic), *Barbastella leucomelas* (rare), *Canis lupus* (V), *Vulpes cana* (K), *Vulpes zerda* (K), *Caracal caracal* (rare), *Felis margarita* (rare), *Capra nubiana* (I), *Gazella gazella* (V) and *G. dorcas* (V). Reptiles: *Coluber sinai* (endemic). Flora: *Paracaryum intermedium*, *Gomphocarpus sinaicus*, *Ephedra alata*, *Centaurea scoparia*.

■ Conservation issues

The Elat Mountains comprise an extensive Nature Reserve and further reserves exist in the valley south of Yotvata. In 1992 a 'Bird Park' plantation of native trees and shrubs was established at the site of a disused garbage tip 3 km north of Elat. The increase in the area's human population and its usage for recreation has made it more hazardous for some migrants. Considerable amounts of biocides used for agriculture may be a factor in the recent disappearance of some breeding species, e.g. *Lanius excubitor*. There is an outfall for semi-screened sewage on the Elat shore, which unless controlled (together with other runoff, etc.) may eventually affect the ecology of the Gulf through nutrient enrichment of seawater. Many *Chlidonias leucopterus* are killed by overhead cables, fast craft at sea can disturb loafing seabirds and ducks, and increasing numbers of all-terrain vehicles are penetrating many new areas inland and destroying the desert crust. Despite the efforts of the Nature Reserves Authority, the question of increased protection for established reserves needs to be addressed. Further tree-planting in the environs of Elat

Globally threatened species

Aquila heliaca	Passage migrant (10–90 in a season) and winter visitor (1–2).
Falco naumanni	Passage migrant (20–100 in a season).
Crex crex	Passage migrant (at least 10 in a season).
Larus leucophthalmus	Passage migrant (1–80 in a season) and winter visitor (1–5).

1% or more of population

	Breeding (pairs)	Wintering	Passage
Pelecanus onocrotalus	—	—	5,850*
Nycticorax nycticorax	—	—	100*
Egretta garzetta	—	—	100*
Casmerodius albus	—	—	80*
Ardea cinerea	—	—	1,000*
Ciconia ciconia	—	—	11,000*
Ciconia nigra	—	—	3,771*
Anas querquedula	—	—	10,000*
Grus grus	—	—	500*
Himantopus himantopus	—	—	hundreds
Tringa stagnatilis	—	—	500
Tringa glareola	—	—	5,000
Chlidonias leucopterus	—	—	50,000

Regionally threatened or declining species

Pernis apivorus	Passage migrant, mainly spring (max. 851,598 in a season).
Neophron percnopterus	Passage migrant, mainly spring (max. 802 in a season).
Gyps fulvus	Passage migrant (5–30 in a season).
Torgos tracheliotus	Rare and declining resident: formerly 20–40 pairs, but last bred 1989.
Accipiter brevipes	Passage migrant (max. 49,836 in a season).
Aquila pomarina	Passage migrant (max. 200 in a season).
Falco concolor	Summer visitor (5–10 pairs) and passage migrant (1–5 in a season).
Falco biarmicus	Resident (0–1 pairs; max. 2 in winter) and passage migrant (1–7 in a season).
Falco cherrug	Passage migrant (0–2 in a season).
Gallinago media	Passage migrant (0–2 in a season).
Carpodacus synoicus	Resident (2–4 pairs) and winter visitor (20–50).

Species restricted wholly or largely to the Middle East

Ammoperdix heyi	Resident.
Glareola nordmanni	Passage migrant (5–80 in a season).
Otus brucei	Winter visitor (3).
Strix butleri	Resident (4–10 pairs).
Oenanthe monacha	Resident.
Turdoides squamiceps	Resident.
Onychognathus tristramii	Resident (10–50 pairs) and winter visitor (usually over 5,000).
Passer moabiticus	Occurs erratically, with up to 10 pairs breeding, up to 100 in winter and up to 5,000 in a passage season.
Serinus syriacus	Winter visitor (0–5) and passage migrant (0–10 in a season).
Emberiza cineracea	Winter visitor (0–15).

would be beneficial. There is a programme for the reintroduction of extinct fauna at Hai-Bar reserve: establishment of *Equus hemionus* has commenced, and *Oryx leucoryx*, *Struthio camelus* and, hopefully, *Torgos tracheliotus* will follow. The number of *Ardea purpurea* migrating through this site has dramatically declined over the last 25 years (hundreds passed through per season ten years ago, now only c.10 per season are recorded), indicating the site's value for monitoring bird populations.

Further reading

Frumkin and Man (1984), Shirihai (1991), Shirihai and Christie (1992), Shirihai *et al.* (1987).

MAIN REFERENCES

AFIK, D. (1984) [Observations on breeding biology of the Arabian Warbler in the Arava valley.] *Tzufit* 2. (In Hebrew, English summary.)

ALON, D. (1987) [Third survey of wintering raptors in Israel 1987.] *Torgos* 13: 25–35, 117–118. (In Hebrew, English summary.)

ALLON, D. AND SHIRIHAI, H. (1991) A survey of wintering raptors in Israel 1987/88. Pp. 46–52 in D. Yekutiel, ed. *Raptors in Israel: passage and wintering populations.* Eilat: International Birdwatching Center Eilat.

ALLON *ET AL.* (1992) [Autumn migration of soaring birds, cross-Samaria and Northern Valleys, 1982–1991.] *Torgos* 20, Vol. 10/1. (In Hebrew.)

ANONYMOUS (1993) *Monthly bulletin of statistics* 44(9). Israel Central Bureau of Statistics.

BAHAT, O. (1985) [The first country-wide survey of wintering raptors in Israel, 1985.] *Torgos* 10. Vol. 5/1. (In Hebrew, English summary.)

BAHAT, O. (1986) [Nesting habits of birds of prey in the Mediterranean region as compared to the desert region in Israel.] *Torgos* 11. Vol. 5/2. (In Hebrew, English summary.)

BAHAT, O. AND LESHEM, Y. (1991) [The owls of Israel.] *Torgos* 18. Vol. 9/1. (In Hebrew, English summary.)

BASET, Y. (1986) [A survey of wintering raptors in the western Negev—January 1986.] *Torgos* 12: 49–60. (In Hebrew, English summary.)

BLITZBLAU, S. (1990a) [Migration of waders along the Carmel Coast, spring 1990.] *Torgos* 17. Vol. 8/2. (In Hebrew, English summary.)

BLITZBLAU, S. (1990b) [The breeding birds of Ein Afeq swamp, 1984–90.] Internal report, Nature Reserves Authority. (In Hebrew, English summary.)

BLITZBLAU, S. (1991) [Breeding waterbirds in the northern coastal plain of Israel, 1983–90.] Internal report, Nature Reserves Authority. (In Hebrew, English summary.)

BRUDERER, B. (1992) Radar studies on bird migration in the south of Israel. BSCE 21, Jerusalem.

CARP, E. (1980) *A directory of western Palaearctic wetlands.* Nairobi: United Nations Environment Programme/Gland (Switzerland): International Union for Conservation of Nature and Natural Resources.

FRUMKIN, R. (1986) Status of breeding raptors in the Israeli deserts, 1980–1985. *Sandgrouse* 8: 42–57.

FRUMKIN, R. (1993) Breeding ecology of the Sooty Falcon (*Falco concolor*) in Israel. Pp. 51–58 in Nichols, M.K. and Clarke, R., eds. *Biology and conservation of small falcons. Proceedings of the 1991 Hawk and Owl Trust Conference.* London: Hawk and Owl Trust.

FRUMKIN, R. AND MAN, S. (1984) [Raptors nesting in the desert areas of Israel 1980–1984.] *Torgos* 9. Vol. 4/2. (In Hebrew, English summary.)

GELLER, S. (1983) [Changes in raptor populations in the north of Upper Galilee since the establishment of the State of Israel.] *Torgos* 6. Vol. 3/1. (In Hebrew, English summary.)

GORNEY, E. (1980) [Breeding birds in Hula Nature Reserve, spring–summer 1980.] Internal report, Nature Reserves Authority. (In Hebrew, English summary.)

GORNEY, E. (1983) [An attempt to introduce White-tailed Eagles in England (with some notes on the attempt to introduce White-tailed Eagles in Hula N.R.—northern Israel).] *Torgos* 6. Vol. 3/1. (In Hebrew, English summary.)

HAREUVENI, I (1985) *Nature Reserves in Israel.* Tel Aviv: Ministry of Defence.

HATZOFE, O. (1988) [A nesting colony of Lesser Kestrels (*Falco naumanni*) in Mussrara, Jerusalem.] *Torgos* 14. Vol. 7/1. (In Hebrew, English summary.)

HORIN, O. (1983) [A survey of wintering raptors in western Negev.] *Torgos* 6, Vol. 3/1. (In Hebrew, English summary.)

HOTER, E. AND EZOV, E. (1991) [The birds of Mount Hermon: a breeding survey, 1990.] *Torgos* 19. Vol 9/2. (In Hebrew, English summary.)

HOVEL, H. (1987) *Check list of the birds of Israel.* Tel Aviv: Tel-Aviv University/Tel Aviv: Society for the Protection of Nature in Israel.

ISRAEL ORNITHOLOGICAL CENTER (1985 onwards) Databanks of unpublished material.

ISRAEL RAPTOR INFORMATION CENTER (1980 onwards) Databanks of unpublished material.

ISRAEL WADER RESEARCH GROUP (1991 onwards) Databanks of unpublished material.

LAVI, N. (1986) [Mutual relation between Cranes and raptors.] *Torgos* 11. Vol. 5.2. (In Hebrew, English summary.)

LEVY, N. AND YOM-TOV, Y. (1991) Activity and status of Cranes *Grus grus* wintering in Israel. *Sandgrouse* 13: 58–72.

LESHEM, Y. (1983) [The status of Falconiformes in Israel.] *Torgos* 6. Vol. 3/6. (In Hebrew, English summary.)

PAZ, U. (1986) *Plants and animals of the land of Israel* Vol. 6 *Birds* (Alon, A., ed.). Tel Aviv: Ministry of Defence.

PAZ, U. (1987) *The birds of Israel*. Christopher Helm, London.

SCHLUTER, P. (1987) [The Brown Fish Owl (*Ketupa zeylonensis*) in Israel.] *Torgos* 13. Vol. 6/2. (In Hebrew, English summary.)

SHIRIHAI, H. (1991) The invasion and breeding of Dunn's Lark *Eremalauda dunni* in the Arava valley, Israel. *Sandgrouse* 13: 7–13.

SHIRIHAI, H. *ET AL.* (1987) *Eilat—an intercontinental highway for migrating birds*. Eilat: International Birdwatching Center Eilat.

SHIRIHAI, H. AND BAHAT, O. (1993) *Birdwatching in the deserts of Israel*. Tel Aviv: Society for the Protection of Nature in Israel/Eilat: International Birdwatching Center Eilat.

SHIRIHAI, H. AND CHRISTIE, D. (1992) Raptor migration at Eilat. *Brit. Birds* 85: 141–186.

SHY, E. (1988–1992) [Winter wildfowl census: summary report.] Internal report, Nature Reserves Authority. (In Hebrew, English summary.)

TSOVEL, A. AND ALLON, D. (1991) Soaring bird migration survey in the Northern Valleys of Israel—Autumns 1988–1990. Pp. 31–45 in Yekutiel, D., ed. *Raptors in Israel: Passage and wintering populations*. Eilat: International Birdwatching Center Eilat.

YOSEF, R. (1991) Foraging habits, hunting and breeding success of Lanner Falcons (*Falco biarmicus*) in Israel. *J. Raptor Res.* 25: 77–81.

ZACHAI, G. (1984) [The reproductive biology of the Mourning Wheatear.] *Tzufit* 2. (In Hebrew, English summary.)

ZUARETZ, S. (1970–1987) [Winter wildfowl census—summary report.] Internal report, Nature Reserves Authority. (In Hebrew, English summary.)

ZUARETZ, S. (1977) [Ten years of breeding waterbird surveys in Israel, 1967–76.] Internal report, Nature Reserves Authority. (In Hebrew, English summary.)

ZUARETZ, S. (1983) [A breeding survey of the birds of Mount Hermon.] Internal report, Nature Reserves Authority. (In Hebrew, English summary.)

■ HASHEMITE KINGDOM OF JORDAN

Dead Sea Sparrow *Passer moabiticus*

GENERAL INFORMATION

The Hashemite Kingdom of Jordan has an area of 89,210 km^2 and is bordered by Syria in the north, Iraq in the north-east, Saudi Arabia to the east and south, and Israel and the West Bank to the west. The country is land-locked except for a 27-km stretch of coastline bordering the Gulf of Aqaba of the Red Sea in the extreme south-west. The human population in 1990 was 4,009,000, with the majority inhabiting the western strip, either in the agriculturally rich Jordan Valley, or in the highlands east of the Rift Valley, including more than 1,000,000 people in the capital Amman itself. The largest urban areas after Amman are Zarqa and Irbid. Apart from some major towns on its fringe (e.g. Ma'an, Mafraq), the desert supports only nomadic pastoralists and a few villages and settlements set widely apart.

The four main physiographic and biogeographic regions of Jordan are (1) the Rift Valley, (2) the scarp and highlands east of the Rift Valley, (3) the desert plateau ('badia') of the eastern three-quarters of the country, (all three of which regions trend north-south) and (4) the marine environment. Most land lies between 500 and 1,000 m, although a few peaks exceed 1,500 m, and the Dead Sea at the bottom of the Rift Valley is the lowest point on Earth, at 400 m below sea-level. The most widespread and dominant land-uses are livestock grazing and agriculture; forestry and mineral extraction (phosphate, potash) are of more local occurrence. About 310,000 ha of Jordan are cultivated, of which 80% is irrigated and 20% is rain-fed.

Rift Valley region

The Dead Sea Rift follows the line of a gigantic fault which extends 370 km from the meeting point of the Yarmuk river with the Jordan river in the north to the Gulf of Aqaba in the south, and is part of the great African Rift Valley. The northern part of the valley, defined by the drainage basin of the Dead Sea, is called the Ghor. The southern part of the valley, draining into the Gulf of Aqaba, is named Wadi Araba.

In the northern Ghor, lying north of the Dead Sea, the country's main river, the Jordan, flows south to the Dead Sea. The northern Ghor is the main agricultural area in Jordan; the principal crops are intensively cultivated fruit and vegetables, irrigated from canals which divert water from the Yarmuk, Zarqa and other rivers. Wadi Araba is mainly composed of stony and gravelly outwash plains and mobile sand-dune desert, with some sabkhah (saline mudflats). There is little cultivation in Wadi Araba, which is mainly used as rangeland and for military purposes.

The natural vegetation of the valley plain and lower scarp slopes has been greatly modified by cultivation and grazing in the Jordan Valley, but is more intact in the stonier Wadi Araba: tropical Sudanian species of tree and dwarf-shrub are prominent in the sparse and very open vegetation, including *Acacia*, *Balanites*, *Tamarix*, *Calotropis*, *Maerua*, *Salvadora*, *Ochradenus* and *Panicum*.

Scarp and highland region

This region of escarpments, mountains, hills and undulating plateaus extends mainly from Irbid in the north to Ras an Naqab in the south, and from the Rift Valley region (see above) in the west to the 'badia' region (see below) in the east. The mountains in the southern half of this region are higher on average, and some range between 1,200 and 1,600 m high. Numerous broad, shallow, gravelly wadis drain the eastern and western flanks of this region. There is also an isolated tract of high mountains between Ras an Naqab and the Saudi Arabian border, including the highest peaks in Jordan, Jabal Rum and Jabal Umm Ishrin, at c.1,750 m.

Mediterranean woodland of pine *Pinus* and oak *Quercus*, with juniper *Juniperus* and cypress *Cupressus* more locally, is believed to have originally covered large tracts of the Jordanian highlands, e.g. between Madaba and Mount Nebo, but millennia of human occupation together with natural climatic change are thought to have resulted in drastic deforestation and replacement of natural vegetation by secondary species. Woodland today covers about 100,000 ha of Jordan, of which about 25,000 ha are natural. The largest remaining areas of natural woodland occur in the highlands between Amman and Irbid, and are dominated by *Pinus halepensis* above 700 m, whilst mixed evergreen/deciduous oak woodland of *Quercus calliprinos* and *Q. ithaburensis* dominates at lower elevations where the original pine-dominated woodland has been degraded. Also in the north-west, between the remaining forested areas and the cultivated areas, are patches of garigue or 'batha', e.g. at Umm Qais near Irbid.

Cultivation of rain-fed wheat is widespread on the plateau between Irbid and Madaba, and olive groves cover a large part of the north-western mountains above 700 m. More than 80% of the Kingdom's cities and villages occur within this region.

Badia or Eastern Desert Plateau region

This comprises the eastern three-quarters of the country and is continuous with the Arabian Desert of Syria, Iraq and Saudi Arabia. It is a gently undulating plateau with an elevation of 500 to 900 m. Two broad habitat-types can be distinguished in the region: (1) the 'hammada' (smooth, gravel/chert plains), which stretches from Ras an Naqab to the Iraqi border in the north-east; and (2) the 'harrat' (black boulder-fields of basalt rock), which extends from south-west Syria, through north-east Jordan, and onwards into Saudi Arabia. Extensive sand-dune desert occurs in the southernmost part of the country, e.g. around Wadi Rum in the Hisma basin. Clay pans lying at the bottom of closed drainage basins in the desert can become flooded after heavy rain, with the water persisting for several months rather than draining away. The best known such area is Qa al Azraq, but the Jafr basin in the south is the largest example in Jordan, very occasionally forming a huge, temporary lake.

This largely treeless region is dominated on its western fringe, adjoining the Highlands region, by Irano-Turanian species of small shrub and bush such as *Artemisia*, *Retama*, *Anabasis* and *Ziziphus*. The majority of the region, to the east of this highland fringe, has an even poorer plant-cover dominated by Saharo-Arabian species, including *Achillea*, *Artemisia*, *Phlomis*, *Stipa*, *Astragalus* and *Trigonella*. The badia is the main rangeland of Jordan, but the range quality is deteriorating due to very heavy grazing and due to widespread ploughing for cultivation of rain-fed barley, which has led to loss of plant cover and accelerated soil erosion and degradation through wind and water erosion. The only other major cultivation is of pivot-irrigated wheat, vegetables and alfalfa around Disi and Abu Suwana in the Hisma basin, using fossil groundwater.

Marine region

The Gulf of Aqaba is narrow and very deep, averaging 10–20 km wide and bordered by precipitous slopes plunging down to 1,800 m depth. Salinity is higher than average at 4.2%, and tidal amplitude is slight at 0.5–0.6 m. There is a seasonal marine upwelling off Aqaba, due to the prevailing north-to-south surface currents in the Gulf of Aqaba. There are two well-developed fringing reefs to the south of Aqaba.

The annual rainfall decreases from west to east, and from north to south, being affected also by the physical features of the country. About 90% of the country is semi-arid to arid, mostly receiving less than 200 mm of rain per year. The more elevated, western part of Jordan has a typical Mediterranean climate with six months of rainy season (November–April, up to 800 mm of rain per year) and a long, hot rainless summer. The highest areas experience cool summers and cold, wet winters with occasional snow. Mean monthly temperatures range from 14 to 32°C in the Rift Valley, 4 to 28°C in the uplands and 10 to 30°C in the eastern deserts. The Rift Valley is the hottest area in Jordan, throughout the year.

ORNITHOLOGICAL IMPORTANCE

Jordan has a wide diversity of bird habitat-types due to its varied topography and climate and its biogeographical position. A total of 363 species have been recorded, of which 141 definitely breed and a further 13 possibly breed. The extensive arid land in the east has the lowest breeding bird diversity, with similar bird communities to the vast desert areas across the border in Syria, Iraq and Saudi Arabia. The highest diversity is found in the highlands and Rift Valley margins in the west of the country.

Accurate population estimates for breeding or wintering birds in Jordan are not yet available, except for a few species. The figures given below are only rough estimates and should be interpreted with caution; it is hoped that their accuracy can be improved in the future.

Jordan supports breeding populations of three globally threatened species: *Marmaronetta angustirostris* (less than 10 pairs), *Falco naumanni* (10–99 pairs) and *Chlamydotis undulata* (although no breeding records have been documented in the last 10 years, there is thought to be a small breeding population, of less than 100 pairs). Remnant populations of some regionally threatened species exist in Jordan (*Francolinus francolinus*) or may still exist (*Gypaetus barbatus*, *Torgos tracheliotus*). Breeding species which are more-or-less restricted to the Middle East and which have important breeding populations in Jordan include *Passer moabiticus* and *Serinus syriacus*. Of great biogeographical interest are the populations of *Ketupa zeylonensis* (highly threatened) and *Carpodacus synoicus*; both are extremely isolated examples of eastern Palaearctic and Asian species respectively, relicts of past climates very different from the present. *Parus caeruleus* is another interesting relict population of a generally more northerly-breeding species.

Jordan lies on the main migration route between Africa and Eurasia of huge numbers of birds, and migrant species dominate the avifauna. The globally threatened *Aquila heliaca* and *Crex crex* occur only on migration, in apparently small numbers. The agricultural plains between Irbid and Madaba appear to be important feeding and resting areas for *Aquila heliaca*, and both of these species appear to concentrate in the Rift Valley whilst on active migration. There is a spectacular spring migration of raptors through Jordan, heading for breeding grounds north and east of the Caucasus mountains, and possibly involving more than 1,000,000 birds, including significant proportions of the world populations of *Buteo buteo*, *Pernis apivorus*, *Aquila nipalensis* and *Accipiter brevipes*. In autumn, thousands of *Aquila nipalensis* also converge at the head of the Gulf of Aqaba on their southward migration, and hundreds of *Circus pygargus* are attracted to drink at the few, isolated water bodies whilst crossing the eastern desert plateau. Most other migrant species probably move across Jordan in a highly dispersed fashion along a broad front, although the Rift Valley appears to be an important flyway for some waterbirds, and spectacular numbers of certain passerine migrants such as *Sylvia curruca* and *S. atricapilla* can regularly be seen in spring. However, many migrants are likely to over-fly the country without stopping or utilizing ground-based resources to any significant degree, especially in the drier autumn period.

Apart from at Azraq, there has not been any extensive survey of wintering birds in Jordan, and published information is sparse; this is perhaps the most obvious gap in Jordan's ornithology. The globally threatened *Aegypius monachus* may once have bred, at least up until the 1960s, but now it is likely to be only a rare winter visitor to agricultural steppe areas in northern Jordan. *Chlamydotis undulata* is likely to winter in significant numbers in the basalt 'harrat' desert in the east, due to the natural protection from human disturbance afforded by the inaccessibility of much of this region. Even so, it appears that the wintering population of this species has declined significantly over the past two decades.

Internationally significant numbers of wildfowl still winter at Qa al Azraq after winters of good rain, although the importance of the permanent marshland at this site (as a rich feeding ground for wildfowl) has declined severely since the 1960s when up to c.350,000 wildfowl could be found in some winters.

CONSERVATION INFRASTRUCTURE AND PROTECTED-AREA SYSTEM

The Ministry of Agriculture is the government body responsible for protecting, conserving and managing wildlife in Jordan, as well as for developing and protecting Jordan's forest resources and rangelands. The Ministry of Agriculture has delegated responsibility for nature conservation, including on-the-ground establishment and management of wildlife reserves, to a non-governmental organization, the Royal Society for the Conservation of Nature (RSCN). There are three categories of protected area relevant to the conservation of areas of national importance for wildlife:

Wildlife Reserve (6 sites covering c.97,000 ha)
Established to protect indigenous fauna and flora (especially threatened species) and their natural habitats, to raise public awareness of and interest in wildlife conservation, to improve socio-economic conditions in the area and to promote tour-

ism. The sites exclude all agriculture, pastoralism, trespass, hunting, fishing, mining, industrial activity and other activities with potential to inflict major damage to the site. Twelve Wildlife Reserves were officially proposed by the RSCN to the government in 1979, of which six have now been established on the ground and in law, and the remaining six are in the process of being established. Seven of the 12 are included in this inventory. In addition, a Marine Reserve is in the process of being established in law.

National Park (3 sites covering c.25,100 ha)
Established by Ministries and municipal authorities for recreation and tourism. Two more sites may be officially proposed in the near future.

Grazing Reserve (18 sites covering c.51,500 ha)
Established by the Department of Forests of the Ministry of Agriculture to restore and improve the plant cover of rangelands through control of grazing; at least 5,000 ha have been planted with fodder shrubs.

Agriculture Law no. 20 of 1973 (Chapter 3, 'Protection of wildlife and birds. Regulations for their hunting', articles 144–155; as amended by Act no. 14 of 1974), and Regulation no. 113 (1973; issued in accordance with article 199 of Agriculture Law no. 20) provide the legal tool for monitoring all hunting activities. The authority for enforcing these laws is delegated by the Ministry of Agriculture to the RSCN, which has divided the country into six hunting areas, and which sets bag limits, close-seasons and permitted hunting frequencies for all game species. The RSCN Hunting Committee meets every month during the hunting season to revise these controls as necessary, depending on species' current status.

INTERNATIONAL MEASURES RELEVANT TO THE CONSERVATION OF SITES

Jordan has ratified the Ramsar Convention, the World Heritage Convention and the Regional Convention for the Conservation of the Red Sea and the Gulf of Aden Environment. It has signed but not ratified the Biodiversity Convention. As of December 1993 it has designated one Ramsar site (7,372 ha; included in this inventory), but no natural World Heritage Sites. Jordan takes part in the UNESCO Man and Biosphere Programme through a National Committee; no Biosphere Reserves have been designated, but at least one is proposed (Burqu).

OVERVIEW OF THE INVENTORY

A total of 17 sites are included in the inventory, covering a total area of about 8,500 km^2 or about 9.5% of Jordan's area. Three of the sites are fully protected by law and five of the sites are partially protected; in addition, two further sites are officially proposed for legal protection. All of the important habitats for birds are covered, with varying degrees of comprehensiveness, including natural and man-made wetlands, the mountainous and biodiversity-rich scarp and fringes of the Rift Valley, and the steppes and deserts of the Rift Valley floor and the eastern plateau (including isolated mountains and the special 'harrat' basalt desert). In the case of the more extensive tracts of homogeneous desert and steppe habitats, large and representative sites have been selected. Few of the sites are under any immediate threat, apart from some of the natural wetlands (Azraq, Qa Hanna, Jordan Valley) which are subject to numerous problems including excessive water-abstraction, salinization and pollution. However, nearly all of the original dry grasslands and shrub-steppes in the less desertic areas have been converted to cultivation, and identification and survey of any remaining fragments of this habitat-type would be very valuable. Many bird species (which Jordan has important populations of) such as breeding raptors, sandgrouse and larks, tend not to congregate but to have scattered distributions. Only a small proportion of their total populations is covered by the inclusion of some representative sites. To conserve these species it is necessary to consider conservation measures for the wider environment, such as regulation of agriculture, forestry and hunting.

ACKNOWLEDGEMENTS

The site accounts were compiled from data-sheets and other information supplied by I. Andrews, A. Sutari and D. M. Shafei (Jordan Natural History Museum), and incorporate comments and amendments by A. Budieri, K. Irani, Dr A. Dajani, Dr M. Masseti and J. F. Stewart. The Introduction was compiled from information supplied by A. Budieri and K. Irani, supplemented by comments from I. Andrews and Dr M. Masseti. The project was coordinated within Jordan by the Royal Society for the Conservation of Nature (A. Budieri).

SITE INVENTORY

Site no.	Site name	Region	Criteria used to select site: 1	2i	2ii	2iii	3	4	5i	5ii	6	0
001	Yarmuk Valley	IB	—	—	—	—	•	•	—	•	—	—
002	Burqu	MF	•	—	—	—	•	•	•	—	—	—
003	Irbid–Mafraq Plains	IB, MF	•	—	—	—	•	•	—	•	—	—
004	Zubiya	IB	•	—	—	—	•	•	—	•	—	—
005	Jordan Valley	IB, BL	•	•	—	•	•	•	—	•	—	—
006	Dibbin Forest	IB	•	—	—	—	—	•	—	•	•	—
007	Khirba as Samra	ZR	—	•	—	•	•	—	—	—	—	—
008	Qa Hanna	ZR	—	—	—	—	—	—	—	•	—	•
009	Azraq Oasis	ZR	•	•	•	—	•	•	—	•	•	—
010	Shaumari Area	ZR	•	•	—	—	•	•	•	—	•	—
011	Hisban–Madaba Plains	AM	•	—	—	—	—	—	—	•	—	—
012	Wadi Mujib	AM, KK	•	—	—	•	•	•	—	—	•	—
013	Wadi Dana–Finan	MN, TF	•	—	—	•	•	•	—	—	•	—
014	Petra Area	MN	•	—	—	•	•	•	•	—	•	—
015	Wadi Araba	MN	•	—	—	—	•	•	—	—	—	—
016	Hisma Basin	MN	—	—	—	—	•	•	•	—	•	—
017	Aqaba Mountains	MN	•	—	—	•	•	•	•	—	•	—

Key to regions

AM Amman Governorate
BL Balqa Governorate
IB Irbid Governorate
KK Karak Governorate
MF Mafraq Governorate
MN Ma'an Governorate
TF Tafila Governorate
ZR Zarqa Governorate

Key to criteria

1 Regularly holds a significant number of a globally threatened species.
2i Regularly holds 1% or more of a species' biogeographical or flyway or Middle Eastern population (waterbirds and seabirds only).
2ii Regularly holds 20,000 or more waterbirds.
2iii Migratory 'bottleneck' site: more than 3,000 raptors or more than 5,000 storks or more than 2,000 cranes pass in a season.
3 Regularly holds a significant number of a species which is threatened or declining within the Middle East. Only the top five sites for each such species in the country are considered to qualify as IBAs.
4 Regularly holds a significant number of a species whose world population is wholly or largely restricted to the Middle East. Only the top five sites for each such species in the country are considered to qualify as IBAs.
5i Representative example of a habitat, associated with a characteristic assemblage of bird species.
5ii Rare/threatened/unique habitat, associated with a characteristic assemblage of bird species.
6 Site important for bird conservation through education/research/tourism.
0 Selected for other reasons. See 'Comments on the inventory'.

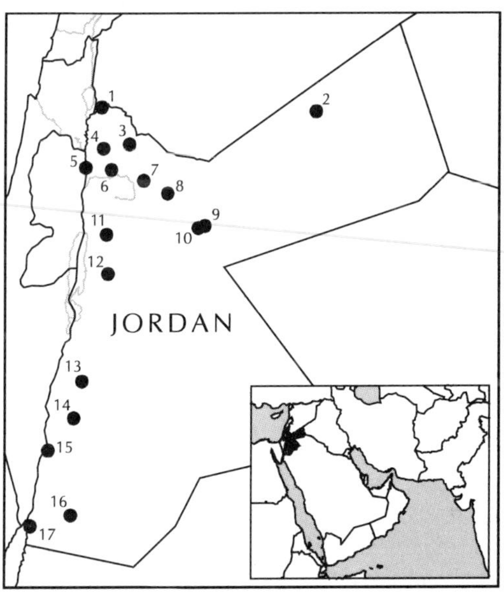

Comments on the inventory

1. The site name has been transliterated from the Arabic, and is sometimes followed by an alternative site name in brackets. This is then followed by the name of the region in brackets. The regions given are the governorates (muhafazat).
2. The majority of the data used in compiling the site accounts was collected during the late 1980s onwards.
3. Information on bird populations is comparatively scant, and even the distribution of some species is not known. One result is a bias in favour of better explored areas, therefore the inventory should be regarded as preliminary.
4. Precise areas are given only for protected areas. Boundaries have not been defined for the non-protected sites, and any areas given in these cases are only crude estimates.
5. Figures in brackets after species' names, and in the boxes, are the maximum daily counts of individuals recorded (not pairs), unless otherwise stated. All counts of wintering birds are from January, unless otherwise stated.
6. It has not been possible to apply 'Top 5 site' criterion in category 4 (as depicted in the above table) for *Ammoperdix heyi*, *Pycnonotus xanthopygos* and *Oenanthe finschii*. These are common and widespread over much of Jordan, and occur commonly in many of the listed sites. However, their presence is generally listed, where known, due to their interest in a Middle Eastern context. The application of the criteria in catego-

ries 3 and 4 is provisional only, due to scarcity of recent or comprehensive information.

7. Certain sites have been chosen as representative of much larger surrounding areas of contiguous habitat, which are generally unexplored and little known, but which may well prove to be of higher habitat quality than the chosen areas due to their isolation and the lack of human impact, after investigation. In particular, sites 014, 016 and 017 come under this description.
8. One site (008) does not meet the criteria and has been chosen for other reasons (see column 0 of above table); it is thought it would qualify if more bird data were available; in addition, it is a seasonal/temporary wetland, and may only be important in occasional years.
9. This inventory should not be regarded as final, since other important bird areas are likely to identified following further surveys of the country's biological resources.
10. One potential site was identified too late for further investigation and possible inclusion in this inventory: Kufr Huda, in the Salt mountains, is a grassland/agricultural area (exact location not known) which supports a breeding colony of the globally threatened *Falco naumanni*. It deserves further investigation as a priority.

Glossary

qa, large, shallow, seasonally flooded basin
sabkhah, saline mudflat
wadi, drainage line or bed of seasonal river

001 Yarmuk Valley (Irbid)

Unprotected

32°44´N 35°44´E
c.3,000 ha

Site description

A steep-sided valley running along the Jordan–Syria border. There are remnants of *Pinus* woodland on the slopes, and lush reedbeds *Phragmites* and oleander *Nerium* thickets along the Yarmuk river, which is the least polluted of Jordan's main rivers. There is a small, spring-fed pool at Birket al Rais. The riverine area is currently a military zone; the main human use of the river is as a water supply to irrigate farmland in the Jordan Valley; local activities include cultivation, fishing, forestry, reed-cutting and mushroom collection.

Birds

See box for key species. Other likely breeding species include *Halcyon smyrnensis*, *Anthus similis*, *Cercomela melanura*, *Acrocephalus stentoreus*, *Cisticola juncidis* and *Nectarinia osea*.

Regionally threatened or declining species	
Gyps fulvus	Possibly breeds (recorded in spring/summer in suitable breeding habitat).
Ketupa zeylonensis	A very rare resident along Yarmuk river (one north of Al Znebneh village, 1986).
Species restricted wholly or largely to the Middle East	
Ammoperdix heyi	Resident.
Oenanthe finschii	Winter visitor.

Other threatened/endemic wildlife

Fish: *Tilapia gallilae* (endemic).

Conservation issues

Access to the military zone is restricted, which provides some indirect protection. Diversion of water to supply irrigation to intensive agricultural projects in the Jordan Valley is a critical problem along the lower course of the river; drainage of wet bank-side habitats is a major problem, and dynamite fishing in the river and excessive soil erosion are occurring locally. The South American rodent *Myocastor coypus* has been introduced; its effects on riverine vegetation are unknown but may be seriously destructive. The Ramtha Wastewater Treatment Plant discharges treated effluent into the river, but this is currently considered to be at an acceptable level. There have long been plans for a large-scale, joint Jordanian—Syrian dam across the Yarmuk river (Wahda or Unity Dam), which would potentially be a critical threat.

Further reading

Pearce (1993).

002 **Burqu** (Mafraq)

Unprotected (proposed Wildlife Reserve)

32°42′N 37°57′E
95,000 ha

■ Site description
Desert landscape of flint/chert plains (hammada) in the east, flattish to gently rolling country covered in black basalt boulders (harrat) in the west, interspersed with siltflats and many shallow wadis. Plant cover is generally sparse, mainly limited to the shallow wadis and dominated by woody perennial herbs such as *Artemisia*, *Anabasis* and *Achillea*. There are no trees or large bushes. Within the reserve there is a near-permanent, spring-fed freshwater pool (200 ha) at Ghadir Burqu which is a major source of water for the livestock of bedouin living in a wide surrounding area. The main land-use is nomadic pastoralism and cultivation is very limited. An ancient Nabataean/Roman castle, Qasr Burqu, lies at the edge of the harrat.

■ Birds
See box for key species. A relatively rich and intact desert bird community. Other proven or probable breeding species include *Buteo rufinus*, *Aquila chrysaetos*, *Alectoris chukar*, *Cursorius cursor*, *Charadrius leschenaultii*, *Ramphocoris clotbey*, *Eremophila bilopha* and *Oenanthe lugens* (a dark morph, endemic to the basalt desert of northern Arabia). Ghadir Burqu is an important water source for large numbers of raptors during autumn migration, e.g. *Circus pygargus* (daily max. 85, September), and a wide variety of waders and passerines are also attracted on migration and in winter. Up to 100 *Grus grus* overwinter around Ghadir Burqu.

■ Other threatened/endemic wildlife
Mammals: *Canis lupus* (V), and possibly *Caracal caracal* (rare) and *Gazella subgutturosa* (rare).

■ Conservation issues
Burqu Wildlife Reserve is currently under establishment; its designation in the future as a (possibly trans-border) Biosphere Reserve is being investigated. Large fauna proposed for re-introduction include *Struthio camelus*, *Acinonyx jubatus*, *Gazella* spp., *Oryx leucoryx* and *Equus hemionus*. Vast areas of the harrat are inaccessible even to four-wheel-drive vehicles due to the bouldery terrain, and are a true refuge for wildlife from hunting and human disturbance. Very intense grazing by camels, sheep and goats is the main environmental problem, this being especially obvious on the hammada. In addition, vehicle access to the hammada plains is virtually unlimited, and the desert crust here has been considerably scarred by tracks. The ease of access facilitates hunting of large animals, which was a major problem at least formerly. Local problems are disturbance of wildlife by military activity, creation of new vehicle-tracks within the harrat (providing increased access to isolated areas locally) and quarrying. At Ghadir Burqu, the trapping of birds of prey is a major problem and bird shooting is often excessive; water extraction by pastoralists for their flocks could have a serious impact on the lake in the near future if current trends continue.

Globally threatened species

Aquila heliaca	Winter visitor or passage migrant.
Chlamydotis undulata	May breed in the inaccessible harrat, and almost certainly winters.

Regionally threatened or declining species

Falco biarmicus	Rare passage migrant/winter visitor.
Falco cherrug	Scarce passage migrant/winter visitor.

Species restricted wholly or largely to the Middle East

Ammoperdix heyi	Resident.
Carpospiza brachydactyla	Irregular passage migrant/winter visitor.

003 **Irbid–Mafraq Plains** (Irbid, Mafraq)

Unprotected

32°27′N 36°01′E
42,500 ha

■ Site description
Agricultural plains between Irbid and Mafraq, with dry and irrigated cultivation of cereals.

■ Birds
See box for key species. Breeding species include *Charadrius leschenaultii*. Wintering species include *Grus grus* and probably *Eudromias morinellus*.

■ Other threatened/endemic wildlife
Flora: *Verbascum transjordanicum* (endemic), *Biarum eximum* (rare) and *Narcissus tazetta* (experiencing collecting pressure).

Globally threatened species	
Aquila heliaca	Scarce passage migrant.
Falco naumanni	Summer visitor or passage migrant.
Crex crex	Passage migrant.
Vanellus gregarius	Passage migrant.
Regionally threatened or declining species	
Gyps fulvus	Non-breeding visitor.
Species restricted wholly or largely to the Middle East	
Oenanthe finschii	Winter visitor.
Serinus syriacus	Winter visitor.

Conservation issues
There may be one or more Grazing Reserves in the area. The area was formerly semi-natural grassland, but little or none is likely to survive now. Expansion and intensification of agriculture, and over-extraction of groundwater for irrigation, are likely to be major problems. The levels of grazing and built development may be very heavy, and abandonment of traditional management may be occurring locally. The site is not well characterized at the moment, and is very little known ornithologically. The lack of surveys to identify the extent of remaining semi-natural grassland, and the composition of the bird community, hinders evaluation of conservation priorities.

004 Zubiya (Irbid)
Wildlife Reserve

32°25′N 35°45′E
1,300 ha

Site description
Hill country in the Jerash–Ajlun mountains between 500 and 900 m with some steep slopes, dominated by a dense Mediterranean woodland of evergreen *Quercus* and *Pistacia*, with an understorey of *Arbutus*, *Juniperus*, *Crataegus*, *Prunus*, *Rhamnus* and *Ceratonia*. The reserve is part of the largest remaining tract of undisturbed oak woodland in the country, and is closely surrounded by villages and farmland; there are scattered patches of cultivation in the area (grapes, olives, wheat, barley).

Birds
See box for key species. A representative assemblage of woodland species characteristic of the hills of the Mediterranean north-west. Other breeding species include *Dendrocopos syriacus* and *Parus caeruleus* (probably; one record of 8+, November).

Other threatened/endemic wildlife
Mammals: re-introduction of *Capreolus capreolus* is ongoing, and is planned for *Dama mesopotamica* (E). Flora: re-introduction of *Iris nigricans* (rare) is planned.

Globally threatened species	
Falco naumanni	Common summer visitor.
Regionally threatened or declining species	
Pernis apivorus	Passage migrant.
Aquila pomarina	Passage migrant.
Species restricted wholly or largely to the Middle East	
Otus brucei	Occurs.
Irania gutturalis	Passage migrant.
Serinus syriacus	Occurs, perhaps as passage migrant.

Conservation issues
The reserve was established in 1988, and now has a warden and has been completely fenced. Fires due to negligence or recreation are a critical threat. Illegal tree-cutting and overgrazing are local threats. Formerly, encroachment by cultivation and heavy grazing of the woodland understorey by livestock were major problems, and many villagers hunted birds in the woodland (especially *Alectoris chukar* and *Streptopelia turtur*), but these practices have now been stopped or very much reduced, apart from hunting of *Streptopelia turtur*.

005 Jordan Valley (Irbid, Balqa)
Unprotected

32°16′N 35°34′E
c.80,000 ha

Site description
A flat, open agricultural plain (below sea-level) with crop fields, market gardens and orchards, gently sloping down to the incised Jordan river in the west. The Jordan river is currently saline. There are small areas of grassland, scrub and bare, eroded badlands,

comprising less than 10% of the area. Remnants of natural vegetation are Afrotropical in character. *Tamarix* woodland and *Phragmites* beds occur along the banks of the Jordan river. This is the main agricultural area in Jordan (mostly irrigated), and population density is relatively high. Livestock grazing, fishponds, hunting, recreation and tourism are secondary land-uses.

Birds

See box for key species. A major migration route and a notable wetland site. Other possible breeding species include *Remiz pendulinus* and *Rhodopechys obsoleta*. During spring passage large numbers of raptors move up the valley before veering eastwards and north-eastwards up tributary wadis, especially *Pernis apivorus* and *Accipiter brevipes* (see box), e.g. at Kafrayn and Ash Shuna Janubbiya. Autumn passage migrants include *Pelecanus onocrotalus* (daily max. 350) and *Ciconia nigra* (daily max. 11), and the latter is also a winter visitor, as is *Eudromias morinellus* (daily max. 50).

Other threatened/endemic wildlife

Fish: *Tilapia gallileae* (endemic).

Conservation issues

The high population density has led to a high impact on the environment. Critical problems include: over-extraction of groundwater and diversion of water from the Zarqa and Yarmuk rivers for irrigation; expansion and intensification of agriculture; toxic pollution from persistent pesticides, herbicides and heavy metals; eutrophication and salinization of soil and water-bodies (including the River Jordan, which is apparently unfit for human use at present). Major problems include: overgrazing; excessive disturbance of birds by human activities; and garbage pollution (especially the plastic mulch used in agriculture).

Globally threatened species

Marmaronetta angustirostris	Very scarce breeder (less than 10 pairs) in reedbeds along Jordan river, e.g. Wadi Damiya area. Also noted in winter in northern part of valley, e.g. Al Adasiyya.
Crex crex	Scarce passage migrant (seasonal total c.100).

1% or more of population

	Breeding (pairs)	Wintering	Passage
Bubulcus ibis	—	300	—
Ciconia ciconia	—	—	5,000

Regionally threatened or declining species

Botaurus stellaris	Rare winter visitor.
Pernis apivorus	Common spring passage migrant (160, May).
Neophron percnopterus	Non-breeding summer visitor (at least 2 pairs).
Accipiter brevipes	Common spring passage migrant (1,680, May).
Francolinus francolinus	Local resident.
Gallinago media	Rare passage migrant.

Species restricted wholly or largely to the Middle East

Ammoperdix heyi	Resident on valley sides.
Passer moabiticus	Common resident (especially between Dead Sea and Damiya).
Serinus syriacus	Rare passage migrant/winter visitor.

006 Dibbin Forest (Irbid)

National Park

32°15'N 35°50'E
1,500 ha

Site description

The best remaining area of mature, natural *Pinus halepensis* forest in the country, on limestone slopes of the highest hill range in northern Jordan, between 550 and 1,000 m. Understorey of *Arbutus* and evergreen *Quercus*. Parts of the forest remain remote from habitation, although there are some pockets of agriculture. The surrounding area has oaks and olive groves as well. There is a much-used recreational area in the centre of the site, with parking spaces, barbecue sites, restaurant and playgrounds.

Birds

See box for key species. A representative bird assemblage of Mediterranean pine woodland, a rare and diminishing habitat in Jordan. Other breeding species include *Dendrocopos syriacus*, *Phylloscopus bonelli* and *Parus caeruleus* (the only known breeding site in Jordan for the latter two species), and other species observed during the breeding season in suitable habitat include *Circaetus gallicus*, *Accipiter nisus*, *Falco subbuteo* and *Nectarinia osea*. *Lullula arborea* winters in small numbers. Large numbers of migrating raptors have been reported in spring, but no details are known.

Globally threatened species

Aquila heliaca	Rare passage migrant.

Species restricted wholly or largely to the Middle East

Serinus syriacus	Rare passage migrant.

■ Other threatened/endemic wildlife

Mammals: *Sciurus anomalus* (relict population). Flora: rare/endemic plants include *Verbascum transjordanicum*, *Orchis collina*, *Biarum eximum* and *Globularia arabica*; in addition, *Cupressus sempervirens*, *Tulipa agensis* and *Cyclamen persicum* are experiencing cutting or collecting pressure.

■ Conservation issues

Part of Dibbin Forest is a National Park (5,000 ha) managed by the Forestry Department of the Ministry of Agriculture, but this designation is in recognition of the forest's value for public recreation, and no management for wildlife conservation occurs. Critical threats are from forest-fires due to negligence and recreation, and from piecemeal clearance and conversion of forest to olive groves. Intense disturbance from picnicers (with attendant litter and burning) is a problem locally.

007 Khirba as Samra (Zarqa)

Unprotected

32°10′N 36°10′E
300 ha

■ Site description

A large area of open, man-made pools in a broad depression close to Wadi Dhulayl (a tributary of the Zarqa river), surrounded by rather bare limestone desert. Amman's main sewage works; pools range from sludge to 'fresh' water, with rocky shores. There is very little natural vegetation. The water is used to irrigate olive groves.

■ Birds

See box for key species. A man-made wetland, but extremely attractive to migrant birds in autumn as the only permanent waterbody in a vast surrounding area, now that Azraq oasis is all but dry. The site's main importance is in the large number of *Ciconia ciconia* which regularly rest and roost during autumn passage (see box). Breeding species include *Himantopus himantopus* (possibly), *Vanellus spinosus* (min. 14 pairs), *Sylvia conspicillata*, and possibly *Charadrius dubius*, *Charadrius alexandrinus*, *Motacilla citreola* and *Rhodopechys obsoleta*. Other passage migrants include *Anas querquedula* (230, September), *Calidris minuta* (500, August), *Tringa ochropus* (110, July), *Chlidonias leucopterus* (150, August) and *Emberiza caesia*.

1% or more of population

	Breeding (pairs)	Wintering	Passage
Ciconia ciconia	—	—	6,000 (Aug)

Regionally threatened or declining species

Aythya nyroca	Passage migrant (2, August).

■ Other threatened/endemic wildlife

None known to BirdLife International.

■ Conservation issues

Threats are few—shooting is insignificant at present, but could rapidly become a problem if the high number of birds present becomes well known. The area is very busy, and numbers of birds are probably much lower than the maximum possible if parts of the site were managed specifically to attract birds. Wildlife-friendly management regimes have been planned and proposed to the operators by a consultant in the late 1980s.

008 Qa Hanna (Zarqa)

also known as Qa Khanna
Unprotected

32°04′N 36°25′E
c.4,500 ha

■ Site description

A seasonal playa-lake in the desert, c.15 × 3 km, which floods in years of good rain and which can then last for several months. After rain, crustaceans and toads *Bufo viridis* proliferate. A large farm has been established in the surrounding steppe desert, irrigated from the qa; the rest of the area is used as rangeland. There is a military base near the site.

■ Birds

The site is not well-known ornithologically. Breeding species include *Charadrius leschenaultii*. Passage migrants include *Grus grus* (200, spring).

■ Other threatened/endemic wildlife

Mammals: possibly *Caracal caracal* (rare).

■ Conservation issues

Critical threats include agricultural intensification and expansion using the qa's water reserves, and excessive/irresponsible hunting; very heavy grazing pressure in the surrounding desert has degraded the vegetation. Excessive soil erosion and destruction of the desert crust are occurring more locally.

009 Azraq Oasis (Zarqa Governorate)

Wildlife Reserve (1,255 ha)

31°49′N 36°48′E
c.12,000 ha
Ramsar site (7,372 ha)

Site description

The only permanent, natural wetland in the Jordanian desert, 85 km east of Amman, and one of very few such sites in the Arabian peninsula. A (formerly) permanent, spring-fed marshland near the village of South Azraq (Azraq Wetland Reserve, 31°50′N 36°50′E, 1,255 ha) with a large, adjacent, seasonal playa-lake to the south-east (Qa al Azraq, 30°50′N 36°53′E, c.6,000 ha). The site also includes some artesian pools with associated marshland (31°51′N 36°50′E, 50 ha) and fishpools (31°49′N 36°48′E, 100 ha).

Until heavily degraded in recent years (see 'Conservation issues'), the Azraq Wetland Reserve was a flat area of pools, marshes, water meadows and silt dunes. Plant cover was very varied, including dense stands of *Juncus*, *Carex*, *Typha*, *Scirpus*, *Cyperus* and *Arundo* in the wetland, and bushes of *Nitraria* and *Tamarix* on the silt dunes. Similar marshland also formerly occurred around the springs at the village of North Azraq.

Qa al Azraq is a low-lying, enclosed basin which is seasonally flooded by c.10 wadis after winter rains over a catchment area of c.13,000 km². A temporary, shallow, freshwater lake (max. depth 1.25 m) is formed, with a flat, muddy margin of up to 35 km circumference and scattered islands (the mounds of dry-season saltworkings). The water never overspills into the adjacent freshwater marsh of the Wetland Reserve, and the lake does not drain into and recharge the underlying aquifer, instead remaining for several months (good aquatic invertebrate populations develop during this time) while becoming increasingly brackish as it dries out to form a siltflat, usually by mid-May. The basin is barren of vegetation when dry, except for salt-tolerant herbs (*Halopeplis*, *Halocnemum*) around the edges.

The artesian pools are an variable area of standing water of variable extent, fed by a small artesian borehole drilled in 1963 and still flowing. There is a small area of *Tamarix* bushes surrounded by damp to wet meadow/marshland with grass and other low vegetation. The fishpools were recently excavated in low-relief, silt desert on the edge of Qa al Azraq, with muddy shore and islands, fringed with reeds *Phragmites* when water levels are not high.

The oasis is a major crossroads for highways running between Amman, Syria, Saudi Arabia and the Gulf, and Iraq, and the level of human activity is high, there being two large settlements, North Azraq (formerly called Druze) and South Azraq (formerly Shishan), as well as a military base. The oasis is a major social and economic resource to Jordan, being one of the largest and most exploited sources of water for human consumption in the country. Cultivation is extensive in former silt desert surrounding the wetlands, irrigated from private wells. Qa al Azraq supports a substantial salt industry; regulated wildfowl hunting occurs in winter. Large numbers of sheep, goats and camels are watered and grazed in the remains of the marshland at Azraq Wetland Reserve and the artesian pools. Small-scale fish farming occurs at the fishpools.

Birds

See box for key species. Other species which currently breed (mostly less than 10 pairs for the waterbirds) include *Rallus aquaticus*, *Charadrius dubius*, *C. leschenaultii*, *Vanellus spinosus*, *V. leucurus*, *Sterna nilotica*, *S. albifrons*, *Pterocles senegallus*, *Caprimulgus aegyptius*, *Ramphocoris clotbey*, *Calandrella brachydactyla*, *C. rufescens*, *Eremophila bilopha*, *Oenanthe deserti* and *Rhodopechys obsoleta*. Large numbers of birds of prey are attracted to drink at the pools on autumn migration, including *Pernis apivorus* (14, September) and *Circus pygargus* (66, September). Currently, Qa al Azraq still supports internationally important numbers of wintering and spring migrant waterfowl in years of good rain (e.g. more than 20,000 waterfowl in winter 1991/2). The artesian pools and fishpools support important numbers of a few species of non-breeding waterbirds, especially during spring migration, and are the only remaining permanent wetland habitat now that the Wetland Reserve is almost dry. They are thus very attractive to all kinds of passage migrants, especially during the very dry autumn period. Azraq has been relatively well-studied and over 300 species have been recorded, a very high total.

The Wetland Reserve is currently lacking importance for waterbirds, due to the drying up of the springs. In the 1960s, before the permanent marshland was so severely degraded, the Wetland Reserve was an important breeding site for many waterbird species and together with Qa al Azraq supported up to c.350,000 wintering wildfowl, predominantly *Anas penelope*, *A. crecca*, *A. acuta* and *Fulica atra*. However by the 1978/79 winter only 2,500 wildfowl were present in the reserve, and by the 1990/91 winter less than 100–200.

The site was listed as a wetland of international importance by Carp (1980).

Globally threatened species

Marmaronetta angustirostris	One pair bred at fishpools, 1990.
Aquila heliaca	Winter visitor (max. 3).
Chlamydotis undulata	Formerly a resident in less disturbed areas of desert just east of Qa al Azraq; may still occur as an occasional winter visitor, although there are no recent documented records.

1% or more of population

	Breeding (pairs)	Wintering	Passage
Tadorna tadorna	1	3,490	—
Grus grus	—	2,500	—
Himantopus himantopus	465	—	—
Recurvirostra avosetta	20	—	300
Glareola pratincola	10	—	—
Charadrius alexandrinus	25	—	2,000
Calidris minuta	—	—	3,000
Philomachus pugnax	—	—	3,500
Chlidonias leucopterus	—	—	1,500

Regionally threatened or declining species

Botaurus stellaris	Very rare winter visitor.
Gallinago media	Rare passage migrant.

Species restricted wholly or largely to the Middle East

Glareola nordmanni	Rare passage migrant.
Oenanthe finschii	Scarce winter visitor.
Hippolais languida	Scarce spring passage migrant.

■ Other threatened/endemic wildlife

Mammals: *Canis lupus* (V); *Caracal caracal* (rare) and *Gazella gazella* (V) are thought to be recently extinct. Reptiles: *Varanus griseus* (rare) occurred in the surrounding desert, at least formerly. Formerly the Wetland Reserve supported a relatively rich fauna and flora, including important and highly isolated or endemic populations of fish, invertebrate and plant species; many species may not have survived the ongoing degradation of the marsh.

■ Conservation issues

Azraq Wetland Reserve was established in 1977 with all-round fencing and a resident warden, and a management plan was produced in 1979. However, the ecological character of the spring-fed wetlands at Azraq has greatly deteriorated over the last 15–20 years, although the playa lake of Qa al Azraq still qualifies as an internationally important wetland under Ramsar Convention criteria. Excessive pumping of water from Azraq's upper aquifer to supply Amman and Irbid with drinking water, and to irrigate private farmland locally, has lowered the water-table and completely dried up the springs at North Azraq and South Azraq (in the Wetland Reserve); in the 1960s the latter were discharging 12.4 million cubic metres of water per year. The previously permanent pools, marshes and water meadows have dried out completely, and most of the aquatic vegetation has died off. Any remaining important species of aquatic fauna and flora are now in imminent danger of extinction. Until recently the remnants of the aquatic vegetation were very heavily grazed by livestock, and by feral horses and water-buffalo (now removed), and were regularly burnt to promote growth for grazing. Large quantities of rubbish have been dumped in the Reserve, due to its fence being in great disrepair. The over-exploitation of the aquifer has now led to increasing salinization of its water as well as of soils. The Ramsar site was subject to the Ramsar Monitoring Procedure in 1990, which resulted in specific recommendations to halt and reverse the deterioration of the Wetland Reserve. A project agreement to rehabilitate the Wetland Reserve has recently been signed by the Jordanian government, the RSCN and the UNDP, with funding from the Global Environment Facility.

Qa al Azraq is unprotected, being almost completely outside the Wetland Reserve boundary, but c.1,000 ha is part of the Ramsar site. Although the qa is still capable of flooding to full capacity, as for example in 1990/91 and 1991/92, Wadi Rajil (considered to be the main source of floodwater) has been dammed in several places upstream in Syria since the 1970s and also recently in Jordan 45 km north of Azraq, all of which is thought to have generally reduced the extent of flooding of the qa. Extraction of clay minerals may occur in the future and might be a local threat.

The artesian pools and fishpools also lie outside the Azraq Wetland Reserve boundary fence, close to the town, and are unprotected. Overexploitation of the regional aquifer is also drying out the artesian marsh, and since the fishpools are supplied from the same source, any further pumping to supply Amman is a critical threat to both areas. Excessive disturbance by hunters, herders and livestock is a major problem at both areas.

■ Further reading

Andrews (1991), Conder (1981a,b, 1982), Jones and Clarke (1990), Mountfort (1965), Nelson (1973, 1985), Wallace (1982, 1983).

010 Shaumari Area (Zarqa)
Wildlife Reserve, Grazing Reserve

31°48′N 36°49′E
34,200 ha

Site description
Low-relief, chert 'hammada' desert at 500–600 m intersected by broad, sandy wadi spreads draining into Qa al Azraq and only flowing after occasional winter or spring floods. Shaumari Wildlife Reserve (31°48′N 36°49′E, 2,200 ha) is strongly fenced to exclude domestic livestock and trespassers, and the vegetation is in markedly better condition than in the adjacent Azraq Desert Grazing Reserve (32,000 ha) and other surrounding, grazed areas. The Grazing Reserve was also fenced but this is now in disrepair. Wadis are dominated by sparse scrub of *Tamarix*, *Retama*, *Amygdalus*, *Artemisia*, *Achillea* and *Atriplex*, which however forms relatively luxuriant bushland within the Wildlife Reserve; there are flat gravel and silt areas in between wadis. Wadi al Butm (31°50′N 36°35′E, 1,000 ha; also called Wadi Usaymir), in the Grazing Reserve, is notable for the mature *Pistacia atlantica* trees which line it, and has occasional flood-pools in winter. The HQ of the Wildlife Reserve has many eucalyptus and casuarina trees. Main human activities are nomadic pastoralism, tourism (frescos at Qasr Amra) and picnicing.

Birds
See box for key species. A representative desert bird community, with potentially up to nine breeding lark species including *Ramphocoris clotbey* and *Eremophila bilopha*. Other known or probable breeding species include *Buteo rufinus*, *Alectoris chukar*, *Cursorius cursor*, *Pterocles orientalis*, *P. alchata*, *Tyto alba*, *Oenanthe deserti*, *O. moesta*, *Scotocerca inquieta*, *Lanius excubitor*, *Rhodopechys githaginea* and *R. obsoleta*. Winter visitors include *Eudromias morinellus*, *Columba oenas* (500, December), *Asio otus* (a roost at the HQ) and *Miliaria calandra* (300, January); the wintering flock of *Grus grus* (see box) also frequents Azraq oasis (see site 009). The area is visited by a wide variety of migrants, including *Circus pygargus* (8, September), *Streptopelia turtur* (150, May), *Oenanthe cypriaca* (one record) and *Emberiza caesia*. Reintroduction of *Struthio camelus* is ongoing.

Globally threatened species

Aquila heliaca	Winter visitor (5, December) and passage migrant (max. 1, March).
Falco naumanni	Passage migrant (max. 22, March–April).
Chlamydotis undulata	In the 1970s it was an unconfirmed breeder (2+ pairs) and winter visitor (max. 10); there are no more recent documented records.

1% or more of population

	Breeding (pairs)	Wintering	Passage
Grus grus	—	1,000	—

Regionally threatened or declining species

Torgos tracheliotus	Presumably extinct: the only Jordan record is of 1 at Wadi al Butm, 1963.
Accipiter brevipes	Irregular passage migrant (max. 200, April).

Species restricted wholly or largely to the Middle East

Oenanthe finschii	Frequent winter visitor.
Serinus syriacus	Rare winter visitor (max. 1).

Other threatened/endemic wildlife
Mammals: *Caracal caracal* (rare); reintroduction of extinct fauna such as *Oryx leucoryx* (currently c.130 individuals), *Gazella subgutturosa* and *Equus hemionus onager* is ongoing. Reptiles: *Varanus griseus* (rare) probably occurs.

Conservation issues
Shaumari Wildlife Reserve was established in 1975, and is managed by the RSCN as a re-introduction site for previously extinct fauna, as well as a wildlife education centre for school-children and tourists. Azraq Desert Grazing Reserve was established in 1987 by the Department of Forests of the Ministry of Agriculture in order to extend the available area for future re-introduction of *Oryx leucoryx* and other extinct desert ungulates. There are probably no threats to the Wildlife Reserve, but the surrounding desert in the Grazing Reserve is heavily grazed by sheep and goats and soil erosion is exacerbated. The *Pistacia* trees in Wadi al Butm are heavily browsed by goats and camels, and cutting of branches for bedu fires and picnic fires is unsustainable.

Further reading
Clarke (1980, 1982).

011 Hisban–Madaba Plains (Amman)

Unprotected

31°45′N 35°47′E
c.4,500 ha

Site description

Plains of former steppeland, e.g. between Jiza and Hisban and between Rabba and Shihan, now almost wholly converted to dry cultivation of cereals. There is also some irrigated agriculture.

Birds

See box for key species. The area has been little investigated ornithologically. Winter visitors include *Eudromias morinellus* (formerly very common, now possibly much reduced).

Globally threatened species	
Aegypius monachus	Scarce winter visitor.
Aquila heliaca	Scarce passage migrant/winter visitor (seasonal total 10).
Crex crex	Uncommon spring migrant (seasonal total 50).
Chlamydotis undulata	Potentially a rare winter visitor to uncultivated areas.

Other threatened/endemic wildlife

Flora: *Colchicum tunicatum* (endemic), *Romulea bulbocodium* (rare), *Globularia arabica* (rare).

Conservation issues

Expansion and intensification of agriculture, and over-extraction of groundwater for irrigation, are all critical problems. The very heavy level of grazing and built development are major problems, as is abandonment of traditional management locally. The site is not well characterized at the moment, and is very little known ornithologically. The lack of surveys to identify the extent of remaining semi-natural grassland, and the composition of the bird community, hinder evaluation of conservation priorities in Jordan.

012 Wadi Mujib (Amman, Karak)

Wildlife Reserve

31°27′N 35°48′E
21,200 ha

Site description

Mountainous, rocky, sparsely vegetated desert (up to 800 m), with cliffs, gorges and deep wadis cutting through plateaus. Perennial, spring-fed streams flow down wadis to the shores of the hypersaline Dead Sea at 400 m below sea-level, and are lined with a narrow strip of *Nerium* scrub. Otherwise the slopes are very sparsely vegetated, with a steppe-type vegetation on plateaus. Groundwater seepage occurs rarely on rocky ground near the Dead Sea shore, especially at the hot springs of Zara, which support a luxuriant thicket of *Acacia*, *Tamarix*, *Phoenix* and *Nerium*, and a small marsh. The less-steep slopes of the higher elevations are mainly used as rangeland by pastoralists (for sheep/goats). The hot springs at Zarqa Ma'in (outside the site) are heavily used for tourism/recreation. The military have a temporary camp in the south of the reserve. Wadi Wala, upstream of Wadi Hidan and outside the reserve, is now a major water-extraction source for Amman.

Globally threatened species	
Falco naumanni	Summer visitor (min. 10 pairs).
Regionally threatened or declining species	
Gypaetus barbatus	Recorded breeding in the last century; possibly still occurs (one or more undocumented sightings during the 1980s).
Neophron percnopterus	Possibly breeds.
Gyps fulvus	Probably breeds (min. 1–5 pairs).
Accipiter brevipes	Common spring passage migrant (8,000, April).
Falco concolor	Rare summer visitor (recorded from Zara hot springs and from Ma'in in 1990).
Carpodacus synoicus	Winter visitor (max. 5).
Species restricted wholly or largely to the Middle East	
Ammoperdix heyi	Common resident.
Strix butleri	Resident.
Oenanthe finschii	Common winter visitor (max. 20).
Oenanthe monacha	Resident.
Turdoides squamiceps	Resident.
Onychognathus tristramii	Resident.
Passer moabiticus	Resident (10 pairs).

Birds

See box for key species. A rich breeding bird assemblage of unusually mixed biogeographical origins. At least nine raptors breed, including *Circaetus gallicus*, *Buteo rufinus*, *Hieraaetus fasciatus* and *Falco pelegrinoides*, and other proven or probable breeding species include *Alectoris chukar*, *Charadrius alexandrinus*, *Vanellus spinosus*, *Apus affinis*, *Halcyon smyrnensis*, *Coracias garrulus*, *Melanocorypha calandra*, *Cercomela melanura*, *Oenanthe lugens*, *Corvus rhipidurus*, *Petronia petronia*, *Rhodopechys obsoleta*, *R. githaginea* and *Emberiza striolata*. There is a strong raptor migration in April, especially of *Accipiter brevipes* (see below), *Buteo buteo* (175), and *Falco tinnunculus* (50). *Emberiza caesia* occurs on passage (15, April) and *Lullula arborea* is a winter visitor in small numbers (max. 12). *Ciconia ciconia* is said to favour the shores of the Dead Sea for resting while on autumn passage.

Other threatened/endemic wildlife

Mammals: *Canis lupus* (V), *Capra nubiana* (I) and *Gazella gazella* (V); *Caracal caracal* (rare) and *Panthera pardus* (rare) are reputed to occur. Flora: *Himantoglossum affine* (rare).

Conservation issues

Wadi Mujib Wildlife Reserve was established in 1987. *Capra nubiana* is being bred in an enclosure for re-introduction. Ongoing construction of a major highway along the Dead Sea shore is greatly increasing public access to this formerly remote area. Much of the steppe vegetation on higher plateaus has been destroyed by ploughing and overgrazing. Current problems are few in the rocky desert, but the vegetation at Zara is suffering heavily from burning, grazing and conversion to cultivation. The flow of water in Wadi Hidan, within the reserve, is potentially threatened by the planned damming of Wadi Wala (i.e. the upper reaches of Wadi Hidan, east of and outside the reserve).

013 Wadi Dana–Finan (Ma'an, Tafila)

Wildlife Reserve

30°37′N 35°32′E
15,000 ha

Site description

A scenically beautiful, major wadi flowing from the rugged Sharrah mountains at 1,200 m down to the Rift Valley floor at sea-level. Bare, rounded mountains and sandstone cliffs occur at the head of the wadi, giving way to metamorphic rock at the base of the escarpment, where the wadi opens out onto a gravelly outwash plain with mobile sand-dunes (60–70% within the reserve). At higher elevations, there is evergreen *Quercus* woodland on steeper slopes, mixed with *Pinus halepensis*, *Pistacia* and scattered *Juniperus* and *Cupressus*, and extensive areas of herbs and scrub; steppe-like *Artemisia* dominates on gentler slopes and also with *Anabasis* at lower elevations. Along the wadi there is a considerable amount of lush vegetation and trees, including *Phragmites*, *Nerium* and *Pistacia*. There is no cultivation apart from traditional orchards at Dana village. Outside the reserve there is a local irrigation project at Qurayqira on the Rift Valley floor. The main land-uses are wildlife conservation, research and tourism. There are at least several Roman antiquity sites (soon to be excavated), including copper mines at Finan.

Birds

See box for key species. A very diverse assemblage of breeding birds of unusually mixed biogeographical origins. Other breeding species include *Circaetus gallicus*, *Buteo rufinus*, *Hieraaetus fasciatus*, *Falco pelegrinoides*, *Otus scops*, *Eremalauda dunni*, *Lullula arborea*, *Oenanthe lugens*, *Sylvia hortensis* (probably), *Nectarinia osea*, *Corvus rhipidurus* and *Petronia petronia*. *Emberiza caesia* is a scarce passage migrant. There is a huge spring migration of raptors, which may total up to 250,000 birds per season, but it has not been investigated in depth; species include *Buteo buteo* (700, April) and *Aquila nipalensis* (35, April).

Globally threatened species	
Aquila heliaca	Rare passage migrant (1, April).
Falco naumanni	Localized summer visitor (5+ pairs).
Regionally threatened or declining species	
Gypaetus barbatus	Vagrant: one undocumented record during the 1980s (Fujeij agricultural station).
Neophron percnopterus	Possibly breeds.
Gyps fulvus	Resident (min. 4 pairs).
Torgos tracheliotus	There are undocumented sightings, post-1980 (e.g. Wadi Dahil).
Carpodacus synoicus	Resident.
Species restricted wholly or largely to the Middle East	
Strix butleri	Rare resident (min. 1 pair).
Oenanthe monacha	Local resident.
Hippolais languida	Possibly breeds.
Sylvia leucomelaena	Resident.
Turdoides squamiceps	Resident.
Onychognathus tristramii	Resident.
Passer moabiticus	Resident or winter visitor (10, December).
Serinus syriacus	Scarce resident (at least 2 pairs breed; 20 in winter).

Other threatened/endemic wildlife

Mammals: *Canis lupus* (V), *Meles meles* (rare), *Panthera pardus* (rare; last unconfirmed report 1987), c.200 *Capra nubiana* (I) and *Gazella gazella* (V); other likely species are *Felis margarita* (rare) and

Caracal caracal (rare). Flora: there is a grove of 15 ancient *Cupressus sempervirens* trees, unique in Jordan.

Conservation issues

The establishment of Dana Wildlife Reserve started in 1989; the area of the reserve extends downwards beyond the originally proposed 400 m contour, down onto the Wadi Araba plain at 200 m at Finan. Re-introduction of *Capra nubiana* and *Panthera pardus* is being investigated. The Fujeij Grazing Reserve (1,000 ha) lies adjacent to the reserve, at the top of the escarpment. The main environmental problems were formerly overgrazing and hunting of larger animals, but these have now been brought under control. An agreement is due to be signed to avert the possibility of any copper/manganese mining re-starting in the Finan area.

Further reading

Biewers (1993).

014 Petra Area (Ma'an)

National Park (20,000 ha)

30°20′N 35°27′E
50,000 ha

Site description

High-relief, rocky, sandstone mountains (700–1,450 m) overlooking Wadi Araba, on the western edge of the Sharrah Mountains, with high cliffs, caves and numerous gorges and dry wadis which flow down to Wadi Araba during storms. Rain falls mainly in winter (100–300 mm; average 180 mm p.a.), when there can be snow; there are two springs. Vegetation-types include *Artemisia* steppe on rocky plateaus, typical Saharo-Arabian desert wadi-spread with *Acacia* and *Calotropis*, lush growth at springs and remnants of formerly more extensive Mediterranean *Quercus–Juniperus* woodland on mountain slopes; more than 200 plant species have been recorded. Petra is a world-famous antiquities site, and tourism is the major land-use in the National Park; however nomadic pastoralists also graze livestock in the wider area.

Birds

See box for key species. An unusually diverse assemblage of at least 50 breeding or probably breeding species of highly mixed biogeographical origins, including *Circaetus gallicus* (possibly), *Aquila chrysaetos* (possibly), *Buteo rufinus*, *Hieraaetus fasciatus*, *Falco pelegrinoides*, *Alectoris chukar*, *Anthus similis* (pre-1983), *Oenanthe lugens*, *Scotocerca inquieta*, *Nectarinia osea*, *Lanius nubicus*, *Petronia petronia*, *Emberiza caesia* (possibly) and *Emberiza striolata*. There is an important raptor migration in spring, especially by *Pernis apivorus* (650, May), *Milvus migrans* (200, April) and *Buteo buteo* (2,000+, April); *Sylvia curruca* (90, April) and *Sylvia atricapilla* (100, April) are also very common spring migrants.

Globally threatened species	
Aquila heliaca	Passage migrant.
Falco naumanni	Possibly breeds.
Regionally threatened or declining species	
Pernis apivorus	Passage migrant (see above).
Neophron percnopterus	Bred before 1983; no recent evidence.
Gyps fulvus	Bred before 1983; no recent evidence.
Falco concolor	Probably breeds (probable family party, October 1979).
Carpodacus synoicus	Resident.
Species restricted wholly or largely to the Middle East	
Ammoperdix heyi	Resident.
Strix butleri	Scarce resident (min. 5 pairs).
Turdoides squamiceps	Resident.
Onychognathus tristramii	Resident.
Serinus syriacus	Rare winter visitor.

Other threatened/endemic wildlife

Flora: *Iris petrana* (endemic), *Verbascum transjordanicum* (endemic), *Cupressus sempervirens* (experiencing cutting pressure).

Conservation issues

Over-exploitation by tourism of the core antiquities area (6,500 ha) within the National Park is potentially a threat, through over-disturbance of wildlife and damage to desert by vehicles. Other, similar areas of habitat are inaccessible and will presumably remain more pristine. Up until 1987 populations of birds of prey and gamebirds were in a reduced state due to (formerly?) heavy hunting. Bedouin flocks exert very heavy grazing pressure on the vegetation.

Further reading

Wittenberg (1987).

015 Wadi Araba (Ma'an)

Unprotected

30°05′N 35°11′E
c.150,000 ha

Site description

An extensive 'wilderness' area of desert sand-dunes, gravel outwash plains and mudflats, c.160 km long by up to 25 km wide (widest between Jabal Fidan and Umm Muthla). There is some open bushland of *Acacia tortilis*, *A. raddiana* and *Ziziphus*; *Tamarix* and *Phragmites* occur locally in the lowest areas. Main land-use is nomadic pastoralism, with a minor but increasing amount of irrigated cultivation. Large areas are military zones.

Birds

See box for key species. *Eremalauda dunni* breeds in large numbers after good rains. *Neophron percnopterus*, *Gyps fulvus*, *Onychognathus tristramii* and *Carpodacus synoicus* breed in the hills bordering the wadi, adjoining this site.

Globally threatened species

Chlamydotis undulata	Probably a rare resident or winter visitor (4 seen to the north near Fifa in winter 1982).

Regionally threatened or declining species

Neophron percnopterus	Non-breeding summer visitor (min. 1 pair, 1989).
Gyps fulvus	Non-breeding visitor (up to 30, 1986).
Torgos tracheliotus	There are undocumented sight-records (post-1980); formerly it may have bred.

Species restricted wholly or largely to the Middle East

Ammoperdix heyi	Resident.
Sylvia leucomelaena	Resident.
Turdoides squamiceps	Resident.
Onychognathus tristramii	Resident.
Carpodacus synoicus	Winter visitor.

Other threatened/endemic wildlife

Mammals: *Canis lupus* (V), *Felis margarita* (rare), *Caracal caracal* (rare) and *Gazella dorcas* (V). Reptiles: *Varanus griseus* (rare).

Conservation issues

About 10,000 ha of the Wadi Dana Wildlife Reserve (see site 013) is in Wadi Araba, and is included in that site. Public access to large areas of the wadi is restricted by military zones, thus providing some indirect protection. Overgrazing and over-browsing of the vegetation is a major problem. More local problems are agricultural intensification, salinization of soil due to intensive water-pumping, and tree-cutting.

016 Hisma Basin (Ma'an)

Proposed Wildlife Reserve (50,000 ha)

29°35′N 35°25′E
200,000 ha

Site description

An isolated tract of huge, precipitous, sandstone and granite mountains, ranging up to 1,754 m (Jabal Rum, the highest point in Jordan), separated from each other by flat, sandy 'corridor'-wadis (at 800 m), and surrounded by a desert of extensive siltflats and mobile dunes. The predominant desert vegetation is a scanty shrub-steppe of *Haloxylon*, *Anabasis*, *Retama*, *Artemisia* and *Acacia tortilis* bushes. *Amygdalus arabicus* bushes are common in sandy wadis and in gorges leading into the mountains. Vegetation on the high and inaccessible peaks of the mountains is poorer than in wadis, including scattered *Acacia tortilis* and *Juniperus* trees, which also occur along seepage lines in Wadi Rum at the base of Jabal Rum, together with patchy, remnant vegetation of *Pistacia*, *Ficus*, *Olea* and *Phoenix* palms. The main land-uses are nomadic pastoralism (sheep, goats and camels), a Ministry of Agriculture irrigation project on the siltflats (centred on Disi and Abu Suwana) and 'wilderness tourism'.

Birds

See box for key species. An unusually varied assemblage of desert and mountain birds. As well as species listed below, possible or known breeders include *Circaetus gallicus*, *Buteo rufinus*, *Aquila chrysaetos* (outside the Reserve), *Aquila verreauxii*, *Hieraaetus fasciatus*, *Falco pelegrinoides*, *Alectoris chukar*, *Bubo ascalaphus*, *Pycnonotus xanthopygos*, *Oenanthe lugens*, *O. leucopyga*, *Nectarinia osea*, *Corvus rhipidurus* and *Emberiza striolata*. Quite large numbers of migrating *Buteo buteo* have been seen irregularly (max. 100, April). Two key species, now apparently extinct, are the globally threatened *Chlamydotis undulata* (formerly a rare winter visitor) and the regionally threatened *Gypaetus barbatus* (formerly a rare resident).

Globally threatened species

Aquila heliaca	Rare passage migrant (max. 1, November).
Falco naumanni	Uncommon passage migrant (max. 9, April).

Regionally threatened or declining species

Gypaetus barbatus	Resident; breeding in the 1960s, but no records since, and may be extinct.
Neophron percnopterus	Fairly common, especially subadults; possibly breeds.
Gyps fulvus	Uncommon, and possibly breeds.
Falco concolor	Rare summer visitor (min. 1 pair).
Falco biarmicus	Very rare resident.
Falco cherrug	Rare winter visitor.
Carpodacus synoicus	Very common resident.

Species restricted wholly or largely to the Middle East

Ammoperdix heyi	Resident.
Strix butleri	Rare resident (min. 1 pair).
Oenanthe monacha	Resident.
Turdoides squamiceps	Resident.
Onychognathus tristramii	Common resident.
Carpospiza brachydactyla	Irregular passage migrant/winter visitor.

■ Other threatened/endemic wildlife

Mammals: *Felis margarita* (rare), *Capra nubiana* (I) and *Gazella subgutturosa* (rare).

■ Conservation issues

Establishment of Wadi Rum Wildlife Reserve started in 1989 and is continuing, although it has not yet been gazetted; re-introduction of *Oryx leucoryx* is planned. Grazing pressure on the desert steppe vegetation is very heavy and pivot-irrigated agriculture using fossil groundwater is expanding on the siltflats (wheat, alfalfa, vegetables). Although the difficult terrain has tended to protect against over-hunting of larger animals, the increasing and unregulated off-road vehicle traffic due to tourism is degrading and disturbing sensitive fauna and flora locally, e.g. on sand-dunes.

■ Further reading

Mountfort (1965).

017 Aqaba Mountains (Ma'an)

Unprotected

29°30′N 35°00′E
c.130,000 ha

■ Site description

Jordan's only coastline: Aqaba is a port town at the head of the very deep Gulf of Aqaba (2,000+ m) of the Red Sea. The coastal plain is very limited, and alluvial fans spread from the inland mountains to the shore, which is composed mainly of rock and sand/gravel beaches, fringed in part with coral reefs. Most habitats in the area have been substantially altered by man; freshwater springs along the coast support irrigated market gardens and native palm groves (near the beach), and some natural scrub vegetation survives near the Israeli border. There is some undisturbed desert to the south of the area. A very important area economically for Jordan, with port, industries, and tourism; fisheries are secondary in importance.

■ Birds

See box for key species. A migratory bottleneck site also holding a breeding bird community representative of the Rift Valley. The enormous spring passage of raptors just across the border at Eilat only occasionally passes over Aqaba, as indicated by the relatively small maximum daily counts: *Buteo buteo* (105, April) and *Accipiter brevipes* (75, September). Generally raptors cross the Rift Valley into Jordan further north up Wadi Araba (see site 013), but spring passage at Aqaba undoubtedly exceeds 50,000 raptors per season nevertheless. Raptor passage in autumn is relatively insignificant, however.

Other spring migrants occurring in good numbers include *Nycticorax nycticorax*, *Ardea cinerea*, *Sterna hirundo*, *Chlidonias leucopterus*, *Sylvia curruca*, *S. atricapilla*, *Passer hispaniolensis* and *Emberiza hortulana*. *Falco pelegrinoides* and *Corvus rhipidurus* are resident and the town has a small population of *Corvus splendens* (min. 10–20 pairs).

Globally threatened species

Larus leucophthalmus	Non-breeding summer visitor in small numbers (12, October).

Regionally threatened or declining species

Gypaetus barbatus	Vagrant: at least one record in 1980s, and it possibly breeds in the mountains.
Accipiter brevipes	Passage migrant (max. 75, September).
Falco concolor	Possibly breeds in nearby mountains.
Falco biarmicus	Possibly breeds in nearby mountains.
Carpodacus synoicus	Possibly breeds in nearby mountains.

Species restricted wholly or largely to the Middle East

Sterna repressa	Uncommon non-breeding summer visitor.
Strix butleri	Presumed rare resident in nearby mountains (feathers found).
Oenanthe monacha	Resident in nearby mountains.
Sylvia leucomelaena	Resident.
Turdoides squamiceps	Resident.
Onychognathus tristramii	Resident in nearby mountains.

A diverse selection of non-breeding seabirds occurs offshore between spring and autumn due to an upwelling at the head of the Gulf; species appear to occur only in small numbers although there has been no detailed investigation (daily max. less than 20 unless stated) and include *Calonectris diomedea* (50+, June), *Puffinus pacificus*, *P. griseus*, *Sula leucogaster*, *Stercorarius pomarinus*, *S. parasiticus* (75, June), *S. longicaudus*, *Larus leucophthalmus*, *Sterna repressa* and *S. anaethetus*, as well as vagrant pelagic species.

■ Other threatened/endemic wildlife

The reefs have a relatively high diversity of corals and support a moderately diverse reef-fish community, including the Red Sea endemic *Paracheilinus octotaenia*.

■ Conservation issues

Port expansion, and coastal development for industrial, military and touristic uses, are a critical problem around Aqaba due to lack of space. A new highway, giving access to the port, now crosses the formerly undisturbed Aqaba hinterland. Little natural coastline will remain unless some conservation action is taken soon. Overgrazing and excessive hunting are problems locally inland. Offshore, marine habitats are being degraded by pollution from phosphate dust, chemical and hot water effluent, and sewage, and by anchor damage. A marine National Park has been proposed, to cover the central third of the Jordanian coast including mountain hinterland areas, and feasibility studies are underway.

■ Further reading

UNEP/IUCN (1988).

MAIN REFERENCES

AHMAD, A. A. (1989) *Jordan environmental profile: status and abatement*. Amman, Jordan: Privately published.

ANDREWS, I. J. (1991) Is Azraq still an oasis? *Orn. Soc. Middle East Bull.* 27: 13–19.

BIEWERS, M. (1993) *L'habitat traditionnel du sud de la Jordanie: les villages de 'Aima, Dana et Khirbet Nawafleh*. Amman: Ambassade de France/Ministère du Tourisme de Jordanie.

CARP, E. (1980) *A directory of western Palaearctic wetlands*. Nairobi: United Nations Environment Programme/Gland (Switzerland): International Union for Conservation of Nature and Natural Resources.

CLARKE, J. E. (1979) *A proposal for wildlife reserves in Jordan*. Amman, Jordan: Royal Society for the Conservation of Nature.

CLARKE, J. E. (1980) The avifauna of Shaumari Wildlife Reserve, Jordan. *Sandgrouse* 1: 50–70.

CLARKE, J. E. (1982) The Houbara Bustard in Jordan. *Sandgrouse* 4: 111–113.

CONDER, P. J. (1981a) Birds of the Azraq Wetland Reserve, Jordan: January and February 1979. *Sandgrouse* 2: 22–32.

CONDER, P. J. (1981b) Water extraction at Azraq. *Orn. Soc. Middle East Bull.* 6: 8.

CONDER, P. J. (1982) Azraq Wetland Reserve, Jordan. *Orn. Soc. Middle East Bull.* 8: 4–5.

JONES, T. A. AND CLARKE, J. E. (1990) Azraq oasis, Jordan. Ramsar Convention Monitoring Procedure (Report no. 16). IUCN/IWRB, Gland, Switzerland.

MMRAE (Ministry of Municipal and Rural Affairs and the Environment) (1991) *National Environment Strategy for Jordan*. IUCN—The World Conservation Union, Gland, Switzerland.

MOUNTFORT, G. (1965) *Portrait of a desert*. Collins, London.

NELSON, J. B. (1973) *Azraq: desert oasis*. Allen Lane, London.

NELSON, J. B. (1985) Return to Azraq. *Oryx* 19: 22–26.

PEARCE, F. (1993) Peace pact promises unity in the desert. *New Scientist* 1891: 4.

WALLACE, D. I. M. (1982) Observations on migrant birds at Azraq in north-east Jordan, up to April 1967. *Sandgrouse* 4: 77–99.

WALLACE, D. I. M. (1983) The breeding birds of the Azraq oasis and its desert surround, Jordan, in the mid-1960s. *Sandgrouse* 5: 1–18.

WITTENBERG, J. (1987) Zur Vogelfauna einer semi-ariden Gebirgsregion in Süd-Jordanien (Petra und Umgebung) (Aves). *Verh. naturwiss. Ver. Hamburg* 29: 5–49.

RSCN (1982) *Introduction to the marine life of Aqaba, H. K. of Jordan*. Amman, Jordan: Royal Society for the Conservation of Nature.

UNEP/IUCN (1988) *Coral reefs of the world. Volume 2: Indian Ocean, Red Sea and Gulf*. IUCN, Gland, Switzerland and Cambridge, U.K./UNEP, Nairobi, Kenya.

■ STATE OF KUWAIT

Crab Plover *Dromas ardeola*

GENERAL INFORMATION

Kuwait occupies the north-eastern part of the Arabian peninsula bounded on the north and west by Iraq, on the west and south by Saudi Arabia, and on the east by the Arabian Gulf. It has approximately 550 km of coastline, of which the main feature is the large embayment of Kuwait Bay. Kuwait has a surface area of approximately 18,000 km^2 and extends between 28°30´N and 30°05´N and between 46°33´E and 48°36´E. At the start of 1990 the total population was 2,086,000, the average population density was 110 persons per km^2 and Kuwaitis constituted about 40% of the population. However, only 4% of the country is permanently inhabited, the rest being relatively barren desert with permanent or even intermittent water streams lacking. The State has a number of offshore islands of which only Failaka is inhabited. The islands of Bubiyan, Warba, Mishan, Umm Al-Nammel, Auhha, Kubbar, Qaruh and Umm Al-Maradim are not inhabited except for a few police outposts on some islands and oil drillers on Bubiyan, the largest island.

The general topography is flat to gently undulating, rising gradually from the shores of the Arabian Gulf up to 300 m in the extreme south-west of the country. The Jal Az-Zor escarpment is the most striking topographical feature in Kuwait and borders the northern shore of Kuwait Bay; it extends for some 80 km and reaches a height of 145 m above sea-level, with the upper 30–45 m having bold relief. The Ahmadi ridge runs parallel to the coast south of Kuwait City and separates the Burgan plain in the west from Al-Adan along the Gulf coast to the east. Lower and less conspicuous ridges occur in the central and north-western parts of the country, gravel-capped and rising imperceptibly above the level of the surrounding country. These were extensively quarried for gravel prior to the Iraqi invasion. Low elongated sand-dunes or ridges extend along the Gulf coast south of Kuwait City. The northern and western parts of the country are dissected by a number of wadis of different sizes and patterns which drain mostly to the north-east; except for Wadi Al-Batin, they are usually shallow.

The climate of Kuwait is characterized by its very hot, dry summers and cool to mild, rainy winters. The mean temperatures are 37°C for July and August and 14°C for January. The absolute maximum and minimum are 49°C for July and August, and –3°C for January; relative humidity is highest in January and lowest in June. Rainfall is erratic and inconsistent and shows great temporal and spatial variation (averaging 23–206 mm per year between stations), with most rain usually falling between November and May, although occasional showers may fall in October, and June to August are practically rainless. Fog occurs particularly in the winter months, forming during the very early hours and disappearing by mid-morning. Evaporation far exceeds rainfall throughout the year. On the coast, climatic extremes are probably less than inland. The maximum tidal range on the mainland coast is 3.5–4.0 m; seawater temperature varies widely, from 12°C (January) to 34°C (July), and salinity from 3.8 to 4.2%.

The vegetation of Kuwait is a species-poor, open scrub of dwarf-shrubs, dominated by *Rhanterium* and *Haloxylon*, with perennial herbs and ephemerals; only in favoured sites such as drainage lines can taller shrubs be found. In years of above-average rainfall, the desert is covered with a rich, green mantle, while years of meagre rainfall usually witness partial or complete failure of the vegetation. The length of the rainy season generally determines the length of the growth season, and best growth is noticeable if the first rains are early (October–November), called 'wasm', when warm temperatures help seed germination and bud development. Saltmarshes occur along the coast, particularly along the south-western and the northern shores of Kuwait Bay and also on Bubiyan and Warba islands. They are associated with deltaic, intertidal flats of sandy to silty clays, and sandbanks.

Nomadic and semi-nomadic pastoralism is the main land-use, and overgrazing by goats, sheep and camels is widespread. In years of good rainfall, animals usually find a sufficiency of food during the growing season, but continue to denude the land throughout the long, dry season so that the rich green mantle in the spring and early summer contrasts markedly with the poor, almost bare, desert aspect of summer and autumn. In bad years, grazing makes a bad situation worse and the land is degraded almost past recovery. The perennial vegetation and especially the more palatable species are grazed down to the ground. In 1989 an Act was passed banning all types of grazing in an area covering almost half of Kuwait.

The urban setting for Kuwait was developed according to an ambitious Master Plan made in the mid-1950s. The plan was revised and updated in 1970 and 1983; the latest draft was finalized in June 1990 just before the invasion by the Iraqi troops. Urban development has been mostly along Kuwait Bay and has extended along the shores of the Gulf to the south. The major constraints include the exclusive rights of the oil companies, the location of ground-water fields, and the areas suitable for agriculture. Recreation has featured as a major land-use in the Master Plan and its subsequent reviews.

ORNITHOLOGICAL IMPORTANCE

Located at the south-east corner of the western Palearctic realm, Kuwait possesses a fairly rich avifauna despite its small size and harsh climate, with more than 280 species having been recorded; however, probably only 16 species breed on the mainland and only eight of them regularly, the rest being passage migrants or winter visitors. Species from the adjacent Indo-Malayan and Afrotropical realms form minor components of the avifauna, but which may be more significant than past records indicate.

Kuwait is on the cross-roads of several major bird migration routes between continents. The high ranges of the Caucasus, the Elburz and the Zagros Mountains and the wide expanses of the Black Sea, the Caspian Sea and the Gulf, all present natural barriers to bird migration. Thus, one of the major routes that passes through Kuwait is from eastern Europe along the river valleys of Turkey, Syria and Iraq, across the head of the Gulf eastwards along the western edge of the Zagros mountains to Pakistan and India. The second important route runs east of the Caspian Sea and Elburz Mountains then south-westwards through passes in the Zagros across Kuwait and the Arabian peninsula into eastern and central Africa via the Bab Al-Mandab straits.

Only about 10% of the country's avifauna are resident throughout the year but in summer their numbers are augmented by the arrival of several species, mainly terns, four species of which breed on Kubbar Island.

The climate during the winter months is relatively mild and in addition to the passage migrants many birds travel from northern latitudes to spend the entire winter here. Harsh winter conditions in the north will oblige even hardy species to travel further south than usual, which accounts for sporadic, rare occurrences in some winters. If there is scant winter rainfall in the Arabian peninsula, migrants that have crossed the region will be induced to rest in Kuwait.

The number and variety of migratory birds stopping off to 're-fuel' in Kuwait are greater in spring than in autumn, since a good food supply is ensured by the cool, wet months of winter which permit the growth and fruiting of plants and encourage insects to flourish. Of particular conservation importance is the spring migration of the globally threatened *Falco naumanni*, which concentrates around the migratory 'bottleneck' posed by the Gulf in general and by Kuwait Bay in particular. Between the 1940s and 1960s, several thousands per day passed over Kuwait City during peak passage in April, but the numbers are smaller today, with a marked decline having been noted by the 1970s.

CONSERVATION INFRASTRUCTURE AND PROTECTED-AREA SYSTEM

Conservation of nature has been prominent in the environment policy adopted by the Council of Ministers. The Environment Protection Council (EPC) is the government body responsible for the protection of the environment in general. A number of sites have been identified by the Kuwait Institute for Scientific Research (KISR) as potential terrestrial reserves, based on their overall ecological importance. The main law governing the conservation of natural habitats is Decree Law No. 62 (1401H, 1404H; 1980, 1983), which provides for designation of two categories of protected area (number of sites as of June 1993; all are included in this inventory).

National Park (1 site) Primary objectives and functions are to preserve natural and ecological components, provide education with proper land-use, provide areas for environmental and ecological research, and provide facilities for education and training. Livestock grazing is restricted by fencing, and hunting is not permitted.

A major proposal in the Kuwait Master Plan was for the whole of the northern coast to be designated as a National Park. In 1983 a coastal conservation zone was designated covering the Doha peninsula and the east-facing shore of Kuwait Bay as far as Subiya. However, upon designation in 1990 the National Park was reduced in area in recognition of military requirements. The National Park is included in this inventory and is intended to be a multi-purpose resort for conservation, recreation and education. It is proposed to open up the Park to outdoor camping with minimal service facilities.

Nature Reserve (2 sites) Primary objectives and functions are to preserve all natural and ecological components of the desert environment and provide areas for environmental and ecological research (including into the feasibility of restoring extinct wildlife). The Environment Protection Council has designated two nature reserves so far, both of which are in this inventory and both are managed by the Public Authority for Agriculture Affairs and Fish Resources, an active member of the EPC. No access is allowed during certain periods to avoid disturbance by the public. Prohibited activities include introduction of any foreign animals or plants, livestock grazing, motor traffic, hunting, use of firearms, killing animals, uprooting plants, littering or any other kind of waste disposal.

A special Act for nature conservation (including the designation of other protected areas in the future) has been drafted and is currently awaiting official ratification by the Council of Ministers. In particular, it is hoped that the coral islands and the submerged coral reefs will be declared as protected areas and the necessary legislation passed for the protection of nesting seabirds, sea-turtles and the coral reefs.

INTERNATIONAL MEASURES RELEVANT TO THE CONSERVATION OF SITES

Kuwait is not yet a party to any of the international area-based conservation conventions, although it has signed the Biodiversity Convention. It is a party to the Regional Convention for Cooperation on the Protection of the Marine Environment from Pollution, and to the Action Plan for the Protection and Development of the Marine Environment and the Coastal Areas.

OVERVIEW OF THE INVENTORY

This inventory contains eight sites, covering a total area of c.900 km^2, or about 5% of the land area of the country. The sites cover, with varying degrees of representativeness, all of the important habitats for birds, including intertidal mudflats for wintering and migrating waterbirds, seabird colonies on offshore islands, extensive desert plains, scarps and wadi systems, and man-made freshwater wetlands and agricultural areas. The land around Kuwait Bay is an important 'bottleneck' for migrating raptors in spring, and the extensive desert area of Jal Az-Zor provides important roosting habitat for these birds. Three of the sites are legally protected (totalling c.260 km^2, or c.30% of the area of the sites in this inventory) and two more have been officially proposed for protection. It is likely that further intertidal areas, important for waterbirds, remain to be identified, and this inventory should be considered provisional. In particular, the mudflats in the Bay of Kuwait and the Khiran area to the south would qualify as a Wetland of International Importance under the criteria of the Ramsar Convention. Some important bird species (which Kuwait has important populations of) such as sandgrouse and larks, tend not to congregate but to have scattered distributions. Only a small proportion of their total populations is covered by the inclusion of some representative sites. To conserve these species it is necessary to consider conservation measures for the wider environment, such as regulations covering important land-uses such as agriculture (especially concerning the grazing of rangeland) and recreation. Hunting birds is a traditional pastime in Kuwait and is now largely directed towards passage migrants. *Struthio camelus* has been eliminated through the use of modern weapons, and the globally threatened *Chlamydotis undulata* virtually so in recent times.

ACKNOWLEDGEMENTS

The information used in compiling the introduction and site accounts was contributed by Prof. C. Pilcher of Kuwait University and M. Shehab of the Museum of Natural Science, who have carried out an extensive investigation sponsored by the Environment Protection Council (EPC) of Kuwait. They place on record their appreciation for the painstaking efforts of the Head and staff of the Public Authority for Agriculture Research and Fish Resources in running the existing Jahra Pool Nature Reserve. The compiler thanks Dr M. Y. Abdulraheem (Secretary General, EPC) for provision of information and assistance.

SITE INVENTORY

Site no.	Site name	Criteria used to select site: 1	2i	2ii	2iii	3	4	5i	5ii	6	0
001	Jal Az-Zor	•	—	—	—	—	—	—	—	—	—
002	Dawhat Kazima	—	—	—	—	—	•	—	—	—	—
003	Ad-Doha Nature Reserve	—	•	—	—	—	•	—	—	—	—
004	Al-Abraq Al-Khabari	•	—	—	—	—	—	—	—	—	—
005	Sulaibikhat Bay	—	•	—	—	—	•	—	—	—	—
006	Al-Jahra Pool Nature Reserve	•	—	—	•	—	—	—	—	—	—
007	Al-Batin 'Park'	•	—	—	—	—	—	—	—	—	—
008	Kubbar Island	—	•	—	—	—	•	—	—	—	—

Key to criteria

1 Regularly holds a significant number of a globally threatened species.

2i Regularly holds 1% or more of a species' biogeographical or flyway or Middle Eastern population (waterbirds and seabirds only).

2ii Regularly holds 20,000 or more waterbirds.

2iii Migratory 'bottleneck' site: more than 3,000 raptors or more than 5,000 storks or more than 2,000 cranes pass in a season.

3 Regularly holds a significant number of a species which is threatened or declining within the Middle East. Only the top five sites for each such species in the country are considered to qualify as IBAs.

4 Regularly holds a significant number of a species whose world population is wholly or largely restricted to the Middle East. Only the top five sites for each such species in the country are considered to qualify as IBAs.

5i Representative example of a habitat, associated with a characteristic assemblage of bird species.

5ii Rare/threatened/unique habitat, associated with a characteristic assemblage of bird species.

6 Site important for bird conservation through education/research/tourism.

0 Selected for other reasons. See 'Comments on the inventory'.

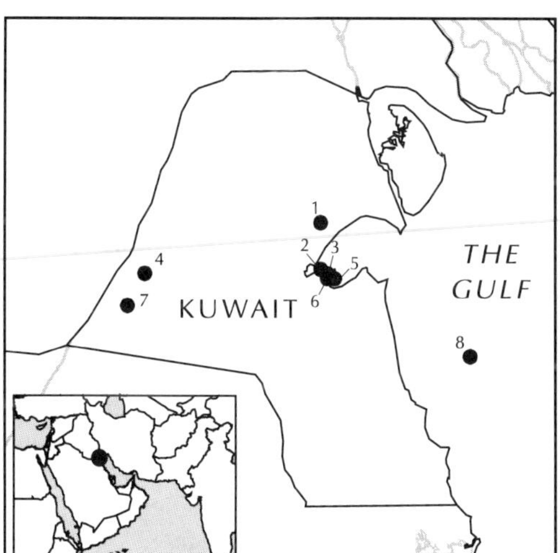

Comments on the inventory

1. The site name has generally been translated from the Arabic, and is sometimes followed by an alternative site name in brackets. This is then followed by the name of the region in brackets, where appropriate.
2. The majority of the bird data used in compiling the site accounts was collected during the 1980s.
3. Application of the criteria is provisional, due to the scarcity of ornithological information. This scarcity has led to a bias towards better explored areas
4. Precise areas are given only for protected areas and some of the sites which have been well documented. Boundaries have not been defined for the non-protected sites, and any areas given in these cases are only crude estimates.
5. Figures in brackets after species' names, and in the boxes, are the maximum daily counts of individuals recorded (not pairs), unless otherwise stated. All counts of wintering birds are from the month of January, unless otherwise stated.
6. The areas given for offshore island sites (important for breeding seabirds) generally do not include the area of the surrounding seas which are

important as feeding grounds, generally because the latter have not been identified with sufficient accuracy as yet.

7. The application of the criterion in category 4 (as depicted in the above table) is provisional, due to unavoidable lack of access to a previously compiled, national ornithological data-bank. Some landbird areas have been chosen to include a representative cross-section of bird habitats.
8. The formerly uninhabited islands of Bubiyan and Warbah (29°45′N 48°12′E) were, at least in the 1920s, a very important breeding site for *Pelecanus onocrotalus*, *Phoenicopterus ruber*, *Dromas ardeola*, *Larus genei* and large numbers of terns, amongst other waterbirds. They are not included in this inventory since there is a complete lack of recent ornithological information, and the islands are also now inhabited, making it unlikely that any breeding colonies remain.
9. The areas given for sites 002 and 005 are those at high tide; however, these sites also cover the expanse of intertidal mudflat exposed at low tide.

Glossary

dawhat, embayment
jal, scarp
khawr, tidal inlet or coastal lagoon
ra's, point or headland
sabkha, saline mudflat
wadi, drainage line or bed of seasonal river.

001 Jal Az-Zor (Al-Jahra)

also known as Jal az Zawr
National Park

29°33′N 47°47′E
25,000 ha

■ Site description

A rocky escarpment rising steeply to 116 m from the coastal mudflats and associated saltmarshes and sand-dunes on Kuwait Bay. A gravel plain extends northwards from the escarpment ridge and gives rise to the extensive wadi system of Ar-Rimam. Most of the park is sandy desert, with much gravel in northern areas. Dunes of the coastal zone are dominated by *Zygophyllum*, higher areas of sand by *Rhanterium* and *Cyperus*, whilst on the gravel plains *Stipa* grass is dominant. In spring, the playas are covered in *Gynandriris* irises. Soil fertility is very low and the site has no agricultural value; the site was much used during winter and spring for prolonged recreational camping activities before the recent conflict.

■ Birds

See box for key species. A representative desert bird community (seven breeding species). An important raptor migration occurs, including *Aquila clanga* (10, March and October–November), as well as species listed below. At least 190 species have been recorded. There have been proposals to reintroduce *Chlamydotis undulata*.

Globally threatened species	
Aegypius monachus	Passage migrant (daily max. 2, March and October).
Aquila heliaca	Passage migrant (daily max. 14, March and October–November).
Falco naumanni	Passage migrant (daily max. 28, March–April).

■ Other threatened/endemic wildlife

None known to BirdLife International.

■ Conservation issues

Prior to the Gulf conflict, the park had been completely enclosed but much of the fencing was destroyed or removed during the Iraqi occupation. The Park management and protection schemes have not yet been re-instated. Without a resumption of these measures, the area will again be subjected to former major problems: excessive hunting/falconry, destruction of desert crust by vehicles, overgrazing and browsing, and, more locally, excessive soil erosion. There have been proposals to reintroduce *Oryx leucoryx* and *Gazella subgutturosa*.

002 Dawhat Kazima (Al-Jahra)

29°23'N 47°47'E
1,660 ha

also known as Dohat Kadhma or Bay of Kazima/Kadhma
Unprotected

Site description

A shallow, relatively well-sheltered bay, part of the larger Kuwait Bay system, with extensive intertidal mudflats (c.890 ha). The site is important for economically valuable shrimp nurseries, and supports both recreational and traditional fishing with fixed traps (hadra). A close season operates for shrimp catching.

Birds

The site is important for coastal waterfowl during winter and on passage, including *Ardea cinerea* (62, January) and *Recurvirostra avosetta* (70, January). Mixed-species flocks of several thousand waterfowl occur during migration seasons but accurate counts of species and individuals have not been made. At least 66 species have been recorded.

Species restricted wholly or largely to the Middle East

Dromas ardeola	Common winter visitor (280, January).

Other threatened/endemic wildlife

Invertebrates: the crab *Cleistostoma kuwaitense* (endemic).

Conservation issues

There are no serious threats at present: some local oil pollution occurs from power stations on Doha peninsula, and toxic outflow from Jahra Pool destroyed extensive stands of *Salicornia* in early 1980s. The site has been inaccessible since the 1990–1991 Iraqi occupation because of unexploded ordnance, which gives some *de facto* protection from human disturbance.

003 Ad-Doha Nature Reserve (Al-Jahra)

29°22'N 47°49'E
450 ha

Nature Reserve

Site description

A sandy sabkhah, some of which is flooded by exceptional tides, with salt-tolerant vegetation; associated intertidal mudflats are considered as part of site 005. Drainage water from a few nearby private chalets or an Entertainment Park flows across part of the site and supports 0.5 ha of *Phragmites* reedbed. The reserve is bisected by a public lane to the chalets, and within it there is also a major outlet for seawater coolant used by Doha power-stations. Previously the site was used at weekends for picnics and recreation.

Birds

See box for key species. The salt-tolerant vegetation provides a favoured roost site for waders, especially in winter and during migration seasons. Important January counts include *Ardea cinerea* (90), *Recurvirostra avosetta* (85) and *Larus genei* (900). About 70 species have been recorded; the site is not well-watched by local standards.

1% or more of population

	Breeding (pairs)	Wintering	Passage
Larus cachinnans/L. argentatus	—	900	—

Species restricted wholly or largely to the Middle East

Dromas ardeola	Common winter visitor (290, January).

Other threatened/endemic wildlife

None known to BirdLife International.

Conservation issues

The entire reserve is fenced on the landward sides but some sections of fencing are broken at present and gates are permanently open. Some protection from hunters is provided on the seaward side by barbed wire of Iraqi defences, which remain in place.

004 Al-Abraq Al-Khabari (Al-Jahra)

29°22′N 46°56′E
130 ha

also known as Al-Abraq Al-Habari
Unprotected

Site description
Private farmland, formerly well irrigated, on sparsely vegetated desert plateau (altitude 235 m) at northern end of the Ad-Dibdibbah gravel plain which extends southwards into Saudi Arabia; well sheltered by 10 m high windbreaks of *Tamarix*, and annually planted with a variety of vegetable and grain crops. There is a small area of sparsely irrigated scrub/bushland.

Birds
See box for key species. This is an attractive area for migrants, and relatively well watched; 168 species have been recorded.

Other threatened/endemic wildlife
None known to BirdLife International.

Globally threatened species

Falco naumanni	Passage migrant (max. 17).

Regionally threatened or declining species

Neophron percnopterus	Passage migrant (max. 2).
Accipiter brevipes	Passage migrant (max. 1).

Species restricted wholly or largely to the Middle East

Hippolais languida	Passage migrant (max. 4).
Sylvia mystacea	Passage migrant (max. 5).
Sylvia minula	Passage migrant (max. 3).

Conservation issues
Excessive and indiscriminate bird hunting and the cessation of irrigation during and ever since the 1990–1991 Iraq conflict are critical problems.

005 Sulaibikhat Bay (Al-Jahra)

29°21′N 47°51′E
4,845 ha

Unprotected

Site description
A shallow, relatively well-sheltered bay, part of the larger Kuwait Bay system, with extensive intertidal mudflats (c.2,250 ha); reportedly the most productive shore in Kuwait, and an economically valuable shrimp nursery. Traditional fishing by fixed traps ('hadra') and recreational fishing occur; the hadra (on the intertidal flats) appear to be in poor repair, and may have been abandoned because of Iraqi mine-laying in the area.

Birds
See box for key species. The site is important for coastal waterfowl during winter and on passage, especially *Ardea cinerea* (90, January) and *Recurvirostra avosetta* (95, January). It is fairly well watched by local standards, and at least 70 bird species have been recorded.

Other threatened/endemic wildlife
Invertebrates: the crab *Cleistostoma kuwaitense* (endemic).

1% or more of population

	Breeding (pairs)	Wintering	Passage
Larus genei	—	1,500	—

Species restricted wholly or largely to the Middle East

Dromas ardeola	Common winter visitor (320, January).

Conservation issues
Land-claim destroyed 500 ha of mudflat in the early 1980s, and a resumption of this policy would be disastrous for the site. There is some local oil pollution from power stations on Doha peninsula and from Mina Shuwaikh port. About 3 km of shore in the south-west corner of bay, adjacent to this site, is a Nature Reserve (see site 003). A proposal was made in 1987 to protect the entire area from shooting (potentially a local problem), whilst allowing traditional and recreational fishing to continue.

006 Al-Jahra Pool Nature Reserve (Al-Jahra)

Nature Reserve

29°21′N 47°49′E
250 ha

Site description

The only significant area of non-marine wetland in the country, man-made by effluent (sewage plus a variety of pollutants) coming from Al-Jahra town and flowing across sandy sabkhah to the sea, forming stagnant, open, shallow pools and extensive beds of *Phragmites*. There are scattered halophytes on the sabkhah, and some old plantations of *Tamarix* in poor condition. The site has great value as a potential field study centre for all educational levels up to university research, and if properly zoned could also provide for recreation. Part of the site is a designated camping area.

Birds

See box for key species. A wet and green area attracting a very wide variety of migrants and winterers, and providing an important refuge from hunting: 220 species have been recorded. An important raptor migration bottleneck, with a maximum daily passage total of 410 (17 species), and estimated spring/autumn totals of 2,000–3,000, including *Buteo buteo* (85, September), *Aquila clanga* (10, March and October), *Aquila nipalensis* (343, March and October) and *Circus aeruginosus* (5, September and October).

Globally threatened species

Aegypius monachus	Passage migrant (max. 2, March and October).
Aquila heliaca	Passage migrant (max. 14, March and October).
Falco naumanni	Passage migrant (max. 28, April).
Crex crex	Passage migrant (max. 2, May and September).

Other threatened/endemic wildlife

None known to BirdLife International.

Conservation issues

Within the reserve, 70 ha are robustly fenced and signs state that this is for protection of birds. An official management plan exists but has not yet been fully re-implemented. Two full-time guards have been employed since February 1993 which should reduce trespassing. Military patrols expel shooters for security reasons and thus provide some unintentional protection. Destruction of vegetation by campers was common before mid-1990; shrubs were used for firewood and vehicles damaged the desert crust. This may recur as confidence grows that the site is safe from unexploded ordnance.

007 Al-Batin 'Park' (Al-Jahra)

Unprotected

29°15′N 46°51′E
57,500 ha

Site description

The area is part of a flat, desert plateau of hard-packed gravelly sand with numerous playas, at 240 m. Its northern side is bordered by Wadi Al-Batin, where the land falls away some 45 m and is characterized by shallow, rocky gullies. The plateau is dominated by *Haloxylon* and, in spring and early summer, by *Stipa* grass. In rocky gullies *Zilla* is common, and many annuals flourish including *Diplotaxis* species. Traditionally the area has been used for grazing, hunting and recreational camping; the main economic value of the land probably lies in its underground water reserves.

Birds

See box for key species. Until overgrazing severely damaged the vegetation in the early 1980s, a representative breeding bird community occurred, comprising *Cursorius cursor*, *Bubo ascalaphus*, *Athene noctua*, *Eremophila bilopha*, *Alaemon alaudipes*, *Ammomanes deserti*, *Ammomanes cincturus*, *Melanocorypha bimaculata* and *Galerida cristata*. Proper management could see a return of these species.

Globally threatened species

Aquila heliaca	Passage migrant (max. 12, March and October–November).
Chlamydotis undulata	Formerly bred.

Regionally threatened or declining species

Neophron percnopterus	Passage migrant (max. 2, April and September–October).

Species restricted wholly or largely to the Middle East

Sylvia minula	Passage migrant (max. 10, March and October).

Other threatened/endemic wildlife

None known to BirdLife International.

Conservation issues

Overgrazing in the last 12 years seriously reduced the wildlife value of the area, and movement of military vehicles during the 1990–1991 conflict with Iraq caused major damage to vegetation and desert crust. At present much scattered, unexploded ordnance is deterring grazing activity, and anecdotal reports from military pilots suggest that the area is fast becoming revegetated. A study was carried out by the Kuwait Institute for Scientific Research and Kuwait Municipality to designate the area as a National Park.

008 Kubbar Island

Unprotected (proposed Marine Park)

29°04′N 48°30′E
18 ha

Site description

One of a small group of coral islets and associated reefs. Part of the island is covered in salt-tolerant bushes, other areas are dominated by *Seidlitzia* annuals, and there are patches of bare ground. Beaches are mainly sandy with some rocky stretches. A favourite recreational area for weekend trippers, scuba divers and fishermen. A small solar energy plant provides power for a beacon in the centre of the island.

Birds

See box for key species. An important breeding colony for *Sterna bengalensis* and *Sterna anaethetus*. Also breeding are *Sterna repressa* and *Sterna bergii* (min. 7 pairs).

Other threatened/endemic wildlife

Reptiles: a former nesting area for the sea-turtles *Chelonia mydas* (E) and *Eretmochelys imbricata* (E).

1% or more of population

	Breeding (pairs)	Wintering	Passage
Sterna bengalensis	270	—	—
Sterna anaethetus	820	—	—

Species restricted wholly or largely to the Middle East

Sterna repressa Summer visitor (max. 285 pairs).

Conservation issues

Disturbance and wilful killing are major problems at the seabird colonies. The island was included in a Marine Park proposed by the Kuwait Institute for Scientific Research in 1988, and included together with several submerged coral reefs in the draft Nature Conservation Act submitted by the Environment Protection Council.

MAIN REFERENCES

Cowan, P. J. (1990) The Crab Plover in Kuwait and the northern Arabian Gulf; a brief review and some new counts. *Orn. Soc. Middle East Bull.* 25: 6–9.

Stuart, B. and Pilcher, C. (1983) Birds. In D. Clayton and C. Pilcher, eds. *Kuwait's natural history: an introduction.* Kuwait: Kuwait Oil Company.

■ REPUBLIC OF LEBANON

White Storks *Ciconia ciconia*

GENERAL INFORMATION

Lebanon is a small country of 10,450 km² with a Mediterranean coastline 225 km long. It is bordered by the Syrian Arab Republic to the north and east, and by Israel to the south. The human population is about 4 million, with a natural increase of 2.2% per annum. Beirut, the capital, stands midway along the coast.

The Lebanon Mountains, overlooking the Mediterranean to the west and the Beka'a valley to the east, run parallel to the coast and rise to more than 3,000 m. The western slopes up to 300 m support evergreen maquis, with *Quercus calliprinos*, *Ceratonia* and *Pistacia*. Remnants of *Pinus halepensis* woodland (replaced by *P. brutia* in the north) occur from sea-level to 1,200 m; the higher slopes were formerly covered with forests of pine *Pinus nigra*, cedar *Cedrus libani* and oak *Quercus calliprinos* which have now been reduced to less than 5% of their original extent by wars, logging, charcoal production and firewood-collection. Large and powerful springs are found high up on the mountains, allowing widespread cultivation on the slopes. The alluvial plains of the Beka'a valley lie at c.900 m and separate the Lebanon Mountains from the parallel Anti-Lebanon range to the east; the valley is the source of two rivers, the Asi (Orontes) and the Litani (Leontes), which flow north and south respectively. The Anti-Lebanon mountains rise to more than 2,600 m, together with their southern continuation, Mount Hermon, which reaches 2,814 m. These mountains are drier, lying in the rain-shadow of the Lebanon Mountains, and have *Amygdalus–Pistacia* scrub and fragmented deciduous forests on their western slopes, together with remnants of steppe-coniferous forests with *Abies cilicica*, *Cedrus libani* and *Juniperus excelsa*. There are subalpine and alpine plant communities above 2,500 m on all the mountains in Lebanon.

Overstocking of sheep and goats and poor agricultural practices have led to severe degradation of Lebanon's remaining forests, and to widespread deterioration of the soil and vegetation cover generally. A recently completed review gives further details of the current status of the environment in Lebanon (Fawaz *et al.* 1992).

ORNITHOLOGICAL IMPORTANCE

Lebanon is rich in numbers and variety of migrating species. Millions of soaring birds, especially birds of prey, storks and pelicans, pass through or over the skies of Lebanon, especially during the autumn migration to Africa when the dominant species are *Pernis apivorus*, *Accipiter brevipes* and *Aquila pomarina*; huge numbers of *Ciconia ciconia* occur in spring. Millions of larks migrate through the northern Beka'a valley each year, where unfortunately most of them are shot for they are considered gamebirds in Lebanon and the hunting law still sets no bag limits for any hunted species.

In the Beka'a valley waterbirds are attracted to the only major natural wetland in Lebanon, Ammiq Swamp, and to Qaraoun Lake (a dam on the Litani river). Waterfowl such as herons, ducks and rails breed at Ammiq whenever permitted by hunters. Ammiq Swamp is of national and regional importance to migrating birds especially waterbirds since it is the only sizeable wetland between Turkey and Israel.

The recently established Palm Islands Marine Reserve off the coast of Tripoli in northern Lebanon is a potentially important site for breeding seabirds, where the globally threatened *Larus audouinii* used to breed along with several other species of seabirds in good numbers.

CONSERVATION INFRASTRUCTURE AND PROTECTED-AREA SYSTEM

National parks and protected areas are created in compliance with two legislative decrees, Decree No. 8371 (30 December 1961, Articles 17 and 19) and Decree No. 1631 (30 April 1984, Articles 111 and 130). Ministry of Agriculture Law 1/127 (23 October 1991) was used to create Barouk Cedars Forest Reserve, and Law 121 (9 March 1992) was used to declare the Marine Nature Reserve of Palm Islands Park as well as Ehden Forest Reserve/Natural Park.

The management of protected Forest Reserves is covered by regulations of the Ministry of Agriculture. But since the recent re-establishment of a Ministry of Environment, protected areas and hunting are the joint responsibility of both Ministries. For example, the Barouk Cedar Forest Reserve is under the jurisdiction of the Ministry of Agriculture, whereas the Palm Islands Reserve and the Ehden Forest Reserve are under the Ministry of Environment in cooperation with local municipalities and environmental NGOs. The Ministry of Environment, SPNL, IUCN and UNDP are working on a proposal to the Global Environment Facility to develop a Department for Protected Areas and Wildlife within the Ministry of Environment.

New bird hunting legislation was ratified on 16 March 1993 (Decree 1/64), banning all hunting in Lebanon between 15 March and 15 September henceforth, and protecting the nationally endangered *Alectoris chukar* for five years.

INTERNATIONAL MEASURES RELEVANT TO THE CONSERVATION OF SITES

Lebanon is a party to the World Heritage Convention and has signed the Biodiversity Convention, but has not signed the Ramsar or Bonn Conventions. Lebanon is a party to the Barcelona Convention and has ratified the protocol concerning Mediterranean Specially Protected Areas.

OVERVIEW OF THE INVENTORY

This inventory contains four sites, covering a total area of at least 880 ha. There is a good coverage of the most important wetland and offshore island habitats for birds and other wildlife, but only two representative sites cover the forest and mountain habitats, and these cover only small core areas that in themselves are not large enough to sustain viable or fully diverse bird communities: delimitation of the proper boundaries of these sites awaits further survey. There is no doubt that further important forest, scrub and mountain sites will be discovered or be re-surveyed in future, if extensive ornithological surveys can be carried out. Steppe, semi-desert and agricultural habitats (in the Beka'a Valley) also deserve investigation. Two of the four sites have recently been declared as legally protected (since 9 March 1992), namely the Palm Islands and Ehden Forest. However these still lack adequate management and protection, and all the sites in this inventory are facing problems or threats, in particular the wetland of Ammiq Swamp (drainage) and the Palm Islands (human disturbance). Most of Lebanon can be considered as a huge 'bottleneck' for migratory raptors and storks, therefore despite the intense shooting that populations of these birds endure in Lebanon, it would be meaningless to define any particular sites for protection in isolation. To conserve these species, wide-scale enforcement of the current hunting regulations is necessary.

ACKNOWLEDGEMENTS

The site accounts and introduction were compiled mainly from information provided by A. Serhal (Society for Protection of Nature and Natural Resources). Data-sheets submitted by A. M. Macfarlane to the Ornithological Society of the Middle East's Sites Register Scheme were also incorporated. D. J. Brooks researched the existing literature and assisted with the compilation of data.

SITE INVENTORY

Site no.	Site name	Region	Criteria used to select site: 1	2i	2ii	2iii	3	4	5i	5ii	6	0
001	Palm Islands	NL, TP	•	—	—	—	—	—	—	•	—	—
002	Ehden Forest	NL	•	—	—	—	•	—	•	—	•	—
003	Barouk Cedars	SM	•	—	—	—	•	•	•	—	•	—
004	Ammiq Swamp	BV	•	—	—	•	•	—	—	•	•	—

Key to regions

BV	West Beka'a Valley
NL	North Lebanon
SM	Shouf Mountain
TP	Tripoli

Key to criteria

1 Regularly holds a significant number of a globally threatened species.
2i Regularly holds 1% or more of a species' biogeographical or flyway or Middle Eastern population (waterbirds and seabirds only).
2ii Regularly holds 20,000 or more waterbirds.
2iii Migratory 'bottleneck' site: more than 3,000 raptors or more than 5,000 storks or more than 2,000 cranes pass in a season.
3 Regularly holds a significant number of a species which is threatened or declining within the Middle East. Only the top five sites for each such species in the country are considered to qualify as IBAs.
4 Regularly holds a significant number of a species whose world population is wholly or largely restricted to the Middle East. Only the top five sites for each such species in the country are considered to qualify as IBAs.
5i Representative example of a habitat, associated with a characteristic assemblage of bird species.
5ii Rare/threatened/unique habitat, associated with a characteristic assemblage of bird species.
6 Site important for bird conservation through education/research/tourism.
0 Selected for other reasons. See 'Comments on the inventory'.

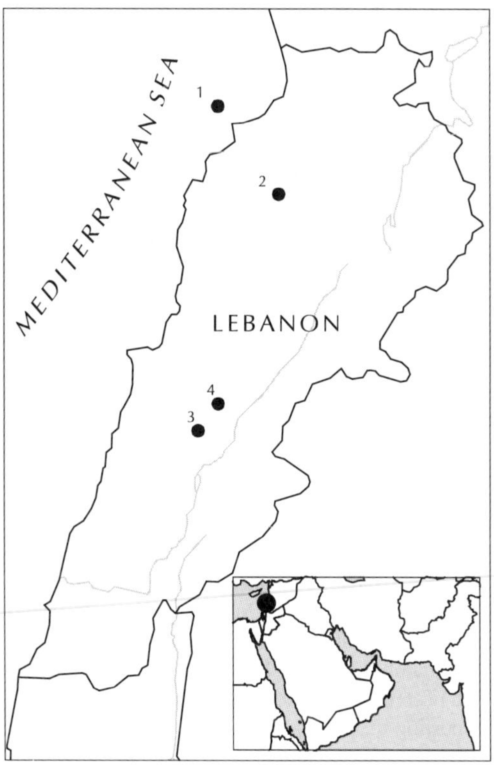

Comments on the inventory

1. The site name is sometimes followed by an alternative site name in brackets. This is then followed by the name of the region in brackets, where appropriate.
2. The majority of the data used in compiling the site accounts was collected in the 1960s and early 1970s.
3. Application of the criteria is provisional, due to the scarcity of ornithological information. This scarcity has led to a bias towards better explored areas
4. Precise areas are given only for protected areas and some of the sites which have been well documented. Boundaries have not been defined for the non-protected sites, and any areas given in these cases are only crude estimates.
5. Figures in brackets after the species' names, and in the boxes, are the maximum daily counts of individuals recorded (not pairs), unless otherwise stated. All counts given of wintering birds are from the month of January, unless otherwise stated.
6. No area is given for one site (002) because its boundaries have not been determined.
7. The area given for the offshore island site (001; important for breeding seabirds) does not include the area of the surrounding seas which are important as feeding grounds, because the latter have not been identified with sufficient accuracy as yet.
8. The application of the criteria in categories 3 and 4 as depicted in the above table is provisional only, due to scarcity of recent or comprehensive information. Some landbird areas have been chosen to include a representative cross-section of bird habitats.
9. The site descriptions provided are tentative outlines only for most sites, in the absence of more detailed information based on ornithological surveys.
10. One potential site was identified too late for fur-

ther investigation and possible inclusion in this inventory: the ruins at Baalbek formerly held a breeding colony of the globally threatened *Falco naumanni*, and deserve further investigation.

Glossary

MSPA, Mediterranean Specially Protected Area

jazirat, island

001 Palm Islands (North Lebanon/Tripoli)

also known as Iles des Lapins
Marine Reserve

34°30′N 35°46′E
c.500 ha
MSPA (unknown area)

■ Site description

A group of three flat, rocky islands of eroded limestone pavement (rising to 6 m), c.13 km offshore and north-west of Tripoli, together with their surrounding seas. Palm Island (Jazirat al-Nakhl or Ile du Palmier) is the largest (20 ha), and has a sand beach on its north and east sides, and a central depression where rainwater accumulates in winter. Parts of the islands are flooded with seawater during storms. There is some very stunted maquis-type vegetation in clefts in the limestone but the islands are otherwise relatively bare, except in spring when carpeted in wildflowers. On Palm Island there are also some small ponds, boggy areas and stands of reed *Phragmites*. The islands are commonly visited by picnicers, tourists, hunters, school parties and fishermen. There is a freshwater well on Palm Island, as well as some half-built concrete buildings and some ruins from antiquity. There is a lighthouse on Ramkin Island. The third island is called Sanani.

■ Birds

See box for key species. The islands were formerly an important seabird breeding site, known as the 'Bird Islands' in the last century. *Larus audouinii* (see below), *L. cachinnans*, *Sterna bengalensis*, *S. hirundo* and *S. albifrons* were all breeding on Palm Island at the end of the 19th century at least, but currently no species breed, apart from *L. cachinnans* possibly, due to high levels of disturbance. *L. cachinnans* has been declining for a long time (80–90 pairs in 1956, 50 birds in 1973, at least 15 pairs in 1975, no birds present in April 1993) and may be extinct. The site would make an excellent observatory for monitoring the large, visible migration of waterbirds along the coast (egrets, ducks, waders, gulls etc.) and for observation and ringing of passerine migrants; over 300 species of migrants had been recorded by 1974, including vagrants such as *Haliaeetus albicilla*, *Falco eleonorae*, *F. pelegrinoides* and *Vanellus gregarius*. The site was listed as a wetland of international importance by Carp (1980).

Globally threatened species

Larus audouinii	Formerly bred (until at least the end of 19th century), and still occasionally present; 18 adults recorded in April 1973, but none in May 1975; no records since.

■ Other threatened/endemic wildlife

Mammals: old records of *Monachus monachus* (E), perhaps up until the 1960s. Reptiles: old records of sea-turtles *Chelonia mydas* (E) and *Caretta caretta* (E) nesting on the sand beaches. Flora: some wildflower species are nationally endangered or extinct along the mainland coast, or otherwise unusual, e.g. *Euphorbia pithyusa*, *Cressa cretica*.

■ Conservation issues

Although declared a Marine Reserve on 9 March 1992 (Law 121), the law is not enforced. The reserve was recently also designated as a Mediterranean Specially Protected Area. Critical problems presently are extreme disturbance of birds by all visitors, the large numbers of illegal hunters, deliberate persecution of birds, and over-collection of eggs and young of nesting seabirds in the past. Dynamite fishing has been frequent offshore in the last decade, and oil and garbage pollution from Tripoli are problems. Introduction of non-indigenous fauna/flora has occurred. Some half-built buildings occur on Palm Island; before 1975–1976 there were proposals to develop the islands for tourism, potentially a critical threat.

■ Further reading

Carp (1980), Haber *et al.* (no date), Tohmé (1973), Tohmé and Neuschwander (1974).

002 Ehden Forest (North Lebanon)
Forest Reserve/Natural Park

34°17′N 35°58′E
Area undefined

Site description
A forest of cedars *Cedrus libani*, firs *Abies* and oak *Quercus*, in a rocky, mountainous area at c.1,500 m; usually covered in snow during December–April. The main land-use is hunting, but the site is also important for shepherds and loggers, and is visited by tourists and for recreation.

Birds
See box for key species. Other breeding species include *Gyps fulvus* and *Alectoris chukar*.

Globally threatened species	
Falco naumanni	Passage migrant.
Regionally threatened or declining species	
Pernis apivorus	Passage migrant.
Gyps fulvus	Breeds.

Other threatened/endemic wildlife
Flora: there are many endemic plants.

Conservation issues
Although declared a Forest Reserve on 9 March 1992 (Law 121), protective measures are not enforced. Illegal bird hunting, and associated excessive disturbance and deliberate persecution of birds, is a critical problem. There is no forest management plan, and logging occurs locally. Air pollution is widespread. Potential threats, at least locally, include overgrazing (sheep and goats), fire and built development.

003 Barouk Cedars (Shouf Mountain)
Forest Reserve

33°42′N 35°42′E
100 ha

Site description
The best remaining stand of cedar *Cedrus libani* forest in Lebanon, in a mountainous, rocky area at 1,750 m, covered in snow between December and March. The forest is relatively open, with much scrub, and about 10% of the area is under cultivation. Currently the area is primarily used for hunting, tourism and recreation, secondarily for forestry, rangeland and wildlife conservation.

Birds
See box for key species. Other breeding species include *Alectoris chukar* (if not extinct), *Lullula arborea*, *Eremophila alpestris*, *Anthus similis*, *Oenanthe oenanthe*, *O. hispanica*, *Sylvia hortensis*, *Parus lugubris*, *Pyrrhocorax graculus* (possible), *Emberiza cia* (possible) and *E. caesia*. Migrants include *Ciconia ciconia*.

Globally threatened species	
Aquila heliaca	Passage migrant.
Falco naumanni	Passage migrant.
Regionally threatened or declining species	
Pernis apivorus	Passage migrant.
Gyps fulvus	Passage migrant.
Accipiter brevipes	Passage migrant.
Aquila pomarina	Passage migrant.
Falco cherrug	Passage migrant.
Species restricted wholly or largely to the Middle East	
Oenanthe finschii	Summer visitor.
Serinus syriacus	Summer visitor.
Rhodopechys sanguinea	Resident.

Other threatened/endemic wildlife
Mammals: *Canis lupus* (V), *Sciurus anomalus* (relict). Flora: there are many endemic plants.

Conservation issues
Major problems include persecution and excessive hunting and disturbance of birds, abandonment of traditional forest management, excessive soil erosion and a fungal disease attacking the cedars. Drought, fire, logging and overgrazing are also causing forest loss and degradation locally. There is no forest management plan. A national nature education center is planned, given the site's great potential for tourism, recreation and education in the future. The area has been nominated as a natural World Heritage Site by the Lebanese government.

004 Ammiq Swamp (West Beka'a Valley)

33°46′N 35°46′E
280 ha

Unprotected

Site description

The largest remaining freshwater wetland in Lebanon, lying at 865 m on the western side of the Beka'a valley, fed by the El Rhabe stream from springs high up in the Lebanon Mountains. It is bordered to the south by the straight-cut, canalized Riachi river, and to the north by the Houjier river. The main area floods markedly beyond 280 ha (especially towards the north-east) in February–March due to late winter rain and melting snow, but dries out between August and November each year. There are extensive *Phragmites* beds, interspersed with open fields of coarse pasture, and there are trees along the Litani and Riachi rivers; native *Salix* have almost died out, but *Populus* and *Cupressus* have been introduced. The site is a major water resource for people locally, and large flocks of goats and sheep are moved into the swamp for grazing during the dry period of August–November. Other main land-uses are hunting (hunters come from all over Lebanon, all year but especially between autumn and spring), tourism and recreation. More locally the site is used for cultivation and fishing.

Birds

See box for key species. Breeding species include *Tachybaptus ruficollis*, *Ixobrychus minutus*, *Nycticorax nycticorax*, *Anas querquedula* (possible), *Circus aeruginosus* (occasional), *Rallus aquaticus*, *Porphyrio porphyrio* (possible; one record, February 1977), *Calandrella rufescens*, *Cettia cetti*, *Cisticola juncidis*, *Prinia gracilis*, *Locustella luscinioides* (common), *Acrocephalus melanopogon*, *A. palustris* (possible), *A. scirpaceus*, *A. arundinaceus* and *Emberiza melanocephala* (probable). Wintering species include *Casmerodius albus*, *Egretta garzetta*, *Anas crecca*, *Circus cyaneus* and *Fulica atra*; the grazing fields which are flooded in late winter attract many waterfowl. A 'pair' of *Remiz pendulinus* has been recorded in February. Notably common passage migrants include *Ciconia nigra* (7, May), *Anas querquedula*, *Porzana porzana* and *Fulica atra*. Due to the site's position on the Rift Valley migration route, large numbers of pelicans, *Ciconia ciconia*, raptors (e.g *Aquila clanga*, *Pandion haliaetus*) and swifts pass overhead in spring and autumn. The site was listed as a wetland of international importance by Carp (1980).

Globally threatened species	
Crex crex	Regular passage migrant, especially in spring (3, May).
Regionally threatened or declining species	
Botaurus stellaris	Winter visitor.
Aythya nyroca	Possibly breeds: two records of 1–2 birds, June and August 1974.
Pernis apivorus	One recorded on passage.
Aquila pomarina	One recorded on passage.
Gallinago media	Regular passage migrant, especially in spring (2, April).
Species restricted wholly or largely to the Middle East	
Glareola nordmanni	Passage migrant; one record (12, April).

Other threatened/endemic wildlife

Mammals: *Lutra lutra* (rare) recently went extinct.

Conservation issues

There are many critical problems, most associated with abandonment of traditional management for agricultural intensification, and with direct impacts on birds. The wetland formerly covered most of the central and western Beka'a valley north up to Zahle, but has now been reduced to one tenth of its former area. Since at least 1970, farmers around the site have been draining its margin (into the Litani river) for conversion to farmland, and a project was planned for 1973 which would have drained the entire marsh, though this was deferred. The water supply also suffers from over-extraction and diversion for irrigation elsewhere. The marsh vegetation is overgrazed/browsed by livestock in the dry season, when it also suffers from drought and fire, especially the trees which are deliberately burnt off by farmers. Deliberate persecution of birds, hunting, general disturbance and over-exploitation by trapping of birds are all occurring at excessive levels. Other major problems are garbage dumping and introduction of non-indigenous flora/fauna, whilst toxic pollution and damming also occur locally. The land is privately owned although access is unrestricted; negotiations are underway to protect the remaining habitat as a bird sanctuary.

Further reading

Carp (1980), Macfarlane (1978), Tohmé and Neuschwander (1974).

MAIN REFERENCES

BIJLSMA, R. G. (1987) *Bottleneck areas for migratory birds in the Mediterranean region: an assessment of the problems and recommendations for action.* Cambridge, U.K.: International Council for Bird Preservation (Study Rep. 18).

CARP, E. (1980) *A directory of western Palaearctic wetlands.* Nairobi: United Nations Environment Programme/Gland (Switzerland): International Union for Conservation of Nature and Natural Resources.

FAWAZ, M., MALLAT, H. AND KHAWLIE, M. (1992) *Environment and development in Lebanon. National report on environmental status in Lebanon in view of UNCED Agenda 21 concept of sustainability.* Beirut: United Nations Development Programme.

HABER, R., SEMAAN-HABER, M. AND RECKITT, R. (no date) *Palm Islands Park.* Tripoli, Lebanon: Committee for Environmental Protection.

HOLLOM, P. A. D. (1959) Notes from Jordan, Lebanon, Syria and Antioch. *Ibis* 101: 183–200.

KHAYRALLAH, N. H. (1985) Raptor migration over Bhamdoun, Lebanon; autumn 1981. *Lebanese Sci. Bull.* 1: 73–81.

KHAIRALLAH, N. H. (1991) Notes on the autumn raptor migration over the Lebanon in 1981. *Sandgrouse* 13: 34–41.

MACFARLANE, A. M. (1978) Field notes on the birds of Lebanon and Syria 1974–77. *Army Bird-watching Soc. Per. Publ.* 3.

TOHMÉ, G. (1973) Projet de transformation de l'île du Palmier (Tripoli, Liban) en réserve naturelle. *Congrès international des parcs méditerranéens côtiers,* Castellabate and Malta, 18–25 June 1973.

TOHMÉ, G. AND NEUSCHWANDER, J. (1974) Nouvelles données sur l'avifaune de la République Libanaise. *Alauda* 74: 243–257.

■ SULTANATE OF OMAN

Arabian Partridge *Alectoris melanocephala*

GENERAL INFORMATION

The Sultanate of Oman has a total land area of 309,500 km^2. A national census was completed for Oman in 1993, putting the human population at just over 2 million, increasing at a rate of 3.5% per annum. The Sultanate shares borders with the United Arab Emirates, the Kingdom of Saudi Arabia and the Republic of Yemen. Oman lies on the southern flank of the great belt of arid deserts which stretches from western Africa to China, but has a favourable position along the eastern seaboard of the Arabian peninsula, with its shoreline stretching for more than 1,700 km from the Arabian Gulf and the Gulf of Oman to the Arabian Sea. The distance from mainland Oman to the mainland of the Islamic Republic of Iran across the Gulf of Oman is 55 km.

The Sultanate stretches in a huge crescent from its most northerly point at Jazirat as Salamah south-westwards to its southern border with the Republic of Yemen, except for a 90-km-wide corridor of the United Arab Emirates (UAE) which lies between the Musandam region and the rest of Oman. A small enclave of the Sultanate of Oman, called Mahda, lies within this corridor. In over 10 degrees of latitude, mostly within the tropics, it bridges much of the gap between the huge landmasses of Asia and Africa, and thus between the Indo-Malayan and Afrotropical biogeographic realms.

Oman can be divided into seven biological zones according to topography and climate as follows.

Northern mountains

The mountains of the northern part of Oman commence in the Musandam Peninsula and the Ruus al Jibal('Heads of the Mountains', up to 2,087 m) of the mainland of the Musandam region, and emerge from the UAE corridor as the western and eastern Hajar ranges (Al Hajar al Gharbi and Al Hajar ash Sharqi), extending in an arc 500 km long almost to the coast at the easternmost point of Oman. They are dominated by the huge limestone massif of Al Jabal al Akhdar (up to 2,980 m), the highest mountain in eastern Arabia; the rest are mostly jagged igneous and metamorphic rocks and are generally sparsely vegetated, although small patches of alluvium produce rich, grassy pastures. Many villages nestle in the wadis wherever perennial water is available.

Coastal plains

Plains occur along the coast wherever the mountains or plateaus do not reach the sea, and unless backed by mountains they are very arid. One of the most important is the Batinah, which curves from the UAE border in the north, some 270 km south-eastwards nearly to Muscat, varying from 3 to 30 km in width. Further to the south-east the well-vegetated plain of the Jaalan in the Ash Sharqiyah Region reaches the sea between the Hajar ash Sharqi mountains and the Ramlat al Wahaybah (Wahiba Sands). One of the drier coastal plains is the Sahil al Jazir, which lies west-south-west of Ra's Madrakah. Further south-west, in the Dhofar Governorate, the narrow and extensively cultivated Salalah plain extends for 50 km from Taqah westwards to Raysut.

Northern pediment

This is an alluvial gravel plain lying inland between the Hajar al Gharbi mountains and the sand desert near the border with UAE on the west. It stretches from Al Buraymi in the Jaww district south-westwards through the A'Dhahirah and Ad Dakhliyah Regions until it meets the central gravel desert to the south. Wadi beds cross the region towards the west and south, draining the rare floods into sand desert or saline depressions. The Umm as Samim is one such depression, a vast salt-lake when flooded and a treacherous sabkha (saline mudflat) at other times.

Central gravel desert

This is an arid steppe in the centre of the country, with an elevation of 100–200 m, which continues south from the northern pediment, then south-west across the Nejd north of the Dhofar highlands, to the border with Yemen. It is the largest and driest of the biological zones of Oman distinguished here, experiencing extremes of heat and cold. Vast, flat expanses of gravel are interrupted by small hills, by many drainage lines in which sand collects and in which vegetation is concentrated, and by the Jiddat al Harasis, a limestone plateau. Scattered over the whole region are some oases watered from artesian wells.

Sand desert

Sand deserts occur wherever any blown sand accumulates in sufficient quantities to cover a wide area or to form dunes. Best known are the mobile dunes, some over 30 m high, in the sand sea of Ar Rub al Khali (the Empty Quarter), which reaches into Oman over the border with Saudi Arabia. Occasional storm waters drain north from the Dhofar highlands into these sands, and form permanent water-holes in places such as Wadi Muqshin. The Ramlat al Wahaybah (Wahiba Sands) is an isolated sand sea bordering the east coast.

Dhofar highlands

The Dhofar highlands start near Hasik on Al Halaaniyaat Bay (formerly Kuria Muria Bay), and continue westward for 290 km as a chain comprising Jabal Samhan (1,812 m), Jabal al Qara (960 m) and Jabal al Qamar (1,400 m) to the Yemen border. Along its northern side, the range slopes gently to the desert interior of the Nejd, with much steeper slopes facing south or south-east towards the sea. Thick deciduous woodland covers these south-facing slopes in a very narrow and easily damaged belt, and grassland covers the top of Jabal al Qara seasonally, both being sustained by fog moisture from the south-west monsoon of summer. Traditional cattle and goat pastoralism has increased in scale, aggravated by thousands of camels, severely threatening the woodland. Where out of range of the fog and the occasional rainstorm the hills are arid, though spectacularly eroded and dissected by the rainfall of previous epochs; the canyons thus formed are refuges for animals. Springs occur at the foot of the escarpments, but the flows are diminishing.

Coasts

Apart from coastal cliffs such as those in the Musandam region, the coastline is emergent, often with a shelf reef exposed at low water, and backed by small dunes of calcareous sand bound by grasses and other halophytes. Intertidal flats are very extensive between the Barr al Hikman peninsula and Masirah island, south of the Ramlat al Wahaybah, and also occur in the Ad Duqm area and to a lesser extent in the creeks (khawrs)—the mouths of wadis which flood occasionally—of which there are many. Khawrs include those that are wide, shallow and surrounded by sabkha and halophytes, and those with deep narrow channels lined with mangrove *Avicennia* or with reeds *Phragmites*, bulrushes *Typha* and other aquatic vegetation. Some are saline and strongly tidal, but others become lagoons when sealed temporarily from the sea by a sandbar until wadi-flood or tide bursts through, and their waters are partly fresh at the inland end when this is fed by subsurface or very occasional surface flow. Examples are found along most of Oman's coastline.

Oman's largest offshore island is Masirah, in the Arabian Sea. The two other major island groups are the Juzor al Halaaniyaat (formerly the Kuria Muria islands) in the Arabian Sea in the south, and the Juzor ad Daymaniyat off the Batinah plain in the Gulf of Oman. There are many steep-sided islands and rock stacks in the Musandam region, as well as small islands or island groups elsewhere, notably off Ra's as Sawadi, between Muscat and Ra's Abu Da'ud, and the isolated rock stack of Hamar an Nafur. The inhabited islands of Oman are Masirah, Al Hallaniyah, the largest of the Juzor ad Daymaniyat, and Didamar (Jazirat Quwayn as Saghir).

In Oman there are two distinct climatic periods: the cool winter months (approximately late November to March), when northerly winds affect much of the country and most rain falls in the northern parts; and the hot summer (May to September), when a south-west monsoonal airflow affects most of the country, and when significant deposition of fog moisture occurs in parts of the Dhofar highlands.

Rainfall is very uneven in its distribution, and in most parts of Oman is irregular and unpredictable in its timing and quantity, with droughts of several years duration being experienced in some parts. Even the intensity of the summer monsoon varies annually.

The effects in coastal Dhofar are unique. The south-west trade winds begin to blow across the Indian Ocean in May, reaching the Dhofar coast as the warm moist monsoon (but inland the wind comes from Africa and is hot and dry). By July and August these winds reach a peak of 20–30 knots parallel to the coast, setting up a strong current from Somalia to western India. Deep, cold water wells up, particularly off Dhofar, and, being several degrees colder than the air passing over it, cools the air to dew-point. A bank of fog and ragged cloud then forms over the sea and a temperature inversion tends to prevent its dispersal, though daily changes occur. Where the Dhofar highlands face the wind, the fog and cloud press against them, riding to the top of Jabal al Qara, but rarely over Jabal Qamar; the moisture condenses on objects (especially plants) and sometimes occurs as drizzle. The upwelling of nutrient-rich cold water during the monsoon is also responsible for a rise in marine productivity, which attracts large numbers of seabirds, fish and cetaceans.

ORNITHOLOGICAL IMPORTANCE

A total of 430 bird species have been recorded in the Sultanate, a high number in relation to the country's land area. Oman, perhaps alone amongst all countries, can claim an avifauna composed from no less than four of the world's principal faunal regions. Northern Oman is firmly Indo-Malayan in its land avifaunal affinities. Southern Oman—the Dhofar region—is distinctly linked, by way of Yemen, with the Afrotropical bird fauna. These two areas are divided by a c.800 km stretch of gravel desert whose bird affinities are strongly Palearctic. In addition, large numbers of many species of Palearctic migrants are supported throughout Oman during ten months of the year. Finally, the upwelling in the Arabian Sea during the summer monsoon sustains large numbers of non-breeding seabirds from Antarctica and the southern oceans.

Oman's coastal zone supports huge numbers of wintering and migrating waterbirds and of breeding and non-breeding seabirds. Midwinter counts by a modest number of people covering only a fraction of the Sultanate's coastline give a total mid-winter population of 300,000–500,000 waterbirds of 90–110 species, with the majority of individuals being shorebirds and at a single site, the Barr al Hikman. Recent records (a minimum of three birds, January 1990) suggest that the globally endangered *Numenius tenuirostris* may winter in this area regularly in significant numbers. Other waterbirds which winter in especially large numbers are as follows (all figures are approximate and are likely to be underestimates).

- More than 80% of the world population of *Larus hemprichii* (34,000)
- More than 50% of the flyway populations of *Calidris tenuirostris* (1,200 birds), *Limosa lapponica* (55,000) and *Sterna sandvicensis* (50,000)
- More than 10% of the population of the subspecies *Charadrius mongolus atrifrons* (9,000)
- More than 10% of the flyway or biogeographical populations of *Egretta gularis* (3,000), *Haematopus ostralegus* (12,000), *Calidris minuta* (17,000), *Calidris alpina* (60,000+), *Larus ridibundus* (45,000), *Larus genei* (55,000) and *Sterna bergii* (7,000).

In addition, substantial numbers of the following waterbirds occur in winter, but estimates of the total flyway populations are not yet available and the exact significance of the counts cannot yet be judged, although they are obviously important: *Ardea cinerea* (1,500), *Charadrius alexandrinus* (5,000), *Limicola falcinellus* (5,000), *Numenius arquata* (3,000), *Tringa totanus* (c.14,000), *Larus ichthyaetus* (3,000), *Larus cachinnans/L. argentatus* (6,500) and *Sterna caspia* (1,700).

The offshore islands and islets of Oman are very important as breeding places for many seabirds. With few exceptions they have the characteristics of natural nature reserves and deserve protection as such. Particularly significant are the populations of *Phalacrocorax nigrogularis* (3,000–5,000 pairs; only breeding in the Arabian Sea and Arabian Gulf), *Phaethon aethereus* (min. 200 pairs), *Sula dactylatra* (8,000–13,000 pairs of the western Indian Ocean subspecies *S. d. melanops*), *Larus hemprichii* (11,000 pairs), *Sterna anaethetus* (min. 31,000 pairs), *Sterna repressa* (min. 2,000 pairs) and *Sterna bergii* (min. 4,000 pairs). Two seabirds may breed only in Oman: the only known breeding site for *Puffinus persicus* is at Al Hallaniyah island in the Arabian Sea, and the breeding grounds of *Bulweria fallax* have not yet been found but are suspected of lying in Oman. Good numbers of *Pandion haliaetus* (min. 40 pairs) and *Falco concolor* (min. 60 pairs) breed on the offshore islands and to a much lesser extent on mainland cliffs; the population of the latter species, threatened or declining in the Middle East, is important in a regional context. The only known breeding site for the very isolated and threatened subspecies *Todirhamphus chloris kalbaensis* (max. c.50 birds) is at Khawr Kalba (shared with the United Arab Emirates). In addition, an isolated, coastal population of *Zosterops abyssinicus* may prove to be a new subspecies.

Huge feeding concentrations of seabirds occur in the upwelling off Oman's Arabian Sea coast during the summer, many species being non-breeding visitors from the southern oceans and Antarctica. Although quantitative estimates are not available, it would appear that most of the world populations of *Bulweria fallax* and *Puffinus persicus* depend on these waters throughout the year, and substantial populations of *Puffinus carneipes*, *Fregetta tropica* and *Oceanites oceanicus* also occur. In winter, a significant proportion of the world population of *Phalaropus lobatus* is likely to winter within Oman's marine territory in the Arabian Sea.

The richest breeding avifauna on land is found in the Dhofar highlands and coast in the south of Oman, where many Afrotropical species breed. Relatively large numbers of the globally threatened *Aquila heliaca* winter or migrate through Oman; largest numbers are found in Dhofar, where the coastal khawrs and moist inland areas support up to seven birds per site in winter. Oman's mountains support a breeding population of *Torgos tracheliotus* significant in the Middle Eastern context (since the species is threatened or declining in the region) as well as major populations of some species with world ranges wholly or largely confined to the Middle East: *Alectoris melanocephala*, *Oenanthe lugentoides* and *Rhynchostruthus socotranus* in the Dhofar highlands, and *Oenanthe alboniger* in the northern mountains.

The desert plains of Oman support a notably healthy breeding population of the globally threatened *Chlamydotis undulata* (a minimum of 10–100 pairs), and this relatively large resident population is further swelled by migrants from the north during winter. The former south Arabian population of *Struthio camelus*, whose range included Oman, may also have been a distinctive subspecies, but is now extinct. Other notable breeding species of the desert avifauna are four sandgrouse *Pterocles* species and six lark (Alaudidae) species.

In Oman there is no tradition of falconry and no attempts are made to capture birds of prey. As a result Oman supports healthy populations of breeding and wintering raptors. Apart from those birds of prey mentioned already, other species whose breeding or wintering populations are probably important on a Middle Eastern scale include *Neophron percnopterus*, *Aquila chrysaetos* and *Aquila verreauxii*.

Numerous passerine birds migrate through Oman's airspace but on the whole they do not regularly make landfalls concentrating in large numbers at particular sites. An exception is *Acrocephalus palustris*: hundreds of thousands pass through Oman northbound in May, and a significant proportion of the global population must be involved.

CONSERVATION INFRASTRUCTURE AND PROTECTED-AREA SYSTEM

Legislation in the form of a Ministerial Decision by the Ministry of Regional Municipalities and Environment protects all wildlife, including birds, throughout the Sultanate, as of August 1993. A system of Nature Conservation Areas was proposed in 1986, and a Coastal Zone Management Plan was prepared during 1986–1992. These proposals are now the responsibility of the Ministry of Regional Municipalities and Environment, and legislation which will enable this Ministry to designate Nature Conservation Areas is currently being studied.

The Juzor ad Daymaniyat and the Turtle Reserve at Ra's al Junayz are protected by order of the Diwan of Royal Court and administered by the Ministry of Regional Municipalities and Environment; guards on the Juzor ad Daymaniyat are from the Coastguard Section of the Royal Oman Navy. The bird sanctuaries at Khawr Salalah, Al Qurm and Khawr Kashmir, the White Oryx Project on the Jiddat al Harasis and the Wadi Sarin Tahr Reserve in the Hajar ash Sharqi mountains are all under the control of the Office of the Adviser for the Conservation of the Environment of the Diwan of Royal Court; all are proposed National Nature Reserves and are monitored by guards.

INTERNATIONAL MEASURES RELEVANT TO THE CONSERVATION OF SITES

The Sultanate has ratified the World Heritage Convention and the Action Plan of the Regional Convention for Co-operation on the Protection of the Environment from Marine Pollution, and has signed the Biodiversity Convention, but it is not a signatory to the Ramsar Convention or the Bonn Convention. Oman has not designated any natural World Heritage Sites or Biosphere Reserves; however a large area of the central desert region has been proposed as a natural World Heritage Site.

OVERVIEW OF THE INVENTORY

The inventory covers 33 sites with a total area of c.75,000 km^2, or about 23% of the total area of Oman. Only four of the sites—Khawr Salalah, Al Qurm, Khawr Kashmir and the Juzor ad Daymaniyat—are currently protected, but almost all of the sites lie within the proposed system of Nature Conservation Areas and/or have been identified and incorporated within the proposed Coastal Zone Management Plan.

A large proportion of the sites are coastal, with an excellent coverage of Oman's seabird breeding areas and the mainland khawrs. Mountain and desert habitats are covered by a smaller number of much larger, representative sites.

ACKNOWLEDGEMENTS

The introduction and site accounts were compiled from material supplied by the Office of the Adviser for Conservation of the Environment of the Diwan of Royal Court (R. H. Daly) and by the Oman Bird Records Committee of the Oman Bird Group (R. H. Daly, M. D. Gallagher, Dr J. Eriksen, Prof. C. H. Fry and M. Cummins). The text was reviewed and revised by the Department of Awareness and Guidance of the Ministry of Regional Municipalities and Environment, and incorporates amendments by the Department's experts, coordinated by Dr S. A. Al Muscati (Director General of Public Relations and Guidance) and assisted by the National Survey Authority. The major assistance of the Office of the Adviser for Conservation of the Environment of the Diwan of Royal Court is gratefully acknowledged. S. Albrecht assisted with the initial compilation of data.

SITE INVENTORY

Site no.	Site name	Region	Criteria used to select site: 1	2i	2ii	2iii	3	4	5i	5ii	6	0
001	Musandam Islands	MD	—	•	—	—	•	•	—	—	—	—
002	Musandam Area	MD	—	—	—	—	—	•	—	—	—	—
003	Khawr Kalba	BT	—	—	—	—	•	—	—	—	—	—
004	Khawr Shinas and Khawr Liwa	BT	—	•	—	—	•	—	—	—	—	—
005	Sun Farms, Sohar	BT	•	—	—	—	•	—	—	—	—	—
006	Al Batinah Coast	BT	—	•	—	—	—	—	—	—	—	—
007	Juzor ad Daymaniyat	MS	—	•	—	—	•	•	—	—	—	—
008	Ra's as Sawadi–Juzor as Sawadi	BT	—	—	—	—	•	—	—	—	—	—
009	Jazirat al Fahl	MS	—	—	—	—	•	—	—	—	—	—
010	Al Qurm	MS	—	—	—	—	—	—	•	—	•	—
011	Bandar Jussah	MS	—	—	—	—	•	•	—	—	—	—
012	Ra's Abu Da'ud	MS	—	—	—	—	•	•	—	—	—	—
013	Quriyat–Daghmar	MS	•	•	—	—	•	•	—	—	—	—
014	Al Jabal al Akhdar	DK, BT	—	—	—	—	•	•	—	—	—	—
015	Ra's al Hadd	SH	—	•	—	—	—	•	—	—	—	—
016	Barr al Hikman	WS, SH	•	•	•	—	•	•	—	—	—	—
017	Masirah	SH	•	•	•	—	•	•	—	—	—	—
018	Hamar an Nafur	WS	—	•	—	—	—	•	—	—	—	—
019	Jiddat al Harasis	WS	•	—	—	—	—	—	—	—	—	—
020	Ad Duqm	WS	—	•	—	—	—	•	—	—	—	—
021	Khawr Dhirif	WS	•	•	—	—	•	•	—	—	—	—
022	Ar Rub al Khali	DF, WS	—	—	—	—	—	•	•	—	—	—
023	Khawr Ghawi	WS	—	•	—	—	—	—	—	—	—	—
024	Juzor al Halaaniyaat	DF	—	•	—	—	—	•	—	—	—	—
025	Jabal Samhan	DF	—	—	—	—	—	•	—	—	—	—
026	Wadi Darbat	DF	•	•	—	—	•	•	—	—	—	—
027	Khawr Rawri	DF	•	•	—	—	•	•	—	—	—	—
028	Khawr Hassan	DF	•	•	—	—	—	•	—	—	—	—
029	Khawr ad Dahariz	DF	•	•	—	—	•	•	—	—	—	—
030	Khawr Salalah	DF	—	•	—	—	•	—	—	—	•	—
031	Jazirat Hino	DF	—	•	—	—	—	•	—	—	—	—
032	Khawr al Mughsayl	DF	•	•	—	—	•	•	—	—	—	—
033	Jabal al Qamar	DF	—	—	—	—	—	•	—	—	—	—

Key to regions

BT Al Batinah Region
DF Dhofar Governorate
DK Ad Dakhliyah Region
MD Musandam Governorate
MS Muscat Governorate
SH Ash Sharqiyah Region
WS Al Wustta Region

Key to criteria

1 Regularly holds a significant number of a globally threatened species.
2i Regularly holds 1% or more of a species' biogeographical or flyway or Middle Eastern population (waterbirds and seabirds only).
2ii Regularly holds 20,000 or more waterbirds.
2iii Migratory 'bottleneck' site: more than 3,000 raptors or more than 5,000 storks or more than 2,000 cranes pass in a season.
3 Regularly holds a significant number of a species which is threatened or declining within the Middle East. Only the top five sites for each such species in the country are considered to qualify as IBAs.
4 Regularly holds a significant number of a species whose world population is wholly or largely restricted to the Middle East. Only the top five sites for each such species in the country are considered to qualify as IBAs.
5i Representative example of a habitat, associated with a characteristic assemblage of bird species.
5ii Rare/threatened/unique habitat, associated with a characteristic assemblage of bird species.
6 Site important for bird conservation through education/research/tourism.
0 Selected for other reasons. See 'Comments on the inventory'.

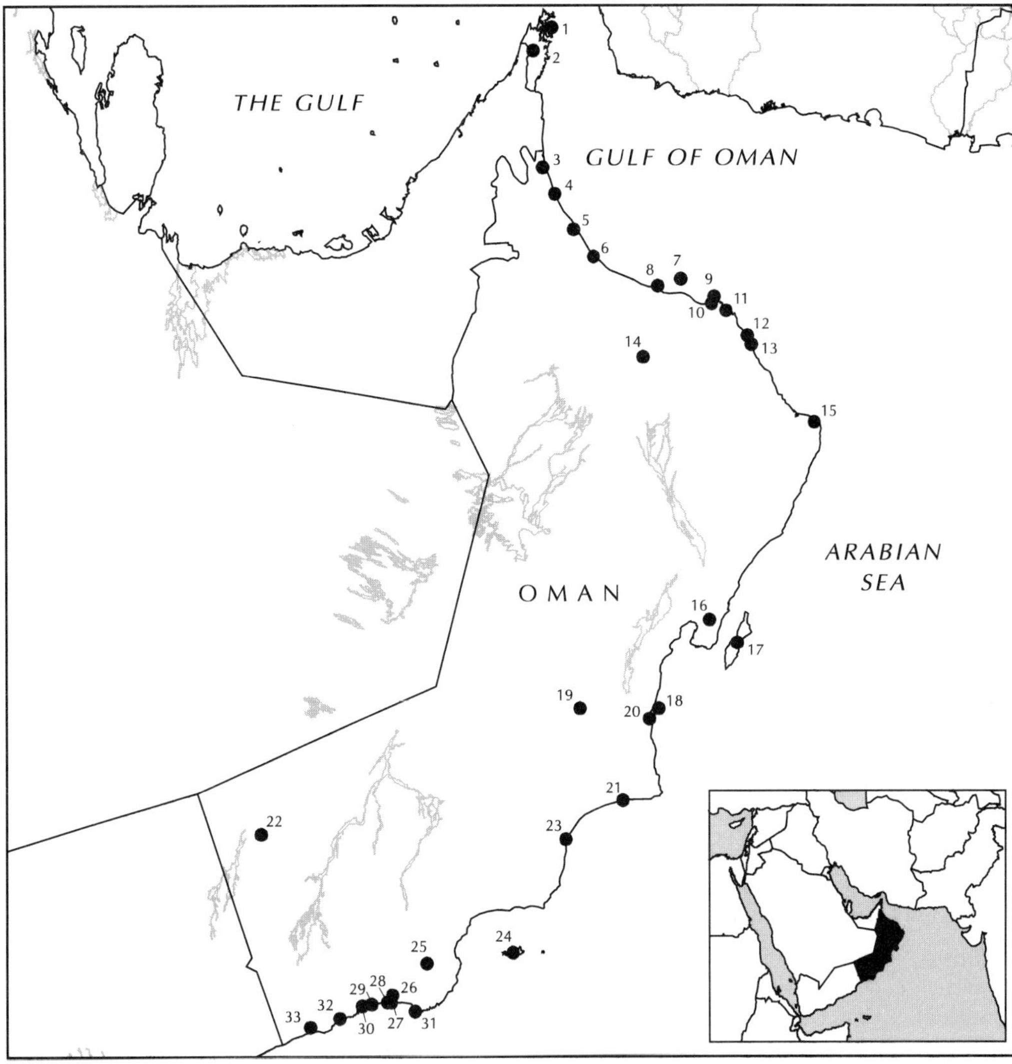

Comments on the inventory

1. All counts/figures are daily maximum counts of individuals (not pairs) seen, unless otherwise stated; winter counts are from the month of January, unless otherwise stated.
2. Due to the proximity of major tanker lanes, major oil pollution is potentially a threat to virtually all coastal sites, especially seabird feeding sites, near seabird breeding sites, and at extensive intertidal flats/sheltered areas. Small-scale oil pollution from tanker-washings and release of ballast is frequent along the Omani coast. These factors should be taken into account when reading the accounts for coastal sites.
3. The great majority of the ornithological data quoted in the inventory date from the 1980s onwards.
4. The daily maximum counts for concentrations of seabird species feeding or moving offshore (usually associated with areas of upwelling) are likely to be severe underestimates of the total sizes of the populations involved.
5. Arabic place names have been used wherever possible, following especially the 1:1,300,000 National Survey Authority map (Series Oman Misc. 06, edition 03–NSAO [1992]).

Glossary

bandar, bay
ghubbat, gulf
jabal, mountain
jazirat, island
jibal, mountains
juzor, islands
khawr, tidal inlet or coastal lagoon
ra's, point or headland
sabkha, saline mudflat
wadi, drainage line or bed of seasonal river

001 **Musandam Islands** (Musandam Governorate)

Unprotected (proposed Nature Conservation Areas)

26°13′N 56°29′E
c.1,000 ha

Site description

At least 16 rugged, rather barren islands offshore of the Musandam region (mainly to the north and east), together with their surrounding seas. See 'Conservation issues' for names and areas.

Birds

See box for key species. Jazirat Umm al Fayyarin is the most important seabird breeding island in the Musandam region, but six of the other islands add significantly to the diversity of breeding seabirds covered by the proposed system of Nature Conservation Areas. Notable concentrations of feeding seabirds also occur in the rich seas offshore during migration seasons and in winter. *Sterna anaethetus* nests in important numbers on Jazirat Umm al Fayyarin, and other breeding species include *Phaethon aethereus* (confirmed or suspected on all of the islands; daily max. 100 birds, outside breeding season in January), *Egretta gularis* (20 pairs, on Jazirat Lima), *Pandion haliaetus* (c.30 pairs on all Musandam islands; 8–9 pairs on the seven most important breeding seabird islands), *Falco concolor* (2 pairs) and abundant *Apus pallidus*. Notable passage migrants include *Larus ridibundus* (abundant in winter) and *Larus genei* (min. 450, November).

Other threatened/endemic wildlife

None known to BirdLife International.

Conservation issues

There are (or were) feral goats on Bu Rashid (Tawakkul). The speed and volume of small boat traffic apparently disturbs feeding flocks of *Phalacrocorax nigrogularis* significantly. Oil pollution from tanker washings is frequent despite the efforts of Coastguards to prevent violation of the international maritime legislation to which Oman is a signatory; the site lies next to a major tanker lane. Six of the seven most important islands for breeding birds are proposed National Nature Reserves (totalling 630 ha), as follows (proposed areas include sea and sublittoral habitat 200 m beyond low water mark): Jazirat Abu Sir (Jazirat Fujar, 150 ha), Jazirat al Khayl (Jazirat Kun, 300 ha), Bu Rashid (Tawakkul, As Suwayq, 50 ha), Jazirat as Salamah (Jazirat Quwayn al Kabir, 60 ha), Fanaku (20 ha) and Jazirat Umm al Fayyarin (50 ha). The seventh such island, Jazirat Lima (c.40 ha), is not part of a proposed Nature Conservation Area.

Regionally threatened or declining species

Phalacrocorax nigrogularis	Thousands of non-breeding birds roost on ledges of coastal cliffs (mainland and islands) during spring and summer. The maximum count of 2,000 (October) is an underestimate of the numbers present.
Falco concolor	Scarce summer visitor (2 pairs).

Species restricted wholly or largely to the Middle East

Puffinus persicus	Common passage migrant, feeding offshore (min. 325, November).
Phalacrocorax nigrogularis	Common non-breeding visitor (see above).
Sterna repressa	Common passage migrant (max. 1,500, October).

1% or more of population

	Breeding (pairs)	Wintering	Passage
Phaethon aethereus	?20+	100	—
Sterna hirundo	—	—	326 (Nov)
Sterna anaethetus	4,000–5,000	—	—

002 **Musandam Area** (Musandam Governorate)

Unprotected (proposed Nature Conservation Areas)

26°00′N 56°15′E
163,500 ha

Site description

A mountain landscape (up to 2,087 m) of stark grandeur, with a tortuous peninsula at the northern end where the mountains sink precipitously into the Strait of Hormuz, creating a tortuous coastline with fjord-like drowned valleys. The mountains contain plateaus and flat-bottomed wadis with some cultivation. Surface water is very scarce. Vegetation above 1,000 m is dominated by shrubs *Dodonaea viscosa* and *Amygdalus arabica* and a relict *Artemisia* steppe. Below 1,000 m the slopes have a thin covering of grass, and a sparse shrubland of *Acacia tortilis*, *Ficus salicifolia* and *Ziziphus spina-christi* occurs along drainage lines. Human settlement is limited to several, small coastal villages and mountain localities, some seasonally occupied. Local Shihuh and Kumzari people still follow their traditional ways of life based on fishing; the Shihuh also practise opportunistic pastoralism, with some subsistence farming inland in the mountains during the hotter months. There is also some irrigation cultivation in wadis. The road system has been much expanded in recent years.

Birds

See box for key species. There is a good selection of restricted-range birds. Other species known or expected to breed (not all proven) include *Alectoris chukar* (common resident; the only site in Oman) and *Anthus similis*. Other wintering birds include large numbers of *Alcedo atthis* on the rocky shores. Raptor migration is known to occur in spring and autumn on at least a small scale, but has not been investigated in detail (it is unclear whether more than 3,000 birds pass per season); the main species involved appears to be *Aquila nipalensis*. At least 180 species occur overall; coverage of the area has been limited.

Other threatened/endemic wildlife

Mammals: *Panthera pardus* (rare), *Caracal caracal* (rare), *Gazella gazella* (V) and possibly *Canis lupus* (V). Species or subspecies that are endemic or near-endemic to Oman are particularly common, including at least two plants and four lizards.

Species restricted wholly or largely to the Middle East	
Ammoperdix heyi	Uncommon resident (30, November).
Otus brucei	Probably resident (3, November).
Oenanthe xanthoprymna	Common winter visitor.
Oenanthe picata	Regular winter visitor (6, December).
Oenanthe monacha	Probably a scarce resident (1, November).
Oenanthe alboniger	Common resident.
Phylloscopus neglectus	Winter visitor (20, December).
Carpospiza brachydactyla	Occasionally common breeding summer visitor (70+ birds, April) and common passage migrant.

Conservation issues

The difficult terrain, isolation and low human population density have so far largely protected the area from human impact. This site comprises four proposed Nature Conservation Areas: Musandam Peninsula National Scenic Reserve (15,800 ha), Jabal Letub National Nature Reserve (8,900 ha), Sal al A'la National Nature Reserve (6,800 ha) and Musandam National Resource Reserve (132,000 ha).

003 **Khawr Kalba** (Al Batinah Region)

Unprotected

24°54′N 56°22′E
c.50 ha

Site description

A tidal inlet on the Oman/UAE border on the northern Batinah coast, lined with extensive mangrove *Avicennia*. Most of the site is in the UAE, but the southern end extends into Oman at Khatmat Milahah.

Birds

See box for key species. *Todirhamphus chloris kalbaensis* is resident, and endangered due to its total dependence on the mangrove habitat. *Hippolais rama* probably breeds.

Other threatened/endemic wildlife

None known to BirdLife International.

Regionally threatened or declining species	
Todirhamphus chloris	Resident. The subspecies *T. c. kalbaensis* has a world population of perhaps less than 50 birds and is virtually confined to this site.

Conservation issues

Despite the efforts of the local municipality, garbage dumping occurs in some khawrs. Awareness efforts or other measures will be intensified in the future to prevent tree-cutting, land-claim and disturbance of birds.

Further reading

Cowles (1980).

004 **Khawr Shinas and Khawr Liwa** (Al Batinah Region)

Khawr Liwa also known as Khawr Nabr

Unprotected (proposed Nature Conservation Areas)

24°39′N 56°31′E
4,400 ha

Site description

Two extensive tidal inlets on the northern Batinah coast, which support extensive mangrove *Avicennia*, and are near the towns of Shinas and Liwa respectively.

Birds

See box for key species. The endangered subspecies *Todirhamphus chloris kalbaensis* occurs irregularly in the mangrove as a non-breeder. *Hippolais rama* probably breeds. Roosting *Larus ichthyaetus* (max. 103), *L. ridibundus* and *L. cachinnans*/*L. argentatus* occur at the khawrs and on nearby beaches in winter. A total of 118 species has been recorded.

1% or more of population

	Breeding (pairs)	Wintering	Passage
Larus ridibundus	—	c.2,500	—
Larus cachinnans/L. argentatus	—	c.1,400	—

Regionally threatened or declining species

Todirhamphus chloris	The subspecies *T. c. kalbaensis* occurs irregularly (eight records, all of single birds), but is not suspected of breeding; otherwise known only from Khawr Kalba, site 003).

Other threatened/endemic wildlife

None known to BirdLife International.

Conservation issues

Despite the efforts of the local municipality, garbage dumping still occurs in some khawrs. The area is covered by two proposed Nature Conservation Areas: Khawr Shinas National Nature Reserve (2,100 ha) and Khawr Nabr National Nature Reserve (2,300 ha).

005 **Sun Farms, Sohar** (Al Batinah Region)

Unprotected

24°19´N 56°45´E
500 ha

Site description

Large agricultural fields irrigated by rotary gantries on the Batinah coast.

Birds

See box for key species. Large numbers of birds are attracted to the water, greenery and spilt grain during migration and winter; at least 149 species occur. Other notable species wintering or dispersing after the breeding season include *Melanocorypha bimaculata* (200, February), *Calandrella brachydactyla* (500, January) and *Emberiza striolata* (60, December). Notable species on passage or during the post-breeding season include *Falco amurensis* (133, April–May), *Pterocles exustus* (1,000, August), *Coracias benghalensis* (500, November), *Merops superciliosus* (400, August) and *Anthus campestris* (100, November).

Globally threatened species

Aquila heliaca	Winter visitor (3, January).
Falco naumanni	Common spring passage migrant (66, May).
Vanellus gregarius	Winter visitor (3, January).

Regionally threatened or declining species

Neophron percnopterus	Passage migrant (22, September).

Other threatened/endemic wildlife

None known to BirdLife International.

006 **Al Batinah Coast** (Al Batinah Region)

c.50 ha protected (proposed Nature Conservation Areas)

24°03´N 57°02´E
c.9,000 ha

Site description

About 300 km of exposed, sand beach facing the Gulf of Oman, extending from As Seeb north-west to Shinas. Khawrs (creeks) frequently occur at the mouths of drainage lines; most are transitory, appearing and disappearing according to the occurrence of strong tides and wadi-floods. The following major khawrs occur within this area, but are dealt with separately due to their ornithological importance: Kalba (site 003), Shinas and Liwa (004), Ra's/Juzor as Sawadi (008) and Al Qurm (010).

Birds

See box for key species. Important numbers of waterbirds occur in winter, especially large numbers of *Calidris alba* and roosting gulls and terns; the latter often concentrate at the small khawrs.

1% or more of population

	Breeding (pairs)	Wintering	Passage
Calidris alba	—	2,500+	—
Larus hemprichii	—	800	—
Larus ichthyaetus	—	3,800	—
Larus ridibundus	—	c.35,000	—
Larus genei	—	1,600	—
Larus canus	—	1,700	—
Larus cachinnans/L. argentatus	—	c.4,000	—
Sterna bengalensis	—	850	—
Sterna sandvicensis	—	900	—

Other threatened/endemic wildlife

None known to BirdLife International.

Conservation issues

Khawr Kashmir is maintained as a bird sanctuary by the Office of the Adviser for the Conservation of the Environment of the Diwan of Royal Court. There are seven proposed Nature Conservation Areas within this site, totalling 860 ha: three National Nature Reserves, three National Resource Reserves, and one National Scenic Reserve.

007 **Juzor ad Daymaniyat** (Muscat Governorate) 23°51´N 58°05´E
Land area (<100 ha) protected (proposed Nature Conservation Area) 20,300 ha (mainly sea)

Site description
A group of 13 islands extending westward from Jazirat ad Dimaniyah (23°50´N 58°10´E) to Jazirat Jun (23°50´N 57°59´E), in the Gulf of Oman north-west of As Seeb, with surrounding coral reefs, shoals and rocky outcrops. The islands themselves have a total area of less than 100 ha.

Birds
See box for key species. The second most important seabird breeding colonies in Oman after the Juzor al Halaaniyaat (site 024). Other breeding species include *Phaethon aethereus* (6–13 pairs; max. 32 birds offshore in July), *Egretta gularis* (6 pairs), *Pandion haliaetus* (min. 4 pairs), *Sterna bergii* (2+ pairs) and *Anous stolidus* (c.30 pairs; max. 200 birds offshore, May).

1% or more of population

	Breeding (pairs)	Wintering	Passage
Larus hemprichii	110–200	—	—
Sterna dougallii	70–135	—	—
Sterna anaethetus	6,800–9,300	—	—

Regionally threatened or declining species

Falco concolor	Summer visitor. The most important breeding site in Oman (27–35+ pairs, with some evidence of decline since a 1978 survey; daily max. 70 birds, September).
Sterna dougallii	Summer visitor (see above). The most important breeding site in Oman and Arabia.

Species restricted wholly or largely to the Middle East

Larus hemprichii	Resident (see above).
Sterna repressa	Summer visitor (580–1,125 pairs).

Other threatened/endemic wildlife
Reptiles: sea-turtles *Eretmochelys imbricata* (E) and *Chelonia mydas* (E) nest on beaches.

Conservation issues
General public access during the seabird and sea-turtle breeding season (May–October) is banned by order of the Diwan of Royal Court; licenses to visit are issued by the Ministry of Regional Municipalities and Environment. Guards are stationed on the largest island, but in spite of this overexploitation of seabird and sea-turtle eggs for food by fishermen continues to be a major problem, with resulting excessive disturbance of colonies. Visits by small boats for recreation are frequent (causing disturbance to breeding birds). Introduction of feral cats *Felis* is a critical threat. The site is a proposed National Nature Reserve.

008 **Ra's as Sawadi–Juzor as Sawadi** (Al Batinah Region) 23°47´N 57°48´E
Unprotected (proposed Nature Conservation Areas) 1,500 ha

Site description
A headland north-west of As Seeb, with a khawr and a beach, and sandbars and a group of eight islands offshore. Extensive mudflats occur in the khawr, and the headland is surrounded by sabkha and flat, sandy terrain. There are important archaeological sites of settlement on the two largest islands, more than 4,000 years old.

Birds
See box for key species. The islands are an important site for breeding *Falco concolor*. Other island-breeding species include *Egretta gularis* (c.25 pairs) and *Pandion haliaetus* (at least 2 pairs). The mudflats hold fair numbers of wintering and passage waterbirds, especially roosting gulls and terns (Laridae).

Regionally threatened or declining species

Falco concolor	Summer visitor (14–16 pairs).

Other threatened/endemic wildlife
There are some high quality coral reefs around the islands.

Conservation issues
The site (including the islands) is a very popular recreation spot; people can wade across to the islands at low tide, and excessive disturbance of nesting birds is a critical problem: the increasing number of visitors threatens the survival of the nesting colonies of *Egretta gularis* and *Falco concolor*, whose nests are destroyed or their eggs taken by fishermen. Building development is encroaching on the mainland. The area is a proposed National Scenic Reserve.

009 **Jazirat al Fahl** (Muscat Governorate)

Unprotected (proposed Nature Conservation Area)

23°41′N 58°30′E
c.600 ha

Site description

A rocky island, 77 m high, near Muscat. There is a navigation beacon on top.

Birds

See box for key species. An important site for breeding *Falco concolor*; other breeding species include *Phaethon aethereus* (8 pairs).

Regionally threatened or declining species	
Neophron percnopterus	Breeds (1 pair).
Falco concolor	Common summer visitor (6–20 pairs).

Other threatened/endemic wildlife

The sea between the island and the mainland has a particularly high coral diversity and is included within the site's area. Mammals: unidentified baleen whales *Balaenoptera* are occasionally seen feeding around the island.

Conservation issues

Disturbance of nesting birds by human activities is not significant, due to the precipitous nature of the island. The proposed Qurm–Fahal National Nature Reserve (1,000 ha) would cover both this site and the two khawrs at Al Qurm (site 010) nearby on the mainland.

010 **Al Qurm** (Muscat Governorate)

Protected (proposed Nature Conservation Area)

23°37′N 58°28′E
c.100 ha

Site description

Two rather deep and narrow tidal inlets at the mouth of Wadi Adai, within the city of Muscat, with well-developed mangrove *Avicennia* and large, sandy expanses of salt-tolerant bushes in between. There is a rocky cliff on the east side.

Birds

See box for key species. Fair numbers of waterbirds occur on passage and during winter, including *Ardea purpurea* (70, September). At least 172 species have been recorded.

Globally threatened species	
Falco naumanni	Occasional spring passage migrant (max. 35 roosting in mangrove, May).

Other threatened/endemic wildlife

None known to BirdLife International.

Conservation issues

The area is bounded by a wall-cum-fence. The proposed Qurm–Fahal National Nature Reserve (1,000 ha) covers both this site and the island of Jazirat al Fahl (site 009) close offshore.

011 **Bandar Jussah** (Muscat Governorate)

Unprotected (proposed Nature Conservation Area)

23°33′N 58°39′E
700 ha

Site description

An island and adjacent headland coastline south-east of Muscat. There are interesting archaeological sites of settlement in the proposed reserve, some more than 3,000 years old.

Birds

See box for key species. Other breeding species include *Phaethon aethereus* (4–11 pairs). The terns *Sterna* breed only on the offshore island, but *Falco concolor* also nests on the mainland cliffs, uniquely in Oman.

Regionally threatened or declining species	
Falco concolor	Summer visitor (4–5 pairs).
Sterna dougallii	Summer visitor (a few pairs).
Species restricted wholly or largely to the Middle East	
Sterna repressa	Summer visitor (several hundred pairs).

Other threatened/endemic wildlife

Reptiles: sea-turtles *Eretmochelys imbricata* (E) and *Chelonia mydas* (E) nest on small beaches on the mainland.

Conservation issues

Collection of the terns' eggs for food by local people is a critical problem; instances of the entire colony being robbed have been recorded. The area is a proposed National Scenic Reserve.

012 Ra's Abu Da'ud (Muscat Governorate)

Unprotected (proposed Nature Conservation Area)

23°19′N 58°55′E
1,500 ha

Site description

An offshore island and adjacent mainland cliffs, north-west of Quriyat. There is an as-yet-unstudied archaeological site on the island.

Birds

See box for key species.

Regionally threatened or declining species

Falco concolor	Summer visitor (3–6 pairs).

Species restricted wholly or largely to the Middle East

Sterna repressa	Summer visitor (several hundred pairs).

Other threatened/endemic wildlife

None known to BirdLife International.

Conservation issues

Eggs from the tern colony are often heavily harvested by local people, and excessive disturbance is a major threat to nesting birds. The area is a proposed National Scenic Reserve.

013 Quriyat–Daghmar (Muscat Governorate)

Unprotected (proposed Nature Conservation Area)

23°14′N 58°58′E
c.1,000 ha

Site description

A 12-km stretch of flat coastline from Quriyat south-east to Daghmar, bounded by rocky hills and backed by sabkha with sand-dunes. About five khawrs are scattered along the coarse-sand beach, of which the one on the north side of Quriyat is the largest and has the most extensive mangrove *Avicennia*. The khawr immediately to the south of Quriyat has the most extensive mudflats.

Birds

See box for key species. Other breeding species include *Vanellus indicus* (5–10 pairs). A total of 181 species has been recorded.

Globally threatened species

Aquila heliaca	Winter visitor (max. 2, February).

1% or more of population

	Breeding (pairs)	Wintering	Passage
Larus hemprichii	—	min. 450	—
Larus ichthyaetus	—	700 (Feb)	—
Larus ridibundus	—	2,800	—
Larus cachinnans/L. argentatus	—	1,300	—

Regionally threatened or declining species

Neophron percnopterus	Non-breeding visitor (max. 61, February).

Species restricted wholly or largely to the Middle East

Alectoris melanocephala	Fairly common resident in nearby hills.
Oenanthe xanthoprymna	Common winter visitor to nearby hills (max. 20, November).
Oenanthe alboniger	Common resident in nearby hills (max. 12, December).

Other threatened/endemic wildlife

Mammals: *Gazella gazella* (V).

Conservation issues

The town of Quriyat is developing and expanding rapidly, potentially threatening the integrity of the site. There is potential for conservation education, tourism and research at the khawrs next to Quriyat, given the site's proximity to Muscat. The southernmost khawr, Khuwayr, is part of the proposed Wadi Hawir National Nature Reserve (3,300 ha), but the most important khawrs around Quriyat and the rest of the coastline are not proposed as parts of Nature Conservation Areas.

014 Al Jabal al Akhdar (Ad Dakhliyah and Al Batinah Regions)

23°07′N 57°37′E
187,000 ha

Unprotected (proposed Nature Conservation Areas)

■ Site description

A huge tabular mass of uplifted and greatly hardened limestone which dominates the Hajar mountains of northern Oman, ranging from 600 m up to the twin peaks of Jabal Shams at 2,980 m, the highest in eastern Arabia. The sloping strata of this anticline form pavements which end abruptly in the precipitous northern face. The southern slopes are dissected by deep gorges and there are several springs. The *Acacia tortilis* parkland of the lowest altitudes gives way to *Euphorbia larica* shrub slopes, then on broken ground above 1,350 m to *Monotheca–Olea* woodland, and above 2,300 m to the summit zone of large *Juniperus* trees and perennial tussock grasses. Many small villages and other settlements occur in the mountains where there are adequate sources of perennial water; formerly remote, they are now being increasingly linked by graded roads. The larger settlements cultivate extensive date-palm plantations, sometimes on terraces, except at Sayq, where there are other crops, e.g. rose gardens. Pastoralism is practised wherever possible.

■ Birds

See box for key species. Other breeding species include *Circaetus gallicus* (occasional), *Hieraaetus fasciatus*, *Pterocles lichtensteinii*, *Columba palumbus*, *Anthus similis* and *Emberiza striolata*.

Regionally threatened or declining species

Neophron percnopterus	Widespread but scarce resident; large post-breeding roosts occur, e.g. 50 on Jabal Shams.
Torgos tracheliotus	Rare resident (max. 3 pairs); post-breeding roosts of up to 15 birds occur (Jabal Shams, August).

Species restricted wholly or largely to the Middle East

Alectoris melanocephala	Fairly common resident.
Ammoperdix heyi	Common resident.
Otus brucei	Scarce resident (max. 6, January).
Oenanthe monacha	Scarce resident.
Oenanthe alboniger	Widespread and common resident.

■ Other threatened/endemic wildlife

The mountain provides an important refuge for endemic and relict species: at least 14 plant species, eight reptile and three fish species or subspecies endemic, near-endemic or apparently endemic to Oman are known. Mammals: the rare ungulate *Hemitragus jayakari* (V), endemic to the northern mountains of northern Oman, still occurs as do *Gazella gazella* (V) and *Canis lupus* (V), though all are threatened.

■ Conservation issues

The area of interest encompasses five proposed Nature Conservation Areas: Wadi Bani Ghafir National Nature Reserve (37,000 ha), Jabal Shams National Nature Reserve (6,000 ha), Sayq Plateau National Nature Reserve (15,000 ha), Jabal Nakhl National Nature Reserve (46,000 ha) and Al Jabal al Akhdar National Scenic Reserve (83,000 ha).

■ Further reading

Gallagher (1977).

015 Ra's al Hadd (Ash Sharqiyah Region)

22°30′N 59°45′E
c.2,000 ha

Unprotected (proposed Nature Conservation Area)

■ Site description

Two major tidal inlets with mangrove *Avicennia*, Khawr al Jaramah and Khawr al Hajar, part of the major headland east of Sur. The intertidal flats at Khawr al Jaramah are particularly extensive.

■ Birds

See boxes for key species. Other notable wintering species include *Ardea cinerea* (89) and *Calidris alba* (800). In autumn, large numbers of migrant *Ciconia ciconia* (150, September) and *Larus argentatus* (1,600, September) rest on the intertidal flats. Marine upwelling offshore provides rich feeding grounds

1% or more of population

	Breeding (pairs)	Wintering	Passage
Haematopus ostralegus	—	470	—
Phalaropus lobatus	—	—	10,000 (May)
Larus hemprichii	—	860	—
Larus ichthyaetus	—	1,000	—
Larus ridibundus	—	3,500	—
Larus genei	—	4,700	—
Larus cachinnans/L. argentatus	—	8,000	—
Sterna bergii	—	1,200	—
Sterna sandvicensis	—	2,400	600 (Sep)
Sterna saundersi	—	—	400 (Mar)

Species restricted wholly or largely to the Middle East

Puffinus persicus	Non-breeding visitor, feeding offshore (1,000, August).
Larus hemprichii	Winter visitor (see above).
Sterna saundersi	Passage migrant (see above).

(especially in June–August) for non-breeding and passage seabirds, with large numbers of *Puffinus persicus* (see box), *Oceanites oceanicus* (400, July) and *Phalaropus lobatus* (see box). A total of 87 species has been recorded.

Other threatened/endemic wildlife

Reptiles: the most important nesting beach in Oman for the sea-turtle *Chelonia mydas* (E) lies immediately adjacent to the the south (and is protected by the Ministry of Regional Municipalities and Environment).

Conservation issues

The area lies within a proposed National Scenic Reserve (8,000 ha).

016 Barr al Hikman (Al Wustta and Ash Sharqiyah Regions)

Unprotected (proposed Nature Conservation Area)

20°38′N 58°26′E
290,000 ha

Site description

A raised, rocky limestone peninsula west of Masirah island (site 017), with c.160 km of coastline fringed by extensive inland sabkha, at least c.12,000 ha of intertidal flats and shallow seas. There are five tidal inlets; Khawr Barr al Hikman, at c.4,000 ha, is the largest khawr in Oman and the most important for birds. Up to 7 km width of mudflats is exposed at low tide; the major area (south of Khawr Barr al Hikman) is called Bayad Dimnah. Inland near the coast there are also areas of sand/gravel plain and of sand-dunes. The richest and most extensive seagrass beds in Oman grow in the bay of Ghubbat Hashish. There is much coral offshore, and the mudflats are fringed with reefs at very low tide. The area is rather isolated and sparsely populated. Fishing is the major human activity, predominantly in winter, and especially prawn fishing in Ghubbat al Hashish. Many people migrate to tend date groves north and inland in summer, when prevailing very strong, cold winds make fishing very difficult.

Birds

See boxes for key species. One of the most important coastal areas for wintering waterbirds (other than wildfowl) in western Asia, especially for waders. A survey between December 1989 and January 1990 counted at least 220,678 waterbirds of 52 species. Although the situation has not been investigated comprehensively during the migration seasons, even larger numbers of waterbirds are expected to occur in autumn than in winter, and numbers in spring are also likely to be very important. Other notable counts in winter include *Platalea leucorodia* (182), *Circus aeruginosus* (28), *Pandion haliaetus* (44), *Falco peregrinus* (8) and *Recurvirostra avosetta* (64); the peak count for *Charadrius mongolus*/*C. leschenaultii* is 10,083. On the island of Mahawt there is an isolated breeding population of *Zosterops abyssinicus*, possibly of an undescribed subspecies. A total of 119 species has been recorded.

Globally threatened species

Numenius tenuirostris	Rare winter visitor (min. 3); presumed to occur regularly.

1% or more of population

	Breeding (pairs)	Wintering	Passage
Phalacrocorax carbo	—	8,200	—
Phalacrocorax nigrogularis	—	15,000	—
Egretta gularis	c.90	1,800	—
Casmerodius albus	—	340	—
Ardea cinerea	—	c.600	—
Phoenicopterus ruber	—	c.9,300	—
Haematopus ostralegus	—	10,700	—
Dromas ardeola	—	c.3,000	—
Charadrius alexandrinus	—	c.3,500	—
Charadrius mongolus	—	c.5,000	—
Charadrius leschenaultii	—	800	—
Pluvialis squatarola	—	2,600	—
Calidris tenuirostris	—	c.1,200	—
Calidris alba	—	11,000	—
Calidris minuta	—	15,500	—
Calidris ferruginea	—	15,300	—
Calidris alpina	—	60,000	—
Limicola falcinellus	—	5,000	—
Limosa lapponica	—	50,000	—
Numenius phaeopus	—	950	—
Numenius arquata	—	1,750	—
Tringa totanus	—	c.13,200	—
Tringa nebularia	—	3,200	—
Tringa cinerea	—	c.600	—
Arenaria interpres	—	c.1,700	—
Larus hemprichii	—	28,500	—
Larus ichthyaetus	—	1,500	—
Larus genei	—	50,000	—
Larus cachinnans/L. argentatus	—	22,000	—
Sterna caspia	—	c.1,400	—
Sterna bergii	—	c.4,100	—
Sterna bengalensis	—	3,000	—
Sterna sandvicensis	—	45,000	—
Sterna hirundo	—	3,000	—
Sterna anaethetus	1,500–2,500	—	—

Regionally threatened or declining species

Phalacrocorax nigrogularis	Winter visitor in large numbers. This the most northerly locality known for the Arabian Sea population.
Sterna dougallii	Summer visitor (c.10 pairs).

Species restricted wholly or largely to the Middle East

Phalacrocorax nigrogularis	Winter visitor (see above).
Dromas ardeola	Common winter visitor (see above).
Larus hemprichii	Resident (75–100 pairs).
Sterna saundersi	Breeds on the mainland (c.20 pairs).

Other threatened/endemic wildlife

Mammals: *Gazella gazella* (V) and probably *G. subgutturosa* (rare). Reptiles: the area is an important feeding ground for at least four species of sea-turtle: *Caretta caretta* (V), *Chelonia mydas* (E), *Eretmochelys imbricata* (E), *Lepidochelys olivacea* (E) and probably *Dermochelys coriacea* (E). Offshore there is a vast monospecific reef of cabbage coral *Montipora foliosa*, possibly unique in the world.

Conservation issues

No current problems are known, and potential threats appear to be few, due to the relative isolation and low human population density of the area. The whole area is proposed as a National Nature Reserve (288,000 ha), apart from 2,000 ha of the west coast of Ghubbat Hashish.

Further reading

Green *et al.* (1992).

017 Masirah (Ash Sharqiyah Region)

Unprotected (proposed Nature Conservation Areas)

20°25′N 58°47′E
109,500 ha

Site description

Masirah is a large island c.20 km off the east coast of Oman in the Arabian Sea. The land is gently undulating with a central spine of hills (up to c.280 m) and peripheral coastal plains. The site includes the small islands of Jazirat Shaqaf (J. A'Shaghah), Jazirat ash Shi'inzi (J. Thu Khayr) and Jazirat Kalban (Qa'ad Kalban), as well as all other associated islets. The central and northern parts of the west coast have the most extensive mudflats. The east coast is mostly exposed ocean beach. Trees are few, and the plant cover is almost entirely composed of dwarf shrubs such as *Limonium*, *Suaeda* and *Arthrocnemum*. About 5,000 people live on the island, mostly in the north. Fishing is the mainstay of the local economy.

Birds

See boxes for key species. Together with the adjacent Barr al Hikman (site 016), this is one of the most important sites for wintering and migrating waterbirds in the Middle East (excepting wildfowl). Other notable species in winter include *Circus aeruginosus* (21) and *Pandion haliaetus* (58). Concentrations of feeding and moving seabirds occur off the east coast, especially during the monsoon-induced upwelling in June–August: *Bulweria fallax* (see box), *Puffinus carneipes* (200, August), *Puffinus persicus* (see box), *Oceanites oceanicus* (500, November), *Stercorarius pomarinus* (30, July), *S. parasiticus* (30, July), *Anous tenuirostris* (48 at roost, July) and *A. stolidus* (106 at roost, July). Interesting 'falls' or concentrations of Palearctic migrants occur, e.g. *Otus scops* (25, Octo-

Globally threatened species

Crex crex	Passage migrant (11 records, all but one of singles).
Chlamydotis undulata	Regular passage migrant in autumn according to local people (daily max. 4, October).

1% or more of population

	Breeding (pairs)	Wintering	Passage
Egretta gularis	20–30	424	—
Ardea cinerea	—	217	—
Ciconia ciconia	—	—	50 (Nov)
Haematopus ostralegus	—	3,000 (Dec)	—
Dromas ardeola	85	2,000 (Dec)	—
Charadrius mongolus	—	6,443	—
Charadrius leschenaultii	—	—	5,250 (Aug)
Pluvialis squatarola	—	505	1,600 (Oct)
Calidris alba	—	479	—
Calidris ferruginea	—	—	800 (Aug)
Limosa lapponica	—	2,442	—
Numenius arquata	—	620	—
Numenius phaeopus	—	278	2,000 (Aug)
Tringa totanus	—	—	2,000 (Aug)
Tringa nebularia	—	—	112 (Aug)
Arenaria interpres	—	629	—
Phalaropus lobatus	—	—	2,000 (Sep)
Larus hemprichii	5,200	3,923	—
Larus ichthyaetus	—	723	620 (Mar)
Larus genei	—	1,730	—
Larus cachinnans/L. argentatus	—	5,562	—
Sterna caspia	—	170	100 (Aug)
Sterna bergii	300	1,720	—
Sterna sandvicensis	—	1,037	4,000 (Oct)
Sterna dougallii	c.160	—	—
Sterna repressa	1,200	—	70,000 (Oct)
Sterna anaethetus	15,500	—	—
Sterna saundersi	200	—	600 (Sep)

Regionally threatened or declining species

Aythya nyroca	Passage migrant (5, November).
Neophron percnopterus	Resident (c.12 pairs).
Sterna dougallii	Local summer visitor (see above).

Species restricted wholly or largely to the Middle East

Bulweria fallax	Non-breeding visitor, feeding offshore (11, April).
Puffinus persicus	Common non-breeding visitor, feeding offshore (1,000, May).
Dromas ardeola	Breeds locally; common winter visitor (see above).
Larus hemprichii	Common resident (see above).
Sterna repressa	Local summer visitor; abundant passage migrant (see above).
Sterna saundersi	Resident (see above).

ber), *Caprimulgus europaeus* (50, October), *Merops superciliosus* (300, April–May), *Coracias garrulus* (87, April), *Acrocephalus palustris* (310, May) and *Phylloscopus sibilatrix* (30, September). A total of 298 species has been recorded, including many vagrants.

Other threatened/endemic wildlife

Mammals: *Gazella gazella* (V), *Lepus capensis jefferyi* (endemic to Masirah). Reptiles: the island is a sea-turtle breeding ground of global importance; four species breed: *Caretta caretta* (V), *Chelonia mydas* (E), *Eretmochelys imbricata* (E) and *Lepidochelys olivacea* (E). Two restricted-range lizards endemic to Oman are present.

Conservation issues

Large numbers of tern and gull eggs and gull chicks are collected for food by local people (especially from the islets of Shagaf and Shi'inzi), and given that recent reports suggest that nesting populations of most seabirds breeding on and around Masirah are declining, it would appear that over-exploitation of this resource may be a problem, as is excessive disturbance at the colonies, especially at very low tide when Shagaf and Shi'inzi can be reached by vehicles and motorcycles. Feral cats occur on the main island. The area of interest is covered by three proposed National Nature Reserves: East Masirah (4,500 ha, north-east coast and sea), South Masirah (19,000 ha, southern half of island plus sea) and Masirah Straits (86,000 ha, west coast of island and eastern half of straits, including Jazirat Shagaf).

Further reading

Curry *et al.* (1980), Pomeroy (1980), Rogers (1988).

018 Hamar an Nafur (Al Wustta Region)

Unprotected (proposed Nature Conservation Area)

19°48′N 57°48′E
12 ha

Site description

A small, isolated island rising abruptly from the sea to 98 m, 6 km due east of the village of Nafun on the mainland. The island is uninhabited and now unused by man, although guano used to be extracted.

Birds

See box for key species. *Phaethon aethereus* breeds (probably at least 7 pairs).

1% or more of population

	Breeding (pairs)	Wintering	Passage
Phalacrocorax nigrogularis	—	10,000–15,000	—

Regionally threatened or declining species

Phalacrocorax nigrogularis	Roosts in large numbers in winter at night. There are few (if any) other comparably safe roosting areas in a very wide surrounding area.

Species restricted wholly or largely to the Middle East

Phalacrocorax nigrogularis	Common winter visitor (see above).

Other threatened/endemic wildlife

Invertebrates: the seabird tick *Ornithodoros muesebecki* occurs (endemic to islands of eastern Arabia).

Conservation issues

No problems or threats are known. The site is a proposed National Nature Reserve.

Further reading

Gallagher (1993).

019 **Jiddat al Harasis** (Al Wustta Region)
Protected (proposed Nature Conservation Area)

19°48′N 56°49′E
2,750,000 ha

Site description
A limestone plateau with sandy depressions, sand/gravel plains, karst, sand-dunes, hills and escarpments, ranging from 20 to 200 m elevation. There are occasional trees and bushes of *Acacia ehrenbergiana*, *Acacia tortilis* and *Prosopis cineraria*, but the vegetation consists mainly of sparse, low shrubs and ephemeral grasses. The area is relatively well-vegetated, given the low average annual rainfall, due to regular condensation of fog moisture blowing in off the sea. Al Huqf is a low, discontinuous escarpment marking the boundary between the Jiddat al Harasis and the depression of sabkha and low hills which continues eastward to the coast; water seepages occur along it. Al Huqf is an important refuge for animals, permitting the penetration far northward of some species otherwise limited to Dhofar. The main land-use is nomadic pastoralism. There are major oilfields south-west of the area.

Birds
See box for key species. A diverse assemblage of desert breeding birds, including *Aquila chrysaetos*, *Chlamydotis undulata*, *Burhinus capensis*, *Pterocles coronatus*, *P. exustus*, *Tyto alba*, *Athene noctua*, *Eremopterix nigriceps*, *Eremalauda dunni*, *Ammomanes cincturus* and *Alaemon alaudipes*.

Globally threatened species

Chlamydotis undulata	Frequently recorded resident and winter visitor; thought to be the most important breeding site in Oman.

Other threatened/endemic wildlife
Mammals: *Canis lupus* (V), *Caracal caracal* (rare), *Capra nubiana* (I), *Gazella gazella* (V), *G. subgutturosa* (rare) and *Oryx leucoryx* (re-introduced). Reptiles: the endemic lizard *Uromastyx thomasi* occurs. Flora: several plants endemic to Oman are virtually restricted to this site.

Conservation issues
The White Oryx Project, based at Jaaluni since 1979, is operated by the Office of the Adviser for Conservation of the Environment of the Diwan of Royal Court. *Oryx leucoryx* has been successfully reintroduced at this site and is now breeding freely in the wild; the oryx are guarded by patrols of rangers recruited from the local people, which gives protection to bird populations. The area is a proposed National Nature Reserve and part of the proposed natural World Heritage Site (see also sites 021, 023).

020 **Ad Duqm** (Al Wustta Region)
Unprotected

19°42′N 57°41′E
c.1,000 ha

Site description
A shallow, sandy bay (Ghubbat Quwayrat) with coastal lagoons and extensive intertidal flats, and sand/gravel terrain of low hills, ridges and escarpments inland. There are relatively few and small settlements in this region, apart from the town of Ad Duqm (which is developing and expanding, away from the coast), and human population density is low. Major human uses of the area are fishing and pastoralism (goats).

Birds
See box for key species. An important site for wintering waterbirds (apart from wildfowl), even though this coast is little known ornithologically. Other notable wintering species include *Casmerodius albus* (30), *Platalea leucorodia* (212, February), *Phoenicopterus ruber* (3,000), *Pandion haliaetus* (31) and *Recurvirostra avosetta* (175). A total of 77 bird species has been recorded.

1% or more of population

	Breeding (pairs)	Wintering	Passage
Phalacrocorax nigrogularis	—	15,000	—
Egretta gularis	—	250	—
Ardea cinerea	—	253	—
Larus hemprichii	—	1,200	—
Larus ichthyaetus	—	820	—
Larus genei	—	5,000 (Feb)	—
Larus cachinnans/L. argentatus	—	3,000 (Dec)	—
Sterna sandvicensis	—	2,300	—
Sterna caspia	—	196	—
Sterna bergii	—	620	—

Regionally threatened or declining species

Phalacrocorax nigrogularis	Winter visitor in large numbers (see above).

Species restricted wholly or largely to the Middle East

Phalacrocorax nigrogularis	Winter visitor (see above).
Larus hemprichii	Winter visitor in large numbers.

Other threatened/endemic wildlife
None known to BirdLife International.

021 Khawr Dhirif (Al Wustta Region)

Unprotected (proposed Nature Conservation Area)

18°56′N 57°21′E
100 ha

Site description

A major lagoon (900 × 600 m) on the Sahil al Jazir coastal plain, land-locked and predominantly freshwater, and surrounded by flat, sandy terrain including dunes. Aquatic vegetation includes *Potamogeton* and *Ruppia*; salt-tolerant dwarf shrubs and woody-based herbs are abundant around the site, becoming sparse away from the water. Human population density is low. Nomadic pastoralism is widely practised, and fishing is important in the coastal people's economy.

Birds

See box for key species. The site is rich in duck and roosting seabirds and shorebirds in winter and during migration. Up to c.600 duck occur in winter (the highest number in central Oman), including *Aythya nyroca* (see box), as well as good numbers of gulls and terns: *Larus cachinnans/L. argentatus* (140, January), *Sterna nilotica* (50, November), *S. caspia* (80, January), *S. bergii* (300, May) and *S. sandvicensis* (350, January). At least 121 species have been recorded, though the site is rather underwatched due to its remoteness.

Globally threatened species

Chlamydotis undulata — Rare winter visitor in the surrounding desert (2, October).

1% or more of population

	Breeding (pairs)	Wintering	Passage
Aythya nyroca	—	—	15 (Nov)

Regionally threatened or declining species

Aythya nyroca — Passage migrant (see above).

Species restricted wholly or largely to the Middle East

Larus hemprichii — Winter visitor (300).
Sterna saundersi — The only confirmed mainland nesting area (max. 60 birds, May).

Other threatened/endemic wildlife

Mammals: *Gazella gazella* (V) is regularly seen. Flora: the terrestrial vegetation shows a high degree of endemism.

Conservation issues

The area is part of the proposed North Jazir National Nature Reserve (15,000 ha) which is part of the proposed natural World Heritage Site (see also sites 019 and 023).

022 Ar Rub al Khali (Dhofar Governorate and Al Wustta Region)

Unprotected (proposed Nature Conservation Area)

18°37′N 52°48′E
3,430,000 ha

Site description

Sand desert of linear and crescent dunes up to 70 m high with broad swales between dunes, and gently undulating plains and low hills of sand and gravel along the margins. Dominant vegetation is a sparse, low shrubland of *Prosopis cineraria*; after good rains the dunes support a good cover of perennials such as *Calligonum* bushes, *Tribulus*, sedges *Cyperus* and grass *Stipagrostis*. There are no permanent settlements apart from artificial oases at Montasar (Montesar) (19°27′N 54°37′E) and Dawkah (Dauka) (18°40′N 54°04′E) which are fed by permanently flowing boreholes (the water is sulphurous and unsuitable for agriculture). Similar pools are also found at Fasad (South) and in the Muqshin area. Nomadic pastoralism is the dominant human activity. Major oilfields and important archaeological sites occur in the area.

Birds

See box for key species. A representative desert bird community. The following species are known or presumed to breed in the area (counts in brackets refer to individuals unless stated otherwise): *Buteo rufinus* (30–34), *Aquila chrysaetos* (7–8), *Pterocles coronatus* (250+), *P. senegallus* (5,000–6,500), *P. exustus* (100, April) and *Eremalauda dunni* (8 pairs, March). There is a strong passage of *Acrocephalus palustris* in spring. There was an intensive ringing study of bird migration at Dawkah in spring 1992.

Species restricted wholly or largely to the Middle East

Hippolais languida — Spring passage migrant in good numbers (daily max. 15).
Carpospiza brachydactyla — Irregular passage migrant (2–3, May).

Other threatened/endemic wildlife

Mammals: *Gazella gazella* (V) and *G. subgutturosa* (rare) occur; the latter is the more common.

Conservation issues

The area is a proposed National Resource Reserve.

Further reading

Ash and Nikolaus (in prep.)

023 Khawr Ghawi (Al Wustta Region)

18°34´N 56°38´E
c.1,000 ha

also known as Khawr Shumayr
Unprotected (proposed Nature Conservation Area)

Site description

A 6-km-long tidal inlet parallel to the coast, open to the sea at the northern end and protected by a long, sandy barrier beach, with extensive intertidal mudflats and minimal build-up of fresh water. The site is sheltered by dunes with much shrubby salt-tolerant vegetation, otherwise the surroundings are very flat and sandy. Human population density is generally low in the region, although the small, new township of Al Kahil is nearby. People fish offshore for local markets, and there may be some recreational use by expatriates from southern oil-fields.

Birds

See box for key species. The site supports far greater numbers of wintering and passage waterbirds than any khawr further south in Oman. Other notable wintering species include *Platalea leucorodia* (max. 110), *Phoenicopterus ruber* (1,500, November), *Pandion haliaetus* (21, February), *Recurvirostra avosetta* (104), *Calidris ferruginea* (3,000, December) and *Arenaria interpres* (234). The site is rather underwatched due to its remoteness.

1% or more of population

	Breeding (pairs)	Wintering	Passage
Egretta gularis	—	1,121	—
Ardea cinerea	—	124	—
Calidris alba	—	1,500 (Dec)	—
Calidris minuta	—	1,500 (Dec)	—
Calidris alpina	—	4,000 (Nov)	—
Larus genei	—	2,100	—
Larus cachinnans/L. argentatus	—	500 (Dec)	—
Sterna caspia	—	191	—

Other threatened/endemic wildlife

None known to BirdLife International.

Conservation issues

The area is part of the proposed South Jazir National Nature Reserve (18,000 ha) which is part of the proposed natural World Heritage Site (see also sites 019 and 021).

024 Juzor al Halaaniyaat (Dhofar Governorate)

17°30´N 55°58´E
10,200 ha

formerly known as Kuria Muria Islands
Unprotected (proposed Nature Conservation Areas)

Site description

A group of four main islands of mostly very rugged topography off the Dhofar coast, up to 500 m high, although there are some flat areas. There is a massive limestone cliff on the north-east point of Al Hallaniyah island. Most of the land is bare or supports only a very sparse, low shrub layer; the islands of Jazirat al Qibliyah and Jazirat al Hasikiyah are lightly covered in bird guano. The islands are in the centre of a zone of strong upwelling of cold, nutrient-rich water during the south-west monsoon of May–September (especially June–August), when seas are very rough and very strong winds, driving spray and mist prevail. The only habitation is a village at the western end of Al Hallaniyah (c.150 people), with an airstrip. Local people have boats and visit all the islands, weather permitting.

Birds

See box for key species. A very important breeding site for seabirds, and the surrounding seas also provide very important feeding grounds for pelagic species visiting from the southern oceans. Other breeding species include *Pandion haliaetus* (8+ pairs), and *Bulweria fallax* may breed (see below). Non-breeding seabirds attracted to the upwelling include *Puffinus carneipes* (common), *P. pacificus* (infrequent), *Oceanites oceanicus* (abundant) and *Sula leucogaster* (rare). The site is not visited very often due to its isolation, remoteness and the difficulty of access during the hazardous south-west monsoon, and knowledge is thus incomplete.

Other threatened/endemic wildlife

Mammals: large numbers of cetaceans occur offshore, including a probable breeding population of *Megaptera novaeangliae* (V). Reptiles: a few sea-turtles *Chelonia mydas* (E) nest on the beaches. Flora: three plant species with very restricted ranges (apparently endemic to Oman) occur, as does a rare lichen *Simonyiella*.

Conservation issues

Islanders and visiting fishermen take eggs and adults

1% or more of population

	Breeding (pairs)	Wintering	Passage
Phaethon aethereus	300	—	—
Sula dactylatra	8,250–13,250	—	—
Phalacrocorax nigrogularis	3,000-5,000	—	—
Larus hemprichii	5,000–10,000+	—	—
Sterna bergii	c.3,100	—	—
Sterna anaethetus	c.2,000	—	—

Regionally threatened or declining species

Phalacrocorax nigrogularis	The only known breeding site in Oman (see above).

Species restricted wholly or largely to the Middle East

Bulweria fallax	Occurs offshore in large numbers (max. 200, May) and it is possible that it breeds at this site between June and November. However several searches have failed to find any evidence at all.
Puffinus persicus	The only known breeding site for this species is the cliffs on Al Hallaniyah; numbers of breeders are unknown, but many thousands occur offshore during the summer monsoon, the presumed breeding season.
Phalacrocorax nigrogularis	The only known breeding site in Oman (see above).
Larus hemprichii	Resident (see above).
Oenanthe lugentoides	Resident.

of *Sula dactylatra* and *Sterna bergii* and eggs of *Phalacrocorax nigrogularis* and *Larus hemprichii* for food: this over-exploitation may have reached critical levels, with attendant disturbance and persecution of nesting birds. Introduced mammals are a major problem and include feral goats (on Al Hallaniyah: supported by brackish seepages inland), feral cats (on Al Hallaniyah and Jazirat as Sawda) and rats (*Rattus norvegicus* on Jazirat al Hasikiyah and *Rattus rattus* on Al Hallaniyah). At present there are no control or removal measures in place. The area comprises four proposed National Nature Reserves (defined areas include surrounding seas to 500 m beyond the low water mark): Jazirat al Qibliyah (800 ha), Al Hallaniyah (7,000 ha), Jazirat as Sawda (2,000 ha) and Jazirat al Hasikiyah (400 ha). The proposed reserves cover all the important seabird nesting sites.

Further reading

Bailey (1966), Gallagher (1985).

025 Jabal Samhan (Dhofar Governorate)

Unprotected (proposed Nature Conservation Area)

17°24′N 54°53′E
346,000 ha

Site description

A tract of elevated limestone highlands, rising abruptly as an escarpment from the coastal plain and sloping more gently towards the interior plains, everywhere deeply incised by tortuous canyons and ravines, up to 1,000 m deep and often very steep or vertical. Elevations range from sea-level up to c.1,800 m. The mountain lies parallel to the south-west monsoon winds of summer, and the vegetation does not benefit as much from their moisture as the mountains of Jabal al Qara and Jabal al Qamar to the west. The vegetation is mostly a sparse, low shrub layer typified by *Euphorbia balsamifera*, with grass and occasional trees or bushes of *Acacia*, *Commiphora*, *Boswellia*, *Boscia* and *Dracaena*. This is unusually wild and uninhabited country, with no settlements and few motorable tracks: most of the area is impassable by road and is relatively little used by pastoralists (otherwise the main land-use in the region). There are at least two antiquity sites.

Birds

See box for key species. A very important natural wildlife refuge. It is mostly unexplored due to the extreme difficulty of access.

Species restricted wholly or largely to the Middle East

Alectoris melanocephala	Fairly common resident.
Rhynchostruthus socotranus	Uncommon resident (one of the largest populations in Oman).

Other threatened/endemic wildlife

Flora: there is a high degree of endemism. Mammals: the major Omani populations of *Panthera pardus* (rare) and *Capra nubiana* (I) are here. *Vulpes cana* (K), *Gazella gazella* (V) and possibly *Canis lupus* (V) also occur.

Conservation issues

The area is a proposed National Nature Reserve.

026 **Wadi Darbat** (Dhofar Governorate)

Unprotected (proposed Nature Conservation Area)

17°06′N 54°27′E
78,000 ha

Site description

A wadi in the eastern sector of Jabal al Qara in the Dhofar highlands, feeding into Khawr Rawri on the coast. Habitats include a plateau of low annual grasslands (seasonal), well-wooded highlands on either side of the wadi (rising to 1,500 m) and coastal escarpment watered mainly by monsoon rainfall in summer. The wadi is unusually attractive scenically: its sides are thickly wooded and there are one to three permanent lakes in its floor (depending on rainfall/water-levels), narrow (30 m) and long (c.3 km overall). At the southern end of the site, the wadi terminates abruptly at high cliffs (occasionally waterfalls). There are very large *Ficus* trees along the banks of the wadi. There are numerous small, permanent settlements in the area. The mainstay of the local economy is cattle husbandry, and rangeland is heavily grazed; there is very little cultivation.

Birds

See box for key species. A rich assemblage of breeding species of wetland, woodland and cliffs, including many Afrotropical species; other notable breeding species include *Tachybaptus ruficollis* (50–100 pairs), *Hieraaetus fasciatus*, *Treron waalia*, *Chrysococcyx caprius*, *Otus scops pamelae*, *Halcyon leucocephala*, *Mirafra cantillans* and *Terpsiphone viridis*. In winter there are good numbers of *Ciconia ciconia*, wildfowl (for example up to 160 *Tachybaptus ruficollis*) and eagles (up to 2 *Aquila clanga* and 10 *Aquila nipalensis*). *Philomachus pugnax* is common on passage (max. 400, October). At least 134 species have been recorded.

Globally threatened species

Aquila heliaca	Relatively common winter visitor (max. 6, November).

1% or more of population

	Breeding (pairs)	Wintering	Passage
Aythya nyroca	—	17	—

Regionally threatened or declining species

Aythya nyroca	Winter visitor (see above).

Species restricted wholly or largely to the Middle East

Alectoris melanocephala	Common resident.
Sylvia leucomelaena	Uncommon resident.
Oenanthe lugentoides	Common resident.
Oenanthe monacha	One record, October.

Other threatened/endemic wildlife

Flora: the vegetation of the Dhofar highlands is amongst the richest in Oman; the tree *Anogeissus dhofarica* (endemic to Dhofar) is common, and a variety of other plants endemic or near-endemic to Oman may also occur more scarcely, as well as Afrotropical plants rare in Arabia such as baobab *Adansonia digitata*. Mammals: *Canis lupus* (V), *Genetta felina* (rare) and *Capra nubiana* (I).

Conservation issues

The area is a proposed National Scenic Reserve.

027 **Khawr Rawri** (Dhofar Governorate)

Unprotected (proposed Nature Conservation Area)

17°02′N 54°26′E
1,100 ha

Site description

One of the largest coastal lagoons in Oman, c.2.6 km long, on the Salalah coastal plain east of and close to the town of Taqah. There is substantial but variable freshwater inflow from Wadi Darbat. Its sandbar is occasionally breached, when the lagoon becomes temporarily tidal. The khawr is cliff-girt along its central part, and a small hill occurs at either side of its mouth. The water surface is partly open, with a dense fringe of *Juncus*, *Phragmites*, *Typha* and sedges and grasses. There are beds of water-weed *Chara*. An important antiquity site lies just east of the lagoon. A road leads to the mouth of the khawr from Taqah, and the sandbar is open to the public. The vegetation is heavily grazed and browsed by camels, cattle and goats.

Birds

See box for key species. The most important khawr in Dhofar for wintering and passage waterbirds, with a greater diversity of species and larger numbers of birds present than at other khawrs. Other wintering species include wildfowl (up to 1,200 birds of 16 species), *Aquila clanga* (max. 3, November) and *Hydrophasianus chirurgus* (50, February). Large numbers of *Ardea cinerea* (40, April) and *Ciconia ciconia* (150, November) occur on migration. The number of species recorded overall (203) is high,

Globally threatened species

Haliaeetus leucoryphus	Vagrant or very rare winter visitor (one record).
Aquila heliaca	Winter visitor (2, November).

1% or more of population

	Breeding (pairs)	Wintering	Passage
Aythya nyroca	—	30 (Feb)	—

Regionally threatened or declining species

Botaurus stellaris	Winter visitor (2, November).
Aythya nyroca	Winter visitor (see above).

Species restricted wholly or largely to the Middle East

Alectoris melanocephala	Common resident on nearby rocky hills.
Sylvia leucomelaena	Uncommon resident on nearby rocky hills.

reflecting the occurrence of many migrant species, a wide variety of breeders including Afrotropical species, and scarce or vagrant freshwater waterbirds.

Other threatened/endemic wildlife

Flora: at least three species on the Salalah coastal plain are endemic or near-endemic to Oman, and some may be present at this site.

Conservation issues

The close presence of Salalah could lead to an increase in uncontrolled recreational use in the future, with potentially detrimental effects on birds through disturbance. The area is a proposed National Nature Reserve.

028 Khawr Hassan (Dhofar Governorate)

17°02′N 54°23′E
300 ha

also known as Khawr Hassan Mubarak or Khawr Taqah
Unprotected (proposed Nature Conservation Area)

Site description

A disparate, complex coastal lagoon on the Salalah coastal plain, immediately west of the town of Taqah. There is substantial but variable freshwater inflow, said to be at least partly from a freshwater spring at the north end, where the shore is rocky. The barrier beach is low and sandy. The water surface is mostly open but with a dense fringe of *Phragmites* (abundant), *Juncus*, *Typha* and sedges. There are some minor pools to the west. There are patches of sabkha and scrub around the site. The marginal vegetation is heavily browsed by camels, and some cutting of *Typha* occurs. Tree-planting has occurred to the northwest.

Birds

See box for key species. *Ixobrychus minutus* may breed in some years (1+ pairs). Other notable species in winter or on passage include *Nycticorax nycticorax* (max. 63, March) and *Ardea cinerea* (56, January; 60, March). Large roosts of non-breeding seabirds occur on the barrier beach in summer. At least 193 species occur, including a wide variety of waterbirds and breeding Afrotropical species such as *Mirafra cantillans*. *Coracias garrulus* (100, May) can be a notable passage migrant in the vicinity of the creek.

Globally threatened species

Aquila heliaca	Winter visitor (2, January).

1% or more of population

	Breeding (pairs)	Wintering	Passage
Larus hemprichii	—	—	1,330 (Jun)
Larus ridibundus	—	3,300	—
Sterna bergii	—	—	920 (Jun)
Sterna hirundo	—	—	500 (Sep)

Regionally threatened or declining species

Larus hemprichii	Non-breeding visitor (see above).
Sterna dougallii	Non-breeding visitor (37, July).

Species restricted wholly or largely to the Middle East

Larus hemprichii	Non-breeding visitor (see above).
Carpospiza brachydactyla	Irregular passage migrant (30, March).

Other threatened/endemic wildlife

Flora: at least three species on the Salalah coastal plain are endemic or near-endemic to Oman, and some may be present at this site.

Conservation issues

The area is a proposed National Nature Reserve.

029 **Khawr ad Dahariz** (Dhofar Governorate)

17°01′N 54°11′E
150 ha

also known as East Khawr
Unprotected (proposed Nature Conservation Area)

Site description

A long (c.2 km), thin coastal lagoon by Salalah town, broadening inland and fed by substantial but variable freshwater inflow from Wadi Sahnut. A gravel road crosses the sandbar which separates the lagoon from the sea, though this is still sometimes breached. The water surface is partly open, with the margins mostly rocky and lined with dense *Phragmites*, *Juncus* and sedges, but also with some open, sandy, grassy banks. The east side is busy with sardine-drying activity, and the site is surrounded by developed or fenced land. The marginal vegetation is heavily browsed by camels.

Birds

See box for key species. Other notable wintering species include *Bubulcus ibis* (64), *Ardea cinerea* (75), *Circus aeruginosus* (5) and *Larus ridibundus* (1,100). Other notable passage migrants include *Aquila clanga* (6, March), *Pluvialis fulva* (80, March) and *Calidris alba* (300, April). A total of 189 species has been recorded, including a very wide variety of waterbirds.

Other threatened/endemic wildlife

Flora: at least three species on the Salalah coastal plain are endemic or near-endemic to Oman, and some may be present at this site.

Globally threatened species

Aquila heliaca	Passage migrant and winter visitor (1).

1% or more of population

	Breeding (pairs)	Wintering	Passage
Aythya nyroca	—	2	16 (Oct)
Larus hemprichii	—	1,300	—
Sterna bergii	—	—	600 (Jul)
Sterna hirundo	—	—	300 (Sep)

Regionally threatened or declining species

Botaurus stellaris	Passage migrant (max. 2, October)
Aythya nyroca	Passage migrant and winter visitor (see above).
Neophron percnopterus	Passage migrant and resident (max. 25, November).
Sterna dougallii	Non-breeding summer visitor, roosting on offshore sandbanks (30, June).

Species restricted wholly or largely to the Middle East

Puffinus persicus	Non-breeding summer visitor, feeding offshore (50, August).
Phalacrocorax nigrogularis	Predominantly a winter visitor (max. 2,000, January), always offshore.
Larus hemprichii	Predominantly a winter visitor (see above).

Conservation issues

Encroachment from road-widening and pipe- and track-laying, and pollution from sewage and other waste, have occurred locally in the past. The area is a proposed National Nature Reserve.

030 **Khawr Salalah** (Dhofar Governorate)

17°00′N 54°04′E
200 ha

Protected

Site description

A predominantly freshwater coastal lagoon (c.1.1 km long) in the built-up municipal area of Salalah, fed by seepage from a tributary wadi; the sand barrier is occasionally breached by wadi floods. There are extensive stands of *Phragmites*, *Juncus* and sedges. Freshwater inflow has been controlled as part of measures to reduce flood damage in the town.

Birds

See box for key species. Other notable species in winter and on migration are *Philomachus pugnax* (400, October) and *Tringa stagnatilis* (48, November). A wide variety of waterbirds occur, including interesting numbers of unusual species such as *Nettapus coromandelianus* (14, April), *Hydrophasianus chirurgus* (20, February) and *Pluvialis fulva* (106, November). At least 148 species have been recorded.

Globally threatened species

Haliaeetus leucoryphus	Vagrant or very rare winter visitor (one record).

1% or more of population

	Breeding (pairs)	Wintering	Passage
Larus cachinnans/argentatus	—	1,000 (Feb)	1,000 (Mar)

Regionally threatened or declining species

Botaurus stellaris	Passage migrant (2, October).
Aythya nyroca	Passage migrant and winter visitor (8, October).

Other threatened/endemic wildlife

Flora: at least three species on the Salalah coastal plain are endemic or near-endemic to Oman, and some may be present at this site.

Conservation issues

The area is property of the Diwan of Royal Court and is maintained as a bird sanctuary by the Office of the Adviser for Conservation of the Environment of the Diwan of Royal Court. It is fenced (apart from the ocean-facing barrier beach side) and guarded, and public access is restricted by permit. Two guards patrol the site, and two hides have been constructed. More hides and a visitor information display centre are planned.

031 **Jazirat Hino** (Dhofar Governorate)

Unprotected (proposed Nature Conservation Area)

16°57′N 54°44′E
c.50 ha

Site description

An island off Hino, c.7 km south-east of Marbat, lying within the zone of strong upwelling during the summer monsoon.

Birds

See box for key species. There is a report of large numbers of terns nesting on the island. Notable numbers of feeding and/or moving seabirds occur offshore, e.g. *Puffinus persicus* (see box).

Other threatened/endemic wildlife

Unusual beds of kelp *Ecklonia radiata* with abalones *Haliotis mariae* and the spiny lobster *Panulirus homarus* occur offshore.

1% or more of population

	Breeding (pairs)	Wintering	Passage
Larus hemprichii	200	—	—

Species restricted wholly or largely to the Middle East

Puffinus persicus	Non-breeding visitor offshore (360, May).
Phalacrocorax nigrogularis	Large feeding concentrations occur offshore.
Larus hemprichii	Resident (see above).

Conservation issues

Over-exploitation of eggs for food with resulting disturbance of nesting birds is reported to be a major problem. The area is part of the proposed Marbat National Nature Reserve (26,000 ha).

032 **Khawr al Mughsayl** (Dhofar Governorate)

Unprotected (proposed Nature Conservation Area)

16°53′N 53°47′E
100 ha

Site description

A 700-m-long coastal lagoon set between low hills, c.45 km west of Salalah, and blocked from the sea by a pebbly bar which is traversed by a tarmac road. The water is fresh or only slightly brackish, and inflow of fresh water is variable though not substantial. A severe flood in 1989 caused effluent pollution. The water surface is largely open, and the banks are sandy and dominated by grasses, with only small areas of marginal fringing vegetation (*Phragmites*). Shoals of small fish occur at the seaward end. A culvert has been built under the road to allow passage of strong tides and wadi-floods. The bankside vegetation is heavily grazed by livestock. The site is near a fishing village and housing extends right up to it.

Birds

See boxes for key species. Used extensively by a wide variety of feeding waterbirds, and large roosts of gulls and terns occur on the barrier beach. Another notable species in winter is *Ardea cinerea* (41, February). Large numbers of seabirds feed offshore during spring/summer: *Puffinus persicus* (see box), *Phaethon aethereus* (50, July) and *Sula dactylatra* (200, May). At least 170 species have been recorded.

Globally threatened species

Aquila heliaca	Passage migrant/winter visitor (1).

1% or more of population

	Breeding (pairs)	Wintering	Passage
Phaethon aethereus	—	—	50 (Jul)
Larus hemprichii	—	2,200 (Dec)	—

Regionally threatened or declining species

Aythya nyroca	Winter visitor (7, December).

Species restricted wholly or largely to the Middle East

Puffinus persicus	Non-breeding summer visitor, feeding offshore (60, June).
Phalacrocorax nigrogularis	Common winter visitor (2,000, January; offshore).
Larus hemprichii	Common winter visitor (see above).
Sterna repressa	Common passage migrant offshore (1,000, September).

Other threatened/endemic wildlife

Flora: at least three species on the Salalah coastal plain are endemic or near-endemic to Oman, and some may be present at this site.

Conservation issues

The area is a proposed National Scenic Reserve.

033 Jabal al Qamar (Dhofar Governorate)

Unprotected (proposed Nature Conservation Areas)

16°48′N 53°25′E
65,100 ha

Site description

The steep, south-facing slopes of the western sector of the Dhofar highlands, west of Salalah, ranging from sea-level up to 1,100 m elevation. High cliffs occur where the mountain meets the coast. The southern slopes receive the full impact of the moist, southwesterly winds of the summer monsoon, and are very verdant at this time. Dense deciduous woodland occurs at the base of the mountain, seasonal grasslands along the top, and a mixture in between on the slopes. The main land-use is cattle husbandry, and cultivation is very local. The rangeland is heavily used.

Birds

See box for key species. An interesting and diverse breeding community with many Afrotropical species, including *Aquila verreauxii*. Non-breeding *Sula dactylatra* roost on the coastal cliffs together with *Phalacrocorax nigrogularis*.

Species restricted wholly or largely to the Middle East

Phalacrocorax nigrogularis	Forms large non-breeding roosts on coastal cliffs.
Alectoris melanocephala	Fairly common resident.
Rhynchostruthus socotranus	Uncommon resident (one of the largest populations in Oman).

Other threatened/endemic wildlife

Mammals: *Canis lupus* (V), *Genetta felina* (rare), *Panthera pardus* (rare) and *Capra nubiana* (I). Flora: there are many rare and/or endemic species.

Conservation issues

The area comprises three proposed Nature Conservation Areas: the Dalkut National Nature Reserve (1,600 ha), the Wadi Nhart National Nature Reserve (5,500 ha) and the Jabal Qamar National Scenic Reserve (58,000 ha).

MAIN REFERENCES

Ash, J. S. and Nikolaus, G. (in prep.) Spring bird migration in Oman. *Sandgrouse*.

Bailey, R. S. (1966) The seabirds of the southeast coast of Arabia. *Ibis* 108: 224–264.

Cowles, G. S. (1980) A new subspecies of *Halcyon chloris* from an isolated population in eastern Arabia. *Bull. Brit. Orn. Club* 100: 226–230.

Curry, A. C., Etheridge, B. and Bodley, D. W. (1980) The Royal Air Force Ornithological Society's expedition to Masirah island. *Royal Air Force Orn. Soc. J.* 11 [unpaginated].

DGNS (Directorate General of National Statistics) (1992) *Statistical Year Book 1991 A.D. 1412 A.H.* Muscat: DGNS, Development Council General Secretariat.

Fry, C. H. and Eriksen, J. (1993) *Khawrs and birdlife.* Unpubl. report to Plan. Comm. Devel. and Environm. of Dhofar Governorate, Salalah.

Gallagher, M. D. (1977) Birds of the Jabal Akhdar. In: The scientific results of the Oman Flora and Fauna Survey 1975. *J. Oman Stud. Spec. Rep.* 1: 27–58.

Gallagher, M. D. (1985) Seabirds of the Kuria Muria islands. *Sea Swallow* 34: 5–18.

Gallagher, M. D. (1988) The Ostrich in Oman. *Sandgrouse* 10: 97–101.

Gallagher, M. D. (1993) Socotra Cormorants on Jazirat Hamar an Nafur. *Oman Bird News* 14: 15–17.

Gallagher, M. D. and Brown, M. R. (1982) The Golden Eagle breeding in Oman, eastern Arabia. *Sandgrouse* 4:

100–107.

GALLAGHER, M . AND WOODCOCK, M. W. (1980) *The birds of Oman*. Quartet, London.

GREEN, M. G., MCGRADY, M., NEWTON, S. AND UTTLEY, J. D. (1992) *The shorebirds of Barr al Hikman and Ghubbat al Hashish, Oman*. West Asian Shorebird Survey, unpublished report.

IUCN (1986) *Proposals for a system of nature conservation areas*. Gland, Switzerland: International Union for Conservation of Nature and Natural Resources.

JENSEN, R. A. C. AND SALM, R. V. (1992) *Coastal birds in the Sultanate of Oman*. Unpubl. report to Min. Commerce and Industry, Muscat.

LEES-SMITH, D. T. (1986) Composition and origins of the south-western Arabian avifauna: a preliminary analysis. *Sandgrouse* 7: 70–91.

POMEROY, C. A. (1980) RAFOS Masirah Island Expedition (1979) 22nd October to 26th November 1979. *Royal Air Force Orn. Soc. J.* 13 [unpaginated].

ROGERS, T. D. (1988) *A new list of birds of Masirah island, Sultanate of Oman*. Muscat: Oman Bird Records Committee.

■ STATE OF QATAR

Socotra Cormorant *Phalacrocorax nigrogularis*

GENERAL INFORMATION

Qatar is a northward-extending peninsula, c.160 km long and up to 90 km wide, situated halfway along the west coast of the Arabian Gulf and with an area of 11,437 km^2. It is bounded to the south by Saudi Arabia. (The sovereignty of the Hawar islands, off the west coast of Qatar, is disputed with Bahrain, and the issue is currently before the International Court of Justice.) The population of Qatar was estimated at 400,000 in 1990, most of whom reside in Doha, the capital city. The terrain is predominantly low-lying, flat, stony desert, with some hills (up to 40 m above sea-level) in the western and northern parts of the country and sand-dunes in the south-east. Natural vegetation is sparse, limited in any abundance largely to the north of the country where there are open desert scrub communities dominated by *Acacia* trees and *Lycium* bushes, especially in depressions and small wadis. Land-use is 4.5% pasture and 0.3% cropland with the remainder being semi-desert, grazed by numerous herds of livestock in spring after good rains; almost all of the land is more-or-less modified or degraded by human activity. The coastal waters of the peninsula are fairly shallow (average depth less than 20 m) and salinity is higher than average; there are a number of offshore islands, and coral reefs, extensive seagrass beds and several areas of mangrove also occur around the coast. Terrestrial wildlife species diversity is low and there are few, if any, endemics. The desert climate is hot in summer (25–46°C) and relatively warm in winter with little rain. The prevailing winds come from the north-west and south-east.

ORNITHOLOGICAL IMPORTANCE

Most of Qatar, with its flat desert and scanty vegetation, supports only a sparse and restricted avifauna. Of 255 species recorded in the country, about 23 breed, 78 are winter visitors and 104 are more-or-less regular migrants; the rest are vagrants or are rarely recorded. Seabirds breed on the offshore islands, possibly in internationally significant numbers, but the colonies have not been comprehensively surveyed; the species include *Phalacrocorax nigrogularis*, *Egretta gularis*, *Sterna caspia*, *S. bengalensis*, *S. repressa* and *S. anaethetus*. Parts of the low, rocky coast have broad intertidal flats of sand or mud, but coastal waterbirds are generally found at low densities except in certain spots, mostly on the more sheltered east coast. Outside the breeding season, the coastal zone of Qatar supports internationally important numbers of *P. nigrogularis* and, possibly, of *Dromas ardeola*.

CONSERVATION INFRASTRUCTURE AND PROTECTED-AREA SYSTEM

Responsibility for nature conservation issues rests with the Environment Protection Committee (EPC), which is attached to the Cabinet, although the Scientific and Applied Research Centre of Qatar University also supports projects studying the flora and fauna of the country. The EPC has wide-ranging powers to develop environmental policy and to draft legislation and regulations, to conduct environmental assessments and monitoring, approve development projects and educate the public. There are no protected areas with the primary purpose of nature conservation.

INTERNATIONAL MEASURES RELEVANT TO THE CONSERVATION OF SITES

Qatar is a contracting party to the World Heritage Convention but has not designated any natural World Heritage Sites. It has signed (but not ratified) the Biodiversity Convention, and is a party to the Regional Convention for Cooperation on the Protection of the Marine Environment from Pollution, and to the Action Plan for the Protection and Development of the Marine Environment and the Coastal Areas.

OVERVIEW OF THE INVENTORY

The inventory covers five sites with a total area of about 150 km^2, or 1.3% of the land surface of Qatar. All of the sites are coastal, comprising three offshore islands important for breeding seabirds, and two mainland intertidal areas important for feeding and roosting waterbirds. None of the sites are formally protected. Although no sites appear to be imminently threatened, the seabird colonies on the islands must be considered under permanent threat of introduction of non-native mammalian predators and/or excessive disturbance by human activities, as shown by the past loss of rich seabird colonies on Halul island. Further Important Bird Areas may be identified in the future if comprehensive coastal surveys are undertaken; in particular, the intertidal flats in the embayments north of Dukhan on the west coast of Qatar, and the very long sandbar and islands at Ra's Umm Laiji on the east coast, deserve further investigation for their wintering waterfowl and for breeding/feeding tern populations respectively.

ACKNOWLEDGEMENTS

The site accounts and introduction were compiled mainly from data-sheets and other information supplied by R. Nation and by the staff of the Environment Protection Committee (EPC). The assistance of the EPC with survey logistics is gratefully acknowledged. M. Gallagher and F. E. Warr assisted with provision of references and other information.

SITE INVENTORY

Site no.	Site name	Criteria used to select site									
		1	2i	2ii	2iii	3	4	5i	5ii	6	0
001	Al-Dhakira Mangrove	—	—	—	—	—	—	•	—	—	—
002	Al-Aliyah Island	—	—	—	—	—	•	—	—	—	—
003	Shara'awh Island	—	—	—	—	—	•	—	—	—	—
004	Al-Ashat	—	—	—	—	—	•	—	—	—	—
005	Khor al-Udeid	—	—	—	—	—	—	•	—	—	—

Key to criteria

1 Regularly holds a significant number of a globally threatened species.

2i Regularly holds 1% or more of a species' biogeographical or flyway or Middle Eastern population (waterbirds and seabirds only).

2ii Regularly holds 20,000 or more waterbirds.

2iii Migratory 'bottleneck' site: more than 3,000 raptors or more than 5,000 storks or more than 2,000 cranes pass in a season.

3 Regularly holds a significant number of a species which is threatened or declining within the Middle East. Only the top five sites for each such species in the country are considered to qualify as IBAs.

4 Regularly holds a significant number of a species whose world population is wholly or largely restricted to the Middle East. Only the top five sites for each such species in the country are considered to qualify as IBAs.

5i Representative example of a habitat, associated with a characteristic assemblage of bird species.

5ii Rare/threatened/unique habitat, associated with a characteristic assemblage of bird species.

6 Site important for bird conservation through education/research/tourism.

0 Selected for other reasons. See 'Comments on the inventory'.

Comments on the inventory

1. Sovereignty over the Hawar Islands off western Qatar, which qualify as an Important Bird Area, is formally disputed between Qatar and Bahrain, and the issue is currently before the International

Court of Justice. Since Bahrain currently administers the site, the account for this site can be found in that country (site 004).

2. The data used in compiling two of the site accounts dates from the 1990s (sites 001 and 002), whilst those used for the other three sites dates from the 1970s and early 1980s (in the absence of more recent information).
3. The site name is sometimes followed by an alternative site name in brackets.
4. No area is given for three sites because fieldwork is required before their boundaries can be determined.
5. The only area given for offshore island sites (important for breeding seabirds) does not include the area of the surrounding seas which are important as feeding grounds, because the latter have not been identified with sufficient accuracy as yet.
6. The site descriptions provided are tentative outlines only for most sites, in the absence of more detailed information based on ornithological surveys.
7. Figures in brackets after species' names, and in the boxes, are the maximum daily counts of individuals recorded (not pairs), unless otherwise stated. All counts of wintering birds are from the month of January, unless otherwise stated.
8. Information on bird populations is comparatively scant, and even the distribution of some species is not known. One result is a bias in favour of better explored areas, therefore the inventory should be regarded as preliminary.

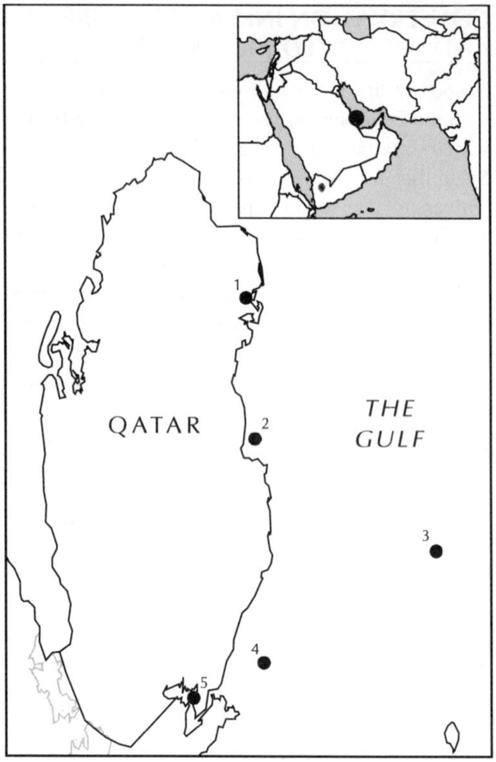

Glossary

khor, tidal inlet or coastal lagoon

wadi, drainage line or bed of seasonal river

001 Al-Dhakira Mangrove

Unprotected

25°45′N 51°32′E
3,000 ha

■ Site description

A sheltered set of bays adjacent to the town of Al-Dhakira, with dense stands of mangrove *Avicennia marina* (c.1,000 ha or less), broad mudflats (tidal amplitude is less than 2 m) and saltmarsh vegetation. The bay is largely protected from open sea to the east by a spit. Longshore drift is north to south. Possibly an important spawning and nursery area for economically valuable fish and shrimp stocks. Some artisanal fishing occurs, and the mangrove is grazed by camels.

■ Birds

The site has not yet been comprehensively surveyed, but it may be important for wintering or passage waterbirds, including *Platalea leucorodia* (max. 22), *Phoenicopterus ruber* (max. 'low hundreds'), duck (max. 'low hundreds'), and, offshore, *Sterna anaethetus* (max. 'low hundreds').

■ Other threatened/endemic wildlife

None known to BirdLife International.

Conservation issues

The site has been protected with booms during major oil spills in the past, but the site has no formal recognition or protection as a wildlife conservation area. Camel-grazing of the mangrove is a problem locally; in the future, land reclamation and recreational disturbance may become problems as the adjacent town grows to support a new industrial town to the north, and oil spills are always a threat although the topography of the site provides fairly good protection.

002 Al-Aliyah Island

Unprotected

25°21′N 51°34′E
65 ha

Site description

A small, low, rocky outcrop 3 km offshore, within 5 km of the northern outskirts of Doha. Surface is loose, weathered limestone rock with uneven cover of salt-tolerant bushes (*Zygophyllum*, *Limonium*). A sand-spit extends south for about 2 km at low tide, and there are broad intertidal flats to south and east, and coral reefs nearby. The island is occasionally visited by fishermen and authorized falcon-trappers.

Birds

See box for key species. Surveys in 1992 and 1993 found *Phalacrocorax nigrogularis* (350 pairs), *Egretta gularis* (17 pairs), and secondhand reports of *Sterna bengalensis* (75 pairs), *S. repressa* (see box) and *S. anaethetus* (50 pairs). None of these populations exceed the 1% population levels, but the figures for terns are probably underestimates.

Species restricted wholly or largely to the Middle East	
Sterna repressa	Summer visitor (25 pairs).

Other threatened/endemic wildlife

None known to BirdLife International.

Conservation issues

No conservation measures have been taken, although the nearby presence of a security area restricts the number of visitors and thus provides some unintentional protection from disturbance. Visitors are also monitored to some extent by the Coast Guard at Doha, 13 km to the south. No signs of shooting or disturbance were found during a visit in December 1993. However *Phalacrocorax nigrogularis* did not breed in the winters of 1991/92 and 1992/93, and the current status of the tern *Sterna* breeding colonies is not known and excessive disturbance and over-exploitation of seabird eggs may be occurring. Formal protection for the site was suggested in 1986, and new proposals are now under consideration. The site has potential for education and research, and is part of the most significant remaining natural marine habitat close to Doha.

Further reading

ABCS (1986), Planning Dept. (1992).

003 Shara'awh Island

also known as Shara'iwah or Sharaawh
Unprotected

25°02′N 52°15′E
30 ha

Site description

An island 65 km due east of the mainland of Qatar, just less than 1 km long and c.500 m wide. A hill with crags, slopes and undulating sand with a good cover of salt-tolerant bushes.

Birds

See box for key species. Details of only two visits are known; breeding species in October 1973 included *Phalacrocorax nigrogularis* (old nests and mummified chicks found), *Pandion haliaetus*, *Sterna bengalensis* (traces of nesting) and *Sterna repressa* (traces of nesting). *Phaethon aethereus* may nest.

Species restricted wholly or largely to the Middle East	
Phalacrocorax nigrogularis	Bred 'abundantly' in the early 1970s or before.
Sterna repressa	Abundant summer visitor; breeding in 1973.

Other threatened/endemic wildlife

Reptiles: *Eretmochelys imbricata* (E) nests, but numbers are reported to be very low.

Conservation issues

The current status of the seabird breeding colonies is unknown.

Further reading

Gallagher *et al.* (1984), UNEP/IUCN (1988).

004 Al-Ashat

Unprotected

24°43´N 51°36´E
1 ha

Site description

A group of small islands c.10 km off the south-east coast of Qatar.

Birds

See box for key species. Breeding species in 1970–1972 included *Phalacrocorax nigrogularis* (dead chicks found).

Species restricted wholly or largely to the Middle East
Phalacrocorax nigrogularis Breeds, presumably only in small numbers.

Other threatened/endemic wildlife

None known to BirdLife International.

Conservation issues

The lack of recent surveys makes it difficult to judge whether the island is under any threat.

Further reading

Gallagher *et al.* (1984).

005 Khor al-Udeid

also known as Khawr al-'Udayd
Unprotected

24°37´N 51°20´E
c.12,000 ha

Site description

A very large tidal inlet with sandy islands, in the south-east corner of Qatar.

Birds

Breeding species include *Pandion haliaetus* and *Sterna caspia* (1 pair, October 1981). In winter, large concentrations of *Phoenicopterus ruber* are reported to occur, and significant numbers of other waterbirds may also occur, including *Phalacrocorax carbo*, *P. nigrogularis*, waders and gulls *Larus* and terns *Sterna*.

Other threatened/endemic wildlife

Mammals: unidentified whales recorded, possibly *Balaenoptera edeni* (K). The area may be an important feeding ground for dolphins. Reptiles: the site may be an important feeding ground for sea-turtles (globally threatened).

Conservation issues

Commercial fishing was banned in 1993. The southern shores are now controlled by Saudi Arabia. There is some recreational disturbance by campers and four-wheel drive vehicles, but otherwise there are no obvious threats apart from oil pollution.

Further reading

Gallagher *et al.* (1984).

MAIN REFERENCES

ABCS (1986) *Doha West Bay Lagoon Development–Environmental Studies: Part 2: Technical Annexes.* Report to Ministry of Municipal Affairs and Agriculture by Aquatic Biological Consultancy Services Ltd.

Clarke, J. E. (1987) *Consultancy report on a UNESCO mission to Qatar.* Report to UNESCO, Paris.

El-Hinnawi, E. (1987) *National State of the Environment Report. 1. Qatar.* Second edition. Nairobi, Kenya: United Nations Environment Programme.

Gallagher, M. D. (1985) A brief survey of ornithological habitats of the State of Qatar. *Qatar National Mus. J. (Arrayan)* 10: 120–188.

Gallagher, M. D., Scott, D. A., Ormond, R. F. G., Connor, R. J. and Jennings, M. C. (1984) The distribution and conservation of seabirds breeding on the coasts and islands of Iran and Arabia. Pp. 421–456 in J. P. Croxall, P. G. H. Evans and R. W. Schreiber, eds. *Status and conservation of the world's seabirds.* Cambridge, U.K.: International Council for Bird Preservation (Techn. Publ. 2).

Planning Dept. (1992) *Conceptual Plans for West Bay Lagoon.* Planning Department, Ministry of Municipal Affairs and Agriculture.

UNEP/IUCN (1988) *Coral reefs of the world*, 2: *Indian Ocean, Red Sea and Gulf.* Gland, Switzerland: International Union for the Conservation of Nature and Natural Resources/Nairobi: United Nations Environment Programme (Regional Seas Directories and Bibliographies).

■ KINGDOM OF SAUDI ARABIA

White-eyed Gull *Larus leucophthalmus*

GENERAL INFORMATION

The Kingdom of Saudi Arabia covers an area of 2,144,969 km^2 and comprises over 70% of the Arabian peninsula. It is the largest country in the Middle East, with significant lengths of coastline on both the Arabian Gulf and Red Sea, and common borders with all other countries on the peninsula (Kuwait, Qatar, United Arab Emirates, Oman, Yemen) and with both Jordan and Iraq in the north. A causeway connects Saudi Arabia with the island state of Bahrain in the Gulf. The human population was estimated at 11.5 million in 1988 but is more likely to approach 14–15 million now (at the time of writing the 1993 census results are not yet available), the majority concentrated in a few large urban areas: Dammam–Dhahran–al-Khobar and Jubail on the Gulf coast, together with the neighbouring oasis town of Hofuf; the capital Riyadh and Buraydah in the central part of the country; various cities on the Red Sea coast, principally the centrally placed Jiddah–Makkah area, with Yanbu further to the north and Jizan in the south near the Yemen border. There are several cities along the western mountains, commencing with Al-Madinah in the north, running south through Taif, al-Baha, Abha–Khamis Mushayt and ending with Najran. Ha'il, Tabuk and Sakakah are the major centres of population in the northernmost part of the Kingdom.

Topographically and geologically the country can be divided into five major regions, though each often consists of several, fairly varied, dominant land forms. These regions are described in more detail below, following a south-west to north-east transect from the Red Sea to the Gulf coast.

The Red Sea coastal plain or Tihamah

This is generally up to 50 km wide for most of its length between Yanbu and the Yemen border; to the north it tends to be much narrower. For the most part, it is fairly uniformly flat and sandy, and is formed by wide, sometimes extensively cultivated, flood-plains with central, often silty, wadis, draining from the mountainous country to the east. Large gravel plains with savanna-like *Acacia* scrubland occur in the southern part. Dense thickets of doum palms *Hyphaene thebaica* and *Salvadora persica* often line the wadi beds. Sabkhah and saltflats with sparse salt-tolerant vegetation can be extensive immediately inland of the coast. The actual coastline is varied, with combinations of low coral cliffs, sand beaches, lagoons (often hypersaline) and tidal inlets in close proximity. Several lagoons and tidal inlets are lined with stands of mangrove, notably *Avicennia marina*. There are numerous scattered offshore islands, ranging in size from a few hectares to the largest island in the Farasan archipelago (Farasan

Kabir) at 381 km^2. Most are fairly barren with low fossil-coral cliff lines, though some more stabilized islands such as Umm al-Qamari have a dense cover of *Salvadora persica* and *Suaeda*, and mangrove stands can be extensive with both *Avicennia marina* and *Rhizophora mucronata* present.

The western mountains

The main block of mountainous country in Saudi Arabia runs in a fairly narrow band 50–100 km wide parallel to the Red Sea coast. This terrain, often called the Sarawat mountains, is usually divided into the Hijaz mountains in the north and the Asir mountains in the south. There is no universally accepted boundary and in this account Hijaz is applied to the more broken chain of generally lower mountains to the north of Taif, while Asir is used for those between Taif, Abha and Najran. On a west–east axis through the Asir, three sub-zones can be identified: the foothills, the main escarpment and highlands, and the inland plateau. The foothills rise from the Tihamah coastal plain to 500–1,500 m: they are mostly fairly arid, though cut by well-vegetated wet wadi systems running towards the sea. Exceptionally, geologically distinct massifs (often granite plutons) may rise to as much as 2,000 m. Good examples include Jabal Shada near al-Mikwah and Jabal Faifa near Bani Malik, and here increased moisture and rainfall have considerably increased floral and faunal diversity to levels akin to the main escarpment/highland area slightly further east. The escarpment itself is a spectacular feature running more or less the length of the Asir. There is a dominant west-facing fault scarp that is considered the headwall of the north-easternmost part of the Red Sea/Great African Rift Valley. The escarpment often rises from foothill wadis around 1,000–1,200 m to more than 3,000 m in the Jabal Sawdah area near Abha; for most of its length, the lip is at or above 2,000 m. The climate in this sub-zone is near-temperate; the south-west monsoon brings in oceanic moisture-laden clouds and frequent rainfall in summer, but rain also regularly occurs at other times of year. The flora can be lush and the highest slopes are covered with largely Afroalpine vegetation climaxing in evergreen cloud-forest of *Juniperus excelsa*, *Lavandula* and *Euryops arabicus* scrub on north-facing slopes and with *Aloe sabae* and *Euphorbia* on the more barren south-facing slopes. The highland plateau forms broken hilly country descending from the escarpment lip to altitudes of c.1,500 m and becoming increasingly arid and barren inland. Some wadis, rising near the escarpment, flow inland and in places support lush vegetation, though the majority are dry through most of the year. *Acacia* woodland can be extensive in places. The Hijaz mountains north of Taif tend to occur as more isolated ranges usually rising from relatively low altitudes. Several approach or exceed 2,000 m and support *Juniperus phoenicea* scrub, e.g. Jabal al-Fiqrah (1,900 m) and Jabal al-Lawz (2,549 m).

The west-central and northern plains

This inland plateau generally ranges between 700 and 1,500 m in altitude. Fairly monotonous gravel plains predominate with sparse vegetation unless grazing by domestic livestock is under control. The plains are often interrupted by large areas of raised black volcanic lava desert, the harrats. Fields of black basaltic boulders make these harrats almost inaccessible in many parts and create specific micro-habitats leading to an increased diversity of fauna and flora. Seven major harrats are found in the western and northern part of the Kingdom. Harrat al-Harrah, covering c.13,000 km^2 in the extreme north, is contiguous with similar landscape over the border in Jordan and is a well-known example. Several mountain ranges rise above the plains, usually rounded exfoliation domes of granite rock types. Good examples are Jabal Aja' and Jabal Salma in the Ha'il region in the north and the more centrally located Jibal al-Humrah/Majami al-Hadb range.

Sandy deserts

These cover vast tracts of the east and south of the Kingdom. Although more or less continuous, several distinct areas are recognized: the large an-Nafud desert in the north and north-east is connected to the vast Rub' al-Khali (Empty Quarter) in the south and south-east by a corridor of similar sandy terrain known as the ad-Dahna' desert. All are characterized by a variety of dune landscapes. However, an arc of limestone cliffs and plateaus, the Tuwayq escarpment, runs for c.800 km through this corridor area from the vicinity of Qassim in the north through Riyadh to the al-'Arid/Najran area in the south. Vegetation throughout both sandy desert and limestone landscapes is exceedingly sparse, though canyons in the latter area can support *Acacia* scrub/woodland.

The eastern lowlands

This region flanks the Arabian Gulf and is mostly devoid of major topographical features. Although the landscape can be varied, it is predominantly sandy with large areas of sabkhah near the coast and bordered by numerous rocky outcrops towards the west. Important concentrations of natural artesian springs have here created some of the Kingdom's most important oases, such as the al-Hasa oasis with its major town Hofuf, and the numerous scattered oases around Qatif, which formed the first important human settlements in this region. The outflow of excess water of the al-Hasa oasis has created a system of natural pools and lagoons from Abqaiq to al-'Uqair in the Gulf of Salwah. Nutrient-rich run-off from the Qatif oases to the Gulf is largely responsible for the increased productivity of the extremely rich intertidal zone in Tarut Bay. The intertidal flats and saltmarshes of the Gulf are generally more extensive than on the Red Sea coast. North of Ras Tanurah the coastline is very exposed to the wind and intertidal flats and saltmarshes in this area are restricted to some large enclosed embayments such as Dawhat ad-Dafi and Dawhat al-Musallimiyah north of Jubail. Further south, the coastline is more protected from wind and waves and in this sector an increased sedimentation of fine mud particles has created the richest intertidal areas, such as in Tarut Bay. Large parts of these bays are lined with stands of mangrove *Avicennia marina* and extensive areas of saltmarsh. In the recent past, these intertidal zones were subject to considerable attrition from industrial reclamation. The intertidal zone of the enclosed, shallow Gulf of Salwah consists largely of sand and rockflats. Several slightly elevated portions of the mainland have been cut off by present water levels in the Gulf, forming inshore islands such as Zakhnuniyah and Judhaym in the Gulf of Salwah, and Abu Ali and Jinnah north of Jubail. These inshore islands mostly consist of sandy habitats similar to the mainland but generally have a denser vegetation of low-growing salt-tolerant shrubs. In places coral reefs in the shallow Gulf have accumulated sandbanks on their flattened tops, forming elongated islands. Six such islands, ranging from 2 to 120 ha in size, occur offshore in northern Saudi Arabian Gulf waters at distances of 35–90 km from the mainland. The central parts of the larger, more stable islands are covered with salt-tolerant vegetation.

Until recently, three principal types of traditional agricultural land-use predominated across the Kingdom: pastoral livestock husbandry (mostly sheep, goats and camels), arable/cereal production and fruit-growing (mainly dates).

The Tihamah and foothills have traditionally supported both livestock grazing and cereal production, with sorghum and millet the chief crops. Irrigation is used in some areas, while in others, often in wadi beds, large earth bunds are constructed around fields to hold rainwater. Most dates are grown in the vicinity of wadis and in some places bananas are a common crop. With its high rainfall, the main escarpment and highland area was, until c.1970–1980, the chief wheat-growing region in Saudi Arabia, and narrow terraced fields have been constructed over many hundreds of years on the more gentle slopes of the western highland plateaus and escarpment. Fruit (often apricots, pomegranates or water melons) and some vegetables are also grown in the benign climate. Livestock-rearing is possibly less important. The arid eastern flanks of the mountains and the west-central plains of the Kingdom are the principal areas for livestock, although with water-trucks easily available and with the distribution of vast quantities of subsidized feed, many former bedouin are more sedentary now and herds can be exceptionally large. Consequently, grazing pressure has increased dramatically in most areas and vegetation is often very stunted. The resulting soil erosion is becoming a serious threat to huge areas of rangeland which once used to be very important in supporting the nomadic lifestyle of the bedouin population. Some unpalatable non-native weeds have become very persistent and can cover vast areas. The same factors have enabled livestock herders to penetrate ever further into sandy desert areas, leaving very little pristine habitat in the country.

The southern and western margins of the an-Nafud and ad-Dahna' deserts are the centre of an intensive modern agricultural industry. Cereal fields are irrigated by centre-pivot, using easily available fossil groundwater. These fields are packed into the area running from Ha'il in the north, through Qassim to Riyadh, a belt 700 km long and often c.50 km wide. Smaller agricultural outposts occur in the Tabuk–Sakakah area and to the east and south of Riyadh. Wheat is the principal crop, though hay and alfalfa are also important. More ambitious farmers are diversifying and the extent of fruit orchards and vegetables is probably increasing.

In the east of the country, the oases of Qatif and Hofuf still support large date plantations, in the shade of which numerous vegetables, fruits and fodder plants are grown on small irrigated fields. More recently, pivot-irrigated fields have been established at several locations in the eastern desert. The Gulf coast area is still home to some traditional livestock-grazing bedouin, but it is also the heart of the Saudi Arabian petrochemical industry.

ORNITHOLOGICAL IMPORTANCE

Geographers usually consider the Arabian peninsula as Asian in character. However, birds—amongst other taxa—clearly show that zoogeographically the area has affinities to the western Palearctic, Oriental and Afrotropical regions, with no easily definable boundaries. As the major landmass connecting Africa and Eurasia, Saudi Arabia has a pivotal role in the lives of many migrating species, contains representative populations from all these faunal regions, and additionally has a small number of Arabian endemic species, mostly confined to the south-west.

The major deserts and plains of Saudi Arabia are a central and contiguous part of the Saharo-Sindian arid zone that stretches from the Atlantic eastwards to Pakistan. The breeding avifauna includes important populations of *Chlamydotis undulata* and *Torgos tracheliotus* and the most diverse lark community found in the Middle East with up to eight species in the northern part of the Kingdom. Saudi Arabia probably supports large parts of the breeding ranges of *Eremalauda dunni* and *Eremophila bilopha* and is also one of the few areas with breeding *Ramphocoris clotbey*. Various sandgrouse and wheatear species are important components of the arid-zone avifauna. The Arabian Gulf and the Red Sea support internationally important concentrations of seabirds, especially *Phalacrocorax nigrogularis*, *Sterna bengalensis* and *S. anaethetus*, together with significant numbers of *S. bergii* and *S. repressa* in the Gulf and *Sula leucogaster*, *Pelecanus rufescens*, *Larus hemprichii*, *L. leucophthalmus* and *Anous stolidus* in the Red Sea.

The Tihamah and the Asir/Hijaz mountains, together with Yemen, hold the bulk of the world ranges of the south-west Arabian endemics. *Passer euchlorus* is typically present in the cultivated areas of the Tihamah, whereas the remainder are more frequent in mountain and wadi habitats. *Alectoris philbyi*, *Oenanthe lugentoides* and *Serinus menachensis* are most numerous in the more barren and rocky habitats; *Dendrocopos dorae* and *Sylvia leucomelaena* are largely restricted to relatively intact tracts of *Acacia* woodland, although together with *Serinus rothschildi* and *Estrilda rufibarba* they may also be found in more open and scrubby areas with some cultivation. The majority of the endemics can be considered typical of the montane juniper woodland (*Alectoris melanocephala*, *Turdus menachensis*, *Parisoma buryi*, *Pica pica asirensis*, *Carduelis yemenensis* and *Rhynchostruthus socotranus*), though with continued loss of woodland they can be widespread in secondary habitats. Endemics aside, the area is predominantly Afrotropical in character, and distinctive Arabian races have evolved in many cases. Afrotropical breeding species include *Scopus umbretta*, several species of raptor (*Terathopius ecaudatus*, *Aquila verreauxii*, *Accipiter badius*, *Micronisus gabar*, *Melierax metabates*), *Ardeotis arabs*, *Numida meleagris*, *Tockus nasutus*, *Coracias abyssinica* and many passerines; an isolated population of *Caprimulgus poliocephalus* was recently discovered in the Asir mountains.

The creation of several inland wetlands, most notably near Riyadh, has extended the breeding range of several wetland species well into the heart of Arabia, in particular *Nycticorax nycticorax*, *Ardeola ralloides*, *Ardea purpurea*, *Aythya nyroca* and *Acrocephalus scirpaceus*.

During winter and passage periods, Saudi Arabia's wetlands, both coastal and inland, support internationally important numbers of a wide variety of species. The northern Gulf is important for *Podiceps cristatus*, *P. nigricollis*, *Phalacrocorax carbo*, *P. nigrogularis*, *Limicola falcinellus* and *Sterna saundersi*, whereas the Red Sea harbours significant numbers of *Dromas ardeola* and *Larus genei*. Inland waters hold internationally important numbers of wintering *Plegadis falcinellus* and *Ciconia nigra*. The recent creation of numerous dams, reservoirs, irrigation channels and sewage ponds inland, as well as the enrichment of intertidal areas by sewage outfalls from coastal urban areas (e.g. Jiddah, Jizan, Dammam, Dhahran) has undoubtedly led to an increase in total numbers of wintering waterfowl in many areas.

The interior deserts and plains provide wintering habitat for significant populations of small passerines, especially wheatears (*Oenanthe isabellina*, *O. deserti*, *O. lugens*, *O. xanthoprymna*) and *Sylvia* warblers (*S. nana*, *S. mystacea*, *S. minula*), while considerable numbers of *Aquila nipalensis* and *A. heliaca* swell the resident community of scavenging raptors.

Vast numbers of passerines and near-passerines pass through the country during both spring and autumn en route between sub-Saharan Africa and the Palearctic. From these groups it would appear that migration over the Red Sea occurs on a broad front and the widespread small breeding colonies of *Falco concolor* on many islands capitalize on this phenomenon. Although very few species of these groups appear to fly non-stop over the Kingdom, numbers of migrants may vary considerably between years, depending on when and where falls of migrants occur. The Asir/Hijaz mountains are relatively lush and no doubt provide good refuelling habitat—as do various artificial wetlands, gardens and irrigated agricultural areas, here and in most other areas. Although there has been relatively little systematic monitoring of raptor migration, autumn passage, especially down the western mountains, appears to be heavy with large numbers of *Buteo buteo* and *Aquila nipalensis* heading for the narrow crossing point to Africa at the Bab al-Mandab straits. In spring, most raptors return via the northern Red Sea crossing around Suez, though there is a broad-front movement of large numbers of *Circus*, *Milvus migrans*, *Falco tinnunculus* and *F. naumanni* through the country. Due to the extremely favourable conditions for soaring, many raptors may pass through most of the Kingdom at altitudes which make chances for detection from the ground very slim. Recently the main migratory flyway of African-wintering *Grus virgo* was located, with more than 6,000 passing over the central Red Sea, Jiddah and Ha'il in spring.

CONSERVATION INFRASTRUCTURE AND PROTECTED-AREA SYSTEM

Local community-controlled conservation of natural resources has been a long-standing tradition in Saudi society through the 'hima' system. More recently, however, the system has become seriously undermined by several factors, notably rapid population growth, increasing wealth and recreation time, subsidized livestock fodder, and easy availability of water, water trucks and firearms. Consequently, the specific interest of HRH Prince Saud Al-Faisal in conservation led to the establishment of the National Commission for Wildlife Conservation and Development (NCWCD) by Royal Decree (No. M/22) in 1986, and this is now the principal government agency dealing especially with wildlife conservation and the establishment and management of protected areas. The Ministry of Agriculture and Water is peripherally involved in conservation through management of the single National Park (Asir) in the country, though the Park is more of an umbrella organization promoting tourism and recreation in a generally unprotected area of outstanding natural beauty. The Meteorology and Environmental Protection Administration (MEPA) was established in 1980 and is largely responsible for marine conservation and environmental protection through setting up policy guidelines and standards for pollution control (both aquatic and atmospheric).

The NCWCD System Plan for Protected Areas outlines a logical rationale for the creation of a representative system of effectively protected areas and defines procedures to proclaim and properly manage these areas as reserves. It defines five categories of reserve, but definitions for this essentially artificial division have been deliberately kept rather flexible.

Special Nature Reserve (SNR) Large prime sites of high biological excellence in which the conservation of biodiversity is the main aim. Settlement, fishing, domestic stock and cultivation are totally excluded with the exception of acceptable small-scale, traditional activities that were already established when the SNR was created. These areas are open for scientific research, education and strictly regulated outdoor recreation, including controlled hunting. SNRs are managed and controlled by the NCWCD and concentrate on preservation and restoration of natural communities of plant and animal species indigenous to the area.

Natural Reserve (NR) This category is proposed for: (a) relatively small areas of high natural excellence, or larger areas of lower natural excellence than SNRs, that are managed directly by the NCWCD; (b) areas of very high natural excellence, managed by an authority other than the NCWCD; (c) areas of high to very high natural excellence which, because of human settlement or land-uses within them, are managed by the NCWCD in cooperation with other authorities; and (d) areas of any size that are of very high biological importance, including areas of modified habitats such as artificially created wetlands or ecological field research stations, that are managed by the NCWCD or in cooperation with other agencies. Management guidelines for NRs are very similar to those of SNRs, but with a greater freedom of public access.

Biological Reserve (BR) These small-scale reserves fulfil a range of very important conservation functions, including (a) strategically located sites for rangeland reclamation, managed as seedbanks and as demonstration areas on the effects of overgrazing, (b) water catchment areas and (c) areas of specific significance to key habitats and/or to individual animal species, such as mangrove, coral reefs, sea-turtle nesting beaches, vulture colonies, etc. They should be fully protected from any form of man-related disturbance and are preferably managed by the local communities and/or authorities other than the NCWCD.

Resource Use Reserve (RUR) Relatively large areas in which the emphasis of conservation is on sound resource management rather than on the conservation of biological diversity, although this will also benefit from the management regime. RURs offer a holistic approach to land and resource use which are managed in terms of sustainability by the local communities, but in early stages the Government may have to initiate them through the NCWCD.

Controlled Hunting Reserve (CHR) This category is suggested for areas in which wildlife is managed with the aim of providing improved sustainable hunting at some time in the future when game populations have recovered. To provide sanctuary for hunted populations CHRs should include at least one fully protected breeding area in which there is no grazing by livestock and public access is rigidly controlled. As such, all other categories are also *de facto* CHRs.

For management purposes most protected areas are subdivided into zones of permissible use, and this is easily accommodated by allocating a different reserve classification to each zone. As such, most 'protected areas' consist of a cluster of different types of 'reserve'.

The System Plan listed 56 terrestrial and 42 marine sites as priority areas for protection and nature conservation (in fact, 55 marine sites are listed, but several are grouped together under one heading and there are only 42 actual site descriptions). To date, 10 sites have been legally declared as protected areas and several more are in the pipeline. In addition, the al-Ha'ir wetland reserve near Riyadh is managed by the Riyadh Development Authority, but is wardened by NCWCD rangers. Currently, the established protected-area network is rather biased towards establishing sanctuaries for native ungulate populations (ibex and gazelles) or sites suitable for the reintroduction of the these and of captive-bred *Oryx leucoryx*.

Established protected areas are delineated on the ground by signs and ranger camps, and generally patrolled by vehicle-based rangers, though in some cases this is supported by fixed-wing aircraft. One reserve has been fenced in its entirety (Mahazat as-Sayd).

INTERNATIONAL MEASURES RELEVANT TO THE CONSERVATION OF SITES

Saudi Arabia acceded to the World Heritage Convention in 1978, but at present has not notified any natural sites. The Kingdom is planning to ratify the Ramsar Convention, and the first site to be nominated is likely to be the Gulf Coral Islands. The country is a Contracting Party to the Bonn Convention, and although this does not make any obligations to provide protection for sites, it does influence species conservation policies. At present (August 1993) the Kingdom is preparing an Agreement under this Convention to improve the international conservation status of the Asian populations of *Chlamydotis undulata*. Saudi Arabia is also a signatory to the Regional Convention for the Conservation of the Red Sea and Gulf of Aden Environment, and to the Regional Convention for Cooperation on the Protection of the [Gulf] Environment from Marine Pollution together with the Action Plan for the Protection and Development of the [Gulf] Marine Environment and the Coastal Areas, but has not signed the Biodiversity Convention.

OVERVIEW OF INVENTORY

A total of 39 sites is included in this inventory. For a country the size of Saudi Arabia, this may seem a small number. However, blocks of homogeneous habitats cover vast tracts of land and many sites listed are very large and thus representative. Additionally, several single-site entries comprise amalgamations of several islands or of mountains and adjacent wadi systems which could be listed separately, but for conservation management purposes in the Kingdom they are treated as one entity. So far, only three out of a total of ten formally protected reserves have been created because of their ornithological importance: Harrat al-Harrah, Raydah Escarpment and Umm al-Qamari. Although more than 100 sites have been earmarked for protection in the NCWCD System Plan for Protected Areas, most are very poorly known ornithologically, but ultimately may prove worthy of Important Bird Area status. Within the inventory, wetlands, especially coastal ones, predominate. This is mainly attributable to the existence of a well-established wetland monitoring scheme which contributes data annually to the Asian Waterfowl Census. Conversely, monitoring of terrestrial bird populations is in its infancy and, unlike ungulates, these cannot be surveyed from the air. Desert, montane and woodland biotopes are very poorly represented in the inventory and more information on such habitats is urgently needed. Several new desert protected areas, assigned for ungulate reintroduction programmes, have still yet to be assessed thoroughly for their bird populations, and some may well prove of importance for birds. Furthermore, many montane areas in the Asir support woodland fragments and are likely to be globally important for species such as *Turdus menachensis* and other south-west Arabian endemics. Further survey work in this area is likely to identify additional Important Bird Areas in the future. As it stands, the inventory includes eight formally protected areas and another five which are in the pipeline; the proximity of three sites to the Royal Commission cities of Jubail and Yanbu effectively renders them protected. Many bird species (which Saudi Arabia has important populations of) such as breeding raptors, gamebirds, sandgrouse, and larks, tend not to congregate but to have scattered distributions. Only a small proportion of their total populations is covered by the inclusion of some representative sites. To conserve these dispersed species it is necessary to integrate conservation measures for the wider environment into regulations which govern land-uses such as agriculture and forestry.

ACKNOWLEDGEMENTS

The site accounts were compiled from data-sheets and other information provided on behalf of the National Commission for Wildlife Conservation and Development (NCWCD) by S. F. and A. V. Newton, P. Symens (Wildlife Sanctuary for the Gulf Region), P. Gaucher, B. S. Meadows, A. J. Stagg and M. C. Jennings, and with assistance from M. Shobrak, A. Suhaibani, M. al-Salamah, D. James, G. and H. Welch, X. Eichacker, J.-M. Thiollay, and staff and students from Manchester Metropolitan University during field surveys. The participants gratefully acknowledge the continued support of Prof. Dr A. H. Abuzinada, Secretary General of the NCWCD, and Mr Y. al-Wetaid, Head of the NCWCD Research and Monitoring Department. S. F. Newton wrote the introduction on behalf of NCWCD, with assistance from P. Symens. D. J. Brooks assisted with the compilation of data.

SITE INVENTORY

Site no.	Site name	Region	Criteria used to select site: 1	2i	2ii	2iii	3	4	5i	5ii	6	0
001	Harrat al-Harrah	JW, DR	•	—	—	—	—	—	•	•	•	—
002	Dawmat al-Jandl	JW	—	—	—	—	—	—	—	•	—	—
003	At-Tubayq	DR	—	—	—	—	•	•	•	—	—	—
004	Jabal al-Lawz	TB	—	—	—	—	•	—	•	—	—	—
005	King Faisal Airbase, Tabuk	TB	—	•	—	—	•	—	—	—	—	—
006	Jabal Aja and Northern Ha'il	HL	—	—	—	•	•	—	•	—	—	—
007	Gulf Coral Islands	EP	—	•	•	—	•	•	•	•	•	—
008	Abu Ali	EP	—	•	—	—	—	—	—	—	—	—
009	Sabkhat al-Fasl Lagoons	EP	—	•	•	—	—	—	—	—	•	—
010	Tarut Bay	EP	—	•	•	—	—	—	•	—	—	—
011	Al-Wajh Bank	TB	•	•	—	—	—	—	•	—	—	—
012	Al-Hasa lagoons	EP	•	•	•	—	•	—	—	—	—	—
013	Gulf of Salwah	EP	—	•	•	—	—	—	•	•	—	—
014	Al-Ha'ir	RD	•	•	—	—	—	—	—	•	•	—
015	Hima al-Fiqrah	MD	—	—	—	—	—	•	•	—	—	—
016	Madinat Yanbu al-Sinaiyah	MD	—	—	—	—	•	•	—	—	—	—
017	Hawtat Bani Tamim	RD	—	—	—	—	—	—	•	—	—	—
018	Wadi Rabigh	MK, MD	—	—	—	—	—	—	—	•	—	—
019	Mahazat as-Sayd	MK	•	—	—	—	•	•	•	—	•	—
020	Jiddah South Corniche and Port	MK	—	•	—	—	—	—	—	—	—	—
021	Makkah Waste-water Stream	MK	—	•	—	—	—	—	—	—	•	—
022	NWRC, Taif	MK	•	—	—	—	—	—	—	—	•	—
023	Taif Escarpment	MK	•	—	—	•	•	—	•	—	—	—
024	Wadi Turabah and Jabal Ibrahim	MK	—	•	—	—	•	•	•	•	—	—
025	Qishran Bay	MK	—	—	—	—	•	•	•	—	—	—
026	Umm al-Qamari	MK	—	•	—	—	—	—	—	•	—	—
027	Shallal ad-Dahna	AS	—	—	—	—	—	—	—	•	•	—
028	Al-Habrow al-Arabi	MK, AS	—	—	—	—	•	•	•	—	—	—
029	Khawr 'Amiq	AS	—	—	—	—	•	—	—	•	—	—
030	Raydah Escarpment	AS	•	—	—	—	•	•	—	•	•	—
031	Kutambil Island	JZ	—	•	—	—	•	—	—	—	—	—
032	Shuqaiq Mangrove	AS	•	—	—	—	•	—	—	•	—	—
033	Jabal Qaha	JZ	—	—	—	—	—	—	—	•	—	—
034	Jabal Faifa	JZ	—	—	—	—	•	•	•	—	—	—
035	Malaki Dam	JZ	•	•	—	—	—	—	•	—	•	—
036	Wadi Jawwah	JZ	—	—	—	•	•	—	•	•	—	—
037	Jizan Bay	JZ	•	•	•	—	—	—	•	—	—	—
038	Farasan Islands	JZ	•	•	—	—	•	—	•	—	•	—
039	Khawr Wahlan	JZ	—	—	—	—	—	—	•	•	—	—

Key to regions

AS	Asir Emirate
DR	Durayyat Emirate
EP	Eastern Province Emirate
HL	Ha'il Emirate
JW	Al-Jawf Emirate
JZ	Jizan Emirate
MD	Al-Madinah Emirate
MK	Makkah Emirate
RD	Ar-Riyadh Emirate
TB	Tabuk Emirate

Key to criteria

1 Regularly holds a significant number of a globally threatened species.

2i Regularly holds 1% or more of a species' biogeographical or flyway or Middle Eastern population (waterbirds and seabirds only).

2ii Regularly holds 20,000 or more waterbirds.

2iii Migratory 'bottleneck' site: more than 3,000 raptors or more than 5,000 storks or more than 2,000 cranes pass in a season.

3 Regularly holds a significant number of a species which is threatened or declining within the Middle East. Only the top five sites for each such species in the country are considered to qualify as IBAs.

4 Regularly holds a significant number of a species whose world population is wholly or largely restricted to the Middle East. Only the top five sites for each such species in the country are considered to qualify as IBAs.

5i Representative example of a habitat, associated with a characteristic assemblage of bird species.

5ii Rare/threatened/unique habitat, associated with a characteristic assemblage of bird species.

6 Site important for bird conservation through education/research/tourism.

0 Selected for other reasons. See 'Comments on the inventory'.

Comments on the inventory

1. The majority of the data used in compiling the site accounts was collected in the late 1980s and early 1990s. Information on bird populations is regionally uneven. One result is a bias in favour of better explored areas, therefore the inventory

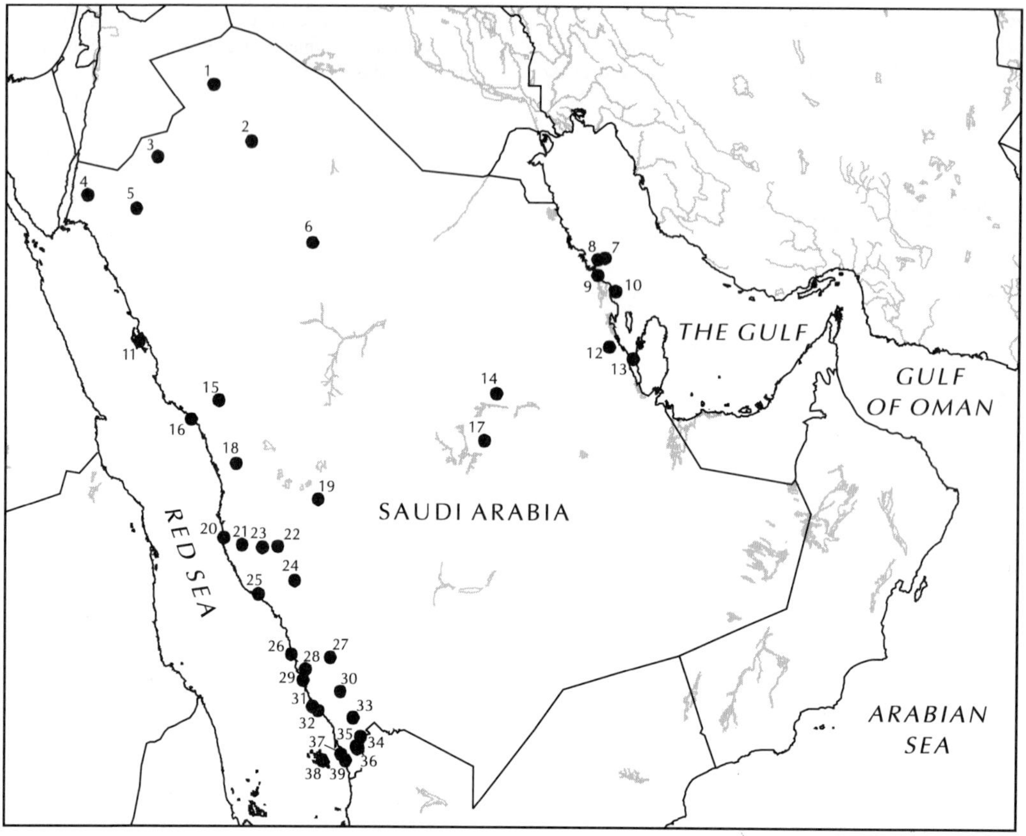

should be regarded as preliminary.

2. The site name has been transliterated from the Arabic, and is sometimes followed by an alternative site name in brackets. This is then followed by the name of the region in brackets, where appropriate. The regions given are the emirates.
3. Precise areas are given only for protected areas and some of the sites which have been well documented. Boundaries have not been defined for the non-protected sites, and any areas given in these cases are only crude estimates. No area is given for one site because its boundaries have not been determined. The areas given for some offshore island sites (important for breeding seabirds) do not include the area of the surrounding seas which are important as feeding grounds, because the latter have not been identified with sufficient accuracy as yet.
4. Figures in brackets after species' names, and in the boxes, are the maximum daily counts of individuals recorded (not pairs), unless otherwise stated. All counts of wintering birds are from the month of January, unless otherwise stated.
5. The following species (wholly or largely confined to the Middle East) are widespread and common over much Saudi Arabia, and their presence generally has not been used when applying the 'Top 5 site' criterion in category 4 (as depicted in the above table), since identification of sites for them would be of negligible conservation value: *Pycnonotus xanthopygos*, *Oenanthe lugentoides*, *Sylvia minula*, *Turdoides squamiceps* and *Onychognathus tristramii*. They are however mentioned in the site accounts, due to their interest in a Middle Eastern context.

Glossary

dawhat, embayment
harrat, volcanic region
hima, traditional natural resource conservation area
khawr, tidal inlet or coastal lagoon
jabal, mountain
jibal, mountain range
madinat, town
sabkhah/sabkhat, saline mudflat
wadi, watercourse (usually seasonally dry) or valley.

001 Harrat al-Harrah (Al-Jawf, Durayyat)

Special Nature Reserve

31°00′N 38°50′E
c.1,377,500 ha

■ Site description

A huge desert area of northern Saudi Arabia, close to the border with Jordan, and 80 km north-west of Sakakah. Undulating, black, basalt boulder-fields with numerous volcanic cones and frequent low hills, interspersed with siltflats and some sabkhah. Wadis are generally shallow. Rainfall is seasonal (every winter) but varies greatly in amount between years. There is rarely any surface water except for a permanent reservoir at Dawmat al-Jandl (see site 002) near the southern edge of the reserve. Except for a very few stunted palms the vegetation is devoid of trees, and is sparse except after good winter/spring rains, although drainage features contain a reasonable cover of small shrubs (*Artemisia*, *Haloxylon*, *Zilla*).

■ Birds

See box for key species. The site holds the most diverse breeding community of larks in the Middle East: *Eremalauda dunni*, *Ammomanes cincturus*, *A. deserti*, *Alaemon alaudipes*, *Ramphocoris clotbey*, *Calandrella rufescens*, *Galerida cristata* and *Eremophila bilopha* are regular, and *Melanocorypha bimaculata* and *Calandrella brachydactyla* may breed in some years after good rains. Other breeding species include *Aquila chrysaetos*, *Buteo rufinus*, *Falco tinnunculus*, *F. pelegrinoides* (probably), *Alectoris chukar* (now possibly extinct), *Cursorius cursor*, *Bubo ascalaphus* and *Athene noctua*. A concentration of 10,000–15,000 sandgrouse (70% *Pterocles orientalis*, 30% *P. alchata*) has been recorded at the eastern edge of the reserve in winter, and other wintering species include *Falco columbarius* (relatively common) and *Sylvia conspicillata* (regular). The site was one of the last places that *Struthio camelus* occurred in Saudi Arabia before being hunted to extinction; the last documented record from the area was in January 1930.

Globally threatened species

Aquila heliaca	Scarce winter visitor.
Falco naumanni	Passage migrant and probably an occasional summer visitor (2 pairs).
Chlamydotis undulata	Breeds (c.50 nests) and winters (max. 570, November).

1% or more of population

	Breeding (pairs)	Wintering	Passage
Eudromias morinellus	—	1,500–3,000	—

Regionally threatened or declining species

Falco cherrug	Regular passage migrant.

Species restricted wholly or largely to the Middle East

Ammoperdix heyi	Common resident.
Strix butleri	Uncommon resident.
Oenanthe finschii	Common winter visitor.
Carpospiza brachydactyla	Uncommon summer visitor and occasionally common passage migrant.

■ Other threatened/endemic wildlife

Mammals: *Canis lupus* (V), *Vulpes rueppelli* (K), *Felis margarita* (K), *Gazella subgutturosa* (rare) and possibly *G. gazella* (V).

■ Conservation issues

The site is an established NCWCD reserve and among the best protected, with a large staff of rangers and an aerial patrol. Nomadic pastoralists and their sheep and goats are excluded, but free-ranging camels are not, and in years of average rainfall the area still verges on being overgrazed. There is still some poaching of *Chlamydotis undulata* and gazelles by illegal hunters and by those given 'permits' to attend their camels.

■ Further reading

Goriup (1989), Goriup *et al.* (1992), Green (1984), Jennings (1988), Symens (1988).

002 Dawmat al-Jandl Wetland (Al-Jawf)

Non-hunting Zone

29°48′N 39°53′E
c.2,500 ha

■ Site description

This site, on the north-east side of Dawmat al-Jandl town, is one of the very few remaining wetland habitats in the northern desert. Until 1983–1984 it was a medium-sized natural lake surrounded by a large marsh of reeds and sedges (900 ha overall), but this has now been drained and converted to agricultural smallholdings; the water is pumped to an elevated basin in the hills overlooking the former marsh, forming a reservoir (150 ha). From here water flows through a number of irrigation channels back to the agricultural areas, where there are some very small, scattered remains of marshland. The reservoir is used for recreation in summer, and fish *Tilapia* have been introduced.

■ Birds

See box for key species. There is little detailed information at present, although a January 1993 count found 2,294 waterbirds including 1,346 *Fulica atra*, and up to 10,000 *F. atra* were present in the colder winter of 1991–1992, when some unidentified *Cygnus* sp. were also present. Flocks of over 1,000 *Chlidonias leucopterus* have occurred in late April.

■ Other threatened/endemic wildlife

Mammals: *Vulpes rueppelli* (K).

■ Conservation issues

The site is situated in the non-hunting zone which extends around NCWCD's large, northern reserves but shooting nevertheless occurs, and this and other disturbance seem to be the major threats for the birds on the reservoir, which have no alternative sites in the vicinity. Over-extraction of water is a potential threat.

Globally threatened species

Oxyura leucocephala	Possible presence in cold winters needs confirmation (one recorded on the former lake, October–November 1983).
Haliaeetus leucoryphus	One found shot, January 1990.

Regionally threatened or declining species

Falco cherrug	One seen in April.

■ Further reading

Green (1984).

003 At-Tubayq (Durayyat)

Special Nature Reserve, Biological Reserve and Resource Use Reserve

29°28′N 37°15′E
500,000 ha

■ Site description

This huge area is a raised platform of old, dark sandstone rising 300–400 m above the undulating sandy plain which surrounds it. The ramparts are extremely broken and rocky, precipitous in places, but the plateau is flat. There is no permanent water and, apart from a flush of ephemeral plant growth after rains, vegetation is limited to drought-resistant shrubs (e.g. *Haloxylon*) and grasses with a few stunted *Acacia* trees.

■ Birds

See box for key species. Other breeding species include *Buteo rufinus*, *Aquila chrysaetos* (probably 2–3 pairs), *Cursorius cursor* and *Rhodopechys githaginea*. This is one of the last areas in Arabia where *Struthio camelus* occurred and might be a possible reintroduction site.

■ Other threatened/endemic wildlife

Mammals: *Capra nubiana* (I).

Globally threatened species

Aegypius monachus	Has been recorded and may breed.

Regionally threatened or declining species

Neophron percnopterus	Probably a scarce breeder.
Torgos tracheliotus	Probably at least 10 pairs breeding.

Species restricted wholly or largely to the Middle East

Ammoperdix heyi	Resident.
Oenanthe monacha	Scarce but widespread breeder.

■ Conservation issues

The site is an NCWCD reserve (established primarily for *Capra nubiana*) with a permanent staff of rangers; 240,000 ha have full protection as Special Nature Reserve and Biological Reserve. Being such a remote area and one which does not offer good grazing, the region is little-visited by nomadic pastoralists and no important threats have been identified.

■ Further reading

Jennings (1992).

004 Jabal al-Lawz (Tabuk)

Unprotected

28°40′N 35°15′E
30,000 ha

■ Site description

A group of granitic mountains with at least 20 peaks over 2,000 m, rising from 700 m to a maximum of 2,549 m (Jabal Fayhan, the tallest mountain in northern Arabia and high enough to have snow in winter). There is some permanent running water and the rocky high mountain habitats are densely vegetated in places, with clear zoning. *Retama raetam* scrub dominates the wadis; trees include *Pistacia*, *Ficus*, *Salix* and (on the summit) some stunted *Juniperus*. *Acacia* trees/bushes are only found below 1,200 m. The area is remote and very sparsely populated.

Birds

See box for key species. Other residents include *Aquila verreauxii* (min. one pair), *Alectoris chukar* (numerous; the only site in Saudi Arabia), *Cercomela melanura*, *Nectarinia osea*, *Lanius excubitor*, *Corvus rhipidurus* and *Rhodopechys githaginea*.

Regionally threatened or declining species

Gypaetus barbatus	Probably resident.
Neophron percnopterus	Resident.
Gyps fulvus	Resident.
Carpodacus synoicus	Common resident.

Species restricted wholly or largely to the Middle East

Ammoperdix heyi	Common resident.
Strix butleri	Resident.
Oenanthe finschii	Winter visitor.
Turdoides squamiceps	Resident.
Onychognathus tristramii	Common resident.

Other threatened/endemic wildlife

Mammals: *Canis lupus* (V), *Capra nubiana* (I) and possibly *Gazella gazella* (V). Flora: the site is of high botanical interest; species include wild date palm *Phoenix dactylifera*, wild almond *Prunus dulcis* (only site in Arabia), wild tulip *Tulipa biflora* (one of two sites in Arabia).

Conservation issues

The site is threatened by grazing, tree-cutting, road construction and military development. It is proposed as a Natural Reserve, Biological Reserve and Resource Use Reserve in the NCWCD System Plan for Protected Areas. The area is relatively little-known biologically and further surveys would be advantageous.

Further reading

Jennings (1989).

005 King Faisal Airbase, Tabuk (Tabuk)

Unprotected

28°23′N 36°38′E
Area not defined

Site description

Sewage settling lagoons within the airbase which support large reedbeds *Phragmites*, though these are subject to cutting and burning. The lagoons are bordered partly by sand and scrub desert, partly by areas with irrigated trees (mainly *Eucalyptus*), shrubs and grass. About 10 km from the base and c.5 km from Military City is a reservoir of c.100 ha in an area of desert bordered by military training grounds. The Tabuk area, surrounded on three sides by mountains, was formerly desert but is now intensively cultivated.

Birds

See box for key species. Breeding birds of the sewage lagoons include *Ixobrychus minutus* (possible), *Rallus aquaticus*, *Porzana parva*, *P. pusilla* (possible), *Charadrius dubius*, *Acrocephalus stentoreus* and *Rhodopechys obsoleta* (10–15 pairs). The importance of the reservoir is not yet known as it has been visited only twice, in March and April 1990, when birds present included grebes, c.1,000 ducks, c.700 *Fulica atra*, waders and c.400 *Chlidonias leucopterus*.

1% or more of population

	Breeding (pairs)	Wintering	Passage
Aythya nyroca	4–9	—	—

Regionally threatened or declining species

Aythya nyroca	Breeds at sewage lagoons (see above).

Other threatened/endemic wildlife

None known to BirdLife International.

Conservation issues

The area is not protected, but is within a military zone and as such receives some unintended protection from disturbance and hunting. It seems likely that the sewage system will eventually be upgraded, and the lagoons may well then disappear. Part of the site is included in the NCWCD System Plan for Protected Areas.

Further reading

Stagg (1989).

006 Jabal Aja and Northern Ha'il (Ha'il)

Unprotected

27°40′N 41°38′E
400,000 ha

■ Site description

Jabal Aja (27°30′N 41°30′E, 200,000 ha) lies west and south-west of Ha'il city and is an extensive outcrop of granite mountains with deep valleys. The site is extended north-east to the edge of the Nafud Desert to include an area used for surveys of migrant *Grus virgo* (Jibal at-Tuwal and Dilan al-Jilf, 27°50′N 41°45′E, 200,000 ha)—an area of flattish semi-desert and sandstone hills, punctuated by medium-altitude granitic mountains with deep valleys. The climate is fairly benign (altitude 800–1,550 m), and the area is one of the greenest in northern Arabia; in wet springs the desert and sandstone hills bloom, and many ephemeral pools and lakes are formed. Valleys in granite mountains are often lined with many *Acacia* trees. Much of the crane survey area is under wheat cultivation by pivot irrigation systems.

■ Birds

See box for key species. The site is crucially important for two species. It seems to lie at the centre of the spring flyway for the threatened African-wintering population of *Grus virgo*, and may be the best site for assessing the population size; flocks use both desert and agricultural habitats. Other breeding species include *Tachymarptis melba* (probable), *Eremalauda dunni*, *Eremophila bilopha*, *Passer hispaniolensis*, *Rhodopechys obsoleta* and *R. githaginea*. A wide range of raptors passes through in spring, and migration of swifts and passerines (especially larks, hirundines and wheatears) can be spectacular; migrants are attracted to agricultural areas in dry years, but otherwise prefer natural habitats.

1% or more of population

	Breeding (pairs)	Wintering	Passage
Grus virgo	—	—	5,600

Regionally threatened or declining species

Neophron percnopterus	Resident on Jabal Aja (10–100 pairs).
Gyps fulvus	Resident (perhaps 100 pairs): possibly the largest population in Saudi Arabia, despite what seems to have been a considerable decline since the mid-1980s.
Falco cherrug	Spring passage migrant (seasonal total 3).
Grus virgo	Common spring migrant (see text).

Species restricted wholly or largely to the Middle East

Ammoperdix heyi	Abundant resident.
Strix butleri	Resident (recorded at nearby Jabal Selma).
Pycnonotus xanthopygos	Common resident.
Irania gutturalis	Spring passage migrant.
Oenanthe finschii	Spring passage migrant and winter visitor.
Sylvia mystacea	Winter visitor, probably in considerable numbers, and common spring passage migrant.
Sylvia minula	Winters in considerable numbers; common on spring passage.
Turdoides squamiceps	Common resident in mountain wadis.
Carpospiza brachydactyla	Irregular summer visitor (possibly 1,000 pairs in 1993).
Emberiza cineracea	Spring passage migrant.

■ Other threatened/endemic wildlife

Mammals: *Felis margarita* (K), *Canis lupus* (V) and *Capra nubiana* (I). Flora: the site is of high botanical interest. Reptiles and amphibians: the area may have functioned as a Pleistocene refuge during ice-ages.

■ Conservation issues

Jabal Aja is proposed as a Special Nature Reserve, Natural Reserve, Resource Use Reserve and Controlled Hunting Reserve, and establishment is proceeding. A management plan is being developed by local government, NCWCD and King Abdulaziz University, while NCWCD has established a monitoring programme for key species. The proximity of Jabal Aja to Ha'il city makes it popular for recreation, and there are threats from uncontrolled road and house building. Feral donkeys are present but probably affect bird populations relatively little. Semi-desert areas adjacent to agricultural zones are heavily grazed but seem able to recover after wet winters/springs.

■ Further reading

Newton and Symens (1993), Newton *et al.* (1993), Symens *et al.* (1992).

007 Gulf Coral Islands (Eastern Province)
Unprotected

27°22´N 49°52´E
c.2,000 ha

Site description
Five uninhabited coral islands (Harqus 27°56´N 49°41´E, Karan 27°44´N 49°50´E, Kurayn 27°39´N 49°50´E, Jana 27°22´N 49°54´E, Jurayd 27°11´N 49°52´E) in the northern Arabian Gulf, 35–90 km offshore. Island areas range from 2 to 120 ha (total c.190 ha), with a maximum elevation of 3–4 m, and they are surrounded by extensive, shallow coral reefs. There are wide, sand beach platforms, and the central parts of the larger islands are well-vegetated with *Salsola* and *Suaeda*, and *Mesembryanthemum* after good rains. The islands support local fisheries, and are valuable for recreational diving.

Birds
See box for key species. The site is considered to be the most important breeding site for *Sterna bengalensis* in the world. See box for key species (numbers of terns are 1991–1993 three-year-averages). Other breeding species include *Galerida cristata*, *Melanocorypha bimaculata* (irregular) and *Calandrella brachydactyla* (irregular). The islands are used as a stopover site by considerable numbers of passage migrants (mainly passerines), especially in spring.

Globally threatened species

Crex crex	Passage migrant in good numbers.

1% or more of population

	Breeding (pairs)	Wintering	Passage
Sterna bergii	c.3,500	—	—
Sterna bengalensis	c.24,250	—	—
Sterna repressa	c.10,400	—	—
Sterna anaethetus	c.34,400	—	—

Regionally threatened or declining species

Phalacrocorax nigrogularis	Breeds on Kurayn (av. 30 nests, 1991–1993); the only surviving colony north of Bahrain.

Species restricted wholly or largely to the Middle East

Phalacrocorax nigrogularis	See above.
Glareola nordmanni	Good numbers occur on spring passage.
Sterna repressa	Abundant summer visitor (see above).
Sterna saundersi	Summer visitor (50, June); breeds irregularly (2–3 pairs).
Irania gutturalis	Passage migrant in good numbers.
Hippolais languida	Passage migrant in good numbers.
Sylvia mystacea	Passage migrant in good numbers.
Sylvia minula	Passage migrant in good numbers.
Sylvia althaea	Passage migrant in good numbers.

Other threatened/endemic wildlife
Reptiles: important breeding populations of sea-turtles *Eretmochelys imbricata* (E) and *Chelonia mydas* (E). Invertebrates: the surrounding coral reefs are thought to be the best-developed and most diverse in the Gulf.

Conservation issues
The site is included in the NCWCD System Plan for Protected Areas, and establishment as a Special Nature Reserve and Resource Use Reserve is proceeding. It has also been mentioned as a potential Ramsar Site. Disturbance from fishermen, recreational divers and the military is increasing. Egg collecting by fishermen occurs regularly, but is not a major threat. Plans exist to build coastguard facilities on Kurayn and an oil installation on Jana. Another island, al-Arabiyah, has already lost all its breeding seabirds and sea-turtles due to the construction of a coastguard station. Oil pollution is a permanent threat. Feral mice *Mus musculus* occur on most islands and can be extremely damaging when their population peaks coincide with the tern breeding season; a rat was found on Karan in 1992 and a feral cat on Jana in 1991 (both were removed); the increasing rate of visiting of the islands by fishing boats and other craft increase the risk of further damaging introductions. The monitoring of terns has led to a wide awareness of the value of the islands, and conservation measures should include strict control of access during breeding seasons, a ban on military activity, control or extermination of introduced mice and complete avoidance of introduction of other non-indigenous species, and the inclusion of the islands as priority sites in oil contingency plans. There should be continued monitoring of terns' breeding activity and an assessment of the islands' importance for migrating passerines. Guided tours and other activities could be used to educate those who use the islands (fishermen, divers, coastguards).

Further reading
Basson *et al.* (1981), Symens and Evans (1993).

008 Abu Ali (Eastern Province)

Unprotected

27°20´N 49°40´E
c.12,500 ha

■ Site description

Two long, elevated inshore Gulf islands (Abu Ali and Batinah) north-east of Jubail, linked to each other and to the mainland by causeways. They consist largely of sabkhah and sandsheets, the latter becoming very well-vegetated with grasses and herbs after winter rains. The exposed northern shores are mainly sand beach with fringing reefs in places, while on the sheltered south side there are intertidal flats of sand and sand-mud, bordered by large saltmarshes. A shallow, brackish pond is present near the eastern tip and there are several smaller islands in the enclosed southern bay. There are oil installations and small traditional fishing camps, and the site is used for weekend recreation.

■ Birds

See box for key species. Vast numbers of *Sterna saundersi/S. albifrons* congregate to moult after the breeding season, as do large numbers of other tern species (see box). Breeding birds include *Charadrius alexandrinus*, *Alaemon alaudipes*, *Calandrella rufescens* and possibly *Pandion haliaetus*. Other wintering species include *Larus genei* (1,267). Numerous migrating passerines use the site as a stop-over in spring, and good numbers are present in winter.

1% or more of population

	Breeding (pairs)	Wintering	Passage
Phalacrocorax carbo	—	8,000	—
Sterna bengalensis	—	—	4,800
Sterna sandvicensis	—	—	2,000–3,000
Sterna repressa	120–250	—	8,000+ (Sep)
Sterna saundersi/albifrons	8–12	—	c.14,000

Species restricted wholly or largely to the Middle East

Dromas ardeola	Passage migrant (max. 135).
Sterna repressa	Common passage migrant, especially in autumn (see above); small numbers breed.
Sterna saundersi/albifrons	Post-breeding, moulting birds congregate in huge numbers (see text); small numbers breed.

■ Other threatened/endemic wildlife

None known to BirdLife International.

■ Conservation issues

The site is proposed as a Resource Use Reserve in the NCWCD System Plan for Protected Areas, and establishment is proceeding. At present large areas are fenced and protected as a military area, and access to the whole site is strictly controlled; the consequent lack of grazing greatly benefits the vegetation. The configuration of the coastline renders the site particularly vulnerable to major oil spills in the northern Gulf, and the eastern tip of the islands is increasingly used by the oil industry. The proximity of the expanding Jubail Industrial City may increase disturbance from recreational activities in the near future.

■ Further reading

Evans and Keijl (1993a,b).

009 Sabkhat al-Fasl Lagoons (Eastern Province)

Unprotected

27°00´N 49°40´E
c.500 ha

■ Site description

Evaporation lagoons on the south-west border of Jubail Industrial City. The site consists of a large sabkhah area surrounded by landfill and divided up by sand dams, fed by excess treated organic wastewater which produces a large biomass of microflora and -fauna. The water is very shallow (0–30 cm) and is influenced by wind, creating a tidal effect as wind direction changes. Rainwater is a secondary source of water; after heavy winter rains the water surface can be more than doubled, occasionally reaching 2,500 ha. Water is fed into the site only from October to May, and the lagoons can dry out from the end of July, but in years with good rains a water area of c.100–150 ha remains all summer. Three large concrete reservoirs (c.100 ha) are included in the site. These, and some parts of the edge of the sabkhah, are vegetated with reedbeds *Phragmites* and *Tamarix* scrub.

■ Birds

See box for key species. Other breeding species include *Phoenicopterus ruber* (unsuccessful attempts) and *Acrocephalus scirpaceus* (suspected).

Other wintering species include *Phoenicopterus ruber* (1,200) and more than 5,000 ducks, including *Anas penelope*, *A. strepera*, *A. crecca*, *A. platyrhynchos*, *A. acuta* and *A. clypeata*. The site is used by large numbers of waders on passage (see box), including *Calidris alba* (657, April–May) and *Tringa stagnatilis* (184, August–October), and *Falco peregrinus* is a regular passage migrant (max. seasonal total 20) and winter visitor (daily max. 1–3).

1% or more of population

	Breeding (pairs)	Wintering	Passage
Recurvirostra avosetta	45	420	—
Charadrius alexandrinus	70	2,800	3,500
Charadrius mongolus	—	—	1,800 (Apr–May)
Calidris minuta	—	—	4,850 (Oct–Nov)
Calidris ferruginea	—	—	3,100 (Apr–May)
Calidris alpina	—	5,900	11,350 (Aug–Oct)
Limicola falcinellus	—	—	700 (Apr–May)
Philomachus pugnax	—	—	2,650 (Apr–May)
Arenaria interpres	—	—	650 (Apr–May)
Larus cachinnans/argentatus	—	600–1,200	—

Other threatened/endemic wildlife

None known to BirdLife International.

Conservation issues

In the planning of Jubail Industrial City this area was mapped as a permanent buffer zone between the industrial and urban zones, and was included in the NCWCD System Plan for Protected Areas as part of a larger coastal reserve. At present it is a core area in the proposed Natural Reserve of Dawhat ad-Dafi and Dawhat al-Musallamiyah: the site had great value as a refuge for small waders (*Charadrius* and *Calidris*) after the oil pollution of adjacent intertidal areas during the 1991 Gulf War oil spills, and it is well placed for utilization in educational projects on the importance of the Gulf for waterfowl and on the importance of man-made wetlands. Declaration and establishment of the reserve are proceeding. As a man-made site the lagoons may be only temporary and are threatened by changes to their water supply. The effluent of the water treatment plant is normally used to irrigate urban plantations, and only the excess is fed into the site for evaporation, but the continuing expansion of Jubail city may mean that no excess water is available in the near future. Deliberate persecution of birds and falcon-trapping occur regularly.

Further reading

Evans and Keijl (1993a,b).

010 Tarut Bay (Eastern Province)

Unprotected

26°40′N 50°10′E
c.41,000 ha

Site description

A clear, shallow, predominantly sandy bay with extensive seagrass beds; Qatif is on its west side and Dammam on the south. Local factors make the intertidal zone the richest in the Saudi Arabian sector of the Gulf: the bay is well-protected from winds and from water currents, allowing sedimentation of the finest particles, and a large nutrient input is provided by run-off from the Qatif oases and by organic waste effluent. The extensive intertidal flats of sand-mud and mud were formerly fringed by extensive mangrove and saltmarshes, but much of these have now been destroyed by land-claim. The bay is an important nursery for shrimps and fish and sustains several traditional fishing communities. It contains one of the largest oil facilities in the world and includes several important archaeological sites.

Birds

See boxes for key species. The bay is the most important site for wintering and migrating waders and other waterbirds on the Saudi Arabian Gulf coast, with a total of c.58,000 waterbirds wintering in 1991/92, and more than 20,000 present in April–May 1991. See box for key species: breeding species nest on Za'l, a small island; winter figures are for February 1993; migration figures are incomplete through lack of comprehensive surveys in autumn, but most of the key wintering species, plus additional waterfowl, are likely to migrate through in significant numbers, especially the waders. Other wintering species include *Aquila clanga* (6; much declined since 1983 when c.20 present, perhaps due to land-claim of mangrove) and *Pandion haliaetus* (11).

Globally threatened species

Haliaeetus leucoryphus	Very rare winter visitor (2, November 1979; January 1987).
Haliaeetus albicilla	Very rare winter visitor (1, July 1950; 1, October 1978).

Species restricted wholly or largely to the Middle East

Sterna repressa	Breeds (c.1,250 pairs).

1% or more of population

	Breeding (pairs)	Wintering	Passage
Phalacrocorax carbo	—	4,850	—
Egretta gularis	186	435	—
Casmerodius albus	—	121	—
Ardea cinerea	—	467	—
Himantopus himantopus	—	390	—
Charadrius alexandrinus	—	2,755	—
Charadrius mongolus	—	2,160	2,580
Charadrius leschenaultii	—	901	—
Pluvialis squatarola	—	1,708	1,469
Calidris tenuirostris	—	—	108
Calidris alpina	—	7,800	—
Limicola falcinellus	—	645	281
Limosa lapponica	—	1,795	5,136
Numenius phaeopus	—	183	188
Numenius arquata	—	1,820	—
Tringa totanus	—	4,900	—
Tringa cinerea	—	1,670	2,895
Arenaria interpres	—	1,104	1,505
Larus genei	—	4,480	—
Larus cachinnans/L. argentatus	—	2,840	—
Sterna nilotica	—	419	—
Sterna caspia	—	236	—
Sterna bengalensis	114–250	—	—
Sterna anaethetus	c.10,000	—	—

■ Other threatened/endemic wildlife

Mammals: *Dugong dugon* (V). Reptiles: *Chelonia mydas* (E; important feeding area).

■ Conservation issues

This coast is subject to large-scale urban expansion and to agricultural intensification. Land-claim continues to destroy large parts of the intertidal zone, and much of the bay itself has been dredged. Bird-trapping with mistnets occurs frequently in the remaining mangrove. The oil facilities at Ras Tanurah provide a permanent threat of oil pollution, smaller and medium-sized spills having occurred frequently in the past. There is heavy disturbance from recreational activities at weekends. The site is proposed as a Resource Use Reserve in the NCWCD System Plan for Protected Areas but is not accepted as a potential Ramsar Site. The strict and immediate protection of several relatively intact, smaller-scale, core areas would seem to be a high priority.

■ Further reading

Basson *et al.* (1981), Evans and Keijl (1993a).

011 Al-Wajh Bank (Tabuk)

Unprotected

25°35′N 36°45′E
c.288,000 ha

■ Site description

A group of northern Red Sea islands lying off the coast between al-Wajh and Umm Lajj, with a mixture of rocky or sandy, and vegetated (mangrove *Avicennia* and salt-tolerant bushes *Salicornia*) or barren habitats. There are some low cliffs of less than 5 m, and seagrass beds offshore.

■ Birds

See box for key species. The islands are important for their breeding population of *Falco concolor* (see box) and probably for their breeding seabirds (which are very little-known, however) including *Sula leucogaster* (100+ pairs, August/September 1982), *Sterna caspia* (3+ pairs, February) and *S. bengalensis*; *Pandion haliaetus* (106 birds) and *Sterna anaethetus* have been seen in October and may breed. The site is of low value for wintering waterbirds.

■ Other threatened/endemic wildlife

Mammals: *Dugong dugon* (V). Reptiles: sea-turtles (globally threatened) nest.

Globally threatened species

Larus leucophthalmus	Summer visitor (last confirmed breeding was in 1982).

Regionally threatened or declining species

Falco concolor	At least 40 pairs breed.

Species restricted wholly or largely to the Middle East

Dromas ardeola	Breeds.
Larus hemprichii	Breeds (15 pairs).
Larus leucophthalmus	Breeds (see above).
Sterna repressa	Summer visitor.

■ Conservation issues

No threats are known, but there have been no proper surveys of breeding seabirds, and collection of seabird eggs probably occurs. The site is proposed as a Resource Use Reserve in the NCWCD System Plan for Protected Areas. Summer surveys for breeding seabirds are urgently needed.

■ Further reading

Evans (1987).

012 Al-Hasa Lagoons (Eastern Province)
Unprotected

25°30′N 50°00′E
c.7,500 ha

Site description
A long, narrow, man-made river, the only large-scale freshwater habitat in the Eastern Province, running east-south-east from Hofuf and Abqaiq towards al-'Uqair. It is formed by run-off from al-Hasa oasis and sewage effluent from Hofuf, Abqaiq and numerous small towns, and frequently disappears under sand-dunes, to surface again a few kilometres further on. There are numerous pools of up to c.250 ha, often surrounded by large reedbeds. The rest of the area consists of sandy gravel plain and sand-dunes interspersed with sabkhahs and aeolian sand-fields.

Birds
See box for key species. There is little information on the site at present. Other breeding species include *Ixobrychus minutus* (possible, in low numbers), *Tadorna ferruginea* (possible), *Cursorius cursor*, *Acrocephalus melanopogon* (only Saudi Arabian breeding site) and *Locustella luscinioides* (probable). Large numbers of wintering and migrating waterbirds have been observed during several aerial surveys: *Ardea cinerea* (50–60), *Egretta garzetta* (100), 10,000–15,000 ducks including *Tadorna ferruginea* (50), *Grus grus* (22), and small flocks of *Philomachus pugnax* and *Limosa limosa*.

Other threatened/endemic wildlife
None known to BirdLife International.

Globally threatened species

Chlamydotis undulata — Regular in small numbers on migration and in winter, according to local people.

1% or more of population

	Breeding (pairs)	Wintering	Passage
Himantopus himantopus	Breeds	200	—

Regionally threatened or declining species

Botaurus stellaris — Winter visitor and passage migrant.
Aythya nyroca — Breeds in unknown but possibly significant numbers.
Francolinus francolinus — Possibly resident; species may be extinct in Saudi Arabia.

Conservation issues
Some of the pools are reasonably well protected through their inaccessibility, being surrounded by sabkhah and sand-dunes, but many are regularly disturbed by hunters and sport-shooters and the area is widely used for recreation by people from the al-Hasa region at weekends. An increasing demand for waste-water is reducing the amount of run-off and the watercourse is often diverted for agriculture or for development projects. The site is proposed as a Special Nature Reserve, Biological Reserve and Resource Use Reserve in the NCWCD System Plan for Protected Areas.

013 Gulf of Salwah (Eastern Province)
Unprotected

25°15′N 50°40′E
62,500 ha

Site description
The western sector of a shallow, enclosed bay between Saudi Arabia, Bahrain and Qatar, from al-'Uqair south to Salwah on the border with Qatar (c.100 km of coastline). It is bordered by a generally well-vegetated sandy coast where the high level of groundwater allows the growth of date palms and reedbeds at the edge of the sea, with reeds *Phragmites* often extending into the seawater. The area contains large sabkhahs and elevated peninsulas surrounded by shallow, hypersaline lagoons, and the intertidal zone consists largely of flats of sand and sand-rock. Marine substrates are sand and rock supporting extensive seagrass beds. Elevated parts have been isolated by the present water level, forming islands close to the coast (e.g. Zakhnuniyah, Samamik, Judhaym). These are often muddier than the mainland, support a good growth of salt-tolerant vegetation, and seabird colonies are found on sandier parts. Unaybir, a small island at the southern tip of the gulf, consists of elevated fossil coral rock. Small-scale traditional fishing occurs, with a small fishing settlement on Zakhnuniyah. The mainland supports major rock quarrying operations and is used for camel grazing. The ruins of al-'Uqair are of considerable historical value.

Birds
See box for key species. The gulf holds the main breeding sites in Saudi Arabia of *Phalacrocorax*

nigrogularis (see box). There are important breeding numbers of three species of tern (see box), as well as the only known breeding *Sterna caspia* on the Saudi Arabian Gulf coast (3–5 pairs). There are many wintering *Larus ichthyaetus* (189 in January 1993) and *L. cachinnans/L. argentatus*, largely associated with breeding colonies of *P. nigrogularis*. Other winter counts include 1,260 *Larus genei*.

1% or more of population

	Breeding (pairs)	Wintering	Passage
Podiceps cristatus	—	1,086	—
Podiceps nigricollis	—	2,378	—
Phalacrocorax nigrogularis	11,000	—	—
Egretta gularis	100	486	—
Ardea cinerea	—	156	—
Larus cachinnans/argentatus	—	2,500	—
Sterna bengalensis	2,000	—	—
Sterna repressa	thousands	—	—
Sterna anaethetus	thousands	—	—

Regionally threatened or declining species

Phalacrocorax nigrogularis	Breeds in winter on Judhaym (over 10,000 pairs) and Unaybir (over 1,000 pairs).

Species restricted wholly or largely to the Middle East

Phalacrocorax nigrogularis	Breeds in winter (see above).
Sterna repressa	Abundant summer visitor (see above).

Other threatened/endemic wildlife

Mammals: *Dugong dugon* (V; globally important population).

Conservation issues

The marine environment is relatively undisturbed, but would act as an oil trap in the case of a large spill to the north. Chicks from the *Phalacrocorax nigrogularis* colonies are occasionally harvested by people from the Hofuf and Dammam areas. Quarrying is a major threat to large parts of the elevated coastline, and vegetation on some parts has been removed for the creation of recreational beaches. At present there is only a small area of land-claim near al-'Uqair, but plans exist to create a large recreational and residential complex with marinas and artificial beaches. The site is proposed as a Resource Use Reserve in the NCWCD System Plan for Protected Areas.

014 Al-Ha'ir (Ar-Riyadh)

Special Nature Reserve, Natural Reserve (500 ha)

24°30′N 46°50′E
2,500 ha

Site description

An artificial, permanently flowing river of treated effluent run-off, running for 50 km along Wadi Hanifah, 25 km south of Riyadh. The river flows mostly between rocky cliffs, incorporating many pools fringed with reeds and *Tamarix*. In several places wide lagoons are formed between sand-dunes, and there are some adjacent small and medium-sized pivot-irrigation farms.

Birds

See box for key species. Other breeding species include *Ixobrychus minutus*, *Ardeola ralloides*, *Ardea purpurea* and *Acrocephalus scirpaceus*. Other wintering species include *Ciconia nigra*, *Aquila clanga* (20) and *Circus aeruginosus* (17). Over 220 species have been recorded.

Globally threatened species

Marmaronetta angustirostris	Scarce visitor.
Aquila heliaca	Winter visitor in small numbers.
Falco naumanni	Passage migrant and winter visitor in variable numbers.
Crex crex	Rare passage migrant.
Vanellus gregarius	Rare passage migrant and winter visitor.

1% or more of population

	Breeding (pairs)	Wintering	Passage
Nycticorax nycticorax	breeds	130	—
Egretta garzetta	—	340	—
Ardea cinerea	—	366	—
Aythya nyroca	breeds	69	—
Himantopus himantopus	—	236	—

Regionally threatened or declining species

Aythya nyroca	Fairly common resident (see above).

Other threatened/endemic wildlife

None known to BirdLife International.

Conservation issues

Part of the river is an established NCWCD protected area, patrolled by NCWCD rangers on behalf of the Riyadh Development Authority since 1988. Agricultural development in the area often changes the natural water flow, and plans exist to use the effluent for other purposes which would cut the water supply to the wadi by over 80%.

Further reading

Stagg (1987).

015 Hima al-Fiqrah (Al-Madinah)

Unprotected

24°20′N 39°00′E
124,000 ha

Site description

A mountain with surrounding foothills at 1,700–2,000 m in the Hijaz range, west of al-Madinah. The vegetation is open *Juniperus phoenicia* climax woodland with associated Mediterranean-type flora. Lichens and ferns occur on the wetter slopes. The *Juniperus* zone is easily accessible, unlike anywhere else in the central Hijaz. There is an ancient agricultural terrace system, now abandoned. Bee-keeping is an important local activity; secondary human activities are agriculture and recreation.

Birds

See box for key species. Other breeding species include *Aquila verreauxii* (min. 1 pair), *Buteo rufinus* (min. 1–2 pairs), *Hieraaetus fasciatus*, *Tachymarptis melba* (possible), *Apus pallidus*, *Rhodopechys githaginea* and *Emberiza striolata*.

Other threatened/endemic wildlife

Mammals: *Canis lupus* (V; unconfirmed), *Panthera pardus* (rare) and *Capra nubiana* (I).

Conservation issues

The site is proposed as a Special Nature Reserve, Natural Reserve, Resource Use Reserve and Controlled Hunting Reserve in the NCWCD System Plan for Protected Areas, and establishment is proceeding. The mountain is a 'hima' (traditional protected area) for bee-keeping, and grazing animals have long been excluded. Possible abandonment of this system in the future is a major threat to the presently good condition of the vegetation. Agricultural intensification, involving rehabilitation of terraces and construction of new houses and roads, is currently a major problem. Water supplies are now being brought in by tanker to permit this otherwise unsustainable development.

Regionally threatened or declining species

Gyps fulvus	Resident.

Species restricted wholly or largely to the Middle East

Alectoris melanocephala	Resident (probably less than 10 pairs).
Ammoperdix heyi	Abundant resident.
Dendrocopos dorae	Resident.
Oenanthe xanthoprymna	Common winter visitor.
Sylvia leucomelaena	Resident.
Onychognathus tristramii	Abundant resident.
Serinus rothschildi	Resident.

016 Madinat Yanbu al-Sinaiyah (Al-Madinah)

Biological Reserve

23°56′N 38°14′E
c.700 ha

Site description

Three nearby areas of mangrove *Avicennia marina* (the densest on the northern Red Sea coast of Saudi Arabia) covering c.11 km of coast on the 'delta' of Wadi Farrah, in the midst of a port and harbour complex serving the new industrial city of Madinat Yanbu al-Sinaiyah (25 km south of Yanbu al-Bahr). There are associated coral flats, sand beaches, saltmarsh, sabkhah, and an offshore islet.

Birds

See box for key species. The site has a representative mangrove avifauna. Other breeding species include *Ixobrychus minutus* (probable), *Nycticorax nycticorax* (possible), *Butorides striatus* (min. 2 pairs), *Egretta gularis* (two colonies), *Ardea cinerea* (possible), *A. purpurea* (max. 3 pairs), *Pandion haliaetus* (3 pairs), *Acrocephalus baeticatus* (c.45 pairs) and *A. stentoreus* (c.10 pairs).

Other threatened/endemic wildlife

None known to BirdLife International.

1% or more of population

	Breeding (pairs)	Wintering	Passage
Tringa cinerea	—	700	—

Regionally threatened or declining species

Ardea goliath	Occurs, and possibly breeds.

Species restricted wholly or largely to the Middle East

Dromas ardeola	Winters (max. 200).
Sterna repressa	Breeds (c.15 pairs).
Sterna saundersi	Breeds (c.30 pairs).

Conservation issues

The three areas have been established as, and are managed as, Conservation Areas by the Royal Commission for Jubail and Yanbu, and will be retained in their natural state and protected from disturbance. There are plans for an environmental awareness centre with a marine laboratory.

Further reading

Anon. (in press), Ash *et al.* (1989), Baldwin and Meadows (1988), Meadows (1986, in press).

017 Hawtat Bani Tamim (Ar-Riyadh)

23°30′N 46°30′E
236,900 ha

Special Nature Reserve, Natural Reserve, Resource Use Reserve and Controlled Hunting Reserve

Site description

A massive, isolated hill on the Tuwayq escarpment, in desert 200 km south of Riyadh.

Birds

See box for key species. The avifauna is representative of that of the Tuwayq escarpment. Other known or possible breeders include *Circaetus gallicus*, *Bubo ascalaphus*, *Oenanthe leucopyga* and *Corvus rhipidurus*.

Globally threatened species

Chlamydotis undulata	Rare non-breeding visitor.

Regionally threatened or declining species

Gyps fulvus	Resident in small numbers.

Species restricted wholly or largely to the Middle East

Ammoperdix heyi	Very common resident.
Pycnonotus xanthopygos	Common resident.
Hypocolius ampelinus	Rare winter visitor.
Oenanthe xanthoprymna	Rare winter visitor.
Hippolais languida	Common passage migrant.
Sylvia minula	Common winter visitor.
Sylvia mystacea	Common winter visitor.
Turdoides squamiceps	Common resident.

Other threatened/endemic wildlife

Mammals: *Canis lupus* (V) and *Capra nubiana* (I), as well as reintroduced *Gazella gazella* (V).

Conservation issues

The reserve was established by NCWCD to protect *Capra nubiana* and is patrolled by rangers; 90,000 ha are fully protected as Special Nature Reserve and Natural Reserve. Some parts have been fenced off to prevent grazing by camels, though controlled camel grazing is permitted in other parts. Grazing by sheep and goats is prohibited, as are hunting and built development. Camping and wildlife viewing are encouraged.

018 Wadi Rabigh Springs (Makkah, Al-Madinah)

23°00′N 39°30′E
35 ha

Unprotected

Site description

A natural lake near Haggag in Wadi Rabigh (c.35 km inland), fringed with reeds *Phragmites* and fed by several permanent freshwater springs. Such natural wetland habitat is unique on the Tihamah north of Jiddah. Fish are abundant. Surrounding land is primarily used for grazing, less so for agriculture. There is some recreational use by picnicers.

Birds

Breeding species include *Ixobrychus minutus* (1 pair), *Glareola pratincola* (1 pair), *Sterna albifrons* (possibly 1 pair) and *Alcedo atthis* (possibly 1 pair). Fourteen *Ciconia nigra* were present in mid-winter 1991–1992. The site is situated along the autumn raptor flyway to the Bab al-Mandab; *Buteo buteo* is especially common, and raptors roost on the cliffs adjacent to the springs.

Other threatened/endemic wildlife

None known to BirdLife International.

Conservation issues

The site is included in the NCWCD System Plan for Protected Areas. Hunting, damming and water diversion are currently problems on a minor scale. Recreational use, and consequent disturbance, by people from Jiddah, Rabigh and Yanbu is likely to increase, and the area has potential for agricultural development.

019 Mahazat as-Sayd (Makkah)

22°15′N 41°50′E
c.219,000 ha

Special Nature Reserve

Site description

A fairly level, sandy plain at 900–1,100 m with a few rock outcrops, 175 km north-east of Taif and south of al-Muwayh. Rainfall in 1992 was 96 mm, mainly in August, and temporary pools can form. Following fencing, the site is moderately to well vegetated, in parts with *Acacia tortilis*, *Indigofera* and *Salsola* as dominant shrubs/trees; dense grass (e.g. *Panicum*) often covers sandier areas, and some dry shallow wadis have large *Maerua* trees.

Birds

See box for key species. There is a diverse and, at times, abundant community of breeding larks, including *Eremalauda dunni*. *Torgos tracheliotus* breeds, and the largest non-breeding concentrations in Arabia have been recorded (see box). The reserve will probably be the first release site for the reintroduction of *Struthio camelus*. About 115 species have been recorded.

Other threatened/endemic wildlife

Mammals: *Felis margarita* (K) and *Vulpes rueppelli* (K); the reserve is a key reintroduction site for *Oryx leucoryx* (E) and *Gazella subgutturosa* (rare).

Conservation issues

The site is an NCWCD reserve, completely fenced in 1989, and there are no threats to it, although reintroduction of *Oryx*, *Gazella* and *Chlamydotis undulata* have priority over general conservation of wild birds. School parties visit regularly, and increased supervised access by the public is likely in future.

Further reading

Newton and Newton (1993), Newton and Shobrak (1993), Weigeldt and Schulz (1992).

Globally threatened species

Aegypius monachus	One recorded, January.
Aquila heliaca	Almost certainly a winter visitor.
Falco naumanni	Passage migrant.
Crex crex	Passage migrant.
Chlamydotis undulata	Being reintroduced (a few wild birds winter).

1% or more of population

	Breeding (pairs)	Wintering	Passage
Glareola pratincola	—	—	300

Regionally threatened or declining species

Neophron percnopterus	Non-breeding visitor (max. 51, October).
Gyps fulvus	Non-breeding visitor (max. 8, October).
Torgos tracheliotus	Resident (min. 15 pairs); 162 birds have been recorded in October.

Species restricted wholly or largely to the Middle East

Hypocolius ampelinus	Winter visitor in small numbers.
Irania gutturalis	Passage migrant in small numbers.
Oenanthe finschii	Recorded in March.
Oenanthe xanthoprymna	Winter visitor in small numbers.
Hippolais languida	Spring and autumn passage migrant in small numbers.
Sylvia mystacea	Abundant winter visitor.
Sylvia minula	Abundant winter visitor.
Turdoides squamiceps	Common resident.
Carpospiza brachydactyla	Spring and autumn passage migrant (max. 25).

020 Jiddah South Corniche and Port (Makkah)

Unprotected

21°26′N 39°09′E
c.900 ha

Site description

The site comprises the coastal lagoons just north of Jiddah port (21°30′N 39°10′E) and along the South Corniche road (21°23′N 39°07′E), south of the military area. It contains extensive sandy and muddy intertidal flats and shallow lagoons with sandy islands/peninsulas. All the surrounding area has been landfilled and urbanized, and the whole landward side of the site is bordered by roads.

Birds

See box for key species. This is the richest area of the central Red Sea coast for wintering waterbirds, and has a high density of migrating and wintering waders due to the presence of sewage outlets from Jiddah. In 1990 dozens of nests of *Phoenicopterus ruber* were present as were large numbers of displaying birds, although the colony disappeared after the site was flooded by spring tides.

1% or more of population

	Breeding (pairs)	Wintering	Passage
Platalea leucorodia	—	277	—
Ardea cinerea	—	139	—
Egretta gularis	—	337	—
Larus genei	—	5,475	—
Sterna caspia	—	118	—

Other threatened/endemic wildlife

None known to BirdLife International.

Conservation issues

The South Corniche is a busy recreational site at weekends, though the port area is relatively well protected from disturbance due to its proximity to the heavily guarded port. The mudflats at the port show signs of severe eutrophication, and in 1992 the South Corniche area was hit by an oil spill. The entire site is threatened by expanding urbanization and industrial development. Part of the site is proposed as a Natural Reserve in the NCWCD System Plan for Protected Areas.

021 Makkah Waste-water Stream (Makkah)

Unprotected

21°17′N 39°41′E
c.300 ha

Site description

A stream of treated sewage effluent, flowing 20–30 km south-west from Makkah into the largely flat sandy desert of the Tihamah. The flow is rather erratic, being strongest for the first 12–15 km, after which satellite pools tend to be ephemeral. The water is often densely lined with *Calotropis*, *Phragmites* and grasses.

Birds

See box for key species. A wide range of ducks and waders uses the site in winter. Other migrants include small numbers of *Grus grus* and *G. virgo*. *Pterocles lichtensteinii* and *P. exustus* can be very common in the area.

1% or more of population

	Breeding (pairs)	Wintering	Passage
Plegadis falcinellus	—	—	600
Himantopus himantopus	6	980	—
Glareola pratincola	—	—	540

Regionally threatened or declining species

Ardeotis arabs	There are historical records in the general area, though disturbance levels are probably too high for them now.

Species restricted wholly or largely to the Middle East

Irania gutturalis	Passage migrant.
Hippolais languida	Passage migrant.

Other threatened/endemic wildlife

See Gasperetti (1989).

Conservation issues

Not proposed as a protected area and not threatened, although waterfowl may be shot where the site runs close to the Makkah bypass. 'No hunting' signs could be placed on the adjacent roadside.

Further reading

Felemban and Al-Banna (1993), Gasperetti (1989).

022 National Wildlife Research Center and Environs, Taif (Makkah)

Natural Reserve

21°15′N 40°42′E
3,000 ha

Site description

Fairly flat, sandy/gravelly desert fringe at 1,450 m on the edge of the north-east Asir foothills, c.40 km south-east of Taif. There are a few gneiss inselbergs and dry wadis. The site is a fenced captive breeding centre, and the previously overgrazed vegetation is rapidly recovering to grassland and scrub bushland. Wadis just outside the boundary fence have many *Acacia iraqensis* trees and one has been dammed with some water usually present. Large semi-natural enclosures contain ungulates or are ungrazed.

Birds

See box for key species. Large numbers of *Chlidonias leucopterus* have occurred at the dam on migration (seasonal total 26,000; see box).

Other threatened/endemic wildlife

None known to BirdLife International.

Conservation issues

Virtually the only threat is that the Center's 'green island' character renders it vulnerable to locust plagues, which only occur irregularly and infre-

Globally threatened species

Geronticus eremita	Rare spring passage migrant (24 in 1991, 2–3 in 1992). The site encompasses the feeding and roosting areas of *Geronticus eremita*.
Falco naumanni	Occasionally common winter visitor.
Crex crex	Passage migrant in small numbers.

1% or more of population

	Breeding (pairs)	Wintering	Passage
Chlidonias leucopterus	—	—	26,000

Species restricted wholly or largely to the Middle East	
Ammoperdix heyi	Common resident.
Dendrocopos dorae	Resident (at least one pair).
Pycnonotus xanthopygos	Common resident.
Hypocolius ampelinus	Common but irregular winter visitor (max. 850).
Irania gutturalis	Passage migrant (max. 7).
Oenanthe xanthoprymna	Common but irregular winter visitor.
Oenanthe lugentoides	Winter visitor.
Sylvia mystacea	Common winter visitor.
Sylvia leucomelaena	Probably resident in small numbers.
Sylvia minula	Common winter visitor.
Turdoides squamiceps	Common resident.
Carpospiza brachydactyla	Common but irregular passage migrant (thousands).
Serinus rothschildi	Occasional non-breeding visitor.

quently. The surrounding area is seriously overgrazed, with attendant spread of the exotic weed *Argemone mexicana*, and a new camel farm has caused considerable damage to the *Acacia iraqensis* woodland used by *Dendrocopos dorae*.

Further reading

Newton and Newton (1993), Schulz and Schulz (1992), Symens (1989). Also monthly, quarterly and annual reports are available at the National Wildlife Research Center (Taif) and the National Commission for Wildlife Conservation and Development (Riyadh).

023 Taif Escarpment (Makkah)

Unprotected

21°14′N 40°16′E
c.40,000 ha

Site description

A 40-km-long by 10-km-wide stretch of the west-facing granitic escarpment of the northern Asir mountains, rising from 500 m in Wadi Nu'man to the peaks of Jabal Daka and Jabal Barad at 2,600 m (from 21°22′N 40°15′E south to 21°06′N 40°18′E). The climate is reasonably moist at higher levels but dry in the wadi. Much of the site is rocky and rather barren, but a narrow wooded zone along the escarpment lip is the only locality in Arabia where Mediterranean *Juniperus phoenicia* and Afrotropical *J. excelsa* overlap to any extent; shrubs are dominated by *Euryops* and *Lavandula*. Valleys east of the scarp have *Acacia iraqensis* woodland and patches of endangered tree *Euphorbia* and *Aloe*. Foothills, wadis and the lower slopes to the west have various *Acacia* species. There is considerable agricultural terracing and grazing; traditional activities include honey production and rose-growing, and the area is a major recreational resort.

Birds

See box for key species. Other breeding species include *Aquila verreauxii*. A passage of raptors occurs in autumn, with maximum daily totals in October of 4,000 *Buteo buteo* and 500 *Aquila nipalensis*.

Globally threatened species	
Turdus menachensis	Resident in fair numbers.
Regionally threatened or declining species	
Gypaetus barbatus	Very scarce and declining resident.
Gyps fulvus	Resident: up to 6 small colonies, not all used every year.
Caprimulgus poliocephalus	Probably resident in small numbers.
Species restricted wholly or largely to the Middle East	
Alectoris melanocephala	Scarce resident.
Alectoris philbyi	Moderately common resident.
Dendrocopos dorae	Common resident.
Oenanthe lugentoides	Common resident.
Onychognathus tristramii	Common resident.
Estrilda rufibarba	Recorded here at its northern limit, though its status is uncertain.
Serinus rothschildi	Resident.
Serinus menachensis	Possibly resident.
Carduelis yemenensis	Common resident in *Juniperus*.

Other threatened/endemic wildlife

Mammals: *Papio hamadryas* (endemic), *Canis lupus* (V), *Genetta felina* (rare), *Caracal caracal* (rare).

Conservation issues

Part of the site is included in the NCWCD System Plan for Protected Areas, and a major management plan for a nature reserve and recreation area has been compiled by NCWCD and King Abdulaziz University. There is high pressure on land for housing development, and, as the area was re-opened to built development by government decree in 1990, continued deterioration is likely. Terracing may be increasing, at the expense of *Juniperus* woodland, and there is fairly high grazing pressure and doubtless some illegal hunting.

Further reading

Anon. (1991), Symens (1989), Welch and Welch (1991).

024 Wadi Turabah and Jabal Ibrahim (Makkah)

Unprotected

20°32′N 41°11′E
c.5,000+ ha

Site description

The site lies 80 km north of al-Baha and 150 km south-east of Taif, between the Bani Saad–al-Baha escarpment road and the Taif–al-Baha road. Jabal Ibrahim (Jabal Batharah, 5,000 ha, up to 2,604 m) is a granite mountain rising c.1,000 m above the surrounding rocky hills and giving rise to several streams which provide a permanent flow for Wadi Turabah and its tributaries (west end 20°27′N 41°05′E, east end 20°37′N 41°18′E). Habitats include: bare granite domes and slabs; well-vegetated granite boulder slopes with montane woodland, including *Juniperus*; wadis with abundant *Ficus* and *Ziziphus* trees; and *Acacia* woodland.

Birds

See box for key species. The site's location and interesting mix of habitats provide an avifauna with Afrotropical elements as well as most of the south-west Arabian endemics, and breeding birds thus include *Scopus umbretta* (c.30 birds present), *Aquila verreauxii*, *Halcyon leucocephala*, *Monticola rufocinereus*, *Phylloscopus umbrovirens* and *Emberiza tahapisi*. Up to 20 *Ciconia nigra* overwinter.

Other threatened/endemic wildlife

Mammals: *Papio hamadryas* (endemic) and several (heavily persecuted) large carnivores. Fish: *Cyprinion mahalensis*, *Garra buettikeri* and *Barbus apoensis* (all endemic). Flora: Jabal Ibrahim is of high botanical interest.

Conservation issues

The site is proposed as a Natural Reserve, Biological Reserve and Resource Use Reserve in the NCWCD System Plan for Protected Areas. Some nature conservation public awareness activities have been undertaken, but large numbers of visitors and hunters are not reached by this method. Many camps of nomadic pastoralists are now appearing more permanent and buildings are being erected, even though ownership of the area remains unknown, and the complexities of land ownership and utilization mitigate against rapid establishment of a protected area. There is a threat from overgrazing locally, as from settlement and building in key areas.

Globally threatened species	
Turdus menachensis	Resident.
Regionally threatened or declining species	
Botaurus stellaris	Passage migrant.
Neophron percnopterus	Resident (a few pairs).
Gyps fulvus	Resident.
Falco biarmicus	One record, March.
Caprimulgus poliocephalus	Probably resident (c.5 pairs).
Species restricted wholly or largely to the Middle East	
Alectoris melanocephala	Probably resident.
Alectoris philbyi	Common, probably resident.
Ammoperdix heyi	Common resident.
Dendrocopos dorae	Resident (c.5–10 pairs).
Pycnonotus xanthopygos	Common resident.
Oenanthe lugentoides	Common resident.
Sylvia leucomelaena	Probably resident.
Turdoides squamiceps	Common resident.
Onychognathus tristramii	Common resident.
Estrilda rufibarba	Apparently resident.
Serinus rothschildi	Resident.
Serinus menachensis	Recorded occasionally; status uncertain.
Carduelis yemenensis	Probably resident.
Emberiza cineracea	Spring passage migrant.

Further reading

Eichacker (1990), Newton and Newton (1993), Schulz *et al.* (undated).

025 Qishran Bay (Makkah)

Unprotected

20°15′N 40°10′E
c.400,000 ha

Site description

A shallow bay of 15 × 35 km, almost closed by a long narrow island, and containing eight other islets. It is situated at a point where the Asir mountains run close to the Red Sea. Most of the islets are surrounded by mangrove *Avicennia* trees and clothed with dense *Salicornia*, and there are seagrass beds in the bay.

Birds

See box for key species. The site holds the densest population of *Falco concolor* in Saudi Arabia and probably in the world, and at least 50 pairs of *Sterna anaethetus* breed. The coastal topography concentrates migrants moving down the coast.

Regionally threatened or declining species

Ardea goliath	Rare summer visitor.
Falco concolor	Common summer visitor (c.40 pairs).
Falco biarmicus	Passage migrant.
Falco cherrug	Passage migrant.
Todirhamphus chloris	One recorded in summer.

Species restricted wholly or largely to the Middle East

Dromas ardeola	Occurs all year round and may breed (a burrow possibly attributable to this species has been found).

Other threatened/endemic wildlife

Mammals: *Dugong dugon* (V). Reptiles: the sea-turtles *Eretmochelys imbricata* (E) and *Chelonia mydas* (E) breed.

Conservation issues

Trapping of migrant birds (especially falcons) between mid-September and mid-November is a tradition, and average numbers of falcons caught per year are c.30 *Falco biarmicus*, c.15 *F. cherrug*, c.40 *F. peregrinus* and c.30 *F. pelegrinoides*. In one year, three adult *F. concolor* were known to have been trapped and a nest robbed, and a leaflet explaining the importance of the *F. concolor* population is to be distributed to falcon trappers. The site is proposed as a Special Nature Reserve in the NCWCD System Plan for Protected Areas.

Further reading

Gaucher *et al.* (in press).

026 Umm al-Qamari (Makkah)

Special Nature Reserve

18°59′N 41°06′E
14.7 ha

Site description

Two small, flat, fossil-coral islands in the Red Sea (12 ha and 2.7 ha), south-west of Qunfudah town. Rainfall is light and erratic, but there is often a heavy dew and the islands are exceedingly well vegetated, with thickets up to 3 m tall of *Salvadora* and *Suaeda*; on more open ground there is *Cyperus*, *Atriplex* and *Zygophyllum*.

Birds

See box for key species. Other breeding birds include *Butorides striatus* (2 pairs), *Egretta gularis* (7 pairs), *Pandion haliaetus* (2 pairs) and *Streptopelia roseogrisea* (c.500 pairs). Small numbers of *Pelecanus rufescens* roost on the beaches in winter.

Other threatened/endemic wildlife

None known to BirdLife International.

Globally threatened species

Larus leucophthalmus	Small numbers roost on the beaches in winter.

1% or more of population

	Breeding (pairs)	Wintering	Passage
Bubulcus ibis	65	—	—
Platalea leucorodia	10–15	—	—

Species restricted wholly or largely to the Middle East

Larus hemprichii	Resident (50–100 pairs in two colonies; up to 100 birds in winter).

Conservation issues

The islands have long been protected by traditional hunting laws, and are now also formally protected by NCWCD. It is not known whether hunting and egg-collecting occur, nor whether there is disturbance by other visitors.

027 Shallal ad-Dahna (Asir)

also known as Shallal Tanoma or an-Numas
Unprotected

18°55′N 42°12′E
5,000 ha

Site description

Shallal ad-Dahna lies 90 km north of Abha on the road to Taif and comprises broken granite hill country at 2,400–2,700 m covered with *Juniperus* and *Acacia* scrub. The site contains one of the very few permanent waterfalls of the country, and a pool.

Birds

See box for key species. The main interest is the presence of the isolated and distinctive endemic race *Pica pica asirensis* (3 pairs). Other breeding species include *Phylloscopus umbrovirens*, *Ploceus galbula* and *Corvus rhipidurus*. Further surveys would be advantageous.

Regionally threatened or declining species

Gypaetus barbatus	One record.
Gyps fulvus	Non-breeding visitor.

Species restricted wholly or largely to the Middle East

Alectoris melanocephala	Resident.
Ammoperdix heyi	Resident.
Strix butleri	Resident.
Dendrocopos dorae	One record.
Pycnonotus xanthopygos	Resident.
Oenanthe lugentoides	Resident.
Turdoides squamiceps	Resident.
Onychognathus tristramii	Resident.
Serinus rothschildi	Resident.

Other threatened/endemic wildlife

The fauna is unusually rich in Palearctic relict species; vertebrate species include the shrew *Crocidura russula*, the snake *Eirenis coronella fennelli*, the toad *Bufo viridis*, and the frogs *Rana ridibunda* and *Hyla savignyi*.

Conservation issues

The site is included in the NCWCD System Plan for Protected Areas. The hills are severely grazed, and other threats are drainage, the planting of exotic trees, refuse dumping and visitor pressure. New roads and car parks (for a picnic area) are being developed near the waterfall.

028 Al-Habrow al-Arabi (Makkah, Asir)

Unprotected

18°40′N 41°30′E
c.250,000 ha

Site description

A diverse section of the hot, humid coastal Tihamah centred on Kiyad and including the Makhshush sabkhah/outwash fan and Wadi Hali and Wadi Qarnayn with their permanent pools, as well as adjacent lava fields, wooded savanna and rocky foothills. Sandy coastal areas support *Salvadora* bushes but more inland vegetation is dominated by *Acacia tortilis*, *A. ehrenbergiana* and *A. asak* trees. Sparse shrubs and herbs include *Dipterygium*, *Heliotropium*, *Indigofera*, *Malva* and *Euphorbia*. The whole area is very heavily grazed by domestic stock, but rains can produce a good cover of grasses *Pennisetum* and *Panicum*. There is considerable cultivation, mainly of sorghum and millet, and charcoal production is practised in the foothills.

Birds

See box for key species. The area has not been well studied in summer, but other known or presumed breeding species include *Scopus umbretta*, *Melierax metabates*, *Aquila verreauxii*, *Pterocles exustus*, *Coracias abyssinica* and *Tockus nasutus*, and other species regularly present all year or in winter and which may breed include *Pelecanus rufescens*, *Terathopius ecaudatus* and *Circaetus gallicus*.

Globally threatened species

Haliaeetus leucoryphus	One winter record.
Aquila heliaca	Winter visitor (max. 2).
Chlamydotis undulata	Regular winter visitor in small numbers.

Regionally threatened or declining species

Neophron percnopterus	Resident in small numbers.
Gyps fulvus	May breed.
Ardeotis arabs	A maximum of five was present in the winter of 1989/90, but there is no proof of breeding and numbers have declined, with none seen in 1991/92.

Species restricted wholly or largely to the Middle East

Alectoris melanocephala	Resident.
Ammoperdix heyi	Abundant resident.
Pycnonotus xanthopygos	Common resident.
Hypocolius ampelinus	Irregular winter visitor (max. 30).
Oenanthe lugentoides	Uncommon resident in foothills.
Sylvia leucomelaena	Apparently resident.
Turdoides squamiceps	Common resident.
Passer euchlorus	Probably common breeding species.

Other threatened/endemic wildlife

Mammals: *Caracal caracal* (rare), *Canis lupus* (V) and *Gazella gazella cora* (V; at Makhshush).

Conservation issues

The regular presence of NCWCD personnel conducting bustard research has done much to gain local support for wildlife protection. However, habitat degradation (overgrazing, wood-cutting, charcoal burning) combined with severe pressure from illegal hunting will probably eliminate *Ardeotis arabs* and the gazelles in the near future, since most hunting is probably done by non-local people. The Makhshush outwash fan is proposed as a Special Nature Reserve, Natural Reserve, Biological Reserve and Resource Use Reserve in the NCWCD System Plan for Protected Areas, on account of its gazelles. Rahmani and Shobrak (1992b) suggested that the whole site as described here (not just Makhshush) be designated a Resource Use Reserve containing several smaller areas strictly protected for bustards and gazelles; the wider area would have stricter control of hunting, tree-felling, etc., but would otherwise not infringe too much on current land-use. The appointment of rangers from the relatively poor local community would bring some direct benefit from conservation.

Further reading

Rahmani and Shobrak (1992a,b), Shobrak and Rahmani (1991, 1993).

029 Khawr 'Amiq (Asir)

also known as Amq
Unprotected

18°26′N 41°26′E
c.150 ha

Site description

An area of mangrove on the southern Red Sea shore, 30 km north-west of al-Birk. A shallow, muddy bay with large stands of *Avicennia marina*. The subtidal zone is sandy with seagrass beds. There is a local fishery.

Birds

See box for key species. Other breeding species include *Butorides striatus* and *Pandion haliaetus*, and possibly *Pelecanus rufescens* (also winters: max. 21), *Platalea leucorodia*, *Acrocephalus stentoreus* and *A. baeticatus*.

Regionally threatened or declining species	
Todirhamphus chloris	Resident (3–5 pairs).

Other threatened/endemic wildlife

Mammals: *Dugong dugon* (V).

Conservation issues

There are presently local threats from small-scale cutting of mangrove and grazing by camels. The area is a proposed Resource Use Reserve in the NCWCD System Plan for Protected Areas.

Further reading

Stagg (1984a).

030 Raydah Escarpment (Asir)

Special Nature Reserve

18°12′N 42°30′E
c.900 ha

Site description

Lying c.15 km west of Abha, the site is a very steep west-facing slope with crags, falling from 2,700 to 1,600 m in less than 3 km. The soil is very thin. There are permanent streams and the climate is generally cool and wet, the area being frequently cloud-covered. The escarpment supports a more-or-less intact forest, predominantly *Juniperus excelsa*, with *Olea europea* on upper and north-facing slopes and more deciduous trees (*Nuxia*, *Ficus*, *Acacia*) lower down and in valleys and gullies. The bottom third and south-facing slopes are often dominated by *Buddleja* and by tree aloes *Aloe sabaea* and other succulents. Bee-keeping is a common human activity and there is moderate to heavy use of the area for recreation.

Birds

Possibly the most important compact site in Saudi Arabia for south-west Arabian endemic, and other,

Globally threatened species	
Turdus menachensis	Resident (c.550 pairs).
Regionally threatened or declining species	
Gyps fulvus	Resident in the reserve.
Micronisus gabar	Resident in the reserve or vicinity.
Caprimulgus poliocephalus	Resident (at least 10 pairs).
Species restricted wholly or largely to the Middle East	
Alectoris melanocephala	Resident (c.50–100 pairs).
Alectoris philbyi	May breed at top of escarpment.
Strix butleri	Resident (2–5 pairs).
Dendrocopos dorae	Resident (at least 2 pairs).
Parisoma buryi	Resident (100–500 pairs).
Onychognathus tristramii	Resident (10–20 pairs).
Estrilda rufibarba	Resident.
Serinus rothschildi	Common resident (100–500 pairs).
Serinus menachensis	Probably resident.
Rhynchostruthus socotranus	Possibly resident.
Carduelis yemenensis	Resident (over 1,000 pairs).

woodland species. See box for key species. Other breeding species include *Accipiter badius* (1–2 pairs), *Aquila verreauxii*, *Columba arquatrix* (probable), *Streptopelia lugens*, *Treron waalia*, *Otus scops pamelae*, *Monticola rufocinereus*, *Phylloscopus umbrovirens*, *Terpsiphone viridis*, *Zosterops abyssinicus* and *Pica pica asirensis*. There may be a considerable raptor passage through the area, and many *Sylvia* (especially *S. atricapilla*) stop off on migration. Many warblers winter, especially *Phylloscopus collybita*.

Other threatened/endemic wildlife

Mammals: *Papio hamadryas* (endemic), *Caracal caracal* (rare) and *Canis lupus* (V).

Conservation issues

The site is an established NCWCD Special Nature Reserve with two rangers, but there is no control over livestock grazing, vehicular access and road maintenance. A road recently bulldozed along the steep slope requires frequent clearance due to continuing rock fall, and spoil from this has destroyed large areas of forest. Soil-water retention is probably reduced by the road, and most *Juniperus* are in poor condition. A small, previously abandoned farm within the reserve has been reoccupied, and this may encourage illegal agricultural development.

Further reading

Jennings *et al.* (1988), Symens (1990).

031 Kutambil Island (Jizan)

Unprotected

17°53′N 41°42′E
c.8 ha

Site description

An island lying 5 km off the coast of south-west Saudi Arabia, midway between Shuqaiq and al-Birk. It is dominated by a mound of volcanic clinker rising to 100 m; a few trees (up to 3 m high) grow on its slopes, and there is a good growth of salt-tolerant bushes along its base on the south and south-east side abutting a flat and sandy area. Offshore are rich coral reefs. There is a small 7-m-high rock outcrop 200 m to the south.

Birds

See box for key species. An important breeding area for *Platalea leucorodia* (of the Red Sea subspecies *P. l. archeri*); however the site has only once been surveyed in the breeding season, in 1982. Other breeding species included *Egretta gularis* (9 pairs), *Butorides striatus* (2 pairs) and *Pandion haliaetus* (1 pair). Small numbers of wintering waterfowl include *Pelecanus rufescens* (9), *Sula leucogaster* (30), gulls *Larus* (200) and terns *Sterna* (200).

1% or more of population

	Breeding (pairs)	Wintering	Passage
Platalea leucorodia	60	—	—

Regionally threatened or declining species

Falco concolor At least 2 pairs probably breed.

Other threatened/endemic wildlife

None known to BirdLife International.

Conservation issues

About 50% of the eggs or young of *Platalea leucorodia* were almost certainly taken by visiting people in 1982. Hundreds or even thousands of feral pigeons *Columba livia* have been recorded in winter, and may compete with breeding seabirds for nest-sites in summer.

Further reading

Stagg (1984b).

032 Shuqaiq Mangrove (Asir)

also known as Sharm at-Ta'nah or ad-Darb
Unprotected

17°48′N 41°52′E
c.200 ha

Site description

An area of mangrove on the southern Red Sea shore, c.20 km north-west of the town of Shuqaiq (west of ad-Darb). A shallow bay with large intertidal mudflats, stands of mangrove *Avicennia* and offshore seagrass beds. There is a local fishery.

Birds

See box for key species. Other breeding species include *Butorides striatus* and *Pandion haliaetus*, and possibly *Pelecanus rufescens* (also winters: max. 35), *Platalea leucorodia*, *Acrocephalus stentoreus* and *A. baeticatus*.

Globally threatened species

Larus leucophthalmus	Winter visitor (max. 45, February).

Regionally threatened or declining species

Todirhamphus chloris	Resident (2–5 pairs).

Other threatened/endemic wildlife

Mammals: *Dugong dugon* (V).

Conservation issues

There are presently local threats from small-scale cutting of mangrove and grazing by camels, but plans to develop shrimp farms in the future are a critical threat to the mangrove. The area is not proposed for protection in the NCWCD System Plan for Protected Areas.

Further reading

Stagg (1984a).

033 Jabal Qaha (Jizan)

Unprotected

17°39′N 42°52′E
c.3,750 ha

Site description

A rugged mountain with an extensive summit plateau of sedimentary rock at c.1,800–2,000 m, c.80 km south-south-east of Abha. Just to the south is the very deep, steep-sided Lajb gorge. There was apparently thriving *Juniperus* woodland on the plateau until a series of drought years in the 1960s killed off most of the trees, which have been left standing however. The main human activities are livestock grazing and small-scale terraced agriculture.

Birds

The site has been little investigated, but there is known to be an important population of the isolated endemic race *Pica pica asirensis* (at least 30 pairs), and many of the other high-altitude south-west Arabian endemics presumably also occur.

Other threatened/endemic wildlife

Mammals: *Panthera pardus* (rare; possibly extinct).

Conservation issues

The site was only recently discovered, and there is an urgent need for surveys to investigate conservation values, threats and needs. It is not known how the death of most or all of the juniper trees actually affected the population of *Pica pica*, since all ornithological and botanical investigations occurred only after the die-off, but the current habitat seems to be highly attractive to *Pica pica*, which occurs at high densities.

034 Jabal Faifa (Jizan)

Unprotected

17°15′N 43°05′E
c.5,000 ha

Site description

An isolated steep-sided jabal on the western side of the Asir mountains (above 500 m). The temperate summit area (c.2,000 m) is heavily built up and cultivated, with *Juniperus* in parts too steep for terracing, as well as various broadleaved shrubs and bushes, *Ficus* and a few *Dracaena* trees, as well as introduced *Eucalyptus* and *Opuntia*. At lower altitudes *Adenium obesum* and *Commiphora* occur. The western slopes have considerable rainfall but there is very little permanent water on the summit area and supplies for crops are brought up by bowser.

Birds

The mountain and its foothills hold c.70 breeding species. See box for key species; other breeding species include *Terathopius ecaudatus*, *Melierax metabates*, *Falco pelegrinoides*, *Streptopelia lugens*, *Treron waalia*, *Cypsiurus parvus*, *Halcyon leucocephala*, *Merops albicollis*, *Coracias abyssinica*, *Tockus nasutus*, *Anthus similis*, *Oenanthe bottae*, *Monticola rufocinereus*, *Phylloscopus umbrovirens*,

Muscicapa gambagae, *Anthreptes metallicus*, *Nectarinia habessinica*, *N. osea*, *Zosterops abyssinicus*, *Tchagra senegala*, *Cinnyricinclus leucogaster* and *Emberiza tahapisi*.

Regionally threatened or declining species

Neophron percnopterus	Resident; possibly breeds in small numbers.
Gyps fulvus	Resident; breeds in adjacent mountains.

Species restricted wholly or largely to the Middle East

Alectoris melanocephala	Resident.
Dendrocopos dorae	Resident.
Oenanthe lugentoides	Resident.
Sylvia leucomelaena	Resident.
Turdoides squamiceps	Resident.
Estrilda rufibarba	Resident.
Serinus rothschildi	Resident.
Carduelis yemenensis	Resident.

■ Other threatened/endemic wildlife
Mammals: the only Saudi Arabian site for several small species. Reptiles: the only Saudi Arabian site for several species, including *Varanus yemenensis* (endemic). Flora: the site is of very high botanical interest; features include a grove of the tree *Mimusops laurifolia* (rare), the largest trees in Saudi Arabia.

■ Conservation issues
The grove of *Mimusops laurifolia* has been scheduled as a site of special interest by the NCWCD, but the mountain is otherwise unprotected. Urban development is continuing on the summit area. There is little or no grazing on the mountain, and the dry, scrub-covered eastern side seems not to be threatened.

035 Malaki Dam (Jizan)
17°03′N 42°58′E
2,500 ha

also known as Malakiyah, Wadi Jizan Dam or Hakima Dam
Unprotected

■ Site description
Malaki Dam lies at 120–250 m on the edge of the Asir foothills, c.15 km east of Abu Arish. The reservoir, used for flood control and irrigation, is fed by the four major wadis of the extreme south-west of Saudi Arabia, with a catchment area extending well into Yemen. High rates of sedimentation have occurred in the reservoir, reducing its depth and expanding the water surface to c.10 km^2 at high-water levels. To the north the reservoir is bordered by basaltic lava plains, and several rocky outcrops with hot springs are found on the south side and between the main wadis such as Ain Wakrah. There are a variety of marshy areas near the reservoir and in the lower runs of the four wadis, and huge banks of silt have isolated some permanent and semi-permanent pools from the main reservoir. Many of these banks are covered with *Tamarix* woodland edged by a lush growth of weeds and sedge. Similar vegetation borders the main wadis, while the wadi beds are cultivated with sorghum whenever the water level allows it. Some of the rocky outcrops are vegetated by palms *Phoenix reclinata* and *Hyphaene*, succulent *Adenium obesum* and the rare tree *Acacia alba*. Isolated *Dobera* trees, *Acacia* scrub and *Salvadora* bushes are the main vegetation on more open, sandy areas. Much of the surrounding hill area is grazed by livestock.

■ Birds
See box for key species. The dam and its immediate area have one of the highest diversities of breeding birds in Arabia and hold a community representative of the lower Tihamah foothills, including many of the African elements: *Terathopius ecaudatus*, *Turnix sylvatica*, *Burhinus capensis*, *Streptopelia semitorquata*, *Oxylophus jacobinus*, *Centropus superciliosus*, *Caprimulgus nubicus*, *Cypsiurus parvus*, *Coracias abyssinica*, *Mirafra cantillans*, *Anthreptes metallicus*, *Tchagra senegala* and *Emberiza tahapisi*. Winter visitors include *Ciconia nigra* (21), *Platalea leucorodia* (84) and *Limosa limosa* (233), and large

Globally threatened species

Haliaeetus leucoryphus	Presumably a rare but regular winter visitor: since 1987 there have been three records of single long-staying birds.

1% or more of population

	Breeding (pairs)	Wintering	Passage
Plegadis falcinellus	—	986	3,500
Aythya nyroca	—	83	—

Regionally threatened or declining species

Micronisus gabar	Resident.
Aythya nyroca	Winter visitor.

Species restricted wholly or largely to the Middle East

Strix butleri	Resident.
Passer euchlorus	Occurs occasionally.
Estrilda rufibarba	Common resident (300+ birds).
Serinus rothschildi	Common resident.

numbers of *Ciconia ciconia*, *Grus grus* (187), *Plegadis falcinellus* and *Bubulcus ibis* use the site as a roost, feeding mainly on the surrounding agricultural areas and/or rubbish dumps. At least 287 species have been recorded.

Other threatened/endemic wildlife

Mammals: *Genetta felina* (rare), *Canis lupus* (V). Reptiles: *Coluber manseri* (endemic). Fish: the wadi system holds endemic fish which are threatened with local extinction by the large numbers of introduced *Tilapia* in the reservoir.

Conservation issues

The site is presently managed by the Ministry of Agriculture through the FAO Agricultural Development Centre, but without major concern for its ecological values. The demands of a growing human population require cultivation of an increasing amount of the land, and large amounts of scrub have been and still are being bulldozed. A newly constructed road to al-Arida has opened the area for development. No data are available on the local use of agricultural pesticides, but there is regular spraying in and around the reservoir to eradicate malaria, and this may threaten the ecosystem. The site is proposed as a Natural Reserve, Biological Reserve and Resource Use Reserve in the NCWCD System Plan for Protected Areas, and was proposed for declaration in 1991, but procedures are presently frozen. This is one of the prime sites for a protected area in Saudi Arabia, and its value to waterbirds could still increase considerably if the water level was managed more sympathetically.

036 Wadi Jawwah (Jizan)

17°00′N 43°00′E
c.5,500 ha

also known as Wadi Juwah
Unprotected

Site description

Wadi Jawwah lies at 100–300 m in the foothills east of Abu Arish and south of al-Arida, inland from Jizan. It consists of a sandy and clay bed surrounded by often steep volcanic rocky slopes, and there is a small artificial dam, behind which lies a small lake for most of the year. Scattered *Dobera* and *Ficus* trees dominate the landscape and there are many remnant patches of *Acacia* and *Salvadora* scrub. The rocky outcrops and bordering slopes are only sparsely vegetated with *Acacia* and succulents but can have a surprising cover of grasses after heavy rain. The wadi is densely populated and most of it is cultivated with sorghum and millet.

Birds

See box for key species. The wadi has one of the highest diversities of breeding species known in Arabia, some in the highest densities known in the country, including *Terathopius ecaudatus*, *Coturnix delegorguei*, *Numida meleagris* (the single most important site in Saudi Arabia: c.350 birds in 1988 and over 1,000 in 1990), *Burhinus capensis*, *Streptopelia roseogrisea*, *Treron waalia*, *Centropus superciliosus*, *Bubo africanus*, *Caprimulgus inornatus*, *Halcyon leucocephala*, *Merops albicollis*, *Coracias abyssinica*, *Tockus nasutus*, *Anthreptes metallicus*, *Tchagra senegala*, *Cinnyricinclus leucogaster* and *Emberiza tahapisi*. The lake has breeding *Tachybaptus ruficollis*, and wintering waterbirds have included *Plegadis falcinellus* (72). There is a colony of 1,200–1,500 pairs of *Bubulcus ibis* 50 km to the south at Tuwal, nearby but outside the site. There is a strong autumn migration of raptors, including *Circaetus gallicus* (18), *Buteo buteo vulpinus* (975), *Aquila nipalensis* (650) and *Hieraaetus pennatus* (12).

Globally threatened species	
Aquila heliaca	Frequent autumn passage migrant (daily max. 36).
Regionally threatened or declining species	
Neophron percnopterus	Resident.
Gyps fulvus	Resident.
Micronisus gabar	Resident.
Species restricted wholly or largely to the Middle East	
Ammoperdix heyi	Resident.
Strix butleri	Resident.
Dendrocopos dorae	Resident.
Pycnonotus xanthopygos	Resident.
Oenanthe lugentoides	Resident.
Sylvia leucomelaena	Resident.
Turdoides squamiceps	Resident.
Passer euchlorus	Resident.
Estrilda rufibarba	Resident.
Serinus rothschildi	Resident.

Other threatened/endemic wildlife

None known to BirdLife International.

Conservation issues

The local Emir traditionally protects *Numida meleagris* against hunting and, more recently, against egg-collecting. The rapidly rising population is leading to increased pressure on natural scrubland for agricultural development; there is heavy grazing by goats and camels, as well as wood gathering. The site is proposed as a Special Nature Reserve, Natural Reserve, Biological Reserve and Resource Use Reserve in the NCWCD System Plan for Protected Areas, and was proposed for declaration in 1991, but this has been frozen.

037 **Jizan Bay** (Jizan)

also known as Ra's Tarfa'
Unprotected

16°53´N 42°32´E
200 ha

■ Site description

A 4-km-long by 500-m-wide stretch of muddy and mud-sand intertidal flats, from Jizan Port to the northern edge of the city. The flats, enriched by sewage outfall from Jizan city, were in the past fringed by mangrove, but all such areas have now been lost to land-claim.

■ Birds

See box for key species. This site is a core area in a region of generally good wader habitat from Jizan south to the Yemen border. Densities are on average much higher than at neighbouring sites, due to the sewage outfalls of Jizan city. There is a peak January count of 20,053 waterbirds, though this was in 1992, an unusually cold winter, and may therefore be higher than typical; 10,000–15,000 waterbirds were present in December 1992.

Globally threatened species

Numenius tenuirostris — One record of a single bird, January 1990; the species may occur more regularly in this general area than is presently known.

1% or more of population

	Breeding (pairs)	Wintering	Passage
Dromas ardeola	—	480	—
Pluvialis squatarola	—	2,232	—
Charadrius mongolus	—	1,125	—
Limicola falcinellus	—	311	—
Numenius phaeopus	—	94	—
Limosa lapponica	—	2,740	—
Tringa totanus	—	1,647	—

Species restricted wholly or largely to the Middle East

Dromas ardeola — Winter visitor (see above).

■ Other threatened/endemic wildlife

None known to BirdLife International.

■ Conservation issues

The site is severely threatened by pollution from oil, organic domestic effluent and garbage, and especially by large-scale land reclamation for urban expansion. Fishing activities and the proximity of the large city of Jizan result in frequent human disturbance of birds. Part of the site is proposed as a Special Nature Reserve in the NCWCD System Plan for Protected Areas. Immediate action should be taken to stop further loss of intertidal habitat, and pollution should be monitored. Regular counts during winter and migration seasons are required.

038 **Farasan Islands** (Jizan)

Special Nature Reserve, Natural Reserve, Resource Use Reserve and Controlled Hunting Reserve

16°45´N 42°00´E
c.620,000 ha

■ Site description

A Red Sea coral archipelago, 40 km offshore, with dozens of low-lying islands and islets. Some islands are bare and surrounded by coral, while others are sandy. The largest island, Farasan Kabir (c.39,500 ha), is 120 km long and up to 75 m high; inland vegetation comprises *Acacia-Commiphora* bushland with *Ziziphus* and *Salvadora*, as well as *Euphorbia* thickets and dense, 3-m-high *Asparagus* bushland. There are several dense stands of mangrove (mostly *Avicennia* but also *Rhizophora*). Some islands are fringed with salt-tolerant bushes. Farasan Kabir, Saqid (the only other large island: 15,600 ha) and Qummah are permanently inhabited (c.7 villages), but there are Coastguard stations and/or temporary fishing camps on other islands. There is a pearl fishery, a small amount of cultivation (dates and sorghum), and a few herds of goats.

■ Birds

See box for key species. The islands are important mainly for breeding seabirds and raptors, but have

Globally threatened species

Larus leucophthalmus	Summer visitor (300 birds, June–July).

1% or more of population

	Breeding (pairs)	Wintering	Passage
Sula leucogaster	150	—	—
Ardea goliath	1–10	—	—
Platalea leucorodia	10	—	—
Larus hemprichii	545 birds	—	—
Sterna repressa	8,300 birds	—	—
Sterna anaethetus	12,150 birds	—	—
Sterna saundersi	20	591	—
Anous stolidus	10,000	—	—

Regionally threatened or declining species

Ardea goliath	Probably resident; recorded all year round, daily max. 12 birds (see above).
Neophron percnopterus	Common resident (c.65 pairs, one of the highest concentrations in Arabia).
Falco concolor	Common summer visitor (32 pairs).

Species restricted wholly or largely to the Middle East

Dromas ardeola	Common resident (110 pairs; max. 324 in winter).
Larus leucophthalmus	Summer visitor (see above).
Larus hemprichii	Common resident (see above).
Sterna repressa	Common summer visitor (see above).
Sterna saundersi	Common resident (see above).

only been incompletely surveyed. Other breeding species include *Phaethon aethereus* (6–12 pairs), *Pelecanus rufescens* (40+ pairs), *Egretta gularis*, *Ardea purpurea*, *Pandion haliaetus* (40 pairs) and *Sterna bergii* (100 pairs). There are important concentrations of wintering waterbirds on the southern beach of Farasan Kabir, including *Arenaria interpres* (335).

Other threatened/endemic wildlife

Mammals: *Gazella gazella farasani* (endemic); *Asellia patrizii* (only site in Arabia). Reptiles: *Coluber insulans* (endemic); many sea-turtles (globally threatened) breed.

Conservation issues

The islands are managed as an established protected area by the NCWCD, and rangers patrol the two main islands to prevent poaching; 15,500 ha are fully protected as Special Nature Reserve and Natural Reserve. Seabirds' eggs are taken and are being over-exploited, and feral cats are a problem for nesting seabirds on some islands. Large numbers of migrant shrikes are trapped to extract their fat (for cooking); the impact of this on the migrant populations has not been studied. On the two main islands there are threats to the habitat from uncontrolled grazing and the possible exploitation of potash in the future.

Further reading

Jennings (1988a,b), Symens (1988).

039 Khawr Wahlan (Jizan)

also known as Sawarma

Unprotected

16°45′N 42°40′E
c.3,000 ha

Site description

A large stretch of intertidal mudflats on the southern Red Sea coast, c.40 km south of Jizan. The flats are fringed in places with mangrove *Avicennia* and saltmarsh, and an upwelling of fresh water in the marsh creates the only known coastal wet grassland (c.800 ha) in the region. The area is favoured for grazing by camels.

Birds

See box for key species. This is the only known regular wintering site for *Pluvialis fulva* in Saudi Arabia (January max. 36). The site has been visited only for Asian Waterfowl Census counts, and virtually nothing is known of its breeding species or of its importance for waders during migration. Aerial surveys have indicated that the intertidal zone from Jizan southwards is the most important wader area along the Saudi Arabian Red Sea coast, and this site is a good representative of this almost untouched coastal habitat.

Species restricted wholly or largely to the Middle East

Dromas ardeola	Common winter visitor (349).

Other threatened/endemic wildlife

None known to BirdLife International.

Conservation issues

The wet grassland (and to some extent the mangrove and saltmarsh) are heavily grazed and trampled by camels, leading to habitat destruction and disturbance. The site is a proposed Special Nature Reserve in the NCWCD System Plan for Protected Areas.

MAIN REFERENCES

ANON. (1991) *Al Taif escarpment nature reserve and recreation area: report and master plan with guidelines.* Riyadh: National Commission for Wildlife Conservation and Development/Jiddah: Dept. Landscape Architecture, King Abdulaziz Univ.

ANON. (in press) Shorebird numbers. In *Ecology of the Red Sea: investigations at Yanbu, 1981–1992*. Riyadh: Royal Commission for Jubail and Yanbu.

ASH, J. S., PEARSON, D. J., NIKOLAUS, G. AND COLSTON, P. R. (1989) The mangrove reed warblers of the Red Sea and Gulf of Aden coasts, with description of a new subspecies of the African Reed Warbler *Acrocephalus baeticatus*. *Bull. Brit. Orn. Club* 109: 36–43.

BALDWIN, P. J. AND MEADOWS, B. S. (1988) *Birds of Madinat Yanbu Al-Sinaiyah and its hinterland.* Riyadh: Royal Commission for Jubail and Yanbu.

BASSON, P. W., BURCHARD, J. E., HARDY, J. T. AND PRICE, A. R. G. (1981) *Biotopes of the western Arabian Gulf.* Second edition. Dhahran: Aramco.

BUNDY, G., CONNOR, R. J. AND HARRISON, C. J. O. (1989) *Birds of the Eastern Province of Saudi Arabia*. London: Witherby/Dhahran: Saudi Aramco.

CHILD, G. AND GRAINGER, J. (1990) *A system plan for protected areas for wildlife conservation and sustainable rural development*. Riyadh: National Commission for Wildlife Conservation and Development.

COLES, S. L. AND MCCAIN, J. C. (1989) The marine environment of the Saudi Arabian Gulf: baseline information and management considerations. Unpublished paper presented at *National Commission for Wildlife Conservation and Development workshop on ecological imperatives for the conservation and sustainable use of the flora and fauna of Saudi Arabia, 1989*. Riyadh.

EICHACKER, X. (1990) First breeding record of Verreaux's Eagle *Aquila verreauxii* in Saudi Arabia. *Sandgrouse* 12: 53–54.

EVANS, M. I. AND KEIJL, G. O. (1993a) Spring migration of coastal waders through the Saudi Arabian Gulf in 1991. *Sandgrouse* 15: 56–84.

EVANS, M. I. AND KEIJL, G. O. (1993b) Impact of Gulf War oil spills on the wader populations of the Saudi Arabian Gulf coast. *Sandgrouse* 15: 85–105.

EVANS, P. G. H. (1987) Sea birds of the Red Sea. Pp. 315–338 in A. J. Edwards and S. M. Head, eds. *Key Environments: Red Sea*. Oxford: Pergamon Press.

FELEMBAN, H. M. AND AL-BANNA, A. H. (1993) The occurrence of birds in Makkah sewage water outflow area. *Biol. Sci.* 2: 69–80.

GASPERETTI, P. R. (1989) Mammals of the Makkah by pass. *J. Saudi Arabian Nat. Hist. Soc.* 2 (9): 21–27.

GAUCHER, P. *ET AL.* (in press) Ecology of Sooty Falcon in Saudi Arabia. *Proc. IV World Conf. Birds of Prey, Berlin 1992*.

GORIUP, P., ED. (1989) Houbara Bustard field research project: report on activities 1989. Internal report, National Commission for Wildlife Conservation and Development.

GORIUP, P. *ET AL.* (1992) Houbara Bustard field research project: report on activities 1990. Internal report, National Commission for Wildlife Conservation and Development.

GREEN, A. A. (1984) The avifauna of the Al Jawf region, northwest Saudi Arabia. *Sandgrouse* 6: 48–58.

IUCN (International Union for Conservation of Nature and Natural Resources) (1987) *Saudi Arabia: an assessment of biotopes and management requirements for the Saudi Arabian Gulf coast*. Unpublished report (in draft) to Meteorology and Environmental Protection Administration (Jiddah).

JENNINGS, M. C. (1981) *The birds of Saudi Arabia: a check-list*. Whittlesford, U.K.: Jennings.

JENNINGS, M. C. (1986) The distribution of the extinct Arabian Ostrich *Struthio camelus syriacus* Rothschild, 1919. *Fauna of Saudi Arabia* 8: 447–461.

JENNINGS, M. C. (1988a) A note on the birds of the Farasan Islands, Red Sea, Saudi Arabia. *Fauna of Saudi Arabia* 9: 457–467.

JENNINGS, M. C. (1988b) Farasan Islands, Red Sea, Saudi Arabia. *Phoenix* 5: 8–9.

JENNINGS, M. C. (1988) The Harrat al Harrah Reserve, northern Saudi Arabia. *Phoenix* 5: 8.

JENNINGS, M. C. (1989) Sites of Interest: Jebel Al Lawz (BA 34), north west Saudi Arabia. *Phoenix* 6: 8–9.

JENNINGS, M. C. (1992) Summary report of an ornithological survey of northern Saudi Arabia: April–May 1992. *Desert Rambler* 13 (3): 6–14.

JENNINGS, M. C. AND FRYER, R. N. (1984) Birds of Saudi Arabia. The occurrence of the Lappet-faced Vulture *Torgos tracheliotus* (J. R. Forster) in the Arabian peninsula, with new breeding records from Saudi Arabia. *Fauna of Saudi Arabia* 6: 534–545.

JENNINGS, M. C., AL SALAMA, M. I. AND FELEMBAN, H. S. (1988) Report on an ornithological survey of the Asir National Park, Saudi Arabia 29 June to 18 July 1987. Internal report, National Commission for Wildlife Conservation and Development.

MEADOWS, B. S. (1986) Sites of interest: mangrove conservation areas at Yanbu Al-Sinaiyah, Saudi Arabia. *Phoenix* 3: 3–4.

MEADOWS, B. S. (in press) On the occurrence of Palaearctic land migrants in Red Sea mangrove stands. *Proc. VII Pan-Afr. Orn. Congr.*

METEOROLOGY AND ENVIRONMENTAL PROTECTION ADMINISTRATION (1987) *The Red Sea: an assessment of management requirements for the Saudi Arabian Red Sea coastal zone*. Jiddah: MEPA Coastal Marine Management Ser. Rep. 2.

NEWTON, S. F. AND NEWTON, A. V. (1993) The birds of Wadi Turabah, with some comments on threats, conservation and management. Internal report, National Wildlife Research Center.

NEWTON, S. F. AND NEWTON, A. V. (1993) Birds recorded at NWRC, Taif, December 1991–December 1992. Internal report, National Wildlife Research Center.

NEWTON, S. F. AND NEWTON, A. V. (1993) The birds of Mahazat As Said reserve: surveys and observations February 1992–January 1993. Internal report, National Wildlife Research Center.

NEWTON, S. F. AND SHOBRAK, M. (1993) The Lappet-faced Vulture *Torgos tracheliotus* in Saudi Arabia. *Proc. VIII Pan-Afr. Orn. Congr.* 111–117.

NEWTON, S. AND SYMENS, P. (1993) A survey of African

Demoiselle Cranes *Anthropoides virgo* migrating through Saudi Arabia in spring 1992. *Proc. VIII Pan-Afr. Orn. Congr.* 595–596.

NEWTON, S. F., NEWTON, A. V., GREEN, M., SUHAIBANY, A. AND LLEWELLYN, O. (1993) Report of the second Demoiselle Crane survey in Ha'il 17 March-4 April 1993. Internal report, National Commission for Wildlife Conservation and Development.

PERENNOU, C. AND MUNDKUR, T. (1991) *Asian Waterfowl Census 1991*. Slimbridge, U.K.: International Waterfowl and Wetlands Research Bureau.

PERENNOU, C. AND MUNDKHUR, T. (1992) *Asian and Australasian Waterfowl Census 1992*. Slimbridge, U.K.: International Waterfowl and Wetlands Research Bureau.

PERENNOU, C., ROSE, P. AND POOLE, C. (1990) *Asian Waterfowl Census 1990*. Slimbridge, U.K.: International Waterfowl and Wetlands Research Bureau.

RAHMANI, A. R. AND SHOBRAK, M. (1992a) Birds of the Tihamah coastal plains of Saudi Arabia. Internal report, National Commission for Wildlife Conservation and Development.

RAHMANI, A. R. AND SHOBRAK, M. (1992b) The Arabian Bustard in Saudi Arabia: final report. Internal report, National Commission for Wildlife Conservation and Development.

SCHULZ, H. AND SCHULZ, M. (1992) New records of the Bald Ibis (*Geronticus eremita*) from Saudi Arabia. *J. Orn.* 133: 165–172.

SCHULZ, H., SCHULZ, M., GAUCHER, P. AND EICHACKER, X. (undated) Freshwater fishes of Wadi Turabah—water parameters, distribution and morphometrics. Internal report, National Commission for Wildlife Conservation and Development.

SHOBRAK, M. AND SHOBRAK, M. AND RAHMANI, A. (1991) Notes on the Arabian Bustard *Ardeotis arabs* in Saudi Arabia. *Sandgrouse* 13: 14–23.

SHOBRAK, M. AND RAHMANI, A. R. (1993) Conservation of the Arabian Bustard. *Proc. VIII Pan-Afr. Orn. Congr.*: 350–357.

STAGG, A. J. (1984a) Birds of Saudi Arabia. A note on the White-collared Kingfisher. A new species for Saudi Arabia. *Fauna of Saudi Arabia* 6: 549–550.

STAGG, A. J. (1984b) Birds of Arabia: a note on the breed birds of Kutambil island on the Red Sea coast of Saudi Arabia. *Fauna of Saudi Arabia* 6: 546–548.

STAGG, A. J. (1984c) *The birds of S. W. Saudi Arabia: an annotated checklist*. Riyadh: Stagg.

STAGG, A. J. (1987) *Birds of the Riyadh region: an annotated checklist*. Riyadh: Stagg.

STAGG, A. J. (1989) Tabuk airbase lagoons, north west Saudi Arabia. *Phoenix* 6: 7–8.

SYMENS, P. (1988) Houbara Bustard survey in Harrat al Harrah 1988. Internal report, National Wildlife Research Center.

SYMENS, P. (1988) Birds of the Farasan Islands. Internal report, National Wildlife Research Center.

SYMENS, P. (1989) Birds of Taif. Internal report, National Wildlife Research Center.

SYMENS, P. (1990) Notes on birds of the NCWCD protected areas of south west Saudi Arabia. Internal report, National Wildlife Research Center.

SYMENS, P. AND EVANS, M. I. (1993) Impact of Gulf War oil spills on Saudi Arabian breeding populations of terns *Sterna* in the Arabian Gulf, 1991. *Sandgrouse* 15: 18–36.

SYMENS, P., LLEWELLYN, O., NEWTON, S. AND SHOBRAK, M. (1992) Report of the Demoiselle Crane survey in Ha'il 20–31 March 1992. Internal report, National Commission for Wildlife Conservation and Development.

WEIGELDT, C. AND SCHULZ, H. (1992) Counts of Lappet-faced Vultures *Torgos tracheliotus* at Mahazat As Said (Saudi Arabia), with a discussion of the species' taxonomy. *Sandgrouse* 14: 16–26.

WELCH, G. AND WELCH, H. (1991) Research report: raptor migration along the Al Hada escarpment (Taif, Saudi Arabia). Internal report, National Wildlife Research Center.

ZWARTS, L., FELEMBAN, H. AND PRICE, A. R. G. (1991) Wader counts along the Saudi Arabian Gulf coast suggest that the Gulf harbours millions of waders. *Wader Study Group Bull.* 63: 25–32.

■ SYRIAN ARAB REPUBLIC

Syrian Serin *Serinus syriacus*

GENERAL INFORMATION

Syria is situated on the eastern shore of the Mediterranean and covers 185,180 km². It borders Turkey in the north, Iraq in the east, Jordan in the south, Lebanon and Israel in the south-west, and is flanked by the Mediterranean Sea to the west. The country is mountainous in the west and south-west (Mount Hermon, Jibal al-Sharqi and Jibal al-Nusayriyah), but otherwise largely flat. The Syrian Desert covers the east and south-east.

With 10.5 million inhabitants, Syria has a low population density compared with European and other Middle East countries (an average of 56.7 people per km²), but the population density strongly reflects the amount of precipitation: it is highest in the coastal area and in the mountain chains close to the Mediterranean, but decreases rapidly to the east. Thus more than 50% of the surface area has a population density less than 3 people per km². The average annual precipitation in 90% of Syria is less than 500 mm. Most of Syria's flora comprises Mediterranean and Irano-Turanian elements, the latter mainly confined to the Syrian Desert. Six landscape types are distinguishable, as follows.

Mediterranean west

The geology, geomorphology, climate and vegetation of western Syria are similar to other Mediterranean countries. The main subregions (all parallel and trending north–south) are the coastal plain, the karst mountain range of the Jibal al-Nusayriyah (Jabal al-Ansariyah or Alawite mountains) further inland, and the flat, rift valley floor of the Al-Ghab basin to the east of this range. There are 180 km of coastline, mostly rocky with narrow sand beaches; islands offshore are few, small and rocky, the best known being Arwad off Tartus. The coastal plain generally very narrow but up to 40 km wide and is intensively cultivated, with citrus fruits and olives among the main crops. There are remnant areas of species-rich, evergreen maquis scrub.

The Jibal al-Nusayriyah range (up to 1,562 m) is 15–20 km wide with a narrow crest, and stretches from the Turkish border south to the Homs Gap just north of Lebanon. The western slopes are gentle but the eastern are very steep. There are remnant (but apparently still extensive) woodlands of *Abies*, *Quercus* and *Arbutus*, with *Cedrus* at the higher elevations (especially in the northern parts), and *Sarcopterium* maquis scrub and *Astragalus* thorn scrub on lower slopes. Numerous permanent streams and rivers flow to the Mediterranean or inland. In the 1940s there appear from maps to have been c.650 km² of forest. Overall, the coastal plain and the mountains currently possess c.1,200 km² of woodland and pasture, and c.2,150 km² of cultivated land.

To the east of the mountains, the Al-Asi (Orontes) river flows north along the flat depression of Al-Ghab, which formerly supported a wetland complex of spring-fed marshes and small lakes of major biodiversity importance, but which was drained between 1954 and 1968 to be replaced by irrigated cultivation (mainly of cotton, sugar-beet, vegetables and wheat), livestock husbandry stations and fish-farms. There are now many irrigation and drainage channels, with small patches of *Phragmites*.

Agricultural area of the north Syrian plateau

This region lies to the east of the Mediterranean zone and extends from the Turkish border in the north to the basin of Homs in the south. Limestone plains are the main geological feature, and are deeply dissected by wadis and rivers. Areas of intensive, irrigated agriculture are scattered like islands, the largest being the plain of Halab (Aleppo) in the north and the plains of Hamah and Homs in the south. The main water body is the Al-Asi river; its water is extracted for irrigation, and it almost runs dry in summer for this reason. The other major waterbodies are Bahrat Homs, an artificial barrage lake on the Al-Asi river dating from Roman times, and the large, flat salt-lake of Sabkhat al-Jabbul near Halab (Aleppo).

Mountains and irrigated oases of west-central Syria

West-central Syria is characterized by a series of parallel mountain ranges with intermediate valleys. The main ranges are the Jibal al-Sharqi (Karamun or Anti-Lebanon mountains, up to 2,424 m) and Jabal al-Shaykh (Haramun or Mount Hermon, up to 2,814 m). West-central Syria is situated in the rain-shadow of the Lebanese mountains, and the average annual precipitation is much lower than in the north and south of the country. Deserts and steppes extend up to the foot of the mountains; the latter support *Pistacia–Amygdalus* scrub and remnants of steppe-coniferous woodland, with *Abies*, *Pinus* and *Quercus*, now much depleted. Subalpine and alpine plant communities are found above 2,000 m. About 1,700 km^2 of this region are cultivated, of which c.700 km^2 are irrigated, mainly from karstic springs. The largest and most famous oasis is the Ghouta of Damascus where c.350 km^2 are under cultivation, including extensive orchards and *Populus* plantations.

Southern basalt areas

About 18,000 km^2 of the south-east of Syria (north-west to the edge of the Ghouta of Damascus) are covered in boulder-fields of black basalt, which extend continuously south through Jordan into Saudi Arabia. The Syrian basalt area can be subdivided into three regions. The Golan Heights (700–1,000 m) in the west are very stony and thus little-cultivated, and most of the area is used for grazing livestock; most of this area has been occupied by Israel since 1967. The fertile Hauran (500–700 m), east of the Golan, is known as Syria's granary. The largest areas of basalt are adjoining to the east, and include Jabal Druze, the land of the Druze people, an isolated mountain (reaching 1,800 m).

Rivers and agricultural plains of the north-east

The River Euphrates (Al-Furat) is the main freshwater body in Syria, with the Balikh and Khabur rivers joining it from the north. A large section of the Syrian Euphrates valley was dammed and flooded in the 1970s, creating Buhayrat al-Assad (Lake Assad).

The fertile steppe of the north-east extends east of the River Euphrates all along the Turkish border south to the isolated hill range of Jabal Abdul Aziz, and is part of the Jazirah region. The southern boundary of this landscape class marks the traditional limit of rain-fed cultivation, but vast areas have now been converted to more intensive, irrigated cultivation. There is a network of springs which feed the Khabur, Balikh and Jaghjagha rivers (now much depleted by water extraction for irrigation), and the River Tigris flows along the shared border with Iraq in the far east. The summers are very hot with daily mean temperatures of about 40°C in July and August; the winters are cold. The climate is of Mediterranean-type, with an average annual precipitation between 250 and 500 mm.

Deserts and steppes

This region in the south-east of the country is a northward extension of the vast Arabian desert plateau, but the precipitation is still relatively high at 70–80 mm per year, supporting a sparse vegetation of *Artemisia* shrub-steppe, with scattered *Pistacia* and *Amygdalus* trees in the least arid areas. There are a number of isolated hill ranges in the desert, notably Jabal Shumriyah, Jabal Bishri, Jabal al-Bilas, Jabal Sha'ir and Jabal Abu Rujmayn. The plant cover is threatened by the very heavy grazing of nomadic pastoralists' livestock (sheep, goats and camels), which can penetrate even the remotest areas now, due to the construction of wells and of roads which allow the transportation of water in tankers.

ORNITHOLOGICAL IMPORTANCE

Syria is poorly known ornithologically. Many parts of the country have never been visited by birdwatchers, and there has been almost no systematic fieldwork. Knowledge up to the mid-1960s was summarized by Kumerloeve (1967–1969), with more recent major contributions by Macfarlane (1978) covering 1974–1977 and Baumgart and Stephan (1986, 1987) covering 1980–1983. Since then, ornithological fieldwork has been only sporadic.

The number of bird species and their population densities are both relatively low. West Palearctic species predominate, and most of the species from this group which breed are confined to the Jibal al-Nusayriyah and Jibal al-Sharqi ranges, the distribution of many extending down to the altitude of Damascus.

The semi-natural and cultivated steppes and semi-deserts of much of Syria are very important for grassland and wetland birds. *Tetrax tetrax*, *Chlamydotis undulata* and *Otis tarda* are all globally threatened and seem to winter and/or breed in notable numbers in these habitats, though lack of extensive surveys means that total population sizes and overall distributions are still unclear. Similarly, the globally threatened *Aegypius monachus* may be a more common winter visitor to the northern steppes and isolated desert mountains than the few records suggest. This area may once also have been an important wintering or staging ground for the globally threatened *Vanellus gregarius*, for which there are similarly few recent records. The cultivated steppes are particularly important feeding areas for large numbers of ducks and geese, which have never been censused however. Two regionally threatened species are of note in this region. *Falco biarmicus* appears to breed in good numbers in the semi-desert of central Syria, probably associated with the frequent, isolated hill ranges found there, and *Torgos tracheliotus* appears to have been recorded in the same area but it is not known whether it still occurs, and if so, regularly.

Syria has relatively few major wetlands, but they are all important for globally threatened species. Of greatest value is the Euphrates valley, where *Phalacrocorax pygmeus* winters and migrates, and may breed. *Marmaronetta angustirostris* may also breed and/or winter in significant numbers along the Euphrates valley and its tributaries, although records are few, and it occurs in small numbers at Sabkhat al-Jabbul and Bahrat Homs. The latter site is important for wintering *Oxyura leucocephala*, which is otherwise very scarce. Large numbers of wintering ducks and geese and migrating waterbirds feed and roost at these wetlands. None of the main, permanent lakes of Syria—Buhayrat al-Assad, Bahrat Homs and Sabkhat al-Jabbul—have rich bank-side vegetation (although this is now developing at Sabkhat al-Jabbul due to a recent change in its hydrology), and they are thus not suitable for a wide range of breeding waterbirds. No cormorants, herons or egrets are known to currently breed in Syria.

The globally threatened *Falco naumanni* is likely to still breed very locally in small numbers in steppe and agricultural areas in the less arid western half of the country, but had apparently disappeared from all of its known breeding colonies by the 1980s, for reasons that are unclear but which may be related to the very widespread intensification of agriculture in Syria. *Geronticus eremita*, a species imminently threatened with global extinction in the wild, used to breed in the remote semi-desert wadis and hills north of a line between Al Qaryatayn and Tadmur, but the last known colony was at Jabal Abu Rujmayn in 1928. However, it is just possible that the species may still breed in Syria, given the continuing existence of a Middle Eastern population in winter in Arabia even after the extinction in 1989 of the only breeding colony known to remain (at Birecik in Turkey), and since the Syrian breeding colonies appear to have never been re-surveyed since 1928.

Despite heavy persecution and hunting for the taxidermy trade (between 10,000 and 100,000 are estimated to be shot each year), Syria supports good populations of breeding raptors (Baumgart 1991a, b): *Circaetus gallicus* (30–50 pairs), *Accipiter gentilis* (1–5 pairs), *Buteo rufinus* (500–1,000 pairs), *Buteo buteo* (5–10 pairs), *Aquila chrysaetos* (5–10 pairs), *Neophron percnopterus* (50–100 pairs), *Gyps fulvus* (100–200 pairs), *Falco biarmicus* (less than 50 pairs), *Falco subbuteo* (30–50 pairs), *Falco tinnunculus* (1,000–2,000 pairs), *Tyto alba* (200–300 pairs), *Otus scops* (200–300 pairs), *Bubo bubo* (100–200 pairs), *Athene noctua* (3,000–5,000 pairs) and *Strix aluco* (30–50 pairs). Raptor migration, whilst mostly 'broad-front' and at high altitude except along the Jibal al-Nusayriyah, probably involves more than 2,000,000 birds per year; the most important species are *Pernis apivorus*, *Milvus migrans*, *Neophron percnopterus*, *Gyps fulvus*, *Circaetus gallicus*, *Accipiter brevipes*, *Buteo buteo*, *Aquila pomarina*, *A. nipalensis* and *Hieraaetus pennatus*.

Serinus syriacus is endemic to the western mountains of the Levant, and Syria probably harbours a significant proportion of the world population, although there have been very few ornithological surveys in the relevant areas. *Lanius nubicus* and *Hippolais languida* also both have small world ranges with important populations in the highlands of western Syria.

CONSERVATION INFRASTRUCTURE AND PROTECTED-AREA SYSTEM

Syria has no area-based environmental laws or protected-area system dedicated explicitly towards conserving biodiversity. However, the Ministry of State for Environmental Affairs is currently drafting a nature conservation law, and there is a system of protected forests and rangelands.

Enclosed Rangeland Reserves (2 sites covering 42,000 ha) These are administered by the Directorate of Rangeland and Countryside of the Ministry of Agriculture and Agrarian Reform, with the aim of developing vegetation cover in order to ameliorate and prevent land degradation in arid and desert areas, by controlling grazing intensity of livestock and by afforestation schemes. A third site of 40,000 ha has been proposed.

State Forest Protection Zones These are administered by the Directorate of Forests and Afforestation of the Ministry of Agriculture and Agrarian Reform. The total number of sites is not known to BirdLife International; at least two are included in this inventory (Jabal Slenfeh and Jabal al-Bilas).

Afforestation projects, administered by a special office of the Ba'ath Party, are said to be ongoing at, or planned for, five areas: Jabal Shumriyah, Jabal Bishri, Jabal Abdul Aziz, Jabal Sha'ir and Jabal Abu Rujmayn.

Hunting occurs throughout Syria and is said to be increasing; the hunting laws (Legislative Decree No. 152 of 22 July 1970) are considered to be strict, but despite the efforts of the authorities many hunters hunt illegally.

INTERNATIONAL MEASURES RELEVANT TO THE CONSERVATION OF SITES

Syria is a Party to the World Heritage Convention and to the Barcelona Convention (and has signed the Protocol concerning Mediterranean Specially Protected Areas). No natural World Heritage Sites or Mediterranean Specially Protected Areas have been designated as yet, but designation of seven of the latter sites is currently under consideration by the government. Syria has not signed the Ramsar, Biodiversity or Bonn Conventions. There is an active National Committee of the UNESCO Man and Biosphere Programme; no Biosphere Reserves have been designated.

OVERVIEW OF THE INVENTORY

A total of 22 sites are contained in the following inventory, with a combined area of about 6,300 km^2 or about 3.5% of the country's area. The inventory covers, to a more-or-less comprehensive degree, all the major habitats of importance for birds: rivers, salt-lakes, permanent lakes and reservoirs, steppes and traditionally farmed agricultural lands, semi-desert, forests, oases, cliffs, and the coastal and high mountain zones. It is believed that all of the permanent and seasonal wetlands that are most important for waterbirds have been included in the inventory, and that important parts of the largest remaining blocks of forest remaining in Syria have been identified and included. However the important steppe and semi-desert sites in the north, east and centre of Syria have been chosen on the basis of the small amount of ornithological information available, and should be considered as representative rather than definitive examples of these habitats, pending further surveys. The coastal and high mountain zones are limited in extent, and the sites covering these habitats in the inventory are likely to be adequately representative, if not the most important. Cliffs used by breeding raptors are without doubt under-represented in the inventory due to the paucity of field surveys. A number of sites of potential importance for bird populations have been identified which may qualify as Important Bird Areas but for which there is at present no significant, up-to-date ornithological information available. These include: the former breeding colonies of the globally threatened *Geronticus eremita* north of Al-Qaryatayn (there may have been no surveys since the 1920s); the Jabal Druze; the isolated high mountains around Tadmur (Jabal al-Nasrani, Jabal al-Khanazir, Jabal Shumriyah, Jabal Sha'ir, Jabal al-Abyad and Jabal Abu Rujmayn); the extensive basalt desert and clay pans of the Badiyat al-Sham in the south-east; and the large saline mudflats in the east on the border with Iraq (including Sabkhat al-Barghut and Sabkhat Shamlan). Many bird species (which Syria has important populations of) such as raptors, bustards, sandgrouse and larks, tend not to congregate but to have scattered distributions. Only a small proportion of their total populations is covered by the inclusion of some representative sites. To conserve these dispersed species it is necessary to integrate conservation measures for the wider environment into regulations governing important land-uses such as agriculture and forestry.

ACKNOWLEDGEMENTS

The site accounts were compiled from data-sheets and other information supplied by Dr I. Hanna, Dr A. M. Agha, Dr R. Sabbagh, Dr M. A. Kabbani, Dr M. Masseti, W. Attar, B. Attar, M. Abbasi, J. J. Dumas, M. Kasparek and J. Davies. The data-sheets originally submitted by A. M. Macfarlane to the Ornithological Society of the Middle East's Sites Register Scheme were also incorporated. The introduction was compiled from information supplied by M. Kasparek and Dr M. Masseti. S. Zaiane translated all the Arabic data-sheets into English, and additional assistance and advice was provided by Dr A. Khatib, Dr E. Bailey, Dr M. al-Nimeh, the University of Aleppo, Dr M. A. Nour, Z. al-Jabbawi, Dr S. Bottema, G. Keijl, I. Andrews and A. Jeudy de Grissac. D. J. Brooks researched the existing literature and compiled the first draft of most site accounts.

SITE INVENTORY

Site no.	Site name	Region	Criteria used to select site 1	2i	2ii	2iii	3	4	5i	5ii	6	0
001	Ras al-Ayn	HK	•	—	—	—	•	•	•	—	—	—
002	Wadi al-Radd	HK	—	—	—	—	—	—	—	•	—	•
003	Tual al-'Abba	RQ	•	•	—	—	•	—	•	•	—	—
004	Jabal Abdul Aziz	HK	•	—	—	—	•	—	—	—	—	—
005	Buhayrat al-Khatuniyah	HK	•	—	—	—	•	—	•	•	—	—
006	Sabkhat al-Jabbul	HB	•	•	•	—	•	•	—	—	—	—
007	Buhayrat al-Assad	RQ, HB	•	•	•	—	•	•	—	—	—	—
008	Baath Lake	RQ	—	—	—	—	—	—	—	—	—	•
009	Umm al-Tuyyur	LK	—	—	—	—	•	—	•	—	—	—
010	Euphrates Valley	HB, RQ, DZ	•	—	—	—	—	•	—	—	—	—
011	Jabal Slenfeh	LK	—	—	—	•	•	—	•	—	—	—
012	Wadi al-Azib	HM	•	—	—	—	•	•	—	—	—	—
013	Jabal al-Shuah	LK	—	—	—	—	—	—	•	—	—	•
014	Jabal al-Bishri	RQ, DZ, HS	•	—	—	—	•	•	—	—	—	—
015	Jabal al-Bilas	HS	•	—	—	—	•	•	—	—	—	—
016	Buhayrat al-Laha	TR	—	—	—	—	—	—	—	•	—	•
017	Bahrat Homs	HS	•	•	•	—	•	—	—	—	—	—
018	Tadmur and Sabkhat Muh	HS	•	•	—	—	•	•	—	—	—	—
019	Abu Zad	DM	—	—	—	—	•	•	—	—	—	—
020	Wadi al-Qarn–Burqush	DM	—	—	—	—	•	•	—	—	—	—
021	Jabal Sis	DM	•	•	—	—	—	•	•	—	—	—
022	Yarmuk Valley	DR	—	—	—	—	•	•	—	•	—	—

Key to regions

DM	Dimashq
DR	Dar'a
DZ	Dayr al-Zawr
HB	Halab
HK	Al-Hasakah
HM	Hamah
HS	Hims
ID	Idlib
LK	Al-Ladhiqiyah
RQ	Al-Raqqah
TR	Tartus

Key to criteria

1 Regularly holds a significant number of a globally threatened species.

2i Regularly holds 1% or more of a species' biogeographical or flyway or Middle Eastern population (waterbirds and seabirds only).

2ii Regularly holds 20,000 or more waterbirds.

2iii Migratory 'bottleneck' site: more than 3,000 raptors or more than 5,000 storks or more than 2,000 cranes pass in a season.

3 Regularly holds a significant number of a species which is threatened or declining within the Middle East. Only the top five sites for each such species in the country are considered to qualify as IBAs.

4 Regularly holds a significant number of a species whose world population is wholly or largely restricted to the Middle East. Only the top five sites for each such species in the country are considered to qualify as IBAs.

5i Representative example of a habitat, associated with a characteristic assemblage of bird species.

5ii Rare/threatened/unique habitat, associated with a characteristic assemblage of bird species.

6 Site important for bird conservation through education/research/tourism.

0 Selected for other reasons. See 'Comments on the inventory'.

Comments on the inventory

1. The Golan Heights of Syria are currently occupied by Israel. This region qualifies as an Important Bird Area, but is treated in the Israel site inventory (see site 003 in that chapter), since it is currently administered by Israel.
2. The majority of the data used in compiling the site accounts dates from the 1970s, with a minority from the 1980s/1990s and from the 1950s/1960s.
3. The site name has been transliterated from the Arabic, and is sometimes followed by an alternative site name in brackets. This is then followed by the name of the region in brackets, where appropriate. The regions given are the governorates (muhafazat).
4. Precise areas are given only for protected areas and some of the sites which have been well documented. Boundaries have not been defined for the rest of the sites, and any areas given in these cases are only crude estimates. No area is given for site 010 because further fieldwork is required before the most important areas within this site can be identified and their boundaries determined.
5. The area given for the only offshore island site (part of 009; important for breeding seabirds) does not include the area of the surrounding seas which are important as feeding grounds, because the latter have not been identified with sufficient accuracy as yet.
6. The site descriptions provided are tentative outlines only for most sites, in the absence of more detailed information based on ornithological surveys.
7. Figures in brackets after species' names, and in the boxes, are the maximum daily counts of individuals recorded (not pairs), unless otherwise stated. All counts of wintering birds are from the month of January, unless otherwise stated.
8. Four sites do not meet the site-selection criteria (see column 0 of above table), either because they have only been visited by ornithologists once (site 008) or not at all (sites 002, 013 and 016). Three are wetlands (sites 002, 008 and 016)

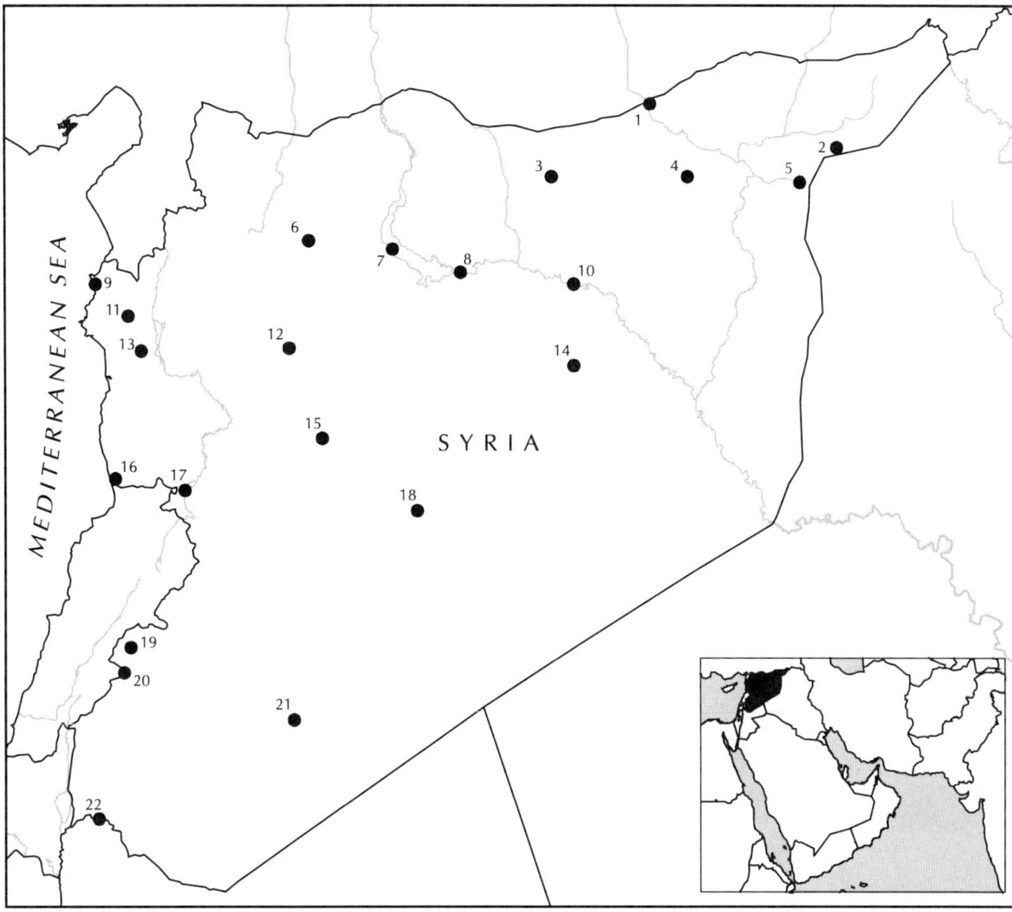

believed to be of importance for large numbers of waterfowl, and in the case of site 008, a count of 800 *Anser albifrons* was close to the 1% population level. Site 013 is thought to be the largest remaining tract of Mediterranean woodland in Syria, and may also be an important raptor migration 'bottleneck' site.

Glossary

ayn, spring
buhayrat, bahrat, lake
jabal, mountain
jazirat, island
jibal, mountain range
nahr, river
ras, headland, point, cape
sabkhat, saline mudflat
tell, hill
wadi, valley, drainage line.

001 Ras al-Ayn (Al-Hasakah)

also known as Tell Halaf
Unprotected

36°50´N 40°05´E
100,000 ha

Site description

A vast area of steppe around the border settlement of Ras al-Ayn, through which the seasonal Khabur river flows in winter and spring, north-west of Al-Hasakah. Much of the steppe along the Khabur valley is now under irrigated cultivation of wheat and cotton. Trees and scrub occur along the Khabur river, especially at Ras al-Ayn where there is a patch of c.100 ha of dense *Salix* bushes, fed by a very powerful, sulphurous hot spring.

Birds

See box for key species. *Streptopelia turtur* is a passage migrant in large numbers at Ras al-Ayn. *Anser albifrons* occurs in winter. There is almost no information on the site since the mid-1970s. Likely species are indicated by extrapolating from the adjacent Ceylanpinar area in Turkey (see Grimmett and Jones 1989). Other likely breeding species include *Buteo rufinus*, *Aquila chrysaetos*, *Burhinus oedicnemus*, *Pterocles alchata* and *Merops superciliosus*, as well as a variety of waterfowl along the Khabur river.

Globally threatened species

Otis tarda	Likely to be an important wintering area for this species.
Tetrax tetrax	Likely to be a winter visitor.

Regionally threatened or declining species

Botaurus stellaris	Passage migrant in Khabur valley.
Neophron percnopterus	Likely to be a non-breeding summer visitor.
Francolinus francolinus	Common resident in Khabur valley.

Species restricted wholly or largely to the Middle East

Ammoperdix griseogularis	Likely to be a resident.
Passer moabiticus	Ras al-Ayn holds part of a colony which extends over the Turkish side of the border (Ceylanpinar). In 1968 there appeared (as seen from Turkey) to be 10–12 nests within the Syrian part of the colony.
Carpospiza brachydactyla	Likely to occur.

Other threatened/endemic wildlife

Mammals: *Gazella subgutturosa* (rare) may still occur. Reptiles: *Varanus griseus* (rare) may still occur.

Conservation issues

The widespread conversion since the 1970s of semi-natural steppe or traditional dryland farming areas to permanent, irrigated cultivation of wheat and cotton monoculture, with associated use of pesticides, has probably led to declines in bustard populations, as it has elsewhee. In the mid-1970s 10,000 ha in this area were irrigated and a further 39,000 ha were earmarked for irrigation. The Khabur river is apparently now saline, presumably as a result of wastewater discharge from irrigation projects. The *Salix* woodland at Ras al-Ayn is considered likely to be still intact.

Further reading

Grimmett and Jones (1989), Kumerloeve (1969, 1970).

002 Wadi al-Radd (Al-Hasakah)

Unprotected

36°35′N 41°30′E
48,000 ha

Site description

A steppic basin in the Jazirah, 60 km long by 10 km wide, near Al-Qamishli and a few kilometres north of the border with Iraq. Numerous small drainage lines descend from Jabal Sinjar in Iraq and from the Turkish mountains to the north. The basin used to flood in winter and spring, the extent depending on the season's rain and snowfall. By December 1971 the area had been converted to intensive cultivation (wheat and cotton), and there was no standing water apparent in that year, but even in the 1990s smaller parts of the original area are considered still liable to winter flooding.

Birds

The site was 'known to attract large numbers of duck on passage, but its importance as a wintering area is uncertain' (Savage 1968). *Phoenicopterus ruber* has been recorded in the last few years, indicating that relatively deep and prolonged flooding may still occur. Otherwise, there is no other ornithological information available.

Other threatened/endemic wildlife

No information.

Conservation issues

Despite the almost-certain conversion of this steppeland site to intensive cultivation, any remaining winter-flooded parts are likely to still be important feeding areas for migrating and wintering waterfowl. However there is no information on the current state of the site's habitats. Hunting is apparently not controlled.

Further reading

Dijksen and Koning (1972), Savage (1968).

003 Tual al-'Abba (Al-Raqqah)
Unprotected

36°25′N 39°20′E
30,000 ha

Site description
An extensive area of steppe to the west of Jabal Abdul Aziz and to the east and south-east of Skiro village (36°25′N 39°05′E), bounded by the Balikh valley to the west. In the 1960s there were seasonally inundated fresh and saline marshes in the Balikh valley, e.g. at Ali Bajiliyah, c.100 km north of Al-Raqqah. In the 1970s, there were extensive reedbeds and some open water at Skiro, and about 10 km north along the road from Skiro on the western side was Al-Sharkrak pond (c.1 ha). In the early 1980s there was an area of small permanent lakes (c.50 ha) called Waz Göl (36°31′N 39°01′E), fed by springs at Ayn al-Arus. Vegetation here, and probably elsewhere in the valley, consisted of *Salix* trees/bushes and stands of *Phragmites*, *Lythrum*, *Carex* and *Luzula*. However by 1992 (and perhaps as early as 1984) the lakes, springs, and river itself were all dry due to major and unsustainable water abstraction from the Balikh river for irrigation in Turkey and Syria. The continued existence of other wetland areas in the valley, of which the above are only representative examples, is thus in doubt. The majority of the steppe is cultivated with cereals and cotton and otherwise very heavily grazed by livestock; crop failures are common during droughts.

Birds
See box for key species. The site is ornithologically little-known. Possible breeding species in the Balikh valley in the 1970s included *Glareola pratincola*, *Sterna albifrons*, *Merops superciliosus* and *Cercotrichas galactotes*. Wintering species in the 1970s and early 1980s included an excellent diversity of waterfowl, including *Anser albifrons* and *Grus grus*. Ducks were reported to occur at Ali Bajiliyah in summer and 'large numbers' were present in winter (Savage 1968). Passage migrants in autumn in the 1980s included *Tachybaptus ruficollis* (200), *Netta rufina*, *Circus aeruginosus* (5) and *Vanellus leucurus*.

Globally threatened species

Phalacrocorax pygmeus	Recorded in October (1).
Marmaronetta angustirostris	A flock of 20, October; may breed or have bred.
Oxyura leucocephala	Recorded in October (1).
Chlamydotis undulata	Said to have been a former visitor to the region, driven away by excessive hunting.
Otis tarda	Winter visitor (max. 16, March 1976). Formerly may have bred, but disturbance is probably too great now.
Vanellus gregarius	Possibly regular passage migrant or winter visitor; recorded in October (1).

1% or more of population

	Breeding (pairs)	Wintering	Passage
Aythya nyroca	—	—	20 (Oct)

Regionally threatened or declining species

Aythya nyroca	Recorded in October (see above).
Falco cherrug	Recorded in October (1).

Other threatened/endemic wildlife
No information.

Conservation issues
The drainage of wetlands in the Balikh valley and the conversion of steppe to rain-fed and irrigated farmland, with associated intensification of agriculture, use of agrochemicals and increased levels of human disturbance, are critical problems. Hunting pressure on waterfowl and gamebirds, including *Otis tarda*, is apparently intense and uncontrolled. *Phragmites* reedbeds are burned to encourage regrowth for cattle grazing. If irrigation practises upstream become more sustainable in the future, it is possible that some of the valley wetlands might be rehabilitated. In the meantime, excessively heavy grazing, encroachment by cultivation, and associated human disturbance continue to degrade or destroy what little remains of these critically threatened wetlands and steppes.

Further reading
Bottema (1985), Macfarlane (1978), Savage (1968).

004 Jabal Abdul Aziz (Al-Hasakah)
Unprotected

36°25′N 40°22′E
45,000 ha

Site description
A mountain range (up to 920 m) lying west of Al-Hasakah and running for c.50 km east–west. The southern slopes are gentle, but the northern slopes are a very steep, linear scarp with frequent cliffs. Numerous small wadis drain the slopes. The steppe

vegetation includes *Pistacia*, *Prunus* and *Rhamnus* scrub, with extensive shrubs of *Artemisia*, *Atriplex*, *Helianthemum* and *Teucrium*. There is an extensive and ongoing afforestation project, planting *Pistacia*, *Pinus brutia* and *P. halepensis*

Birds
See box for key species. As well as species listed below, *Pterocles alchata* is a common resident.

Globally threatened species	
Aegypius monachus	Presumed winter visitor (specimen in Halab University); may breed.
Chlamydotis undulata	Resident.
Regionally threatened or declining species	
Neophron percnopterus	Breeds (c.15 pairs).
Gyps fulvus	Breeds (c.4 pairs).
Francolinus francolinus	Common resident.

Other threatened/endemic wildlife
Mammals: *Canis lupus* (V), *Gazella subgutturosa* (rare); *Equus hemionus hemippus* (V) survived in this area until the 1930s. Flora: many endemics are confined to the isolated mountains in the Syrian Desert.

Conservation issues
As a preliminary to a program for preventing soil erosion, a decree has been issued prohibiting the grazing and agricultural development by which the area is threatened, and there is an afforestation scheme underway (see above). However, illegal cutting of trees and other vegetation still occurs despite the efforts of the authorities. There is overgrazing by livestock and feral donkeys, and a threat from conversion of land to cereal cultivation and consequent wind-erosion. Hunting of *Alectoris chukar* and *Gazella* is prohibited.

005 Buhayrat al-Khatuniyah (Al-Hasakah)

36°23′N 41°13′E
80,000 ha

also known as Khatounia Lake, Bahrat Hatuniya or Buhayrat al-Hul
Unprotected

Site description
A mesotrophic, spring-fed, natural lake (its area is variously quoted as being from 50 ha to c.800 ha) together with the surrounding 'clay' desert, c.50 km east of Al-Hasakah and between the small settlements of Khatuniyah and Al-Hul (6 km from the international border). The mean depth of the lake is or was 8 m, and the vegetation includes *Tamarix*. The lake is used for fishing, hunting and recreation, and the surrounding area for grazing.

Birds
See box for key species. Other breeding species include *Alectoris chukar* and *Pterocles alchata*, and small numbers of *Anser albifrons* and ducks are present in winter. Passage migrants include *Tachybaptus ruficollis*, and large numbers of *Streptopelia turtur*.

Globally threatened species	
Chlamydotis undulata	Resident.
Regionally threatened or declining species	
Gyps fulvus	Resident; presumed to nest (c.4 pairs) on Jabal Sinjar, 12 km to the west-southwest in Iraq.
Falco cherrug	May breed.

Other threatened/endemic wildlife
Mammals: *Canis lupus* (V), *Gazella subgutturosa* (rare).

Conservation issues
Despite the lack of recent ornithological information and the conversion to cultivation of very large areas of steppeland and wetlands in the Jazirah region, these wetlands are known to still exist. No site protection measures are known to have been taken. The governorate authorities have banned or restricted the hunting of *Alectoris chukar* and *Pterocles alchata*; however, some uncontrolled hunting is said to still occur. There is over-fishing, and the surrounding area is heavily grazed by feral donkeys. *Tilapia* fish have been introduced. The site was proposed as a Project Aqua conservation site by the Ministry of Agriculture and Agrarian Reform in the late 1960s.

Further reading
Luther and Rzóska (1971).

006 Sabkhat al-Jabbul (Halab)

also known as Jabbul Salt-Lake
Unprotected

36°03'N 37°29'E
c.15,00 ha

Site description

A large, shallow salt-lake in a closed basin of c.37,500 ha, lying just south of Jabbul village, 35 km east-south-east of Halab (Aleppo). In the 1970s the lake was filled entirely by local run-off of winter/spring rainfall and its extent was highly variable from year to year, reaching a maximum of c.3,000 ha and with at least a little standing water at most times of the year. A levée built on the east side by the 1970s prevented flooding of the majority of the salt-flat in the east of the basin. However, in 1988 large, new irrigation projects on the nearby steppe started discharging surplus water into the lake on a substantial scale; it is not known how saline the inflow is nor whether it is seasonal or perennial. This appears to have led to a higher and more stable water level than in the past, since the lake currently measures up to 20 km long and 5 km wide (c.10,000 ha), and although in the 1970s the flat and sandy banks had little or no marginal vegetation, they are now locally lined by extensive *Phragmites* reedbeds, on the southern and south-eastern shores at least. At least two large islands are created at times of high flooding. Around the lake shore there is turf, close-cropped by sheep. The surrounding steppe has a sparse shrubland of *Haloxylon* and *Artemisia*. Primary uses of the area are salt extraction, wildfowl hunting, and livestock grazing on the surrounding steppe by nomadic pastoralists; in the 1970s the sabkhah to the east was an artillery firing range.

Birds

An important wetland for wintering, migrating and breeding waterbirds. See box for key species. Other confirmed or probable breeding species include *Alectoris chukar*, *Himantopus himantopus*, *Recurvirostra avosetta*, *Cursorius cursor*, *Charadrius leschenaultii*, *Sterna nilotica*, *S. caspia*, *S. albifrons*, *Pterocles alchata* and *Rhodopechys obsoleta*. According to local people *Phoenicopterus ruber* sometimes breeds; 700+ were present in April 1993. In the 1970s the number of wintering waterfowl depended on the water level (maximum recorded was 'tens of thousands'), numbers of *Phoenicopterus ruber* having varied from none to c.8,000. Currently the higher and apparently more stable water level is probably supporting even larger waterfowl numbers than in the 1970s. Other wintering species include *Pelecanus onocrotalus*, *Ciconia nigra*, *Cygnus olor*, *Anser albifrons* (2,030, December 1972), *A. anser*, *Anas crecca* (thousands), *A. acuta* (1,000+), *Fulica atra* (10,000), *Grus grus* (155, December 1972), *Calidris minuta* (many hundreds) and *Ceryle rudis* (200). Other migrating species in spring (April) include *Podiceps nigricollis* (100) *Platalea leucorodia* (70), *Tadorna tadorna* (300), *Himantopus himantopus* (200), *Philomachus pugnax* (thousands) and *Larus genei* (100). The site was listed as a wetland of international importance by Carp (1980).

Globally threatened species

Branta ruficollis	Recorded by hunters; of uncertain status, but presumably a rare winter visitor or vagrant.
Marmaronetta angustirostris	Passage migrant (1, April); the recent development of extensive marginal vegetation favours breeding.
Oxyura leucocephala	Passage migrant (3, April); the recent development of extensive marginal vegetation favours breeding.
Chlamydotis undulata	Resident on surrounding steppe.

1% or more of population

	Breeding (pairs)	Wintering	Passage
Phoenicopterus ruber	?	8,000	—
Tadorna ferruginea	?	300	400
Calidris minuta	—	hundreds	3,000

Regionally threatened or declining species

Gyps fulvus	Recorded in the area by hunters.
Falco biarmicus	Passage migrant (1, April).

Species restricted wholly or largely to the Middle East

Glareola nordmanni	Formerly a summer visitor; no recent information.
Otus brucei	Summer visitor.

Other threatened/endemic wildlife

Mammals: *Canis lupus* (V), *Gazella subgutturosa* (rare).

Conservation issues

The long-term impact of the changes to the lake's hydrology on its value for waterfowl and other wildlife is unclear. Wildfowl shooting is relatively intense throughout the winter, and bag limits and hunting seasons are not enforced; however the large size and openness of the lake give some natural protection.

Further reading

Bodenham (1944), Carp (1980), Clarke (1924), Hollom (1959).

007 Buhayrat al-Assad (Al-Raqqah, Halab)

36°00′N 38°07′E
70,000 ha

also known as Bahrat Assad or Lake Assad
Unprotected

Site description

Buhayrat al-Assad is a huge reservoir of more than 63,000 ha created by a dam on the River Euphrates (Al-Furat) near the town of Al-Thawra, and occupies c.80 km of the valley (north-west end at 36°18′N 38°10′E, south-east end at 35°49′N 38°28′E). The shores are mainly steep and rocky, and the water appears oligotrophic, being very clear and without sediment. Much of the surrounding area is dry, stony, and almost devoid of vegetation. However, the Ministry of Agriculture and Agrarian Reform has recently afforested large areas on the southern shore and around Al-Thawra with *Olea*, *Cupressus*, eucalyptus and *Amygdalus*, including an offshore island (Jazirat al-'Ayd or Jazirat al-Thawra) which is being established as a nature park with a tourist centre and a network of vehicle tracks. The island is linked to the mainland by a causeway with a gate. Sugar-cane and cereals are cultivated in the south-east. The dam is used for hydro-electric power generation. Jabbar Castle is a historical site on the east side of the lake near the dam.

Birds

See box for key species. An important roosting site for large numbers of wintering wildfowl which feed on the surrounding steppes. At least two areas of ornithological interest were identified in the 1970s: (1) the western bank at the northern end, 30 km south-east of Manbij, and (2) the south-east corner 8 km south-west of the dam. Breeding species include *Tachybaptus ruficollis*, *Athene noctua* (very common), *Larus melanocephalus* (possibly breeds: max. 20 adults, June 1975), *L. genei* (said to breed at or near an island called Tell al-Abyad near the dam; 130 adults nearby, April 1993), *Ceryle rudis* and *Rhodopechys obsoleta* (possibly). Huge numbers (said to be hundreds of thousands) of geese, ducks and other waterfowl currently winter in the area, feeding on the surrounding steppe and roosting at the site; *Anser albifrons* (min. 250), *Tadorna tadorna* and *Anas platyrhynchos* are especially common. In the 1970s other common species included *Fulica atra* (10,000, November). Notable species on passage include *Podiceps nigricollis*, *Phalacrocorax carbo*, *Egretta garzetta*, *Casmerodius albus*, *Larus fuscus*, *Emberiza caesia* and *Rhodopechys obsoleta*.

Globally threatened species

Phalacrocorax pygmeus	Passage migrant (1, April 1993).
Pelecanus crispus	Passage migrant (2, March 1976).
Falco naumanni	Probable summer visitor: a group of 5 frequenting some ruins in April 1993.
Vanellus gregarius	Passage migrant (40, September 1974).

1% or more of population

	Breeding (pairs)	Wintering	Passage
Casmerodius albus	—	100 (Nov)	—
Ardea cinerea	—	225	—
Larus cachinnans	—	2,000 (Nov)	—

Regionally threatened or declining species

Gyps fulvus	Present all year.

Species restricted wholly or largely to the Middle East

Ammoperdix griseogularis	Resident at the north-west end of the lake, near the extreme west of the species' range.

Other threatened/endemic wildlife

Mammals: *Canis lupus* (V).

Conservation issues

Unauthorized entry of vehicles or people to Jazirat al-'Ayd is not allowed; there is a guard at the gate. Nevertheless some hunters still enter. Management of this area is geared primarily towards public recreation. Hunting elsewhere is common.

008 Baath Lake (Al-Raqqah)

35°52′N 38°38′E
c.100+ ha

Unprotected

Site description

A shallow, 10-km-long lake formed by a dam on the Euphrates (Al-Furat) at Mansurah, less than 10 km to the east of and below the main dam of Buhayrat al-Assad (Lake Assad) at Tabqa. The upper reaches are particularly shallow with a number of islands fringed by *Phragmites* reedbeds.

Birds

Thousands of roosting and loafing wildfowl occur in winter, especially ducks. The site has been surveyed only once in any detail, in November 1992, when wintering or migrating species included *Ardea cinerea* (80), *Anser albifrons* (800), *Anas penelope* (900), *A. strepera* (700), *Fulica atra* (5,000), *Larus* sp. (1,000–2,000), *Alcedo atthis* (40), *Ceryle rudis* (40) and *Merops superciliosus* (800).

Other threatened/endemic wildlife
Mammals: *Canis lupus* (V).

Conservation issues
No conservation measures are known to have been proposed. Hunting is permitted.

009 Umm al-Tuyyur (Al-Ladhiqiyah)
Unprotected

35°48′N 35°51′E
c.12,000 ha

Site description
A 12-km stretch of mainly rocky coast c.30 km north-north-east of Al-Ladhiqiyah (Lattakia) on the road to Al-Basit, extending north from the sheer limestone cliffs of Jabal Tarnajah (Ras al-Janzir) to the rocky headland of Ras al-Basit. There are 2 km of sand beach with seagrass beds offshore, and the 10-km-deep hinterland comprises well-wooded hills and narrow river valleys and plains. The area itself is also well-wooded, with coastal slopes covered in garigue, and there are a number of small, dammed lakes, including Ballouran Dam (25 ha). About 2,000 people live in and around Umm al-Tuyyur village, which is surrounded by a cultivated plain. Some fishing occurs offshore.

Birds
Breeding species include *Tachybaptus ruficollis* (less than 10 pairs), *Pernis apivorus* (probable), *Circaetus gallicus*, *Accipiter gentilis* (probable), *Buteo buteo* (possibly breeding in 1980s), *Falco subbuteo* (possibly breeding in 1980s), *Larus cachinnans* (c.15–30 pairs on a small island off Ras al-Basit: the only colony in Syria), *Apus affinis*, *Hippolais olivetorum* and *Emberiza cia*. *Falco eleonorae* is a non-breeding summer visitor in small numbers (3–5, June). The area is known locally to be especially attractive to migrant birds, of unspecified type, due to the good cover of woodland.

Regionally threatened or declining species	
Neophron percnopterus	Resident in good numbers in the early 1980s, but not found in 1991.
Gyps fulvus	Resident in the general area.

Other threatened/endemic wildlife
No information.

Conservation issues
In 1991 large areas of forest were destroyed by a fire (Baumgart 1991b). Sand extraction for the building trade occurs on the coast, as well as illegal dynamite fishing offshore. There is some hunting. The coastal zone (c.500 ha) was proposed as a nature conservation area by a Task Force of the UNEP Regional Activity Centre for Mediterranean Specially Protected Areas in 1989 (Jeudy de Grissac 1989), including a strict nature reserve within it.

Further reading
Baumgart (1991b), Baumgart and Kasparek (1992), Jeudy de Grissac (1989).

010 Euphrates Valley (Halab, Al-Raqqah, Dayr al-Zawr)
Unprotected

35°48′N 39°30′E
c.420 km

Site description
The entire valley of the River Euphrates (Al-Furat), from its entry from Turkey at 36°49′N 38°02′E to its exit into Iraq at 34°29′N 40°56′E, apart from Buhayrat al-Assad (see site 007) and Baath Lake (see site 008). The valley lies 80–250 m below the surrounding plains, varying in width from 2 to 12 km. The river still flows in its original bed and is rich in islands, meanders, pools, oxbow lakes, alluvial cliffs, gravel pits and silted old water courses where the river has shifted, many of these being covered in *Phragmites* reedbeds. The water level used to flood 3–4 m higher in spring than in autumn, due to snowmelt in the Turkish uplands, but the completion during the last decade of several large dams in Turkey has now greatly reduced this annual flood. Natural vegetation includes riverine thickets of *Populus euphratica*, *Tamarix*, *Salix* and *Typha*. Intensive agriculture is carried out along its banks in 'mazara', vast areas of irrigated cotton and cereals with orchards and plantations of *Populus* and *Pinus halepensis*. The heavily cultivated steppe of the

Jazirah region lies to the east and the Syrian Desert to the south-west. Gravel extraction occurs locally.

Birds

See box for key species. An excellent diversity of breeding, wintering and passage waterfowl occur. Only three small sites in this huge area have recently been investigated ornithologically in any detail: (1) Shumaytiyah (35°28´N 39°59´E, 50 ha), an oxbow lake c.20 km north-west of Dayr al-Zawr, sandwiched between the Al-Raqqah to Dayr al-Zawr road and a 50 m cliff; (2) Mayadin Pool (35°00´N 39°28´E, 300 ha), a shallow pool between the Euphrates and the Dayr al-Zawr–Abu Kamal road, 2 km south-east of Mayadin; and (3) Halabiyat Zulbiyat, c.40 km north-west of Dayr al-Zawr, on the right bank of the river. Breeding species include *Tachybaptus ruficollis* (c.500 birds at Shumaytiyah), *Tadorna ferruginea*, *Porphyrio porphyrio* (possible), *Vanellus spinosus*, *V. leucurus*, *Chlidonias hybridus*, *Pterocles alchata*, *Merops superciliosus*, *M. apiaster* and *Riparia riparia*. Important wintering species include *Tachybaptus ruficollis* (c.2,000 at Shumaytiyah), *Ciconia nigra* (c.30 at Shumaytiyah), *Anser albifrons* (350 at Mayadin); 3,500 and 2,375 waterfowl were recorded at Shumaytiyah and Mayadin respectively in the January 1993 International Waterfowl Census. There are good numbers of wintering birds of prey such as *Circus macrourus* and *Asio flammeus* on the surrounding steppe. Passage migrants in large numbers include *Ciconia ciconia*, *Himantopus himantopus*, *Glareola pratincola*, *Charadrius dubius*, *Philomachus pugnax*, *Tringa stagnatilis*, *T. hypoleucos*, *Sterna hirundo* and *Chlidonias hybridus*. The few observations indicate that the valley is also a very important migration route for several non-waterbird species, including *Streptopelia turtur* (hundreds of thousands gather on the islands in the river in spring and autumn) and *Lanius minor* (abundant, May). The site was listed as a wetland of international importance by Carp (1980).

Globally threatened species

Phalacrocorax pygmeus	Said to be common around Dayr al-Zawr in the 1980s (and possibly breeding), and noted in small numbers elsewhere along the river.
Marmaronetta angustirostris	One seen on two dates in June 1975 at Shumaytiyah; probably a widespread breeding species in the valley.
Falco naumanni	One at Shumaytiyah in July 1976; may breed locally.
Chlamydotis undulata	Breeds on the steppe in vicinity of Dayr al-Zawr.

Regionally threatened or declining species

Aythya nyroca	Passage migrant and winter visitor.
Gyps fulvus	Non-breeding visitor.
Francolinus francolinus	Locally common resident.

Species restricted wholly or largely to the Middle East

Otus brucei	Resident.

Other threatened/endemic wildlife

Mammals: *Canis lupus* (V) and *Gazella subgutturosa* (rare).

Conservation issues

The river flow has been reduced during the last decade as newly completed large dams upstream in Turkey continue to fill, and further dams are under construction. Once the associated irrigation projects planned for these dams are constructed and begin functioning, the river flow will be diminished further. Other problems (despite the efforts of the authorities) include illegal tree-cutting (for fuelwood), agricultural expansion into semi-natural riparian habitats, and illegal and irresponsible hunting. There is much human disturbance of birds locally.

Further reading

Carp (1980), Dijksen and Koning (1972), Koning and Dijksen (1973), Macfarlane (1978).

011 Jabal Slenfeh (Al-Ladhiqiyah)

State Forest Protection Zone

35°37´N 36°06´E
c.4,000 ha

Site description

A relatively well-wooded mountain area, centred on the village of Slenfeh c.20 km north-east of Al-Ladhiqiyah (Lattakia), on the western slopes of the Jibal al-Nusayriyah range. The woodland is dominated by *Abies* and *Cedrus*. The area is generally densely populated with small settlements.

Birds

Pyman (1953) estimated ('probably conservatively') that several hundred large raptors per day passed south through the area during late September. The raptor stream observed here is presumably a continuation of that which passes through the bottleneck site of Belen in southern Turkey, where at least

30,000 raptors and more than 100,000 *Ciconia ciconia* pass through per autumn (Sutherland and Brooks 1981), and birds have been seen moving on south from Jibal al-Nusayriyah into the Lebanese mountains. The predominant raptors in September are *Pernis apivorus*, *Aquila pomarina* and *Accipiter brevipes*. The raptor migration also occurs in spring. Breeding species include *Hieraaetus fasciatus* (common in the 1940s but no recent records), *Alectoris chukar*, *Coturnix coturnix*, *Tachymarptis melba*, *Lullula arborea*, *Luscinia megarhynchos*, *Sylvia communis*, *Lanius nubicus* (very common), *Corvus corax*, *Emberiza caesia* and *E. melanocephala*.
Regionally threatened or declining species:
Gyps fulvus Resident.

Other threatened/endemic wildlife

No information available to BirdLife International.

Conservation issues

The site is a State Forest Protection Zone administered by the Directorate of Forests and Afforestation of the Ministry of Agriculture and Agrarian Reform. Hunting is a widespread activity in the Jibal al-Nusayriyah range. Shooting of migratory raptors is common in Syria (Baumgart 1991a, 1991b, Bijlsma 1987). The area was proposed as a managed nature reserve or multiple-use management area by a Task Force of the UNEP Regional Activity Centre for Mediterranean Specially Protected Areas in 1989 (Jeudy de Grissac 1989).

Further reading

Bijlsma (1987), Jeudy de Grissac (1989), Pyman (1953), Sutherland and Brooks (1981).

012 Wadi al-Azib (Hamah)

35°26′N 37°20′E
24,200 ha

also known as Wadi Ghrib, Wadi al-Ghareeb or Wadi al-Gharrah
Enclosed Rangeland Reserve (20,000 ha)

Site description

A stony, semi-desert plain, c.120 km east of Hamah. Vegetation includes sparse *Pistacia* trees and shrub-steppe with *Salsola*, *Atriplex* and *Artemisia*. There is said to be a north-south trending depression at 35°22′N 38°00′E which floods in some winters (extent of water up to c.1,000 ha); although this could not be found on maps, there is an area of sabkhah basins (totalling c.5,000 ha) centred on 35°40′N 37°30′E. There are many small settlements and wells, and cultivation is probably extensive.

Birds

See box for key species. Other breeding species include *Pterocles alchata*. *Anser albifrons* is a winter visitor (1,000) and passage migrant (1,500), and at least c.500 ducks have also been noted in winter.

Globally threatened species

Chlamydotis undulata	Resident.
Tetrax tetrax	Occurs; status unclear, but likely to be a winter visitor in small numbers.

Regionally threatened or declining species

Neophron percnopterus	Breeds.
Gyps fulvus	Resident.

Species restricted wholly or largely to the Middle East

Ammoperdix heyi	Resident.

Other threatened/endemic wildlife

Mammals: *Canis lupus* (V). There is a gazelle *Gazella* captive-breeding and release project.

Conservation issues

The site was established as a Enclosed Rangeland Reserve by the Ministry of Agriculture and Agrarian Reform in 1968 to conserve vegetation resources for grazing, and there have since been proposals to designate it as a 'game management area' or nature reserve, with nature conservation as the main management objective. Known threats comprise hunting, overgrazing, fuelwood-gathering and soil erosion.

Further reading

Abou Ja'fer (1984), IUCN (1991).

013 **Jabal al-Shuah** (Al-Ladhiqiyah)
Unprotected

35°25′N 36°12′E
20,000 ha

■ Site description
The eastern slope of the Jibal al-Nusayriyah range is a very steep scarp, lining the western edge of the Al-Ghab basin. A 1977 map based on surveys in the 1940s suggests that c.20,000 ha of woodland existed along the scarp at that time. The current extent of woodland is unknown but is still likely to be sizeable, since the steep slopes have presumably inhibited clearance for agriculture or other uses. The woodland is dominated by *Abies cilicica*, with *Carpinus orientalis* and *Ostrya carpinifolia*.

■ Birds
There is no specific information available to BirdLife International, but the breeding bird community is likely to be very similar to Jabal Slenfeh (see site 011), and large numbers of migrating raptors of similar species to Jabal Slenfeh may pass down this scarp in autumn, arriving from the north-east from the Caucasus Mountains (Macfarlane 1978). As such, this forest site is likely to be very important as a rare example of a threatened and diminishing habitat in the Levant.

■ Other threatened/endemic wildlife
No information available to BirdLife International.

■ Conservation issues
Hunting is a widespread activity in the Jibal al-Nusayriyah range. Shooting of migratory raptors is common in Syria (Baumgart 1991a, 1991b, Bijlsma 1987).

■ Further reading
Bijlsma (1987), Macfarlane (1978).

014 **Jabal al-Bishri** (Al-Raqqah, Dayr al-Zawr, Hims)
Unprotected

35°20′N 39°30′E
c.20,00 ha

■ Site description
An isolated mountain in the semi-desert 80 km west of Dayr al-Zawr, rising to 851 m. There are occasional cliffs. The vegetation includes trees and bushes of *Pistacia*, *Rhamnus*, *Prunus* and *Amygdalus*, and is presumably a sparse steppe-woodland.

■ Birds
See box for key species. Other breeding species include *Pterocles alchata* (common).

Globally threatened species	
Chlamydotis undulata	Resident.
Tetrax tetrax	Occurs; status unclear, but likely to be a winter visitor in small numbers.
Regionally threatened or declining species	
Neophron percnopterus	Breeds.
Gyps fulvus	Resident.
Species restricted wholly or largely to the Middle East	
Ammoperdix heyi	Resident.

■ Other threatened/endemic wildlife
Mammals: *Canis lupus* (V). Flora: many endemics are confined to the isolated mountains in the Syrian Desert.

■ Conservation issues
As a preliminary to a program for preventing soil erosion, a decree has been issued (but so far not implemented) prohibiting the grazing and agricultural development by which the area is threatened. An afforestation programme is to be undertaken in the near future. Hunting occurs.

015 **Jabal al-Bilas** (Hims)
Unprotected

34°55′N 37°35′E
40,000 ha

■ Site description
An isolated mountain (up to 1,105 m) lying c.70 km north-west of Tadmur (Palmyra). The landscape is eroded and the scant vegetation includes scattered trees/bushes of *Pistacia*, *Prunus* and *Rhamnus*, and shrubs of *Artemisia*, *Atriplex*, *Salsola* and *Anabasis*.

There is some unspecified waterfowl habitat, presumably caused by winter flooding of depressions.

Birds

See box for key species. Other breeding species include *Buteo rufinus* and *Pterocles alchata*, and wintering waterfowl include c.500 *Anser albifrons* and c.400 ducks.

Globally threatened species

Chlamydotis undulata	Breeds, and also a winter visitor.

Regionally threatened or declining species

Neophron percnopterus	Resident.
Gyps fulvus	Resident.
Falco biarmicus	Occurs, probably breeds.

Species restricted wholly or largely to the Middle East

Ammoperdix heyi	Resident.

Other threatened/endemic wildlife

Mammals: *Canis lupus* (V) and *Gazella subgutturosa* (rare). Flora: many endemics are confined to the isolated mountains in the Syrian Desert.

Conservation issues

Known threats comprise hunting, fuelwood gathering, grazing and excessive erosion by wind and water. An Enclosed Rangeland Reserve of 40,000 ha has been proposed by the Ministry of Agriculture and Agrarian Reform, and c.20,000 ha may already be a State Forest Protection Zone.

Further reading

Ketene (1991).

016 Buhayrat al-Laha (Tartus)

Unprotected

34°41′N 36°00′E
c.50 ha

Site description

The only remaining natural coastal wetland, south of Hamidiyah and only c.2 km north of the Lebanese border. The coast is low and predominantly sandy, with some permanent rivers; settlements are few and small.

Birds

The site is said to be very important for migratory birds of unspecified type, presumably waterfowl.

Other threatened/endemic wildlife

No information.

Conservation issues

The site is threatened by drainage for cultivation, pesticide run-off and hunting. The lack of knowledge of the site's exact ornithological value hampers any formulation of conservation measures for the site. It was proposed as an ornithological and/or nature conservation reserve by a Task Force of the UNEP Regional Activity Centre for Mediterranean Specially Protected Areas in 1989 (Jeudy de Grissac 1989).

Further reading

Jeudy de Grissac (1989).

017 Bahrat Homs (Hims)

also known as Lake Qattiné or Lake Homs
Unprotected

34°37′N 36°32′E
5,300 ha

Site description

A semi-artificial, eutrophic reservoir lying 15 km south-west of Homs and just west of Qattiné, formed by impoundment of the Nahr al-Asi (Orontes river). The banks of the north-eastern half are steep, while the very flat south-western shores, together with the influx of water from snow-melt in spring and subsequent evaporation during the summer, lead to the extent of open water varying from 3,000 ha in summer to 5,300 ha in winter; water depth is 4–8 m. There are some islands, but not suitable for breeding birds. The shores are generally bare mud, and the lake's marginal and aquatic vegetation is very limited; bankside vegetation includes *Tamarix*, *Salix*, *Nerium*, *Phragmites* and *Typha*. The surroundings are very open, with no trees of any size but still generally green and verdant. To the south the land is fertile and cultivated, but to the north is a large area of lava flow. Villages are scattered around the lakeside; the main human activity is farming, though there is considerable fishing, plus large factories near Qattiné.

Birds

See boxes for key species. More than 20,000 waterfowl occur in winter (e.g. 22,420 of 14 species in January 1993), including (counts mainly from the 1970s) *Pelecanus onocrotalus* (200), *Egretta garzetta* (100), *Casmerodius albus* (70), *Anser albifrons* (c.600), *Anas crecca* (4,000, October), *A. strepera* (c.700), *Anas* sp. (c.10,000), *Netta rufina* (250), *Aythya ferina* (7,000), *Fulica atra* (9,000) and unidentified waders (c.4,000). Counts of passage birds have included several hundred *Chlidonias* terns. *Pelecanus onocrotalus*, *Egretta garzetta*, *Casmerodius albus* and *Porphyrio porphyrio* have been recorded in the breeding season, but they are not likely to breed.

Globally threatened species

Marmaronetta angustirostris	Recorded in summer, but breeding not proven.
Oxyura leucocephala	Regular but apparently declining winter visitor (100 in the 1970s; 30 in the 1990s); recorded in summer, but breeding not proven.

1% or more of population

	Breeding (pairs)	Wintering	Passage
Podiceps nigricollis	—	250	—
Ardea cinerea	—	—	100
Marmaronetta angustirostris	—	20	—
Aythya fuligula	—	8,000	—
Aythya nyroca	—	—	250

Regionally threatened or declining species

Botaurus stellaris	Passage migrant (1, November).
Aythya nyroca	Winter visitor and passage migrant (250-300, October 1982).

Other threatened/endemic wildlife

Mammals: *Canis lupus* (V; possibly occurs).

Conservation issues

There is phosphate and urea pollution from factories near Qattiné, heavy shooting of wildfowl, much disturbance from recreational use (water sports), fishing and generally due to the high human population density. Pressure on fish stocks is very high; Common Carp *Cyprinus carpio* have been introduced. The lake was proposed as a Project Aqua conservation site by the Ministry of Agriculture and Agrarian Reform in the late 1960s.

Further reading

Kumerloeve (1967–1969), Luther and Rzóska (1971), Macfarlane (1978).

018 Tadmur and Sabkhat Muh (Hims)

34°30′N 38°18′E
45,000 ha

Tadmur also known as Palmyra
Unprotected

Site description

An area of steppe-desert around Tadmur in the centre of Syria, 150 km east of Homs, in a closed basin (c.70 × 35 km), surrounded by limestone and marl hills. There is an isolated oasis to the south of the town with extensive date-palm gardens, and Sabkhat Muh, a seasonally flooded salt-lake up to c.20 km long, lies to the south of the oasis. There are some scattered *Tamarix* trees around its fringe, and the steppe-desert surrounds are sparsely vegetated with perennial tussock-grass, Chenopodiaceae and *Artemisia*. The T-3 pumping station (34°31′N 38°45′E), 40 km east of Tadmur on the Iraq–Lebanon oil pipeline, is a small, man-made oasis with a plantation of mature *Eucalyptus* (c.2 ha), a garden and a sewage pond (c.0.5 ha). The main land-use is grazing livestock. The area is famous for its Roman ruins.

Birds

A representative assemblage of characteristic desert species, with added interest due to the isolated oasis, surrounding hills and seasonal wetland. See boxes for key species. Other probable or confirmed breeding species include *Buteo rufinus*, *Aquila chrysaetos*, *Cursorius cursor*, *Charadrius leschenaultii*, *Pterocles alchata*, *Bubo bubo*, *Athene noctua*, *Ammomanes deserti*, *Alaemon alaudipes*, *Eremophila bilopha*, *Oenanthe deserti*, *O. lugens*, *Pycnonotus leucotis* (c.450 km west of its main range in Iraq) and *Corvus corax*. The oasis at Tadmur provides the only substantial shelter for migrant birds for 150 km to the north and west and for much further to south and east, and a very wide variety of species are attracted; the oasis is especially important for migrating raptors, e.g. *Pernis apivorus*, *Buteo buteo* (roost of 1,500, April), *Milvus migrans* (roost of 87, April), *Circus*

Globally threatened species

Aegypius monachus	Presumably a winter visitor; there is a specimen in Tadmur Museum, said to have been collected in this region, and local people report that 'large, black vultures' formerly bred (and perhaps still do) in the mountains around Tadmur (Baumgart 1991b).
Falco naumanni	Common summer visitor in 1948–1950, breeding in the ruins at Tadmur, but it was apparently not present in 1976–1977 or subsequently.
Tetrax tetrax	Occurs; status unclear, but likely to be a winter visitor in small numbers.
Chlamydotis undulata	Apparently breeds in the surrounding desert.
Otis tarda	Occurs; status unclear.

1% or more of population

	Breeding (pairs)	Wintering	Passage
Eudromias morinellus	—	200 (Nov)	—

Regionally threatened or declining species

Neophron percnopterus	Resident; 4 in June 1991.
Gyps fulvus	Bred in the mountains c.15 km north of Tadmur in 1943 (c.8 pairs), with 4 birds seen there in 1974; also recorded in the 1980s in the area.
Torgos tracheliotus	Possibly resident; two specimens at Tadmur Museum are said to have been collected in the surrounding region (possibly as early as 1920–1942); see also *Aegypius monachus* (above).
Falco biarmicus	Presumably breeds in the desert; 21, including at least 5 immatures, seen in July 1976 along the 130 km between T3 and the next pumping station to the east.
Falco cherrug	Passage migrant.

Species restricted wholly or largely to the Middle East

Irania gutturalis	Scarce passage migrant.
Oenanthe finschii	Winter visitor.
Hippolais languida	Scarce passage migrant.
Carpospiza brachydactyla	Passage migrant (100+, April).

macrourus and *C. pygargus*. Wintering species at the salt-lake include *Phoenicopterus ruber* (90, November) and *Grus grus*.

■ Other threatened/endemic wildlife

Mammals: *Canis lupus* (V; probably occurs), *Caracal caracal* (rare) and *Gazella subgutturosa* (rare).

■ Conservation issues

The area is fairly remote and few threats are apparent. However in the 1970s pastoralists were increasingly penetrating formerly little-visited and isolated regions of the steppe-desert to graze their livestock, facilitated by water bowsers, and as a result of the loss of these traditional constraints the rangeland may now be under heavy pressure; any degradation is likely to reduce the value of the desert for important steppe species of birds and other wildlife. The ruins at Tadmur are much visited by tourists; it is not known whether this explains the apparent disappearance of the *Falco naumanni*.

■ Further reading

Baumgart (1991a,b), Kinzelbach (1986), Macfarlane (1978), Peters (1956).

019 Abu Zad (Dimashq)

Unprotected

33°43′N 36°07′E
10,000 ha

■ Site description

An upland area at the southern end of the Jibal al-Sharqi (Anti-Lebanon) range, 50 km by road from Damascus, and centred on Abu Zad, a small village with small orchards and very small fields lying at 1,500 m above the resort village of Bludan. The nearby village of Halbun is at 1,700 m. To the west, vertical cliffs fall to Zabadani far below, and mountains to the north-east rise steeply to 2,462 m within c.10 km. The land above the village is open, with sparse grassland, scattered scrub and bare rock, and is snow-covered in winter.

■ Birds

See box for key species. A diverse assemblage of breeding species characteristic of upland Mediterranean habitats which are rare and local in the Middle East. Other confirmed or probable breeding species include *Circaetus gallicus*, *Buteo rufinus*, *Aquila chrysaetos*, *Alectoris chukar*, *Hirundo rupestris*,

Regionally threatened or declining species

Gyps fulvus	A colony at Halbun, active in the early 1980s, was empty in June 1991, possibly deserted.
Neophron percnopterus	Regular in good numbers at Halbun in the early 1980s but not found in 1991.

Species restricted wholly or largely to the Middle East

Irania gutturalis	Probably breeds.
Oenanthe finschii	Probably breeds.
Hippolais languida	Common summer visitor.
Sylvia mystacea	Summer visitor.
Carpospiza brachydactyla	Summer visitor.
Serinus syriacus	Local summer visitor.
Rhodopechys sanguinea	Resident.

Melanocorypha bimaculata, *Lullula arborea*, *Eremophila alpestris*, *Monticola saxatilis*, *Sylvia hortensis*, *Lanius collurio*, *Pyrrhocorax graculus* (seen in winter 1938/39), *Rhodopechys githaginea* and *Emberiza melanocephala*. Winter visitors include *Prunella collaris*.

Other threatened/endemic wildlife
No information.

Conservation issues
In the mid-1970s there was some shooting of passerines in the orchards, but the uplands appeared under no threat. The area around Bludan is a popular site for second homes, and built development is increasing: Bludan has grown enormously in the last 20 years and is now joined to Zabadani below.

Further reading
Baumgart and Kasparek (1992), Macfarlane (1978).

020 Wadi al-Qarn–Burqush (Dimashq)
Unprotected

33°34′N 36°00′E
4,500 ha

Site description
The main Damascus–Beirut road runs through Wadi al-Qarn (Karn) which runs south-east from the frontier post at Jdeideh (1,275 m). The area of interest in this wadi is the steep hillside above the road on the northern side of the wadi, along the last 1–2 km at the north-west end just before the valley opens out to the area of the frontier post, and includes the small Zarzer reservoir at the lower end (1,175 m) of the wadi 6 km from Jdeideh. The upper reaches are vertical cliffs, below which are rocky slopes with grass, scrub and stunted trees. The area is used for recreation in summer, and people fish at the reservoir. Burqush is an upland site on the slopes of Jabal al-Shaykh (Mount Hermon), 10 km north-west of Qatana, with similar habitat. The area is very close to the steep mountains of Maloula, where there are Christian monasteries.

Regionally threatened or declining species	
Neophron percnopterus	Apparently breeds.
Gyps fulvus	Resident (max. 9–10, January).
Falco biarmicus	Passage migrant.
Species restricted wholly or largely to the Middle East	
Irania gutturalis	Relatively common summer visitor.
Oenanthe finschii	Probably summer visitor.
Hippolais languida	Probable summer visitor.
Sylvia mystacea	Probable summer visitor.
Carpospiza brachydactyla	Probable summer visitor.
Serinus syriacus	Breeds in good numbers.

Birds
See box for key species. Other proven or probable breeding species include *Circaetus gallicus*, *Buteo rufinus*, *Bubo bubo*, *Lullula arborea*, *Eremophila alpestris*, *Phoenicurus ochruros*, *Monticola solitarius*, *Sylvia conspicillata*, *S. hortensis*, *Parus lugubris*, *Sitta neumayer* and *Emberiza caesia*. In winter the reservoir often holds small numbers of waders and occasionally ducks.

Other threatened/endemic wildlife
No information.

Conservation issues
Lying in the frontier zone, the site is not much visited on foot, though there is much shooting and fishing at the reservoir. Traffic is heavy along this, the only road across the Jibal al-Sharqi (Anti-Lebanon) range, but there is no detrimental effect on the birds.

Further reading
Macfarlane (1978).

021 Jabal Sis (Dimashq)
Unprotected

33°18′N 37°22′E
40,000 ha

Site description
A huge, extinct volcanic crater, the largest of many within a huge basalt lava field which covers much of southern Syria and northern Jordan. Jabal Sis (Sies) lies near the eastern edge of the basalt, 100 km east-south-east of Damascus and 55 km south of the main road running east from Damascus to Iraq. The volcano rises about 100 m above the surrounding plain.

Spring rain lies in small lakes and pools in scattered pans of impermeable clay, and there is a rain-fed lake at the foot of Jabal Sis itself. Vegetation is sparse. The terrain is impassable to vehicles except along tracks, of which there are few. Nomadic pastoralists graze large flocks in the area in spring and early summer.

Birds

See box for key species. Proven or probable breeding species include *Cursorius cursor* (common), *Charadrius leschenaultii* (see box; large numbers have been seen at rain-flooded pans in March and May: almost certainly a breeding summer visitor), *Eremophila bilopha*, *Oenanthe deserti*, *Corvus ruficollis* and *Rhodopechys githaginea*. The area also holds a thinly spread resident population of a dark form of *Oenanthe lugens*, which occurs only on the basalt plains of Syria, Jordan and northern Saudi Arabia. *Pterocles orientalis* (150, December) and *P. alchata* (c.300, March) occur in good numbers in winter/spring.

Other threatened/endemic wildlife

No information.

Globally threatened species

Chlamydotis undulata — Adult seen in May 1976; certain to be breeding.

1% or more of population

	Breeding (pairs)	Wintering	Passage
Charadrius leschenaultii	100 birds	—	—

Regionally threatened or declining species

Torgos tracheliotus — Possibly resident; a specimen was collected 'east of Damascus' in 1968 (Baumgart and Kasparek 1992).

Species restricted wholly or largely to the Middle East

Ammoperdix heyi — Resident.

Conservation issues

The area is too remote and inhospitable to be much threatened, though the bringing in of water in barrels has increased grazing and there is some shooting of sandgrouse in winter.

Further reading

Macfarlane (1978).

022 Yarmuk Valley (Dar'a)

Unprotected

32°44′N 35°52′E
20,000 ha

Site description

The Yarmuk river runs along part of the Syria–Jordan frontier, at the southern end of the Golan Heights, and is joined by other streams in this region, e.g. near Heite by the Nahr al-Allan running from the north and by Wadi al-Thahab from the east. The watercourses lie in steep, narrow wadis cutting through a plateau with well-watered farmland (cereals), and though the sides of the valleys are barren the bottoms are full of lush vegetation including *Phragmites* reedbeds and oleander *Nerium*. The lower valleys are below sea-level. There are a few houses by the river below Heite. Lake Muzayrib (32°42′N 36°01′E, 2 ha) lies in a shallow depression on the plateau (Wadi al-Thahab), just west of Al-Muzayrib village and c.12 km north-west of Dar'a: a natural, spring-fed, mesotrophic lake of 2.5 m mean depth, with banks of grazed turf and at least one reedbed *Phragmites*. The lake is much used for irrigation, fishing, fish-farming and recreation (picnicing, etc.), and is surrounded by agriculture and many houses.

Birds

See box for key species. The avifauna resembles that of the Jordan Valley more than does that of any other region in Syria. Breeding species (presumed) include *Halcyon smyrnensis*, *Anthus similis*, *Cercomela melanura*, *Acrocephalus melanopogon*, *A. stentoreus*, *A. arundinaceus*, *Cisticola juncidis* and *Nectarinia osea*. *Remiz pendulinus* and *Passer hispaniolensis* have been recorded in winter.

Regionally threatened or declining species

Gyps fulvus — Almost certainly breeds here (max. 16).

Species restricted wholly or largely to the Middle East

Oenanthe finschii — Winter visitor.
Passer moabiticus — Occurs at Lake Mzerib and may breed.

Other threatened/endemic wildlife

Fish: *Tilapia gallilae* (endemic).

Conservation issues

No conservation measures are known to have been taken. There is some bird shooting locally. There are plans for a large-scale, joint Jordanian-Syrian dam across the Yarmuk river (Wahda or Unity Dam), which would potentially be a critical threat. Fish (*Cyprinus carpio* and *Tilapia*) have been introduced into Lake Muzayrib, where intensification of fish production was cited as a problem or potential threat in the late 1960s. Lake Muzayrib was proposed as a Project Aqua conservation site by the Ministry of Agriculture and Agrarian Reform in the late 1960s.

Further reading

Kumerloeve (1972), Luther and Rzóska (1971), Macfarlane (1978), Pearce (1993).

MAIN REFERENCES

ABOU JA'FER, M. (1984) *National parks and national reserves in the Arab countries.* Tunisia: Arab Organization for Culture, Sciences and Education. (English translation from Arabic by M. Geha.)

BAUMGART, W. (1991a) Gegenwärtiger Status und Gefährdungsgrad von Greifvögeln und Eulen in Syrien. *Birds of Prey Bull.* 4: 119–131.

BAUMGART, W. (1991b) Raptor problems in Syria. *Newsl. World Working Group Birds of Prey and Owls* 14: 15–16.

BAUMGART, W. AND KASPAREK, M. (1992) Notes on some summer birds of Syria. *Zool. Middle East* 6: 13–19.

BAUMGART, W. AND STEPHAN, B. (1986) Ergebnisse ornithologischer Beobachtungen in der Syrischen Arabischen Republik, Teil 1: Non-Passeriformes. *Mitt. zool. Mus. Berlin* 62. *Suppl. Ann. Orn.* 10: 69–110.

BAUMGART, W. AND STEPHAN, B. (1987) Ergebnisse ornithologischer Beobachtungen in der Syrischen Arabischen Republik, Teil 2: Passeriformes. *Mitt. zool. Mus. Berlin* 63. *Suppl. Ann. Orn.* 11: 57–95.

BIJLSMA, R. G. (1987) *Bottleneck areas for migratory birds in the Mediterranean region: an assessment of the problems and recommendations for action.* Cambridge, U.K.: International Council for Bird Preservation (Study Rep. 18).

BODENHAM, K. L. (1944) Some bird notes from northern Syria and northern Palestine during the winter of 1943–1944. *Zool. Soc. Egypt Bull.* 6 (Syria/Palestine Suppl.): 26–32.

BOTTEMA, S. (1985) Vogelwaarnemingen in de Syrische Djezireh. *Vogeljaar* 2: 82–88.

CARP, E. (1980) *A directory of western Palaearctic wetlands.* Nairobi: United Nations Environment Programme/Gland, Switzerland: International Union for the Conservation of Nature and Natural Resources.

CLARKE, G. VON H. (1924) Some notes on birds found breeding in the neighbourhood of Aleppo in 1919. *Ibis* (11) 6: 101–110.

DIJKSEN, L. J. AND KONING, F. J. (1972) Report on IWRB Mission to Syria, December 1971. *IWRB Bull.* 33: 34–37.

GRIMMETT, R. F. A. AND JONES, T. A. (1989) *Important Bird Areas in Europe.* Cambridge, U.K.: International Council for Bird Preservation (Techn. Publ. 9).

HOLLOM, P. A. D. (1959) Notes from Jordan, Lebanon, Syria and Antioch. *Ibis* 101: 183–200.

JEUDY DE GRISSAC, A. (1989) *Integrated management plan of the Syrian Coastline. RAC/SPA contribution: potential marine and coastal protected areas for Syria, draft report.* Tunis: UNEP Regional Activity Centre for Specially Protected Areas (SPA DOC 0076B).

KATTINGER, E. (1970) Vogelbeobachtungen im vorderen Orient: Syrien und unteres Niltal. *Ber. Naturfor. Ges. Bamberg* 45: 57–79.

KETENE, M. S. (1991) *Training and manpower requirements for wildlife and protected areas in the Arab world.* Rome: Food and Agriculture Organization.

KINZELBACH, R. (1986) The White-cheeked Bulbul, *Pycnonotus leucogenys*, a resident of the Palmyra oasis, Syria. *Zool. Middle East* 1: 73–74.

KONING, F. J. AND DIJKSEN, L. J. (1973) Report on IWRB Mission to Iraq and Syria, December 1972. *IWRB Bull.* 35: 57–62.

KUMERLOEVE, H. (1967–1969) Recherches sur l'avifaune de la république arabe syrienne essai d'un aperçu. *Alauda* 35: 243–266, 36: 1–26, 190–207, 37: 43–58, 114–134, 188–205.

KUMERLOEVE, H. (1969) The Dead Sea Sparrow: a second nesting-place on Turkish and the first-known breeding-place on Syrian territory. *Ibis* 111: 617–618.

KUMERLOEVE, H. (1970) Zur Vogelwelt im Raume Ceylanpinar (türkisch-syrisches Grenzgebiet). *Vogelkunde* 16: 239–249.

KUMERLOEVE, H. (1972) Liste comparée des oiseaux nicheurs de Turquie méridionale, Syrie et Liban. *Alauda* 40: 353–366.

LUTHER, H. AND RZÓSKA, J. (1971) *Project Aqua: a source book of inland waters proposed for conservation.* Oxford, U.K.: Blackwell Scientific (International Biological Programme Handbook 21).

MACFARLANE, A. M. (1978) Field notes on the birds of Lebanon and Syria 1974–1977. *Army Bird-watching Soc. Per. Publ.* 3.

MACLAREN, P. I. R. (1944) Isolated field notes, north Syria, autumn and winter 1943–1944. *Zool. Soc. Egypt Bull.* 6 (Syria/Palestine Suppl.): 33–38.

PEARCE, F. (1993) Peace pact promises unity in the desert. *New Scientist* 1891: 4.

PETERS, J. L. (1956) Birds from station T-3, Syria. Pp. 78–79 in H. Field *An anthropological reconnaissance in the Near East, 1950. Pap. Peabody Mus. Archaeol. Ethnol.* 48 (2).

PYMAN, G. A. (1953) Autumn raptor migration in the eastern Mediterranean. *Ibis* 95: 550–551.

SAVAGE, C. D. W. (1968) The wildfowl and wetland situation in the Levant. Pp. 134–138 in *Proceedings of a technical meeting on wetland conservation, Ankara-Bursa-Istanbul, 9–16 October 1967.* Morges, Switzerland: IUCN/ICBP/IWRB (IUCN Publ. New Ser. 12).

SUTHERLAND, W. J. AND BROOKS, D. J. (1981) The autumn migration of raptors, storks, pelicans and spoonbills at the Belen pass, southern Turkey. *Sandgrouse* 2: 1–21.

■ UNITED ARAB EMIRATES

Houbara Bustard *Chlamydotis undulata*

GENERAL INFORMATION

The United Arab Emirates (UAE) is a confederation of seven states situated at the south-east end of the Arabian Gulf, and bordered by the Kingdom of Saudi Arabia to the south and the Sultanate of Oman to the east. The country has a land area of c.83,000 km^2 and had a human population of 2.1 million in 1992.

The UAE's southern and western areas sit astride some of the world's largest oil reserves, which combined with a dynamic business community have led to the country experiencing one of the world's fastest economic growth rates. One consequence is that much of the coastal belt has been changed from a landscape of sparsely inhabited desert to one of fast-growing towns and garden suburbs linked by wide motorways. The 160 km of sand desert between Abu Dhabi and Dubai in particular is undergoing a continuing transformation as these two large cities expand their infrastructure, with the construction of large-scale housing schemes, power stations, desalination plants, an aluminium smelter and the world's largest man-made port, Jebel Ali. Fortunately, much of the ecologically delicate intertidal and coastal land south and west of Abu Dhabi is currently not of great economic value, and is relatively undeveloped, although there are some military installations and luxury residences. Numerous offshore islands have been and are being affected by oil-related development.

Much of inland UAE, with its thousands of square kilometres of dune and sand desert, sabkhah and gravel plains, and mountains, has remained largely undeveloped, though used extensively by nomadic pastoralists. The south and west of the country, extending to the edge of the great Rub al Khali desert and the Umm al Samim basin, on the border with Oman, consists of high, wind-blown sand-dunes interspersed with flat areas of stony plain and sabkhah. Where there is groundwater, obtained by pumping from artesian wells, cultivation and settlements occur, most notably at Liwa oasis. Irrigation is transforming desert areas into fodder fields, large areas of woodland of *Prosopis* and other evergreen desert trees, cultivations and date-palm plantations, so changing the natural desert ecology. Large, new, desert towns are also being established. The northern Emirates are more fertile, with rainfall being greater and more regular than in the south, and the sand-dunes are gentler. Natural parklands of ghaf trees *Prosopis cineraria* are widespread, associated with *Acacia tortilis* trees and *Lycium* bushes, though these are usually subjected to heavy browsing by camels and goats. Areas with better soils support irrigated cultivation, most notably around Al Ain oasis.

The east and far north of the country is rather mountainous, with peaks rising to 1,000 m. Within UAE, the Hajar mountains stretch in a chain 35 km wide from the Oman border in the south to the Musandam peninsula in the north. The mountains consist of steep ridges and valleys of impervious volcanic ophiolites with some Cretaceous shale outcrops which appear pale amongst the dark peaks. Jebel Hafit is an isolated outcrop to the south of the Hajar mountains, on the border with Oman. There is some cultivation in wadis and hollows where soil and water accumulate. The mountains are reasonably untouched by development by virtue of their inaccessibility and hold many varied and interesting species of birds, animals and plants.

ORNITHOLOGICAL IMPORTANCE

At any one time during migration periods (April—May and July–November) probably in excess of 250,000 waders are present on intertidal areas of the country's Gulf coast. Taking into account the likely turnover of shorebirds on this Eurasian/West Asian—Arabian Gulf–African flyway, the mudflats of the southern Gulf probably support several million individuals over the course of a year.

Individual sites are regionally important for wader species, namely Abu al Abyadh for its *Dromas ardeola* colony and migratory populations of *Charadrius alexandrinus*, *C. mongolus*, and *Pluvialis squatarola*, Khor Dubai for its high densities of *C. alexandrinus*, *C. mongolus*, *C. leschenaultii* and *Limicola falcinellus*, and Khor al Beidah for its large wintering population of *Dromas ardeola* and parties of up to 90 wintering *Calidris tenuirostris*. The summer population of *Dromas ardeola* is estimated at over 1,200 birds, shared between Abu al Abyadh and another colony on the island of Umm Amin, while the largest wintering population of over 500 birds is at Khor al Beidah.

The current UAE population of *Phalacrocorax nigrogularis* is around 200,000 birds, which is a substantial proportion of the total world population, estimated at 500,000 to 1 million or more birds (Symens *et al.* 1993). Persecution is a problem as this is the only bird species which may be hunted under UAE law, due to a perceived threat to fish stocks. However, the species may in fact be a vital component in nutrient cycling within Gulf waters, actually maintaining fish stocks rather than reducing them. A number of this species' island breeding sites have been lost since 1980 and only three are now known to remain.

Several islands hold important populations of breeding seabirds and all are (or were) important in some way. Siniyah, Yasat and Ghaghah islands hold large *Phalacrocorax nigrogularis* populations, Qarnayn island alone has breeding *Phaethon aethereus*, *Larus hemprichii* and several tern species, and other islands in the south-west hold exceptional numbers of *Sterna bengalensis*, *S. repressa* and *S. anaethetus*. *Pandion haliaetus* has practically disappeared from its former mainland nesting sites, and breeding is now confined almost exclusively to islands, where its numbers appear healthy. Between 40 and 44 pairs were found on Yasat and Ghaghah islands alone in spring 1993.

Of passerines, populations of many Middle Eastern species with restricted ranges appear healthy. In the Hajar mountains to the east *Oenanthe alboniger* and *Pycnonotus xanthopygos* are common residents, with *O. xanthoprymna*, *O. picata* and *Phylloscopus neglectus* widely distributed in winter. The mangrove-lined creek at Khor Kalba holds the country's only population of *Todirhamphus chloris*; these birds are of the endangered endemic subspecies *T. c. kalbaensis*, with a population of only c.50 birds and only breeding at this site. Khor Kalba is also the only UAE breeding site of *Hippolais rama*.

CONSERVATION INFRASTRUCTURE AND PROTECTED-AREA SYSTEM

At present (November 1993) there is only one legally protected nature reserve, at Khor Dubai (see site 009), established by individual decree and protected by Dubai Municipality. The President has ordered the protection of two sites in Abu Dhabi, the Eastern Lagoon and Al Ghar Lake, but implementation of the order has not yet been successfully undertaken. There is one National Park (Mushrif, included in this inventory), which is primarily managed for public recreation, although restricted land-use protects the vegetation from threats such as overgrazing.

The Federal Environmental Agency (FEA), due to begin operations in 1994, has the designation and protection of nature reserves as part of its mandate. The FEA Board is considering applying for membership of the IUCN—The World Conservation Union.

INTERNATIONAL MEASURES RELEVANT TO THE CONSERVATION OF SITES

The UAE has signed but has not ratified the Biodiversity Convention, and is not a party to the Ramsar, World Heritage or Bonn Conventions. It has ratified some parts of the Regional Convention for Cooperation on the Protection of the Marine Environment.

OVERVIEW OF THE INVENTORY

There are 20 sites included in the inventory, covering a total area of about 2,600 km^2, or about 3% of the area of the country. One site is legally protected for nature conservation. Most are coastal and offshore-island sites. The islands, for which much new information became known in early 1993, are well represented, and are of importance to breeding seabird populations regionally and, in the case of *Dromas ardeola* on Abu al Abyadh and *Phalacrocorax nigrogularis* colony on Siniyah island, of international importance. Natural coastal wetlands are also well represented, the most important being Khor Dubai and Khor al Beidah, while others such as Ramtha Lagoons are entirely man-made. There is clearly a place in the UAE for formal management of man-made wetlands to ensure a future for their well-established bird populations. Due in part to the rapidly increasing human population, development has been especially fast in the coastal zone, often with insufficient consideration paid to wildlife, partly due to lack of meaningful data and lack of representation of nature conservation interests. In some instances, coastal sites suspected to have high importance for conservation of natural resources have been destroyed before their value could ever be confirmed. The chance of obtaining advance warning of development or activities likely to affect adversely or to destroy the wildlife of island sites is remote, hence the need for the production of an integrated coastal zone management plan. Comprehensive surveys would need to be made first, followed by regular monitoring.

Terrestrial habitats have not been well surveyed as yet, and the inventory includes six sites covering a large, representative desert area (Baynunah), *Acacia* and *Prosopis* savannah plains (including cultivated areas) and rocky, mountain habitats. Widespread and major problems include (a) the development by government land-use projects of vast expanses of former deserts and plains with generally no regard for the impact on indigenous wildlife, and (b) excessively heavy and damaging grazing and browsing of the natural plant cover by livestock. Herds of goats and camels inhibit new growth or regeneration of *Prosopis* and *Acacia* trees and other perennials, and branches of trees are regularly lopped and in some cases trees are pulled over to allow the tops to be grazed clean. This has already had an effect on *Turdoides squamiceps*, which, through lack of low cover, has become scarce in many areas where it was formerly more common. Other important species which rely on these trees include breeding *Torgos tracheliotus*, *Otus brucei* and *Petronia xanthocollis*, wintering *Oenanthe xanthoprymna*, *O. picata*, *Sylvia minula* and *Phylloscopus neglectus*, and migrating *Hippolais languida* and *Sylvia althaea*. Additionally, more local degradation of plant cover is being caused by increasing use of four-wheel-drive vehicles off the roads, which destabilizes the fragile desert crust and exposes soil to excessive wind erosion.

ACKNOWLEDGEMENTS

The site accounts were compiled from data-sheets and other information supplied by C. Richardson (who also coordinated the compilation of data), S. Aspinall and Dr P. Osborne of the National Avian Research Center (NARC), and R. P. Morris. The introduction was compiled from a draft by C. Richardson, S. Aspinall and P. Hellyer, who are grateful for the help and enthusiasm of those who have contributed to knowledge of the country's birdlife. Many have made important contributions to the individual site sections, including the staff of NARC and the members of the Dubai and Emirates Natural History Groups. F. E. Warr provided invaluable help throughout.

SITE INVENTORY

Site no.	Site name	Region	Criteria used to select site: 1	2i	2ii	2iii	3	4	5i	5ii	6	0
001	Al Jazirah Khor	RK	—	•	—	—	—	—	—	—	—	—
002	Digdaga–Hamraniyah	RK	•	—	—	—	—	•	—	—	—	—
003	Siniyah Island	UQ	—	•	—	—	—	•	—	—	—	—
004	Masafi–Tayibah Area	RK	—	—	—	—	—	•	•	—	—	—
005	Khor al Beideh	UQ	—	•	—	—	—	—	—	—	—	—
006	Ramtha Lagoons	SH	—	—	—	—	—	•	•	—	•	—
007	Mushrif National Park	DB	—	—	—	—	—	•	•	—	•	—
008	Zabeel Ponds	DB	—	—	—	—	—	—	—	—	•	—
009	Khor Dubai	DB	—	•	•	—	—	—	•	—	•	—
010	Khor Kalba	SH	—	—	—	—	•	—	—	•	•	—
011	Qarn Nazwa	SH	—	—	—	—	—	•	—	•	—	—
012	Qarnayn Island	AD	—	•	—	—	—	•	—	•	—	—
013	Delma	AD	—	—	—	—	•	—	—	—	—	—

Key to regions

AD Abu Dhabi
DB Dubai
RK Ras al Khaimah
SH Sharjah
UQ Umm al Quwain

Site no.	Site name	Region	Criteria used to select site: 1	2i	2ii	2iii	3	4	5i	5ii	6	0
014	Ghaghah	AD	—	•	—	—	—	•	—	—	—	—
015	Islands off Sir Bani Yas Island	AD	—	•	—	—	—	•	—	—	—	—
016	Yasat Islands	AD	—	•	—	—	—	•	—	—	—	—
017	Abu al Abyadh Island	AD	—	•	—	—	—	•	—	—	—	—
018	Umm Amin	AD	—	•	—	—	—	•	—	—	—	—
019	Jebel Hafit	AD	—	—	—	—	•	•	—	—	—	—
020	Baynunah	AD	•	—	—	—	—	•	•	—	•	—

Key to criteria

1 Regularly holds a significant number of a globally threatened species.

2i Regularly holds 1% or more of a species' biogeographical or flyway or Middle Eastern population (waterbirds and seabirds only).

2ii Regularly holds 20,000 or more waterbirds.

2iii Migratory 'bottleneck' site: more than 3,000 raptors or more than 5,000 storks or more than 2,000 cranes pass in a season.

3 Regularly holds a significant number of a species which is threatened or declining within the Middle East. Only the top five sites for each such species in the country are considered to qualify as IBAs.

4 Regularly holds a significant number of a species whose world population is wholly or largely restricted to the Middle East. Only the top five sites for each such species in the country are considered to qualify as IBAs.

5i Representative example of a habitat, associated with a characteristic assemblage of bird species.

5ii Rare/threatened/unique habitat, associated with a characteristic assemblage of bird species.

6 Site important for bird conservation through education/research/tourism.

0 Selected for other reasons. See 'Comments on the inventory'.

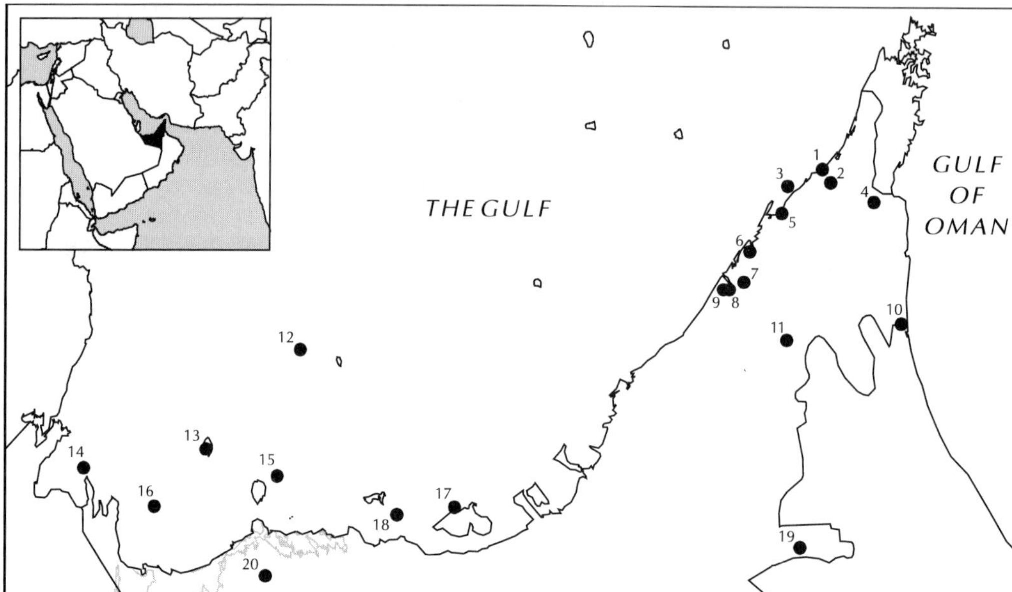

Comments on the inventory

1. The majority of the data used in compiling the site accounts was collected in the late 1980s and early 1990s.
2. The site name has been transliterated from the Arabic, and is sometimes followed by an alternative site name. This is then followed by the name of the region in brackets. The regions given are the emirates.
3. Precise areas are given only for protected areas and some of the sites which have been well documented. Boundaries have not been defined for

the other sites, and any areas given in these cases are only crude estimates. The areas given for offshore island sites (important for breeding seabirds) generally do not include the area of the surrounding seas which are important as feeding grounds, because the latter usually have not been identified with sufficient accuracy as yet.

4. Figures in brackets after species' names, and in the boxes, are the maximum daily counts of individuals recorded (not pairs), unless otherwise stated. All counts of wintering birds are from the month of January, unless otherwise stated.
5. Information on bird populations is regionally uneven, and the distribution of some species is not well known. One result is a bias in favour of better explored areas, therefore the inventory should be regarded as preliminary.
6. It has not been possible to apply 'Top 5 site' criterion in category 4 (as depicted in the above table) for the following species: *Oenanthe xanthoprymna*, *Sylvia mystacea* and *S. minula*. All of these are common and widespread over much of the United Arab Emirates, and occur commonly in many of the listed sites. However, their presence is always listed, where known, due to their interest in a Middle Eastern context. The application of the criteria in categories 3 and 4 is provisional only, due to scarcity of recent or comprehensive information. Some landbird areas have been chosen to include a representative cross-section of bird habitats.

Glossary

jebel, mountain
khor, tidal inlet or coastal lagoon
qarn, hill
ra's, point or headland
sabkhah, saline mudflat
wadi, drainage line or bed of seasonal river.

001 Al Jazirah Khor (Ras al Khaimah)

Unprotected

25°45′N 55°50′E
c.500 ha

Site description

A large bay c.15 km long with extensive intertidal mudflats, sandbars and islets, lying c.10 km south of Ras al Khaimah town. High (30 m) sand-dunes guard the bay to the south-east. Above the tideline there is salt-tolerant scrub, and mature *Prosopis* trees on the dunes, heavily grazed by camels and goats. The whole area is very scenic and is much frequented by picnicers at weekends.

Birds

See box for key species. The site has been little investigated but holds at least c.3,500 waterbirds in autumn (based on a single survey). About 100 *Egretta gularis* have been counted in winter.

1% or more of population

	Breeding (pairs)	Wintering	Passage
Tringa cinerea	—	—	745 (Sep)

Regionally threatened or declining species

Sterna dougallii One bird recorded, October–November.

Other threatened/endemic wildlife

None known to BirdLife International.

Conservation issues

There is no legal protection. Dumping of sewage and solid waste is occurring and there is construction development on the dunes. The vegetation is overgrazed.

Further reading

Uttley *et al.* (1988).

002 Digdaga–Hamraniyah (Ras al Khaimah)

Unprotected

25°40′N 55°55′E
c.2,000 ha

Site description

The most established man-made habitat in the country: a broad, cultivated belt on a sand/gravel plain south of Ras al Khaimah, bordered by sand desert to south and west and by high mountains to the east. The natural vegetation was a parkland savannah of *Prosopis cineraria* trees with large thickets of *Calotropis*, but c.90% has now been replaced by cultivation (fodder-fields irrigated with underground water), although some *Prosopis* trees have been left standing.

Birds

See box for key species. Important for migrant and wintering raptors, of which 20 species have been recorded. The only known breeding site for a number of usually more northerly species.

Globally threatened species

Falco naumanni	Regular spring passage migrant in large numbers (max. 100, March); winter visitor in small numbers (max. 5, 1991/92).
Chlamydotis undulata	Formerly a regular winter visitor to nearby Jiri plain, but no records since 1980.
Vanellus gregarius	Winters in small numbers (3–4, November–February); may be regular.

Regionally threatened or declining species

Falco biarmicus	Two records (migrants).

Species restricted wholly or largely to the Middle East

Otus brucei	Possibly breeds (has bred nearby).
Oenanthe xanthoprymna	Winter visitor.
Oenanthe picata	Winter visitor.
Phylloscopus neglectus	Winter visitor.
Turdoides squamiceps	Resident.

Other threatened/endemic wildlife

None known to BirdLife International.

Conservation issues

No conservation measures have been taken. Over-exploitation of groundwater for irrigation has led to a water shortage, and many fields are left unwatered in some years. Some tree-cutting occurs locally.

Further reading

Richardson (1991).

003 Siniyah Island (Umm al Quwain)

Unprotected

25°39′N 55°40′E
1,000+ ha

Site description

A flat island, 12 km × 1 km, situated 2 km north-east of Umm al Quwain town, and mainly composed of low sand-dunes, saltflats, and some shallow hollows, with sparse salt-tolerant scrub. The sheltered inland side is much dissected by tidal inlets, with associated mudflats; apart from some mangrove *Avicennia* the island is tree-less. Tidal amplitude is 1 m. Khor al Beidah (site 005) lies opposite on the mainland.

Birds

See box for key species. The site is of global importance as one of the largest remaining colonies of *Phalacrocorax nigrogularis* in the world; numbers fluctuate annually and the site has never been aerially surveyed, so the cumulative breeding population over an entire season may be much higher.

1% or more of population

	Breeding (pairs)	Wintering	Passage
Phalacrocorax nigrogularis	c.40,000	—	—

Regionally threatened or declining species

Phalacrocorax nigrogularis	Huge numbers breed in winter (see above).

Species restricted wholly or largely to the Middle East

Phalacrocorax nigrogularis	See above.

Other threatened/endemic wildlife

Mammals: gazelles *Gazella* have been introduced, and there are now c.50–100 on the island, mostly *G. gazella* (V) with some *G. dorcas arabica* (V).

Conservation issues

The owner of the island has been advised of the importance of the island's *Phalacrocorax nigrogularis* colony, and has given assurance of its protection, but no formal measures are known to have been taken. A track between a royal palace at the south end of the island and a fishing cottage at the north end was built through the middle of the *Phalacrocorax nigrogularis* colony site in 1990. Fortunately the birds appear tenacious and moved their colony north beyond the buildings. Other ongoing disturbance by humans during the breeding season, e.g. over-flights by microlight aircraft or boats visiting from the mainland, causes havoc amongst nesting birds, exposing eggs to predation by gulls *Larus* spp. and risking desertion. The introduction of non-indigenous mammals, especially predators such as feral cats *Felis*, is a constant and critical potential threat. Overgrazing is a local problem.

Further reading

Howe (1989), Richardson (1987–1993), Richardson (1993), Symens *et al.* (1993).

004 Masafi–Tayibah Area (Ras al Khaimah)

Unprotected

25°35′N 56°10′E
c.2,000 ha

Site description

Shale foothills (400–600 m) divided by gravel plains and small wadis with scattered *Acacia tortilis* and *Ziziphus spina-christi* trees; the site is surrounded by more barren ophiolitic mountains. These savannah plains, set amidst a dramatic mountain landscape, are one of the most natural, unspoilt and beautiful environments in the UAE.

Birds

See box for key species. A typical example of a bird community rare elsewhere in UAE. Other confirmed or probable breeding species include *Hieraaetus fasciatus*, *Pterocles lichtensteinii*, *Bubo ascalaphus* and *Anthus similis*.

Other threatened/endemic wildlife

Butterflies: *Neohipparchis parisatis* (confined to the Hajar mountains in Arabia).

Species restricted wholly or largely to the Middle East	
Ammoperdix heyi	Resident.
Pycnonotus xanthopygos	Resident.
Oenanthe xanthoprymna	Winter visitor (20+).
Oenanthe picata	Winter visitor (5+).
Oenanthe alboniger	Fairly common resident.
Hippolais languida	Small numbers regular on passage.
Sylvia mystacea	Small numbers regular on passage.
Sylvia minula	Fairly common winter visitor.
Phylloscopus neglectus	Regular winter visitor in small numbers.
Turdoides squamiceps	Resident.
Carpospiza brachydactyla	Flocks of up to 30 on passage, March–April (may breed).

Conservation issues

The main Masafi–Dibba road divides the site. Overgrazing (goats) is a problem locally, as is tree-cutting, built development and rubbish dumping, but there do not appear to be any major threats at present.

005 Khor al Beidah (Umm al Quwain)

Unprotected

25°32′N 55°38′E
c.5,000 ha

Site description

A sheltered lagoon north-east of Umm al Quwain, containing intertidal mudflats (up to 400 m wide), islands and sparse mangrove *Avicennia* bounded inland by sabkhah and rolling dunes with salt-tolerant scrub. The area is difficult of access. Siniyah island (site 003) lies offshore. The site is used for small-scale fishing and for recreation.

Birds

See box for key species. The site has been little investigated but held c.10,000 waterbirds in October–November 1986. The wintering *Dromas ardeola* are believed to breed on Abu al Abyadh island (site 017). At least 30 pairs of *Egretta gularis* breed on the adjacent island of Ghubbah.

1% or more of population	Breeding (pairs)	Wintering	Passage
Egretta gularis	30	100	170 (Oct/Nov)
Dromas ardeola	—	600	350 (Oct/Nov)
Charadrius mongolus	—	1,124	—
Calidris tenuirostris	—	90	—
Numenius arquata	—	—	1,300 (Oct/Nov)

Species restricted wholly or largely to the Middle East	
Dromas ardeola	Common non-breeding visitor (see above).
Sterna repressa	An unknown number breed on the adjacent island of Ghubbah.
Sterna saundersi	An unknown number breed on the adjacent island of Ghubbah.

Other threatened/endemic wildlife

None known to BirdLife International.

Conservation issues
There is no formal protection, but the site is monitored regularly and the ruler of Umm al Quwain would be advised in the event of any threats, though none appear imminent. The inaccessibility of the area may protect it somewhat, though there is a danger of destruction of the desert crust and some low-flying by micro-light aircraft from a nearby airfield.

Further reading
Uttley *et al.* (1988).

006 Ramtha Lagoons (Sharjah)
also known as Al Wasit lagoons
Unprotected

25°22′N 55°27′E
c.250 ha

Site description
A series of man-made lagoons resulting from regular dumping of liquid sewage waste onto a sand-dune/sabkhah area since the early 1980s; some lagoons are deep enough for diving waterbirds, and contain fish. Existing salt-tolerant scrub is being colonized by *Prosopis* and *Tamarix* trees, and there are large *Phragmites* reedbeds. There is potential for wildlife education/research.

Birds
See box for key species. *Vanellus indicus* is resident (c.10 pairs) and *Charadrius dubius* breeds. Winter visitors include *Nycticorax nycticorax* (40), *Egretta gularis* (150), *Phoenicopterus ruber* (400) and *Vanellus leucurus* (rare). Passage migrants include *Egretta gularis* (c.150, August–November). At least 118 species recorded.

Globally threatened species

Aquila heliaca — Rare visitor.

1% or more of population

	Breeding (pairs)	Wintering	Passage
Himantopus himantopus	min. 50	—	370 (Oct)

Regionally threatened or declining species

Threskiornis aethiopicus — Vagrant.
Falco biarmicus — Rare visitor.

Species restricted wholly or largely to the Middle East

Sterna saundersi — A passage migrant, using the area as a moulting site (max. 200).

Other threatened/endemic wildlife
None known to BirdLife International.

Conservation issues
Management is not conservation-orientated and severe changes in water level and destruction of developing habitats occur regularly. Oil sludge and other toxins are often dumped, and outbreaks of botulism regularly kill dozens of birds in summer. The ruler of Sharjah has instructed the Sharjah Municipality to manage the site more sympathetically. The current building of a new sewage works in Sharjah will obviate the need for sewage dumping at this site, so the site seems to have only a limited future anyway.

007 Mushrif National Park (Dubai)
National Park

25°14′N 55°25′E
600 ha

Site description
A sheltered dip amongst rolling sand-dune desert, with 100 ha of natural 'ghaf' *Prosopis cineraria* tree parkland, interspersed with scrub. The whole park is fenced to exclude grazing by camels and goats, and is mainly used for recreation by families and domestic tourists. The park centre is landscaped (grass, pathways) with a leisure complex, and a road system extends throughout the area.

Birds
See box for key species. One of the most important areas of natural woodland in the UAE. Other breeding species include *Upupa epops* and *Petronia xanthocollis*, and *Sylvia hortensis* is a winter visitor.

Species restricted wholly or largely to the Middle East

Otus brucei — Several records in breeding season; may breed.
Turdoides squamiceps — Resident (c.5 pairs).
Sylvia mystacea — Winter visitor (c.10–20).
Sylvia minula — Winter visitor (c.100).

■ Other threatened/endemic wildlife
None known to BirdLife International.

■ Conservation issues
The site is a National Park, but the emphasis is on public recreation and there is no management or protection for nature conservation.

008 Zabeel Ponds (Dubai)

Unprotected

25°12′N 55°18′E
50 ha

■ Site description
Four deep settlement ponds (each 200 × 80 m) with associated sludge beds, constructed in c.1982 to recycle treated effluent for irrigating nearby palace garden, and located 2 km south of Khor Dubai (site 009), on the side of an escarpment overlooking unspoilt desert scrub for 2 km south of the site. The ponds are bordered by *Prosopis* trees, *Calotropis* bushes and *Typha* beds, and frequent overflow of effluent from these onto adjacent sabkhah supports extensive vegetation including 1 ha of *Phragmites* reedbeds. The ponds are also used for fish-farming.

■ Birds
See box for key species. A nationally important waterbird site, especially for wintering grebes, herons, ducks and raptors. *Charadrius dubius* breeds, and this is the only breeding site in the UAE for *Nycticorax nycticorax* (2 pairs) and *Acrocephalus scirpaceus* (c.5 pairs). In winter and on passage up to 60 *Ardea cinerea* occur and *Burhinus oedicnemus* is said to be common in desert to the south in winter. Flocks of up to 45 *Nycticorax nycticorax* occur on passage. 170 species have been recorded, including *Vanellus leucurus* and many other rare migrants.

Globally threatened species

Aquila heliaca	Rare migrant.
Chlamydotis undulata	Said to be common in winter in desert to south.

Regionally threatened or declining species

Aythya nyroca	Rare migrant.

■ Other threatened/endemic wildlife
Mammals: six *Gazella gazella* (V) were released in the area around 1988.

■ Conservation issues
The site is protected by the owner as a private nature reserve, with water levels managed accordingly; however, there is no legal protection. Regular police patrols minimize disturbance from the public. However, shooting and persecution of large raptors are common during September–March when the falconry season is at its peak nearby. This is a prime site for future urban development, but this is probably not a potential threat due to the site's proximity to the palace. The scrub area is being encroached upon by roads locally.

009 Khor Dubai (Dubai)

also known as Dubai Creek
Wildlife Sanctuary

25°12′N 55°20′E
c.300 ha

■ Site description
The head of a 10-km-long tidal creek which penetrates 7 km inland from the Gulf through Dubai city, containing tidal mudflats (maximum low-water extent c.150 ha) and a lagoon with maximum depth of 2 m and tidal range of 1.0–1.5 m. Flat sabkhah surrounds the intertidal area; there is some salt-tolerant scrub above the high-tide line, and some *Tamarix* in disturbed areas. The intertidal zone supports an abundant invertebrate fauna, but in late 1993 most of the 50-cm-deep top layer of mud was scoured off and a network of channels created, after which most of the area was densely planted with mangrove saplings. There is nutrient enrichment from irrigation run-off and treated sewage effluent. Seawards of the mudflats the creek has been dredged for shipping, and much is bounded by commercial development. The land is under the authority of the Coastguard,

but is owned by the Government of Dubai/His Highness Sheikh Mohammed.

Birds

See box for key species. The most important mudflat area in the UAE, supporting a more varied assemblage of waterbird species at much higher densities than any other sites in the coastal zone, especially in winter and during passage periods. Especially important for *Limicola falcinellus*; no other significant concentrations have been found elsewhere in the country. The site is well-known for its population of *Phoenicopterus ruber*, which is present all year but is largest in winter (January av. max. 1,400, 1989–1992; peak 2,300 in February 1990); another notable winter visitor is *Pluvialis fulva* (max. 40). Large numbers of *Larus ridibundus* roost in winter (see box).

1% or more of population

	Breeding (pairs)	Wintering	Passage
Ardea cinerea	—	175 (Dec)	—
Charadrius hiaticula	—	500	344 (Sep)
Charadrius alexandrinus	—	3,990	—
Charadrius mongolus	—	3,000	—
Charadrius leschenaultii	—	500	—
Pluvialis squatarola	—	1,000	727 (Oct)
Limicola falcinellus	—	450–600	4,050 (Oct)
Tringa totanus	—	1,000	—
Larus ridibundus	—	49,000	—

Other threatened/endemic wildlife

None known to BirdLife International.

Conservation issues

The Government of Dubai/His Highness Sheikh Mohammed declared the area a Wildlife Sanctuary in 1985, giving protection from interference (only) at his discretion. Police patrol the area to protect *Phoenicopterus ruber* from close approach by the public during daylight hours. Hundreds of mangrove *Avicennia* saplings were planted in mudflats in 1991, but only a few survived. A more recent attempt to establish mangrove saplings is still ongoing and is much larger in scale; the extensive measures to change the hydrology of the site, together with the loss of open mudflat habitat if the mangrove is successfully established, will almost certainly combine to significantly reduce the number of waterfowl feeding and using the area. In addition, edges of mudflats are being encroached upon by dumping of builders' rubble, and building activity has reached the nearest road, but no further building development is thought likely to take place on the creek side of road. Other problems or changes locally are eutrophication, excessive disturbance of birds, and discharge into the shallows of very saline groundwater from nearby cultivated areas. The wintering population of *Phoenicopterus ruber* has been steadily declining in numbers since monitoring began c.10 years ago, for unknown reasons: the peak count for the winter of 1992/93 was only 267 (January 1993). All-round fencing of the area has been proposed, possibly including hides.

Further reading

DSP (1987), Smart *et al.* (1983), Uttley *et al.* (1988).

010 Khor Kalba (Sharjah)

Unprotected

25°00′N 56°20′E
600 ha

Site description

A tidal inlet stretching inland then parallel to the coast for 5 km southward, with three main channels lined with the oldest and most extensive *Avicennia marina* mangrove woodland in the UAE, and with extensive mudflats. The southern end of the inlet extends across the border into Oman at Khatmat Malahah. Gravel plains with *Acacia tortilis* savannah (part of the extensive Batinah coastal plain) stretch 5 km inland of the khor, rising towards the Hajar mountains. The primary human activity is recreation/leisure; some fishing and grazing of livestock occur to a lesser extent. Crabs are harvested in large numbers in the mangrove.

Birds

See box for key species. Other breeding species include *Himantopus himantopus* (up to 10 pairs, 1988–1989), *Merops superciliosus* (summer visitor, probably less than 100 pairs), and *Hippolais rama* (c.10 pairs; the only proven breeding site on the Arabian peninsula). Winter visitors include *Ardeola grayii* (max. 10; the only regular site in the UAE), and *Merops superciliosus* is also common on autumn passage (max. 500 at roost, September).

Regionally threatened or declining species

Todirhamphus chloris	The only breeding locality in the world for the subspecies *T. c. kalbaensis* (c.15–20 pairs).

Other threatened/endemic wildlife
Mammals: the dolphins *Tursiops truncatus* and *Sousa chinensis* (K) feed in the khor. Reptiles: sea-turtles feed in the creek, including *Chelonia mydas* (E) and *Eretmochelys imbricata* (E), and possibly *Caretta caretta* (V).

Conservation issues
Kalba Municipality has been instructed by the ruler of Sharjah to take 'necessary measures' to protect wildlife. The main problems are excessive disturbance (e.g. vehicles drive all over the mudflats at low tide, also damaging valuable invertebrate habitat) and deliberate persecution of birds. Encroachment by nearby agricultural projects and by development of leisure facilities are locally problems, potentially major in the future; other local threats include tree-cutting, overgrazing and oil pollution. Careful proposals for conservation should be drawn up as soon as possible.

011 **Qarn Nazwa** (Sharjah)
Unprotected

24°59′N 55°40′E
c.250 ha

Site description
A large, rocky outcrop (300 m × 2 km) of shale rising up to 80 m above surrounding stony gravel plain, one of a series of ridges parallel to and west of the Hajar mountains. The rock surface is pitted with hundreds of small to large caves and cracks. Scattered *Acacia tortilis* grow throughout the site, and small shrubs grow on sand-dunes blown up on the south-east side. Camels and goats graze the area, which is a favourite picnic site (there is an adjacent highway). The caves and cracks in the rock surface probably support a vertebrate fauna (e.g. bats, foxes, rodents and snakes) unusual in the UAE.

Birds
See box for key species. Other breeding species include *Buteo rufinus* (irregularly) and *Bubo ascalaphus* (1–2 pairs).

Species restricted wholly or largely to the Middle East

Oenanthe xanthoprymna	Winter visitor.
Oenanthe picata	Winter visitor (daily max. 4).
Hippolais languida	Passage migrant.
Sylvia minula	Winter visitor.
Sylvia althaea	Rare passage migrant (one record, November).
Turdoides squamiceps	Resident.

Other threatened/endemic wildlife
None known to BirdLife International.

Conservation issues
No conservation measures have been taken. Major problems are the building of new road-side shops on the north side, and over-grazing. More locally, picnicers cut trees for firewood, and rubble-dumping from road construction and gravel-mining occur. The recent fencing of the boundary of the adjacent dual carriageway (to ward off straying camels) may inhibit picnicing and the spread of shop buildings in the future.

012 **Qarnayn Island** (Abu Dhabi)
Unprotected

24°56′N 52°51′E
c.300 ha

Site description
A 2-km-long island in the southern Arabian Gulf between Qatar and the UAE, 180 km west-north-west of Abu Dhabi city. It is mostly composed of sabkhah and fairly flat sand, and there are two rocky peaks about 50 m high at the north end, with an outer shelf of limestone rock around the edge of the island, as well as patchy coral reef offshore. The low and level southern area of blown shell-sand is relatively well-vegetated (low shrubs of *Suaeda* and *Salsola*) but this becomes sparse in the undulating hillocks of the north due to the barren subsoil and the former presence of a *Phalacrocorax nigrogularis* roost/colony. There is some habitation with a small permanent population, including a desalination plant and a navigation station.

Birds
A very important seabird breeding site: see box for key species (data are from 1984). Other breeding species include *Sterna bergii* (100 pairs) and *Pandion haliaetus* (one pair).

1% or more of population

	Breeding (pairs)	Wintering	Passage
Phaethon aethereus	50–200	—	—
Larus hemprichii	215	—	—
Sterna bengalensis	min. 500	—	—
Sterna repressa	c.4,000	—	—
Sterna anaethetus	800	—	—

Regionally threatened or declining species

Phalacrocorax nigrogularis 10,000 birds were present in February 1975, and a few hundred pairs were found nesting in the mid-1980s, but none since.

Species restricted wholly or largely to the Middle East

Phalacrocorax nigrogularis	See above.
Larus hemprichii	Breeds (see above).
Sterna repressa	Common summer visitor (see above).

Other threatened/endemic wildlife

Reptiles: important for the breeding sea-turtles *Chelonia mydas* (E), *Caretta caretta* (V) and *Eretmochelys imbricata* (E).

Conservation issues

The island's owners are keen to ensure the survival of terns, *Phaethon aethereus* and sea-turtles. The present level of development is not injurious to bird populations, although the *Phalacrocorax nigrogularis* colony has been displaced. Some harvesting of *Larus hemprichii* eggs by fishermen occurs but this is not a particular problem at the present level. Rats *Rattus* and mice *Mus musculus* are now established, though no evidence of feral cats *Felis* was found in May 1993. Unrestricted driving, off established tracks, is damaging the soil and vegetation. A report including proposals for conservation was submitted to the island's owner in 1989 (Hellyer 1989).

Further reading

Foxall (1985), Hellyer (1989), Richardson (1989).

013 **Delma** (Abu Dhabi)

Unprotected

24°30′N 52°18′E
c.500 ha

Site description

An arid and sparsely vegetated island c.50 km offshore western UAE. The terrain is rocky, with mounds, hillocks, water-worn gullies and low crags and inland cliffs. The southern part of the island (outside the area of the site) has woodland plantations and cultivation, and an important fishing fleet is based there.

Birds

See box for key species. There is a small colony of *Falco concolor* and a pair of *Pandion haliaetus* breeds.

Regionally threatened or declining species

Falco concolor	Summer visitor (at least 5 pairs).

Other threatened/endemic wildlife

None known to BirdLife International.

Conservation issues

There is no legal protection. Disturbance and physical destruction of the cliffs are possible threats.

Further reading

Aspinall (in prep.).

014 **Ghaghah** (Abu Dhabi)

Unprotected

24°25′N 51°35′E
800 ha

Site description

Flat, arid islands in the Arabian Gulf close to the Saudi Arabia and Qatar borders. The islands were formerly inhabited and cultivated.

Birds

See box for key species. A major breeding and wintering (roosting) site for *Phalacrocorax nigrogularis*. Seven pairs of *Pandion haliaetus* breed and c.30 birds are present in winter.

Other threatened/endemic wildlife

None known to BirdLife International.

1% or more of population

	Breeding (pairs)	Wintering	Passage
Phalacrocorax nigrogularis	1,900–2,500	44,000	—

Regionally threatened or declining species

Phalacrocorax nigrogularis Breeds and winters in large numbers (see above).

Species restricted wholly or largely to the Middle East

Phalacrocorax nigrogularis See above.

Conservation issues

No information.

Further reading

Aspinall (in press).

015 Islands off Sir Bani Yas Island (Abu Dhabi)

Unprotected

24°23′N 52°43′E
190 ha

Site description

These three islands in the south-eastern Arabian Gulf are north and east of the large inshore island of Sir Bani Yas. Umm al Kirkum is low and rocky, c.2 km long in a U-shape. The mouth of the U is partly closed off by a sandbar, forming a lagoon where a few mangrove *Avicennia* trees grow; the remainder of the island is covered in sparse salt-tolerant shrubs and grass. Ghasha is low, flat and sandy, with slab sandstone rocks on its eastern and northern aspect. Most of this island is fairly thickly covered in salt-tolerant bushes, with some sparse grass; the centre of the island is more thinly vegetated. Umm Qaser is 2 km east of Umm al Kirkum and is more or less circular, surrounded by a 3–4 m high rocky cliff and a few narrow, steep sand beaches. All the islands are ringed by coral reefs.

Birds

See box for key species. These islands are an important seabird breeding site, although only once surveyed in any detail (July 1991). *Pandion haliaetus* also breeds (min. 2 pairs).

Other threatened/endemic wildlife

None known to BirdLife International.

Conservation issues

For the most part the conservation situation has not been investigated, and almost nothing is known regarding specific threats or problems. However, *Phalacrocorax nigrogularis* have been shot on Ghasha in the past, perhaps in an attempt at eradication. In addition a breeding colony of feral *Columba livia* (c.500 pairs) on Ghasha may be displacing breeding *Sterna anaethetus*. The islands are apparently little used at present by man: there is some seasonal use by fishermen and other occasional visitors.

1% or more of population

	Breeding (pairs)	Wintering	Passage
Sterna bengalensis	c.250	—	—
Sterna repressa	2,250	—	—
Sterna anaethetus	c.2,800	—	—

Regionally threatened or declining species

Phalacrocorax nigrogularis Breeds in winter/spring: a 'sizeable' colony on Ghasha, and 400 birds on Umm al Kirkum in March were probably breeding.

Species restricted wholly or largely to the Middle East

Phalacrocorax nigrogularis See above.
Sterna repressa Summer visitor (see above).
Sterna saundersi Summer visitor to Ghasha (20 pairs) and Umm al Kirkum (a few pairs).

Further reading

Chapman (1991).

016 Yasat Islands (Abu Dhabi)

Unprotected

24°15′N 52°00′E
c.2,000 ha

Site description

Three islands up to 36 m high in the south-east Arabian Gulf, 35 km north of Abu Dhabi mainland and 70 km west of Sir Bani Yas island. North Yasat is uninhabited. The islands are fringed by coral reefs.

Birds

See box for key species. This is a very important

seabird breeding site, judging by the only two surveys in May 1990 and March–April 1993. Other breeding species include *Egretta gularis* (7 pairs), *Pandion haliaetus* (17–20 pairs), *Charadrius alexandrinus*, *Sterna anaethetus* ('large colonies' were found forming on all three islands in May 1990, and a group of 250 birds was on North Yasat in April 1993), *Eremopterix nigriceps* and *Alaemon alaudipes*.

1% or more of population	Breeding (pairs)	Wintering	Passage
Phalacrocorax nigrogularis	c.2,000	—	10,000

Regionally threatened or declining species

Phalacrocorax nigrogularis	150 pairs still nesting within a colony of 2,000 old and new nests, March 1993, North Yasat; most nests were probably not used that season. There was also a roost of 10,000 birds (see above).

Species restricted wholly or largely to the Middle East

Phalacrocorax nigrogularis	See above.
Sterna repressa	In May 1990 large colonies were forming on all three islands, and birds were present in April 1993.
Sterna saundersi	Summer visitor: 10–20 pairs on North and South Yasat, March 1993.

■ Other threatened/endemic wildlife

Mammals: dolphins *Tursiops truncatus* and *Sousa chinensis* (K) occur, and sea-turtles *Chelonia mydas* (E) probably nest.

■ Conservation issues

There is no legal protection and no measures for nature conservation have been taken. There is no sign of feral cats *Felis* on the islands, and the distance from the mainland and the proximity to the border with Saudi Arabia probably help to minimize human disturbance.

■ Further reading

Aspinall (in press), Chapman (1990), Hellyer (1993).

017 Abu al Abyadh Island (Abu Dhabi)

Unprotected

24°15′N 53°45′E
c.60,000 ha

■ Site description

A large, low-lying island (20 km by 30 km, up to 10 m elevation) of calcareous sands and sabkhah, with very little natural vegetation; there are small areas of salt-tolerant scrub and irrigated cultivation. The coast is fringed with extensive intertidal sandflats and mature mangrove *Avicennia* woodland.

■ Birds

See box for key species. The main interest lies in a breeding colony of *Dromas ardeola* (200–300 pairs, probably c.280); this population seems to winter at Khor al Beidah (site 005). Peak counts of passage waders exceed 6,000 at any one time, and other species include *Pluvialis squatarola* (200, March) and *Arenaria interpres* (370+, September).

1% or more of population	Breeding (pairs)	Wintering	Passage
Egretta gularis	—	—	180 (Sep)
Dromas ardeola	c.280	—	—
Charadrius mongolus	—	—	1,190 (May)
Calidris tenuirostris	—	—	31 (Mar)

Species restricted wholly or largely to the Middle East

Dromas ardeola	Summer visitor (see above).
Sterna repressa	Summer visitor (300+ pairs).
Sterna saundersi	Summer visitor (c.50 pairs).

■ Other threatened/endemic wildlife

Mammals: dolphins *Tursiops truncatus* and *Sousa chinensis* (K) are numerous, and *Dugong dugon* (V) probably occurs; there are large numbers of introduced ungulates (including *Gazella gazella* (V), *G. dorcas* (V) and *G. thompsoni*). Reptiles: *Chelonia mydas* (E) is numerous inshore, with occasional *Eretmochelys imbricata* (E), though no sea-turtles have yet been proved to breed.

■ Conservation issues

The breeding site of *Dromas ardeola* is protected by the owner of the island as a private nature reserve (c.20 ha) and is fenced off, and there are presently no threats to the unprotected intertidal flats and mangrove. Artificial propagation of mangrove *Avicennia marina* is being carried out on unvegetated sabkhah (which has little or no intrinsic value to wildlife), and thus this activity is of net benefit to *D. ardeola* and other bird species of the mangrove community.

■ Further reading

Morris (1992).

018 Umm Amin (Abu Dhabi)

Unprotected

24°13′N 53°25′E
c.50 ha

Site description

An uninhabited, low, sandy island with sparse, salt-tolerant vegetation, mainly *Salsola*. The island is surrounded by intertidal sandflats on the south and east sides and a coral shelf elsewhere.

Birds

See box for key species. At least 30 pairs of *Egretta gularis* also breed.

Other threatened/endemic wildlife

None known to BirdLife International.

Conservation issues

The National Avian Research Center is to submit a proposal for protection of the site. There is some collection of the eggs of *Sterna anaethetus* and *Egretta gularis* by visitors, and a risk of accidental damage to the burrows of *Dromas ardeola* (whose eggs appear not to be taken by humans).

1% or more of population

	Breeding (pairs)	Wintering	Passage
Sterna anaethetus	2,000	—	—

Species restricted wholly or largely to the Middle East

Dromas ardeola	Summer visitor (35–38 pairs).
Sterna repressa	Summer visitor (c.100 pairs).

019 Jebel Hafit (Abu Dhabi [Al Ain])

Unprotected

24°05′N 55°45′E
c.1,600 ha

Site description

An isolated massif on the UAE/Oman border, 20 km to the west of the main Hajar range. The barren, arid slopes are deeply incised by wadis full of scree. A road runs up the western flank to the summit (1,300 m), whilst the east flank is very steep. There are no rivers: all rain (mainly storms in early spring) runs off immediately. Vegetation is very sparse: *Ziziphus* and *Acacia* bushes grow on the lower flanks. Most of the mountain is inaccessible and seldom visited.

Birds

See box for key species. An important site for raptors and for some Middle Eastern speciality species. Other interesting species include *Aquila chrysaetos* (one record, November), *Hieraaetus fasciatus* (recorded outside breeding season) and *Falco pelegrinoides* (probably breeds).

Other threatened/endemic wildlife

Mammals: *Hemitragus jayakari* (V): an isolated population formerly occurred on the mountain; there were probably less than 20 in 1980. None has been seen more recently and they are generally believed to be extinct.

Conservation issues

No conservation measures have been taken. Several areas around the summit have been developed (for a transmitter), palaces/hotels have been built on two places on the slopes, and a major road has been constructed from base to summit with several branch roads. Further development as a tourist attraction is anticipated. The Omani half of the mountain by contrast still appears pristine. Development so far has probably had no net detrimental effect on bird populations except perhaps for *Ammoperdix heyi*; other species may have benefited from the increased availability of permanent water.

Further reading

Tourney *et al.* (1982).

Regionally threatened or declining species

Neophron percnopterus	A few nests known; 60–100 birds regularly roost on summit.
Gyps fulvus	Scarce non-breeding visitor, September–April.
Torgos tracheliotus	One breeding pair in 1981/82; current breeding status unknown (ones and twos recorded throughout the year).
Falco concolor	One record in November.

Species restricted wholly or largely to the Middle East

Ammoperdix heyi	Common resident.
Pycnonotus xanthopygos	Resident.
Oenanthe monacha	Resident (min. 4 pairs).
Oenanthe alboniger	Resident (min. 20 pairs).

020 Baynunah (Abu Dhabi)

Unprotected

23°57′N 52°39′E
180,000 ha

Site description

A sand-gravel plain with scattered flat-topped outcrops in the extreme west of Abu Dhabi emirate, becoming purer sand and more undulating towards the south (but not forming large dunes), with sabkhah in coastal and more low-lying areas. Climate is very arid with sparse winter rainfall. Land-uses include some grazing (restricted), military training and limited hunting (perhaps two weeks per year). There are some irrigated plantations of native and non-native trees.

Birds

See box for key species. Very little ornithological work has been carried out in the area (and data are only available for winter), but the desert crust and vegetation are relatively intact compared to other parts of the country. Other wintering species include (with estimated mid-winter populations in some cases) *Pterocles exustus*, *Athene noctua*, *Alaemon alaudipes* (7,000), *Calandrella rufescens* (2,000), *Anthus campestris* (1,500), *Oenanthe deserti* (15,000), *Sylvia nana* (12,000) and *Lanius excubitor* (1,000).

Globally threatened species

Chlamydotis undulata	Winter visitor; an unknown number are hunted annually

Species restricted wholly or largely to the Middle East

Oenanthe xanthoprymna	Winter visitor

Other threatened/endemic wildlife

Mammals: *Gazella* sp. occurs (some may be introduced). Reptiles: there is a good diversity, including relatively high numbers of *Uromastyx aegyptius*.

Conservation issues

There are no conservation measures aimed specifically at this site. Hunting is restricted to members of the ruling family and some enforcement is carried out by hunting guards (or trackers). The military use of part of the area and the private enclosure of HH Sheikh Zayed restrict access to some places. The main problems are habitat destruction through military activity, land degradation due to excessive use of vehicles (creating new tracks), and very heavy grazing by camels and goats.

Further reading

Osborne (1992a,b).

MAIN REFERENCES

Aspinall, S. (in press) The birds of Yasat, Ghaghah and Kafai, United Arab Emirates. *Tribulus*.

Aspinall, S. (in prep.) Sooty Falcons on Delma and Sir Bani Yas. *Tribulus*.

Chapman, A. (1990) Bird notes from offshore. *Emirates Natural History Group Bull.* 42.

Chapman, A. (1991) See birds, seabirds and more seabirds. *Emirates Natural History Group Newsletter* [September].

DSP (Dubai Shorebird Project) (1987) *Shorebirds on Khor Dubai: Dubai Shorebird Project 1987*. Unpublished report, University of Durham, U.K.

Foxall, I. (1985) Notes on the birds breeding on Qarneyn island. *Emirates Natural History Group Bull.* 27: 5–8.

Hellyer, P., ed. (1989) *The Qarnein expedition*. Emirates Natural History Group.

Hellyer, P. (1993) Socotra Cormorants breeding in UAE in April. *Oman Bird News* 14: 3–4.

Howe, S. (1989) Socotran Cormorant breeding in the UAE. *Emirates Natural History Group Bull.* 37: 20–22.

Morris, R. P. (1992) Observations on a colony of Crab Plovers *Dromas ardeola* in Abu Dhabi. *Sandgrouse* 14: 34–7.

Osborne (1992a) *Report on a survey of the Houbara Bustard in Abu Dhabi Emirate. Phase 1*. Internal report, National Avian Research Center, Abu Dhabi.

Osborne (1992b) *Report on a survey of the Houbara Bustard in Abu Dhabi Emirate. Phase 2*. Internal report, National Avian Research Center, Abu Dhabi.

Ramadan-Jaradi, G. (1985) Les oiseaux non nicheurs observés en migration dans les Emirats Arabes Unis. *Oiseau et R.F.O.* 55: 1–52.

Ramadan-Jaradi, G. (1987) Analyse écologique de la répartition des oiseaux nicheurs des Emirats Arabes Unis. *Oiseau et R.F.O.* 57: 113–140.

Richardson, C., ed. (1987–1993) *Emirates Bird Rep.* Dubai.

Richardson, C. (1989) Qarnayn island, UAE. *Phoenix* 7: 7–8.

Richardson, C. (1990) *The birds of the United Arab Emirates*. Dubai, UAE: Hobby.

Richardson, C. (1991) Digdaga and Hamraniyah, United Arab Emirates (VB28). *Phoenix* 8: 12–13.

Richardson, C. (1993) A brief survey of Sinayah island, UAE, 19–20 May 1993. *Emirates Bird Rep.* 17.

Satchell, J. E. (1978) Ecology and environment in the United Arab Emirates. *J. Arid Environments* 1: 201–226.

SATCHELL, J. E., MOUNTFORD, M. D. AND BROWN, W. M. (1981) A land classification of the United Arab Emirates. *J. Arid Environments* 4: 275–285.

SMART, I., MILES, G. A. AND WEST, M. (1983) Waders and waterbirds on Dubai Creek. *Wader Study Group Bull.* 37: 29–30.

SYMENS, P., KINZELBACH, R., SUHAIBANI, A. AND WERNER, M. (1993) A review of the status, distribution and conservation of the Socotra Cormorant *Phalacrocorax nigrogularis*. *Zool. Middle East* 8: 17–29.

TOURNEY, G., BROWN, J. N. B. *ET AL.* (1982) The natural history of Jebel Hafit. *Emirates Natural History Group Bull.* [November].

UTTLEY, J. D., THOMAS, C. J., GREEN, M. G., SUDDABY, D. AND PLATT, J. B. (1988) The autumn migration of waders and other waterbirds through the northern United Arab Emirates. *Sandgrouse* 10: 58–70.

■ REPUBLIC OF YEMEN

Arabian Woodpecker *Dendrocopos dorae*

GENERAL INFORMATION

The Republic of Yemen covers an area of over 531,000 km^2 in the south of the Arabian peninsula, bounded by the Red Sea to the west, the Gulf of Aden to the south, Saudi Arabia to the north, and Oman to the east. Yemen contains the highest mountain in Arabia, Jabal al-Nabi Shu'ayb, which reaches 3,666 m—the roof of Arabia. From the high plateau on which sits the capital, Sana'a, a series of peaks and ramparts tumbles towards the Red Sea in the west, the desert sands in the east, and the plains of Aden in the south. The remainder of the southern and eastern part of the country comprises low, semi-arid hills facing the Arabian Sea with desert to the north, and the island of Socotra, part of the Republic, lies to the south in the Indian Ocean, close to the Horn of Africa.

The Republic has a population of over 10 million but large parts of the country are sparsely populated, especially in the east and south. Cultivable land covers only 6% of the country, mainly on the highland terrace system and on the Tihamah (the Red Sea coastal plain). Some 30% of the land area is said to be grazed and 10% is classified as 'woodland', with the remaining 54% being largely desert or barren, rocky hills.

The Republic of Yemen is characterized by a wide variety of broad environmental zones, with distinct geological, climatic and faunistic characteristics. The Tihamah and coastal lowlands form a rim around Yemen between the mountains and the sea. Much of the coast is sandy beach or sabkhah (salt flats) with dunes, while intertidal mudflats vary in extent but are generally poorly represented, being confined to the pseudo-mouths of large wadis. Also at these latter areas, along the Red Sea coast, there are groves of palms *Phoenix* and *Hyphaene* and mangrove *Avicennia marina*, whilst offshore there are more than 25 islands. Inland, the Tihamah comprises sandy wadis, open woodland of *Commiphora* and *Acacia* on stony areas, and extensive cultivation and *Dobera* parkland on the richer soils. In the southern coastlands, to the north and east of Aden, there is extensive *Acacia* savanna which peters out further east into barren sandy and stony plains.

Between the coastal plain and the highland massif of western Yemen rises a staircase of hills that climb up off the Tihamah. These range in elevation from 300 m to 1,000 m and include several major wadi systems with alluvial sediments. This zone has been subject to deforestation due to the high demands for wood, and few areas of forest remain, the most notable being Wadi Rijaf, on Jabal Bura. On higher ground, up to 2,000 m, the hills are dominated by cultivated terracing. The stone-faced terraces, built into the mountainsides, produce a remarkable landscape of traditional agriculture, on which many of Yemen's endemic birds are dependent. At the top of the staircase lies the highland plateau, with extensive areas of heavily cultivated plains (at 2,400–2,600 m) and an increasing reliance on tube-well irrigation.

Eastern Yemen is much drier than the west. It is dominated by sandy and rocky desert, with sporadic rainfall and a very sparse human population. To the south the mountains rarely rise above 1,000 m and are generally devoid of vegetation. Through these hills runs the impressive Wadi Hadramawt with permanent flowing water and extensive agriculture. In the far east, close to the Oman border, lies the Mahra region. These hills catch the south-west monsoon and the extra rainfall allows a relatively luxuriant vegetation to develop, with the coastal slopes densely covered in trees and shrubs.

The island of Socotra is of especial importance due to its endemic birds and other wildlife, and lies c.800 km east of Aden and 350 km from the nearest mainland coastline of the Republic of Yemen. It has an area of 3,607 km^2, measures c.110 km from east to west, 30 km from north to south, has a shoreline of c.330 km, and reaches a maximum altitude of 1,500 m. Together with the neighbouring islands of Al-Ikhwan (The Brothers) and Abd al-Kuri, it is a continuation of the Horn of Africa. It is predominantly limestone, with the granite outcrops of the Hajhir mountains in the north-east. Most of the original vegetation on Socotra, especially on the coastal plains, is thought to have been heavily degraded or destroyed by the heavy grazing of introduced goats. Currently, the coastal plains are mostly semi-desert dwarf shrubland and grassland, with small areas of mangrove and salt-tolerant scrub on the coast. Grassland thickets, succulent shrubland and semi-evergreen bushland (dominated by impressive *Dracaena* trees) occur on the limestone plateau, and on the Hajhir massif there is grassland and evergreen bushland and thicket. The flora is very rich in endemic species (including many succulents), and a high proportion are globally threatened.

The grazing of livestock is the major land-use on Socotra, and there are smaller areas of cultivation. In recent years 'karifs' (water cisterns) have been constructed on the island and are attracting larger grazing stocks than in the past. However, as yet there is no practicable way to provide supplementary fodder, and drought and disease continue to provide their traditional control on livestock numbers.

Currently Socotra's coastal waters are abundantly stocked with fish, and fishing is a widespread activity. Communications from the mainland by air and by boat are severely restricted by lack of harbours, airport facilities and adequate aircraft, and by monsoon conditions which effectively shut the island off for four months every year. Prospecting for minerals and offshore natural gas is occurring. There is very little tourism on the island.

Plans for future development of the island include an asphalt runway, a harbour jetty at Hadibo and extended road infrastructure; tourism is under discussion.

ORNITHOLOGICAL IMPORTANCE

Yemen is one of the richer countries in the Middle East for birds (and other wildlife, especially endemic species), due to (a) its great diversity of habitats, largely the result of wide altitudinal range and climate, (b) its position at the foot of the Arabian peninsula, lying at the centre of a globally important flyway for migrant birds between Eurasia and Africa, and (c) its biological isolation by seas and deserts, which has resulted in the evolution of 13 endemic or near-endemic bird species on the mainland and a further six on the island of Socotra. Over 360 bird species have been recorded in the Republic, including Socotra, of which more than 100 are known, or thought to, breed. The ornithology of Socotra has been particularly poorly studied and many parts of the island, notably in the west, have never been investigated at all: at least 110 bird species have been recorded of which 31 are known, or thought, to breed. While this is a typically impoverished island avifauna, the world ranges of at least six of these 31 species are restricted to Socotra, as well as those of at least 12 subspecies.

The following five groups of birds are of particular importance in Yemen.

Globally threatened species

Eight globally threatened species occur in Yemen in significant numbers: *Geronticus eremita*, *Aquila heliaca*, *Falco naumanni*, *Chlamydotis undulata*, *Numenius tenuirostris*, *Larus leucophthalmus*, *Turdus menachensis* and *Cisticola haesitatus*. Of these, Yemen has a particularly crucial contribution to make to the conservation of *Geronticus eremita* (one of the world's most threatened birds, which may breed in Yemen), *Larus leucophthalmus* (which is a Red Sea endemic, occurring throughout the year and breeding on the offshore islands) and the two restricted-range species, *Turdus menachensis* and *Cisticola haesitatus*.

Regionally threatened or declining species

Yemen has an important role to play in conserving several species which are threatened or declining in the Middle East but which are not currently globally threatened. These include *Aythya nyroca*, *Gypaetus barbatus*, *Neophron percnopterus*, *Gyps fulvus*, *Torgos tracheliotus*, *Terathopius ecaudatus* and

Ardeotis arabs. The last-named species is especially important as it is almost extinct in Arabia apart from a few tiny populations on the Tihamah of Yemen and Saudi Arabia. *Neophron percnopterus* is a common and widespread resident on Socotra, where the breeding population may well exceed 1,000 pairs, making the island perhaps the single most important breeding area for this species in the Middle East.

Species restricted wholly or largely to the Middle East

Mainland Yemen holds significant, and in some cases the major, populations of 13 species whose ranges are wholly or largely restricted to south-west Arabia, with a further six wholly restricted to Socotra. For this reason the country has two Endemic Bird Areas as defined in ICBP (1992), more than any other country in the Middle East. The mainland species are *Alectoris melanocephala*, *A. philbyi*, *Dendrocopos dorae*, *Prunella fagani*, *Oenanthe lugentoides*, *Turdus menachensis*, *Parisoma buryi*, *Passer euchlorus*, *Estrilda rufibarba*, *Serinus rothschildi*, *S. menachensis*, *Rhynchostruthus socotranus*, *Carduelis yemenensis* and, on Socotra itself, *Cisticola incanus*, *C. haesitatus*, *Nectarinia balfouri*, *Onychognathus frater*, *Passer insularis* and *Emberiza socotrana*.

In addition to the narrowly-endemic breeding species, a significant proportion of the world population of several species breeds in, winters in or migrates through Yemen, including *Bulweria fallax*, *Puffinus persicus*, *Phalacrocorax nigrogularis*, *Larus hemprichii*, *L. leucophthalmus*, *Pycnonotus xanthopygos*, *Irania gutturalis*, *Hippolais languida*, *Sylvia mystacea*, *S. leucomelaena*, *Turdoides squamiceps*, *Onychognathus tristramii* and, on Socotra, *Apus berliozi*.

Seabirds

The great productivity of the Arabian Sea, Gulf of Aden and southern Red Sea, caused by upwellings of cold, nutrient-rich waters during the summer monsoon, together with the presence of numerous offshore islands, makes an ideal feeding and breeding area for seabirds, notably *Bulweria fallax*, *Puffinus persicus*, *Phaethon aethereus*, *Sula dactylatra*, *S. leucogaster*, *Phalacrocorax nigrogularis*, *Phalaropus lobatus*, *Larus hemprichii*, *L. leucophthalmus*, *Sterna bergii* and *S. repressa*.

Migrating and wintering birds

In addition to those that breed in Yemen, over 220 species occur on migration or during the winter—birds that are travelling between their breeding grounds in Europe or Asia and wintering grounds in Africa and the Middle East. Of these, particular mention should be made of the birds of prey that travel through Yemen to make a sea crossing at the Bab al-Mandab on their journey to Africa, and of the waders that gather on coastal mudflats, especially in spring and autumn. The limited information available so far suggests that the country is an important flyway, at least in autumn, for *Milvus migrans*, *Buteo buteo*, *Aquila nipalensis* and possibly *Pernis apivorus*.

CONSERVATION INFRASTRUCTURE AND PROTECTED-AREA SYSTEM

The responsibility for wildlife conservation in the Republic of Yemen lies with the Ministry of Agriculture who have created a Department of Wildlife, and with the Environmental Protection Council (EPC). The EPC undertakes a variety of tasks including the preparation of wildlife laws, policy for protection from pollution and the setting up of a general framework for an environmental education programme.

At present, wildlife legislation is in draft and until it is ratified by Parliament a governmental system does not exist for site protection. Traditional resource-reserves or 'mahjur' (e.g. for bee-keeping or grazing) are thought to be scattered throughout the western highlands of the country at least; they offer improved habitat quality for some of the endemic bird species, but their future is not secure in the face of abandonment of traditional land-management practises, at least locally.

On Socotra, traditional controls on timber utilization are still adhered to by the tribespeople throughout the island. Only dead timber may be removed and replanting is practised where appropriate. Range enclosures and controlled grazing systems are used in the Hajhir mountains. Wild fruit trees are protected. This traditional management is threatened only in the immediate vicinity of Hadibo, Qalansiya and the new coastal settlements where incomers do not respect the resident communities' tribal authority. In general, where motorable tracks provide access, wood-gathering occurs more systematically, but follows traditional practices.

INTERNATIONAL MEASURES RELEVANT TO THE CONSERVATION OF SITES

The Republic of Yemen is a party to the World Heritage Convention and has signed (but not ratified) the Biodiversity Convention. It has ratified the Convention for the Conservation of the Red Sea and the Gulf of Aden Environment. It has not designated any natural World Heritage Sites or Biosphere Reserves. The Republic has not signed the Ramsar or Bonn Conventions.

OVERVIEW OF THE INVENTORY

This inventory contains 57 sites, covering a total area of c.7,300 km^2 or about 1.4% of the area of the country. None of the sites are legally protected for nature conservation purposes, although some may be covered by traditional resource-use reserves or 'mahjur'. Several areas have been officially considered for legal protection measures in the past, and Socotra is currently being considered for nomination as a Biosphere Reserve. The inventory covers all of the most important habitat-types for birds, including marine, coastal, wetland, woodland, bushland, traditional agricultural, steppe/savannah, desert and montane biotopes, but generally in a representative rather than comprehensive fashion, due to the almost complete lack of systematic biological surveys of the country. Coastal and offshore-island habitats receive the best coverage, whilst sites for terrestrial habitats have generally been selected purely on the basis of what information was available, and there is therefore a strong bias towards the best-explored areas. In addition, important feeding areas for seabirds are very poorly represented. Relatively few of the sites are subject to severe and immediate problems or are currently undergoing major changes, but the Ta'izz Marshes are an exception, being critically threatened by excessive water extraction and conversion to agriculture. Most of the offshore islands, important for breeding seabirds, are very poorly known, and are under severe threat from the introduction of mammalian predators such as cats and rats. Many bird species (which Yemen has important populations of) such as raptors, gamebirds, bustards, sandgrouse and many passerines, tend not to congregate but to have scattered distributions. Only a small proportion of their total populations is covered by the inclusion of some representative sites. To conserve these dispersed species it is necessary to consider the integration of conservation measures for the wider environment into the regulations governing important land-uses such as agriculture and forestry.

ACKNOWLEDGEMENTS

The site accounts for southern Yemen and Socotra were compiled from information supplied by R. F. Porter, K. Shaw and C. Bradshaw, and the site accounts for Socotra were compiled by R. F. Porter, with assistance from F. Stone; Dr A. Miller (Royal Botanic Garden, Edinburgh) and Dr M. Morris respectively assisted with the habitat and land-use descriptions for Socotra. D. Showler provided information on endemic reptiles in southern Yemen and Socotra. The ornithological and site information for southern Yemen and Socotra was largely gathered during the OSME survey of spring 1993. The site accounts for southern Yemen were reviewed by M. C. Jennings (Coordinator, Atlas of the Breeding Birds of Arabia). Site accounts for most of northern Yemen were compiled by M. I. Evans, with assistance from D. J. Brooks. D. Raydan assisted with Arabic translation. The introduction was compiled mainly from information supplied by R. F. Porter.

SITE INVENTORY

Site no.	Site name	Region	Criteria used to select site									
			1	2i	2ii	2iii	3	4	5i	5ii	6	0
001	Midi–Al-Luhayyah	HD, HJ	•	•	—	—	•	•	—	—	—	—
002	Ma'rib–Naqil Fardah–Baraqish	MB	—	—	—	—	—	•	•	—	—	—
003	Wadi Mawr–Al-Zuhrah	HD	—	—	—	—	•	•	—	—	—	—
004	Islands north of Al-Hudaydah	HD	•	•	—	—	•	•	—	—	—	—
005	Kawkaban–Shibam	MH	•	—	—	—	•	•	—	—	—	—
006	Al-Mahwit	MH	•	—	—	—	•	•	—	—	—	—
007	Bahr Ibn Abbas–Ra's Isa	HD	•	•	—	—	•	•	—	—	—	—
008	Jabal al-Nabi Shu'ayb	SN	—	—	—	—	•	•	—	—	—	—
009	Al-Kadan Area	HD, MH	•	•	—	•	•	•	—	—	—	—
010	Al-'Urj	HD	—	•	—	—	—	•	•	—	—	—
011	Jabal Shibam	SN	•	—	—	—	•	•	—	—	—	—
012	Jaza'ir al-Zubayr	HD	—	•	—	—	—	•	—	—	—	—
013	Al-Murah	HD	—	—	—	—	•	•	—	—	—	—
014	Wadi Rijaf	HD	•	—	—	•	•	•	—	•	—	—
015	Nukhaylah–Ghulayfiqah	HD	•	—	—	—	•	•	•	—	—	—
016	Al-Fazzah	HD	•	•	—	—	—	•	—	—	—	—
017	Jabal Sumarah–Wadi Rafood–Wadi Bana	IB	•	—	—	—	•	•	—	—	—	—
018	Ibb–Dhi Sufal	IB	•	—	—	—	•	•	—	—	—	—
019	Jaza'ir al-Hanish	HD	•	•	—	—	—	•	—	—	—	—
020	Ta'izz Wadis	TZ	•	•	—	—	•	•	—	•	—	—
021	Mafraq al-Mukha	TZ	•	—	—	•	•	•	—	—	—	—

Site no.	Site name	Region	Criteria used to select site 1	2i	2ii	2iii	3	4	5i	5ii	6	0
022	Bab al-Mandab–Mawza	TZ, AD	•	—	—	•	—	•	—	—	•	—
023	The Wooded Mahra	GD	—	—	—	—	—	•	•	—	—	—
024	Abdullah Gharib Lagoons	GD	—	•	—	—	—	•	—	—	—	—
025	Desert west of Al-Ghayda	GD	•	—	—	—	•	—	—	—	—	—
026	Ra's Fartak	GD	—	—	—	—	—	•	—	—	—	—
027	Qishn Beach	GD	—	•	—	—	—	•	—	—	—	—
028	Wadi Hajar	SB	—	—	—	—	—	•	•	•	—	—
029	Wadi Jahr	AB	—	—	—	—	—	•	•	—	—	—
030	Islands off Bir Ali	GD	—	—	—	—	—	•	—	—	—	—
031	Wadi al-Birayn	DM	—	—	—	—	•	•	—	—	—	—
032	Jabal Iraf	TZ	—	—	—	—	—	•	—	•	—	—
033	Aden	AD	•	•	—	—	—	•	—	—	•	—
034	Hiswat al-Hugayma	AD	—	—	—	—	•	•	—	—	—	—
035	Qalansiya Lagoon, Socotra	AD	—	—	—	—	—	•	—	—	—	—
036	Jabal Ma'lih Escarpment/Badiya Qalansiya, Socotra	AD	—	—	—	—	—	—	—	—	—	•
037	Ra's Hebaq, Socotra	AD	—	—	—	—	—	•	—	—	—	—
038	Airport Dunes, Socotra	AD	•	—	—	—	—	•	—	—	—	—
039	Muqadrihon Pass, Socotra	AD	—	—	—	—	—	—	—	—	—	•
040	Shidahah, Socotra	AD	—	—	—	—	—	•	—	—	—	—
041	Wadi Ayhaft, Socotra	AD	—	—	—	—	—	•	—	—	—	—
042	Rewgid and Regid Plateaus, Socotra	AD	—	—	—	—	—	—	—	—	—	•
043	Jabal Jef, Socotra	AD	—	—	—	—	—	•	—	—	—	—
044	Rookib Hills, Socotra	AD	—	—	—	—	—	•	—	—	—	—
045	Hamaderoh Plateau and Scarp, Socotra	AD	—	—	—	—	—	•	—	—	—	—
046	Coast of Bindar Di-Sha'b, Socotra	AD	—	—	—	—	—	—	—	—	—	•
047	Hajhir Mountains, Socotra	AD	•	—	—	—	•	•	—	—	—	—
048	Firjih/Central Socotra	AD	—	—	—	—	—	—	—	—	—	•
049	Di-Ishal Foothills, Socotra	AD	—	—	—	—	—	•	—	—	—	—
050	Diksam, Socotra	AD	—	—	—	—	—	—	—	—	—	•
051	Ra's Momi and Fikhah, Socotra	AD	—	—	—	—	•	•	—	—	—	—
052	Firmihin near Jabal Keseslah, Socotra	AD	—	—	—	—	—	—	—	—	—	•
053	Noged Plain, Socotra	AD	•	—	—	—	—	•	—	—	—	—
054	Sabuniya and Ka'l Fir'awn	AD	—	•	—	—	•	•	—	—	—	—
055	Abd al-Kuri	AD	—	—	—	—	—	•	—	—	—	—
056	Al-Ikhwan	AD	—	—	—	—	•	•	—	—	—	•
057	Al-Mukha–Al-Khawkhah	TZ	•	—	—	—	—	•	—	—	—	—

Key to regions

AB	Abyan	GD	Al-Ghayda	IB	Ibb	SB	Shabwa
AD	Aden	HD	Al-Hudaydah	MB	Marib	SN	Sana'a
DM	Dhamar	HJ	Hajjah	MH	Al-Mahwit	TZ	Ta'izz

Key to criteria

1 Regularly holds a significant number of a globally threatened species.

2i Regularly holds 1% or more of a species' biogeographical or flyway or Middle Eastern population (waterbirds and seabirds only).

2ii Regularly holds 20,000 or more waterbirds.

2iii Migratory 'bottleneck' site: more than 3,000 raptors or more than 5,000 storks or more than 2,000 cranes pass in a season.

3 Regularly holds a significant number of a species which is threatened or declining within the Middle East. Only the top five sites for each such species in the country are considered to qualify as IBAs.

4 Regularly holds a significant number of a species whose world population is wholly or largely restricted to the Middle East. Only the top five sites for each such species in the country are considered to qualify as IBAs.

5i Representative example of a habitat, associated with a characteristic assemblage of bird species.

5ii Rare/threatened/unique habitat, associated with a characteristic assemblage of bird species.

6 Site important for bird conservation through education/research/tourism.

0 Selected for other reasons. See 'Comments on the inventory'.

Comments on the inventory

1. The site name has been transliterated from the Arabic, and is sometimes followed by an alternative site name in brackets. The regions given in brackets after the site name(s) are the governorates (muhafazat).
2. The areas given for offshore island sites (important for breeding seabirds) generally do not include the area of the surrounding seas which are important as feeding grounds, generally because the latter have not been identified with sufficient accuracy as yet.
3. The majority of the ornithological data used in compiling the site accounts for northern Yemen dates from the last 10 years, whereas that for southern Yemen comes mainly from two surveys carried out in the last 5 years, supplemented with some data from the 1950s.
4. Application of the criteria is provisional, especially in categories 3 and 4 as depicted in the

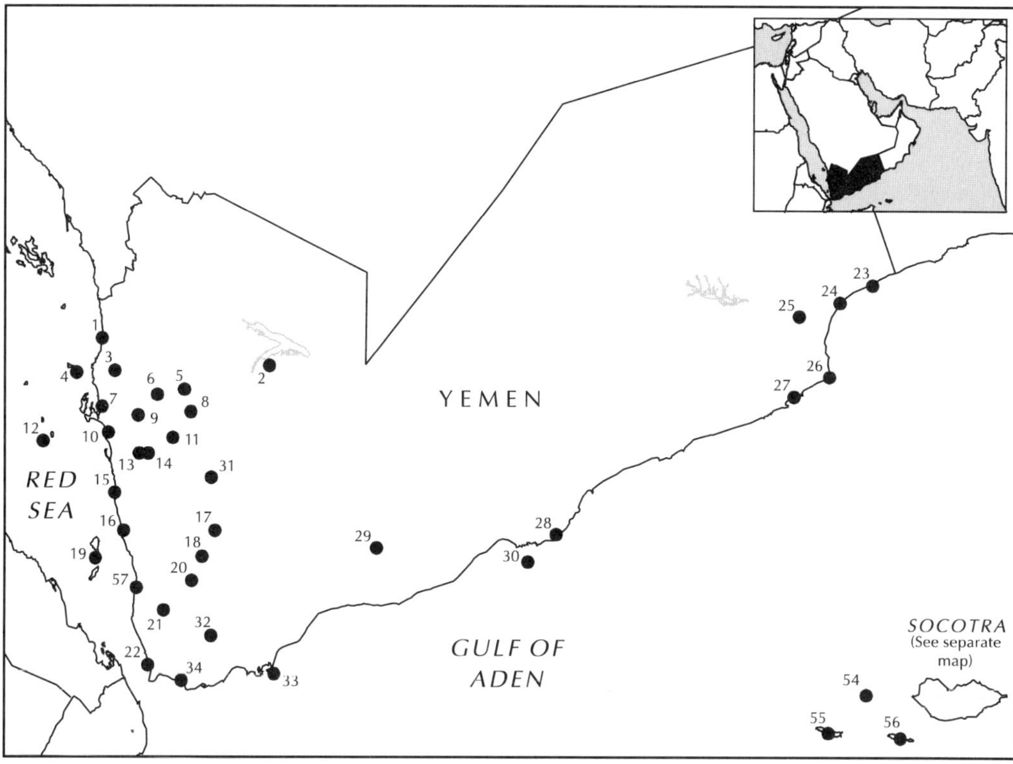

above table, due to the scarcity of ornithological information. This scarcity has led to a general bias towards better explored areas.

5. Figures in brackets after species' names, and in the boxes, are the maximum daily counts of individuals recorded (not pairs), unless otherwise stated. All counts of wintering birds are from the month of January, unless otherwise stated.
6. The following species (wholly or largely confined to the Middle East) are widespread and common over much of Yemen, and their presence generally has not been used when applying the 'Top 5 site' criterion in category 4 (as depicted in the above table), since identification of sites for them would be of negligible conservation value: *Pycnonotus xanthopygos*, *Oenanthe lugentoides* and *Turdoides squamiceps*. However, they are often mentioned in the site accounts, due to their interest in a Middle Eastern context.
7. The majority of the sites on Socotra have been initially selected on the basis of their exceptional botanical interest, due to unusual intactness of vegetational structure and of floristic composition. These areas are likely to be richest in endemic species of invertebrates, and in most cases are known to support good populations of endemic birds and reptiles as well. However, some of these sites, although likely to be important for endemic

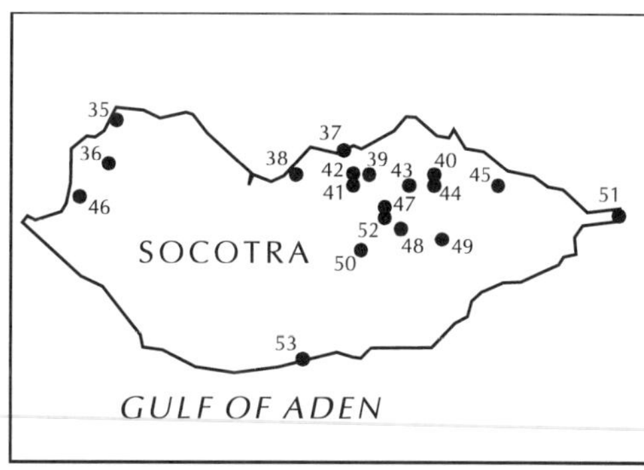

birds, have not yet been ornithologically surveyed (sites 039, 042, 046, 048, 050 and 052), and therefore do not meet the criteria, but are included in this inventory for 'Other reasons' (see column 0 of above table), as is site 056, which may harbour very important colonies of breeding seabirds but has also never been ornithologically surveyed. The following sites on Socotra were chosen purely in accordance with ornithological criteria, without regard to botanical interest: 038, 040, 044 and 049.

8. A number of sites (not included in this inventory) are a high priority for further investigation: they are suspected of meeting the criteria but as yet have not been adequately surveyed for their birds and other wildlife. These sites lie in the following

zones (site names in brackets): Coastal Plain (Lahij–Shaikh Uthman, possibly still has a rich *Acacia* savannah bird community, where 100 years ago *Ciconia abdimii*, *Torgos tracheliotus*, *Terathopius ecaudatus*, *Ardeotis arabs*, *Turnix sylvatica* and *Burhinus capensis* occurred in good numbers), Medium Altitude Western Mountains (Wadi Warazan, and other marshy valleys east and south of Ta'izz; Jabal Jihaf for breeding *Gyps fulvus*), High Altitude Western Mountains (Al-Turbah escarpment for breeding and migrating raptors; juniper woodland of Jabal Aswad and Jabal Lawz). The offshore islands of the southern Farasan group in the Red Sea (including Rumayn, Barri, Sumayr, Jazirat Duqayla, Fasht) are ornithologically completely unknown but are probably important for breeding seabirds and other wildlife—their sovereignty is undetermined or in dispute. No sites have been identified from the High and Medium Altitude Eastern Mountains and Highlands, and only one from the Eastern Desert Plain, zones, due to an almost complete lack of ornithological surveys/information.

9. The major wadi systems on the Red Sea and western Gulf of Aden slopes of western Yemen are cumulatively very important for birds, but to identify particular areas of wadi bed that are potentially protectable is problematic, because of the high human population densities, the lack of surveys, and the highly inter-related and inter-dependent nature of all the constituent parts of such systems. To include a sample selection of several relatively small valley-floor sites from several of the wadi systems is a not a satisfactory approach to the conservation of these areas: a broader approach is needed, and thus no sites of this type appear in this inventory. To summarize the wadis' ornithological importance, their cultivated and wooded floors support very diverse Afrotropical and Arabian-endemic breeding bird communities, and in winter and during migration periods they support large numbers of waterbirds (e.g. *Nycticorax nycticorax*, *Egretta garzetta*, *Ciconia nigra*, *Tringa ochropus*) and many other migratory species.

Glossary

PERSGA, Programme for the Environment of the Red Sea and Gulf of Aden
bab, strait or gorge
bahr, gulf, sea
jabal, mountain
jaza'ir, island group
jazirat, island
jibal, mountains
khawr, tidal inlet or coastal lagoon
naqil, pass
ra's, point or headland
sabkhah, saline mudflat
wadi, drainage line or bed of seasonal river.

001 Midi–Al-Luhayyah (Hajjah, Al-Hudaydah)

Unprotected

16°00′N 42°50′E
30,000 ha

Site description

About 100 km of very flat sabkhah coastline with extensive offshore sandbars and intertidal mudflats (especially at Al-Luhayyah), some sand beaches around Midi, and occasional sand-dunes/cliffs (especially in the northern half). There is a small, rocky hill at Al-Luhayyah (Jabal al-Humara). There are no coral reefs. More than 60 km of the coast is fringed by well-developed mangrove *Avicennia marina*, which becomes very dense between Midi and Buhays: the most extensive mangrove in Yemen. Seagrass beds are few except around Buhays. Coastal terrestrial vegetation (mainly salt-tolerant spiny grass) is very local. Al-Luhayyah is a classic Red Sea port of great cultural, archaeological and historical interest. Fishing is the main human activity, centred on Al-Luhayyah, Midi, Habl and Buhays. Tourism and recreational use occur at low levels.

Birds

See box for key species. The mangrove has not been surveyed, and may hold breeding *Egretta gularis*, *Pandion haliaetus* and endemic Red Sea subspecies of *Todirhamphus chloris*, *Acrocephalus stentoreus* and *A. baeticatus*; *A. stentoreus* is certainly common in winter and spring. Other notable passage migrants include *Egretta gularis* (35++, November), *Recurvirostra avosetta* (20, October), *Charadrius alexandrinus* (hundreds, October), *Tringa cinerea* (200+, October), *Sterna caspia* (60, November),

Globally threatened species

Larus leucophthalmus	Rare but regular passage migrant (max. 5, November) and winter visitor (2).

1% or more of population

	Breeding (pairs)	Wintering	Passage
Platalea leucorodia	?	90+	36 (Nov)
Charadrius mongolus	—	—	1,000+ (Oct)
Limicola falcinellus	—	—	hundreds (Oct)
Numenius arquata	—	—	hundreds (Oct)

Regionally threatened or declining species

Ardea goliath	Rarely recorded throughout the year (max. 3, October), and probably breeds in the mangrove.
Pelecanus rufescens	Frequently recorded throughout the year (100+, October), and probably breeds in the mangrove.

Species restricted wholly or largely to the Middle East

Dromas ardeola	Frequent winter visitor (max. 38, January) and common passage migrant (100, October).
Larus leucophthalmus	Scarce passage migrant (see above).
Sterna repressa	Frequent passage migrant (min. 120, November), and may breed on offshore sandbars.

Tachymarptis melba (2,000+, October) and *Sylvia atricapilla* (abundant, April). Large but unspecified numbers of wintering small waders have been recorded in November.

Other threatened/endemic wildlife

Mammals: *Dugong dugon* (V). Reptiles: *Chelonia mydas* (E).

Conservation issues

No formal conservation measures are known to have been taken. If there are nesting populations of *Pelecanus rufescens*, *Egretta gularis*, *Ardea goliath*, *Platalea leucorodia* and other waterbirds in the mangrove, as seems likely, it is not known whether disturbance of adults and exploitation of eggs occur. Occasional dredging of the shipping channel to Al-Luhayyah may damage mudflats locally. Shrimp-farming is increasing in Yemen, and if so would gravely threaten mangrove habitat.

Further reading

TMRU (1987).

002 Ma'rib–Naqil Fardah–Baraqish (Ma'rib)

Unprotected

15°44′N 45°00′E
c.250,000 ha

Site description

Bare, rocky, sandstone and igneous mountains form an eastward-facing scarp which descends steeply to meet gently undulating silt and gravel plains, which merge into the isolated sand sea of Ramlat al-Sab'atayn towards the south-east (1,000–2,200 m). The plains are locally overlain by black, basalt boulder-fields and areas of mobile sand-dunes, and occasionally punctuated by volcanic ash-cones and low, rocky outcrops. In wadi-spreads close to the hills the scattered vegetation is composed of sizeable *Acacia hamulosa* and *Tamarix* trees (to 5 m), thickets of *Tamarix*, *Salvadora* and *Cadaba*, and also shrubby *Acacia hamulosa*, *Lycium* and *Calotropis*. Perennial herbs, tussock grasses and spiny herbs form the ground layer. To the east, wadi vegetation becomes more open and tree-less, dominated by grass and herbs, with very scattered, shrubby *Acacia tortilis/ ehrenbergiana*. Away from drainage lines, surrounding sandy desert has a very sparse cover of *Acacia ehrenbergiana* and *Panicum* grass. There is a large, man-made reservoir near Ma'rib town, formed by the damming of a wadi at 1,100 m. Below the dam, the former outwash plain of the wadi is now extensively cultivated by irrigation (including millet and *Citrus* orchards). The reservoir mostly abuts steep and rocky hills, so that the shore is only occasionally shallow and muddy. The state of development of the aquatic and marginal vegetation since the reservoir's creation in 1986 is not known. Goats and camels are ranged over the whole area by semi-nomadic pastoralists. There are numerous sites and features of great archaeological, historical and cultural interest.

Birds

See box for key species. The dam has not been comprehensively surveyed for wintering and passage waterfowl, and it is possible that important numbers of herons, diving ducks and waders are now occurring as the new wetland develops. The diverse breeding bird community is well representative of the desert fringe, and includes *Neophron percnopterus*, *Buteo rufinus*, *Hieraaetus fasciatus*, *Falco tinnunculus*, *Pterocles lichtensteinii*, *P. coronatus*, *Streptopelia roseogrisea*, *Tyto alba*, *Athene noctua*, *Merops orientalis*, *Eremopterix nigriceps*, *Eremalauda dunni*, *Ammomanes deserti*, *Hirundo obsoleta*, *H. daurica*, *Cercomela melanura*,

Oenanthe leucopyga, *Scotocerca inquieta*, *Anthreptes metallicus*, *Nectarinia habessinica*, *Ploceus galbula*, *Rhodopechys githaginea*, *Emberiza striolata* and *E. tahapisi*. Other common wintering species include *Cursorius cursor*, *Oenanthe deserti* and *Sylvia nana*.

Other threatened/endemic wildlife

Reptiles: *Uromastyx aegyptius* (rare). Fish: unidentified, possibly endemic, fish live in the wadi and presumably the reservoir.

Conservation issues

No formal conservation measures are known to have been taken. The wadi-spreads on the plains are being rapidly cleared of their currently exceptionally good *Acacia* tree cover, for firewood and charcoal burning.

Regionally threatened or declining species

Falco biarmicus	Scarce resident or winter visitor.

Species restricted wholly or largely to the Middle East

Ammoperdix heyi	Common resident.
Pycnonotus xanthopygos	Common resident in areas with trees.
Hypocolius ampelinus	Scarce passage migrant (April).
Oenanthe xanthoprymna	Local winter visitor.
Oenanthe lugentoides	Local resident.
Oenanthe monacha	Scarce resident.
Sylvia leucomelaena	Fairly common resident.
Sylvia minula	Abundant winter visitor.
Sylvia mystacea	Fairly common winter visitor.
Turdoides squamiceps	Fairly common but local resident.
Onychognathus tristramii	Fairly common but local resident.

003 Wadi Mawr–Al-Zuhrah (Al-Hudaydah)

Unprotected

15°41′N 43°00′E
15,000 ha

Site description

An area of flat wadi-spread on the Red Sea Tihamah plain of western Yemen. Wadi Mawr is the largest wadi on the western watershed of Yemen, and has an enormous catchment area in the mountains of northern Yemen; occasional floods reach far onto the Tihamah. Most of the wadi-spread is heavily cultivated and there are several large, intensive, irrigated agriculture projects, growing crops inside fields enclosed in huge, bulldozed earth bunds. However, there are also extensive areas of uncultivated *Tamarix* woodland, and in the western areas of the site there is well-vegetated, semi-desert dwarf-shrubland, with a low human-population density.

Birds

See box for key species.

Other threatened/endemic wildlife

Mammals: unidentified *Gazella* sp. (V) present in the uncultivated *Tamarix* woodland and western semi-desert areas during the 1980s.

Regionally threatened or declining species

Ardeotis arabs	Fairly common resident (1, October; 7, November).

Species restricted wholly or largely to the Middle East

Passer euchlorus	Common non-breeding visitor to the wadi; breeds in *Acacia* bushes in the western, more desertic part of this site.

Conservation issues

No formal conservation measures are known to have been taken. Intensification of agriculture, especially use of pesticides, may threaten *Ardeotis arabs*, and agricultural expansion may threaten the *Tamarix* woodland.

004 Islands north of Al-Hudaydah (Al-Hudaydah)

Unprotected

15°40′N 42°30′E
c.5,000 ha

Site description

At least 31 islands north and west of Al-Hudaydah on the northern Red Sea shelf (excluding Kamaran, the largest such island, which is part of site 007). Most are low, flat and sandy, elevated only a few metres, but a few of the largest are formed from upraised coral and are higher, up to 36 m on the largest, Tikfash (2,990 ha). Most islands have a fringing coral reef, and usually also have a sand beach, allowing access at least at high tide; the most extensive beaches are on the east coast of Humar and the north coast of Tikfash. Vegetation is sparse on all islands, with thin grass and low, salt-tolerant bushes. There are small areas of mangrove *Avicennia marina* on Tikfash and Humar; Kitamah has a well, surrounded by succulent *Euphorbia* vegetation. Patches of seagrass and reef-rock rubble occur off most islands. Most islands have temporary fishing camps and anchorages, used seasonally, and there are graves on Juwa, Hataban and especially Uqban, where there are also traces of former settlement.

Birds

See box for key species. Other breeding species include *Pandion haliaetus* (min. 2 pairs).

Globally threatened species

Larus leucophthalmus — Common passage migrant (min. 200, October); probably winters and may breed.

1% or more of population

	Breeding (pairs)	Wintering	Passage
Phaethon aethereus	10+	—	—
Sula leucogaster	—	—	100+ (Oct)
Platalea leucorodia	6	—	—
Larus leucophthalmus	?	?	200+ (Oct)
Sterna bengalensis	?	?	1,000+ (Oct)

Regionally threatened or declining species

Falco concolor — Summer visitor (1+ pair).

Species restricted wholly or largely to the Middle East

Dromas ardeola — Passage migrant/winter visitor in small numbers; possibly breeds.

Larus hemprichii — Common passage migrant (min. 300, October); probably winters and may breed.

Larus leucophthalmus — See above.

Sterna repressa — Small colonies (tens of nests, perhaps totalling 100–1,000 pairs) of unidentified terns reported nesting on some of the islands are most likely this species.

Other threatened/endemic wildlife

Mammals: records of dolphins, including *Tursiops* sp., and whales, probably including *Balaenoptera edeni* (K), are frequent, and *Dugong dugon* (V) are said by fishermen to be particularly common. Reptiles: sea-turtles nest, probably in important numbers and including *Chelonia mydas* (E) and *Eretmochelys imbricata* (E). The coral reefs are rich in biodiversity.

Conservation issues

No formal conservation measures are known to have been taken, although the establishment of marine parks has been considered in the past. At the least, Zurbat, Kitamah and possibly Zuraymah are infested with rats, and Juwa and Hataban are infested with mice. Tern (and sea-turtle) eggs are taken by fishermen. Sand extraction for the local building trade from Hamar's beach has occurred and may continue, with attendant disturbance. A baseline-census of the breeding birds, education of fishermen and navy personnel, the erection of signs at key landing points, and the extermination or control of introduced rodents are all highly desirable measures.

Further reading

Evans (1989), Phillips (1982).

005 Kawkaban–Shibam (Al-Mahwit)

Unprotected

15°30′N 43°54′E
c.5,000 ha

Site description

A flat-topped, cliff-girt sandstone massif 35 km north-west of Sana'a, projecting eastwards from the rugged Red Sea escarpment (up to 3,000 m), and surrounded below by montane plains (2,600 m). The bare, treeless, mountain-top plateau is covered mostly by small, terraced fields with scattered water cisterns, interspersed with flat, stony, uncultivated areas and patches of well-grazed sward with a rich Afro-alpine flora. The very steep sides of the massif have a sparse vegetation of low bushes, grass and herbage, richest in the numerous seepage areas and ravines where there are also small *Acacia* trees. The cliffs have numerous ledges. The ancient walled village of Kawkaban lies at the edge of the montane plateau, overlooking the village of Shibam at the base of the massif where there are orchards, as also in the shallow valley of Wadi Mishmish c.4 km to the south-east; there is a well-developed open woodland of *Acacia negrii* here. The montane plains are extensively cultivated with rain-fed sorghum on large, gently sloping terrace fields, while adjacent rocky slopes and stretches of lava rubble are very heavily grazed. The area is historically and archaeologically important, and is very popular with foreign tourists.

Birds

A representative assemblage of breeding species characteristic of the high-altitude mountains and plains of western Yemen, including virtually all Arabian-

Globally threatened species

Aquila heliaca	Scarce winter visitor.
Turdus menachensis	Local resident.

Regionally threatened or declining species

Gypaetus barbatus	Resident (min. 2 pairs).
Gyps fulvus	Resident (max. 45 birds, November).

Species restricted wholly or largely to the Middle East

Alectoris melanocephala	Locally common resident.
Alectoris philbyi	Locally common resident.
Strix butleri	Resident.
Dendrocopos dorae	Local resident.
Prunella fagani	Locally common resident.
Oenanthe lugentoides	Common resident.
Parisoma buryi	Local resident.
Sylvia leucomelaena	One autumn record; probably a non-breeding wanderer.
Sylvia minula	Common winter visitor.
Turdoides squamiceps	Local resident.
Onychognathus tristramii	Common resident.
Serinus rothschildi	Common resident.
Serinus menachensis	Common resident.
Carduelis yemenensis	Common resident.

endemic and Afromontane species. See box for key species; other breeding species include *Buteo rufinus*, *Aquila verreauxii*, *Hieraaetus fasciatus*, *Falco tinnunculus*, *F. pelegrinoides*, *Streptopelia lugens*, *Tachymarptis melba*, *Calandrella cinerea*, *Anthus cinnamomeus*, *A. similis*, *Saxicola torquata*, *Oenanthe bottae*, *Monticola rufocinereus*, *Scotocerca inquieta*, *Phylloscopus umbrovirens*, *Muscicapa gambagae*, *Nectarinia osea*, *Zosterops abyssinicus*, *Corvus rhipidurus* and *Emberiza tahapisi*.

■ Other threatened/endemic wildlife

Mammals: *Meriones rex* (endemic). Reptiles: *Pristurus popovi* (endemic), *Agama yemenensis* (endemic). Butterflies: endemics include *Lasiommata felix* and *Pseudotergumia tewfiki*. Plants: *Acacia negrii* tree (rare, endemic); the Afro-alpine zone harbours many endemics, including *Cichorium bottae*, *Macowania ericifolia*, *Delosperma harazianum*, *Teucrium yemense* and *Crinum yemense*.

■ Conservation issues

No formal conservation measures are known to have been taken. However the traditional land management is favourable to wildlife and probably preserves *Acacia* trees from cutting as far as is possible. Grazing is heavy but probably controlled as far as possible. Despite these traditional measures, the increasing irrigation of the plains from boreholes may lead to a lowering of the water-table in future. Tourist activity is centred on the villages and does not pose any threat; the site attracts a small amount of eco-tourism. Abandonment of traditional land-management practises in future would be a major threat, but currently this seems unlikely.

006 Al-Mahwit (Al-Mahwit)

Unprotected

15°27´N 43°33´E
c.2,500 ha

■ Site description

A wadi at 1,500–1,900 m on the Red Sea escarpment, 2 km west of Al-Mahwit town, including the cliffs of Jabal al-Mahwit. The steep wadi-slopes are extensively terraced and have deep soil. Uncultivated areas are rocky and the wadi bed is seasonally dry, though retaining some permanent pools of water. Sorghum is grown on the terraces, where there is also an open woodland of *Acacia origena* up to 8 m tall, some forming 80% cover on larger terraces; grass is left ungrazed and grown as fodder on the more densely shaded terraces. Other trees on the terraced slopes include frequent *Olea chrysophylla* and occasional *Ziziphus spina-christi*, small *Cordia africana* and clambering *Carissa edulis*. The terrace walls are rich in herbs, grasses, ferns and mosses. Dense coffee groves on narrow terraces in the valley bottom are shaded by huge *Cordia africana* trees (up to 20 m tall) which provide a well-developed canopy.

■ Birds

An excellent representative assemblage of breeding species characteristic of the better-vegetated and higher slopes of the Red Sea escarpment. See box for key species; other confirmed or probable breeding species include *Accipiter badius*, *Hieraaetus fasciatus*, *Falco pelegrinoides*, *Coturnix delegorguei*, *Columba arquatrix* (possible), *Streptopelia lugens*, *Chrysococcyx caprius*, *Otus scops pamelae* (probable), *Bubo africanus*, *Cercomela melanura*, *Monticola rufocinereus*, *Phylloscopus umbrovirens*, *Terpsiphone viridis*, *Nectarinia osea*, *Zosterops abyssinicus*, *Corvus rhipidurus*, *Petronia dentata*, *Ploceus galbula* and *Emberiza tahapisi*. There is a notable raptor migration in autumn; species include *Pernis apivorus*, *Circaetus gallicus*, *Buteo buteo*, *Aquila nipalensis* (max. 35) and *Hieraaetus pennatus*, but the scale of the passage has not been investigated.

Globally threatened species

Aquila heliaca	Passage migrant (1, November).
Turdus menachensis	Locally common resident.

Regionally threatened or declining species

Gypaetus barbatus	Resident.
Gyps fulvus	Resident: 20 pairs nesting on Jabal al-Mahwit in 1979, and 39 birds seen in the area in November 1985.
Emberiza cineracea	Local winter visitor (6–7, November).

Species restricted wholly or largely to the Middle East

Alectoris melanocephala	Locally common resident.
Dendrocopos dorae	Common resident.
Pycnonotus xanthopygos	Resident.
Oenanthe lugentoides	Common resident.
Onychognathus tristramii	Very common resident.
Estrilda rufibarba	Common resident.
Rhynchostruthus socotranus	Scarce resident.
Carduelis yemenensis	Common resident.
Emberiza cineracea	Local winter visitor (6–7, November).

Other threatened/endemic wildlife

No information.

Conservation issues

No formal conservation measures are known to have been taken. However the traditional agroforestry terrace system is fully functional and well-maintained, providing good quality habitat for all the important bird species. The main threat in the future is abandonment of traditional agricultural practises, in particular deterioration of terrace walls and increased tree-cutting; the likelihood of this occurring is difficult to predict, although many examples from elsewhere in Yemen show that the threat is real.

007 Bahr Ibn Abbas–Ra's Isa (Al-Hudaydah)

15°20′N 42°50′E
Unprotected
c.35,000 ha

Site description

Ra's Isa is a headland pointing north-west towards the adjacent island of Kamaran (c.10,000 ha); Bahr Ibn Abbas is the shallow, sheltered bay north of Ra's Isa. Kamaran (15°22′N 42°35′E) is a low, flat, rather bare-looking island, separated from the mainland by a 2.5-km-wide channel less than 100 m deep. The south coast of Ra's Isa is a steep, sand storm-beach, backed by several old, raised beaches of coral debris and with occasional 3+ m-high sand-dunes/cliffs and patches of sabkhah, and with a fringing coral reef close offshore. The north coast of Ra's Isa and of Bahr Ibn Abbas is very flat and dominated by unvegetated sabkhah, broken only by a coral outcrop at the port of Al-Salif and occasional areas of sand-dunes; there are extensive intertidal flats of mud and sand, and some coral reef off Al-Salif and Al-Khawbah. About 10 km of well-developed mangrove *Avicennia marina* fringe a sheltered bay on Kamaran and areas north and south of Ibn Abbas, where appreciable freshwater seepage also supports groves of *Phoenix*/*Hyphaene* palms inland. Seagrass beds are frequent in Bahr Ibn Abbas, especially south of Al-Khawbah. Salt-tolerant bushes (including *Limonium*) grow sparsely on sand on Ra's Isa but are generally absent. Al-Salif is a modern container port and is the Red Sea terminus for a major oil-pipeline. The other major human activity is fishing: Al-Khawbah is a major fishing port and Ibn Abbas is a major fishing village.

Birds

See box for key species. The area is very poorly known ornithologically, and all counts are likely to be severe underestimates. Other breeding species

Globally threatened species

Larus leucophthalmus	Fairly common passage migrant (10+, September; max. 30, October) and uncommon winter visitor (max. 2, February).

1% or more of population

	Breeding (pairs)	Wintering	Passage
Sterna caspia	?	—	100+ (Jul)

Regionally threatened or declining species

Pelecanus rufescens	Resident in small numbers (max. 12, October); the only known breeding colony in Yemen is in mangrove near Ibn Abbas.
Ardea goliath	Rare visitor (1, February); may breed in mangrove.
Falco concolor	Likely to be a non-breeding summer visitor from nearby islands (see site 004), since prey-plucking sites found in July.

Species restricted wholly or largely to the Middle East

Dromas ardeola	Resident in small numbers (max. 34, January); breeding not proved but is possible (max. 22 birds, July).
Larus hemprichii	Common non-breeding resident (max. 140 birds, July).
Sterna repressa	Recorded in summer (max. 125 birds, July): much pre-breeding display observed, but probably breeds on nearby islands (see site 004).

include *Pandion haliaetus* (min. 1 pair) and *Caprimulgus nubicus*. Non-breeding summer visitors to the rich seas offshore include *Sula leucogaster* (max. 100, July), unidentified *Puffinus pacificus*/*Bulweria fallax* (max. 100, July), *Sterna bergii* (max. 20, July), *S. bengalensis* (max. 180, July) and *Anous stolidus* (max. 2, June); some of these species may well breed on adjacent islands (see site 004). *Limicola falcinellus* occurs on autumn passage, in undetermined but probably large numbers (due to the fine-grained intertidal sediment).

■ Other threatened/endemic wildlife

Mammals: there are or were wild *Gazella* on Kamaran, of unknown species: a horn found in 1979 is the last known record. Feeding whales and dolphins are frequent offshore (e.g. *Sousa*); a population of *Dugong dugon* (V) occurs in Bahr Ibn Abbas. Reptiles: the area is probably an important feeding ground for sea-turtles (globally threatened).

■ Conservation issues

No formal conservation measures are known to have been taken, although the establishment of marine parks has been considered in the past, and the area was recommended for special management by a PERSGA survey team. The impact on habitats caused by the construction of the oil terminal at Al-Salif in the late 1980s is not known. Associated development of the Al-Salif area in the future is probably the greatest potential threat to the site, through expansion of industry/housing/human population leading to land-claim, disturbance of nesting birds and pollution. Due to its clear, rich seas and accessible coral reefs, the Ra's Isa area may also become a focus for development of tourism in the future, with potentially major impacts on the birds and other wildlife. Up-to-date base-line surveys of bird populations are urgently needed, especially of the intertidal mudflats and of breeding colonies in the mangrove; the latter may be threatened through human disturbance, deliberate persecution, exploitation of eggs and cutting/lopping of trees for wood and fodder.

008 Jabal al-Nabi Shu'ayb (Sana'a)

Unprotected

15°17′N 43°59′E
6,000 ha

■ Site description

The highest mountain on the Arabian peninsula, 35 km south-west of Sana'a, lying on the crest of the Red Sea escarpment where it meets the high, intermontane plains to the east. The area defined here is the land above the 3,000 m contour to the summit at 3,666 m. The stony slopes are not particularly steep, with numerous small cliffs, boulder screes, and geologically varied outcrops. On the southern and eastern slopes, in the rain-shadow, the general aspect is very bare; there are no trees or woody shrubs, only a sparse, low grassland with numerous alpine, cushion-type herbs. The western and northern slopes have not been investigated, but the former are likely to receive much more rainfall, and the latter may harbour some *Juniperus* scrub in shaded areas. Villages are few and small, and nearly all below 3,000 m. Terrace fields occur locally along shallower valley bottoms up to 3,500 m, but the land is mainly used for grazing goats and sheep. A rough vehicle-track extends up to a small quarry at 3,400 m on the southern slopes, but off-road vehicles can and do drive overland up to the summit. Because of the site's unusual altitude, beautiful scenery and existence as a small area of wilderness within the heavily populated western ramparts, the site is fairly popular with tourists, who generally only frequent the vehicle track.

■ Birds

See box for key species. This is one of the main sites known in Yemen for *Alectoris philbyi*. Other breeding species include *Buteo rufinus*, *Hieraaetus fasciatus*, *Falco pelegrinoides*, *Tachymarptis melba*, *Apus affinis*, *Upupa epops*, *Calandrella cinerea*, *Hirundo obsoleta*, *H. daurica*, *Oenanthe bottae*, *Scotocerca inquieta* and *Corvus rhipidurus*. Common winter visitors include *Monticola solitarius* and *Phoenicurus ochruros*.

Regionally threatened or declining species	
Gypaetus barbatus	Rare resident.
Gyps fulvus	Common resident.
Falco biarmicus	Scarce visitor, possibly breeds.

Species restricted wholly or largely to the Middle East	
Alectoris philbyi	Common resident.
Oenanthe lugentoides	Fairly common resident.
Serinus menachensis	Common resident.
Carduelis yemenensis	Common outside the breeding season.

■ Other threatened/endemic wildlife

Reptiles: *Agama yemenensis* (endemic), *Pristurus popovi* (endemic). Flora: there is a rich Afroalpine vegetation with many endemics.

Conservation issues

No formal conservation measures are known to have been taken. Grazing pressure appears to be heavy. Increasing levels of 'wilderness' tourism in the future may lead to local concentration of predators such as foxes *Vulpes* at picnic/garbage sites, with negative effects on ground-nesting *Alectoris philbyi*, as well as to disturbance of sensitive species such as breeding raptors locally. Any associated infrastructural developments such as upgrading of the track to a hard-surface road might also increase such human pressures on wildlife.

Further reading

Evans (1987).

009 Al-Kadan Area (Al-Hudaydah, Al-Mahwit)

15°15′N 42°18′E

Unprotected

c.6,000 ha

Site description

Rocky foothills of the Red Sea escarpment at the point where the major watercourse of Wadi Surdud flows onto the plain of the western Tihamah, north of Bajil. The foothills are dissected by deep, bouldery wadis, some of which are permanently flowing or at least retain extensive, deep pools of water all year round (e.g. Wadi al-Hawd, 8 km north of Al-Kadan). A fine parkland of *Dobera glabra* trees covers much of the silt plain (especially north of al-Kadan) and extends into the foothills, where there are also scattered trees of *Acacia mellifera*, *A. etbaica* and *Ziziphus*, shrubs (*Anisotis*, *Berchemia*, *Sageretia* and *Carissa*) and succulents (e.g. *Adenium*, *Caralluma*, *Opuntia*), all often festooned with *Cissus* and other climbers. The vegetation is denser along wadi banks and in hollows, where these trees and shrubs form thickets, together with occasional *Trichilia* and *Tamarindus* trees up to 10 m high. Most of the Tihamah plain is cultivated traditionally for rain-fed sorghum and millet, but there is also a large-scale irrigation project comprising large arable fields of maize, sorghum and banana plantations, bounded by massive, earth bunds as well as leys for dairy cattle (centred on the agricultural station at Al-Gerabi, 6 km west of Al-Kadan). The foothills are predominantly uncultivated (some sorghum and bananas), and goats, sheep, camels and cattle range over them as well as on marginal areas on the plain.

Globally threatened species

Geronticus eremita	Very rare but possibly regular non-breeding visitor (two records: one bird in November 1984, and 5–6 in May 1985).
Aquila heliaca	Scarce but regular passage migrant (3, October and November).
Falco naumanni	Common passage migrant (110, October).

1% or more of population

	Breeding (pairs)	Wintering	Passage
Bubulcus ibis	—	170 (Oct)	—

Regionally threatened or declining species

Pernis apivorus	Passage migrant.
Elanus caeruleus	Resident (min. 2 pairs).
Neophron percnopterus	Passage migrant.
Gyps fulvus	Non-breeding visitor (max. 18).
Terathopius ecaudatus	Resident (5–6, April), breeding in *Dobera* trees.
Accipiter brevipes	Scarce autumn passage migrant.
Ardeotis arabs	Scarce resident (nesting confirmed; max. 7 birds).

Species restricted wholly or largely to the Middle East

Alectoris melanocephala	Fairly common but local resident in foothills.
Pycnonotus xanthopygos	Common resident.
Hippolais languida	Fairly common passage migrant.
Sylvia mystacea	Fairly common passage migrant and winter visitor.
Turdoides squamiceps	Locally common resident.
Passer euchlorus	Abundant non-breeding visitor (max. 1,000, October).
Estrilda rufibarba	Locally common resident.

Birds

See box for key species. A diverse assemblage of Afrotropical breeding species, including *Scopus umbretta*, *Ciconia abdimii*, *Milvus migrans*, *Melierax metabates*, *Accipiter badius*, *Buteo rufinus*, *Aquila rapax*, *Aquila verreauxii*, *Hieraaetus fasciatus*, *Falco tinnunculus*, *F. pelegrinoides* (min. 2 pairs), *Coturnix delegorguei*, *Pterocles lichtensteinii*, *P. exustus*, *Streptopelia semitorquata*, *Oxylophus jacobinus*, *Centropus superciliosus*, *Apus affinis*, *Cypsiurus parvus*, *Halcyon leucocephala*, *Coracias abyssinica*, *Tockus nasutus*, *Mirafra cantillans*, *Eremopterix nigriceps*, *Cercotrichas podobe*, *Cercomela melanura*, *Cisticola juncidis*, *Terpsiphone viridis*, *Anthreptes metallicus*, *Nectarinia habessinica*, *Zosterops abyssinicus*, *Tchagra senegala*, *Ploceus galbula*, *Petronia dentata*, *Lonchura cantans* and *Emberiza tahapisi*. Open fields of the Tihamah plain support large numbers of migrants in autumn, including *Circus aeruginosus*, *C. macrourus*, *C.*

pygargus, *Calandrella brachydactyla*, *Anthus campestris*, *Motacilla flava* and *Oenanthe isabellina*. There is a major passage of raptors in autumn along the foothills, mainly of *Buteo buteo* (470, October) and *Aquila nipalensis* (2,025, October), but also with *Circaetus gallicus* (10, October), *Accipiter nisus*, *Aquila clanga* (2, October), *Hieraaetus pennatus* (4, October), *Falco subbuteo* (30, November), and small numbers of *Ciconia nigra* (1, October) and *C. ciconia* (23, November)—all are attracted to rest and feed at irrigated farmland—plus associated *Tachymarptis melba* (100, October) and *A. affinis* (200, October).

■ Other threatened/endemic wildlife
Mammals: *Papio hamadryas* (endemic). Amphibians: *Bufo tihamicus* (endemic), *Euphlyctis ehrenbergii* (endemic).

■ Conservation issues
No formal conservation measures are known to have been taken. Depletion of the water-table and destruction of *Dobera* parkland by expansion of intensive/irrigated agriculture may threaten *Ardeotis arabs* and is leading to a loss of nesting habitat for *Terathopius ecaudatus*.

010 Al-'Urj (Al-Hudaydah)
Unprotected

15°05′N 42°55′E
1,500 ha

■ Site description
A formerly undisturbed 15-km-stretch of coast, with a wide variety of natural habitats in a small area. A steep sand beach dominates, backed mainly by sand-dunes and a few areas of sabkhah. The beach is broken by a tidal inlet c.5 km south of the fishing village of Al-'Urj, at the pseudo-mouth of a wadi, and is backed here by a raised alluvial silt/gravel plain with associated 3+ m-high coastal cliffs, well-developed mangrove (5–10 ha), intertidal mud/sandflats and a sand barrier-beach. Offshore there is a fringing coral reef and seagrass beds are moderately common. The substantial seepage of fresh groundwater at the tidal inlet feeds several brackish wells and small ponds and supports an extensive coastal fringe of doum palm *Hyphaene* and date palm *Phoenix* groves/scrub (c.200 ha) as well as *Odyssea*/*Aeluropus* spiny-grass pastures on the sabkhah by the tidal inlet. The coastal, silt plain is sparsely vegetated with *Suaeda* dwarf-shrubland, grading into sparse *Panicum* grassland further inland. The main human activity is fishing, but the area is also regularly used for recreation/camping; in 1990 there were plans to build a tourist hotel. The mangrove-lined tidal inlet is probably important as a spawning ground and nursery area for shrimps/prawns and fish, and the doum palm woodland is highly valued by local fisherfolk for building/thatching material. The mangrove and spiny-grass flats are grazed by goats and camels.

■ Birds
See box for key species. The mangrove and doum palms support an interesting breeding avifauna, including *Butorides striatus*, *Milvus migrans*, *Pandion haliaetus* (1 pair), *Cypsiurus parvus*, *Acrocephalus stentoreus* (probably), *A. baeticatus* (probably), *Ploceus rueppelli* and *Lonchura cantans*. A very wide variety of coastal waterbirds occur on passage and in winter (a few in good numbers though there have never been any comprehensive counts) including *Pelecanus rufescens* (90, April) and *Sterna bengalensis* (300, October).

1% or more of population

	Breeding (pairs)	Wintering	Passage
Numenius phaeopus	—	—	240+ (Apr)

Species restricted wholly or largely to the Middle East

Dromas ardeola	Resident (max. 166, April), possibly breeding (24+ pairs feeding on mudflats, June), since there are no nearby islands/islets.
Sterna saundersi	Probably breeds (10–20 pairs).

■ Other threatened/endemic wildlife
Mammals: dolphins (probably including *Tursiops*) are frequent offshore; *Genetta felina* (rare). Reptiles: *Chelonia mydas* (E) is common offshore, and *Dermochelys coriacea* (E) has been recorded; other sea-turtle species probably also occur.

■ Conservation issues
No formal conservation measures are known to have been taken, although the establishment of marine parks has been considered in the past, and this area has been recommended for special management by a PERSGA study team in 1985. It is not known whether the planned hotel has been built, and if so, to what extent destruction of habitat, depletion of freshwater supply, pollution through waste disposal, and excessive disturbance of birds has been avoided. Campers' fires have burned down areas of the *Hyphaene* palm woodland locally.

011 Jabal Shibam (Sana'a)
Unprotected

15°02′N 43°45′E
c.5,000 ha

Site description
A relatively well-wooded area of highlands on the Red Sea scarp of western Yemen near the town of Manakhah, with scattered small areas of *Acacia* woodland, well-vegetated mountain meadows, extensive, terraced hillsides and scattered villages on hilltops. Slopes are often steep.

Birds
See box for key species. A good assemblage of Arabian-endemic and Afromontane breeding species, including *Anthus cinnamomeus* and *A. similis*.

Globally threatened species

Turdus menachensis	Fairly common resident.

Regionally threatened or declining species

Gypaetus barbatus	Resident.
Gyps fulvus	Common resident.
Parisoma buryi	Local resident.
Emberiza cineracea	Scarce winter visitor.

Species restricted wholly or largely to the Middle East

Alectoris melanocephala	Fairly common resident.
Prunella fagani	Local resident.
Oenanthe lugentoides	Common resident.
Parisoma buryi	Local resident.
Serinus rothschildi	Common resident.
Serinus menachensis	Common resident.
Carduelis yemenensis	Common resident.
Emberiza cineracea	Scarce winter visitor.

Other threatened/endemic wildlife
Butterflies: the higher slopes are likely to harbour south-west Arabian endemics such as *Cacyreus niebuhri*, *Lepidochrysops arabicus*, *Euchrysops philbyi*, *Lasiommata felix* and *Pseudotergumia tewfiki*.

Conservation issues
No formal nature conservation measures are known to have been taken. Local practises which may benefit nature have not been investigated in depth yet, but it is widely considered that the existing terrace agriculture system greatly benefits wildlife through its low intensity. Abandonment of this system due to emigration of manpower is a problem at least locally, leading to tree-cutting, deterioration of terrace walls, loss of rich topsoil reserves, and overgrazing/browsing. Road building and built development could exacerbate these problems in the future.

012 Jaza'ir al-Zubayr (Al-Hudaydah)
Unprotected

15°00′N 42°04′E
c.3,300 ha

Site description
Rocky, volcanic islands lying near the centre of the Red Sea rift. Major islands include Jabal Zubayr, Centre Peak, 'Great Quoin', 'Little Quoin', Saba and three to four others, as well as the outlying Jabal al-Tayr to the north at 15°30′N 41°47′E. There is a lighthouse on Jabal al-Tayr, and there are navigation aids on 'Little Quoin' with a resident staff to operate them. There are cold upwellings in the seas offshore in the summer, due to inflow of water from the Indian Ocean driven by monsoon winds, and resulting in very rich marine food supplies for birds, fish, cetaceans and other marine wildlife.

Birds
See box for key species. These islands have never been ornithologically surveyed, although important numbers of seabirds have been seen on and around them, and are presumed to breed, including *Phaethon aethereus* (common at Jabal al-Tayr, September [1950s]; a few, October 1975), *Sula dactylatra* (very common in area, June 1945; mostly immatures), *Sula leucogaster* (6,000–10,000 birds, April 1964, including 250 pairs with young) and *Sterna anaethetus* (may breed). Non-breeding species in the rich seas offshore include *Oceanites oceanicus* (several small groups, August 1984).

1% or more of population

	Breeding (pairs)	Wintering	Passage
Phaethon aethereus	?	—	—
Sula dactylatra	?	—	—
Sula leucogaster	3,000–5,000	—	—
Sterna anaethetus	?	—	—

Species restricted wholly or largely to the Middle East

Puffinus persicus	Possibly breeds (several offshore, August 1983).
Larus hemprichii	Probably breeds (common, June 1945).

Other threatened/endemic wildlife
The marine ecosystem offshore is unusual and highly productive. Fish: whale shark *Rhincodon typus* (I).

Conservation issues

No formal conservation measures are known to have been taken, although the establishment of marine parks has been considered in the past. Public access is restricted, which presumably provides some unintentional protection from disturbance. However the spare time activities of the permanent staff on 'Little Quoin' may cause disturbance to seabird breeding colonies. Whether fishermen visit the islands (it seems likely), and how regularly, are unknown. Feral goats exist on 'Great Quoin' and restrict the vegetation cover to a few unpalatable species, inhibiting any nesting of *Sterna anaethetus*. *Sula dactylatra* and *S. leucogaster* are particularly vulnerable to human exploitation and disturbance when nesting; the subspecies *S. d. melanops* is endemic to the western Indian Ocean, and its Yemeni breeding colonies urgently need a baseline-census, protection and monitoring to avoid the fate of similar colonies elsewhere in the Indian Ocean. The lighthouse keepers, if suitably instructed, could act as wardens and recorders. Education of navy personnel and fishermen, and the erection of signs at key landing points, are both highly desirable measures.

Further reading

Bourne (1966), Elliott (1952), Phillips (1947), Yerbury (1896).

013 **Al-Murah** (Al-Hudaydah)

Unprotected

14°53′N 43°19′E
12,500 ha

Site description

An agricultural plain east of Al-Qutay' on the eastern Tihamah (150–250 m), including the isolated outcrop of Jabal al-Maqasi (340 m), and stretching south from the broad, silt wadi-spread of Wadi Siham to the village of Al-Midman. Cultivation is mostly traditional, with many small (1 ha) fields of rain-fed sorghum and millet, bounded by small banks and set in a parkland of *Dobera glabra* trees and occasional *Acacia* and *Ziziphus* bushes. Many fields lie fallow, depending on the local rains. There are patches of more intensive agriculture, including flooded cotton fields enclosed by earth bunds 6 m high as well as irrigated banana plantations in Wadi Siham, where there are also dense thickets of *Salvadora*. To the south, broad, parallel sand-dunes occur. Around Al Midman there is an extensive area (600 ha) of thicket on stonier ground on the plain (and also a similar, smaller area to the north), dominated by mature *Acacia tortilis* trees, *Anisotes* bushes and especially succulents (*Euphorbia*, *Adenium*, *Aloe*, etc.): a rare habitat on the Tihamah. There are many scattered, small villages and homesteads.

Birds

See box for key species. The area supports a rich Afrotropical breeding avifauna, including *Bubulcus ibis* (a colony at Khalifah; see box), *Ciconia abdimii*, *Aquila rapax* (probably), *Coturnix delegorguei*, *Numida meleagris*, *Burhinus capensis*, *Oxylophus jacobinus*, *Caprimulgus nubicus*, *Merops albicollis*, *Coracias abyssinica*, *Mirafra cantillans*, *Cinnyricinclus leucogaster* and *Amandava subflava*. Passage migrants include *Sylvia nisoria* (650+, April).

1% or more of population

	Breeding (pairs)	Wintering	Passage
Bubulcus ibis	min. 100	—	—
Plegadis falcinellus	—	—	200 (Nov)

Regionally threatened or declining species

Micronisus gabar	Scarce resident.
Falco biarmicus	Recorded in May; presumably resident.
Ardeotis arabs	Locally common resident.
Grus virgo	Scarce passage migrant and winter visitor.

Species restricted wholly or largely to the Middle East

Glareola nordmanni	One spring record.
Hippolais olivetorum	One autumn record.
Passer euchlorus	Abundant non-breeding visitor to cultivation.
Carpospiza brachydactyla	One autumn record.
Estrilda rufibarba	Locally common resident or non-breeding visitor (103, October).

Other threatened/endemic wildlife

Mammals: *Papio hamadryas* (endemic).

Conservation issues

No formal conservation measures are known to have been taken. The suitability of such agricultural landscapes for *Ardeotis arabs* will almost certainly be reduced if agricultural practises are intensified, through increasing use of pesticides (especially insecticides), changes in field structure following mechanization, and changes in crops following replacement of traditional methods of irrigation or cultivation. Human activity in the area in 1985 appeared not to cause undue disturbance to *Ardeotis arabs*.

014 Wadi Rijaf (Al-Hudaydah)

also known as Wadi Hudayn, Suq al-Sabt or Sabt al-Mahrab
Unprotected

14°53´N 43°26´E
250 ha

Site description

One of two deep valleys (300–1,000 m) on the west side of Jabal Bura, a granite massif which rises very steeply from the Tihamah foothills to 2,200 m, 60 km east of Al-Hudaydah. The climate is very hot and humid; rain is frequent in summer, and after storms there is continuously flowing water in the wadi for up to a month afterwards. Large pools persist throughout the year. The best and most intact example of Afrotropical 'Sudanian' woodland left in Yemen and perhaps in Arabia. In the valley bottom is gallery forest up to 20 m high, dominated by *Ficus* and *Trichilia* at 400 m, and by *Acacia abyssinica* at 600 m, with other common trees including *Combretum* and *Berchemia*. The bouldery slopes are covered in impenetrable thicket dominated by *Acacia asak*, whilst below 400 m there is a dense shrubland of *Anisotes* bushes with numerous succulent *Euphorbia*, *Caralluma*, *Adenium* and *Aloe*. There is a small human population in the valley (less than 10 families). The wadi provides plentiful fresh water for much of the year. Cows are ranged in the woodland, and goats/sheep graze more open areas. Timber is cut for building material, firewood is gathered, and foliage is cropped for livestock forage. There is a general lack of cultivation, apart from some banana terraces created in recently cleared gallery forest and irrigated by pump. The local Seyid community (c.1,000) on Jabal Bura are especially knowledgeable on use of local plants for medicine. Eco-tourism occurs at a low and sporadic level.

Birds

See box for key species. The most complete and representative breeding assemblage of Afrotropical woodland species known in Yemen, characteristic of the Red Sea foothills. See box for key species. At least 46 species are known or presumed to breed within the site's small area, notably *Numida meleagris*, *Oxylophus jacobinus*, *Caprimulgus inornatus*, *C. nubicus* and *Tchagra senegala*, as well as very high densities of *Streptopelia semitorquata* and *Phylloscopus umbrovirens*. There is a high diversity of resident birds of prey, including *Milvus migrans*, *Accipiter badius*, *Aquila chrysaetos*, *A. verreauxii*, *Hieraaetus fasciatus*, *Falco tinnunculus*, *Otus scops pamelae* and *Bubo africanus*. A major raptor migration route passes over the site in autumn, following the Red Sea foothills and dominated by *Buteo buteo* (daily max. 200, September) and *Aquila nipalensis* (daily max. 200, October); *Pernis apivorus* is also suspected to pass through in large numbers (daily max. 200, September; thought to be this species). The passage has not been studied in detail, but it is certain that its magnitude exceeds 3,000 birds per season. Wintering raptors include *Circaetus gallicus*, *Accipiter nisus* and *Falco peregrinus*; *Terathopius ecaudatus* and *Melierax metabates* are occasional visitors from the Tihamah plain.

Globally threatened species	
Aquila heliaca	Autumn passage migrant (1, November).
Regionally threatened or declining species	
Neophron percnopterus	Scarce resident (1 pair); common passage migrant (70, April; 25, September) and winter visitor (12, January).
Gyps fulvus	Fairly common resident (10, November), breeding elsewhere on the mountain.
Micronisus gabar	Rare resident or non-breeding visitor.
Species restricted wholly or largely to the Middle East	
Alectoris melanocephala	Common resident.
Dendrocopos dorae	Scarce resident or winter visitor from higher altitudes.
Irania gutturalis	Scarce winter visitor (only known site in Yemen).
Oenanthe lugentoides	Local resident.
Sylvia leucomelaena	Winter visitor from lower altitudes.
Pycnonotus xanthopygos	Abundant resident.
Turdoides squamiceps	Common resident.
Onychognathus tristramii	Common resident.
Estrilda rufibarba	Common winter visitor.
Serinus rothschildi	Scarce winter visitor.
Carduelis yemenensis	Scarce winter visitor.

Other threatened/endemic wildlife

Mammals: *Papio hamadryas* (endemic), *Panthera pardus* (rare; one shot in 1989). Reptiles: *Varanus yemenensis* (endemic), *Pristurus flavipunctatus* (endemic), *Agama adramitana* (endemic), *Coluber variabilis* (endemic). Amphibians: *Bufo tihamicus* (endemic), *Euphlyctis ehrenbergii* (endemic). Butterflies: *Charaxes bernstorffi* (endemic). Flora: the '*Acacia abyssinica*' population may be an undescribed species.

Conservation issues

No formal conservation measures are known to have been taken. A rough vehicle track was constructed up the valley in 1983–1984, damaging the small area of gallery forest remaining and leading to erosion of adjacent slopes locally due to the high rainfall. The small banana plantations have also destroyed the gallery forest locally; it is not known whether associated pumping of irrigation water is depleting groundwater levels. Current exploitation of forest products appears to be for local use only and may be at a sustainable level. Any increases in the human population, through for example immigration, may threaten this balance. Local residents recognize and value the unusually intact nature of the forest, and the Local Council of the Bura administrative district is taking steps to ban the commercial cutting of wood, and has pointed out that local residents must be given access to cheap alternatives to firewood, i.e. butane gas cylinders, if the forest is to be preserved in the longer term. One Local Council member has recommended protection of trees and animals, and a ban on hunting.

Further reading

Scholte and Evans (in prep.), Shu' (1989), Wood (1982).

015 Nukhaylah–Ghulayfiqah (Al-Hudaydah)

Unprotected

14°30′N 43°00′E
9,000 ha

Site description

About 90 km of flat coast south from the village of Nukhaylah (c.20 km south of Al-Hudaydah) to the village of Ghulayfiqah, with mostly gentle, sand beaches and large areas of sabkhah, especially near Ghulayfiqah. Intertidal flats occur just north of Nukhaylah (c.350 ha) and at Ghulayfiqah. The narrow, sandy promontory of Ra's al-Shi'b juts 25 km north-north-west and is tipped by two flat, sandy islands. Much freshwater seepage occurs along the coast, supporting extensive date palm *Phoenix* plantations at Nukhaylah and Ghulayfiqah, as well as a c.2 km fringe of patchy mangrove *Avicennia* (associated with a small tidal inlet), doum palms *Hyphaene* and grass-flats (c.80 ha) at Nukhaylah. Coastal sand-dunes are common locally, and there are small amounts of coral reef offshore. Salt-tolerant bushes are locally common above the high water mark. Seagrass beds are particularly well-developed and widespread offshore. The major human activity along the coast is artisanal fishing. There is a deserted Turkish fort 2 km north of Nukhaylah.

Birds

See box for key species. The area has received only brief and incomplete ornithological surveys, and there is good reason to expect that numbers of some coastal waterbird species exceed 1% levels in winter and/or during migration: notable species include *Pelecanus rufescens* (29, October), *Egretta gularis* (31, October), *Platalea leucorodia* (33, January–February), *Charadrius mongolus* (120, February), *C. leschenaultii* (55, October), *Calidris ferruginea* (200, February), *Tringa totanus* (300, January), *Tringa cinerea* (170+, January), *Sterna nilotica* (32, January) and *S. saundersi* (127, October). Breeding species include *Caprimulgus nubicus*.

Globally threatened species	
Larus leucophthalmus	Fairly common passage migrant (max. 10, November).
Regionally threatened or declining species	
Threskiornis aethiopicus	Rare resident or non-breeding visitor (max. 2–4, January–February).
Micronisus gabar	Scarce resident in inland *Acacia*-lined wadis (at least 1 pair).
Species restricted wholly or largely to the Middle East	
Sterna repressa	Passage migrant.

Other threatened/endemic wildlife

No information.

Conservation issues

No formal conservation measures are known to have been taken. Current threats are not known.

016 Al-Fazzah (Al-Hudaydah)

Unprotected

14°08′N 43°07′E
3,500 ha

Site description

A 35-km-stretch of Red Sea coast between the village of Al-Mujaylis and Ra's al-Buqa, centred on the village of Al-Fazzah at the pseudo-mouth of Wadi Zabid. Most of the shoreline is an exposed, sand beach, with a small amount of intertidal mudflats in more sheltered areas. Sand-dunes are common behind the beach, especially around Al-Fazzah, and there are small areas of bare sabkhah. There are no coral reefs, seagrass beds or mangrove. Substantial subsurface seepage of fresh water supports large date palm *Phoenix* plantations at Al-Mujaylis, at Ra's al-Buqa and along Wadi Zabid 'upstream' of Al-Fazzah, as well as extensive grass pastures, *Typha* beds with *Juncus*, *Pandanus* thickets and open, shallow, brackish pools on the coastal flats. There are small areas of salt-tolerant bushes (*Suaeda*/*Zygophyllum*) in sandy areas. Artisanal fishing is the major human activity. The coastal grass flats are heavily grazed by livestock.

Birds

See box for key species. The area has received only brief and incomplete ornithological surveys, and there is good reason to expect that numbers of some coastal waterbird species exceed 1% levels in winter and/or during migration: notable species include *Egretta gularis* (20, November), *Platalea leucorodia* (19, January), *Anas penelope* (586, January), *Recurvirostra avosetta* (32, January), *Charadrius hiaticula* (60+, November) and *Calidris minuta* (200, January). Unusual but apparently regular winter visitors are *Grus virgo*, *Charadrius asiaticus* (11, January) and *Pluvialis fulva* (70, November).

Globally threatened species

Larus leucophthalmus — Fairly common passage migrant (35, November).

1% or more of population

	Breeding (pairs)	Wintering	Passage
Charadrius alexandrinus	?	?	500+ (Nov)

Species restricted wholly or largely to the Middle East

Sterna repressa — Fairly common passage migrant (100+, November).

Other threatened/endemic wildlife

No information.

Conservation issues

No formal conservation measures are known to have been taken.

017 Jabal Sumarah–Wadi Rafood–Wadi Bana (Ibb)

Unprotected

14°08′N 44°18′E
22,500 ha

Site description

One of the highest areas in southern Yemen (1,800–3,000 m), c.30 km north of Ibb and c.15 km south-west of Yarim, at the triple junction between the watersheds of the Red Sea, Indian Ocean and interior desert basin. Steep-sided but fairly flat-topped basalt mountains (up to 3,000 m) with broad slopes of boulder scree, and shallow valleys and rivulets which steepen to become ravines at lower elevations on the Red Sea scarp slope. Flat, cultivated, montane plains of loess (at c.2,400–2,600 m) fringe the north and north-east of the area. The slopes of the Red Sea scarp (down to 1,800 m) are often shrouded in mist and clouds. Traditional, low-intensity agriculture covers the plains and dominates the slopes below the highest peaks (as terraced fields). The higher, rocky slopes are covered with dense patches of low shrubbery such as *Rumex*, *Acanthus* and *Rosa*, interspersed with patchy mat-forming herbs and grasses, whilst scattered *Acacia* trees (often lopped/pollarded) and 'candelabra cactus' *Euphorbia ammak* are frequent to common on terraced slopes lower down. The main crops are sorghum and millet, with some qat *Catha edulis* on lower altitude terraces. Grazing pressure is apparently fairly low. The main Sana'a–Ta'izz road cuts through the area at Naqil Sumarah (2,800 m). The ancient agricultural terrace system is the culmination of an enormous amount of work, and is of great economic, social, cultural and historical significance.

Birds

See boxes for key species. One of the richest known assemblages of south-west Arabian endemic birds. Other notable Afromontane or wider Eritreo-Arabian endemic breeding species include *Streptopelia lugens*, *Chrysococcyx klaas*, *Anthus similis*, *Saxicola torquata*, *Oenanthe bottae*, *Monticola rufocinereus*, *Phylloscopus umbrovirens*, *Muscicapa gambagae*, *Terpsiphone viridis*, *Nectarinia osea*, *Zosterops abyssinicus*, *Corvus rhipidurus* and *Ploceus galbula*. Other raptors likely to breed include *Milvus migrans*, *Buteo rufinus*, *Falco tinnunculus* and *F. pelegrinoides* (1–2 pairs). There is a distinct concentration of migrating raptors in this area in autumn; the magnitude of the movement is unknown, but numbers are suspected to be more than 3,000 per season, and species include *Pernis apivorus*, *Milvus migrans*, *Circaetus gallicus*, *Accipiter nisus*, *Buteo buteo*, *Aquila clanga* and *A. nipalensis*. Small numbers of *Buteo buteo* (10–100) and *Aquila nipalensis* (50–100) overwinter in the area.

Globally threatened species	
Aquila heliaca	Autumn passage migrant (max. 3, November).
Falco naumanni	Common passage migrant in autumn; many hundreds appear to pass through per season (daily max. 50+, October–November), stopping off to feed on the cultivated montane plains of Qa al-Haql and Yarim, to the north.
Turdus menachensis	Uncommon resident.
Regionally threatened or declining species	
Gypaetus barbatus	Resident (min. 2 pairs).
Gyps fulvus	Resident (min. 5–10 pairs; max. 100 birds, November).
Torgos tracheliotus	One possible sighting (September 1983).
Pernis apivorus	Autumn passage migrant.
Falco biarmicus	Uncommon visitor (possibly breeds).
Emberiza cineracea	Passage migrant/winter visitor (3, October).

Species restricted wholly or largely to the Middle East	
Alectoris philbyi	Scarce resident.
Alectoris melanocephala	Fairly common resident.
Dendrocopos dorae	Uncommon resident.
Pycnonotus xanthopygos	Common resident.
Prunella fagani	Fairly common resident.
Oenanthe lugentoides	Common resident.
Parisoma buryi	Scarce resident.
Turdoides squamiceps	Fairly common resident.
Onychognathus tristramii	Common resident.
Estrilda rufibarba	Uncommon resident.
Serinus rothschildi	Fairly common resident.
Serinus menachensis	Fairly common resident.
Rhynchostruthus socotranus	Fairly common but local resident.
Carduelis yemenensis	Common resident.
Emberiza cineracea	Passage migrant/winter visitor (3, October).

■ Other threatened/endemic wildlife
Butterflies: the higher slopes are likely to harbour south-west Arabian endemics such as *Cacyreus niebuhri*, *Lepidochrysops arabicus*, *Euchrysops philbyi*, *Lasiommata felix* and *Pseudotergumia tewfiki*.

■ Conservation issues
No formal nature conservation measures are known to have been taken. Local practises which may benefit nature have not been investigated in depth yet, but it is widely considered that the existing terrace agriculture system greatly benefits wildlife through its low intensity. Abandonment of this system due to emigration of manpower is a problem at least locally, leading to tree-cutting, deterioration of terrace walls, loss of rich topsoil reserves, -and overgrazing/browsing. Road building and built development could exacerbate these problems in the future.

018 Ibb–Dhi Sufal (Ibb)
Unprotected

13°53´N 44°08´E
25,000 ha

■ Site description
A highland area (1,500–3,100 m), from a little north of Ibb to the small town of Dhi Sufal to the south-west, with the town of Jiblah (2,000 m) and Jabal al-Ta'kar (up to 3,100 m) in between. There are steep, rocky slopes and crags of mountains and valley-sides, where terraced fields predominate. The climate is the wettest in Arabia with much cloud and mist (mean annual rainfall is greater than 1,000 mm, and there is more than 2,000 mm in some years). There is a shallowly sloping agricultural plain to the west of Ibb. Major wadis such as Wadi Maytam are broad, shallow and flat, the rocky bed often with pools of standing water. The vegetation is very rich. The commonest trees are pollarded *Acacia gerardii*, *A. origena*, *A. oerfota* and *Ziziphus*, scattered or in dense hedges/patches, and large trees are frequent, including *Cordia africana*, *Trichilia emetica* and *Ficus vasta*. *Euphorbia ammak*, *Opuntia* and other succulents are frequent on stony hillsides at lower altitudes. Low bushes and undershrubs of *Acanthus*, *Rosa*, *Carissa edulis*, *Rumex*, *Solanum* and *Myrsine* are often common on uncultivated slopes. There is a generally high cover of grasses and annual herbs in uncultivated areas. Many crops are grown, especially sorghum, maize, qat and lucerne. Most uncultivated areas are browsed by goats.

■ Birds
See box for key species. Other breeding species of Afrotropical or more narrowly Eritreo-Arabian affinities include *Scopus umbretta*, *Circaetus gallicus* (possible—seen carrying nest material in February), *Melierax metabates*, *Accipiter badius*, *Aquila rapax*, *Streptopelia lugens*, *Treron waalia*, *Chrysococcyx caprius*, *C. klaas*, *Bubo africanus*, *Halcyon leucocephala*, *Tockus nasutus*, *Mirafra cantillans*, *Anthus cinnamomeus*, *A. similis*, *Oenanthe bottae*, *Monticola rufocinereus*, *Phylloscopus umbrovirens*, *Muscicapa gambagae*, *Terpsiphone viridis*, *Tchagra senegala*, *Cinnyricinclus leucogaster*, *Petronia dentata* and *Amandava subflava*. There is an autumn

Globally threatened species

Aquila heliaca	Autumn passage migrant (3, November) and winter visitor (5–10).
Falco naumanni	Passage migrant; possibly winters in small numbers.
Crex crex	Autumn passage migrant (probably in important numbers).
Turdus menachensis	Fairly common but local resident.

Regionally threatened or declining species

Neophron percnopterus	Scarce resident (min. 1 pair).
Gyps fulvus	Resident (max 15 birds).
Falco biarmicus	Scarce resident (min. 1 pair).

Species restricted wholly or largely to the Middle East

Alectoris melanocephala	Locally common resident.
Dendrocopos dorae	Fairly common but local resident.
Pycnonotus xanthopygos	Common resident.
Prunella fagani	Uncommon and local resident.
Oenanthe lugentoides	Common resident.
Parisoma buryi	Locally common resident.
Onychognathus tristramii	Common resident.
Estrilda rufibarba	Locally common resident.
Serinus rothschildi	Common resident.
Serinus menachensis	Uncommon and local resident.
Rhynchostruthus socotranus	Locally common resident.
Carduelis yemenensis	Locally frequent resident.

passage of *Ciconia ciconia*, *Accipiter nisus*, *Buteo buteo* and *Aquila nipalensis*; the magnitude of the passage is unknown, but the raptors stop off and disperse to feed, at notably high densities. There is also a strong autumn passage of *Cuculus canorus*, *Apus apus*, *Merops apiaster*, *Motacilla flava*, *Luscinia megarhynchos*, *Sylvia communis*, *Muscicapa striata* and *Oriolus oriolus*; the area is probably very important as a refuelling zone for migrant passerines in autumn. Wintering species include *Circaetus gallicus* (1–10), *Accipiter nisus*, *Buteo buteo* (10–1,000), *Aquila nipalensis* (10–100), *Hieraaetus pennatus* (1–10), *Coturnix coturnix*, *Apus apus*, and *Motacilla citreola*.

■ Other threatened/endemic wildlife

Mammals: *Papio hamadryas* (endemic). Reptiles: *Chamaeleo arabicus* (endemic), *Chamaeleo calyptratus* (endemic).

■ Conservation issues

No formal conservation measures are known to have been taken. Local practises which may benefit nature have not been investigated in depth yet, but it is widely considered that the existing terrace agriculture system greatly benefits wildlife through its low intensity. Abandonment of this system due to emigration of manpower is a problem at least locally, leading to tree-cutting, deterioration of terrace walls, loss of rich topsoil reserves, and overgrazing/browsing. Road building and built development could exacerbate these problems in the future.

019 Jaza'ir al-Hanish (Al-Hudaydah)

Unprotected

13°52′N 42°45′E
28,000 ha

■ Site description

A group of bare, steep, volcanic islands lying to the east of the central Red Sea rift. There are two major islands, Jabal al-Zuqar (14°00′N 42°45′E, 9,600 ha, rising to over 500 m) and Hanish al-Kabir (13°45′N 42°45′E, 11,640 ha, rising to 645 m), two much smaller islands (Hanish al-Saghir and Al-Mamalih or Suyul Hanish), and numerous associated islets (including Abu Ali). There are cold upwellings in the seas offshore in the summer, associated with monsoon winds and water exchanges with the Indian Ocean, and resulting in very rich marine food supplies for birds, fish, cetaceans and other marine wildlife.

■ Birds

See box for key species. Confirmed breeding species include *Sula dactylatra* (a few nesting, November 1961; a few present, December 1975) and *S. leucogaster* (nesting in large numbers, November 1961; 200 birds, June 1963, possibly nesting; many, October and December 1975). Probable breeding species include *Phaethon aethereus* (present offshore, November 1961) and *Sterna anaethetus* (large flocks, June).

Globally threatened species

Larus leucophthalmus	Present in November 1961 and had possibly nested.

1% or more of population

	Breeding (pairs)	Wintering	Passage
Sula leucogaster	200+?	—	—

Species restricted wholly or largely to the Middle East

Puffinus persicus	Possibly breeds (many offshore, December 1975 or 1976).
Larus hemprichii	Probably breeds (large numbers offshore, June 1945).
Larus leucophthalmus	Possibly breeds (see above).
Sterna repressa	Possibly breeds (large flocks offshore, June 1945).

Other threatened/endemic wildlife

The marine ecosystem offshore is unusual and highly productive. Reptiles: sea-turtles (E) nest. Fish: whale shark *Rhincodon typus* (I).

Conservation issues

No formal conservation measures are known to have been taken. Public access is restricted, thereby providing some unintentional protection from disturbance. Whether fishermen visit (it seems likely), and how regularly, are unknown. *Sula dactylatra* and *S. leucogaster* are particularly vulnerable to human exploitation and disturbance when nesting; the subspecies *S. d. melanops* is endemic to the western Indian Ocean, and its Yemeni breeding colonies urgently need a baseline-census, protection and monitoring to avoid the fate of similar colonies elsewhere in the Indian Ocean; the breeding status of *Larus leucophthalmus* also deserves urgent investigation. Education of navy personnel and fishermen, and the erection of signs at key landing points, are both highly desirable measures. The rich marine resources in the surrounding waters appear intact and unaffected by over-fishing, pollution or mass tourism.

Further reading

Morris (1962), Phillips (1947).

020 Ta'izz Wadis (Ta'izz)

Unprotected

13°39´N 44°00´E
11,000 ha

Site description

Low, stony hills and rocky outcrops dissected by relatively wide, shallow wadis, in an arc 10–15 km north-north-west to east-north-east of Ta'izz, at 1,000–1,400 m. There is a good supply of groundwater in the area, and locally in valley bottoms there are permanently wet grazing marshes of grass and *Juncus* (close-cropped by cattle) with occasional stands (up to 2 ha in extent) of 2-m-high *Typha* in the wettest areas; notable examples are in Wadi al-Malih (Al-Haima Marsh, 13°40´N 44°00´E, c.500 ha), at a former reservoir (13°38´N 44°00´E, 2 ha) whose dam burst in 1986, and at Hidhran (Wadi Dabab, 13°36´N 43°56´E, 25 ha). The marshes have a deep, blackish soil layer, resembling peat and apparently somewhat saline. An important feature is the three sewage settling/evaporation pools (8 ha) created by shallow dams across Wadi al-Malih and filled with semi-treated effluent from Ta'izz; there are extensive stretches of shallow, open shore with scattered grass tussocks and *Tamarix* bushes but little other marginal vegetation, and a few drowned, dead trees offshore. Their water-level remains relatively constant. Vegetation on surrounding hillsides is dominated by dense, low thicket of succulents (including *Euphorbia*, *Caralluma*, *Aloe*, *Adenium* and creepers of *Cissus*) set in sparse *Acacia–Commiphora* bushland (to 2.5 m) with frequent *Anisotis* shrubs. Sorghum cultivation is extensive in wadi bottoms, with fields often being lined with pollarded *Acacia* and *Ziziphus* hedges, and there are some date palm gardens. Human population density is high, with numerous small villages and isolated homesteads throughout the area. The area's groundwater is heavily exploited to supply Ta'izz. Surrounding hills are heavily grazed by sheep and goats, and the *Acacia–Commiphora* bushland is a major source of fuelwood for the region. Hidhran is a popular picnic spot. The main Ta'izz rubbish dump lies immediately north of Hidhran.

Birds

See box for key species. The grazing marshes are extremely important as the only regular wintering area for the eastern population of the globally endangered *Geronticus eremita*, known since 1985. Numbers have been declining since the maximum of 14 was recorded in that year, and the last record is of 2 adults and an immature from at least October to December 1992, with none found in December 1993, suggesting the imminent loss of the species from this site. These wetlands are also important as a representative fragment of a rare and threatened habitat in both Yemen and the Middle East. At least 43 species breed, including: waterbirds such as *Tachybaptus ruficollis* (158 birds, August), *Scopus umbretta*, *Ciconia abdimii* (16, March), *Plegadis falcinellus* (possibly: 'many', June 85) and *Porphyrio porphyrio* (probably: 2+ heard, July); raptors such as *Melierax metabates*, *Aquila rapax* and *Falco pelegrinoides*; and a full complement of Afrotropical species such as *Burhinus capensis*, *Streptopelia lugens*, *Treron waalia*, *Centropus superciliosus*, *Bubo africanus*, *Caprimulgus inornatus*, *Halcyon leucocephala*, *Merops albicollis*, *Tockus nasutus*, *Anthus cinnamomeus*, *Monticola rufocinereus*, *Muscicapa gambagae*, *Tchagra senegala*, *Nectarinia habessinica*, *Cinnyricinclus leucogaster*, *Petronia dentata*, *Amandava subflava* and *Lonchura cantans*. In winter up to 2,000 ducks have been recorded, notably *Anas clypeata*

(800, January), and other waterfowl species include *Tachybaptus ruficollis* (340, February) and *Plegadis falcinellus* (130, February). Notable passage migrants include *Ciconia nigra* (15, October), *Plegadis falcinellus* (143, October), *Himantopus himantopus* (190, October), *Tringa ochropus* (60, August), *T. hypoleucos* (125, August) and *Motacilla citreola* (5+, October). The rubbish dump and surrounding wetlands attract large numbers of post-breeding, migrant and wintering raptors to feed, drink and roost, including *Milvus migrans* (610, October), *Circus aeruginosus* (7, October), *Aquila clanga* (10, March), *A. rapax* (106, July) and *A. nipalensis* (150, March).

Globally threatened species

Geronticus eremita	Rare and declining non-breeding visitor (max. 14, October 1985).
Aquila heliaca	Scarce passage migrant (12, March) and winter visitor (1, January).

1% or more of population

	Breeding (pairs)	Wintering	Passage
Bubulcus ibis	?	100 (Feb)	350 (Oct)
Ciconia ciconia	—	265 (Feb)	150+ (Oct)
Aythya nyroca	?1	150 (Feb)	72 (Nov)

Regionally threatened or declining species

Botaurus stellaris	Not uncommon passage migrant (2+, October).
Aythya nyroca	Regular winter visitor and passage migrant (see above); probably breeds (1 pair, June).
Neophron percnopterus	Scarce passage migrant and winter visitor (3, November).
Gyps fulvus	Non-breeding visitor all year (5, November).
Falco biarmicus	Resident at high density (2+ pairs).
Falco cherrug	Frequent passage migrant (max. 3, October) and winter visitor.

Species restricted wholly or largely to the Middle East

Alectoris melanocephala	Scarce resident.
Oenanthe lugentoides	Scarce resident.
Sylvia mystacea	Scarce winter visitor.
Turdoides squamiceps	Locally common resident.
Estrilda rufibarba	Common resident (hundreds, March).
Serinus rothschildi	Fairly common but local resident.
Rhynchostruthus socotranus	Fairly common resident (max. 25, November).

■ Other threatened/endemic wildlife

Mammals: all specimens of *Gazella bilkis* (E) of known provenance came from this site, during the 1950s; the species is certainly extinct at this site now though (see below), and may well be globally extinct. Reptiles: *Chamaeleo calyptratus* (endemic).

■ Conservation issues

The area is not protected by law and no formal measures for nature conservation are known to have been taken. Details of local, traditional land-use practises and the pattern of land-ownership are not known. The close presence of the expanding city of Ta'izz is placing severe pressure on the natural resources and biodiversity of the site. Lowering of groundwater levels due to excessive water-pumping is a critical problem, which has already led to habitat destruction: boreholes in Wadi al-Malih supply nearby factories, and also possibly drinking water to the Ta'izz region. The large *Typha* marsh and permanent stream at Hidhran dried up between September 1984 and August 1985 (and were reported as completely destroyed by late 1989), for reasons that are unclear, but which presumably relate to water extraction higher up in the watershed. More than 30% of grazing marsh in Wadi Malih has been deep-ploughed for conversion to cultivation since 1985, even though the soil appears to be saline. Large areas of succulent shrubland on hillsides have been, and are being, cleared due to the high regional demand for fuelwood and cultivable land. Harvesting of remaining *Commiphora* trees for fuelwood appears to be at unsustainable levels. The sewage settlement pools were built c.1982 and are likely to disappear if further water treatment works are built in order to reuse the waste-water, e.g. for irrigation. Currently the pools may be providing some local groundwater recharge, albeit possibly polluted. There appears to be no persecution of birds, e.g. *Geronticus eremita* is relatively approachable and apparently untroubled by local human presence.

■ Further reading

Brooks *et al.* (1987), Morris (1993).

021 Mafraq al-Mukha (Ta'izz)

Unprotected

13°22'N 43°38'E
100,000 ha

■ Site description

The area in a 20 km radius of the small town of Mafraq, at the crossroads between Ta'izz, Al-Mukha and Al-Hudaydah. A gently sloping stony plain with numerous rocky outcrops, small foothills and shallow, gravelly wadis, at the eastern edge of the Tihamah (200–500 m). A sparse scattering of *Acacia ehrenbergiana* bushes is the main vegetation, but sometimes quite dense *Acacia–Commiphora* bushland occurs on flatter areas close to the hills.

The main watercourse, Wadi Rasyan, has running water, possibly all year round, and supports large date palm gardens at Al-Barh. Human population density is low.

Birds

An important raptor migration 'bottleneck' in autumn, also with a representative breeding assemblage of species characteristic of *Acacia–Commiphora* bushland. See box for key species. Volume of raptor passage is sure to exceed 3,000 birds per season. Most pass over at high altitude, unless driven low by strong southerly headwinds, but large numbers descend to roost in the area at night, and raptors are attracted to drink at the wadis as well. Species include *Milvus migrans* (273, November), *Buteo buteo* (55, November), *Aquila clanga* (6, November), *A. nipalensis* (168, November), *Accipiter nisus* (50, October) and *A. brevipes* (100, October). Small numbers of *Ciconia ciconia* (11, November) and *Ciconia nigra* (11, November) migrate through, and small numbers of *Ciconia ciconia* winter (60). Large numbers of passerine migrants occur in 'falls' in the area in autumn, including *Cercotrichas galactotes*, *Oenanthe isabellina*, *O. oenanthe* and shrikes *Lanius*. Other breeding species include *Scopus umbretta*, *Falco pelegrinoides*, *Pterocles lichtensteinii*, *Tockus nasutus*, *Nectarinia habessinica* and *Amandava subflava* (possibly).

Globally threatened species	
Aquila heliaca	Frequent passage migrant (6, November).
Falco naumanni	Common passage migrant (80, October).
Regionally threatened or declining species	
Pernis apivorus	Passage migrant (5, September), probably much commoner than figures suggest.
Neophron percnopterus	Passage migrant and non-breeding visitor (60, November).
Gyps fulvus	Resident (24, November).
Terathopius ecaudatus	Scarce visitor, may breed.
Falco biarmicus	Passage migrant (1, November); may breed.
Falco cherrug	Passage migrant (1, November).
Species restricted wholly or largely to the Middle East	
Alectoris melanocephala	Locally frequent resident.
Sylvia mystacea	Winter visitor.
Sylvia leucomelaena	Resident.

Other threatened/endemic wildlife

Mammals: *Genetta felina* (rare).

Conservation issues

No formal conservation measures are known to have been taken. The low population density and the lack of a bird-hunting tradition mean that roosting raptors are relatively safe. Clearance of *Acacia–Commiphora* bushland for irrigated cultivation may occur locally in future.

022 Bab al-Mandab–Mawza (Ta'izz, Aden)

Unprotected

12°50′N 43°26′E
c.100,000 ha

Site description

A rocky promontory jutting out at the south-west extremity of Yemen towards Djibouti. To the east is a broad sand beach stretching c.5 km east to As-Suqayya. To the north-east of Bab al-Mandab a series of well-vegetated wadis dissect the foothills. The barren, mostly rocky island of Perim (also known as Barim or Miyun) lies offshore in the straits. To the north, a relatively undisturbed succession of semi-natural vegetation extends from the coast to the foothills across the stony Tihamah plain, with extensive dwarf-shrubland, grassland and *Acacia–Commiphora* bushland. Dhubab Flats (12°55′N 43°24′E, 100–200 ha) is a stretch of at least 3 km of coastal lagoons and flats extending south from the village of Dhubab and possibly continuing to the Bab al-Mandab.

Birds

See box for key species. This is probably the most important area in Yemen for the study of bird migration. The site is a major bottleneck for soaring, migratory birds, especially birds of prey, flying between Africa and their Eurasian breeding grounds, mainly *Aquila nipalensis* and *Buteo buteo*. This passage has been largely established by observations in Djibouti; there has been little opportunity to survey at Bab al-Mandab. From very limited observations it appears that the promontory and neighbouring areas, particularly the nearby vegetated wadis, are important stop-over points for passerine migrants and at least in spring there are good numbers of *Cercotrichas galactotes*, *Sylvia nisoria*, *S. atricapilla*, *Phylloscopus trochilus*, *Oriolus oriolus* and *Cinnyricinclus leucogaster*. Only one very brief count on a small part of Dhubab Flats has been carried out, and this showed the lagoon/saltflat system to be a good area for waders, notably *Dromas ardeola*, *Limicola falcinellus* and *Tringa cinerea*. A full survey of the whole complex would doubtless show the site to be

Globally threatened species

Larus leucophthalmus	Breeding was recorded on Perim in 1857; current breeding status is unknown, but the species occurs regularly in good numbers offshore as a passage migrant (max. 45).

Species restricted wholly or largely to the Middle East

Puffinus persicus	Large feeding concentrations occur off-shore.
Dromas ardeola	May breed.

one of the richest coastal wetlands in Yemen. Offshore there are major movements of seabirds (notably *Oceanites oceanicus*, skuas, gulls, *Sterna bergii*, and *S. bengalensis*) and of waders (notably *Numenius phaeopus* and *Phalaropus lobatus*).

Other threatened/endemic wildlife

Mammals: *Gazella* sp. (globally threatened). Reptiles: *Chelonia mydas* (E) occurs offshore, and the beach 5 km east of Al-Suqayya may be a nesting locality; *Eretmochelys imbricata* (E) is reported to nest on Perim.

Conservation issues

No formal nature conservation measures are known to have been taken. However, due to military security, the area has apparently been little visited or used, and it continues to receive this unintentional protection.

Further reading

Welch and Welch (1988).

023 The Wooded Mahra (Al-Ghayda)

Unprotected

16°31′N 52°46′E
c.15,000 ha

Site description

A well-wooded escarpment (up to 800 m) extending 30 km from the Omani border west-south-west along the coastline and c.5 km inland. The scarp descends directly down to the sea, and there is little or no coastal plain. The south-west monsoon brings mist and rain to the south-west facing slopes in late summer and autumn, when the mostly deciduous vegetation springs into leaf and the otherwise poor herb layer is transformed. By spring the landscape is brown and arid except where water flows permanently through the few wadis that dissect the hills. The tree cover on hillsides is mainly dense *Anogeissus dhofarica*/*Commiphora habessinica* woodland with abundant *Adenium obesum* and in places *Acacia senegal*. The tree canopy is generally c.3–4 m high and there are occasional *Boscia arabica* and *Steniegia* trees. Vegetation is much richer in wadis, with *Tamarindus* (managed groves), *Anogeissus*, *Acacia nilotica* and palms, with occasional other trees such as *Delonix elata* and *Ficus*. These areas have a rich understorey, and climbing species are notable, e.g. *Jasminum*, *Capparis*, *Cissus*. The human population density is not high, and largely settled pastoralists who use the hills as rangeland.

Birds

There is a rich breeding assemblage of restricted-range and Afrotropical species, often at high densities; see box for key species. Other notable breeding species include *Chrysococcyx caprius*, *Otus scops pamelae*, *Halcyon leucocephala*, *Anthus similis*, *Cercomela melanura*, *Terpsiphone viridis*, *Nectarinia habessinica*, *N. osea*, *Zosterops abyssinicus*, *Tchagra senegala*, *Lonchura cantans* and *Emberiza tahapisi*. The diversity of resident birds of prey does not appear to be high, but *Hieraaetus fasciatus*, *Falco tinnunculus* and *F. pelegrinoides* almost certainly breed.

Species restricted wholly or largely to the Middle East

Alectoris melanocephala	Resident at high density.
Oenanthe lugentoides	Resident.
Sylvia leucomelaena	Resident in good numbers.
Onychognathus tristramii	Resident.
Rhynchostruthus socotranus	Resident at locally high density.

Other threatened/endemic wildlife

Mammals: *Caracal caracal* (rare) and *Canis lupus* (V). Reptiles: *Chamaeleo arabicus* (endemic), *Hemidactylus yerburii* (endemic) and *Coluber thomasi* (endemic); sea-turtles, probably *Chelonia mydas* (E), commonly nest on the sand beaches.

Conservation issues

No formal nature conservation measures are known to have been taken. However it is reported that the tribesmen meet at least annually to discuss the protection of the woodland. The whole of the Mahra woods are heavily grazed by goats, camels and cattle, leading to the paucity of a herb/grass ground flora—though this does not appear to have had an adverse effect on the bird fauna, several species of which are at very high densities. Deforestation is potentially a major threat but the area can cope with the low level of cutting and clearance carried out for fuelwood and animal fodder at the present human population density.

024 Abdullah Gharib Lagoons (Al-Ghayda)

Unprotected — 16°21´N 52°21´E — c.50 ha

Site description

Situated 20 km north-east of Al-Ghayda, these large coastal lagoons lie either side of the village of Abdullah Gharib. They are separated from the sea by sand-dunes, surrounded by extensive fringes of saline mud, and set in a dusty sand and gravel plain with a poor cover of salt-tolerant plants.

Birds

An important feeding and roosting area for gulls and terns, and to a lesser extent waders. See box for key species; smaller numbers of other terns occur, notably *Sterna caspia*. This coast attracts very large numbers of migrant gulls *Larus* in autumn, with 30,000 (80% *L. fuscus*) counted along 50 km in November.

1% or more of population

	Breeding (pairs)	Wintering	Passage
Larus hemprichii	—	—	1,700
Larus fuscus	—	—	c.2,400 (Nov)
Sterna bergii	—	—	1,700
Sterna sandvicensis	—	—	600

Species restricted wholly or largely to the Middle East

Larus hemprichii	Non-breeding visitor (see above).

Other threatened/endemic wildlife

No information.

Conservation issues

No formal nature conservation measures are known to have been taken. The only likely threat to the sites is excessive disturbance of birds by human activity.

025 Desert West of Al-Ghayda (Al-Ghayda)

Unprotected — 16°13´N 51°49´E — 5,000+ ha

Site description

An extensive and largely uninhabited desert plain of silt and gravel, centred c.60 km west of Al-Ghayda, with little vegetation except for occasional patches of *Acacia* scrub and seasonal grasses and herbs.

Birds

This is the only area in Yemen where *Torgos tracheliotus* is known to currently occur. See box for key species. Other breeding species include *Pterocles lichtensteinii*, *P. coronatus* (500, October), *P. exustus* (500, October) and *Cercomela melanura*.

Globally threatened species

Chlamydotis undulata	Reported to have wintered in the area formerly, and may still do so.

Regionally threatened or declining species

Neophron percnopterus	Good numbers in April 1993.
Torgos tracheliotus	Resident (14, April 1993).

Species restricted wholly or largely to the Middle East

Ammoperdix heyi	Resident.
Sylvia leucomelaena	Resident.
Turdoides squamiceps	Resident.
Onychognathus tristramii	Resident.

Other threatened/endemic wildlife

Reptiles: *Pristurus collaris* (endemic).

Conservation issues

No formal nature conservation measures are known to have been taken. The southern part of Yemen is relatively poor for birds of prey and for vultures in particular. The concentration on this plain is therefore likely to signify a regular supply of dead domestic animals not found in other areas. As long as present levels of grazing continue, and poisons are not used, there appear to be no imminent threats.

026 Ra's Fartak (Al-Ghayda)

Unprotected — 15°35´N 52°10´E — c.10,000 ha

Site description

The easternmost prominent headland in Yemen. The climate is assumed to be much like that of the adjacent Dhofar coast of Oman, with strong winds and mist cloaking the coast during much of the summer monsoon. The monsoon winds induce major marine upwelling offshore, especially between July and September. Inland is rocky with *Acacia–Commiphora* bushland.

Birds

A major feeding area for a representative assemblage of pelagic seabirds characteristic of the south Arabian monsoon upwelling, located unusually close to the coast, as identified by extensive ship-based surveys offshore. See box for key species. There are also large, offshore, feeding flocks of seabirds, including *Puffinus carneipes*, *P. pacificus*, *P. persicus* (see box) and *Oceanites oceanicus* during July–September, and of *Phalaropus lobatus* in winter. Other seabirds occurring further offshore are *Pelagodroma marina*, *Oceanodroma monorhis*, *Fregetta tropica*, *Stercorarius pomarinus* and *S. parasiticus*.

Species restricted wholly or largely to the Middle East

Bulweria fallax	Large feeding flocks occur offshore in August.
Puffinus persicus	Non-breeding visitor: large, feeding flocks occur offshore.
Alectoris melanocephala	Resident inland.
Larus hemprichii	Large numbers feed offshore and roost onshore, June–September.
Oenanthe lugentoides	Resident inland.
Sylvia leucomelaena	Resident inland.
Onychognathus tristramii	Resident inland.

Other threatened/endemic wildlife

Mammals: *Capra nubiana* (I) occurs inland.

Conservation issues

No formal nature conservation measures are known to have been taken. There is apparently no immediate threat of over-fishing in the area.

Further reading

Bailey (1966).

027 Qishn Beach (Al-Ghayda)

Unprotected

15°26′N 51°45′E
c.100 ha

Site description

A long, shallow beach c.6 km in length backed by dunes and (close to Qishn village) by cultivated fields and date palm groves. The track to Ras Fartak runs along the ridge of the dunes to the seaward side of which are a few small pools.

Birds

See box for key species. Important for non-breeding and migratory *Larus hemprichii* and may be important for waders on passage; up to 300 *Calidris alba* have been observed. *Sterna nilotica* is probably an abundant passage migrant in autumn (September–December). Other breeding birds of the hinterland include *Cercomela melanura*.

1% or more of population

	Breeding (pairs)	Wintering	Passage
Phalacrocorax nigrogularis	—	30,000	—
Larus hemprichii	—	—	7,800

Species restricted wholly or largely to the Middle East

Phalacrocorax nigrogularis	Flocks numbering up to 30,000 feed and roost along this coast.
Alectoris melanocephala	Resident.
Oenanthe lugentoides	Resident.
Onychognathus tristramii	Resident.

Other threatened/endemic wildlife

Mammals: *Sousa chinensis* (K; common inshore). Reptiles: *Chelonia mydas* (E; possible nesting site).

Conservation issues

No formal nature conservation measures are known to have been taken. The concentration of birds must be a reflection of the richness of the sea for fish.

028 Wadi Hajar (Shabwa)

Unprotected

14°06′N 48°42′E
50–100 ha

Site description

A sandy wadi with permanently running water that drains into the Gulf of Aden, west of Mukalla. The wadi is obviously a very important source of irrigation water and there is much agriculture in the surrounding area. The whole wadi system and its associated sandy fringes have been stabilized by the planting of the introduced shrub *Prosopis juliflora*. The river has been dammed c.3–4 km from its mouth and extensive *Typha* beds have developed. There appears to be much clearance of native trees for firewood and agriculture, and the wadi is much used for local water supply and washing.

Birds

The wadi has an unusual flora and fauna, being one of the few, permanently running freshwater streams in southern Yemen: the wadi bed itself has apparently breeding *Alcedo cristata* (the only known site in Arabia) and *Amaurornis phoenicurus* has been recorded in habitat which could be suitable for breeding. There are high densities of birds typical of the south Yemen lowlands. See box for key species; others include *Streptopelia senegalensis*, *Oena capensis*, *Merops orientalis*, *Cercotrichas podobe*, *Prinia gracilis*, *Anthreptes metallicus*, *Ploceus galbula* and *Corvus rhipidurus*. The site is clearly an important resting and feeding place for migrants, especially warblers.

Species restricted wholly or largely to the Middle East	
Ammoperdix heyi	Resident.
Pycnonotus xanthopygos	Resident.
Sylvia leucomelaena	Resident.

Other threatened/endemic wildlife

Mammals: *Vulpes rueppelli* (K); in the surrounding hills there are said to be *Panthera pardus* (rare), *Canis lupus* (V), *Capra nubiana* (I). Reptiles: *Pristurus ornithocephalus* (endemic), *Stenodactylus pulcher* (endemic). Amphibians: *Bufo dhufarensis* (endemic), *Euphlyctis ehrenbergii* (endemic). Flora: Bankoualé Palm *Livistona carinensis* (rare endemic; the only site in Arabia, at Madi in the upper wadi).

Conservation issues

No formal conservation measures are known to have been taken. However, while the wadi continues as a permanent running water system, the threats to this area are relatively low. The damming of the river c.3–4 km from the mouth has not so far reduced the flow to a level of concern and indeed may have enhanced the wadi through the creation of *Typha* beds, though the ornithological interest of these is not fully known. Agricultural intensification away from the wadi banks is not a serious threat but clearance of native trees may be. Disturbance from human activities is high but the impenetrable nature of the *Prosopis juliflora* scrub mitigates this. Whilst this site is important it should be noted that much of its stability relies on an introduced species of tree.

029 Wadi Jahr (Abyan)

Unprotected

13°58′N 46°23′E
c.500 ha

Site description

A deep rocky wadi up to 1 km wide running east to west at the edge of a rather bare, stony, silt plateau at an altitude of 600 m. The plateau vegetation is dominated by *Acacia–Commiphora* bushland. The gravel floor of the wadi bed is dominated by *Tamarix* with *Acacia* and *Commiphora*, some in dense clumps. Surface water flow along the wadi bed may be permanent and there are some large pools with *Typha* beds. There is some rain-fed agriculture, and honey production is an important activity. The whole area is thinly populated.

Birds

A relatively well-vegetated area with running water in the otherwise barren landscapes of interior southern Yemen. See box for key species; other breeding species include *Scopus umbretta*, *Pterocles lichtensteinii*, *Caprimulgus nubicus* and *Cercotrichas podobe*. Considerable numbers of spring migrant passerines occur.

Species restricted wholly or largely to the Middle East	
Alectoris melanocephala	Resident on the edges of the wadi.
Ammoperdix heyi	Resident on the edges of the wadi.
Sylvia leucomelaena	Good numbers are resident in the *Acacia–Commiphora* bushland.
Estrilda rufibarba	Resident.

Other threatened/endemic wildlife

Amphibians: *Bufo arabicus* (endemic), *Euphlyctis ehrenbergii* (endemic).

Conservation issues

No formal nature conservation measures are known to have been taken. However there is little threat to the area presently. It is important that the tree cover of the wadi bed is not cleared for agriculture though there are no signs that this is likely in the near future.

030 **Islands off Bir Ali** (Al-Ghayda)

Unprotected

13°50'N 48°20'E
c.300 ha

Site description

Three islands (Baraqa, Sikha and Hallaniyah) lying less than 10 km off Bir Ali on the Gulf of Aden coast. Hallaniyah is flat and rocky. There is a trade in guano, the islands being visited by boats from Aden which may take off c.365–730 tonnes per year.

Birds

See box for key species. The apparent scale of the guano trade indicates substantial use of the islands by seabirds, and it is suspected that further surveys will reveal that more than 1% of the populations of *Phalacrocorax nigrogularis* and *Larus hemprichii* breed there.

Species restricted wholly or largely to the Middle East	
Phalacrocorax nigrogularis	Breeding in 1950s on Baraqa and Sikha during the summer; post-breeding flocks of thousands occur offshore in September.
Larus hemprichii	Breeding in 1950s on Halaniya, July–August.

Other threatened/endemic wildlife

No information.

Conservation issues

No formal nature conservation measures are known to have been taken. It is not known whether the site is threatened or facing any problems. The apparently continuing off-take of guano suggests that the seabird populations still breed in considerable numbers—however seabird breeding colonies on offshore islands are very sensitive to a variety of human impacts, and the lack of current information hinders effective conservation of the birds and the economically valuable guano resource.

Further reading

Smith (1956).

031 **Wadi al-Birayn** (Dhamar)

Unprotected

13°39'N 44°15'E
1,000 ha

Site description

A large wadi system (part of the headwaters of Wadi Rima) dissecting the western ramparts in a westerly direction from the Dhamar highland plain, the wadi starting c.20 km north-west of Dhamar and descending through an altitudinal range of c.2,000–2,350 m. Below the rocky cliff faces and slopes that border the wadi, the sides are richly vegetated with trees and scrub (with much montane scrub on the higher slopes), and lower down the wadi bottom and sides support an ancient agricultural terrace system including coffee and orange groves. The lower reaches give way to drier *Euphorbia*-dominated slopes. Scrub, though sparse in places, probably covers less than 60% of the area, with 30% agriculture and 10% woodland, much of the latter in clumps in the deepest part of the wadi ravines. There are small settlements, increasing in size towards lower altitudes. The site is a typical example of a well-managed, terraced wadi system of the western ramparts; the upper slopes are not highly managed for agriculture and would repay further study.

Birds

See box for key species. The wadi supports a good variety of species typical of the western ramparts, including six endemics, and there may well be further endemic species present there and on the higher slopes (see box). Other breeding species include *Hieraaetus fasciatus* and *Falco pelegrinoides*.

Regionally threatened or declining species	
Gypaetus barbatus	Resident.
Gyps fulvus	Resident in moderate numbers and probably nests on the cliffs at c.2,000 m.

Species restricted wholly or largely to the Middle East	
Alectoris melanocephala	Resident.
Dendrocopos dorae	May occur among trees in the wadi clefts.
Prunella fagani	May occur on the higher slopes.
Oenanthe lugentoides	Resident.
Turdus menachensis	May occur among trees in the wadi clefts.
Estrilda rufibarba	Resident.
Serinus rothschildi	Resident.
Serinus menachensis	Resident.
Carduelis yemenensis	Resident.

Other threatened/endemic wildlife

None known to BirdLife International.

Conservation issues

No formal conservation measures are known to have been taken. However, provided the present agriculture practices continue (low-intensity farming on upper slopes of the wadi, becoming more intensive lower down), this site is relatively unthreatened. Tree-cutting and overgrazing are problems locally; further removal of trees, particularly the scattered acacias on the edge of the terraces, would be a major threat. Human persecution of birds of prey does not appear to occur.

032 Jabal Iraf (Ta'izz)

Unprotected

13°07′N 44°15′E
2,000 ha

Site description

A rocky plateau at 1,450–1,680 m, the scarp of which was the former border between northern and southern Yemen and which overlooks the coastal plains to the south. On the plateau itself is possibly the largest remaining area of juniper *Juniperus excelsa* woodland in Yemen. There is a variety of other trees, especially *Acacia*, and the woodland forms c.30% cover. There is a very rich herb and grass layer covering c.50% of the area and in places there is light cultivation. Jabal Iraf is one of the most scenically beautiful places in southern Yemen.

Birds

See box for key species. The relatively undisturbed woodland holds several endemics in good numbers (see box). In addition the densities of *Monticola rufocinereus* and *Phylloscopus umbrovirens* are particularly high for Yemen. *Otus scops pamelae* breeds, as does *Caprimulgus inornatus* (perhaps as many as 10 pairs) and almost certainly *Chrysococcyx klaas*.

Species restricted wholly or largely to the Middle East	
Alectoris melanocephala	Resident (c.20 pairs).
Dendrocopos dorae	Resident (2–3 pairs).
Estrilda rufibarba	Resident (20 pairs).
Serinus rothschildi	Resident (at least 100 pairs).
Rhynchostruthus socotranus	Resident (10–15 pairs).

Other threatened/endemic wildlife

Mammals: *Papio hamadryas* (endemic). Reptiles: *Telescopus dhara* (endemic to the montane periphery of Arabia) and *Pristurus flavipunctatus* (endemic). Amphibians: *Bufo arabicus* (endemic) and *B. dhufarensis* (endemic). Flora: there are many restricted-range or endemic plants.

Conservation issues

No formal nature conservation measures are known to have been taken. Grazing is currently at a low, sustainable level, but if it were to intensify it would almost certainly pose a threat, as would any intensification of cultivation. While tree-cutting for fuelwood by the few people dwelling on the plateau is at only a low level, there are signs that trucks are coming in to log *Juniperus*, and this must represent the greatest threat to the intactness of the area's habitats.

033 Aden (Aden)

Unprotected

12°45′N 45°04′E
c.10,000 ha

Site description

The area of the town and harbour of Aden includes mudflats, saltpans and a beach at Khor Maksar and a large area of rich marshland caused by a long-established sewage outflow at Hiswa. The outer harbour is over 10 m deep at low tide. Steep, rocky, rather barren hills flank either side of Aden harbour, reaching up to c.540 m. There is a refuse tip at Dar Musabein. Little is known about present human activities and uses of the area apart from as a harbour for shipping; possible uses are artisanal fishing, aquaculture, salt production on pans, and recreation.

Birds

An important coastal wetland for wintering and migrating waterbirds; see box for key species. The most important feeding area for waders is the mudflats at Khor Maksar. Other notable wintering and/or migrating waterbird species include *Pelecanus rufescens* (150 non-breeding birds, July), *Plegadis falcinellus* (135, November), *Phoenicopterus ruber* (several thousands, November), *Recurvirostra avosetta* (100, November), *Pluvialis squatarola* (250, November), *Calidris ferruginea* (1,500, January) and *Limosa limosa* (200, November). Some of these species' counts are not far below internationally important levels and might exceed them if coverage was improved. An unidentified species of *Apus* has been recorded fairly regularly over the city in all months between April and July (daily max. 50+), and may be *A. berliozi*, possibly breeding on cliffs nearby or inland. Notable passage migrants include *Aquila clanga* (15–20, November; also a winter visitor in smaller numbers) and *Sterna bergii*, of which 'huge' flocks have been recorded in March, most likely concentrations of pre-breeding birds from the huge colony on the Saba islands (Djibouti) south-west of the Bab al-Mandab. There is a major passage of *Lanius* spp. during April–May. Many rare species have been recorded over the past 100 years, including the globally threatened *Haliaeetus leucogaster* and *Limnodromus semipalmatus*. Many of the bird counts in this account date from the 1950s.

Globally threatened species

Aquila heliaca	Passage migrant (5, March) and winter visitor.
Larus leucophthalmus	Passage migrant and winter visitor in small numbers.

1% or more of population

	Breeding (pairs)	Wintering	Passage
Egretta gularis	—	—	300 (Nov)
Platalea leucorodia	—	—	170 (Sep)
Himantopus himantopus	—	—	300 (Nov)
Charadrius mongolus/leschenaultii	—	900	1,200 (Aug)
Limicola falcinellus	—	60 (Feb)	125 (May)
Tringa totanus	—	—	500 (Aug)
Sterna nilotica	—	200	200 (Nov)
Sterna caspia	—	140	200 (Nov)
Sterna bergii	650	—	1,300 (Aug)

Regionally threatened or declining species

Neophron percnopterus	Non-breeding visitor all year; numbers have greatly declined since c.100 years ago, when up to c.1,350 roosted on the hills above the town in October.
Grus virgo	At least one record of wintering or passage birds in the 1980s (40+ at Hiswa).

Species restricted wholly or largely to the Middle East

Dromas ardeola	Common passage migrant (max. 300, September) and winter visitor.
Larus hemprichii	Abundant in winter and during passage seasons.
Pycnonotus xanthopygos	Resident.
Estrilda rufibarba	Occurred at Hiswa, at least formerly.

Other threatened/endemic wildlife

Reptiles: *Pristurus ornithocephalus* (endemic).

Conservation issues

No formal nature conservation measures are known to have been taken. The intertidal and shallow subtidal areas are presumably threatened by land-claim and dredging, and other problems which may be currently occurring are water pollution and excessive disturbance of waterfowl. However there is almost no current information on the status of the site. The introduced and commensal population of *Corvus splendens* underwent a population explosion during the 1970s and early 1980s, eventually numbering hundreds of thousands and becoming a public health hazard and a major nuisance; a control programme has been partially successful.

Further reading

Ash (1984, 1988).

034 Hiswat al-Hugayma (Aden)

Unprotected

12°41′N 43°52′E
at least 25,000 ha

Site description

Extensive area of gravel plain with well-developed, relatively dense *Acacia* savanna (up to 11 or more trees per ha) east of Bab al-Mandab, stretching from the coast to foothills, and at least from al-Hajaf to beyond Bir Ras al-Ara. The vegetation comprises mostly *Acacia tortilis* woodland with *Panicum* grassland and *Zygophyllum* in gravel areas. Plant cover is densest in shallow wadis and runnels that drain from the inland hills to the coast, where the grassland is best-developed. This area may be the most extensive and intact woodland savanna in Yemen. The area is not highly populated and is used by the local inhabitants for grazing of livestock, notably goats and camels.

Birds

See box for key species. Breeding species in good numbers include *Pterocles lichtensteinii*, *P. exustus*, *Alaemon alaudipes*, and especially *Lanius excubitor* which occurs here probably at a higher density than anywhere else in the country. The site's good cover of vegetation and closeness to the Bab al-Mandab make it a very important stop-over point for migrants.

Regionally threatened or declining species

Ardeotis arabs	Probably occurs in only small numbers, though in the recent past it was apparently much commoner.

Species restricted wholly or largely to the Middle East

Turdoides squamiceps	Resident in good numbers.

■ Other threatened/endemic wildlife

Mammals: unidentified *Gazella* (rare) are reported to occur in the area. Reptiles: *Pristurus ornithocephalus* (endemic), *P. crucifer* (endemic), *P. flavipunctatus* (endemic), *Varanus griseus* (rare).

■ Conservation issues

No formal nature conservation measures are known to have been taken. The sparseness of the grass is clearly due to heavy grazing, which probably has a negative impact on the *Ardeotis arabs* population. Tree-cutting is a problem locally. *Ardeotis arabs* used to be shot in this area and this may still occur. Fire is a potential threat to the habitat.

035 Qalansiya Lagoon, Socotra (Aden)

Unprotected

12°42′N 53°30′E
c.100 ha

■ Site description

A coastal wetland in north-west Socotra, said to be a brackish lagoon in 1964 (thus possibly sealed off from the tide at that time by a sandbar), but it is now used as an alternative, bad-weather harbour for fishing boats and thus must now be a tidal inlet. Inland there is a lowland plain, and the vegetation is mainly *Croton* shrubland (relatively thick and tall in 1964). The fishery is sprats and shellfish.

■ Birds

See box for key species. A variety of waterfowl have been recorded in November 1993, including ducks, herons, waders, gulls (1,500+ roosting) and terns. No other information is available.

Species restricted wholly or largely to the Middle East	
Larus hemprichii	Occurs commonly.

■ Other threatened/endemic wildlife

No information.

■ Conservation issues

See p. 352.

036 Jabal Ma'lih Escarpment/Badiya Qalansiya, Socotra (Aden)

Unprotected

12°38′N 53°29′E
10,000 ha

■ Site description

An upland area of north-west Socotra (600–750 m) with sub-montane, semi-deciduous thicket and montane thicket. This is the main sheep-grazing region in the western part of Socotra; some goats are also present.

■ Birds

See box for key species. No other information: not yet surveyed.

Species restricted wholly or largely to the Middle East	
Phalacrocorax nigrogularis	Said by local people to breed or roost on the cliffs of Ra's Baduwa and to have formerly been taken for food.

■ Other threatened/endemic wildlife

Flora: the escarpment and deep gullies are some of the richest for endemics such as *Aloe squarrosa*, *Punica protopunica* and *Turraea socotrana*.

■ Conservation issues

See p. 352.

037 Ra's Hebaq, Socotra (Aden)

Unprotected

12°39′N 53°58′E
600 ha

■ Site description

A coastal headland on north-west Socotra with cliffs, a limestone escarpment, rocky slopes and limestone hills (to 550 m). It is well vegetated with open *Croton* and *Jatropha* shrubland (a prime example of the 'succulent shrubland' for which the island is famed).

Human activities include grazing/browsing of goats, rock removal for road construction, and constant traffic due to road to airport and to main secondary school of island.

Birds

See box for key species. *Onychognathus blythii* is also present. The site is well-placed for observing seabird passage.

Species restricted wholly or largely to the Middle East

Nectarinia balfouri	Resident.
Onychognathus frater	Resident.

Other threatened/endemic wildlife

Reptiles: *Pristurus sokotranus* and *Mabuya socotrana* are common (both endemic).

Conservation issues

See p. 352.

038 Airport Dunes, Socotra (Aden)

Unprotected

12°37′N 53°52′E
c.200 ha

Site description

A sand and gravel coastal plain in northern Socotra with *Croton* shrubland. Fishing occurs offshore, and shell-middens have been observed.

Birds

See box for key species.

Globally threatened species

Cisticola haesitatus	Uncommon resident, occurring at a higher density than any other part of the island so far investigated.

Species restricted wholly or largely to the Middle East

Cisticola haesitatus	See above.

Other threatened/endemic wildlife

No information.

Conservation issues

See p. 352.

039 Muqadrihon Pass, Socotra (Aden)

Unprotected

12°37′N 54°01′E
200 ha

Site description

The pass lies at c.600 m between the Hadibo plain in the north of Socotra and Wadi Ayhaft (site 041), and is at the junction of the granite Hajhir mountains (site 047) to the south-east and of the limestone of the Regid plateau (site 042) to the north-west. Probably the wettest area on the island, catching monsoon rain (especially June–September) and subjected to very strong, dry winds during the rest of the year. The vegetation is luxuriant, with sub-montane, semi-deciduous thicket dominated by *Buxus hildebrandtii* and with emergent *Dracaena cinnabari*, as well as 11 other trees/shrubs (10 being endemic). A continuation of the dense woodland of Wadi Ayhaft, particularly rich on southern slopes. Human activities include grazing of goats and tourism.

Birds

As for Wadi Ayhaft, but the site has not been surveyed yet.

Other threatened/endemic wildlife

Flora: rare and endangered endemic species present include *Punica protopunica*, *Dorstenia gigas*, *Begonia socotrana* and *Dirachma socotrana*.

Conservation issues

See p. 352. A recent drought led to overgrazing, and more and more livestock have been left to graze untended in recent years. The area would be very vulnerable to any road-building or the digging of new wells; future development programmes pose the main threat.

Further reading

Bazara'a *et al.* (1991).

040 Shidahah, Socotra (Aden)

Unprotected

12°37′N 54°09′E
c.2,200 ha

Site description

Open, stony, limestone foothills (50–100 m) in northern Socotra, well-vegetated with open sub-montane shrubland (often succulent) with emergents and low cushions. By water in this zone, particularly in wadis, there are thickets of *Acacia pennivenia*, *Ficus salicifolia* and *Ziziphus spina-christi*. There is grazing, mainly by goats.

Birds

See box for key species. There are also good populations of *Anthus similis sokotrae*, *Lanius excubitor uncinatus* and *Onychognathus blythii*.

Species restricted wholly or largely to the Middle East

Nectarinia balfouri	Common resident.
Onychognathus frater	Present in small numbers.
Passer insularis	A good population is present.

Other threatened/endemic wildlife

Reptiles: *Pristurus socotranus*, *Mabuya socotranus*, *Coluber socotrae*.

Conservation issues

See p. 352.

041 Wadi Ayhaft, Socotra (Aden)

Unprotected

12°36′N 53°59′E
1,300 ha

Site description

Granite and limestone slopes in northern Socotra, with abundant running water. This is one of the most densely wooded areas of the island, with sub-montane, semi-deciduous thicket (50–300 m) and montane thicket (up to 800 m). There is a military experimental agricultural station and the area is a source of piped water and a site frequented by tourists. Dead wood is collected for timber, and browsing by goats occurs locally. A tree nursery has been proposed in the area.

Birds

See box for key species. The site is also important for *Otus scops socotranus* (probably over 20 pairs).

Species restricted wholly or largely to the Middle East

Cisticola incanus	Resident (c.10 pairs).
Nectarinia balfouri	Resident (over 100 pairs).
Onychognathus frater	Resident (c.15 pairs).
Rhynchostruthus socotranus	Resident (c.50 pairs).

Other threatened/endemic wildlife

Reptiles: *Chamaeleo monachus* (the site may be particularly important for this species), *Pristurus sokotranus*, *Mabuya socotrana* (all endemic).

Conservation issues

See p. 352.

042 Rewgid and Regid Plateaus, Socotra (Aden)

Unprotected

12°36′N 53°59′E
1,450 ha

Site description

Two limestone plateaus at 600–750 m in northern Socotra with sub-montane, semi-deciduous thicket. On Regid (650 ha) there is also dense woodland and open shrubland with woody herb communities. The human population is sparse, but there is access to Rewgid (800 ha) via a new road. Grazing/browsing of goats and the collection of dead timber occur.

Birds

No information: not yet surveyed.

Other threatened/endemic wildlife

No information.

Conservation issues

See p. 352.

043 Jabal Jef, Socotra (Aden)

Unprotected

12°36′N 54°06′E
300 ha

Site description
Rocky granite slopes (to 850 m) in northern Socotra with grass and scattered montane thicket, dense in places. Cattle and goats are grazed/browsed on the grassland, and sheep are new to the area. Timber is taken where there is road access.

Birds
See box for key species. There are also large populations of *Zosterops abyssinicus socotrana* and *Emberiza tahapisi insularis*.

Species restricted wholly or largely to the Middle East	
Apus berliozi	Probably breeds.
Cisticola incanus	Present on the lower slopes.
Nectarinia balfouri	Common resident.

Other threatened/endemic wildlife
Reptiles: *Pristurus insignis*, *P. sokotranus*, *Hemidactylus homoelepis* (all endemics).

Conservation issues
See p. 352.

044 Rookib Hills, Socotra (Aden)

Unprotected

12°36′N 54°09′E
c.300 ha

Site description
Barren, rocky limestone hills (c.500 m) in northern Socotra with sub-montane, semi-deciduous thicket. There is grazing, mainly by goats.

Birds
See box for key species. There is also a good density of *Anthus similis sokotrae* and *Emberiza tahapisi insularis*.

Species restricted wholly or largely to the Middle East	
Emberiza socotrana	Probably at the lower part of its altitudinal range here.

Other threatened/endemic wildlife
Reptiles: *Pristurus sokotranus* and *Mabuya socotrana* (both endemics).

Conservation issues
See p. 352.

045 Hamaderoh Plateau and Scarp, Socotra (Aden)

Unprotected

12°36′N 54°17′E
c.10,000 ha

Site description
Limestone slopes and a rolling limestone plateau (c.500 m) in eastern Socotra, with a vegetation of sub-montane, semi-deciduous thicket and a mosaic of dwarf *Croton* and *Jatropha* shrubland. There is grazing/browsing by goats (mostly), sheep and cattle, with a seasonal influx of stock from other regions, notably from the Hajhir mountains (site 047).

Birds
See box for key species. There is also a good density of *Lanius excubitor uncinatus* and *Onychognathus blythii*, and *Otus scops socotranus* occurs.

Species restricted wholly or largely to the Middle East	
Cisticola incanus	Occurs on the lower slopes.
Nectarinia balfouri	Present.
Onychognathus frater	Present.
Passer insularis	Occurs at a good density.
Rhynchostruthus socotranus	Occurs on the lower slopes.

Other threatened/endemic wildlife
Reptiles: *Pristurus sokotranus*, *P. insignis*, *Hemidactylus homoelepis*, *Mabuya socotrana*, *Mesalina balfouri*, *Ditypophis vivax* (all endemics).

Conservation issues
See p. 352. There are traditional controls on timber collection.

046 Coast of Bindar Di-Sha'b, Socotra (Aden)

12°35′N 53°23′E
1,400 ha

Unprotected

Site description
A coastal area of *Croton* shrubland in western Socotra. The best example known to date of an undisturbed coastal flora, and perhaps the only one remaining. There is fishing and goat grazing.

Birds
No information: not yet surveyed.

Other threatened/endemic wildlife
Flora: endemics present include *Taverniera serichofylla*, *Farsetia socotrana*, *Lachnocapsa spathulata* and *Leucas flagellifolia*.

Conservation issues
See p. 352.

047 Hajhir Mountains, Socotra (Aden)

12°34′N 54°03′E
5,800 ha

also known as Haggar Mountains or Hagghier Mountains
Unprotected

Site description
The Hajhir mountains of Socotra comprise rather barren-looking granite slopes and pinnacles (up to 1,500 m) with montane thicket, though the floristic composition is not well known. Near Adho Dimellus on the south-eastern slopes there is a short-grass plateau at c.850 m with a stream flowing through and with scattered bushes and light scrub. There is grazing/browsing by cattle, goats and camels.

Birds
See box for key species. The area is very little explored ornithologically. Given the altitude and habitat, breeding species may include '*Buteo buteo*', *Otus scops socotranus*, *Cisticola incanus*, *Nectarinia balfouri*, *Onychognathus frater*, *Passer insularis* and *Rhynchostruthus socotranus*.

Other threatened/endemic wildlife
Reptiles: *Pristurus insignoides* (known only from Adho Dimellus), *P. guichardi* (possibly restricted to the uplands).

Globally threatened species	
Cisticola haesitatus	Rare resident: a breeding pair was found near Adho Dimellus in April 1964, but the species was not re-located in the 1993 survey.
Regionally threatened or declining species	
Neophron percnopterus	Common resident; many pairs probably breed on cliffs.
Species restricted wholly or largely to the Middle East	
Apus berliozi	Common resident, breeding on cliffs.
Cisticola haesitatus	See above.
Emberiza socotrana	Rare resident; the only record during the 1993 survey came from this site.

Conservation issues
See p. 352. There are strict traditional controls on the cutting of trees.

Further reading
Ripley and Bond (1966).

048 Firjih/Central Socotra (Aden)

12°32′N 54°05′E
200 ha

Unprotected

Site description
Deep wadis with abundant water, protected by the Hajhir mountains to the north, at 50–100 m. The vegetation is open *Croton* and *Jatropha* shrubland. Many goats browse the area, and former millet terraces have been given over to extensive date palm plantations.

Birds
No information: not yet surveyed. It is said by local people that certain birds come here to shelter from the monsoon winds.

Other threatened/endemic wildlife
No information.

Conservation issues
See p. 352.

049 Di-Ishal Foothills, Socotra (Aden)

Unprotected

12°31′N 54°10′E
c.1,500 ha

Site description

Open, stony grassland at 400–500 m in eastern Socotra, well-vegetated with an open shrubland of *Croton* and *Jatropha* and sub-montane, semi-deciduous thicket. There is grazing by goats, and date palms are grown.

Birds

See box for key species. Also present are *Otus scops socotranus*, *Eremopterix nigriceps forbeswatsoni*, *Zosterops abyssinicus socotrana* and *Onychognathus blythii*; *Pterocles lichtensteinii* occurs at a good density.

Species restricted wholly or largely to the Middle East	
Cisticola incanus	Present.
Passer insularis	Common resident.

Other threatened/endemic wildlife

No information.

Conservation issues

See p. 352.

050 Diksam, Socotra (Aden)

Unprotected

12°30′N 54°00′E
9,000 ha

Site description

Granite and limestone slopes at 550–700 m in central Socotra, with sub-montane, semi-deciduous thicket and montane thicket, distinguished by *Punica protopunica* shrubland. Many cattle are grazed in the area, and some goats.

Birds

No information. Not yet surveyed.

Other threatened/endemic wildlife

Plants: *Punica protopunica* (endemic).

Conservation issues

See p. 352.

051 Ra's Momi and Fikhah, Socotra (Aden)

Unprotected

12°32′N 54°29′E
2,500 ha

Site description

Coastal dunes and flats below steep cliffs in eastern Socotra. The vegetation comprises variably dense *Croton* and *Jatropha* shrubland, and grassland at Ra's Momi. Human activities include fishing, and grazing and browsing of livestock at Ra's Momi (heavy after rains, mainly by sheep) and Fikhah (minimal). Fikhah is a traditional water source for seamen, and has been suggested as a possible site for water extraction.

Birds

See box for key species. Boobies *Sula* apparently roost on the cliffs.

Other threatened/endemic wildlife

No information.

Regionally threatened or declining species	
Bulweria fallax	Common offshore; the cliffs are a potential nesting site.
Phalacrocorax nigrogularis	The cliffs are or were used for roosting.

Species restricted wholly or largely to the Middle East	
Bulweria fallax	See above.
Phalacrocorax nigrogularis	See above.
Apus berliozi	Probably breeds.
Cisticola incanus	Present at a good density in dense vegetation.

Conservation issues

See p. 352. New water cisterns are being built, allowing increased grazing stock. Seabirds (i.e. *Phalacrocorax nigrogularis*, *Sula* spp.) were formerly taken from the cliffs for food.

052 Firmihin near Jabal Keseslah, Socotra (Aden)

Unprotected

12°33′N 54°03′E
900 ha

Site description

An upland area of Socotra (700–800 m), with sub-montane, semi-deciduous thicket, montane thicket and dense *Dracaena cinnabari* woodland. Some grazing (cattle and goats) occurs.

Birds

No information: not yet surveyed.

Other threatened/endemic wildlife

No information.

Conservation issues

See p. 352.

053 Noged Plain, Socotra (Aden)

Unprotected

12°19′N 53°53′E
31,500 ha

Site description

A relatively flat, barren semi-desert plain on the southern coast of Socotra (up to 100 m), traversed by dry wadis. There is sparse *Croton* shrubland with date palm groves. Vegetation in wadis such as Wadi 'Ireh needs further study. Plantations of date palms and melons were formerly present, but the field systems have now collapsed. There are coastal lagoons and tidal inlets (with saltpans), and camels are grazed in the area.

Birds

See box for key species. There are also good breeding populations of *Eremopterix nigriceps forbeswatsoni* and *Onychognathus blythii*. *Cursorius cursor* breeds. Local people say that the plain is important for migrants which differ from those occurring on the northern coast. It is also said that the deep caves with permanent water are frequented by birds.

Globally threatened species

Cisticola haesitatus	Resident in good numbers.

Species restricted wholly or largely to the Middle East

Cisticola incanus	Breeds in good numbers.
Cisticola haesitatus	See above.
Passer insularis	Good numbers are present.

Other threatened/endemic wildlife

No information.

Conservation issues

See p. 352. Bulldozing and widespread disturbance for agricultural development occurred in the 1960s and 1970s, and some plant extinctions were attributable to this.

054 Sabuniya and Ka'l Fir'awn (Aden)

Unprotected

12°33′N 52°42′E
Unknown area

Site description

Two small sea-stacks west of Socotra, both c.80 m high. Sabuniya (12°39′N 53°09′E, 100 ha) consists of three peaks whilst Ka'l Fir'awn (12°27′N 52°07′E) is two rocks separated by a narrow gap of water. These stacks are whitened by guano and are presumably bare of vegetation, but have not yet been surveyed.

Birds

See box for key species. *Sula dactylatra* breeds on both islands (see box). *Phaethon aethereus* almost certainly breeds on Sabuniya. There is no evidence for *Phalacrocorax nigrogularis* breeding.

1% or more of population

	Breeding (pairs)	Wintering	Passage
Sula dactylatra	c.100	—	—

Regionally threatened or declining species

Bulweria fallax	Common offshore and breeding is possible on either island.

Species restricted wholly or largely to the Middle East

Bulweria fallax	See above.

Other threatened/endemic wildlife
No information.

Conservation issues
Breeding seabirds are taken for food by local people, but in the absence of any surveys, it is not known whether this practice is sustainable.

055 Abd al-Kuri (Aden)
Unprotected

12°11′N 52°13′E
13,300 ha

Site description
A large island in the Gulf of Aden to the west of Socotra, c.32 km long, less than 5 km wide and rising to c.570 m, with c.90 km of shoreline. Vegetation is much sparser than on Socotra, dominated by low, open shrubland and dwarf-herb communities containing *Euphorbia*. There is a diminishing permanent human population supported by brackish water only; the main human activities are grazing livestock (goats) and fishing.

Birds
See box for key species. There are unspecified seabirds, probably breeding. It is said that the island is visited by many small birds on summer migration from May to August.

Species restricted wholly or largely to the Middle East

Passer insularis	The island supports an endemic subspecies different to that on Socotra, *P. i. hemileucus*.

Other threatened/endemic wildlife
Reptiles: *Hemidactylus forbesii*, *H. oxyrhinus*, *Pristurus abdelkuri* (all endemic). Flora: there are at least ten endemic species.

Conservation issues
Seabirds are taken for food by local people. No other information is available on current problems or potential threats.

056 Al-Ikhwan (Aden)
also known as The Brothers
Unprotected

12°08′N 53°09′E
c.5,600 ha

Site description
Two rather inaccessible islands lying to the south-west of Socotra in the Gulf of Aden. Both are c.10–15 km long, rather flat-topped and sheer-sided. Jazirat Darsa (12°07′N 53°18′E, 1,640 ha) has low shrubland on the coastal plain and lower slopes, and rises to 385 m. There is c.20 km of shoreline. The higher altitudes in the centre of the island are as yet unsurveyed. There is very little fresh water. The main human activities are fishing (seasonal) and fish-salting on the north shore. Jazirat Semha (12°10′N 53°02′E, 3,980 ha) rises to 780 m, has c.28 km of shoreline and is covered in low, open shrubland and open dwarf-herb communities. Only the coastal plain and foothills have been provisionally surveyed, and the escarpments and plateau are unexplored. There is a village settlement; main human activities are fishing and grazing goats.

Birds
See box for key species. The higher altitudes of Jazirat Darsa are covered with guano, and boobies in great numbers have been seen, presumably nesting *Sula dactylatra* and/or *S. leucogaster*.

Regionally threatened or declining species

Bulweria fallax	Common offshore, and breeding is possible on either island.

Species restricted wholly or largely to the Middle East

Bulweria fallax	See above.

Other threatened/endemic wildlife
Flora: the important Socotran endemic species *Dendrosicyos socotranus* and *Euphorbia arbuscula* occur at the base of the escarpment on Jazirat Semha, indicating a potentially rich flora.

Conservation issues
Jazirat Darsa is infested with rats, which may severely inhibit the nesting success of the boobies. No other information is available on current problems or potential threats.

057 Al-Mukha–Al-Khawkhah (Ta'izz)

Unprotected

13°35′N 43°17′E
c.7,000 ha

Site description

About 70 km of southern Red Sea coastline between the towns of Al-Mukha and Al-Khawkhah, including the fishing villages of Mawshij, Yakhtul and Al-Ru'ays. The northern coast is dominated by narrow sand beaches, the southern by sabkhah areas. At Al-Ru'ays there is a stretch of intertidal mudflats, associated with underground freshwater seepage which supports 10–15 ha of variably dense mangrove *Avicennia* and c.100 ha of variably dense palms (*Phoenix*, *Hyphaene*). Salt-tolerant bushes (*Suaeda*, *Zygophyllum*) and grasses (*Odyssea* and others) are very common along most of the coast, especially on low dunes and fringes of sabkhah. *Salvadora* bushes are locally common inland, and seagrass beds and coral reefs are relatively frequent offshore in the south of the site. Artisanal fishing is widespread all along the coast, and more pelagic fisheries are based at Al-Mukha and Al-Khawkhah; there are also active salt-pans and a power station on the coast at the former town.

Birds

The intertidal zone at Al-Ru'ays provides valuable feeding habitat for non-breeding coastal waterbirds, and large numbers of gulls and terns roost at Al-Mukha and Al-Khawkhah, associated with the fisheries there. Wintering species include *Platalea leucorodia* (19) and *Larus ridibundus* (900). Migrants (all November unless otherwise stated) include *Charadrius mongolus* (100), *Limicola falcinellus* (16), *Tringa cinerea* (44), *Larus fuscus*/*L. argentatus* (200), *Sterna bengalensis* (140), *Sterna hirundo* (50, April) and *Hirundo rupestris* (20). Breeding species of the palms and mangroves include *Butorides striatus*, *Caprimulgus nubicus*, *Acrocephalus stentoreus* (presumed) and *Tchagra senegala*.

Globally threatened species

Numenius tenuirostris	Possibly a very rare passage migrant or winter visitor. There is only one record: two at Al-Mukha and at Al-Khawkhah on consecutive days (October 1988).
Larus leucophthalmus	Regular non-breeding visitor all-year round, peaking in spring (100, April).

Regionally threatened or declining species

Falco concolor	Scarce passage migrant (1, June).

Species restricted wholly or largely to the Middle East

Puffinus persicus	Common non-breeding visitor offshore (100, April).
Dromas ardeola	Passage migrant (130, November) and winter visitor.
Larus hemprichii	Common non-breeding visitor (200, April and November).
Larus leucophthalmus	See above.
Sterna repressa	Passage migrant (170, November) and winter visitor.
Sterna saundersi	Resident (40, April).
Turdoides squamiceps	Local resident.

Other threatened/endemic wildlife

Reptiles: the seagrass beds are an important feeding ground for the sea-turtle *Chelonia mydas* (E), which is common.

Conservation issues

No formal conservation measures are known to have been taken, although the establishment of marine parks has been considered in the past. The area is currently relatively undisturbed. Any major depletion of the freshwater table, caused by wadi-damming or unsustainable pumping of groundwater for irrigation projects inland on the Tihamah, would probably have severe consequences for the mudflat/mangrove/palm-grove habitat (and the associated fishing community) at Al-Ru'ays. No conservation measures are known to have been proposed.

Further reading

Gretton (1991), TMRU (1987).

MAIN REFERENCES

Ash, J. S. (1984) Report of the UNEP ornithologist/ecologist on the advice to the Government of the People's Democratic Republic of Yemen on 'Combating the crow menace'. Rep. NEP/84/0189, United Nations Environment Programme.

Ash, J. S. (1988) Some observations in South Yemen in 1984 and a selected bibliography of the region. *Sandgrouse* 10: 85–90.

Bailey, R. S. (1966) The sea-birds of the southeast coast of Arabia. *Ibis* 108: 224–264.

Bazara'a, M., Guarino, L., Miller, A. and Obadi, N. (1991) *Dirachma socotrana*—back from the brink? *Oryx*

25: 229–232.

BOURNE, W. R. P. (1966) Observations on sea-birds. *Sea Swallow* 18: 9–39.

BROOKS, D. J., EVANS, M. I., MARTINS, R. P. AND PORTER, R. F. (1987) The status of birds in North Yemen and the records of OSME expedition in autumn 1985. *Sandgrouse* 9: 4–66.

ELLIOTT, H. F. I. (1952) Off-season sea-bird distribution on the Suez route to East Africa. *Ibis* 94: 526–528.

EVANS, M. I. (1987) Sites of interest. Jebel Nabi Shu'ayb. *Phoenix* 4: 5.

EVANS, M. I. (1989) Breeding birds on some Red Sea islands off North Yemen. *Orn. Soc. Middle East Bull.* 23: 14–20.

GRETTON, A. (1991) *The ecology and conservation of the Slender-billed Curlew (Numenius tenuirostris).* Cambridge, U.K.: International Council for Bird Preservation.

ICBP (1992) *Putting biodiversity on the map: priority areas for global conservation.* Cambridge, U.K.: International Council for Bird Preservation.

JENNINGS, M. C. (1992) The House Crow *Corvus splendens* in Aden (Yemen) and an attempt at its control. *Sandgrouse* 14: 27–33.

MORRIS, R. O. (1962) Two visits to the Haycocks. *Sea Swallow* 15: 57–58.

MORRIS, R. P. (1993) Important Bird Areas in the Middle East: Ta'izz sewage lagoons and marshes. *Oman Bird News* 14: 8–10.

PHILLIPS, N. R. (1982) Observations on the birds of North Yemen in 1979. *Sandgrouse* 4: 37–59.

PHILLIPS, W. W. A. (1947) The ornithological diary of a voyage of the S. S. Samluzon. *J. Bombay Nat. Hist. Soc.* 46: 593–613.

RIPLEY, S. D. AND BOND, G. M. (1966) The birds of Socotra and Abd-el-Kuri. *Smithsonian Misc. Coll.* 151 (7): 1–37.

SCHOLTE AND EVANS (in prep.) Fauna of Wadi Rijaf, Jabal Bura.

SHU', A. M. (1989) Wahat al-majalis. *Al-Thawra* [newspaper, 23 March].

SMITH, K. D. (1956) On the birds of the Aden Protectorate. *Ibis* 98: 303–307.

TMRU (Tropical Marine Research Unit) (1987) *North Yemen marine conservation survey. Vol. 1. Distribution of habitats and species.* University of York, U.K.: TMRU.

WELCH, G. AND WELCH, H. (1988) The autumn migration of raptors and other soaring birds across the Bab-el-Mandeb straits. *Sandgrouse* 10: 26–50.

WOOD, J. R. I. (1982) The Jabal Bura valley forest community. Unpublished report to GTZ, Germany.

YERBURY, J. W. (1896) Further notes on the birds of Aden. *Ibis* (7) 2: 13–39.

APPENDIX 1: English names of bird species mentioned in the text

SCIENTIFIC NAMES in this book follow Monroe and Sibley (1993), with one exception (*Parisoma buryi* was preferred over *Sylvia buryi*). This has resulted, in a small minority of cases, in the use of scientific names that may be unfamiliar to many Middle Eastern ornithologists and birdwatchers, including the following: *Egretta alba* becomes *Casmerodius albus*; *Clamator jacobinus* becomes *Oxylophus jacobinus*; *Apus melba* becomes *Tachymarptis melba*; *Halcyon chloris* becomes *Todirhamphus chloris*; *Ptyonoprogne fuligula* becomes *Hirundo obsoleta*; *Anthus novaeseelandiae* becomes *Anthus cinnamomeus*; *Petronia brachydactyla* becomes *Carpospiza brachydactyla*; *Euodice* becomes *Lonchura*; and *Bucanetes* becomes *Rhodopechys*. For these and other, more minor, cases the familiar names are provided in brackets in the following list.

Accipiter badius Shikra
Accipiter brevipes Levant Sparrowhawk
Accipiter gentilis Northern Goshawk
Accipiter nisus Eurasian Sparrowhawk
Acridotheres tristis Common Myna
Acrocephalus agricola Paddyfield Warbler
Acrocephalus arundinaceus Great Reed Warbler
Acrocephalus baeticatus African Reed Warbler
Acrocephalus concinens Blunt-winged Warbler
Acrocephalus griseldis Basra Reed Warbler
Acrocephalus melanopogon Moustached Warbler
Acrocephalus palustris Marsh Warbler
Acrocephalus scirpaceus Eurasian Reed Warbler
Acrocephalus stentoreus Clamorous Reed Warbler
Aegithalos leucogenys White-cheeked Tit
Aegypius monachus Cinereous Vulture
Alaemon alaudipes Hoopoe Lark
Alauda gulgula Oriental Skylark
Alcedo atthis Common Kingfisher
Alcedo cristata Malachite Kingfisher
Alectoris chukar Chukar
Alectoris melanocephala Arabian Partridge
Alectoris philbyi Philby's Partridge
Amandava subflava Zebra Waxbill
Amaurornis phoenicurus White-breasted Waterhen
Ammomanes cincturus Bar-tailed Lark
Ammomanes deserti Desert Lark
Ammoperdix griseogularis See-see Partridge
Ammoperdix heyi Sand Partridge
Anas acuta Northern Pintail
Anas clypeata Northern Shoveler
Anas crecca Common Teal
Anas penelope Eurasian Wigeon
Anas platyrhynchos Mallard
Anas querquedula Garganey
Anas strepera Gadwall
Anhinga rufa African Darter
Anous stolidus Brown Noddy
Anous tenuirostris Lesser Noddy
Anser albifrons Greater White-fronted Goose
Anser anser Greylag Goose
Anser erythropus Lesser White-fronted Goose
Anser indicus Bar-headed Goose
Anthreptes metallicus Nile Valley Sunbird
Anthus campestris Tawny Pipit
Anthus cinnamomeus (*A. novaeseelandiae*) African Pipit (Richard's Pipit)
Anthus roseatus Rosy Pipit
Anthus similis Long-billed Pipit
Anthus spinoletta Water Pipit
Anthus trivialis Tree Pipit
Apus affinis Little Swift
Apus apus Common Swift
Apus berliozi Forbes-Watson's Swift
Apus pallidus Pallid Swift
Aquila chrysaetos Golden Eagle
Aquila clanga Greater Spotted Eagle
Aquila heliaca Imperial Eagle
Aquila nipalensis Steppe Eagle
Aquila pomarina Lesser Spotted Eagle
Aquila rapax Tawny Eagle
Aquila verreauxii Verreaux's Eagle
Ardea cinerea Grey Heron
Ardea goliath Goliath Heron
Ardea purpurea Purple Heron
Ardeola grayii Indian Pond Heron
Ardeola ralloides Squacco Heron
Ardeotis arabs Arabian Bustard
Arenaria interpres Ruddy Turnstone
Asio flammeus Short-eared Owl
Asio otus Long-eared Owl
Athene brama Spotted Owlet
Athene noctua Little Owl
Aythya ferina Common Pochard
Aythya fuligula Tufted Duck
Aythya nyroca Ferruginous Duck

Botaurus stellaris Great Bittern
Branta ruficollis Red-breasted Goose
Bubo africanus Spotted Eagle Owl
Bubo ascalaphus Pharaoh Eagle Owl
Bubo bubo Eurasian Eagle Owl
Bubulcus ibis Cattle Egret
Bucephala clangula Common Goldeneye
Bulweria fallax Jouanin's Petrel
Burhinus capensis Spotted Thick-knee
Burhinus oedicnemus Eurasian Thick-knee
Burhinus (*Esacus*) *recurvirostris* Great Thick-knee (Great Stone Plover)
Butastur teesa White-eyed Buzzard
Buteo buteo Common Buzzard
Buteo rufinus Long-legged Buzzard
Butorides striatus Striated Heron

Calandrella acutirostris Hume's Lark
Calandrella brachydactyla Short-toed Lark
Calandrella cinerea Red-capped Lark
Calandrella raytal Indian Short-toed Lark

Calandrella rufescens Lesser Short-toed Lark
Calidris alba Sanderling
Calidris alpina Dunlin
Calidris ferruginea Curlew Sandpiper
Calidris minuta Little Stint
Calidris tenuirostris Great Knot
Callacanthis burtoni Spectacled Finch
Calonectris diomedea Cory's Shearwater
Caprimulgus aegyptius Egyptian Nightjar
Caprimulgus europaeus Eurasian Nightjar
Caprimulgus inornatus Plain Nightjar
Caprimulgus mahrattensis Sykes's Nightjar
Caprimulgus nubicus Nubian Nightjar
Caprimulgus poliocephalus Mountain Nightjar
Carduelis spinoides Yellow-breasted Greenfinch
Carduelis spinus Eurasian Siskin
Carduelis yemenensis Yemen Linnet
Carpodacus rhodochlamys Red-mantled (Blyth's) Rosefinch
Carpodacus rubicilla Great Rosefinch
Carpodacus synoicus Sinai Rosefinch
Carpodacus thura White-browed Rosefinch
Carpospiza (Petronia) brachydactyla Pale Rock Sparrow
Casmerodius albus (Egretta alba) Great (White) Egret
Centropus superciliosus White-browed Coucal
Cercomela melanura Blackstart
Cercotrichas galactotes Rufous-tailed Scrub-robin
Cercotrichas podobe Black Scrub-robin
Certhia himalayana Bar-tailed Treecreeper
Ceryle rudis Pied Kingfisher
Cettia cetti Cetti's Warbler
Chaimarriornis leucocephalus White-capped Water-Redstart
Charadrius alexandrinus Kentish Plover
Charadrius asiaticus Caspian Plover
Charadrius dubius Little Ringed Plover
Charadrius hiaticula Common Ringed Plover
Charadrius leschenaultii Greater Sand Plover
Charadrius mongolus Lesser Sand Plover
Chlamydotis undulata Houbara Bustard
Chlidonias hybridus Whiskered Tern
Chlidonias leucopterus White-winged Black Tern
Chrysococcyx caprius Didric Cuckoo
Chrysococcyx klaas Klaas's Cuckoo
Ciconia abdimii Abdim's Stork
Ciconia ciconia White Stork
Ciconia nigra Black Stork
Cinclus cinclus White-throated Dipper
Cinclus pallasii Brown Dipper
Cinnyricinclus leucogaster Violet-backed Starling
Circaetus gallicus Short-toed Eagle
Circus aeruginosus Western Marsh Harrier
Circus cyaneus Hen Harrier
Circus macrourus Pallid Harrier
Circus pygargus Montagu's Harrier
Cisticola haesitatus Island Cisticola
Cisticola incanus Socotra Cisticola
Cisticola juncidis Zitting Cisticola
Clamator glandarius Great Spotted Cuckoo
Columba arquatrix African Olive Pigeon
Columba eversmanni Eastern Stock Dove
Columba leuconota Snow Pigeon
Columba livia Rock Pigeon
Columba oenas Stock Dove
Columba palumbus Common Woodpigeon
Columba rupestris Hill Pigeon
Coracias abyssinica Abyssinian Roller
Coracias benghalensis Indian Roller
Coracias garrulus European Roller
Corvus corax Common Raven
Corvus frugilegus Rook
Corvus macrorhynchos Large-billed Crow
Corvus rhipidurus Fan-tailed Raven
Corvus ruficollis Brown-necked Raven
Corvus splendens House Crow
Coturnix coturnix Common Quail
Coturnix delegorguei Harlequin Quail
Crex crex Corncrake
Cuculus canorus Common Cuckoo
Cursorius cursor Cream-coloured Courser
Cygnus columbianus Tundra Swan
Cygnus cygnus Whooper Swan
Cygnus olor Mute Swan
Cypsiurus parvus African Palm Swift

Delichon dasypus Asian House Martin
Dendrocopos assimilis Sind Pied Woodpecker
Dendrocopos dorae Arabian Woodpecker
Dendrocopos leucopterus White-winged Woodpecker
Dendrocopos major Great Spotted Woodpecker
Dendrocopos medius Middle Spotted Woodpecker
Dendrocopos syriacus Syrian Woodpecker
Dicrurus leucophaeus Ashy Drongo
Dicrurus macrocercus Black Drongo
Dromas ardeola Crab Plover
Dryocopus martius Black Woodpecker

Egretta garzetta Little Egret
Egretta gularis Western Reef Heron
Elanus caeruleus Black-winged Kite
Emberiza bruniceps Red-headed Bunting
Emberiza buchanani Grey-necked Bunting
Emberiza caesia Cretzschmar's Bunting
Emberiza cia Rock Bunting
Emberiza cineracea Cinereous Bunting
Emberiza citrinella Yellowhammer
Emberiza hortulana Ortolan Bunting
Emberiza leucocephalos Pine Bunting
Emberiza melanocephala Black-headed Bunting
Emberiza pusilla Little Bunting
Emberiza schoeniclus Reed Bunting
Emberiza socotrana Socotra Bunting
Emberiza stewarti Chestnut-breasted Bunting
Emberiza striolata House Bunting
Emberiza tahapisi Cinnamon-breasted Bunting
Eremalauda dunni Dunn's Lark
Eremophila alpestris Horned Lark
Eremophila bilopha Temminck's Lark
Eremopterix nigriceps Black-crowned Finch-lark
Erithacus rubecula European Robin
Estrilda rufibarba Arabian Waxbill
Eudromias (Charadrius) morinellus Eurasian Dotterel

Falco amurensis Amur Falcon
Falco biarmicus Lanner
Falco cherrug Saker
Falco columbarius Merlin
Falco concolor Sooty Falcon
Falco eleonorae Eleonora's Falcon
Falco jugger Laggar

Falco naumanni Lesser Kestrel
Falco pelegrinoides Barbary Falcon
Falco peregrinus Peregrine
Falco subbuteo Eurasian Hobby
Falco tinnunculus Common Kestrel
Ficedula parva Red-breasted Flycatcher
Ficedula semitorquata Semicollared Flycatcher
Francolinus francolinus Black Francolin
Francolinus pondicerianus Grey Francolin
Fregetta tropica Black-bellied Storm-petrel
Fringilla coelebs Chaffinch
Fulica atra Common Coot

Galerida cristata Crested Lark
Gallinago gallinago Common Snipe
Gallinago media Great Snipe
Gallinula chloropus Common Moorhen
Garrulax albogularis White-throated Laughingthrush
Garrulus glandarius Eurasian Jay
Garrulus lanceolatus Black-headed Jay
Geronticus eremita Northern Bald Ibis
Glareola nordmanni Black-winged Pratincole
Glareola pratincola Collared Pratincole
Grus grus Common Crane
Grus leucogeranus Siberian White Crane
Grus (Anthropoides) virgo Demoiselle Crane
Gypaetus barbatus Lammergeier
Gyps bengalensis White-rumped Vulture
Gyps fulvus Eurasian Griffon Vulture
Gyps himalayensis Himalayan Griffon Vulture

Haematopus ostralegus Eurasian Oystercatcher
Halcyon leucocephala Grey-headed Kingfisher
Halcyon smyrnensis White-throated Kingfisher
Haliaeetus albicilla White-tailed Eagle
Haliaeetus leucoryphus Pallas's Sea-eagle
Hieraaetus fasciatus Bonelli's Eagle
Hieraaetus pennatus Booted Eagle
Himantopus himantopus Black-winged Stilt
Hippolais icterina Icterine Warbler
Hippolais languida Upcher's Warbler
Hippolais olivetorum Olive-tree Warbler
Hippolais rama (H. caligata) Sykes's Warbler (Booted Warbler)
Hirundo daurica Red-rumped Swallow
Hirundo fluvicola Streak-throated Swallow
Hirundo obsoleta (Ptyonoprogne fuligula) Pale Crag-martin
Hirundo (Ptyonoprogne) rupestris Eurasian Crag Martin
Hirundo smithii Wire-tailed Swallow
Hydrophasianus chirurgus Pheasant-tailed Jacana
Hypocolius ampelinus Grey Hypocolius

Irania gutturalis White-throated Robin
Ixobrychus minutus Little Bittern

Jynx torquilla Eurasian Wryneck

Ketupa zeylonensis Brown Fish-owl

Lanius collurio Red-backed Shrike
Lanius excubitor Great Grey Shrike
Lanius isabellinus Isabelline Shrike
Lanius minor Lesser Grey Shrike
Lanius nubicus Masked Shrike
Lanius schach Long-tailed Shrike
Lanius vittatus Bay-backed Shrike
Larus argentatus Herring Gull
Larus armenicus Armenian Gull
Larus audouinii Audouin's Gull
Larus brunnicephalus Brown-headed Gull
Larus cachinnans Yellow-legged Gull
Larus canus Common Gull
Larus fuscus Lesser Black-backed Gull
Larus genei Slender-billed Gull
Larus hemprichii Sooty Gull
Larus ichthyaetus Great Black-headed Gull
Larus leucophthalmus White-eyed Gull
Larus melanocephalus Mediterranean Gull
Larus minutus Little Gull
Larus ridibundus Common Black-headed Gull
Leucosticte brandti Black-headed Mountain-finch
Leucosticte nemoricola Plain Mountain-finch
Limicola falcinellus Broad-billed Sandpiper
Limnodromus semipalmatus Asian Dowitcher
Limosa lapponica Bar-tailed Godwit
Limosa limosa Black-tailed Godwit
Locustella luscinioides Savi's Warbler
Locustella naevia Common Grasshopper Warbler
Lonchura (Euodice) cantans African Silverbill
Lonchura (Euodice) malabarica White-throated Munia
Lophophorus impejanus Himalayan Monal
Lullula arborea Woodlark
Luscinia megarhynchos Common Nightingale
Luscinia svecica Bluethroat
Lymnocryptes minimus Jack Snipe

Marmaronetta angustirostris Marbled Teal
Melanocorypha bimaculata Bimaculated Lark
Melanocorypha calandra Calandra Lark
Melanocorypha leucoptera White-winged Lark
Melierax metabates Dark Chanting Goshawk
Mergellus (Mergus) albellus Smew
Mergus merganser Common Merganser
Mergus serrator Red-breasted Merganser
Merops albicollis White-throated Bee-eater
Merops apiaster European Bee-eater
Merops orientalis Little Green Bee-eater
Merops superciliosus Blue-cheeked Bee-eater
Micronisus gabar Gabar Goshawk
Miliaria calandra Corn Bunting
Milvus migrans Black Kite
Milvus milvus Red Kite
Mirafra cantillans Singing Lark
Monticola rufocinereus Little Rock Thrush
Monticola saxatilis Rufous-tailed Rock Thrush
Monticola solitarius Blue Rock Thrush
Montifringilla nivalis White-winged Snowfinch
Montifringilla theresae Afghan Snowfinch
Motacilla cinerea Grey Wagtail
Motacilla citreola Citrine Wagtail
Motacilla flava Yellow Wagtail
Muscicapa gambagae Gambaga Flycatcher
Muscicapa ruficauda Rusty-tailed Flycatcher
Muscicapa sibirica Dark-sided Flycatcher
Muscicapa striata Spotted Flycatcher
Mycerobas carnipes White-winged Grosbeak
Mycerobas icterioides Black-and-yellow Grosbeak
Myiophonus caeruleus Blue Whistling Thrush

Nectarinia asiatica Purple Sunbird
Nectarinia balfouri Socotra Sunbird
Nectarinia habessinica Shining Sunbird
Nectarinia osea Palestine Sunbird
Neophron percnopterus Egyptian Vulture
Netta rufina Red-crested Pochard
Nettapus coromandelianus Cotton Pygmy-goose
Nucifraga caryocatactes Spotted Nutcracker
Numenius arquata Eurasian Curlew
Numenius phaeopus Whimbrel
Numenius tenuirostris Slender-billed Curlew
Numida meleagris Helmeted Guineafowl
Nycticorax nycticorax Black-crowned Night Heron

Oceanites oceanicus Wilson's Storm-petrel
Oceanodroma monorhis Swinhoe's Storm-petrel
Oena capensis Namaqua Dove
Oenanthe alboniger Hume's Wheatear
Oenanthe bottae Red-breasted Wheatear
Oenanthe cypriaca Cyprus Wheatear
Oenanthe deserti Desert Wheatear
Oenanthe finschii Finsch's Wheatear
Oenanthe hispanica Black-eared Wheatear
Oenanthe isabellina Isabelline Wheatear
Oenanthe leucopyga White-crowned Black Wheatear
Oenanthe lugens Mourning Wheatear
Oenanthe lugentoides South Arabian Wheatear
Oenanthe moesta Red-rumped Wheatear
Oenanthe monacha Hooded Wheatear
Oenanthe oenanthe Northern Wheatear
Oenanthe picata Eastern Pied Wheatear
Oenanthe xanthoprymna Red-tailed Wheatear
Onychognathus frater Socotra Starling
Onychognathus tristramii Tristram's Grackle
Oriolus oriolus Eurasian Golden Oriole
Otis tarda Great Bustard
Otus brucei Striated Scops Owl
Otus scops Common Scops Owl
Oxylophus (Clamator) jacobinus Jacobin Cuckoo
Oxyura leucocephala White-headed Duck

Pandion haliaetus Osprey
Panurus biarmicus Bearded Tit
Parus ater Coal Tit
Parus bokharensis Turkestan Tit
Parus caeruleus Blue Tit
Parus flavipectus Yellow-breasted Tit
Parus lugubris Sombre Tit
Parus major Great Tit
Parus melanolophus Black-crested Tit
Parus rufonuchalis Dark-grey Tit
Passer euchlorus Arabian Golden Sparrow
Passer hispaniolensis Spanish Sparrow
Passer insularis Socotra Sparrow
Passer moabiticus Dead Sea Sparrow
Passer pyrrhonotus Sind Jungle Sparrow
Pelagodroma marina White-faced Storm-petrel
Pelecanus crispus Dalmatian Pelican
Pelecanus onocrotalus Great White Pelican
Pelecanus rufescens Pink-backed Pelican
Perdix perdix Grey Partridge
Pericrocotus ethologus Long-tailed Minivet
Pernis apivorus European Honey Buzzard
Petronia dentata Bush Petronia
Petronia petronia Rock Sparrow
Petronia xanthocollis Yellow-throated Sparrow
Phaethon aethereus Red-billed Tropicbird
Phalacrocorax carbo Great Cormorant
Phalacrocorax nigrogularis Socotra Cormorant
Phalacrocorax pygmeus Pygmy Cormorant
Phalaropus lobatus Red-necked Phalarope
Phasianus colchicus Common Pheasant
Philomachus pugnax Ruff
Phoenicopterus ruber Greater Flamingo
Phoenicurus erythrogaster Güldenstädt's Redstart
Phoenicurus erythronotus Eversmann's Redstart
Phoenicurus ochruros Black Redstart
Phylloscopus bonelli Bonelli's Warbler
Phylloscopus chloronotus Pale-rumped Warbler
Phylloscopus collybita Common Chiffchaff
Phylloscopus griseolus Sulphur-bellied Warbler
Phylloscopus inornatus Inornate Warbler
Phylloscopus magnirostris Large-billed Leaf Warbler
Phylloscopus neglectus Plain Leaf Warbler
Phylloscopus occipitalis Western Crowned Warbler
Phylloscopus sibilatrix Wood Warbler
Phylloscopus subviridis Brooks's Leaf Warbler
Phylloscopus trochiloides Greenish Warbler
Phylloscopus trochilus Willow Warbler
Phylloscopus tytleri Tytler's Leaf Warbler
Phylloscopus umbrovirens Brown Woodland Warbler
Pica pica Black-billed Magpie
Picus viridis Eurasian Green Woodpecker
Platalea leucorodia Eurasian Spoonbill
Plegadis falcinellus Glossy Ibis
Ploceus galbula Rüppell's Weaver
Pluvialis fulva Pacific Golden Plover
Pluvialis squatarola Grey Plover
Podiceps cristatus Great Crested Grebe
Podiceps grisegena Red-necked Grebe
Podiceps nigricollis Black-necked Grebe
Podoces pleskei Pleske's Ground Jay
Porphyrio porphyrio Purple Swamphen
Porzana parva Little Crake
Porzana porzana Spotted Crake
Porzana pusilla Baillon's Crake
Prinia criniger Striated Prinia
Prinia gracilis Graceful Prinia
Prunella atrogularis Black-throated Accentor
Prunella collaris Alpine Accentor
Prunella fagani Yemen Accentor
Prunella fulvescens Brown Accentor
Prunella himalayana Rufous-streaked Accentor
Prunella modularis Hedge Accentor
Prunella ocularis Radde's Accentor
Prunella strophiata Rufous-breasted Accentor
Psittacula himalayana Slaty-headed Parakeet
Psittacula krameri Ring-necked Parakeet
Pterocles alchata Pin-tailed Sandgrouse
Pterocles coronatus Crowned Sandgrouse
Pterocles exustus Chestnut-bellied Sandgrouse
Pterocles lichtensteinii Lichtenstein's Sandgrouse
Pterocles orientalis Black-bellied Sandgrouse
Pterocles senegallus Spotted Sandgrouse
Pucrasia macrolopha Koklass Pheasant
Puffinus carneipes Flesh-footed Shearwater
Puffinus griseus Sooty Shearwater
Puffinus pacificus Wedge-tailed Shearwater
Puffinus persicus (P. lherminieri) Persian Shearwater

Pycnonotus leucotis (*P. leucogenys*) White-eared Bulbul (White-cheeked Bulbul)
Pycnonotus xanthopygos Yellow-vented Bulbul
Pyrrhocorax graculus Alpine Chough
Pyrrhocorax pyrrhocorax Red-billed Chough
Pyrrhula pyrrhula Eurasian Bullfinch

Rallus aquaticus Water Rail
Ramphocoris clotbey Thick-billed Lark
Recurvirostra avosetta Pied Avocet
Remiz coronatus White-crowned Penduline Tit
Remiz pendulinus Eurasian Penduline Tit
Rhodopechys githaginea (*Bucanetes githagineus*) Trumpeter Finch
Rhodopechys mongolica (*Bucanetes mongolicus*) Mongolian Trumpeter Finch
Rhodopechys (*Rhodospiza*) *obsoleta* Desert Finch
Rhodopechys sanguinea Crimson-winged Finch
Rhyacornis fuliginosus Plumbeous Water Redstart
Rhynchostruthus socotranus Golden-winged Grosbeak
Riparia paludicola Brown-throated Sand Martin
Riparia riparia Sand Martin

Saxicola caprata Pied Bushchat
Saxicola macrorhyncha Stoliczka's Bushchat
Saxicola rubetra Whinchat
Saxicola torquata Common Stonechat
Scolopax rusticola Eurasian Woodcock
Scopus umbretta Hamerkop
Scotocerca inquieta Scrub Warbler
Serinus menachensis Yemen Serin
Serinus pusillus Red-fronted Serin
Serinus rothschildi Arabian Serin
Serinus syriacus Syrian Serin
Sitta cashmirensis Kashmir Nuthatch
Sitta leucopsis White-cheeked Nuthatch
Sitta neumayer Western Rock Nuthatch
Sitta tephronota Eastern Rock Nuthatch
Stercorarius longicaudus Long-tailed Skua
Stercorarius parasiticus Arctic Skua
Stercorarius pomarinus Pomarine Skua
Sterna albifrons Little Tern
Sterna anaethetus Bridled Tern
Sterna bengalensis Lesser Crested Tern
Sterna bergii Great Crested Tern
Sterna caspia Caspian Tern
Sterna dougallii Roseate Tern
Sterna hirundo Common Tern
Sterna (*Gelochelidon*) *nilotica* Gull-billed Tern
Sterna repressa White-cheeked Tern
Sterna sandvicensis Sandwich Tern
Sterna saundersi Saunders' Little Tern
Streptopelia decaocto Eurasian Collared Dove
Streptopelia lugens Dusky Turtle Dove
Streptopelia orientalis Oriental Turtle Dove
Streptopelia roseogrisea African Collared Dove
Streptopelia semitorquata Red-eyed Dove
Streptopelia senegalensis Laughing Dove
Streptopelia turtur European Turtle Dove
Strix aluco Tawny Owl
Strix butleri Hume's Tawny Owl
Struthio camelus Ostrich
Sturnus pagodarum Brahminy Starling
Sturnus roseus Rosy Starling
Sula dactylatra Masked Booby
Sula leucogaster Brown Booby
Sylvia althaea Hume's Lesser Whitethroat
Sylvia atricapilla Blackcap
Sylvia buryi Yemen Warbler
Sylvia communis Common Whitethroat
Sylvia conspicillata Spectacled Warbler
Sylvia curruca Lesser Whitethroat
Sylvia hortensis Orphean Warbler
Sylvia leucomelaena Arabian Warbler
Sylvia minula Desert Lesser Whitethroat
Sylvia mystacea Ménétries's Warbler
Sylvia nana Desert Warbler
Sylvia nisoria Barred Warbler
Syrrhaptes paradoxus Pallas's Sandgrouse

Tachybaptus ruficollis Little Grebe
Tachymarptis (*Apus*) *melba* Alpine Swift
Tadorna ferruginea Ruddy Shelduck
Tadorna tadorna Common Shelduck
Tarsiger cyanurus Red-flanked Bluetail
Tchagra senegala Black-crowned Tchagra
Terathopius ecaudatus Bateleur
Terpsiphone viridis African Paradise Flycatcher
Tetrao mlokosiewiczi Caucasian Black Grouse
Tetraogallus caspius Caspian Snowcock
Tetraogallus himalayensis Himalayan Snowcock
Tetrax tetrax Little Bustard
Threskiornis aethiopicus Sacred Ibis
Tichodroma muraria Wallcreeper
Tockus nasutus African Grey Hornbill
Todirhamphus (*Halcyon*) *chloris* Collared Kingfisher
Torgos tracheliotus Lappet-faced Vulture
Treron waalia Bruce's Green Pigeon
Tringa cinerea (*Xenus cinereus*) Terek Sandpiper
Tringa erythropus Spotted Redshank
Tringa glareola Wood Sandpiper
Tringa (*Actitis*) *hypoleucos* Common Sandpiper
Tringa nebularia Common Greenshank
Tringa ochropus Green Sandpiper
Tringa stagnatilis Marsh Sandpiper
Tringa totanus Common Redshank
Troglodytes troglodytes Winter Wren
Turdoides altirostris Iraq Babbler
Turdoides caudatus Common Babbler
Turdoides squamiceps Arabian Babbler
Turdus menachensis Yemen Thrush
Turdus merula Eurasian Blackbird
Turdus philomelos Song Thrush
Turdus rubrocanus Chestnut Thrush
Turdus torquatus Ring Ouzel
Turnix sylvatica Small Buttonquail
Tyto alba Barn Owl

Upupa epops Eurasian Hoopoe

Vanellus gregarius (*Chettusia gregaria*) Sociable Plover
Vanellus (*Hoplopterus*) *indicus* Red-wattled Plover
Vanellus leucurus (*Chettusia leucura*) White-tailed Plover
Vanellus (*Hoplopterus*) *spinosus* Spur-winged Plover
Vanellus vanellus Northern Lapwing

Zosterops abyssinicus White-breasted White-eye
Zosterops palpebrosus Oriental White-eye

APPENDIX 2: English names of mammal species mentioned in the text

Acinonyx jubatus Cheetah
Apodemus hermonensis Mount Hermon Mouse
Asellia patrizii De Beaux's Trident Leaf-nosed Bat
Axis axis Indian Axis Deer (Spotted Deer)

Balaenoptera edeni Bryde's Whale
Barbastella leucomelas Arabian Barbastelle

Canis lupus Wolf
Capra falconeri Markhor
Capra nubiana Nubian Ibex
Capra hircus aegagrus Persian Wild Goat
Capra ibex Eurasian Ibex
Capreolus capreolus Roe Deer
Caracal caracal Caracal
Cervus elaphus Red Deer

Dama mesopotamica Mesopotamian Fallow Deer
Dugong dugon Dugong

Equus hemionus Asiatic Wild Ass
Erythronesokia bunnii Mesopotamian Bandicoot-rat

Felis margarita Sand Cat
Funambulus pennanti Western Palm Squirrel

Gazella dorcas Dorcas Gazelle
Gazella gazella Mountain Gazelle (Idhmi)
Gazella bilkis Queen of Sheba's Gazelle
Gazella thompsoni Thompson's Gazelle
Gazella arabica Red Sea Gazelle
Gazella subgutturosa Goitered Gazelle (Reem)
Gazella bennetti Chinkara
Genetta felina Small-spotted Genet
Gerbillus mesopotamiae Harrison's Gerbil

Hemitragus jayakari Arabian Tahr
Hylopetes fimbriatus Flying squirrel

Lepus capensis Brown Hare
Lutra perspicillata Smooth-coated Otter
Lynx lynx Northern Lynx

Macacca mulatta Rhesus Macaque
Megaptera novaeangliae Humpback Whale
Meriones sacramenti Buxton's Jird
Meriones rex King Jird
Monachus monachus Mediterranean Monk Seal
Moschus sifanicus Alpine Musk Deer

Oryx leucoryx Arabian Oryx
Ovis ammon Wild Sheep (Argali; Red Sheep)
Ovis orientalis Asiatic Mouflon

Panthera leo persica Persian Lion
Panthera tigris virgata Caspian Tiger
Panthera pardus Leopard
Papio hamadryas Hamadryas Baboon
Petaurista petaurista Red Giant Flying Squirrel
Phoca caspica Caspian Seal
Pipistrellus ariel Egyptian Desert Pipistrelle
Pipistrellus bodenheimeri Bodenheimer's Pipistrelle
Prionailurus bengalensis Leopard Cat

Rattus rattus Ship (House, Black) Rat
Rattus norvegicus Common (Norway, Brown) Rat

Sciurus anomalus Persian Squirrel
Selenarctos thibetanus Asiatic Black Bear
Sousa chinensis Indo-Pacific Humpback Dolphin
Spalax leucodon Lesser Mole-rat
Spermophilus fulvus Fulvous Ground Squirrel

Tursiops truncatus Bottle-nosed Dolphin

Uncia uncia Snow Leopard
Ursus arctos Brown Bear

Vulpes zerda Fennec Fox
Vulpes rueppellii Rüppell's Fox
Vulpes cana Blanford's Fox

APPENDIX 3: Occurrence of globally threatened bird species at Important Bird Areas in the Middle East

SITES are listed only if the species regularly occurs in significant numbers. However, for Important Bird Areas where there is no recent information on the status of the site and/or the species, the site is also listed.

Phalacrocorax pygmeus **Pygmy Cormorant**
Iran: 013, 014, 015, 016, 017, 018, 020, 022, 023, 061.
Iraq: 007, 008, 009, 013, 032, 038, 039.
Israel: 002, 004, 007, 008.
Syria: 003, 007, 010.

Pelecanus crispus **Dalmatian Pelican**
Afghanistan: 016.
Iran: 012, 016, 017, 023, 024, 025, 027, 058, 059, 060, 061, 064, 074, 076, 077, 087, 088, 090, 092, 096, 099, 100, 101, 102, 103, 104, 105.
Iraq: 020, 021, 028, 030, 032, 033, 035, 038, 039, 040.
Syria: 007.

Geronticus eremita **Northern Bald Ibis**
Saudi Arabia: 022.
Yemen: 009, 020.

Anser erythropus **Lesser White-fronted Goose**
Afghanistan: 016.
Iran: 004, 006, 007, 016, 017, 019, 020, 023, 024, 025, 026, 059, 060, 074, 076, 077, 090.
Iraq: 020, 030, 036.

Branta ruficollis **Red-breasted Goose**
Iran: 010, 017, 023, 026, 059, 060.
Iraq: 020.
Israel: 002.
Syria: 006.

Marmaronetta angustirostris **Marbled Teal**
Afghanistan: 009, 016.
Iran: 001, 006, 007, 008, 009, 010, 011, 012, 018, 023, 031, 047, 057, 058, 059, 060, 061, 062, 063, 064, 066, 073, 074, 076, 077, 087, 088, 090.
Iraq: 005, 006, 007, 008, 011, 015, 016, 019, 020, 021, 029, 030, 040.
Israel: 002, 003, 005, 007, 008, 012.
Jordan: 005, 009.
Saudi Arabia: 014.
Syria: 003, 006, 010, 017.

Oxyura leucocephala **White-headed Duck**
Afghanistan: 009, 015, 016.
Iran: 005, 007, 008, 010, 012, 016, 017, 020, 022, 023, 025, 026, 028, 047, 074, 076, 078, 088, 090.
Iraq: 016, 039.
Israel: 004, 008, 012.
Saudi Arabia: 002.
Syria: 003, 006, 017.

Milvus milvus **Red Kite**
Iran: 013, 020.

Haliaeetus leucoryphus **Pallas's Sea-eagle**
Iran: 023.
Oman: 027, 030.
Saudi Arabia: 002, 010, 028, 035.

Haliaeetus albicilla **White-tailed Eagle**
Afghanistan: 016.
Iran: 006, 007, 010, 011, 012, 013, 014, 015, 016, 017, 018, 019, 020, 021, 022, 023, 024, 025, 026, 035, 037, 061, 063, 064, 067, 068, 072, 074, 076, 077, 087, 088, 090, 092, 096, 099, 100, 101, 102, 103, 104, 105.
Iraq: 008, 025, 033, 036.
Israel: 002, 008, 012.
Saudi Arabia: 010.

Aegypius monachus **Cinereous Vulture**
Afghanistan: 005, 009, 016.
Iran: 006, 025, 026, 030, 031, 034, 035, 036, 039, 040, 049, 056, 068, 074, 075, 087, 088, 105.
Israel: 003, 008, 017.
Jordan: 011.
Kuwait: 001, 006.
Saudi Arabia: 003, 019.
Syria: 004, 018.

Aquila heliaca **Imperial Eagle**
Afghanistan: 008, 016.
Iran: 004, 013, 016, 017, 019, 020, 021, 023, 024, 025, 026, 029, 031, 032, 034, 035, 059, 060, 062, 064, 068, 074, 076, 077, 087, 088, 090, 105.
Iraq: 020, 025, 028, 029, 030, 032, 033, 038, 039, 040.
Israel: 002, 008, 012, 015, 016, 017, 018.
Jordan: 002, 003, 006, 009, 010, 011, 013, 014, 016.
Kuwait: 001, 006, 007.
Lebanon: 003.
Oman: 005, 013, 026, 027, 028, 029, 032.
Saudi Arabia: 001, 014, 019, 028, 036.
Yemen: 005, 006, 009, 014, 017, 018, 020, 021, 033.

Falco naumanni **Lesser Kestrel**
Afghanistan: 003, 004, 005, 006, 008, 011.
Iran: 013, 021, 023, 024, 029, 030, 031, 035, 036, 042, 074, 076.
Iraq: 007, 008, 009, 016.
Israel: 002, 006, 008, 011, 012, 013, 014, 015, 016, 017, 018.
Jordan: 003, 004, 010, 012, 013, 014, 016.
Kuwait: 001, 004, 006.
Lebanon: 002, 003.
Oman: 005, 010.
Saudi Arabia: 001, 014, 019, 022.
Syria: 007, 010, 018.
Yemen: 009, 017, 018, 021.

Crex crex Corncrake
Iran: 029, 031, 035.
Israel: 002, 004, 007, 008, 009, 012, 014, 015, 016, 017, 018.
Jordan: 003, 005, 011.
Kuwait: 006.
Lebanon: 004.
Oman: 017.
Saudi Arabia: 007, 014, 019, 022.
Yemen: 018.

Grus leucogeranus Siberian White Crane
Afghanistan: 005, 007, 015.
Iran: 019.

Tetrax tetrax Little Bustard
Iran: 004, 023, 024, 028, 035, 056, 059.
Israel: 002, 003, 004, 009, 011, 012, 015.
Syria: 001, 012, 014, 018.

Chlamydotis undulata Houbara Bustard
Afghanistan: 006, 016, 017.
Iran: 023, 032, 034, 036, 056, 059, 069, 072, 074, 077, 079, 080, 081, 083, 084, 085, 086, 087, 088, 092, 102, 105.
Iraq: 007, 008, 009, 013.
Israel: 015, 017.
Jordan: 002, 009, 010, 011, 015.
Kuwait: 007.
Oman: 017, 019, 021.
Saudi Arabia: 001, 012, 017, 019, 028.
Syria: 003, 004, 005, 006, 010, 012, 014, 015, 018, 021.
United Arab Emirates: 020.
Yemen: 025.

Otis tarda Great Bustard
Iran: 006, 007, 008, 010, 011, 023, 037, 038, 043, 046, 049, 050, 051, 052, 053.
Israel: 003.
Syria: 001, 003, 018.

Vanellus gregarius Sociable Plover
Iran: 016, 023.
Iraq: 008, 020.
Israel: 002, 003, 004, 008, 015.
Jordan: 003.
Oman: 005.
Saudi Arabia: 014.
Syria: 003, 007.

Numenius tenuirostris Slender-billed Curlew
Iran: 023.
Iraq: 030, 039.
Oman: 016.
Saudi Arabia: 037.

Larus leucophthalmus White-eyed Gull
Iran: 104.
Israel: 018.
Jordan: 017.
Saudi Arabia: 011, 026, 032, 038.
Yemen: 001, 004, 007, 015, 016, 019, 022, 033.

Larus audouinii Audouin's Gull
Lebanon: 001.

Saxicola macrorhyncha Stoliczka's Bushchat
Afghanistan: 017.

Turdus menachensis Yemen Thrush
Saudi Arabia: 023, 024, 030.
Yemen: 005, 006, 011, 017, 018.

Cisticola haesitatus Island Cisticola
Yemen: 038, 047, 053.

Appendix I of the Bonn Convention lists migratory species which are considered (by the Contracting Parties) to be in danger of extinction throughout all or a major part of their range, and of the above species it includes: *Pelecanus crispus*, *Geronticus eremita*, *Haliaeetus albicilla*, *Grus leucogeranus*, *Numenius tenuirostris*, *Larus leucophthalmus* and *L. audouinii*. In addition, it lists two species which occur in significant numbers in the Middle East but which are not currently considered to be globally threatened (Groombridge 1993). The Important Bird Areas in the Middle East which harbour significant numbers of these two species are listed below.

Pelecanus onocrotalus Great White Pelican
Afghanistan: 015, 016.
Israel: 002, 004, 007, 008, 009, 012, 018.
Iraq: 020, 021, 032, 033, 035, 038, 039.
Iran: 006, 007, 011, 074, 077, 087, 088.

Serinus syriacus Syrian Serin
Israel: 001, 014, 018.
Jordan: 003, 004, 005, 006, 010, 013, 014.
Lebanon: 003.
Syria: 019, 020.

APPENDIX 4: Example of IBA data-sheet, with guidelines for completion

BirdLife International
INTERNATIONAL

BirdLife International
Ornithological Society of the Middle East

IMPORTANT BIRD AREAS IN THE MIDDLE EAST

OSME

DATA-SHEET

NOTE

Please read the accompanying *Guidelines for completion of data-sheet* before attempting to complete this form. Please complete as many sections as possible for each site.

Please return completed data-sheets to:

Middle East IBA, BirdLife International, Wellbrook Court, Girton Road, Cambridge CB3 0NA, U.K.

BirdLife use:

1.Country: **2. Province:**

3. Name of site: **4. Date of compilation:**

5. Name and address of compiler:

6. General location:

7. Geographical coordinates:

8. Area: (in hectares) **9. Altitude**

10. Criteria used to select sites: see *Guidelines for the selection of IBAs*

Put an 'X' in relevant box(es):

- ☐ Globally threatened species
- ☐ 1% or more of a species' population (List 2)
- ☐ 20,000 or more waterfowl
- ☐ Migratory 'bottleneck' site
- ☐ Top 5 site: restricted range species
- ☐ Top 5 site: regionally threatened species
- ☐ Representative bird community
- ☐ Rare/threatened/unique bird community
- ☐ Importance for education/research/tourism
- ☐ Other reasons (specify below)

List 'Other reasons' here:

11. Ornithological importance: see Lists 1-3 in *Guidelines for the selection of IBAs*

Name of species	No. of breeding pairs	Code	No. of birds in mid-winter (individuals)	Code	No. on migration (individuals)	Code

Continue on separate sheet if necessary

Additional information:

12. Topography / climate / hydrology / soils / geology / tides:

13. Habitats / vegetation / flora and non-bird fauna:

Brief description of habitats/vegetation/flora:

Habitats: give % cover of each

- [ ] Marine environment
- [ ] Non-marine wetlands
- [ ] Desert/desert fringe
- [ ] Grassland/steppe
- [ ] Scrub/bushland
- [ ] Woodland/forest
- [ ] Agriculture/cultivation
- [ ] 'Artificial'
- [ ] Other (specify): ...
- [ ] Other (specify): ...

Details of non-bird fauna: (especially globally threatened/endemic)

14. Threats: (give brief summary)

Classify threats as **C** (Critical), **M** (Major) or **L** (Local), where relevant. Potential, rather than actual, threats should be bracketed:

- [ ] Over-exploitation of birds/eggs (food, pets etc.)
- [ ] Excessive or irresponsible hunting/falconry
- [ ] Deliberate persecution of birds
- [ ] Excessive disturbance of birds
- [ ] Introduction of non-indigenous fauna/flora
- [ ] Deforestation/tree-cutting
- [ ] Forestry/afforestation
- [ ] Diversion of water/canalization
- [ ] Drainage
- [ ] Damming
- [ ] Over-extraction of ground-water
- [ ] Irrigation
- [ ] Drought
- [ ] Fire
- [ ] Built development/construction
- [ ] Dredging
- [ ] Land claim/landfill
- [ ] Extraction industry (mines, quarries etc.)
- [ ] Destruction of desert crust
- [ ] Conversion to agriculture/ploughing up
- [ ] Agricultural intensification
- [ ] Abandonment of traditional management
- [ ] Over-grazing/over-browsing
- [ ] Excessive soil erosion/degradation
- [ ] Oil pollution/exploration
- [ ] Toxic pollution
- [ ] Eutrophication
- [ ] Air pollution
- [ ] Debris/garbage pollution
- [ ] Other (specify):
- [ ] ...
- [ ] ...

15. Conservation measures taken: (protected areas/other measures)

16. Conservation measures proposed:

17. Land ownership:

18. Economic, cultural and social values of site:

Current land use(s): classify as **P** (Primary) or **S** (Secondary):

- ☐ Agriculture/cultivation
- ☐ Rangeland (livestock)
- ☐ Water supply
- ☐ Fisheries/aquaculture
- ☐ Forestry
- ☐ Hunting
- ☐ Urban/industrial/utility
- ☐ Tourism
- ☐ Recreation
- ☐ Wildlife conservation/research
- ☐ Other (specify): ...
- ☐ Other (specify): ...

19. References: cite key references in full.

20. Relevant maps available: list map(s) covering the site.

THANK YOU VERY MUCH FOR YOUR HELP

Please return to:
Middle East IBA, BirdLife International, Wellbrook Court, Girton Road, Cambridge, CB3 0NA, U.K.
Telephone: +44-1223-277318 **Fax:** +44-1223-277200 (+44-223- until April 1995)
Email: birdlife@gn.apc.org

BirdLife International
Ornithological Society of the Middle East

BirdLife INTERNATIONAL

IMPORTANT BIRD AREAS IN THE MIDDLE EAST

OSME

GUIDELINES FOR COMPLETION OF DATA-SHEET

Throughout this document, the abbreviation 'IBA' refers to 'Important Bird Area'.

How to fill in the data-sheet

An IBA data-sheet should be completed for each IBA, in English and/or Arabic, preferably typed.

Compilers are urged to fill out as many sections of the data-sheet as possible. In the case of a site which has been well-documented, or which is the subject of a special field investigation, far more information may be available than can be accommodated on the data-sheet. If so, additional information can be provided on separate sheets.

Whenever possible, copies of published or unpublished papers and reports on the site should be appended to the data-sheet, as well as transparencies/slides or photographs of the site.

Please send data-sheets to: Middle East IBA, BirdLife International, Wellbrook Court, Girton Road, Cambridge, CB3 0NA, U.K. Email: birdlife@gn.apc.org
Tel: +44-1223-277318 Fax: +44-1223-277200 (code +44-223- until April 1995)

1. Country:
The name of the country.

2. Province:
The name(s) of the province(s) and/or administrative district(s) in which the site lies.

3. Name of site:
The most widely used name for the site (alternative names should be given in brackets).

4. Date:
The date on which the data-sheet was completed by the compiler.

5. Name and address of compiler:
The full name and address of the person compiling the data-sheet, with any telephone, fax and telex numbers.

6. General location:
A very short description of the general location of the site within the country, e.g. the distance (in a straight line) and compass direction of the site from the nearest significant village, town or city.

7. Geographical coordinates:
The geographical coordinates (latitude and longitude; Greenwich) of the approximate centre of the site, expressed in degrees and minutes. If the site is large, please also give the coordinates of the site's boundary (north-south and east-west spans).

8. Area:
The area of the site in hectares. It is important to specify which map or delineated site boundary this area refers to if more than one boundary configuration has been proposed or has existed for the site in the past.

9. Altitude:
The altitude range in metres above mean sea level, or the average altitude if the terrain is level.

10. Criteria used to select site:
Put a cross 'X' against those criteria which were used to select the site. Please refer to the chapter on 'Site Selection' (pp.20–27) for the full list of criteria.

11. Ornithological importance:
Give counts for those regularly occurring bird species which satisfy the relevant criteria (see the chapter on 'Site Selection', pp.20–27), in the following standardized format whenever possible (so as to allow comparability

of data between different sites); distinguish between maximum and average counts:

Breeding count: give the maximum count of breeding PAIRS, and/or average count (over the most recent 3–5 years), e.g. '70 max.' or '400 av.', etc..

Mid-winter count: give the January maximum count and/or January average count (over the most recent 3–5 years) of INDIVIDUALS, e.g. "1,000 Jan. max." or "4,000 Jan. av.", etc..

Migration count: give the maximum daily count and/or the estimated season's total (spring and/or autumn) of INDIVIDUALS, e.g. "400 daily max." or "900 autumn total". Important counts of moulting birds or oversummering non-breeders should be entered in the 'migration' column, but please specify that this is what the figure refers to.

Where data cannot be given in the above format, please specify how the provided count differs, e.g. for a winter count '1,000 Feb. max.', or for a breeding count '600 minimum', or for a migration count '300 minimum', etc.

In the 'Code' columns, indicate the reliability and accuracy of each count supplied, using the following scale:

1 = rough estimate / no quantitative data available
2 = reasonable estimate / based on incomplete or poor quantitative data
3 = accurate count or estimate / based on reliable quantitative data

If a complete species list for the site is available, please append it to the data-sheet.

Under 'Additional information', give ornithological data of a more general or summarized nature, e.g. the overall total number of raptors migrating through a bottleneck site, the total number of waterfowl wintering at the site, and so on, as well as any other comments, e.g. on how well known the site is, the quality of the data, etc..

12. Topography / climate / hydrology / soils / geology / tides:
Give a brief description of the principal physical features of the site, covering the following points where relevant: geology, soils, topography, hydrology, climate, tides.

13. Habitats / vegetation / flora and non-bird fauna:
Give a brief description of the principal habitats and/or vegetation types present, including any dominant plant species, and give details on any other endemic, rare, threatened or internationally significant numbers of non-bird fauna and flora.

In the boxes, give the approximate % cover of the major habitats at the site, using the following classification:

Marine environment: includes mangroves, intertidal flats, estuaries/deltas, coastal lagoons, offshore islands.

Non-marine wetlands: includes marshes, temporary/seasonal wetlands, natural/man-made wetlands, saline and soda lakes, rivers, streams, swamps, bogs.

Desert/desert fringe: areas that are bare, open, relatively vegetation-less, with very high evaporation compared to precipitation (hyper-arid/arid/semi-arid), and a low and irregular annual rainfall.

Grassland/steppe: areas where grass, herbs, and dwarf shrubs comprise more than 50% of the vegetational biomass. Often difficult to distinguish from previous habitat, but rainfall is more regular and higher.

Scrub/bushland: areas where woody species without obvious trunks (i.e. the species are branching from the base) comprise more than 50% of the vegetational biomass.

Woodland/forest: areas where woody species with trunks comprise more than 50% of the vegetational biomass; includes forestry and crop plantations, orchards, very open wooded savannah habitats, urban wooded parks (but *not* gardens: these are '*Artificial*').

Agriculture/cultivation: includes arable land, permanent pasture and rain-fed 'shifting' cultivation if active.

'Artificial': includes built structures (e.g. buildings, roads, airports, ports, but not reservoirs, dams and other man-made wetlands: these are '*Non-marine wetlands*'), urban areas, non-wooded parks, gardens, garbage dumps and other man-made features that are otherwise difficult to classify.

N.B. Mountainous or 'montane' habitats should be classified according to the above scheme; their 'high altitude' aspect is indicated in section 9, 'Altitude'.

14. Threats:
Briefly summarise any human activities at the site and in the surrounding area, which have had, are having or may have an harmful effect on the natural ecological character of the site, including any proposed changes in land-use and any planned development projects involving the site.

In the boxes, label threats where applicable with **C** (Critical), **M** (Major) or **L** (Local), according to the percentage of the resource which is predicted to be affected negatively if current trends continue:

CRITICAL = more than 50% of resource
MAJOR = 10–50% of resource
LOCAL = less than 10% of resource

The 'resource' could be the water in a lake, the trees in a forest, the population of a threatened bird species at the site, and so on. For threats which could *potentially* occur or which are only *proposed*, rather than actually taking place, it is important that the code (C/M/L) should be placed in *brackets*.

15. Conservation measures taken:
(a) **Protected areas**: give details of any areas protected for nature conservation established at or around the site; especially, define the protected area's boundary on a map if it does not coincide with the IBA boundary, and give the % overlap between the two as well as the protected area's present area. State whether an officially approved management plan exists and whether it has been, or is being, implemented. Also note any unintentional or non-governmental protection (e.g. through an IBA's location in a trans-border security zone, wildlife ranch, private hunting reserve, traditional resource-use reserve [*hema*], community forest, and so on).
(b) **Other conservation measures** taken at the site: give details, e.g. restrictions on development, closures of hunting, management practices beneficial to wildlife.

An assessment of the effectiveness of measures should be given whenever possible.

16. Conservation measures proposed:
Give details of any conservation measures which have been proposed for the site, including any proposals for legislation, protection or management. Make a clear distinction between:
(a) existing proposals, officially submitted by the appropriate governmental body; and
(b) new proposals, not yet endorsed officially, e.g. report recommendations, resolutions from specialist meetings.

17. Land ownership:
Give details of ownership of the site and of the surrounding area, e.g. governmental, private, commercial, religious, communal. Describe grazing rights and water-use rights at the site where possible.

18. Economic, cultural and social values of site:
Specify the principal human activities and main forms of land-use at the site, e.g. importance of resources such as fish, reeds for thatching, traditional grazing of livestock, recreation. Describe any religious, cultural or social values, e.g. religious significance, historical or archaeological associations or structures.

For the 'Current land-uses' list, label boxes with **P** (Primary land-use) and **S** (Secondary land-use) according to their economic/cultural/social importance at the present time.

19. References:
Cite any key references relevant to the site. Reprints or copies of documents should be appended with the data-sheet whenever possible.

20. Relevant maps available:
Important: Please attach copies of any published maps available (preferably of scale 1: 50,000 or more detailed), *with the IBA boundary clearly delineated*, as well as protected area boundaries where these differ. Supply A4 photocopies or colour transparencies if the original maps cannot be attached. Write on the data-sheet the details of the relevant maps (publisher, scale, date, sheet numbers). If there are no published maps, please attach a sketch map, including where possible: site boundaries, distribution of main habitat types, scale, compass North, latitude/longitude, access points.

THANK YOU VERY MUCH FOR YOUR HELP

INDEX OF SITES